Published by the Center for Rural Manpower and Public Affairs and the Cooperative

Territorial Boundaries of Rural Poverty

Profiles of Exploitation

MYRTLE R. REUL

Extension Service, Michigan State University, East Lansing, Michigan

Cover design and illustrations by Bob Brent

To Paul A. Reul—

*My husband friend, confidant, and fellow
traveler on an adventure that for us started in
the days of the Depression and has spanned
every section of the nation; a generous, kind
man whose capacity to understand, accept,
and encourage people regardless of their race,
social position, sex, or age has won and kept
my deepest admiration*

— this book is dedicated.

"For this is the journey that men [people] make; to
find themselves. If they fail in this, it doesn't matter
much what else they find. Money, position, fame,
many loves, revenge are all of little consequence,
and when the tickets are collected at the end of the
ride they are tossed into a bin marked FAILURE.

"But if a man happens to find himself – if he knows
what he can be depended upon to do, the limits of
his courage, the positions from which he will no
longer retreat, the degree to which he can surrender
his inner life to some woman [or she to him], the
secret reservoirs of his determination, the extent of
his dedication, the depth of his feeling for beauty,
his honest and unpostured goals–then he has found
a mansion which he can inhabit with dignity all the
days of his life."

James A. Michener
20th century American author
The Fires of Spring

Acknowledgments

Writing this book and doing the research for it are tasks that have taken place over a number of years in different parts of the country. In the process, I have met and come to know many people to whom I owe deep appreciation.

I am first of all indebted to those whose lives are recounted within these pages, who told their stories so that others might learn.

To the staffs of the Department of Agricultural Economics, their chairman Harold Riley, and the Center for Rural Manpower and Public Affairs at Michigan State University goes my gratitude for their patience in working with me for over two years on a manuscript that never seemed to be finished. I extend my appreciation especially to Dale Hathaway, former Chairman of the Department of Agricultural Economics, Michigan State University, now with the Ford Foundation, New York, who first suggested that I prepare the manuscript; and to various staff members of the Rural Manpower Service of the U.S. Department of Labor for their interest and encouragement.

To the editors—Kathleen Schoonmaker of University Publications, Department of Information Services, and Addiann Hinds of the Department of Agricultural Economics and the Center for Rural Manpower and Public Affairs, both at Michigan State University—goes a special thank you for the final editing, layout, and production arrangements that saw the manuscript into print.

My deep appreciation goes also to Sherry Fuller, who worked untiringly on the preparation of the manuscript through its numerous revisions and whose keen appraisal and questions assisted me immeasurably. Five graduate assistants from the University of Georgia's School of Social Work get special thanks: Herman Harris, William Moon, and Cheryl Mowinckel, who read parts of the manuscript and offered valuable suggestions; Thomas Nosal, who helped in the search for reference material; and Dianne Huchins, who assisted with parts of the indexing.

For their unfaltering belief in rural development, I owe thanks to my Rural Manpower Policy Research Consortium colleagues: Varden Fuller, Department of Agricultural Economics at the University of California; Robert Hunter, Department of Sociology at the University of Colorado; Louis Levine, School of Government Studies at the George Washington University; Ray Marshall, Department of Economics and Director of the Center for the Study of Human Resources at the University of Texas; Gerald Somers, Department of Economics at the University of Wisconsin; and, for her special encouragement, Collette Moser, director of the Consortium and assistant professor of Agricultural Economics at Michigan State University.

To my daughters, M. Santa Schoof and Pauline C. Holland, and my sons-in-law, William L. Holland and Richard J. Schoof, for reading and appraising certain chapters, and to my grandsons, Stephen Lewis and Bradley Jon, who tolerated my dissertation in recent months so that this book could appear, go my love, thanks, and appreciation.

I wish to express my sincere gratitude to the publishing companies and authors, or the families of authors, who gave me permission to quote from their copyrighted materials or to reprint their illustrations. I herewith acknowledge each as they requested:

For the material from *The United States Story of A Free People* by Samuel Steinberg, copyrighted 1954 by Allyn and Bacon, Inc.—
ALLYN AND BACON, INC., permission of the publisher to use maps.

For the material from *Children of Bondage* by Allison David and John Dollard, copyrighted 1940 by American Council on Education—
AMERICAN COUNCIL ON EDUCATION, permission of the publisher.

For the material from *The Negro Immigrant* by Ira De Augustine Reid, copyrighted 1968 by Ams Press—
AMS PRESS, with permission of Ams Press.

For the material from *Toward Understanding Human Personalities* by

Robert Leeper and Peter Madison, copyrighted 1959 by Appleton-Century-Crofts—

APPLETON-CENTURY-CROFTS, reprinted by permission of Appleton-Century-Crofts Educational Division, Meredith Corporation.

For the material from *Disinherited: The Lost Birthright of the American Indian* by Dale Van Every, copyrighted 1966 by Dale Van Every—

AVON LIBRARY BOOKS, with permission of William Morrow and Company, Inc.

For the material from *American Handbook of Psychiatry*, Vol. I and Vol. III, edited by Silvane Arieti, copyrighted 1959 and 1966 by Basic Books, Inc.

BASIC BOOKS, INC., with permission of Basic Books, Inc.

For the material from *War Chief Joseph* by Helen Addison Howard—

THE CLAXTON PRINTERS, LTD., with permission of the Claxton Printers, Ltd.

For the material from *The Invisible Scar* by Caroline Bird, orginally published by David McKay Company, Inc. in 1967; Pocket Book edition published in 1967 by Pocket Books, a division of Simon and Schuster, Inc.—

DAVID McKAY COMPANY, INC., with permission of David McKay Company, Inc.

For the material from *The Souls of Black Folk* by W. E. Burghardt DuBois, copyright by W. E. Burghardt DuBois, 1953—

FAWCETT PUBLICATIONS, INC., with permission of Fawcett Publications, Inc.

For the material from *The Story of Cotton* by Harris Dickson, copyright by Harris Dickson, 1937—

FUNK AND WAGNALLS, INC., with permission of Funk and Wagnalls, Inc.

For the material from "Nikki Rosa" copyrighted 1970 by Nikki Giovanni—

GIOVANNI, NIKKI, with permission of Nikki Giovanni.

For the material from *Strategies of Psychotherapy* by Jay Haley, copyrighted by Grune and Stratton, 1963—

GRUNE AND STRATTON, by permission of the publisher and the author.

For the material from *I Came Out of the Eighteenth Century* by John Andrew Rice, originally published in 1942 by Harper and Brothers—

HARPER AND ROW, PUBLISHERS, INC., with permission of Harper and Row, Publishers, Inc.

For the material from *Black Boy* by Richard Wright, originally published in 1945 by Harper and Brothers—

HARPER AND ROW, PUBLISHERS, INC., with permission of Harper and Row, Publishers, Inc.

For the material from *The Negro in Mississippii 1865–1890* by Lane Wharton, originally published by Harper and Brothers in 1947—

HARPER AND ROW, PUBLISHERS, INC., with permission of Harper and Row, Publishers, Inc.

For the material from *The Puerto Rican Journey* by C. Wright Mills, Clarence Senior, and Rose Kohn Goldsen, originally published in 1950 by Harper Brothers—

HARPER AND ROW, PUBLISHERS, INC., with permission of Harper and Row, Publishers, Inc.

For the material from *Cultural Values of American Ethnic Groups* by Sister Frances Jerome Woods, originally published in 1956 by Harper Brothers—

HARPER AND ROW, PUBLISHERS, INC., with permission of Harper and Row, Publishers, Inc.

For the material from *Major Social Problems* by Earl Raab and Gertrude Jaeger Selznick, copyrighted by Row, Peterson and Company, 1961—

HARPER AND ROW, PUBLISHERS, INC., with permission of Harper and Row, Publishers, Inc.

For the material from *Socio-Economic and Other Variations Related to Rehabilitation of Mexican Americans in Arizona* published in 1969 by Arizona State University—

HARWARD, NAOMI, quoted with permission of the author.

For the material from "Where is Tell?" by Herbert Kubly, in *Holiday Magazine*, July-August 1971—

HOLIDAY, with permission of the publisher.

For the material from *Escape from Freedom* by Erich Fromm, copyright (c) 1941 Rinehart and Company, Inc.—

HOLT, RINEHART AND WINSTON, INC., reprinted by permission of Holt, Rinehart and Winston, Inc.

For the material from *Education of the Disadvantaged* edited by A. Harry Passow, Miriam Goldberg, and Abraham J. Tannenbaum, copyright (c) 1967 by Holt, Rinehart and Winston, Inc.—

HOLT, RINEHART AND WINSTON, INC., permission by Holt, Rinehart and Winston, Inc.

For the material from *Bury My Heart at Wounded Knee* by Dee Brown, copyright (c) 1970 by Dee Brown—

HOLT, RINEHART AND WINSTON, INC., reprinted by permission of Holt, Rinehart and Winston, Inc.

For the material from *Environmental Psychology: Man and His Physical Setting* edited by Harold M. Proshansky, William H. Ittelson, and Leanne G. Rivlin, copyright (c) 1970 by Holt, Rinehart and Winston, Inc.—

HOLT, RINEHART AND WINSTON, INC., permission by Holt, Rinehart and Winston, Inc.

For the material from *Leadership for Action in Rural Communities* by Burton W. Kreitlow, E. W. Aiton, and Andrew P. Torrence, copyright 1960 by the Interstate Printers and Publishers, Inc.—

THE INTERSTATE PRINTERS AND PUBLISHERS, INC., with permission of the publisher.

For the material from *Americans from Japan* by Bradford Smith, copyrighted 1949 by Bradford Smith—

J.B. LIPPINCOTT COMPANY, reprinted by courtesy of J.B. Lippincott Company.

For the material from *Tally's Corner* by Elliot Liebow, copyrighted 1967 by Little, Brown and Company, Inc.—

LITTLE, BROWN AND COMPANY, reprinted by courtesy of Little, Brown and Company.

For the material from *A Cultural History of Education* by R. Freeman Butts, copyright 1947 by the McGraw Hill Book Company, Inc.—

MCGRAW-HILL BOOK COMPANY, INC., used with permission of McGraw-Hill Book Company.

For the material from *North from Mexico* by Carey McWilliams, published by J.B. Lippincott Company, copyright 1948 by Carey McWilliams—

McWILLIAMS, CAREY, quoted with permission of the author.

For the material from "Indian Is Outcast in City of Hope" by Carl Rowan in the *Minneapolis Tribune*, Feb. 9, 1957 and "What Can Society Do to Help Set Free Today's Indians?" by Carl Rowan in the *Minneapolis Tribune*, March 3, 1957—

MINNEAPOLIS TRIBUNE, reprinted by permission of the *Minneapolis Tribune*.

For the material from "Why Women Fear Success" by Vivian Gornick in *Ms.*, Spring, 1972—

MS., with permission of the publishers.

For the material from "Who Are the Poor?" by Herman P. Miller in *The Nation*, June 7, 1965—

THE NATION, with permission of the publishers.

For the material from "Regimented Non-Education: Indian Schools" by Daniel Henninger and Nancy Esposito in *The New Republic*, Feb. 15, 1969—

THE NEW REPUBLIC, reprinted by permission of *The New Republic* (c) 1969, Harrison-Blaine of New Jersey, Inc.

For the cartoon from *Puck*, a magazine of the 1870s—

THE NEW YORK PUBLIC LIBRARY, courtesy New York Public Library.

For the material from *Childhood and Society* by Erik H. Erikson, copyright 1950—

W.W. NORTON AND COMPANY, with permission of the W.W. Norton Company, Inc.

For the material from *Communication: The Social Matrix of Psychiatry* by Jurgen Ruesch and Gregory Bateson, copyright 1951 by W.W. Norton and Company, Inc.—

W.W. NORTON AND COMPANY, INC., with permission of the W.W. Norton and Company, Inc.

For the material from *The Strange Career of Jim Crow* by C. Vann Woodward, copyright 1955 by Oxford University Press, Inc.—
OXFORD UNIVERSITY PRESS, with permission of Oxford University Press.

For the material from *Acculturation in Seven American Indian Tribes* edited by Ralph Linton, copyright 1963 by Peter Smith Publisher, Inc.—
PETER SMITH PUBLISHER, INC., with permission of Peter Smith Publisher, Inc.

For the material from *Marriage and Family among Negroes* by Jessie Bernard, copyright 1966 by Prentice-Hall, Inc.—
PRENTICE-HALL, INC., with permission of Prentice-Hall, Inc.

For the material from *We Who Built America* by Carl Frederick Wittke, 1967 printing by Press of Western Reserve University—
PRESS OF WESTERN RESERVE UNIVERSITY, with permission of Press of Western Reserve University.

For the material from "Making It the Hardest Way" by J. W. Lawrie in *Psychology Today*, Nov. 1969—
PSYCHOLOGY TODAY, with permission of the publisher.

For the material from *The Happy Child: A Psychoanalytic Guide to Emotional and Social Growth* by Irene Milliken Josselyn, copyright 1955 by Irene Milliken Josselyn—
RANDOM HOUSE, with permission of Random House, Inc.

For the material from *One America* by Francis J. Brown and Joseph Slabey Roucek, published in 1945 by Prentice-Hall, Inc.—
ROUCEK, JOSEPH S., with permission of the surviving author.

For the material from *Portrait of Myself* by Margaret Bourke-White, copyrighted 1963 by Margaret Bourke-White—
SIMON AND SCHUSTER, with permission of Simon and Schuster.

For the material from *Killers of the Dream* by Lillian Smith, originally published by W.W. Norton and Company, Inc. in 1949—
SMITH, LILLIAN, ESTATE OF, with permission of the family of Lillian Smith.

For the material from *The Migrant Farmer* by Robert Coles, published in 1965 by the Southern Regional Council—
SOUTHERN REGIONAL COUNCIL, with permission of the Southern Regional Council.

For the material from *Empire Builders of Georgia* by Ruth Elgin Suddeth, Isa Lloyd Osterhout, and George Lewis Hutcheson, copyrighted 1963 by the Steck Company—
STECK COMPANY, with permission of the Steck Company.

For the material from *People in Families* by George Simpson, copyrighted 1960 by Thomas Y. Crowell—

THOMAS Y. CROWELL, with permission of Thomas Y. Crowell.

For the material from "Why Can't We Help Them Help Themselves?" by Myrtle R. Reul in *Shifting Scenes,* Summer 1971 (with agency cases at the end)—

TRAVELERS AID SOCIETY, the cases are partly reprinted with permission of the Travelers Aid Society of America.

For the material from *Mexican Immigration to the United States* by Manuel Gabio, copyrighted 1930 by the University of Chicago Press—

UNIVERSITY OF CHICAGO PRESS, with permission of the University of Chicago Press.

For the material from *Tepoztlan, A Mexican Village: A Study of Folk Life* by Robert Redfield, copyrighted 1930 by the University of Chicago Press—

UNIVERSITY OF CHICAGO PRESS, with permission of the University of Chicago Press.

For the material from *Shadow of the Plantation* by Charles S. Johnson, copyrighted 1934 by the University of Chicago Press—

UNIVERSITY OF CHICAGO PRESS, with permission of the University of Chicago Press.

For the material from *Rebel Voices, an I.W.W. Anthology* by Joyce Kornbluh, copyrighted 1964 by the University of Michigan Press—

UNIVERSITY OF MICHIGAN PRESS, with permission of the University of Michigan Press.

For the material from *Sharecroppers All* by Arthur F. Raper and Ira De A. Reid, copyrighted 1941 by the University of North Carolina Press—

UNIVERSITY OF NORTH CAROLINA PRESS, with permission of the University of North Carolina Press.

For the material from *Across the Tracks: Mexican-Americans in a Texas City* by Arthur J. Rubel, copyrighted 1966 by the Hogg Foundation for Mental Health—

UNIVERSITY OF TEXAS PRESS, with permission of the University of Texas Press.

For the material from *The Southeastern United States* by John Fraser Hart, copyrighted 1967 by Litton Educational Publishing, Inc.—

VAN NOSTRAND REINHOLD COMPANY, reprinted by permission of Van Nostrand Reinhold Company.

For the material from "Communication: Client, Community and Agency" by Edith Varon in *Social Work,* April 1954—

VARON, EDITH, with permission of the author.

For the material from *Brown Americans, The Story of a Tenth of the Nation* by Edwin R. Embree, copyright 1943 by the Viking Press, Inc., renewed copyright 1971 by Kate C. Embree—

THE VIKING PRESS, reprinted with permission of the Viking Press.

For the material from *The Mind of the South* by W. J. Cash, copyright 1941 by Alfred A. Knopf—

VINTAGE BOOKS, with permission of Vintage Books published by Alfred A. Knopf, Inc. and Random House, Inc.

Contents

Figures and Tables

Figures

Tables

PART I

Preview to Understanding

There can be no revolution until the ideas of men become the conscience of the mass, and until the passions of men become a living force, because "it is man and not events which constitute the world."

Bartolemé Mitre, 19th century President
    of Argentina
The Emancipation of South America

1

The Frame of Reference

This book is an attempt to examine rural poverty in various parts of our country. Some of it is a collection of papers and articles in which I mainly describe the everyday tasks of one segment of the rural poor—namely migrant farm laborers. In order to view the territorial boundaries of poor rural residents who migrate to improve their lot in life, one must also view those who remain in home-base areas of rural America; therefore, this book also describes those poor rural residents who do not migrate.

The psychosocial-cultural portraits that I have sketched are intended to convey something of the life styles of farm migrants and poor rural nonmigrants against the backdrop of rural poverty as it is today and as it was in decades past, including those man-made forces that helped create present poverty. The reader will recognize in these analytic sketches versions of middle- and lower-class cultural themes. My aim is to show that, psychologically, people are more alike than they are different and that social class and culture must be variables in all personal and family analysis because personalities and role expectations are molded by social determinants, especially poverty. Another aim of this book is to help point out the great difference between the life styles of various families, even within the same socioeconomic class. My hope is to illustrate what it feels like to be shaped by want or discrimination, as well as to point out the perceptive accuracy of those living under these conditions—a strength of the lower-class person that is often overlooked by those who do research in this area.

For years I have been impatient with those middle-class researchers who tend to classify the poor as apathetic, without moral values or dreams of the future, when most such researchers have never viewed the everyday situation through the eyes of the poor or from the actual experience of the poor. What may appear to be apathy, a valueless existence, and/or an orientation to the present with no thought for the future—or even an orientation to the past—takes on new meaning when seen in light of whether there is food for a meal, a place to sleep at night, clothes for school, medicine for a sick baby, or a way to bury one's dead. Within the living experiences of the rural poor, events occur in far from a random fashion; instead, events within the territorial boundaries of the poor occur in a pattern that molds behavior and emotional reactions. Even individual or family uncertainty is given a customary place in the scheme of things. The family may move from one crisis to another without any period of stability at all.

Depicting such situations is not my sole purpose. I am also concerned with developing a framework for understanding the rural poor—whether they be American Indians, Appalachian and Southern whites, Southern Blacks, or Chicanos. One of my main aims is to better equip those who work with the poor to do their jobs. I hope to show commonalities of culture and dynamics of behavior by applying experiences and episodes to various psychological and sociological theories, or by at least calling the reader's attention to these theories through footnotes so he, or she, may make his, or her, own application. Therefore, I urge a careful examination of the notes at the end of each chapter; otherwise much of the theoretical base or explanations of the situation from the writer's viewpoint will be missed.

The material of this book falls into seven main sections. The first is the introduction, which gives the reader something of my background as it is related to rural poverty. Part 2 is an historical perspective of social determinants that have shaped the lives of the rural poor. The influence of culture and the way it is reflected in some parts of rural America are the main topics for part 3. The reader is provided in part 4 with an opportunity to become a participant observer in the everyday living experiences of farm migrant workers. Part 5 is a continuation of part 4, but the focus is narrowed to experiences related to work. The implications of the life styles of the rural poor for such helping professions as health, education, welfare, and labor are examined in part 6. The seventh section is concerned with the future as it relates to the maximum use of human resources, especially rural resources.

In the chapters of this book are the stories of rural people whom my husband and I know personally. They are mostly minority people. They are newcomers, outsiders. They are so-called socially or educationally disadvantaged, and most of them live in poverty. This book is their story, and yet it is our story. For that reason it may help the reader to understand better the case-study approach I use in these writings if I share something of our backgrounds and our more than three decades of personal experiences with rural poverty in different parts of the country. So I will begin with the years of the Depression and our early involvement with farm migrant workers.

Here with a Loaf of Bread beneath the Bough
A Flask of Wine, a Book of Verse—and Thou
Beside me singing in the Wilderness—
And Wilderness is Paradise enow.

Omar Khayyam, 11th century Persian poet
The Rubaiyat

2

Our Interest in Migrants

Migrant Families of the 1930s

More than thirty years have passed since John Steinbeck's
Grapes of Wrath[1] and Carey McWilliams's *Factories in the Field*[2]
called attention to the plight of migrant farm laborers. The workers
who crowded the migrant streams in 1939 were mainly products of
the Depression.[3] Many were refugees of the Dust Bowl.[4] In the
years between 1933 and 1938, when droughts, dust storms, the
corn borer, and the cotton boll weevil took their major toll,
approximately a quarter of a million destitute farm refugees
entered the state of California.[5] (Figure 1 shows the states of
origin of migrants entering California between 1935 and 1937.)
Thousands more looked for work in the apples of Washington, the
hops of Oregon, the sugar beets of Michigan, and the potatoes of
Maine. (Figure 2 shows the states of origin of 2,300 migrants into
Washington.) These were the families described by Steinbeck and
McWilliams as "forgotten ones." Once, not long before, they had
been taxpayers and property owners, but suddenly they were the

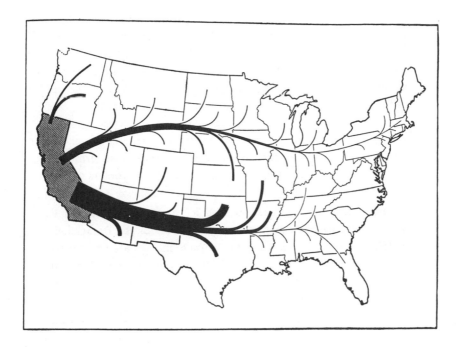

Fig. 1. States of origin of migrants (shown as percentage, by states, of total number reported) to California, June 16, 1935 to November 15, 1937. (Source: Farm Security Administration and California Department of Agriculture. Data on 210,168 immigrants.)

deprived, the disenchanted, the exploited migrant farm workers of the 1930s.

Migrant Families of Today

Thirty-five years later migrant farm-laborer families are still entering the same states searching for work in the same crops. The main difference between migrants of the 1970s and those of the 1920s and 1930s is their ethnic backgrounds. Although there were Mexican workers in the earlier years,[6] today the majority of migrant agricultural workers are Spanish-speaking and either Chicano or Puerto Rican. The next largest number are Southern-born Blacks and whites from the deep South and from the mountains of Kentucky and Tennessee, followed by day-haul workers from cities such as Philadelphia. The migrants of this decade are part of the culture of America's newly discovered poor. While most farm migrants of the Depression knew work as nonmigrant or even nonfarm employees, most of the migrant families of today have never known the security of anything other than seasonal work, whether on a farm or some other place. Some have been raised on welfare for two generations. Some have no legal residence or have never voted, although they, their parents, and their grandparents were born in the United States. Others have never gone to school one day of their lives, and therefore their educational level and training in skills are lower than those of the farm workers of the Depression.

Although there have been marked improvements in living and working conditions of migrants since the years of the Depression, exploitation, discrimination, poor housing, inadequate transportation, as well as other conditions detrimental to family life still

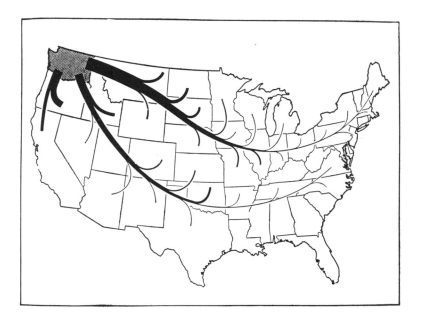

Fig. 2. States of origin of migrants (shown as percentage, by states, of total number reported) to Washington, 1932-36. (Source: Washington State Agricultural Experiment Station.)

exist. There are still conditions that might well have been lifted from the pages of either *Grapes of Wrath* or *Factories in the Field*. Numerous investigations of the conditions of farm migrants have been made since 1939; countless articles have been written; statements of blame have been made and refuted. Even in the 1970s, when those who say such conditions do not exist and when those who claim they do have ceased their accusations, the migrant laborer and his family remain the most disadvantaged of any working segment of the American population, and the American Indian farm workers the most disadvantaged of all.

My Firsthand Knowledge of Migrant Workers

Awareness of the working and living conditions of farm employees is not a new experience for my husband and me. Although we were born in different sections of the country, since our early childhoods we have both known farm workers who represented various cultures.

My husband was born on a truck garden farm in the Midwest. His grandfather and father pioneered in muckland farming in southern Michigan, raising onions, carrots, celery, and head lettuce. Even in the years before World War I, his family had established a reputation for producing unusual vegetables and catering to the Oriental market of Chicago. In the beginning their employees were single men and an occasional tenant family; later their workers, including entire families, were day employees from a nearby city. At that time in the Midwest, most of these "seasonal stable agricultural workers" did not have the same stigma generally applied to migrant workers. The day workers were often nextdoor neighbors or individuals who returned year after year to work for the same farmer. Known to the grower's family, they were accepted because next week the grower's son might be employed in the harvest on a neighbor's farm. Many of these Midwest farmers were poor immigrants themselves or were the sons or grandsons of immigrants who had fled a war-torn Europe in the early years of this century. Some were even recruited to the Midwest to work as farm laborers in the sugar beets.[7]

My first introduction to migratory farm labor was in the wheat lands of Montana. The migrant workers who came to the grain fields of the Great Plains were unattached men and teenage boys.[8] These people referred to each other as "cats." The term *cat* meant a worker who was well fitted to some occupational subculture; for example, a hep cat was a worker who followed a specific occupation and a straw cat was a bundle feeder on a thrashing machine. The expression was also used to mean the threat of a strike. "Turn the cat loose" came to mean "throw something into the machinery" or sabotage the work.[9]

The people of the area called them "wobs" or "wobblies" because they talked of organized labor and wages. A wob, short for wobbly, was a member of the Industrial Workers of the World (IWW).[10] The word *wobbly* was a Chinese mispronunciation of "IWW" as "I Wobbly Wobbly." I suspect that the word *wobbly* in the grain lands was intended to imply an inebriated or unsteady state because workers in the wheat harvest were said to all be alcoholics. The IWWs of the grain lands[11] talked and sang of strikes, and many were "red" card-carrying members.[12] This labor organization became more commonly associated with the slogan "I Want Whiskey and I Won't Work" because of its strikes, or its threats of strikes and acts of sabotage.[13]

Other times the workers in the grain fields were called "bindle stiffs" because they slept fully clothed and carried their earthly possessions on their person or in a bedroll slung across their backs. A bindle was the actual roll of bedding in which personal possessions were wrapped. *Stiff* referred to any kind of hobo worker; for example, a harvest stiff was a migratory agricultural worker. (*Stiff* could also be used to mean corpse.) These migrant workers were looked upon by their employers as a necessary evil, a part of the harvest. They were not trusted; indeed, they often were feared and disliked.

Like most farm migrants of today, the wobblies of yesterday were not part of the community. They were strangers to those for whom they worked. Sometimes they were escorted out of the county by the sheriff and not missed until the next harvest. They were needed and used. They were neither wanted nor liked. No one even knew them or cared to know them.

The Dust Storms[14]

I vividly recall when an empire from north Texas to the Canadian border was laid waste in the most severe drought of the century. Had my parents and I not moved from Montana to Michigan shortly before, we too would have been dust-bowl refugees. The ranch we owned in Montana was stripped of fertility and eddied against fence posts and empty buildings, as was the land of our neighbors who remained. Had we not moved to Michigan, we too would have been part of the more than 70,000 workers stranded in the San Joaquin Valley the summer of 1937.[15] One of those workers was a former neighbor of ours, a man who had once owned a thousand acres of the richest wheat land in Montana. He wrote to us, warning, "Stay in Michigan where you are, the golden dream of California is a lie, there are five men here for every available job. Every day we are told, 'if you don't like what you are being paid, quit.' "

The supply and demand of workers in the San Joaquin Valley forced the payment of pickers like this workman downward until it reached an all-time low of seventeen cents a day. It was a wage that enslaved people. It was enough neither to live on nor to leave on. It was only enough to ensure that the workers would stay, hoping conditions might improve. With the winter of 1938 came heavy rains, and over 50,000 migrant workers were still there, camping in tin shelters, cardboard boxes, their stranded automobiles, or whatever they could find that offered some semblance of protection. Some lived under pieces of cloth or canvas nailed to trees.

The Days of the Depression

Although by moving to Michigan we avoided the dust bowl, we did not avoid the Depression. The employment picture in Michigan for young teenagers and for adults past sixty was as bleak as in any section of the country. People were hungry in Michigan as they were in other places, especially if they were outsiders, newcomers, or those who were too old[16] or had no prior work experience in factories and therefore were not eligible for employment in those factories operating with skeleton crews. The only way such people could buy food was to take whatever odd jobs they could find, often in fields and orchards, even when such work had not been their prior employment. Children worked to help support their families or else to buy their own school books and supplies. By thirteen I was working full days in the cherries and blueberries instead of the occasional half day picking strawberries on shares for my mother to make jam, as I did at ten. In the mid-1930s teenagers, some even younger than the legal age of sixteen, dropped out of school to work full time when the necessity of food, fuel, and rent monies or the support of aging parents became more pressing than any long-range dream of a college education. I too dropped out of ninth grade for that reason and enrolled in evening school and correspondence courses. After two years of working days and going to school at night, I dropped my education altogether for a time.

As newlyweds in the late years of the 1930s, my husband and I worked full time in the crops—not, at that time in our lives, out of research interest, but out of necessity. We picked strawberries, topped onions, and bagged potatoes behind the diggers. We stood on ladders in the apple orchard until the last of the apples was picked in November. Harvesting huckleberries, we stood ankle deep in marsh waters, knocking the ripe fruit with a quick tap of our fingers into bushel baskets tied around our necks. Late at night we poured those huckleberries over a flannel-covered frame and sorted out the leaves and tiny sticks and boxed the fruit for delivery at the early market on our way to the marsh the next morning.

In those days, when we were barely out of our teens ourselves, we knew we were poor, but it was a relative experience. Practically everyone we knew was nearly as poor, although many had not always been so poor. We saw around us those who became disheartened and gave up after long years of struggle and accepted welfare as a way of life, never again motivated to take care of themselves. "The country owes me a living," they said. We saw others become bitter, apathetic, or cynical, losing all faith in God, mankind, or themselves. We saw still others for whom a good education became a means of fighting hunger, both physical and emotional, who saw education as a means of denying that for years they had not known even the bare necessities of life.

In those days of the late Depression, rural Americans all over the country, regardless of race or nationality, were living in shacks without running water, plumbing, or electricity, and sometimes with only an earthen floor. There was need everywhere for more adequate housing, for employment and higher wages, for health and educational services, and even for food. The plight of the agricultural worker was not greatly different from the plight of many others, including farmers and even some growers. There was not, at that time, the sharp contrast between the experiences of the farm worker and nonfarm worker that there would be thirty years later. The great Depression following the crash of 1929 was never solved. It terminated with the attack on Pearl Harbor and the entry of the United States into World War II.[17]

After the Depression

Sometimes we worked for my husband's relatives, other times for neighbors, and still other times for strangers. Sometimes we worked with crews of day-haul workers who walked or hitchhiked from nearby cities. These day-haul workers were mainly Polish-American, Irish-American, and Hungarian-American women, children, and old men. They came to the fields to supplement grocery orders that they received from the welfare department, or else they came to the fields to avoid relief (the 1930's term for public assistance). Sometimes we worked with crews of Chicanos from Texas or Arkansas-Blacks who were part of the central migration stream.

It was hard work, and at night we were weary, but it was a happy time of laughter and songs and a feeling of comradeship. The two of us stood together against a world that suddenly had sunk into the depths of an economic quagmire. Because we were making it on our own, with our own hands, there was also a feeling of accomplishment. We had a firm conviction that for us the only way out was up, because it would not be possible to become much poorer. The medical expenses for the birth of our first child were paid with potatoes raised on shares and traded for service to the hospital and the doctor; the medical expenses for our second child were paid with huckleberries sold at the produce market. Later, huckleberries from that same marsh, together with red raspberries, green beans, and gladioli, paid for tutors and tuition for me to complete the high-school education that I had interrupted to work full time. Money from the same work sources paid most of my tuition to two colleges, which in turn enabled me to further my college education for advanced degrees.

The national work situation improved with World War II; wages spiraled. Former farm workers, both migrant and local, began to find employment in factories, in shipyards, in offices, with transportation lines, and as security guards for new munitions plants. Many men and women went into various branches of the armed services and received specialized training there that would provide for them a new way of life. We, too, with professional training, began a different way of life not related to seasonal farm labor.

The Postwar Period

Our next direct contact with the conditions of migrant farm workers came in 1950 when we spent some time as part of a research project among the vegetable harvesters in the Glades of Florida and with cotton workers in Georgia, Alabama, and Mississippi. We again saw the conditions under which migrant farm laborers lived in 1955 while making a study of child welfare needs in the Midwest. As part of our research we talked with Chicanos in the sugar beets of central Michigan. Although a few camps in that area provided for the safety and health of families, the majority of the sugar beet workers in the mid-1950s lived in shacks, old farm houses, and odds and ends of buildings that were not structurally sound enough for any other purpose.

Materials provided the delegates to the 1960 White House Conference on Children and Youth gave national statistics on migrant farm families. Although the data were fragmentary, they pointed out that the low earning capacity of such parents caused them to regard the work of their children as essential and therefore made migrant children the "largest reservoir of legal and illegal child labor in America." We read the materials with interest in preparation for the Washington, D. C., conference, but none of the information was new. We had heard and seen it all before. Some of it we ourselves had lived. It had been ten years since we sat in a cockroach-infested kitchen in Pahokee, Florida; five years since we stepped gingerly over the rotting floorboards of shacks near Mt. Pleasant, Michigan; twenty years since we had supported ourselves and our two babies by picking apples; and twenty-three years since the bloody riots in the California fields and orchards.[18] During those years working and living conditions for the rest of rural America had changed. For the migrant farm laborer changes had been few and had come, for the most part, grudgingly.

Our Renewed Interest in Migrant Research

After the 1960 White House Conference, we began to have a renewed interest in the conditions of farm workers. We wanted to see firsthand if conditions around the country were as bad as reported. We wanted to see if they were as bad as we had known them personally in the 1930s, '40s, and '50s, or if they had improved as our own personal conditions had improved. We wanted to know how the migrant workers of the 1960s differed from farm workers we had known previously.

These and other questions, both professional and personal, were the motivating factors that led us to take a year and nine months of our lives, financed from our own earnings, to make firsthand observations of the conditions of migrant farm workers and other low-income families in various parts of the United States. The first phase of our study covered fifty-four weeks, from late August 1963 to mid-September 1964. The second phase covered the period from March 1965 to January 1966, six months of which my husband conducted research while I returned to my position on the faculty at Michigan State University. Since the late 1960s we have lived in the deep South, where we have continued our involvement with farm workers.

In the many years of our observations of and direct relationship to the agricultural picture in the United States, we have seen firsthand the contradictions that make it difficult to get an accurate understanding of migrant agricultural workers. We have heard growers, farm superintendents, and process foremen say of migrant farm workers, "None of them are capable of making decisions for themselves. We know better than they do what is good for them." We have heard migrant workers described as alcoholics; as dirty bums; as so destructive that they could not be provided with decent housing; as ignorant animals who were willing to start a fight without provocation; as lazy, tricky, and so dishonest that they would stand beans on end to cover weeds in the bottom of hampers and baskets. We have heard such accusations about farm workers, and we have seen all this behavior on the part of individual farm workers even as we have seen such behavior on the part of individual nonfarm workers. Although we saw such behavior among some workers, it was not the behavior of all, anymore than such behavior is true of the entire population of any community.

The irony in all this is that sometimes the very employer who refers in such derogatory terms to his migrant employees was himself (or his father was) referred to in the same language when he first came to an area as a newcomer, as a foreign worker, or even as an immigrant or refugee. The underlying psychological factor could be that the migrant worker is an unconscious reminder to the employer of what he once experienced and hopes to forget. The migrant worker and his poverty may also be a threat to the grower. There is ever-present in the life of the grower the possibility of crop failures and the unconscious fear of being reduced to poverty. This can be a strong unconscious fear, especially on the part of a grower who has himself risen from poverty.

The employer may also get emotional satisfaction from feeling superior to his employees. His sense of superiority may be enhanced when he can reduce others to the lowest possible denominator by saying, "They are lazy, dishonest; they live like animals; they are not appreciative of the things I work hard to provide for them." Such an employer may gain emotional satisfaction by saying, "I made it on my own; I pulled myself up by my bootstraps; therefore, anyone who really wants to can, especially if they use me as their model." In making such statements an employer is more likely to be responding to his own emotional need to hurt others for the humiliation he once knew, or to hit back at those who do not appreciate him as a person than he is to be describing the migrant worker who harvests his crops.

Our Involvement

We were warned by well-meaning friends and acquaintances as we started our 1963 trip that we were endangering our lives. When we returned from what they assumed to be our first encounter with migrant farm laborers, they asked, "How could you bring yourselves to live with that class of people; how could you talk to them?" Further exploration brought their real questions: "How could you communicate with those who are so illiterate, so ignorant, so mentally degenerate?"

We had very little trouble with communication. There were few barriers, even with people who represented a cross section of humanity. We made certain that they had an opportunity to see us in camp, in the trucks, or working next to them in the fields before we tried to do anything more than speak. Much of our communication was nonverbal. There were some who mistrusted us, as they mistrusted anyone they did not know. Their mistrust was transmitted at the nonverbal level by their attitudes and their behavior. The Indians on the reservations who knew our identity and the reason we were there were the most suspicious; they told us that they did not trust what we might say about the information they shared with us. They tested us daily. They had come through too many long years of painful experiences with members of the dominant race not to be suspicious of anyone who was not of their own tribe or culture.

We knew long before we left home that it is easier for most migrant farm workers to talk about things that concern them when they are busy with their hands. Riding in a bus, hanging clothes on a barbwire fence, picking strawberries, or sorting apples from a conveyor belt were the times we found most people to be comfortable about talking of their fears, hopes, and dreams. We had little trouble communicating because our total way of life was communication. We worked together. Sometimes we ate together. We all traveled or lived under the same conditions. We sweated in the sun, we shivered in the rain and the snow. We too were a family of the open road. The key to communication, we knew, was whether we could do our share of the work, whether we could keep up the pace, whether we could do our work well enough to be healthy competition but not too well to be threatening. Could we mind our business and respect the privacy of others, even in the midst of a lack of privacy? These were the real tests of communication.

The major difference between us and those with whom we worked was that two of us knew there was another way of life to which we could return at any time. We knew there was a distant university campus and an insurance business where life styles were quite different from the trucks, the fields, and the farm camps. Because we had known both ways of life, we were aware that once we too had lived in the daily state of helplessness we saw around us. It was out of this sort of poverty we had once struggled. We knew we could return to the world of affluence and material things, but we also knew why we could emotionally understand the world of the farm worker to which we had returned. We knew at any point in our fifty-four weeks of travel that we could change our clothing and our pattern of speech and open doors which were tightly closed to those who knew only the full-time work of farm migration. At times we were filled with rage by this knowledge. It seems so unfair that only when one has established a respected reputation based on education, publications, positions, or material possessions can he or she become part of the decision-making process; and yet those who live with a problem may be able to make a more accurate assessment of needs and solutions than those who merely have read about the problem. Still the latter is the one usually acclaimed as the true authority.

This was the major difference between us and those in the field, bus, or truck. We had, over the years, established ourselves as part of the decision-making process. We knew the rights and privileges that laws provide for workers, even in agriculture; our fellow migrants were still at the experiencing level. They often did not realize how badly they were exploited. Because we did know these things, we were more sensitive to the hurts, indifferences, and man's inhumanity to man than were many of those who saw one harvest following another as their only way of life and did not always realize how deprived they were on the little end of the American horn of plenty. And because we could not betray our professional identity to those with whom we worked, we had to act as if we did not see what our eyes had taken in or understood what our ears had heard.

What We Found

In our year of travel as migrant workers we found certain conditions worse than we had expected, mostly because the contrast between the migrant farm worker and the nonmigrant worker in the 1960s was greater than it had been in the 1940s and 1930s. We found in the 1960s that the attitude toward farm work, especially stoop labor, was more negative than it had been in earlier periods. The post-World War II stress on college educations and white-collar jobs had given manual labor lower prestige and the harvesting of crops the lowest of all.

The composition of migrant streams had also changed. Although the same races and ethnic groups were involved, greater numbers of Chicanos were finding their way into areas like Florida where migrant workers at one time were predominately Black. Black workers, in turn, were moving from the eastern stream into parts of the central stream where there had been few, if any, Black workers in the past.

We found that conditions like housing, education, and standard of living had improved more for nonmigrants in that period of time than for migrants. Labor unions, policy-making groups, and state laws had brought higher wages and better working conditions into factories, coal mines, and many mills. Workers employed in such places were covered by insurance, sick leave, and benefits pertaining to vacations and retirement. The results were reflected in role expectations and attitudes toward workers. In a work world where an occupational field—agriculture—is omitted from many of the benefits of social security, workmen's compensation, and health and accident insurance, workers are divided into those treated as first-class citizens and those treated as if they were not citizens at all. For example, factory workers receive such fringe benefits automatically, but agricultural workers are seldom if ever even considered and may in some cases even be omitted or counted out entirely by laws which cover all other occupations.

This, then, was how conditions differed in 1963-64 from what we had seen during our first experience with farm workers. In the chapters that follow, I will give examples of working and living conditions which illustrate how migrant farm laborers are now viewed as a result of their occupation and how, within that occupation, they may also experience additional discrimination because of age, race, or sex. Much of this discrimination began with dehumanizing experiences in the early history of this nation. Some of these will be discussed in the next two chapters in an historical perspective of social determinants that have molded role expectations among the rural poor.

NOTES

1. (New York: Viking Press, 1939).

2. (Boston: Little, Brown, and Co., 1939).

3. Caroline Bird, *The Invisible Scar,* Pocket Books (New York: Simon and Schuster, Inc., 1967).

4. Arthur F. Raper and Ira De A. Reid, *Sharecroppers All* (Chapel Hill, N.C.: University of North Carolina Press, 1941).

5. McWilliams, *Factories in the Field* (Boston, Mass.: Little, Brown and Co., 1939), p. 308. *Business Week* for July 3, 1937, said that this influx of people looking for work was "one of the greatest interstate migrations since the gold rush." California attempted to cope with the situation by keeping people out of the state with a border patrol. Police were stationed at various points of entry and were ordered to stop every car that looked as if it might contain "unemployables." If the people could not produce proof of work, they were turned back and not allowed to come into California. The *Monthly Labor Review* for December 1936 reported repercussions of this blockade as far east as El Paso, Texas. A recent publication on this subject is Walter J. Stein, *California and the Dust Bowl Migration* (Westport, Conn.: Greenwood Press, Inc., 1973).

6. See Paul S. Taylor, *Mexican Labor in the United States: Imperial Valley* (1928), *Mexican Labor in the United States: South Texas* (1930), *Mexican Labor in the United States: Chicago and the Calumet Region* (1932), and *Mexican Labor in the United States: Migration Statistics* (1929-34)—all are University of California Publications in Economics (Berkeley, Calif.: University of California Press). See also Charles A. Thompson, "What of the Bracero?" *Survey,* June 1925; and California, State of, Department of Industrial Relations, *Mexicans of California* (California: The Department, 1930).

California farm journals referred to 1920 as the "Mexican Harvest," indicating that half of all migrant labor employed that year was Mexican.

Pacific Rural Press for February 13, 1926, reported that "Mr. S. Parker Frisselle was sent to the United States Congress that year by the growers of the San Joaquin Valley to 'get us Mexicans (workers) and keep them out of our schools and out of our social problems.' " McWilliams describes further how these Mexican workers were viewed and treated in the decade of 1920 to 1930 in *Factories in the Field,* pp. 125-30.

7. Carey McWilliams, *Ill Fares the Land* (New York: Barnes and Noble, Inc., 1967), pp. 257-58.

8. Melvyn Dubofsky describes these workers thus: "Every summer thousands of men and boys would fan out from Chicago, Kansas City, Sioux City, and the twin cities of Minneapolis and St. Paul to follow the wheat harvest from Texas north across the plains to southern Canada. Like migratory farm workers everywhere, they worked long hours for minimal pay and execrable room and board. Most of them traveled by riding the rods or side-door coach, which subjected them to the extortions and the brutalities of trainmen and railroad detectives. On the freights they rode and in the jungles they infested, the wheat harvesters fell prey to holdup men and professional gamblers who, as E. F. Doree put it, 'harvested the harvesters.' After a summer in the field, these migratories often returned to the city for the winter as poor as they had left." *We Shall Be All,* Quadrangle Books (Chicago: New York Times Co., 1969), p. 313.

See also E. F. Doree, "Gathering the Grain," *International Socialist Review,* XV (June 1915), 740-43, and Philip Taft, "The I.W.W. in the Grain Belt," *Labor History,* I (Winter 1960), 53-67.

9. See "Language of the Migratory Worker" (hobo, lumberjack, and mining terms), appendix to *Rebel Voices, an I.W.W. Anthology*, ed. by Joyce L. Kornbluh (Ann Arbor, Mich.: University of Michigan Press, 1964), pp. 405-8.

10. The Industrial Workers of the World was a revolutionary labor organization formed in 1905 in Chicago at what was called the Continental Congress of the Working Class. The attempt of the organization was to combine into one "Big Union" all wage workers: textile workers; grain, fruit, or vegetable harvesters or processors; lumberjacks or miners; section gang workers on railroads or on ship docks; hotel or restaurant workers; or construction workers. As long as they were part of the working class they could be members of the IWW. For more information on the organization's early development see *Proceedings of the First Convention of the I.W.W.*, reported by W. E. McDermutt and revised by William E. Trautmann, secretary of the convention (New York: Labor News Co., 1908).

The preamble of the IWW organization as amended by the 1908 convention states, "The working and the employing classes have nothing in common. There can be no peace so long as hunger and want are found among millions of working people and the few, who make up the employing class, have all the good things of life. . . . Between these two classes the struggle must go on until the workers of the world organize as a class, take possession of the earth and the machinery of production, and abolish the wage system. . . . It is the historic mission of the working class to do away with capitalism. The army of production must be organized, not only for the every-day struggle with capitalists, but also to carry on production when capitalism shall have been overthrown. By organizing industrially, we are forming the structure of the new society within the shell of the old." From the *Proceedings of the 1908 I.W.W. Convention* as reported in the IWW *Industrial Union Bulletin*, November 7, 1908.

The organization was a protest against low wages, long hours, and inadequate housing and living conditions for blue collar workers. The flame of dissatisfaction with working conditions spread among all agricultural workers. The unrest of one worker was contagious until many a hired man, fruit picker, or harvest hand was caught up in the frenzy and joined the organization or took part in a strike simply because he was identified with the working class rather than because he personally had experience with an employer who mistreated him.

In California the IWW was an influential organization until 1912 when the San Diego authorities began to suppress meetings and to stamp out the organization by vigilante tactics. The wobblies staged a demonstration, the object being to force arrest and thus attract national attention to the conditions of agricultural workers. They were physically beaten and jailed. Some died in jail.

The *San Diego Tribune* of March 4, 1908, described the general feeling of the community toward members of the IWW: "Hanging is none too good for them and they would be better off dead for they are the waste material of creation and should be drained off into the sewer of oblivion, there to rot like any other excrement."

Joyce Kornbluh continues the saga:

"Finally, the Agricultural Workers' Industrial Union was completely disorganized when the Federal government cracked down on the I.W.W. in the fall of 1917 and arrested more than one hundred wobblies around the country on charges of violating the Federal Espionage Act.

"Legal suppression of the I.W.W. continued during the postwar period. Throughout the country, I.W.W. organizers and members were arrested and jailed under the terms of state syndicalism laws passed as postwar emergency measures. Postwar demobilization and unemployment created a surplus labor supply which further weakened the union organization.

"However, meeting in September, 1920, the 'one-ten cats' resolved to launch another organizing drive in the Midwest wheat fields. They had spotty success. In Colby, Kansas, for example, wobbly harvesters controlled the town's labor supply for a week when they collectively refused to work at the going wage rates. In some areas the harvest drive was quite successful through the mid-twenties. Elsewhere, however, mechanized harvesters were replacing mobile harvest hands. The combine, developed as a labor-saving device during the war, cut and threshed grain in a single operation. Five men did the work of three hundred and twenty." *Rebel Voices,* p. 233.

Until the early 1930s, however, the fear influence of the IWW could still be felt through the grain lands of Montana. The wobblies' songs, when heard in the fields or the railroad jungles, made growers uneasy lest sometime or other migrant farm laborers, like industrial workers, would be successful in their attempts to unionize and would have their bargaining boards and grievance committees.

11. Dubofsky says, "Much more important to the future of the I.W.W. than the exciting and explosive incidents in Wheatland (California), Butte (Montana), and Salt Lake City (Utah) was the tedious agitating and organizing the Wobblies had begun among the migratory harvesters in the Plains States." *We Shall Be All,* p. 313. Robert L. Tyler points out that "although Wobblies could be found spreading their gospel of discontent among migrant farm workers and hardrock miners, they worked most numerously in the logging camps and secondarily, the lumber mills of the Pacific Northwest." *Rebels of the Woods: The I.W.W. in the Pacific Northwest* (Eugene, Ore.: University of Oregon Press, 1967), p. 5.

12. There were many songs composed by various groups related in different ways to the IWW organization. These songs were printed annually in song books and were sung to the tunes of other well-known songs. The songs covered all kinds of subjects. A few pertaining to the grain harvest were "Harvest War Song" (tune, "Tipperary"); "When You Wear That Button" (tune, "When You Wore a Tulip"); "Pesky Kritters" (tune, "Arrah Wannah"); and "Down in Harvest Land" (tune, "Down in Bom Bom Bay").

Red became the symbolic color of the IWW. The membership cards were red; the standard of the organization was scarlet; and "The Red Flag," the official anthem of the British Labour Party, was first published in the IWW *Industrial Union Bulletin* on July 25, 1908, and became one of the most popular and well-known radical songs in this country.

13. The Industrial Workers of the World endorsed direct action, the general strike, and all forms of sabotage. The word *sabotage* first appeared in the IWW press in *Solidarity,* June 4, 1910. Walker C. Smith indentified it as "to hit the employer in his vital spot, his heart and soul, or in other words his pocketbook." *Sabotage, Its History, Philosophy, and Function* (Spokane, Wash.: By the Author, 1913), p. 8.

"Sabotage included actions which would disable machinery, slacken production, spoil the product, or reduce company profits by telling the truth about the product." Elizabeth Curley Flynn, *Sabotage: The Conscious Withdrawal of the Workers' Industrial Efficiency* (Cleveland, Ohio: I.W.W. Publishing Bureau, 1915), p. 5.

Sabotage symbols for the IWW became a wooden shoe and a black cat and appeared constantly in wobbly illustrations and cartoons. Stickers and circulars showed a hunched black cat showing its claws. The words "sab cat," "kitten," "fix the job" were used to suggest or threaten striking on the job, sabotage, and direct action. (If the reader is interested, many of these cartoons may be found in copies of the *Industrial Worker* and *Solidarity* that appeared between 1910 and 1925.) One example of both the black cat and the wooden shoes appeared in *Solidarity,* September 30, 1916.

The subject of sabotage by IWW workers in the grain fields was used by Zane Grey for a novel, *The Desert of Wheat* (New York: Harper and Bros., 1919), pp. 136-56.

14. See Margaret Bourke-White, *Portrait of Myself* (New York: Simon and Schuster, Inc., 1963), pp. 107-10 for a vivid picture of the dust bowl as seen through the eyes of an internationally known photographer.

15. McWilliams, *Factories in the Field,* pp. 314-23.

16. See Bird, *The Invisible Scar,* p. 188, for those who were discriminated against even by government programs supposed to aid those in need. She states, "The chief beneficiaries of the New Deal were farmers (who still owned their land), union labor, homeowners, bank depositors, debtors— people who had money or jobs to lose." She goes on to identify those discriminated against as "migrants, itinerents; part-time, domestic, or sea- sonal workers who were not covered by Social Security, minimum wages, or unemployment insurance . . . people certified as 'unemployable' because of physical, mental or educational handicaps, farmers too sick, old, poor or ignorant to be risks for loans, big families, sharecroppers, tenants, farm laborers, 'unorganizable' labor."

Contrary to popular opinion, the United States prior to the Depression was not an affluent country for the common man. Incomes were low, the majority of people were poor, and many lived in poverty and pauperism. In 1904 Robert Hunter said that 10 million Americans were in dire need. At that time, his estimate was regarded as exaggerated, but later studies showed it to be extremely conservative. In 1919 the National Bureau of Economic Research estimated that 86 percent of all American families earned less than $2,000 a year. In 1919 the government regarded this income as the least on which a family of five could maintain itself in decent and healthful sur- roundings.

The rich made more money after the First World War, but the poor failed notably to improve their condition. If the income of families in the United States could have been equally divided in 1928, each family of five would have had more than $3,750 a year. As it was, 60 percent of all American families had incomes of less than $2,000, receiving only about one-fourth of the total national income, while the richest 1.2 percent of U.S. families received about the same proportion of the national income. Even in 1928 and 1929, before the Depression, 70 percent of American families did not have income enough to buy sufficient food to maintain good health, and 90 percent could not purchase enough food to constitute what the government itself regarded as a desirable diet.

In the years of the Depression (1930-41), the situation grew worse. In 1933 it was estimated that 12 to 17 million persons were unemployed, and 50 million were living in a state of poverty. Studies made in 1935 show an almost incredible increase of poverty after 1929. As late as the year 1936, two-thirds of all American families were living at or below the poverty line, and more than 10 percent were in a state of pauperism. Government relief kept many families from actual starvation, but the incomes of tens of millions of Americans were below the poverty level.

Even in 1942 millions of Americans were still living far below a decent standard. Labor department studies of 33 cities that year, based on the WPA budget of 1935 brought up to date for December 1941, showed that $29 a week was the minimum income requirement for a worker's family of four. Yet, at that time, the treasury department revealed that 3,324,000 workers were earning only from $5 to $10 a week; 4,975,000 from $10 to $15; 10,747,000 from $20 to $30. In other words, millions of families at the time of Pearl Harbor had insufficient income for bare subsistence.

17. Bird, *ibid.*, pp. 253-54, stated it this way: "Americans hated war, but this one felt like a war of liberation. For millions of men, idle at home, the war meant a job, and a job meant an end to the degrading trade of time for pennies to which so many of them felt reduced. . . . Getting a job was release from pettiness and boredom as well as from privation. It was like getting out of jail. For millions imprisoned by the Depression and poverty, the war meant getting out of the house, out of town, out where the action was. They were needed, and the work was not made up to keep them occupied. . . . Men whose pride had been damaged by unemployment were restored to manhood."

18. McWilliams, *Factories in the Field*, pp. 243-63.

PART II

Forces That Shaped the Territorial Boundaries of the Rural Poor

Historical Events and Man- Made Forces

In the orchard there was a smell of wet bark and the faint promise that winter could not last forever. She knew it would not be long before the trees would put out leaves. And thinking this she felt glad, knowing that like these aged trees, people who lived close to the land became young again with each spring.

Ellen Bromfield Geld, 20th century
Brazilian authoress
A Timeless Place

3

Panorama of Rural America

Writing in the middle of the last century in England, Charles Dickens could well have been prophesying the future instead of describing the events of his country in his own day when he wrote in *A Tale of Two Cities,* "It was the best of times; it was the worst of times. It was the age of wisdom; it was the age of foolishness." He could have been describing the present and the current problems facing rural America. If I might paraphrase Dickens's contrasts, I would add: this is an age of compassion for other people; this is an age of apathy and indifference.

This is the best of times. Never in the history of the world has a

Some of this chapter is from a paper presented at a seminar for the Fruit and Vegetable Industry sponsored by the United States Department of Labor and Michigan State University Center for Rural Manpower and Public Affairs, Department of Agricultural Engineering and Department of Agricultural Economics, held July 21-23, 1969 at Michigan State University, East Lansing, Michigan and published as "Sociology of Rural Deprivation: Implication for the Fruit and Vegetable Industry" in B. F. Cargill and G. E. Rossmiller, editors, *Fruit and Vegetable Harvest Mechanization: Manpower Implications* (East Lansing, Mich.: Center for Rural Manpower and Public Affairs, Michigan State University, 1969), pp. 269-88.

nation had such wealth, knowledge, fertile soil, crop yield, educational and employment opportunities, natural resources, and ease of transportation as that currently found in the United States; never have conditions here been as conducive to abundant rural living as they are today.

Yet this is the worst of times. Automation and mechanical harvesters have reduced the need for agricultural workers. Limited education and job experience make those who desperately need employment an overplus on the manpower market. But at the same time, farmers and growers are having difficulty obtaining dependable employees to manage farms, to work the fields, to operate or repair the mechanical equipment, or even to pick the crops. Small farm owners cannot afford to pay their employees the minimum wage or industrial hourly rate current in their communities. But farm workers cannot afford to live on what they can earn in agricultural employment unless their salaries meet the minimum wage level. It is ironic in the face of surplus food or even wasted and unharvested fruits and vegetables that the continued rising cost of living coupled with inadequate income cause many rural Americans to be malnourished and others to be hungry. It is even more ironic that many of those rural Americans who live in the greatest poverty, who are untrained, illiterate, unemployed, and even hungry, are not eligible (because of age, degree of physical limitation, or age of dependents) for the categorical welfare services that exist for them.

America has only recently discovered its rural poor, the majority of whom have known poverty for a long time—a poverty more complicated and more difficult to correct than that found in any city ghetto. Although an increasing sincere compassion for the problems of poverty exists, often a lack of understanding of the real causes and the extent of rural poverty prevails. This results in efforts to devise instant remedies or to apply programs designed for other populations or other parts of the country, treatment approaches that are now widespread phenomena in America. When such methods are applied to rural poverty they do not work, for there is no instant solution. Because rural areas have uniquely different characteristics, programs designed for urban populations are not usually applicable in rural areas. The poverty problems of rural America were a long time in the making. Furthermore, they are covered with a thick veneer of apathy and indifference, both on the part of the poverty-stricken and those who represent the more affluent parts of our society. Solving these problems may take a long time unless as much concerted effort is directed toward them as is being directed toward the problems of the urban ghettos (whose situations may not be as complex or as rooted in past history as those in remote rural areas).

The poverty problems of rural America are related to a series of historical events and man-made forces. They hinge on attitudes and values, on deep-seated prejudices along racial, sexual, religious, and political lines in counties and districts where change comes more slowly than it does in an urban setting. The purpose of this chapter is to take a closer look at these causative factors as they apply to various rural ethnic groups and to see how historical events and man-made forces are reflected in present-day rural poverty and how they may still influence the way individuals cope with every-day living.

Before we examine the man-made forces that have affected the lives and shaped the personalities of large numbers of our rural population, we need to identify what we mean by that nonhomo-geneous segment of Americans referred to as rural residents. (Figure 3 shows that since 1915 America has been more urban than rural.) For the purpose of this book the United States Census Bureau's definition of rural population is being used. It classifies all individuals not living in urbanized areas or in towns of 2,500 or more as rural residents. The 1970 Census found that 26.6 percent of the population of the United States, or 53,886,996 people, were identified as living in such rural areas.[1] (Figure 4 shows the 1970 population density by states.) Only about one-fourth of those individuals identified as rural actually live on farms or ranches;[2] the remainder live in small towns, villages, hamlets, residential suburban settlements, clusters of houses along highways, or in isolated dwellings scattered over the countryside.

Housing

The lack of homogeneity of the rural population is further illustrated by the style, location, and condition of the housing in which they live. Houses may be white-columned, antebellum plan-

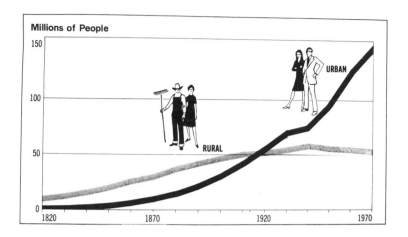

Fig. 3. Urban and rural population in the United States, 1920-70. (Source: United States Bureau of the Census.)

tation manors; tar-paper shacks; rambling two-story wood structures with gingerbread facades; yankee-frame constructions whose weathered sidings have never known a coat of paint; brick ranches or trilevel moderns; cape cods; log cabins whose cracks between the logs are chinked with concrete mud; trailers; corrugated metal sheds; palm-thatched chickees; tents; flat-roofed concrete Spanish *haciendas*; or even junked cars. The house may have been designed and constructed by a nationally known architect or built by the owner himself from cement blocks, used lumber, or salvaged brick, or it may be attached to a barn or other outbuilding, if not surrounded by a fence with an ornate wrought-iron gate. Such a house may be located in a remote section of the Bad Lands, on an Indian reservation, in the cut-over wooded area of the upper Midwest, along the ridge of a mountain, in a hidden cove, in the alkali flats, on the back waters of a river, in a swamp bog, along a red clay road, or within sight of a large city. The rural home may

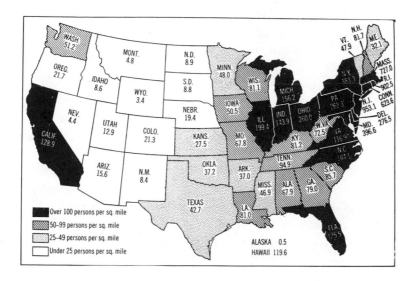

Fig. 4. Density of population per square mile, United States, 1970. (Source: United States Bureau of the Census.)

be in excellent repair or collapsing from neglect and the onslaught of the elements—wind, rain, snow, termites, and oxidation. It may be owned by the occupant, rented, or provided as part of an employment agreement. Regardless of where it is located, it is apt to be substandard. Two-thirds of the nation's substandard housing in 1970 was in rural areas.

Race

Although the rural population is predominately white, 48,975,735 rural poor being of that race, nearly 5 million are nonwhite. The largest number, 4,212,971, are Black. Those remaining—fewer than 1 million—represent several races: 436,992 are Indians; 67,639 are Japanese; 16,283 are Chinese; 50,348 are Filipinos; and 127,028 are classified by the United States Bureau of the Census as "other races."[3] The population of rural America also includes all nationalities and religions as well as ethnic groups such as the Spanish-speaking people of the Southwest and the Amish of Pennsylvania and the Midwest.

Extent of Poverty

Although less than 27 percent of Americans now live in rural America, a much higher percentage of them are poor than of those living in urban areas. This percentage is represented by the whites of Appalachia, the deep South, and the cut-over lands of the Midwest, by the Blacks of the rural South, by the Spanish-Americans and Chicanos of the Southwest, and by the Indians on every Indian reservation in the country. In rural counties, 17.5 percent of the people are poor, compared with 10.6 percent in urban areas. For those rural residents actually related to agriculture and classified in the 1970 census as farm residents, the percentage of poor rises to 20.2 percent.[4]

Writing on rural leadership in 1960, Burton Kreitlow and his associates pointed out some of the complex problems that plague agriculture as an industry and account for the reason that the income for individual farmers may be so low. They said:

> The law of supply and demand plays queer tricks on American farmers. . . . The efficient production which helps several million individual farm families to get the highest possible return from a given market in a given year frequently causes a depressive effect on prices at the market itself. A peculiar feature of the farm market, with its relatively inflexible demand, is that it yields a higher gross return to farm producers when that market is not saturated by excessive offerings. A short crop brings a higher total return to the industry than a full or large crop. . . . One road of individual sacrifice hopefully leads to group welfare. The other road of group freedom may lead to individual ruin.[5]

One reason for the disproportionately low incomes of rural people is their educational level, which is not only shorter in duration but also poorer in quality than is the education of urban persons. There are large numbers of functionally illiterate people living in rural sections who cannot follow written instructions or who may not be able to read or write their own names. As a result, the displaced worker, the school dropout, the unemployed, and the underemployed are more prevalent in rural areas.

Writing on the school dropout, Daniel Schreiber states:

> Rural youth receive an average of one year less education than do their urban counterparts. Rural America has more functional illiterates, fewer educational resources, fewer vocational and technical schools, poorer school buildings and lower-paid teachers. In rural America 1.3 million school-age children are not enrolled in school, and schools are ill-equipped to provide counseling and social services.[6]

Farm, rural nonfarm, and small-town persons—all of whom are rural residents—make up the bulk of the stable poor.[7] They are the low-skilled workers who, even when regularly employed, do not have sufficient incomes to care for large families[8] —another characteristic of the rural population. They tend to have larger nuclear families and to count more dependents within the economic family than do urban families. Geographically most of the rural poor of the nation are found in the South.[9]

Table 1 on personal incomes by states shows that, even in 1970, no Southern state was above the national mean average of $3,921 per capita income. Florida, which has the highest per capita income in the Southeast, is twenty-sixth out of fifty states. The Florida average of $3,642 is 67 percent of the average income of Washington, D.C. Mississippi, the poorest state in the nation, had a per capita income of $2,575 in 1970, which is 56 percent of the 1970 average income in Connecticut, the state reporting the highest personal income average in the country.

According to the United States Department of Commerce Bureau of the Census almost one-half of the nation's poor resided in the South as of 1968, and almost 25 percent of the total population of the country lived in that section. In 1959 it was estimated that 18.6 million Southerners, 11.2 million whites, and 7.4 million Blacks lived in poverty; these figures had declined by 1969 to 11.9 million with 6.7 million being white and 5.2 million Black.[10] Of interest to those concerned with rural poverty is the fact that 63 percent of all Blacks and 65 percent of all whites living in poverty in the South resided in rural areas according to the 1970 Census survey.[11]

TABLE 1
Personal Income, by State

Rank in 1970	State	Per Capita Income	
		1970	1950
. . .	District of Columbia	$5,387	$2,221
1	Connecticut	4,586	1,875
2	New York	4,769	1,873
3	New Jersey	4,598	1,834
4	Alaska	4,592	2,385
5	Nevada	4,562	2,019
6	Hawaii	4,527	1,387
7	Illinois	4,502	1,825
8	California	4,426	1,852
9	Massachusetts	4,360	1,633
10	Delaware	4,324	2,131
11	Maryland	4,225	1,602
12	Michigan	4,059	1,700
13	Washington	3,993	1,674
14	Ohio	3,972	1,620
15	Pennsylvania	3,927	1,541
16	Rhode Island	3,902	1,606
17	Minnesota	3,824	1,410
18	Kansas	3,823	1,443
19	Colorado	3,816	1,487
20	Indiana	3,781	1,512
21	Nebraska	3,751	1,491
22	Oregon	3,705	1,620
23	Missouri	3,704	1,431

continued

Rural Migration

Not only is a higher percentage of rural America's poor found in the South, but also most of the urban poor of this country, both in the South and outside the region, have roots in rural America. The majority of the urban poor migrated to southern, northern, eastern, and western cities from the rural South.[12] Therefore, southern rural poverty is a major issue. In the past ten years more than 1.25 million Blacks have left the deep South, the majority from rural areas, and have taken the trail north to cities like New York, Detroit, Seattle, Philadelphia, and Los Angeles in the greatest single-country migration the world has ever seen. Since 1940 this Black migration, from the Sea Islands off the east coast to west of the Mississippi Delta, has amounted to 3.5 million individuals.

Table 1 (*continued*)

Rank in 1970	State	Per Capita Income	
		1970	1950
24	Wisconsin	3,693	1,477
25	Iowa	3,688	1,485
26	Florida	3,642	1,281
27	Virginia	3,607	1,228
28	Arizona	3,591	1,331
29	New Hampshire	3,590	1,323
30	Wyoming	3,556	1,669
31	Texas	3,531	1,349
32	Vermont	3,465	1,121
33	Montana	3,379	1,622
34	Georgia	3,332	1,034
35	Oklahoma	3,312	1,143
36	Maine	3,257	1,185
37	Idaho	3,240	1,295
38	Utah	3,213	1,309
39	North Carolina	3,207	1,037
40	South Dakota	3,165	1,243
41	New Mexico	3,131	1,177
42	Tennessee	3,085	994
43	Kentucky	3,073	981
44	Louisiana	3,049	1,120
45	West Virginia	3,021	1,065
46	North Dakota	2,995	1,263
47	South Carolina	2,936	893
48	Alabama	2,853	880
49	Arkansas	2,791	825
50	Mississippi	2,575	755
U.S.	Average	$3,921	$1,496

Source: U.S. Department of Commerce

In 1974 the trend has reversed: Blacks have been returning to urban areas of the South in numbers almost equal to those leaving. The movement of poor whites from the rural South has become one of the major movements of the 1970s. They are faced with the same situation as earlier migrants.

Although they have poured into the cities, psychologically they have remained in the Southland. They have brought their cultures and their life styles with them and have tried to mold their new experiences to what they knew in the past. Being Southerners, they all have an inheritance of persecution, real or imagined, stemming from the Civil War and the Reconstruction era. The South lost the

war and paid the price but languished under the heel of Yankee
tyranny for more than a decade, while northern adventurers called
carpetbaggers and their southern helpers called scalawags controlled
the state houses of the South, setting up corrupt governments and
burdening the states with huge debts which the people later had to
pay with tax monies. Out of these humiliating experiences came a
regional prejudice toward the North and toward most Yankees,
which has been kept alive through the years and recalled at every
opportunity. Each time it is recalled psychologically, most Southerners feel afresh the insult of Sherman's march to the sea and
Sheridan's march through the Shenandoah Valley. This culturally
transmitted sense of persecution has caused many Southerners,
both Black and white, to feel that their part of the country has
received a raw deal from the federal government and the industrial
North since the days of the Civil War. Thus many Southerners
living in the North keep strong psychological ties to the South,
refusing to think of themselves as anything other than temporary
residents in Yankee territory and dreaming someday of returning
to their rural Southland.

Many Southerners—white and Black, rural and nonrural, lower
and middle class—are also opposed to Northern industry's desire to
move into the rural South where the new plants would provide
needed jobs. They fear that these branches of Northern companies
are interested only in the exploitation of cheap labor and the
South's natural resources; that outsiders are not interested in
building the Southland. These fears are based on a degree of
reality, but the reality may not be that of the present; it may
instead be of the past. These are fears which should be looked at
honestly for what they are and what they do in the present. It is
rural America which will suffer most if there is rejection and a lack
of trust on the part of those who live in rural America, and also if
there is exploitation and a lack of local involvement on the part of
newcomers.

Need for an Historical Perspective

Because of these many factors, the problems of rural America
are not only more complex than those found in urban areas but
service programs are more difficult to design and deliver because
rural communities differ widely, depending upon the residents

involved and the section of the country. If the problems are to be solved it will be necessary not only to understand the magnitude and complexity of present rural poverty, but also to understand the historical perspective. Knowledge of the causes of historical events, such as the reasons why early immigrants came to this country (whether they were refugees fleeing persecution, whether they came for personal freedom, or whether they were brought as slaves or indentured servants—as well as their treatment after they arrived, whether they were treated as equals, as inferior, or as outsiders) may affect how descendants see themselves today and how they react to authority figures. The historical events or man-made forces that most directly affect rural America today are the exploitation and inconsistent treatment of the American Indians, the lack of economic opportunities and indifference toward genera-tions of Chicanos, and slavery and the aftermath of the Civil War with the open, brutal control of Blacks. Other historical and economic factors that still play an important role today and that directly affected more whites than nonwhites include the pater-nalistic system of coal mining communities, mill towns, plantation farming, and agricultural migrant work crews. Also included in historical events are attitudes toward Orientals and the incarcera-tion of the Japanese-Americans in prisoner-of-war camps during World War II.

Regardless of race, the majority of rural Americans have always been poor, but the poor of 150 years ago or even of 25 years ago were vastly different from those who live in rural poverty today. The poor of the past at least had a history of rather constant work patterns. Today's rural poor have very limited work histories, and some have never held jobs or known parents who worked more than an occasional day at a time. Influences such as always being dependent upon others for financial support or the system of control by others which comes from being a peonage of the soil are reflected in the 1970s when an unemployed rural resident—whether a Black, white, Chicano, or Indian—is afraid to accept even a part-time job for fear of being asked to move, of having his rent increased, or of displeasing the man who is looking after him and his family.

All these man-made forces have left imprints, but the most subtle and influential social determinant is *cultural conflict*. Al-though America is made up of numerous cultures, many individuals are being pushed to give up their cultures. These people may be caught between cultures, and psychologically rootless. Under such circumstances some individuals withdraw into their own cultures and live in the past, while others demand that all cultures conform to one.

The Effect of Cultural Pressure

The culture of a society provides the framework within which the members of that society must operate and the standards to which they must conform. Though cultures are always changing, most behavior patterns show considerable continuity, with the result that successive generations exhibit strikingly similar beliefs and attitudes. Within any culture, however, many values and social images are often incompatible and contradictory, especially when an individual is involved in more than one role. When examined independently, the conflicting demands or expectations of each role may be legitimate, but when experienced simultaneously they may produce undue conflict. Robert Merton and Elinor Barber see this as the social state in which a person in any of many roles—such as wife, husband, farmer, parent, or migrant—faces contradictory, normative expectations of attitudes, beliefs, and behavior which specify how any of these roles or statuses should be defined.[13] Each of the contradictory expectations is often as legitimate as the next. For example, a working wife has the demands and expectations of her employer at the same time she has the demands of her marriage and her home and, if she is a mother, the demands of her children. With each role go certain self-expectations concerning how she sees herself functioning in that role as well as society's expectations of how the role should be performed. These two expectations, of self and of society or dominant culture, may conflict, resulting in ambivalence on the part of the individual.

Role expectations produce real conflicts for the individual when the dominant society in which he or she lives presents a different value system from the cultural framework into which he or she was born. In a country like America, where even the dominant culture with its middle-class values is constantly changing, there is often confusion of role expectations resulting in ambivalence for those minorities who feel pressured to conform, change, or deny their own cultures. The more rapid the demand for a new acculturation the greater the stress on the individual.

Result of Rapid Cultural Change

Anthropologists studying primitive peoples have observed that as long as their social institutions function normally they have a zest for living, even when life, like that of the Eskimo in the frozen North or the Pigmies in Central Africa, seems to be one of constant privation and hardship. On the other hand, when some catastrophe occurs, such as a man-made force which undermines the traditional structure of their society and culture, individuals often lose their natural lust for life. What ego strength they had to cope with hardships is weakened, or their defenses are stripped away until they no longer can handle the problems or details of everyday living. Under such circumstances, a people can be so completely obsessed by a sense of their own inferiority that they lose their identity with their own race or nationality. They become almost culture-free and, chameleon-like, take on and reflect other cultures about them. As far as they are permitted to do so, they may begin to imitate or even overidentify with the dominant culture and deny what they have been.[14] This imitation of other cultural patterns is more a pseudopsychological acceptance than it is a real emotional acceptance. A person in this position has a feeling of emotional emptiness, a sense of betrayal in his or her loss, that is very similar to the grief reaction to death. There is a strong sense of being wronged, a deep sense of shame about personal background, and an even stronger sense of inferiority. This individual is experiencing loss of cultural identity.

Devaluation of a Folk Culture

Such loss of cultural identity today is seen in many American Indians, Chicanos, and others whose culture is in conflict with the value system of what has been identified as the American way of life. In the past there has been little concern over the fact that the migrant or newcomer has always been asked to conform to what he comes into and not to try to change what is there. Minorities are expected to conform to the dominant culture's middle-class values, yet the dominant culture is not expected to realize or consider the psychological results of such conformity on minorities. Too often there is a tendency, in this country, for the dominant society to stamp out folk cultures without understanding what this does to the self-identity of individuals born into those folk cultures.

Although the dominant society has a tendency to devalue folk cultures on the basis that they are "old fashioned" or "non-American" and does not consider the psychological damage to individuals experiencing a loss of cultural identity, the dominant society, at the same time, presents a contradictive picture of denial, projection, and displacement[15] that can only be interpreted as a social-class psychological phenomenon. The contradiction is seen in at least two ways:

1. The first area is the concept that the dominant culture takes precedence over any folk culture and, therefore, even the lone migrant of the dominant culture is expected to impose that culture onto Indian reservations, Chicano neighborhoods, or in remote rural areas because, even in the shadow of their own homes, the Indian, the Chicano, the Oriental, the Amish, the Appalachian highlander, and other minorities are expected to conform to the values and life styles of the dominant society.

2. The dominant American society seems intent upon stamping out folk cultures and forcing all Americans to conform to the dominant society, even though that same dominant society has its roots deep in folk cultures and values very similar to those it now is trying to obliterate. This denial of true cultural roots is difficult to comprehend, unless it can be viewed as a psychological phenomenon which is part of the need for cultural supremacy (very similar to the psychological phenomenon of racial or sexual supremacy).

NOTES

1. U.S., Department of Commerce, Bureau of the Census, *Current Population Reports—Population Characteristics,* Series P-20 (Washington, D.C.: Government Printing Office, January 31, 1972).
2. This figure refers only to the place of residence; it does not mean that the

individuals make a livelihood or even a major part of their livelihood from the farm or ranch.

3. U.S., Department of Commerce, Bureau of the Census, *Current Population Reports—Population Characteristics,* Series P-20 (Washington, D.C.: Government Printing Office, April 1972).

4. Cora Cronemeyer, "A Rural Manpower Strategy" (paper for the U.S. Department of Labor, Manpower Administration Rural Manpower Service, June 1971).

5. Burton W. Kreitlow, E.W. Aiton, and Andrew P. Torrence, *Leadership for Action in Rural Communities* (Danville, Ill.: Interstate Printers and Publishers, Inc., 1960). p. 336.

6. Daniel Schreiber, "The Rural School Dropout," in *Rural Youth in Crisis: Facts, Myths, and Social Change,* ed. by Lee G. Burchinal (Washington, D.C.: U.S. Department of Health, Education and Welfare, 1964), p. 131.

7. Nona Y. Glazer and Carol J. Creedon, *Children and Poverty* (Chicago: Rand McNally Co., 1968), p. 132.

8. Herman P. Miller, Special Assistant, Office of the Director, United States Bureau of the Census, states that an examination of the 1963 census figures shows "about two million families (one-fourth of all the poor) were headed by a person who worked full time throughout the year. This figure dramatizes the fact that low wages are still a major cause of poverty in the United States. Increases in aggregate demand and a full employment economy probably would not benefit these families, except perhaps by providing work for wives, many of whom are already overburdened with large families. About one and one-half million family heads worked at full-time jobs, but did not work throughout the year. The poverty of these families is occasioned largely by unemployment or illness. Although today's poor are frequently presented as psychologically or spiritually handicapped, the fact is that about fifty percent of them are headed by a full-time worker whose wages are simply too low to support a family."

Miller goes on to point out: "The closer we get to the very bottom of the income distribution, the more we encounter the hard-core poor whose incomes largely come from outside the labor market and are not necessarily responsive to the national economic growth. Finally, although economic growth tends to reduce poverty by pushing families above the poverty line, it also tends to increase it in a statistical sense by making it possible for the young and the old to maintain their own homes, thereby creating low-income families by fission." "Who Are the Poor?" *The Nation,* June 7, 1965, pp. 609-10.

9. The states of Alabama, Arkansas, Delaware, Florida, Georgia, Kentucky, Louisiana, Maryland, Mississippi, Missouri, North Carolina, South Carolina, Tennessee, Texas, Virginia, and West Virginia are usually identified as the South. While these states (or geographical area, in the case of West Virginia) were the *South* of the Civil War, the South today has no sharp and clear-cut boundaries. Although the Mason-Dixon Line is usually considered the northern boundary of the South, both Maryland and Delaware are more properly thought of as part of the *megalopolis,* which sprawls from Boston to Washington, than of the South. Likewise, west Texas is not part of the South, as much as it is part of the Southwest, and north Missouri is usually considered to be Midwest rather than South. According to the *1972 Rand McNally United States Atlas,* the South includes Alabama, Arkansas, Delaware, District of Columbia, Florida, Georgia, Kentucky, Louisiana, Maryland, Mississippi, North Carolina, South Carolina, Tennessee, Virginia, and West Virginia. Texas is included in the Southwest and Missouri in the

Midwest. The *Rand McNally* definition of the South is the one used throughout this book.

10. U.S., Department of Commerce, Bureau of the Census, *Current Population Reports—Consumer Income,* Series P-60, No. 76 (Washington, D.C.: Government Printing Office, 1970), p. 72.

11. U.S., Department of Commerce, Bureau of the Census, *Current Population Reports—Special Studies,* Series P-23, No. 33 (Washington, D.C.: Government Printing Office, 1970), p. 73.

12. Roger Bearwood, "The Southern Roots of Urban Crisis," *Fortune,* August 1968.

13. Robert K. Merton and Elinor Barber, "Social Ambivalence," in *Sociological Theory, Values and Sociocultural Change,* ed. by Edward A. Tiryakian (New York: Free Press of Glencoe, 1963), pp. 91-120.

14. An example of the psychological phenomenon of what happens when cultures collide is found in James Houston, *The White Dawn* (New York: Harcourt Brace Jovanovich, Inc., 1971). This book is about three marooned New Bedford whaling men thrust upon the culture of the Eskimo. The men introduced new and strange practices into that culture and, as a result, destroyed many aspects of the Eskimo culture, but in turn added nothing that was helpful to the Eskimo living in the far North.

The dynamics of the psychological factor of loss of cultural identity are seen where individuals are ashamed that they came from a folk culture, such as the folk culture of the Indians, Blacks, Mexicans, Appalachians, Puerto Ricans, Chicanos, Orientals, or from the peasant cultures of Europe.

15. *Denial* is a mechanism of defense whereby the individual treats obvious reality factors as if they did not exist. Fantasy is a form of denial.

Projection is a mechanism of defense whereby painful or objectionable effects or ideas are projected outward upon persons or things in the environment and felt by the individual as being outside of himself. This is one of the most primitive types of mechanism, presumably dating from early infancy. In infancy there is a tendency to consider all *good* or pleasurable things as part of the self and all *bad* or painful things as part of the outside world.

Displacement is a mechanism of defense by which an affect (a strong emotion) which was originally attached to one object is displaced to another. As with other mechanisms of defense, the purpose of displacement is to prevent a painfully conscious situation from developing within the ego. The emotion of hate, fear, distrust, or whatever is displaced from an individual or group in a position of retaliation and is directed to a more innocuous object who is weaker or not in a position to hurt back. This latter individual or group is consciously seen as deserving the anger, hate, or fear while the real source of the emotion is buried in the unconscious of the former, who does not recognize it. Scapegoating is a form of displacement. The object of prejudice is always an innocuous object of displacement.

History is studded with tragedies. . . .

Joan Haslip, 20th century English authoress
The Crown of Mexico

4

Early Immigrants and Indentured Servants

Most American Anglo-Saxons whose ancestral roots go back to this country's early history fantasize that theirs were among the families of the Mayflower which landed at Plymouth Rock, or the Anne which put in at the mouth of the Savannah River. Or they say that their families were among the court friends of Lord Baltimore of the Maryland Colony or were included in the names of the FFVs (First Families of Virginia), which, in terms of numbers alone, could not have been possible. Even where ancestral lines can actually be traced to such beginnings, they still represent a folk culture in most cases. Those first families themselves worked with their hands or may have been just released from prison. According to Ruth Elgin Suddeth and her associates, the first thirty-five families who arrived on the Anne to colonize Georgia were "sober, moral and industrious people . . . consisting of carpenters, bricklayers, farmers, etc. who take (brought) all proper instruments (such as hatchets, hammers, saws, shovels, spades, hoes, grindstones, and others)."[1]

The early roots of folk cultures in this country are spelled out by J. Hector St. John Crèvecoeur in his well-known *Letters,* in which he described conditions in the American colonies in the latter half of the eighteenth century. He wrote:

> The rich stay in Europe; it is only the middling and the poor that emigrate. . . .here they become men; in Europe they were so many useless plants. . . .Formerly they were not numbered in any civil list of their country, except in those of the poor; here they rank as citizens.[2]

The poor came to the New World to escape debtor's prison and in some cases to escape war. They came from prison and off the streets of London where they had begged for their food. Many came in bondage and were slaves and servants to pay their debts. Most of those coming in debt were from a peon culture; few had ever owned any land. In the New World there was "land abundance," and in the South the climate for growing was excellent. While there were fertile land and ideal growing conditions, many of those first settlers were not experienced farmers, and the country's rank vegetation with its almost lush, jungle-like growth made preparation of the fields difficult. W. J. Cash points out that it was 200 years before the growing land in the South could be wrested from the forest "emerging by slow stages from a primitive backwoods community, made up primarily of farmers and laborers" and developed by a few so-called aristocrats. The then close relationship and lack of class distinction between the poor white and the planter or aristocrat of the South are highlighted by Cash:

> Not only is it true that he [the poor white] sprang from the same general sources as the majority of the planters, but even that, in many cases, he sprang from identical sources—that he was related to them by the ties of family. In any given region the great planter who lived on the fertile lands along the river, the farmer on the rolling lands behind him and the cracker on the barren back of both were as often as not kindred.[3]

Many of the poor whites in the South of the past as well as of today had family histories of indentured servitude. Either their ancestors came to this country in bondage or they were sold into bondage after being brought here forcibly.

One man-made force—the indentured servant system with its lasting effect on behavior—has been almost totally ignored by

American historians. The psychological effect of being in bondage to one's own countrymen or one's own race as it related to the early feelings of ethnic and class hostility in this country has never been examined. Behind the tendency of the English to be intolerant of the differences of others, as well as to be hostile toward the waves of impoverished white immigrants who followed them to America,[4] could be the fact that once they themselves had arrived on the shores of America impoverished. A major cause of the cruelty used in enforcing Black slavery could have been related to the fact that many of the slave owners or their near ancestors had once been in servitude. Their anger for their own or their forefathers' suffering was projected onto the newcomers, the weak, or those already in servitude. This psychological phenomenon involving the defense of displacement was often seen on the part of a Black slave put in a position of supervision over other slaves. He was often as cruel to his fellow slaves, both to protect himself and to vent his hostility, as was his white master.

Although the percentage of Anglo-Saxons who came to this country as indentured servants is seldom acknowledged, Marcus Jernegan in *Laboring and Dependent Classes in Colonial America, 1607-1783* points out that "in 1683, about 12,000 persons, or one sixth of the population of Virginia, were indentured. The total for all the colonies (of these redemptioners) was perhaps 250,000."[5]

The term *redemptioner* was applied to those individuals in the Colonial period who served a bondage to pay for their passage from Europe and any debts they may have incurred. At the end of their servitude, for whatever period of time it might be, they redeemed their freedom and thereafter had the rights of any citizen.

More than thirty years after Marcus Jernegan pointed out the percentage of redemptioners in the Virginia Colony, Carl Frederick Wittke wrote about the success of some of the individuals who came to this country in that role.

> Although the redemptioners were victims of the worst features of immigrant traffic. . . . Some became successful. . . . Charles Thomson, secretary of the Continental Congress, and two signers of the Declaration of Independence (Mathew Thornton and George Taylor) began life in America as indentured servants, and Mathew Lyon, "the Hampton of Congress," had been kidnapped and "spirited" into white servitude.[6]

Colonial newspapers contain many advertisements that throw light on this traffic in white indentured servants. "Just imported from Dublin. . .a parcel of Irish Servants both Men and Women, to be sold cheap" was the wording of a typical colonial advertisement.[7] The *American Weekly Mercury* for May 22, 1729, advertised the arrival from Scotland of "a parcel of choice Scotch Servants: tailors, weavers, shoemakers and ploughmen, some for five and others for seven years. . . ."[8] Advertisements for runaway indentured servants appeared frequently,[9] just as advertisements for runaway Black slaves would appear later.

Wittke goes on to discuss the control of indentured servants.

> Punishment. . .involved an extension of the time of service or even a money fine. The master also had the right to inflict corporal punishment or to send the offender to the public workhouse. Marriages by indentured servants required the master's consent, whether the other party to the marriage was a free person or another servant. Marriage sometimes involved a money fine or an extra period of service. In Virginia, ministers who married an indentured couple were subject to fine.[10]

The number of indentured servants gradually declined as the eighteenth century advanced, partly owing to the rise of Black slavery. But as late as 1817 vessels arrived in Philadelphia with hundreds aboard who were "bound out" to pay for their passage. The practice of indenture in Pennsylvania did not actually end until 1831.[11]

While the practice of bringing individuals to the United States as indentured servants ended in the early nineteenth century, the practice of indenturehood did not end at that time. The indenture of white children reached an all-time peak in the decade prior to the outbreak of the Civil War when Charles Loring Brace, a student of theology, and his associates began to send children abandoned on the streets of New York City into the Midwestern and New England states by the trainloads in groups of about a hundred each for distribution to farm families who gathered at designated places to receive them.[12] There is no way of knowing how many of these homeless waifs Charles Loring Brace and his son, who continued his work, disposed of in their sixty-seven years of such work, but it has been estimated that the figure was in the tens of thousands. The work brought both praise and bitter criticism. The praise came mainly from New York City, where it was cited that arrests for juvenile delinquency dropped markedly. The chorus of protests of this system of child placement came mainly from the areas receiving the children. Opponents claimed that the children were dumped without solicitude for their real welfare and that farmers used the children as slaves. They went on to say that even if a farmer wished to be honest and to treat the children decently, he found that they presented behavior problems, often because of their resentment over being kidnapped, and that it was too difficult to handle them without supervision, which often was not available.

Although the vast majority of all indentured servants were white, other races were also included. The *American Annual Cyclopaedia for the Year 1861* reports that in California a law had been passed by the legislature by which large numbers of Indians were nominally indentured to white masters for a long term of years. By the operations of this law Indians of any age under thirty and of either sex, without their consent, or, if they were minors, with the consent of their parents, were "indentured to white masters, who thereupon become entitled to the care, control, custody, and earnings of those thus indentured, whom in consideration thereof, they undertake to feed, clothe, care for and protect";[13] but no security was required that this undertaking should be performed or any penalties prescribed for its violation. As with any form of slavery, the individual indentured was considered property of the master to be treated as he should determine.

NOTES

1. Ruth Elgin Suddeth, Isa Lloyd Osterhout, and George Lewis Hutcheson, *Empire Builders of Georgia* (Austin, Tex.: Steck Co., 1962), pp. 52-53.

2. Quoted in Carl Frederick Wittke, *We Who Built America* (Cleveland, Ohio: Press of Case Western Reserve University, 1967), p. 4.

3. *The Mind of the South,* Vintage Books (New York: Random House, Inc., 1941), p. 27.

4. The first United States census in 1790 showed 60 percent of the population to be of English or Scotch-Irish descent, about 20 percent Negro, and the remaining 20 percent largely German, Dutch, Scandinavian, French, Spanish, and Portuguese. "In the three decades between 1830 and 1860

almost 5 million immigrants came to America . . . the majority being from Germany and Ireland. . . . The Irish immigrants (almost 2 million in three decades) fled absentee landlords, an alien church and stark poverty aggravated by famine. The German immigrants (about 1.5 million) came mainly for economic reasons, although a number of them were political refugees from the unsuccessful revolutions in Germany. . . . The Irish immigrants, who arrived penniless in the big cities of the East and tended to remain there, became the principal objects of nativist displeasure. They offended by being conspicuously poor and devoutly Catholic. . . . The German immigrants . . . offended American opinion by importing strong ideas about social reform and by adhering to continental living habits, which did not include Puritanical observance of the Sabbath. . . . In the forty years between 1880 and 1920, more than 23 million people [arrived] . . . over 4 million from Italy, almost 4 million from Austria Hungry and over 3 million from Russia. . . . The 'new' immigrants came as escapees from poverty, and, particularly in the case of Russian Jews, from religious oppression." Earl Raab and Gertrude Jaeger Selznick, *Major Social Problems* (Evanston, Ill.: Row, Peterson and Co., 1961), pp. 313-17.

5. (Chicago: Frederick Ungar, 1931), pp. 46-48.

6. *We Who Built America*, p. 9.

7. Edward Channing, *History of the United States,* Vol. II (New York: Macmillan Co., 1913), p. 402.

8. V. L. Parrington, *The Colonial Mind, 1620-1800,* Vol. I (New York: Harcourt Brace and Co., 1920), p. 34.

9. Karl F. Geiser, in *Redemptioners and Indentured Servants in the Colony and Commonwealth of Pennsylvania* (New Haven, Conn.: Tuttle, Morehouse and Taylor Co., 1901), p. 80, quotes from the *Maryland Gazette* for March 16, 1769, the following advertisement in rhyme:

> Last Wednesday noon at break of day
> From Philadelphia ran away,
> An Irishman named John McKeohn
> To fraud and imposition prone;
> About five feet, five inches high,
> Can curse and swear as well as lie;
> How old he is I can't engage
> But forty-five is near his age. . . .
> He oft in conversation chatters,
> Of scriptures and religious matters,
> And fain would to the world impart,
> That virtue lodges in his heart;
> But take the rogue from stern to stern,
> The hypocrite you'll soon discern—
> And find (tho' his deportment's civil)
> A saint without, within a devil.
> Who'er secures said John McKeohn
> (Provided I can get my own),
> Shall have from me, in cash paid down,
> Five dollar bills, and half a crown.

10. *We Who Built America*, pp. 11-12.

11. Max J. Kohler, "An Important European Mission to Investigate American Immigration Conditions, and John Quincy Adams' Thereto

(1817-1818)," in *Deutsch-Amerikanische Geschichtsblatter* (Chicago: University of Chicago Press, 1917), pp. 5-27; J.C. Ballagh, "White Servitude in the Colony of Virginia," in *Johns Hopkins University Studies* (Baltimore, Md.: Johns Hopkins University Press, 1895); E. I. McCormac, "White Servitude in Maryland, 1634-1820," in *Johns Hopkins University Studies* (Baltimore, Md.: Johns Hopkins University Press, 1904); and C. A. Herrick, *White Servitude in Pennsylvania* (Philadelphia, Pa.: University of Pennsylvania Press, 1926). An interesting episode in the history of indentures is the pretentious scheme of Dr. Andres Turnbull, who, in the summer of 1768, brought over 1,400 immigrants, including Greeks and southern Italians, to colonize East Florida. The scheme collapsed in a few years. See Wilbur Henry Siebert, "Slavery and White Servitude in East Florida, 1726-1776," *Florida Historical Society Quarterly*, X-XIII (July 1931), 3-25.

12. Henry W. Thurston, *The Dependent Child* (New York: Columbia University Press, 1930), pp. 92-160.

13. *American Annual Cyclopaedia and Register of Important Events of the Year* 1861, Vol. I (New York: D. Appleton and Co., 1862), p. 375.

They made us many promises, more than I can remember, but they never kept but one; they promised to take our land, and they took it.

Red Cloud, or Mahpiua-luta, 19th century chief of the Oglala Sioux

5

American Indians

The major historical events that influenced and molded the poverty of rural America include the separation of Native Americans from the main stream of life onto reservations. This was not only the isolation of a race, but also an attempt to stamp out the culture of a people, even as slavery was an attempt to stamp out the heritage of the Black. The feeling of Indians toward this attempt to destroy their culture was eloquently expressed in the late nineteenth century by Chief Crazy Horse of the Oglala Sioux. He said:

We did not ask you white men to come here. The great Spirit gave us this country as a home. You had yours. We did not interfere with you. The Great Spirit gave us plenty of land to live on, and buffalo, deer, antelope and other game. But you have come here; you are taking my land from me; you are killing off our game, so it is hard for us to live. Now, you tell us to work for a living, but the Great Spirit did not make us to work, but to live by hunting. You white men can work if you want to. We do not interfere with you, and again you say, why

50

do you not become civilized? We do not want your civilization! We would live as our fathers did, and their fathers before them.[1]

The treatment of the American Indian by the dominant society can be said to be, at best, inconsistent. There were periods in which one philosophy prevailed only to be reversed in the next decade. This inconsistency ranged from assuming that the land was actually owned by the Indians and must therefore be purchased with title secure and that the different tribes must be recognized as independent nations with whom treaties should be made (the Dutch philosophy) to viewing the Indians as acceptable neighbors and encouraging intermarriage; to pushing them from the section of the country in which whites wanted to live; to an attempt to annihilate them—"the only good Indian is a dead Indian." This latter philosophy was followed by a period of isolation or forced imprisonment on reservations while control for their well-being remained within the white society. For a time, the policy of encouraging Indians to leave the reservation and become a part of the dominant society prevailed. Finally, re-Indianizing the Indians dominated; they were told to be proud of their culture and to decide themselves if they wanted to live on the reservation or somewhere else.

To understand the significance of the various devices and institutions our government has devised for the control of Indians, we must look in some detail at the inconsistency of the various periods of history and the way Indians were viewed by non-Indians as well as the way Indians were told to view themselves. Byron Brophy has identified these periods and the man-made forces that went into and came out of each.

Colonists' Early Relationship with the Indians

Period of control by community diplomacy, 1607-1778. Our earliest relations with Indians were probably the fairest and most satisfactory we ever had, because the philosophy of force which dominated all our future relations was less expedient when we were not strong (ourselves) and when we were even threatened by the potential interference of foreign nations who fully recognized the value of Indian favor and cooperation.[2]

Had it not been for the Indians of Massachusetts, the members of the Plymouth Colony would have starved the first winter.

A Pemaquid named Samoset and three Wampanoags named Massasoit, Squanto, and Hobomah became self-appointed missionaries to the Pilgrims. All spoke some English, learned from explorers who had touched ashore in previous years . . . they shared corn with [the Pilgrims] from the tribal stores, showed them where and how to catch fish, and got them through the first winter. When spring came they gave the white men some seed corn and showed them how to plant and cultivate it.[3]

Relationship through Treaties

For several years the Indians and their white neighbors lived in peace, but as more white people arrived they became less interested in living as neighbors with the Indians, wanting their land instead. (Figure 5 shows the original location of the various Indian tribes at the time of the first English settlement.)

> *Period of control by treaties, 1778-1891.* Most treaties were forced upon the Indians by one means or another and were made for the purpose of obtaining some advantage, such as land acquisition, right of way, or additional control. In return . . . [the treaties] usually made certain provisions for the Indians. Many of the provisions have never been satisfied, and this fact constitutes a retarding influence of major proportions in Indian development (today).[4]

The extent to which the treaties pushed the Indians around and took from them more and more of their land and freedom is pointed out in an annual report for the year 1867, which is quoted quite fully below.[5] This material is on one of the least known and blackest pages of the history of our country. It is also information that has direct bearing on rural poverty of today. It is only a small part of the disinheritance story of the Native American, whose birthright was appropriated by the white man in a way that stripped the Indian of all that he and his people stood for and gave him nothing in return.

Conditions in 1867

The general causes of hostile outbreaks on the part of the Indians may be traced to the intrusion of settlers upon their reservations, the laying out of lines of travel through their

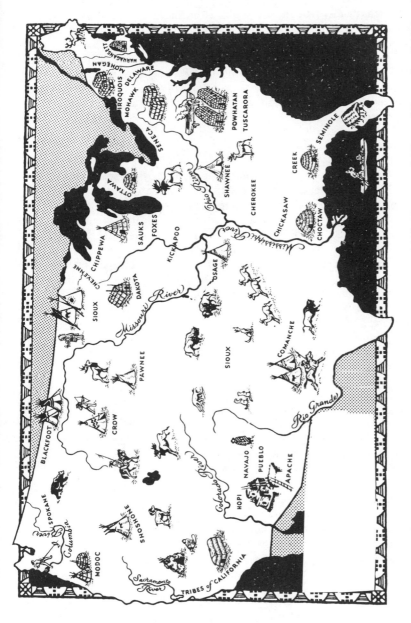

Fig. 5. Original Indian tribes in the geographical area of the United States, 1600. (Courtesy of Allyn and Bacon, Inc. Publishers.)

hunting districts, and a general inefficiency in carrying out treaty stipulations on the part of agents of the United States. The management of Indian affairs is intrusted by the government to the Department of the Interior. This department delegates its authority to a Commissioner of Indian Affairs, to superintendents, special commissioners and agents. It is the duty of Indian agents to reside among the several tribes upon the lands reserved for their use, to pay annuities which have been granted from time to time, and to protect them in the rights, guaranteed by treaty.

Corruption of Indian Agents

Owing partly to the corruption and inefficiency of agents and superintendents, and partly to the difficulty of preserving their lands from the intrusion of pioneers in search of deposits of precious metals, a feeling of distrust and dissatisfaction has long prevailed among many of the tribes to the east of the Rocky Mountains; and a state of destitution, on account of the deminution of game in that region, has tended to increase their irritation and prepare them for the display of open violence in case of strong provocation or temptation.

Gold in California—Immigrants Cross Indian Territory

A rapid glance at the leading events in history for a few years past will assist in obtaining a clear view of the more immediate causes of the hostile outbreaks of the past year. Up to the year 1851 the vast, uninhabited plains eastward of the Rocky Mountains were admitted to be Indian territories, and numerous tribes roamed at will from Texas and Mexico to the northern boundary of the territory of the United States. At that time the discovery of gold in California drew a tide of immigration across this wide reservation thus making a treaty with several tribes. According to the provisions of this treaty a broad highway was opened to California, with the tribes restricted within certain limits, but with the privilege of ranging over the belt reserved as a route of travel in their hunting excursions. The government, moreover, agreed to pay the Indians $50,000 a year for fifteen years in consideration of the privilege granted to immigrants to cross the plains without molestation.

Gold and Silver in Colorado—Indians Give up Territory

The boundaries assigned by this treaty to the Cheyennes and Arapahoes included the larger part of the present Territory of

Colorado, while the Crows and Sioux were to occupy the tract of land now traversed by the Powder River route to Montana. Some years after the treaty mentioned above was made, gold and silver were discovered in Colorado upon the Indian reservations, and settlers poured in regardless of the rights of these tribes; when the lands were in great part taken up by the intruders, another treaty was made to secure them in their possessions. This took place on the 18th of February 1861. By this new treaty these Indians gave up a large extent of territory and agreed to confine themselves to a small district, situated upon both sides of the Arkansas River and along the northern boundary of New Mexico. The United States was to protect them in these possessions and pay an annuity of $30,000 to each tribe for fifteen years and to furnish them with stock and agricultural implements. From this time to April 1864, no difficulties occurred between these tribes and the white inhabitants of Colorado.

Punishment of Indians

During the summer of 1864 complaints were made of Indian depredations and robberies upon the property of settlers. Colonel Chivington, who had command of the troops stationed at Denver, permitted a subordinate officer to set out with a detachment of men to punish the Indians for this offense. The Cheyenne village of Cedar Bluffs was attacked, and 26 Indians killed, 30 wounded, and their property distributed as plunder among the soldiers. After this petty hostilities were kept up during the summer and fall, but the Indians professing a desire for peace applied to the commander of Fort Lyon, Major Wynkoop, to negotiate a treaty to secure it. The Indians were commanded by that officer to collect their people about the fort and were assured of safety. There, under promise of protection, about 500 defenseless men, women and children were attacked by Colonel Chivington and slaughtered without mercy. Known as the Sand Creek massacre, this atrocious affair was perpetrated on the 29th of November 1864. A war with these tribes immediately ensued, which drew 8,000 men from the forces then engaged in suppressing the insurrection in the South and absorbed $30,000,000 of the treasure of the country. No more than fifteen or twenty Indians were killed during the entire campaign of 1865, and the attempt to obtain peace by means of war proved utterly futile. Commissioners were accordingly appointed in the autumn of that year (1865) to procure a council with the hostile tribes and, if possible, settle upon the terms of a treaty.

Indians Give up Arkansas Reservation—Loss of Kansas Lands

The commissioners met the chiefs of the Cheyennes and Arapahoes and other tribes of that region at the mouth of the Little Arkansas in October 1865 and induced them to give up their reservation upon the Arkansas and accept another in the state of Kansas, with the privilege of ranging over the uninhabited plains which had formerly been their own. When this treaty came before the Senate for ratification, it was so amended as to exclude these tribes entirely from the state of Kansas, and they were left with nothing but their hunting privileges on the unsettled lands of the plains. Notwithstanding this material defect in the ratified treaty, the peace was strictly preserved by these southern tribes through the year 1866.[6]

An excellent continuation of the history of the loss of Indian lands is found in Dee Brown's *Bury My Heart at Wounded Knee.*

Settlement of Treaties

Much psychic energy is still spent today by Indians of all ages who still hope to find a way to make the United States government live up to the promises of those early treaties. The prime example is the hope of the Sioux that they will be paid for at least a part of the billions of dollars in gold taken from the Black Hills.

Sometimes the settlement of a claim can be even more discouraging to the Indian than no settlement at all because the amount of money involved is insignificant compared to what the government has spent on the so-called investigation of the claim. The *Minneapolis Tribune* carried a story of a resident of that city who was advised by the Examiner of the Department of the Interior that they had decided to pay her grandfather's pony claim filed against the government May 5, 1891. The amount was $36 to be divided among more than twenty heirs. The Minneapolis resident figured she would receive ninety cents as her share.[7] For more than sixty years this claim had, at various times, been reviewed by numerous examiners, lawyers, and secretaries—each of whom had been involved in writing reports and correspondence which required an outlay of federal monies that would probably have paid for several horses.

The Bureau of Indian Affairs

The Bureau of Indian Affairs was created in 1824 as an arm of the War Department to supplement the efforts of the department to control the Indian. It remained in the War Department for twenty-five years, during which time the philosophy of force was so firmly established that it is still operative in spite of all the efforts of innumerable reformers. The Bureau of Indian Affairs was described by Congressman E. H. Moore:

> From its birth its mission largely was to treat with the Indians for cession of lands and recommend to the War Department (chastisement of the hostiles) when the Indians did not comport themselves agreeable to the Bureau. The public of today cannot know the injustices which have come down to the Indians directly from the department of government the past 160 years.[8]

Indians Pushed Westward

On January 27, 1825, President Monroe recommended to Congress the implementation of a proposal made by his Secretary of War, John C. Calhoun of South Carolina, that

> ... all Indians be required to move west, beyond what was thereafter known as the *Indian Line* and that as an indispensible component of this new national policy, white settlement be forever prohibited west of that line.[9]

In 1829, General Andrew Jackson, a Tennessee frontiersman, took office as President of the United States, and in his first message to Congress recommended that all eastern Indians be removed westward beyond the Mississippi.[10] On May 28, 1830, this recommendation became law. Two years later President Jackson appointed a Commissioner of Indian Affairs to serve in the War Department to see that the new laws affecting Indians were properly carried out. On June 30, 1834, the United States Congress passed *An Act to Regulate Trade and Intercourse with the Indian Tribes and to Preserve Peace on the Frontiers.* This act spelled out Monroe's recommendation to establish the Indian Line, which started at the Canadian border at a point north of the Mississippi

River and followed it to southern Illinois; there it jogged westward around Missouri, Arkansas, and Louisiana. No white person was to be permitted to trade in this Indian country without a license, nor would any white traders of bad character be permitted to reside in Indian country. The military force of the United States would be employed in the apprehension of any white person who was found in violation of provisions of this act.

Even before the laws could be put into effect, however, a new wave of white settlers had swept westward and formed the territories of Wisconsin and Iowa. This meant that the Indian Line had to be shifted westward. When that was accomplished the area was ready for the new refugees: the eastern Indians—the Cherokees, Choctaws, Chickasaws, Creeks, Shawnees, Seminoles, Miamis, Ottawas, Hurons, Delawares, and many other once mighty tribes were rounded up by soldiers and forced to march into Indian country.[11] (Figure 6 shows the forcing of Indians into the territory west of the Mississippi River.) One out of every four Cherokees, or 4,000, died from cold, hunger, or disease in the 800 mile journey westward when they were forced out of Georgia after gold was discovered in the mountains near Dahlonega.[12] This 1829 gold discovery in Cherokee land, which up to that time was not considered important because it was too hilly to be good cotton land, resulted in the greatest gold rush the country had ever experienced.

> The presence of gold in the north Georgia hills immediately increased the value of the Cherokee land which Georgia already had determined to acquire. The discovery of gold helped to bring about the final phase of Indian removal in Georgia.[13]

Prior to the gold discovery, the Cherokees had been considered the best of neighbors. They had the highest degree of acculturation of any American Indians at that time; they had even translated the Bible into Cherokee and used it in their religious services. James Bonner describes their life style.

> In February, 1828, they began a newspaper called the *Cherokee Phoenix,* printed in both English and Cherokee. . . . The Cherokee at this time numbered almost 15,000. They possessed 1,200 slaves, and many of them lived in frame houses and wore the clothing of the white man. The more enterprising Cherokees

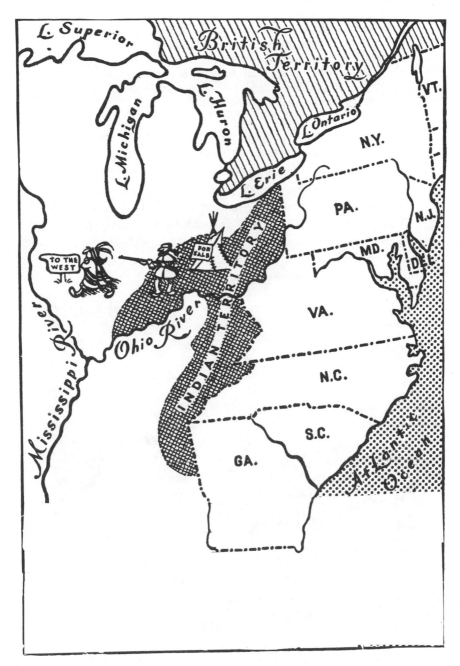

Fig. 6. Forcing the Indian westward, 1832. (Courtesy of Allyn and Bacon, Inc. Publishers.)

cultivated valley farms in the fashion of their white neighbors. Many of their leaders were white blooded and bore English names. John Ross, who became the principal chief of the nation in 1828, was only one-eighth Indian. He lived in a fine house at the head of the Coosa River, where he combined the roles of merchant, planter, and statesman.[14]

A visit to the huge red-brick and white-columned colonial home of Chief James Vann of the Cherokees (see the accompanying photograph) shows the great advances into the white culture made by those Indians at the time they were forced to leave Georgia. A few Cherokees escaped from the soldiers into the mountains of western North Carolina where their descendants are living today as a part of rural America. The majority of the Cherokees, however, went peaceably as Chief James Vann said they would if they were not wanted by their white neighbors.

CHIEF VANN HOUSE. This is the front entrance of the house built by Chief James C. Vann in Spring Place, Georgia and completed in 1805. Known as the finest home in the Cherokee nation, it was owned by Chief Vann's son, Chief Joseph Vann ("Rich Joe") until the removal of the Cherokees westward to Indian territory. (Photograph by Myrtle R. Reul.)

With increasing reports of gold in Appalachia, the state of Georgia pushed to get the Indians out of the area and refused to recognize the Cherokee government (although it was recognized by the federal government), declaring that Georgia law should extend over Cherokee country. This was the second time Indians were forced out of the state of Georgia. Tricked into signing a treaty, the Creek Indians in 1825 were cheated out of 5 million acres of prime cotton land west of the Flint River. "More than 20,000 Georgians . . . received a free lot of two-hundred-two and one-half acres of virgin territory,"[15] which once had been Indian land. (See Figure 7 for a map of Georgia showing the Indian land in 1818.) In the controversy with the Cherokee,

> President Jackson upheld Georgia. The United States Supreme Court upheld the Cherokee. There followed a bitter quarrel between a young state, defining new "rights" to her own advantage and the federal government, which was the lawful protector of the Indians. There [then began] . . . the sorry story of land grabbing in defiance of all law; of bribery and violence; of treaty-breaking; of white greed and Indian stubbornness. But the Cherokees publicly announced that, whatever might happen, they would wage no war, even on any soldier sent to expel them. On June 1, 1830, their laws finally were canceled and those of Georgia substituted. . . . The Cherokee nation gave up its claim to all lands east of the Mississippi for the sum of five million dollars and a track of seven million acres west of the Mississippi River.[16]

And so they began their long walk leaving their beloved mountains where their ancestors were born, their homes, and their crops, and they moved toward the Indian Territory of the west where they were told they would be able to live as they wished, in peace.

John Collier gives the reaction of the president of the United States to what the Cherokee Indians call "the trail of tears."

> While a hundred Cherokees a day were perishing of exhaustion and cold on the dreadful road, President Van Buren on December 3, 1838 addressed Congress: "The measures [for Cherokee removal] authorized by Congress at its last session have had the happiest effects. . . . The Cherokees have emigrated without any apparent reluctance."[17]

The crowning blow in the midst of all of this was that the financial cost for the 7,000 troops used to force the movement of

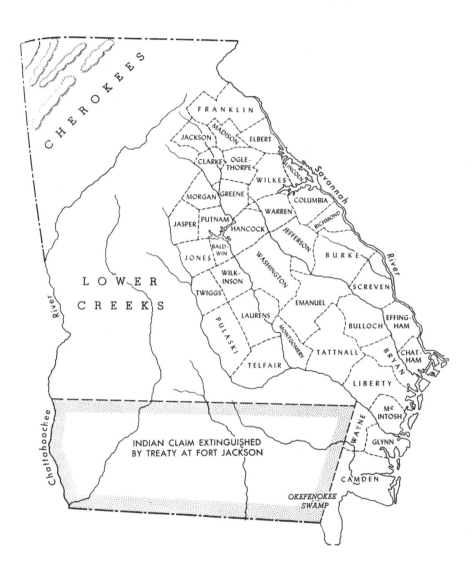

Fig. 7. Area of Georgia held by Indian tribes compared to area held by English settlers, 1818. (Courtesy of American Book Company.)

the Cherokees, the expense of feeding 14,000 Indians who were herded along this journey, and the cost of burial, when this was done, of the 4,000 who died were charged by the government against the funds credited to the tribe pursuant to the fraudulent treaty.

Dale Van Every describes the completeness of the sweep of Indians from the east.

> Aside from a few scattered remnants, such as the Seminole fugitives in Florida swamps, the few mountain Cherokee in North Carolina, the Choctaw residue in Mississippi, and an occasional tiny enclave in the north, every Indian nation which had originally occupied the immense expanse of woodland extending across the eastern part of the United States had been compelled to seek new homes on the plains beyond that woodland's western margin. It had required a persisting effort over a period of fifteen years, distinguished not only by the suffering inflicted upon Indians, but by the virtual disagreements excited among white Americans to give effect to the outwardly plausible policy announced by Monroe and Calhoun in 1825. Removal had been a contemporary success in the sense that the National government had proved able to impose its will and the states concerned had been rid of the unwanted Indian inhabitants. But for the Indians and for the larger interest of the United States, it had been a deplorable failure. The opportunity for Indians to become useful and valued members of American society, an achievement many had seemed on the verge of attaining in 1825, had been heedlessly postponed for more than a century.[18]

As the author of *Bury My Heart at Wounded Knee* points out, these once great eastern nations, after 225 years of acculturation with whites, arrived "as refugees carrying their shabby goods, their rusty farming tools and bags of seed corn . . . poor relations, in the country of the proud and free *Plains Indians*"[19] whose experiences with whites had as yet been very limited.

These refugees had hardly arrived in the "permanent Indian country" when white soldiers engaged in the war with Mexico (1846) began to march across their territory. Afterward, land acquired in the war expanded the territory of the United States to the Pacific Ocean, thus creating a reason for more whites to cross the land which had been identified as belonging only to Indians.

Then in 1848 gold was discovered again, this time in California.

Within a few months fortune-hunting Easterners by the thousands were crossing Indian territory. "To justify these breaches of the earlier acts of Congress, the Washington policy makers 'invented the *Manifest Destiny*' [by which] Europeans and their descendants were ordained by destiny to rule all of America. They were the dominant race and therefore responsible for the Indians—along with their lands, their forests, and their mineral wealth."[20]

"And so only a quarter of a century after passing... [the *Indian Trade and Intercourse Act*] white settlers had driven in both the north and south flanks of the 95th meridian line, and advance elements of white miners and traders had penetrated the center."[21] From the viewpoint of the whites there was now need for pushing the Indians farther back, and so plans for establishing large western reservations were developed.

The next period of Indian control described by Brophy covers the sixteen years from 1871 to 1887. This he calls the

> *Period of control by reservations, segregation, and pauperization.* . . . By 1887 most of the tribes had been separated from their vast areas of land and assigned to particular and restricted reservations. The reservations chosen for them were for the most part in sections of the country then considered unfit for white inhabitation. The lands taken from the Indians were then opened to homestead entry by the federal government.[22]

The Indians of the Black Hills

Article Two of the 1868 treaty between the United States government and the Sioux nation describes the area known as the Rosebud Ridge Reservation to be "set apart for the absolute and undisturbed use and occupation of the Indians." In addition, Article Sixteen states,

> The United States hereby agrees and stipulates that the country north of the North Platte River and east of the summits of the Big Horn Mountains shall be held and considered to be unceded Indian Territory, and also stipulates and agrees that *no white person or persons* shall be permitted to settle upon or occupy any portion of the same.[23]

This vast area of mountains, plains, and badlands was thought to have little value by the white man, but to the Indian this was the place of the gods and holy mountains. In another book I have written about the meaning of the Black Hills to the Indians of that area.

> To the many tribes of the Sioux, the Cheyennes and the Arapahos the Black Hills, or as they called them, the *Paha Sapa*, were sacred. It was in these black pine-covered mountains that the *Indians of the Plains* spent their winters. They found protection there among the trees and rocks from the winds and blizzards. Buffalo could be found in the little valleys even when those great shaggy beasts were scarce in the Platte River Valley or on the open prairies. In the Black Hills hunters could always hear the wild mourn of the wolf and the whistle of the stag. It was here the *Oglala* and the other tribes came to worship *Wakantanka*, the Great Spirit. They felt God in *His* infinite wisdom had looked at the earth and found the *Paha Sapa*, the Black Hills to be the most beautiful of all *His* creations. It was there *He* chose to live. To the early Indians those hills were a cathedral to which they came to worship.[24]

As the Sioux were pushed back into the badlands and the shadow of the Paha Sapa they, like all the other tribes, were told that if they gave up their hunting lands and cooperated they would be taken care of with government rations of food and clothing. Four years after the treaty of 1868, miners were violating the treaty and were searching the Paha Sapa for gold. When the Indians drove them out or killed them, the Army was ordered to make a reconnaissance into the hills; this they did in 1874 without asking Indian permission to enter the area. Led by General George Custer, called "Pahuska" or "Long Hair" by the Sioux, this expedition reported that the hills were filled with gold "from the grass roots down." The trail that Custer and his soldiers opened into the Paha Sapa was called by the Indians the "Thieves' Road." When Red Cloud and other chiefs complained to the federal government, the Army sent soldiers to make another reconnaissance of the Black Hills and found more than a thousand miners in the area. The miners were told that they were violating the law, but no effort was made to force them out. When Red Cloud and Spotted Tail made a stronger protest to Washington, a commission was sent to meet with the chiefs "to treat with the Sioux Indians for the relinquishment of the Black Hills."[25] When Red Cloud, Spotted Tail, Crazy Horse, and the other chiefs refused to sell the Black

Hills for $6 million dollars,[26] because to them the Paha Sapa could not be sold for any price, E. T. Watkins, special inspector for the Indian bureau, recommended that troops be sent against these "uncivilized" Indians "in the winter, the sooner the better, and whip them into subjection."[27] Secretary of War, W. W. Belknap, warned of trouble in the Black Hills "unless something is done to obtain possession of that section for the white miners who have been strongly attracted there by reports of rich deposits of the precious metal."[28]

On December 3, 1875, at a time of the year when travel on the western plains was all but impossible, the Commissioner of Indian Affairs ordered all Indians off reservations to report to their agencies or a "military force would be sent to compel them." When, on February 1, 1876, the time for this travel had expired, the Secretary of the Interior notified the Secretary of War that he was turning the situation over to the military authorities for such action as the Army might deem proper under the circumstances.[29] A week later General Philip Sheridan, whose raids in the Shenandoah Valley of Virginia had played an important part in the North's winning the Civil War, was authorized by the War Department to commence operations against the "hostile Sioux." The next day he ordered military operations to begin moving in the direction of the headwaters of the Powder, Tongue, Rosebud, and Bighorn rivers, "where Crazy Horse and his allies frequented."[30] A little over four months later Chief Sitting Bull and his braves had killed General George Armstrong Custer and all 212 of his soldiers in the Battle of Little Bighorn River (June 25, 1876) in what had turned into the War for the Black Hills.

As punishment for the death of General Custer the Paha Sapa were removed from the possession of the Indians.

> This [was done] without regard to the treaty of 1868, by maintaining that the Indians had violated the treaty by going to war with the United States. This [logic] was difficult for the reservation Indians to understand, because they had not attacked United States soldiers, nor had Chief Sitting Bull's followers attacked them until General Custer sent Major Marcus Reno charging through the Sioux villages.[31]

To intimidate the Indians into giving up the Paha Sapa, a new commission was sent from Washington in September to use whatever tactics they wished, as long as they were successful in forcing the chiefs into signing away their rights to the Black Hills and giving those rights and immeasurable mineral and timber wealth to white owners.

> To break down [the Indians'] opposition, the commissioners dropped strong hints that unless they signed, the *Great Council* [in Washington] in its anger would cut off all rations immediately, would remove them to the Indian Territory in the south, and the Army would take all their guns and horses.[32]

The chiefs signed to save their people more suffering. Red Cloud was the first to sign, and thus the beloved Paha Sapa, the sacred land of the Indian gods with its vast pine forests, its lichen-covered boulders and cold tumbling streams, passed forever from their hands into the hands of the white man. But nothing could ever destroy the deep love that the Indians had for the black pines, the looming, gray, protective peaks, and the grass-green valleys where their ancestors had arranged the teepees of the Seven Council fires long before Columbus sailed for the New World.

Four weeks after the signing of the documents transferring ownership of the Black Hills, all Indian males of the tribes directly involved were "placed under arrest, teepees were searched and dismantled, guns collected, and ponies and horses were rounded up by the soldiers."[33] The women were allowed to keep a few horses for hauling goods; the other horses were taken by the soldiers. The men, including Red Cloud, were forced to walk to Fort Robinson where they were forced to live under the guns of the soldiers.[34] In the months that followed, every opportunity was taken to degrade the Indian prisoners and to break the spirit of those who were called savages by those who claimed to be civilized.

At the same time every effort was made to control all Indians not living at forts and to get them out of any area where gold, silver, or copper were being discovered. Finally, a plan was devised to protect whites who poured west for gold, land, and wealth and, at the same time, to control the Indians. The plan was new only in the amount of land involved; it was to set aside small reservations and force the Indians inside their boundaries. This would free more Indian lands for whites and would get the Indians out of sight. It would also divide them into small numbers so that they would be less apt to try to attack miners and settlers. The new reservations were surveyed, and the Indians were ordered to move inside the new boundaries. So little concern was shown for the Indian national or tribal cultures that groups who previously had been arch enemies, and who were as different from each other culturally as are the French from the Germans, were often placed on the same reservation.[35]

All Indian men, regardless of their nation, were stripped of the life they had known previously. Hunters and warriors were forced to give up their guns and knives and ordered to farm the 140 acres allotted to each Indian, although the Sioux culture, for one, was not a farming culture, and thus it was the Sioux women who harvested the wild berries and grains and planted the squaw corn.[36] Such work as planting and harvesting was not considered worthy work for hunters and warriors. However, not only were the Indians not farmers, but also most of the land allotted for a reservation was the poorest, the least fertile, and the most in need of irrigation of any land in the state.

Indians Are Forced into Farming

That farming for the Indians should prove a failure was to be expected; a more drastic cultural transformation would be harder to envision than to learn the use of money, the principles of commerce, and to acquire a new language, English, as well as the language of agriculture and trading with nothing in the old pattern to serve as a basis upon which to build this new way of life. In hunting and war the Plains Indians were accustomed to constant mobility. Their prestige values centered around warfare and the giving away of goods. To live in permanent, closed dwellings; to engage individually in the steady, plodding routine of farming; to sell produce or grains for profit; to invest in labor with the expectation that at some future time one would be repaid with products that represented a new and unappreciated form of value were completely discordant with the Indians' ingrained attitudes and habitual patterns of behavior. And to do so on the order of a non-Indian government, which neither offered help in instruction or encouragement nor showed any respect or understanding for the needs of the Indians, was to add a guarantee of failure.

Even more important psychologically was the fact that the Indian culture taught that failure meant the supernatural was displeased with the individual. If the hunter was not successful, he had displeased the spirits and must atone. When this same principle was applied to farming, the results were very complicated. As Clark Wissler points out,

> Even when crops were planted, drought, hail, insects and other misfortunes discouraged the Indian, because unlike the white man, he had no folk experience behind him to give him faith in the future and encourage him to expect ultimate success. His philosophy of life led him to expect that "the powers" would protect him from these calamities; but if they did not protect him he accepted such failure as evidence that they disapproved of what he had done, and so there was no use in persisting. . . .[37]

Psychologically, the concept of living was very different for the Indian than it was for the white man. While he was asked to conform to the values and wishes of the white man, such were not his values or wishes, as Chief Luther Standing Bear of the Oglala band of Sioux explained in his autobiography.

> We did not think of the great open plains, the beautiful rolling hills, and winding streams with tangled growth, as "wild." Only to the white man was nature a "wilderness" and only to him was the land "infested" with "wild" animals and "savage" people. To us it was tame. Earth was bountiful and we were surrounded with the blessings of the Great Mystery. Nor until the hairy man from the east came and with brutal frenzy heaped injustices upon us and the families we loved was it "wild" for us. When the very animals of the forest began fleeing from his approach, then it was that for us the "Wild West" began.[38]

Conditions in 1877

The wars of 1876-77 lost for the Teton Sioux tribes the Black Hills and the Powder River Country. The United States government, not satisfied with what remained as Indian lands, changed the western boundary of the Great Sioux Reservation from the 104th to the 103rd meridian. The federal government thus gained a fifty-mile strip adjacent to the Black Hills and the most valuable agricultural lands between the forks of the Cheyenne River. For the Sioux,

> In 1877, after the government drove . . . [them] out of Nebraska, all [the land] that was left to them was an anvil-shaped block between the 103rd meridian and the Missouri River—35,000 square miles of Dakota land which was believed to be virtually worthless by the surveyors who marked off the boundaries.[39]

Scheme to Break up the Great Sioux Reservation

Simultaneously with these happenings the door for immigration into the United States was opening wide, and hundreds of thousands of immigrants from north Europe were encouraged to enter this country. Thousands of these foreign newcomers arrived in the eastern Dakota territory, hoping to buy good land cheap or to obtain land free under the earlier Homestead Act. At Bismark the land-seeking waves of immigrants and the building of the Great Northern Railroad were halted by the Missouri River boundary of the Great Sioux Indian Reservation. Ultimately the railroad would change its plans and take its main line from Saint Paul to Seattle across Canada with lesser lines through the reservation into the newly formed states of Montana, Wyoming, and Idaho. But in 1877 the Great Sioux Reservation, stretching westward from the Missouri River, stood as a barrier to "progress." It prevented the building of another railroad and roads and it stood in the way of agricultural development and the carving out of farms and ranches. Money-hungry white men felt that something needed to be done immediately. "Promoters eager for cheap land to be sold at high profits to immigrants hatched schemes to break up the Great Sioux Reservation."[40]

Chief Sitting Bull in Canada

Meanwhile Chief Sitting Bull, the major chief of the Sioux, was in exile in Canada. Like Geronimo free in Mexico, Sitting Bull, who led the attack on General Custer, was a dangerous symbol of subversion to the federal government. Every attempt was to be made to get him to return to this country to be under the control of the Army. Finally, in the fall of 1877, the War Department arranged with the Canadian government for a special commission to cross the border and promise Sitting Bull "a complete pardon, provided he would surrender all firearms and horses and bring his people back to the Hunkpapa agency at Standing Rock on the Great Sioux Reservation."[41]

Sitting Bull Returns to the United States

The requests for Sitting Bull to return continued, and finally in mid-July of 1881 he and 186 of his followers crossed the border and rode into Fort Buford where he surrendered his Winchester rifle to the commanding officer. At this time the Army broke another promise to the Indians. Instead of allowing their chief to continue to his agency at Standing Rock, they took him as a military prisoner to Fort Randall.

This capture and imprisonment of Sitting Bull drew national attention, and he was visited by many newspapermen who kept his story before the public. Lesser chiefs visited him for consultation on tribal affairs.

In 1882 representatives from the different Sioux agencies came to ask advice concerning a new government proposal to break up the Great Reservation into smaller areas and sell about half the land for white settlement. Sitting Bull advised them not to sell; the Sioux had no land to spare.[42]

Attempts to Get the Land through Fraud

Despite their resistance and attempts to hold onto their land, the Sioux in 1882

... came very near losing 14,000 square miles of territory to a commission headed by Newton Edmunds, an expert at negotiating lands away from Indians. His colleagues were . . . a frontier lawyer, and . . . a brother of the new Secretary of the Interior [the federal agency housing the Bureau of Indian Affairs]. Accompanying them was a "special interpreter," Reverend Samuel E. Hinman, who had been a missionary to the Sioux . . . [and who] believed what the Indians needed was less land and more Christianity.[43]

As the commission traveled from one agency to the other,

Hinman told the chiefs that he was there to lay out different parts of the reservation for the six agencies. This was necessary, he said, so that the different Sioux tribes could claim the areas as their own and have them as long as they lived. "After we have laid out the reservation," Hinman told Red Cloud, "the Great Father will give you 25,000 cows and 1,000 bulls." To obtain the livestock, however, the Sioux had to sign some papers which the commissioners had brought along. As none of the Sioux chiefs could read, they did not know that they were signing away 14,000 square miles of land in exchange for the promised cows and bulls.

At agencies where the Sioux were reluctant to sign anything, Hinman alternately wheedled and bullied them. In order to obtain an abundance of signatures, he persuaded and bribed boys as young as seven years old to sign the papers. (According to the treaty only adult male Indians could sign.) In a meeting at Wounded Knee Creek on the Pine Ridge reservation, Hinman told the Indians that if they did not sign they would not receive any more rations or annuities, and furthermore they would be sent to Indian Territory [Oklahoma territory].[44]

Early in 1883 Edmunds and Hinman journeyed to Washington with their bundle of signatures and succeeded in getting a bill introduced in Congress ceding about half of the lands of the Great Reservation to the United States. Fortunately for the Sioux, they had enough friends in Washington to question the bill and to point out that even if all the signatures were legal, Edmunds and Hinman still had not obtained the names of the required three-fourths of all adult male Sioux.

Another commission, headed by Senator Henry L. Dawes, was immediately dispatched to Dakota to inquire into the methods used by Edmunds and Hinman. Its members soon discovered the chicanery of their predecessors.[45]

Treatment of an Indian Chief

Sitting Bull had been released from Fort Randall and had returned to Standing Rock just before the Dawes commission arrived in Dakota. When the commission arranged for a council to hear testimony, Sitting Bull came to the hearing without an invitation and sat quietly listening to the proceedings. Although he was at that time the most famous of all living Indian chiefs, he was deliberately ignored by the commission while testimony was taken from lesser chiefs. In the protocol of governments, such an act would be comparable to the president of the United States being ignored by a commission of foreign nations while they negotiated for American resources with the assistant secretary to a governor of one of the states. One would expect the president of the United States and the American people to be outraged at such an affront, and yet neither the Dawes commission nor the federal government felt that Chief Sitting Bull should be angry or that his Indian followers should in any way feel insulted when their legally elected leader was ignored as if he were nobody.

When finally Senator Dawes turned to the interpreter and asked if Sitting Bull had anything to say, Sitting Bull is reported to have asked, "Do you recognize me; do you know who I am?" Senator Dawes answered, "I know you as Sitting Bull." The chief asked again, "You say you know I am Sitting Bull, but do you know what position I hold?" Senator Dawes answered, "I do not know any difference between you and the other Indians at this agency."[46] After a few more exchanges Sitting Bull is reported to have made a sweeping motion with his hand, and every Indian in the room arose and followed him out.[47]

Nothing could have dismayed the commissioners more than such an act and the thought of the Sioux rallying around a strong leader like Sitting Bull. However, they could not accept any responsibility for what had happened. They refused to acknowledge that they had insulted a great chief. The Indian leader was at fault. Pressure was put on Sitting Bull; the commissioners said that he had offended them and that his people would lose greatly unless he made amends by apologizing for his behavior. While Sitting Bull was not certain about the trustworthiness of any white man, he did send word to the commissioners that he would like another council. At that meeting he began by saying, "I am here to apologize to you for my bad conduct . . . and to take back what I said. I will take it back because I consider I have made your hearts bad. . . ."[48] He talked on, trying to describe the conditions of the Indians. They had none of the things that white men had. If they were to become like white men they must have tools, livestock, and wagons, since that was how white people made a living.

Instead of accepting Sitting Bull's apology graciously and listening to what he had to say, the commissioners immediately launched an attack. Senator John Logan scolded him for breaking up the previous council. . . . "I want to say further that you are not a great chief of this country." Logan continued, "that you have no following, no power, no control, and no right to any control. You are on an Indian reservation merely at the suffrance of the government. You are fed by the government, clothed by the government, your children are educated by the government, and all you have and are today is because of the government. If it were not for the government you would be freezing and starving today in the mountains. I merely say these things to you to notify you that you cannot insult the people of the United States of America or its committees. . . . The government feeds and clothes and educates your children now, and desires to teach you to become farmers, and to civilize you, and *make you as white men.*"[49]

To speed the process of making the Sioux "as white men," the Indian Bureau assigned James McLaughlin to head the agency at Standing Rock. McLaughlin, or White Hair, as the Indians called him, was a veteran of the Indian service, was married to a half-breed Santee woman, and his superiors were confident that he could efficiently destroy the culture of the Sioux and replace it with the white man's civilization. Every move that White Hair made was calculated to keep Sitting Bull in the background to demonstrate to the Standing Rock Sioux that their old hero was powerless to lead or help them.

White Hair's maneuvers had no effect whatsoever on Sitting Bull's popularity with the Sioux. All visitors to the reservation, Indian or white, wanted to meet Sitting Bull. In 1884 the Secretary of the Interior authorized Sitting Bull to tour fifteen American cities, and his appearance created such a sensation that William F. (Buffalo Bill) Cody decided he must add the famous chief to his Wild West Show. The Indian bureau offered some resistance to the proposal at first, but when White Hair McLaughlin was queried, he was enthusiastic. By all means, he said, let Sitting Bull join the Wild West Show.

Chief Sitting Bull became a major attraction in Buffalo Bill's Wild West Show, which traveled extensively throughout the United States and Canada. The money he received from signed photographs of himself he gave to the "bands of ragged, hungry boys who seemed to surround him wherever he went."[50] He was quoted by Annie Oakley, also a star in the same show, as saying he could not understand how the white man could be so unmindful of their own poor. "The white man knows how to make everything," he is quoted as saying, "but he does not know how to distribute it."[51]

When Buffalo Bill invited him to accompany the show on a tour of Europe in 1887, Sitting Bull declined, saying he was needed by his people. "There is more talk of taking our lands," he explained.

New Attempt to Break up the Great Sioux Reservation

This new attempt to break up the Great Sioux Reservation was a scheme to buy 9 million acres from the Indians for fifty cents an acre. A commission came from Washington to get the required signatures, and when this failed, primarily because of the efforts exerted against it by Sitting Bull, the commissioners returned to Washington recommending that the government ignore the treaty of 1868 and take the land without consent of the Indians. Washington politicians, however, aware of rising concern on the part of some non-Indians about the recent number of broken Indian treaties and afraid of another Indian uprising, preferred to use the psychology of fear and frighten the Indians into believing that they would lose their land if they refused to sell it. The politicians felt that if the Indians were forced to sell, the federal government could do with the land as it wished, without breaking any treaties. The plan was put in motion.

"A new commission was authorized to offer the Indians $1.50 per acre instead of the fifty cents offered by the previous commission."[52] Members of the Congress ordered this new commission to return with the required number of signatures so that the "Indian problem could be settled."

The Great Sioux Reservation Is Broken Up

After days and weeks of pressure and lies, of pitting group against group, of holding secret meetings to which Sitting Bull and Red Cloud were not invited, and with members of the commission afterwards admitting[53] that they, prior to each meeting, had talked (or forced) certain key Indians into speaking in favor of the ratification of the agreement, it was all over. The Indians had signed their land away. The Great Sioux Reservation had been broken into small islands around which would rise the flood of white immigration, most of it foreign immigration. Before Sitting Bull could get away from the grounds where the agreement was made without his signature, a newspaperman is reported to have asked him how the Indians felt about giving up their lands. "Indians!" Sitting Bull shouted. "There are no Indians left but me!"[54]

The Irony of Fate

Thus the Great Sioux Reservation was divided into parcels that fitted the description of the Homestead Act of 1862, granting 160 acres (one-fourth of a section of land) free of charge to any citizen of the United States, or anyone over twenty-one years of age who filed a first paper of intent for citizenship. The only requirement was to settle on the property for five years, build a house, and cultivate the soil. The land could be commuted after six months and bought for $1.25 an acre, which favored land speculation by corporations and individuals who bought up large areas of land to hold until higher prices could be obtained. In much of the area covered by the Great Sioux Reservation, the parcels of land available for homesteads included 320 acres.

The land had been taken from the Indians, who were in no way considered American citizens but to whom the land had belonged for thousands of years. Much of it would be given to immigrants from the countries of north Europe who filed for American citizenship simply for the purpose of having the right to claim homestead lands. These newcomers were encouraged in their homesteading efforts by American big business, especially the new and powerful railroads who saw every immigrant family as potential transportation customers. These new immigrants from Norway, Sweden, Finland, Russia, Denmark, Germany, and Austria were the poor of northern Europe. They were tired of living under war-torn conditions, and they were land-hungry. They were driven by a desire to build a new home in a new country for themselves, their children, and their grandchildren on land provided for them by the government of the United States. They had a love of the earth, a knowledge of farming, and they brought from the "bread basket of Europe" many new kinds of grain seeds for planting.

These foreign immigrants—newcomers to the west—worked hard, and in a few years turned the virgin soil of the western prairies into the great grain lands of America. They made the land of the Great Sioux Reservation productive in a way it had never been productive before. But they and those native to America who tilled the soil of what had been Indian land would create such an adverse condition by turning thousands of acres of open range lands into mile after mile of cultivated fields that the gale-like winds of the mid-1930s would practically denude the land, forcing them and their descendents to flee from the area. Thus, the much-contested lands would revert for nonpayment of taxes to near-bankrupt states.

Indians as Wards of the Government

Part of the promises spelled out in the treaties between the various Indian nations and the United States government implied that the United States government would feed, clothe, and educate the Indians in return for their peaceful withdrawal from the land that they and their ancestors had owned by virtue of having lived, borne their children, and buried their dead upon it.[55] Although the intention of the government was to support the Indians until they could be trained to help themselves, this, in most cases, never materialized—neither the support nor the training. Indians died of starvation or were victimized by Indian agents and exploited by non-Indians. They were kept separate from the mainstream of American life, having to obtain permission to leave their own reservation; yet even on the reservation they were not allowed freedom to handle their own affairs or to develop their culture or even to practice their own religions. They were not allowed to vote until 1924, and then they were often prevented from registering. They were wards of the federal government and yet victimized by that government. At the same time they were looked upon by the general public as something less than human. They were said to be dishonest, dirty, lazy, not worthy of what they were costing the American taxpayers, although they themselves were required to pay taxes.

The result for nearly 100 years has been a passive resistance between the federal government through the Bureau of Indian Affairs on one side, and the American Indian on the other. If Indians on their own initiative try to better their situation, the red tape of bureaucracy (originally set up to protect them) creates such innumerable hurdles that by the time permission is granted from Washington, D. C., it is often too late to implement plans. In turn, because the Bureau of Indian Affairs has always assumed it knew more about what was good for Indians than Indians themselves, there have been countless projects imposed upon the latter. The Indians, in turn, have gone through the motions of implementation with passive hostility in such a way that success has been impossible. These experiences have left them frustrated and angry, but because they could not openly express their feelings toward the white man, they have learned to direct their feelings toward their own race.

Thus, they are jealous and suspicious of others, especially of other Indian tribes or other reservations. Results of such jealousy, suspicion, and distrust are illustrated in the reluctance of Indians until very recently to assume leadership, fearing to set themselves off as better than friends; in hostility and conflict between Indian youths and elders; between full blood and those of mixed blood; and between Indians living on and off the reservations. In all cases jealousy, fear, mistrust, and suspicion all too often prevent Indians from working together effectively.

One example of how the system has victimized and pauperized the Indians is seen in the period identified by Brophy as *Control by legislation: destruction of tribal organizations and seizure of Indian lands under the provision of the Allotment Act, 1887-1934.*

> The Allotment Act[56] provided that eventually every Indian would be given a share of his reservation to be held in trust for a period of twenty-five years, during which time it would not be taxed and could not be sold. After that time he would be given free patent and would be declared competent to manage his own affairs. It is estimated that Indians were separated from . . . more than 60 percent of their holdings, in 1887 as a result of the *Allotment Act.*
>
> Part of the difficulty lay in the restrictions on the sale of the lands. Heirs could not settle their estates except through subdivision . . . Another outcome was the practice of leasing land to whites [which developed when the Indians could not sell]; and the results of this practice still constitute a major problem. . . .[57]

The result has been that many Indians do not know how to manage or make use of their own land. These are skills many have never learned, and as a result they often do not know the true value of the land they may lease to whites for as little as a dollar an acre per year. The effect of the Allotment Act can be seen today on the Pine Ridge Reservation in South Dakota. A report on reservation lands prepared by the Adult Education Department of the Pine Ridge Agency identifies the present area of the reservation as comprising 1,822,349 acres, of which 325,579 acres are tribally owned—that is, they are owned by all members of the tribe; 54,167 acres are government owned; and the remaining 1,442,503 acres are trust allotments, owned by individuals. The trust-allotted acreage is comprised of 5,013 tracts, 1,858 of which have multiple owners, not merely joint ownership between husband and wife. This multiple ownership includes 800 tracts or 375,076.40 acres which, through inheritance, are now owned by six or more heirs, while another 1,058 tracts, or 562,614.90 acres, are owned by from two to five heirs.

The influence of early experiences is seen in the Indian's attitudes about the control of the range lands. It is almost as if he is responding to a conditional stimulus that has been established over the years and that prescribes that the only way he can use his range land is to lease it to non-Indians. The most important economic asset on the Pine Ridge Reservation is the range land, with about 1,349,010 acres devoted primarily to this use. Less than half, or 619,700 acres, is in Indian use.[58] Indians use 400 acres of irrigated land, while 187,964 acres are suitable for hay farming, of which 9,701 acres are used by Indians.[59]

Control of the Indian for the Betterment of the White Man

During this time and in spite of all that was happening, one white type stirred the Indian's imagination to the point of influencing his dress and his children's play: that white role model was the cowboy. The Sioux made a determined and successful attempt to develop a cattle economy from 1900 to 1917. However, the white Midwestern cattle interests from Texas northward pressured Washington to such an extent that a decree was given to the Sioux prohibiting them from being cowboys and raising large numbers of cattle on their allotted land. The loss of their cattle psychologically equalled the earlier loss of the buffalo, and so the Sioux quite readily accepted the theory advanced by some missionaries that they were the lost tribe of Israel—and under God's lasting curse.[60]

But the federal government was not the only exploiter of the Indian. Beginning in the late years of the Depression, the white tourism industry began looking upon the Indian as a diversion and encouraging him to exploit his past for profit. However, the profit for the Indian was very limited and thus bore more similarity to earlier exploitation. For example, Navaho women weaving blankets at home for sale to tourists made an average return of less than five cents an hour. When this fact became known, white men evaluating the situation were apt to comment "that these women enjoy weaving and thereby develop their artistic aesthetic appreciation to their betterment."[61] Because it was felt that the women were developing creativity, it was also felt that they did not need to make a profit on their experience or even to sell their blankets at what the weaving cost them. Because the Indian had had limited contact with the white tourist-buyer, he would place his crafts with the non-Indian owner of the trading post who, for his sales commission, would collect several times the pittance paid the Indian. Adding insult to injury was the employment of Indian clerks in these trading posts to give the impression of Indian ownership and Indian dancers outside as an attraction to bring in tourists.[62]

The Reorganization Act

The next phase of the United States' treatment of Indians was an attempt to motivate racial identification and tribal self-government. Brophy calls this the

> Government attempts at tribal reorganization under the provisions of the Reorganization Act June 18, 1934, 1934-1944. The Indian *Reorganization Act* is another example of control by race legislation. While the *Allotment Act* attempted to *Americanize* the Indians too quickly, the *Reorganization Act* goes to the other extreme and attempts to *Re-Indianize* the Indians.[63]

Under this policy Indian councils were recognized and empowered to undertake political, administrative, and economic self-government. Land allotment was to be stopped, and a system of agricultural and industrial credit was to be provided. Later it was recognized that the *Reorganization Act* had restored some of the self-government of the Indian, but in turn it had tied the Indian more than ever to the reservation.

The next phase of Indian treatment began in the mid-1940s and is still continuing. It consists of the relocation of Indians in work and training experiences off the reservation in an attempt to encourage their break with reservation living and provide them with opportunities for assimilation into the dominant society. Thus the emotional support of the reservation is not always provided. Without this emotional support, most effects of assimilation have been to weaken Indian family ties and to isolate the individual from his relatives and friends. More problems have arisen as a result of this policy as the Indian attempts to cope with the problems created from his being between cultures—neither part of the dominant society, which will not accept him, nor part of his own society from which he has been forced to depart.

Writing about the experiences of one Indian family moving into the city from a Midwest reservation, Carl T. Rowan says,

> Joe Brown's first shock was to find that Minneapolis [like most cities] has an unofficial "reservation" for Indian families. These are dark, squatted, bug-infested dwellings that fit society's ideas of what an Indian wants or deserves.
>
> There was another fact of life that Brown had to face; life on the reservation had not prepared him to compete with other men. He was unskilled, he had no work record, he was stigmatized by the white man's belief that the Indian is unpredictable and lazy and that all Indians go on a lost weekend after their first pay day. . . . For two years, Joe Brown was holding on, not giving in to hopelessness, yet not quite able to take that second step away from the reservation into the bigger, cleaner apartments where his children could see light occasionally. But this winter, the Browns went under, and now a drunken weeping woman just wanted "to forget everything. We came up here because we were sure we could get a new start," Mrs. Brown sobbed. "It seemed so close when the union told my husband he had a job at that lumber mill. But, when they saw this Indian walk in, they turned him away. Now my husband has given up."[64]

Termination Policy

In 1950 the United States government introduced a termination policy that would withdraw federal responsibility for Indian services but which ended in a complete failure. After 1958 a policy was introduced that no tribe would be involuntarily terminated. As a result of the obvious needs of the people, the Indian Resources Development Act was passed in 1967, which was to have given more attention to education, training, and manpower programs and less attention to forcing the breakup of the Indian reservations.

lucation for the Indian

The educational experience for the American Indian has been a continuous battle between parents and the federal government since the establishment of the Bureau of Indian Affairs. Education of Indian children was begun in the last decade of the nineteenth century by the federal government with an approach that lacked appeal to either parents or children.[65] Gordon MacGregor writing in 1946 specifically about the educational experiences of the Sioux, tells how children were virtually kidnapped from their parents and forced into government schools.[66] Their hair was cut and their Indian clothes thrown away. They were forbidden to speak their native language, although the younger children usually could not speak one word of English. The Indian child lived in the school under military discipline, and rules were enforced by corporal punishment.

Even very young children, lonely and homesick for their families, were punished severely if they dared to break a rule. Those children who persisted in clinging to their Indian ways and those who ran away and tried to find their way home to their parents were, if recaptured, thrown into jail. Parents who objected to their children being taken from them or who objected to their children being taught things that were counter to their culture were also jailed for interfering with the operation of the schools. Where possible, children were kept in school year after year to avoid the influence of their families, and parents were told not to visit or contact their children. This attitude persisted into the 1920s. School for the children was a prison from which to escape. Education became a battleground between the federal government and Indian parents, and in the long run it was Indian children who lost.

On the reservation the federal government withdrew rations of food in order to force Indian parents to send their children to school.[67] The force approach to education has resulted in the American Indian being the least well educated of any segment of the entire population, a fact reflected in a 1966 Health, Education and Welfare survey which stated that 16,000 Indian children between the ages of eight and sixteen were not in school. This early attitude toward education is also reflected in a 1969 report that there is a "sixty percent school drop out in the Bureau of Indian Affairs boarding schools as compared with a national average of twenty-three percent."

Parents have always resisted the federal boarding schools where most American Indians have received their education because the curriculum and the attitude of the school personnel have been so opposite to the Indian value system. This situation has not changed markedly over the years. The 1969 report states that the standard curriculum of the Indian schools has nothing to do with the culture of the Indians. Most Indian children speak English poorly or not at all, yet all their classes are conducted in English because only 16 percent of all Bureau of Indian Affairs teachers are Indian. Even when the teachers are Indian they generally are not of the tribe of their students and usually cannot speak or understand their students' home language. They may also be from what historically was an enemy tribe.

A curriculum that does not seem to meet their needs, teachers who do not speak their language or understand their culture, and a boarding-school atmosphere where they are removed from their homes for nine months at a time—all of these constitute what Daniel Henninger and Nancy Espesite identified in their 1968 report as alienation in the name of education. Their report says that although $68 million of the Bureau of Indian Affairs' $240 million were spent in 1968 on the education of 55,000 Indian children, there was little to show for it.

> Estranged from his family, confronted with an alien culture and unable to talk to his teachers, the Indian's academic performance is predictably poor.... For the first few years of school Indian achievement parallels that of white children and then slowly but persistently regresses. An Indian starts to fall behind between the sixth and eighth grades, and if he does not drop out, finishes high school with a 9.5 grade education.[68]

These are some of the man-made forces and historical events which have molded the American Indian and which account for the fact that of all those in rural America today—those whose ancestors owned the land even before Columbus was born—are the poorest. These are some of the factors which account for the difficulty of today's Native Americans having what Erik H. Erikson has called "a sense of identity," which comes from a progressive continuity between what the individual has come to be during the years of childhood and what he or she has promised to become in the future, "between that which he conceives himself to be and that which he perceives others to see in him and to expect of him." The years of disappointment and forced dependence have left the Indians unable to *trust*—to trust the dominant society, to trust members of their own race, and, even more destructive, to have enough self-confidence to *trust themselves.*

Present Conditions among American Indians

There are presently 290 Indian reservations under federal jurisdiction in the United States. They range in size from a few acres to the 14 million acre Navaho reservation in Arizona, New Mexico, and Utah. The Indian human resources are the least used of any segment of the American population; therefore, one-half of all Indian families in the early 1970s had an annual income of less than $2,000, and nearly three-fourths of the families earned less than $3,000. Three-fourths of all Indians live in substandard housing, yet with unemployment on some reservations being more than 70 percent (see Table 2), this has been hard to change.

There has been an increasing attempt on the part of the federal government in the early 1970s to involve Indians in decision making affecting their own welfare. This has been encouraged through local tribal governments as well as through a National Indian Advisory Committee. But as Niles Hansen points out, what is needed more than anything else is "to give the Indian the sociological and psychological preconditions for participation in a disciplined labor force, and then the training corresponding to available job opportunities."[69] Until these changes actually do take place, there will be little significant improvement in economic opportunities for Indians either on or off reservations.

TABLE 2
Percentage of Unemployed on Twenty-five Indian
Reservations, July 1968

Reservation	State	Population	Percentage Unemployed
Fort Berthold	North Dakota	2,657	79.0
Zuni Pueblo	New Mexico	5,000	77.0
San Carlos	Arizona	4,473	74.0
Lower Brule and Crow Creek	South Dakota	1,731	70.5
Rosebud	South Dakota	5,432	61.5
Mescalero	New Mexico	1,559	61.0
Gila River	Arizona	7,197	52.0
Fort Peck	Montana	4,196	51.0
Rocky Boys	Montana	1,149	50.0
Hopi	Arizona	5,556	48.0
Colorado River	Arizona	1,628	47.0
Standing Rock	South Dakota	4,720	47.0
Crow	Montana	4,097	44.0
Fort Apache	Arizona	5,407	43.0
Jicarilla	New Mexico	1,474	43.0
Salt River	Arizona	2,212	43.0
Navajo	Arizona	125,000	39.0
Blackfeet	Montana	6,381	39.0
Red Lake	Minnesota	2,538	38.0
Fort Yuma	Arizona	1,634	35.0
Flat Head	Montana	2,761	34.0
Pine Ridge	South Dakota	10,495	32.0
Fort Belknap	Montana	1,585	30.0
Leech Lake	Minnesota	2,796	26.0

Source: Economic Development Administration

NOTES

1. T. C. McLuhnan, *Touch the Earth* (New York: Outerbridge and Dienstfrey, 1971), p. 67.
2. "The American Indian and Government," in *One America*, ed. by Francis J. Brown and Joseph Slabey Roucek (New York: Prentice-Hall, Inc., 1945), p. 440.

3. Dee Brown, *Bury My Heart at Wounded Knee* (New York: Holt, Rinehart and Winston, Inc., 1970), p. 3.

4. Brophy, "The American Indian and Government," pp. 440-41.

5. *American Annual Cyclopaedia and Register of Important Events of the Year 1867*, Vol. VII (New York: D. Appleton and Co., 1868), pp. 399-400.

6. *Ibid.*

7. "What Can Society Do to Help Set Free Today's Indians?" *Minneapolis Tribune*, March 3, 1957.

8. E. H. Moore, The Honorable, "Extension of Remarks," Senate of the United States, February 25, 1944, as quoted in Brophy, "The American Indian and Government," p. 482.

9. Dale Van Every, *Disinherited* (New York: Avon Library Books, 1967), p. 106.

10. Andrew Jackson, who was called Sharp Knife by the Indians, was said to like nothing better than an Indian hunt. This reputation came out of his treatment of Indians during the Second War for Independence (War of 1812). The Creek Indians in Mississippi Territory, stirred up by Spanish agents from Florida and by a visit from Tecumseh, attacked Fort Mims on the lower Alabama River. General Jackson defeated the Creeks in the Battle of Horseshoe Bend and compelled them to sign the Treaty of Fort Jackson, by which they surrendered to the United States two-thirds of their lands in Alabama.

11. Troops numbering 7,000 were used to move the Cherokee. "Cherokee men, women and children were seized wherever found and without notice removed to concentration camps. Livestock, household goods, farm implements, everything went to the white camp followers; the homes usually were burned. After this the long trek to Arkansas in mid-winter was begun. An eye-witness in Kentucky reported: 'Even aged females, apparently nearly ready to drop into the grave, were traveling with heavy burdens attached to their backs, sometimes on frozen ground and sometimes on muddy streets, with no covering for their feet.' " As quoted by John Collier, *Indians of the Americas*, Mentor Books (New York: New American Library, 1947), p. 124.

12. "In 1837 the federal government established a mint in . . . [Dahlonega]. This mint coined more than one million gold pieces valued at approximately six million dollars . . ." Ruth Elgin Suddeth, Isa Lloyd Osterhout, and George Lewis Hutcheson, *Empire Builders of Georgia* (Austin, Tex.: Steck Co., 1963), p. 154.

13. James C. Bonner, *The Georgia Story* (Oklahoma City, Okla.: Harlow Publishing Corp., 1961), p. 209.

14. *Ibid.*

15. *Ibid.*, p. 205.

16. Suddeth, Osterhout, and Hutcheson, *Empire Builders of Georgia*, pp. 154-55.

17. *Indians of the Americas*, p. 124.

18. *Disinherited*, pp. 273-74.

19. Brown, p. 8.

20. *Ibid.*

21. *Ibid.*, p. 9.

22. "The American Indian and Government," pp. 443-44.

23. Quoted from a copy of the treaty which was given to this writer by a grandson of Chief Red Cloud, the Indian chief who entered into the original treaty with the United States on the part of his people, the Oglala Sioux.

24. Myrtle R. Reul, *Where Hannibal Led Us* (New York: Vantage Press, 1967), p. 188.

25. James H. MacGregor, *The Wounded Knee Massacre* (Baltimore, Md.: Wirth Bros., 1940), p. 22.

26. One-eighth of all the gold in the world has been taken from the Black Hills. Homestake in Lawrence County, South Dakota is the largest producing gold mine. This one Black Hills mine alone has yielded more than $500 million in gold.

27. U.S., Congress, House, *House Executive Document 184,* 44th Cong., 1st sess. (Washington, D.C.: Government Printing Office, 1875), pp. 8-9.

28. U.S., War Department, *War Department Annual Report 1875* (Washington, D.C.: The Department, 1875).

29. *House Executive Document 184,* pp. 10, 17-18.

30. *War Department Annual Report 1875,* p. 441.

31. Brown, *Bury My Heart,* p. 298. Also see pages 90-91 for details of soldiers' atrocities against Indian women and infants. For documentary evidence of atrocities against Indians see the United States Senate Executive Document 26 of the second session of the 39th Congress, pages 73-77, which reports that soldiers fired on a white flag held by a six-year-old Indian girl standing in front of forty women, all of whom were later shot; that they shot unarmed Indian men, women, and children, scalped them, sometimes mutilated their bodies, and even, in some cases, displayed their reproductive organs (especially the women's) on sticks or other objects. In other words, they did the things that the soldiers were accusing the Indians of doing. See also MacGregor, *The Wounded Knee Massacre,* pages 103-139, for sworn legal statements taken from Indian survivors of the December 29, 1890, massacre on the Pine Ridge Reservation in which 90 unarmed Indian men and approximately 200 women and children were killed by members of the Seventh Cavalry, of which General George Armstrong Custer had been the commanding officer. The reason for the massacre was to avenge the death of General Custer.

32. Brown, *Bury My Heart,* p. 300.

33. *Ibid.*

34. At that time, a man of the Sioux culture was not a man without a horse. Psychologically, the most degrading blow a man could receive would be to lose his horse and his role as hunter and warrior. In the Sioux's patriarchal society, with its clearly defined roles for men and women, it was a castrating experience—from which the Sioux would never recover—when the U.S. Army elevated the Sioux women by letting them own the prized animal, the horse, and did not allow the men to ride but made them walk behind as if they were camp followers.

35. An example of this may be seen on the Wind River Reservation in Wyoming. Three socially distinct groups live there. The Shoshoni inhabit the western half, bordering the mountains, the Arapaho the southeastern part, and interspersed among these two groups are a number of white settlers who have purchased or leased Indian allotments. Henry Elkin, in writing about this reservation, says, "A period of sixty years of living together has done little to break down the differences between the Arapaho and Shoshoni. . . . Although reservation life interrupted active hostility, the passive detachment and lack of friendliness between them contrast with the warm feelings both groups extend to Indians from other tribes. Their old fighting days are still remembered, and the Shoshoni still regard their neighbors as interlopers, without proper rights to their share of the reservation." Henry Elkin, "The

Northern Arapaho of Wyoming," in *Acculturation in Seven American Indian Tribes,* ed. by Ralph Linton (Gloucester, Mass.: Peter Smith, 1963), p. 231.

36. Elkin, in his study of the Arapaho, comments that "although agriculture was far from the most feasible economy for the Arapaho, the government never questioned its policy of making the Indians farmers. With their background of nomadic hunting, the Arapaho undoubtedly could more easily have taken over livestock, ideally suited to the resources of the region [Wyoming]. This course, however, was never considered for a number of reasons: it was held that the Indians could be kept under control only if they stopped roaming about and settled; an agricultural economy, moreover, conformed to the traditional White picture of civilized life; then, too, the surrounding Whites could exploit the rich grazing lands on the reservation." *Ibid.,* pp. 232-33.

37. "The American Indian," in *One America,* ed. by Brown and Roucek, p. 24.

38. *Land of the Spotted Eagle* (New York: Houghton Mifflin Co., 1933), p. xix.

39. Brown, *Bury My Heart,* p. 416.

40. *Ibid.,* p. 417.

41. *Ibid.*

42. *Ibid.,* p. 421-22.

43. *Ibid.*

44. This is the same Wounded Knee Creek which was the scene of the December 29, 1890 massacre in which nearly 300 unarmed Sioux men, women, and children were killed by United States soldiers. It is also the same Wounded Knee Creek area where young Indian youth, in the spring of 1973, held out in a seige against the federal government to draw attention to the plight of the American Indian and to demand that something be done to improve that situation.

45. U.S., Congress, Senate, *Senate Report 283,* 48th Cong., 1st sess. (Washington, D.C.: Government Printing Office, 1882), pp. 71-72.

46. Brown, *Bury My Heart,* p. 423.

47. *Senate Report 283,* pp. 71-72.

48. Brown, *Bury My Heart,* p. 424.

49. *Senate Report 283,* pp. 79-81.

50. Brown, *Bury My Heart,* p. 427.

51. Stanley Vestal, *Sitting Bull, Champion of the Sioux* (Norman, Okla.: University of Oklahoma Press, 1957), pp. 251, 255.

52. Brown, *Bury My Heart,* p. 428.

53. James McLaughlin, *My Friend the Indian* (Boston: Houghton Mifflin Co., 1910), p. 285.

54. U.S., Congress, Senate, *Senate Executive Document 51,* 51st Cong., 1st sess. (Washington, D.C.: Government Printing Office, 1886), p. 213.

55. The burial place of ancestors had special meaning, as Chief Joseph of the Nez Perces illustrates when he describes the death of his father Tu-eka-kas in 1871 and the promises he made to the old man. "My father sent for me. I saw he was dying. I took his hand in mine. He said: 'My son, my body is returning to my mother earth, and my spirit is going very soon to see the Great Spirit Chief. When I am gone, think of your country. You are the chief of these people. They look to you to guide them. Always remember that your father never sold his country. You must stop your ears whenever you are asked to sign a treaty selling your home. A few years more, and white

men will be all around you. They have their eyes on this land. My son, never forget my dying words. This country holds your father's body. Never sell the bones of your father and your mother.' I pressed my father's hand and told him I would protect his grave with my life. My father smiled and passed away to the spiritland. I buried him in that beautiful valley of winding waters. I love that land more than all the rest of the world. A man who would not love his father's grave is worse than a wild animal." Helen Addison Howard, *War Chief Joseph* (Caldwell, Idaho: Caxton Printers, Ltd., 1941), p. 84.

The same feeling that the burial spots were sacred had been expressed by earlier Indians, among whom was Chief Seattle of the Dwamish. In 1855, when surrendering his land with a protest speech to Governor Issac Stevens, he said, "To us the ashes of our ancestors are sacred and their resting place is hallowed ground." *Washington Historical Quarterly*, XXII (October, 1931).

56. According to John Collier, United States Commissioner of Indian Affairs, "The Indians of the whole country lost 90,000,000 acres to whites through the direct and indirect workings of land allotment in the years from 1887 to 1933; but in addition, they lost to whites the *use* of most of the alloted land still Indian owned." Collier, *Indians of the Americas*, p. 134.

57. "The American Indian and Government," p. 445.

58. And all of this on a reservation where a *Pine Ridge Agency Report* claims that the unemployment rate is 42 percent (10 percent higher than the Economic Development Administration report of 32 percent), with as many as 800 heads of families being unemployed much of the year. For the 10,495 Indians living on the reservation a figure of something more than $1,500 has been quoted as the average income. This may be misleading because of the relatively large amounts earned by the few Indians who own and operate their own ranches and by those who work for the federal government. Consequently, more than half of the heads of Indian families earn less than $900 a year, and much of this consists of the income from leased lands rented out to non-Indians. Often the Indians fear that if they raise the lease rate to reflect the real value of the land, no one would rent and there would be loss of the few hundred dollars a year which now come from rentals.

As recently as 1966 the gross value of agricultural production—including crop and livestock production as well as direct use of fish and wildlife by Indians on reservations—was about $170 million. Indian operators received $56.6 million of this total, while another $16 million was received by Indians from rents and permits. Income from mineral rentals, bonuses, royalties, and other sources amounted to $31 million during that fiscal year, and the timber sales yielded $15 million. In the same period Indians received $4 million from private developers who leased Indian land for commercial, industrial, and recreational uses. Behind these figures is that fact that while a few reservations have sufficient resources to support their Indian residents, most cannot provide them with even a near-adequate standard of living. U.S., Department of the Interior, Bureau of Indian Affairs, *Answers to Your Questions About American Indians* (Washington, D.C.: Government Printing Office, 1970), pp. 2-3.

59. "Oglala Sioux Reservation Pine Ridge, South Dakota," undated mimeographed report obtained by this writer from the Adult Education Department of the Pine Ridge Agency in 1964.

60. Erik H. Erikson, *Childhood and Society* (New York: W.W. Norton and Co., Inc., 1950), p. 102.

61. Wissler, "The American Indian," p. 25.

62. From personal observations on Indian reservations in various parts of the country. Usually the dancers used to attract the tourists are not paid for

their performances other than the contributions of those who watch, which frequently amount to only a very few dollars a week, and, when divided among all the dancers and drummers, represent very little for any.

63. "The American Indian and Government," p. 445.

64. "Indian is Outcast in City of Hope," *Minneapolis Tribune,* February 9, 1957. Reprinted by permission of the *Minneapolis Tribune.*

65. From personal observations and many discussions in 1964 with Edgar Red Cloud, descendant of Chief Red Cloud, who was the head of the Oglala Sioux when they were located by the federal government on the Pine Ridge Reservation in South Dakota.

66. See MacGregor's *Warriors Without Weapons* (Chicago: University of Chicago Press, 1946) for a complete description of the experiences of Sioux parents with the education of their children by the federal government.

67. Eberet Dale, *The Indians of the Southwest* (Norman, Okla.: University of Oklahoma Press, 1949), p. 181.

68. "Regimented Non-Education Indian Schools," *The New Republic,* February 15, 1969, pp. 18-21.

69. *Rural Poverty and the Urban Crisis: A Strategy for Regional Development* (Bloomington, Ind.: Indiana University Press, 1970), p. 180.

*I was leaving the South to fling myself into
the unknown. . . . Yet, deep down, I knew
that I could never really leave the South,
for there had been slowly instilled into my
personality and consciousness, black
though I was, the culture of the South. So,
in leaving, I was taking a part of the South
to transplant in alien soil, to see if it could
grow differently, if it could drink of new
and cool rains, bend in strange winds, respond to the warmth of other suns, and
perhaps, to bloom. . . .*

Richard Wright, 20th century American author
Black Boy

6

American Blacks

American Indians and white indentured servants were not the
only ones whose life styles and personalities were affected by social
determinants imposed upon them by those who struggled for
control and who saw oppression of a race or a nationality as the
only way for their own position in life to ever be secure. Short of
writing a complete social history on all peoples of this country, it is
impossible to give the entire picture of minority oppression. Therefore, I am considering for inclusion in these chapters only those
races and nationalities most directly involved in rural poverty today.

As we look at the rural population of the 1970s, it becomes
apparent that the oppression of Blacks, Chicanos, Orientals, and
farm workers as well as the regional prejudice and limited educational opportunities for generations of children take on a special
significance never considered at the time these historical events
first occurred.

As C. Vann Woodward explains, writing in the preface of his
book *The Strange Career of Jim Crow*, many Americans, because

of their geographical location, their area of limited experience, or their preoccupation with their own needs and problems, have come to accept many myths and false assumptions. They do not know the length of time that certain conditions have existed in this country, the prevalence of dehumanizing experiences, or the reasons such conditions came about in the first place. Many Americans "have naturally assumed that things have 'always been that way,' or, if not always, then 'since slavery times' or 'since The War,' or 'since Reconstruction.' "[1] Speaking of the Jim Crow laws, Woodward continues,

> Few [Americans] have any clear notion of [the law's] relative recency . . . or any clear notion of how, when, and why the system arose. There is nothing in their history books that gives them much help. And there is considerable in the books that is likely to mislead and confuse them.[2]

Woodward could have been writing about many aspects of rural America—especially rural, nonwhite America.

Blacks in America—The Beginnings

Probably the most apparent historical man-made forces whose influence can currently be seen in rural America are slavery and the treatment of Blacks. In order to obtain a perspective on this present influence, we must look at the role of Blacks throughout American history. It is also impossible to separate the history of American Blacks from the history of whites. They are interwoven. The Black-white relationship had its beginning much earlier than most of us are aware. In writing about the early period, James Weldon Johnson says:

> The history of the Negro in the United States begins definitely with the landing of twenty Africans at Jamestown, Virginia in August, 1619 . . . more than a year before the *Mayflower* landed at Plymouth Rock. These twenty Africans . . . [became] indentured servants . . . [to white masters with a] status . . . practically the same as that of white indentured servants. . . . With the increase of the numbers of Negroes in Virginia and the other colonies . . . there was a transition in this status from indentured to slavery. . . . At the outbreak of the Civil War the total Negro population of the United States amounted to 4,441,830 of which number 488,070 were free.[3]

Also writing on the history of Blacks, Edwin Roger Embree said of the freedman:

> There were over 250,000 freed Blacks living in the slave-owning southern states [in 1860]. Most of the freedmen were in the cities, but even rural Mississippi, in spite of its stringent regulations as to the freeing of slaves, recorded nearly a thousand free persons of color . . . many . . . were persons of considerable property, and a number . . . themselves owned slaves. . . .A free husband purchased his wife or vice versa. Parents purchased their children, and children who had been freed sought out their parents and bought them . . . it seemed safer to hold the relative in slavery than to free him since slaves could be protected from kidnapping more easily than freedmen. . . . But several Negroes, in the earlier decades of the nineteenth century, in Louisiana, South Carolina, Maryland and Virginia owned plantations of slaves and exploited them quite as ruthlessly as white masters.[4]

Also speaking of the freedman, E. Franklin Frazier said:

> A class of free Negroes had existed from the time the first Negroes had served their indenture. . . .But the chief means by which the class of free Negroes had increased was through emancipation. Many of the emancipated slaves were set free by their white fathers and white relatives. About three-eighths of the free Negroes were mulattoes.[5]

Southern Agriculture

The history of agriculture in the South is also the history of Blacks. For example, the first big money crop in America was tobacco. By the early eighteenth century "over one-third of all slaves in the colonies were concentrated in the tobacco fields of Virginia."[6] The century was only four decades old when rice had become an important export, and in 1741 the introduction of indigo created even a greater demand for slave labor. Sugar cane was brought to Louisiana from Barbados together with Blacks who were skilled in its cultivation and harvest. "By 1849, there were 1,536 sugar plantations using 150,000 Negroes."[7]

It was in cotton, however, that the greatest contributions by Black labor were made. With the invention of the cotton gin and the development of a world industry in cotton cloth, cotton growing surged forward as the greatest of all American crops. Its export exceeded all other commodities.[8] To plant and cultivate the fields and pick the crop, more and more slaves were needed. The life and labor of Blacks in the New World grew to revolve around cotton.

Influence of the Plantation System

In the time of slavery it was the plantation system that determined the relationship between Blacks and whites,[9] and even today remnants of this system and its influence can be seen among rural Southern Blacks. In the introduction to Charles S. Johnson's *Shadow of the Plantation*, Robert E. Park claims that, historically, the problems of rural Blacks were tied to two "quite different institutions: (1) the plantation and (2) the Negro peasant family." Park continues his elaboration of the Black family on the plantation:

> . . . in slavery, parents had little or no personal responsibility for the provision and care of their children. . . .The consequence was that natural maternal affection, rather than any common economic interest, constituted the tie that held the family together. The male member of the family did not count for much in this arrangement. . . .With the advent of emancipation the status of the Negro on the plantation had been suddenly transformed from that of a fieldhand to tenant farmer . . . his first conception of freedom was that of a condition in which he would be permanently out of work.[10]

The freed fieldhand did not accidently arrive at the concept that work did not go with freedom. While still a slave, the Black person received the impression that to be free meant no work; it meant to be *lazy*. This concept, too, was part of the myth acquired through limited observation of the white man's world and while listening to the white man's comments about work. Physical labor, according to what the Black thought he heard and saw, was only for Blacks or poor whites who "did not amount to anything." In the South there had always been a casual approach to work which gave rise to the myth of Southern laziness.[11]

The main money crop, cotton, seemed to accommodate itself to this myth and to a more casual attitude toward work than any other agricultural product. Cotton culture took fewer days of actual physical work, from the preparation of the fields for planting until the crop was harvested and sold, than did most other major agricultural crops. Cotton was even called a lazy man's crop because, unlike wheat, corn, cucumbers, or beans where a few hours of delay at the time of harvest could mean the loss of an entire crop, cotton could be picked over a period of several weeks or even months without loss. Not only could the harvest be adapted to the needs of the workers, the total days of applied labor to grow a crop of cotton was about 100, spread from early spring until late fall or even into winter.

The Relationship between Blacks and Whites during Slavery[12]

Understanding why Black slaves were not prepared for the demands of freedom or for living in an integrated society is not difficult since the Black slaves had very limited opportunities to come in contact with whites with whom they could talk. In another book I have described this limitation: "There was almost no contact between fieldhands and any member of the white race with the exception of white overseers who gave work assignments and punished or rewarded for work accomplished."[13]

Jessie Bernard goes into even more detail on the limited relationship between the Black fieldhands, who at that time in history were the vast majority of all Blacks, and the whites with whom they came in contact:

> The field slaves were cut off from the big house. As adults, they had only the most limited contacts with the outside world. They may have watched the comings and goings of their white owners—the carriages, the fine clothes, the elegant balls— perhaps the duels—but it all probably made little sense to them.[14]

Adding to the differences in interpretation of what they saw was the fact that the field slaves themselves represented many African cultures with different customs and dialects.[15] They often had no common language and could not always express their questions to each other. At the same time, each might have some vague distant memory of a tribal custom that he or his grand-parents had known, which gave a different meaning to what he saw among the whites.

On the other hand, the white value standards that the Black slaves did encounter were quite different:

Occasionally there was some contact with the poorest segment of the white population. These poor whites were usually illiterate. They were rejected as "uncouth peasants" by the genteel. Their language was filled with crude and profane expressions. Their behavior included much drinking, fighting and sexual promiscuity. . . .This is what the Black slaves were exposed to and what they learned. Because the field slaves learned from each other, and because they did not always understand, they often misinterpreted the white man's behavior and his expressions. Whether it was an accurate copy of what they saw, or whether it was a misinterpretation of what they thought they saw, this was what they patterned their lives after. So the fears, superstitions, expressions, behavior of the uneducated Black were originally the same as the fears, superstitions, behavior and expressions of uneducated whites.[16]

However, neither did the house servants have role models among the whites which would adequately prepare them for a life of freedom:

House servants had an opportunity to observe the behavior of the so-called refined and more cultured classes. Even there much of the behavior did not offer an adequate blueprint for the Black. Often the slave saw overindulgence, drinking and dueling. The slave saw "gentlemen" who were quick to quarrel and who made use of the dirk, the sword, or the pistol. . . .Violence had already become an accepted part of the Southern culture and would spread to all segments of the population, both white and Black. Betting and horse racing were eagerly entered into. Money was lost easily at cards or on a bet. . . .These things, in the mind of the slave, became associated with freedom. Gambling, drinking, dueling, cutting and lack of concern about the future was the behavior of free men and in turn became the pattern for the Black in his attempt to gain his freedom.[17]

Confusion at the End of the War

The war between the states ended in early April 1865, and although the terms of the surrender agreement presented to General Robert E. Lee provided that cavalry and artillery horses be left to be used "for the spring plowing," as General U. S. Grant put it, the season was already too late for very much cotton planting that year—even had the fields been prepared. This limited crop resulted in a shortage of work for both Blacks and whites. Thus the difficulties of the Reconstruction period had begun even before the war ended.

In addition to viewing freedom as a utopia without the demands of work, the Black slave, according to Robert E. Park, hungering for material ownership, had as "his first impulse and aim to get as deeply in debt as possible."[18] Although millions of Blacks were freed and could no longer be bought and sold, "they had no land, they had no tools, they had no capital, they had no cooking utensils—and they were surrounded by hostile tight-lipped [white] men who were determined to prove the whole thing [freedom for the Blacks] was a mistake."[19] They found themselves in new roles for which nothing in their prior experience had prepared them, anymore than their lives in Africa had prepared them for slavery with white masters. Under the system of slavery, their place as Blacks had been defined by tradition and law. As Lane Wharton states,

> Although the bad feeling between the Negroes and the poor whites already existed, there were few ways during slavery in which it could be expressed. . . .The poor white, at times not so well housed or clothed as the slave, still had two great distinctions to cling to and to preserve. He was a white man, and free; the Negro was black and a slave. With emancipation, only one of these differences remained.[20]

With the end of slavery, the traditional bases of race relations were destroyed and, one might say, the race problems of today were created. The freed Blacks, who had had such hopes for the day of "jubilee,"[21] who had been led to dream of freedom as a utopia, soon found themselves to be pawns in the hands of unscrupulous white men both from the North and within the South. As Frazier describes the situation,

> At first the federal government made a half-hearted attempt to provide land for the freedmen [a mule and forty acres of land]. But in the end, the freedmen were left as dependent upon the white landlords as during slavery. Moreover, the Negro artisan was thrown into competition with the "poor white," who was emancipated from the domination of the plantation system.[22]

This, then, was the long-awaited freedom for nearly 4.5 million Blacks,[23] nine-tenths of whom could neither read nor write.

In the period immediately after the war, thousands of Blacks were hungry. "Crowds of feeble men, women and children were living either in the open air or in rough shelters with brush-covered roofs. A severe epidemic of smallpox spread rapidly through the dirty hovels where people were cramped together in the cities."[24] For Blacks, hungry, sick, without work or a means to support themselves, the fantasy of the "jubilee" had to be forgotten in a world which was fast becoming increasingly hostile toward them. The only answer seemed to be to put aside their dreams and return to work on the land. E. Eric Lincoln describes this decision:

> While vast numbers . . . hungered for an education, they [the Blacks] were faced with the more immediate problem of earning a living. . . .The whites [were left] with land, but without either money or labor to develop it. Since Northern bankers had investment capital, and Negro labor was abundant the major question facing the South was how to bring together the land, the money, and the labor in an economically profitable enterprise.

> Sharecropping was the South's answer to the problem. The financiers lent the farmers money and the farmers in turn, used it to purchase tools, seed and food for the Negro workers. Sharecropping bound the Negro families to the land and to the landowner almost as effectively as had slavery.[25]

As the education of Blacks improved, they became a greater competitive threat. "During the last two decades of the nineteenth century, the Negro artisan and skilled worker [were] eliminated largely from the labor market by the organized efforts of white labor. When the Industrial Revolution came to the South with the appearance of the cotton mill, the Negro worker was excluded entirely from this field of work."[26] The competition between workers increased as did the bitterness and resentment between the poor whites and the Blacks. The only solution to the problem that white men could see was to control the competition through fear. Segregation and lynching were introduced as ways of keeping the Black person "in his place."

> If the psychologists are correct in their hypothesis that aggression is always the result of frustration, then the South . . . was

the perfect cultural seedbed for aggression against the minority race. Economic, political, and social frustrations had pyramided to a climax of social tensions. No real relief was in sight from the long cyclical depression of the 'nineties, an acute period of suffering that had only intensified the distress of the much longer agricultural depression. Hopes for reform and the political means employed in defiance of tradition and at great cost to emotional attachments to effect reform had likewise met with cruel disappointments and frustration. And all along the line signals were going up to indicate that the Negro was an approved object of aggression. These "permissions to hate" came from sources that had formerly denied such permission. They came from the federal courts in numerous opinions, from Northern liberals eager to conciliate the South, from Southern conservatives who had abandoned their race policy of moderation in their struggle against the Populists, from the Populists in their mood of disillusionment with their former Negro allies, and from a national temper suddenly expressed by imperialistic adventures and aggressions against colored peoples in distant lands.[27]

Reconstruction Period

It is impossible to understand the history of Black-white relationships in the South unless thoughtful consideration is given to the Reconstruction Act meted out over the veto of President Andrew Johnson in 1867 by a radical Congress which was determined to punish the ten states that had been part of the Confederacy. The Congressional Reconstruction Act grouped the Southern states into five military districts ruled by a major general of the army and supported by United States troops. The right to vote was denied any white man who had taken a leadership role in the Confederacy, while Blacks who could neither read nor write were pushed to participate on an equal basis with the few eligible whites who had never known prior leadership experience but who were now to help write new constitutions and sit in the new legislative assemblies. This meant that most leading white Southerners could neither vote nor be elected to office; therefore, political power in the South fell into the hands of either the former Black slaves who had no training or experience in self-government or into the hands of the uneducated whites or the whites who came from outside the area for the purpose of graft.[28] In the South Carolina legislature, for example,

There were ninety-eight Negroes to fifty-seven whites, and only twenty-two of the members could read and write. Two-thirds of the members paid no taxes at all, and the rest only trifling amounts; yet they spent the people's money lavishly, voting themselves large salaries, installing expensive furnishings in the capitol[29] and wasting millions on projects for railroads, canals, and public works, from which they reaped large sums in graft. The debt of the state increased from five million dollars in 1868 to nearly twenty million dollars in 1872.[30]

The message of President Johnson to the Congress on December 2, 1867, identified these kinds of dangers and even predicted the outcome should the Congressional Reconstruction Act be put into effect. He said:

It is true this military government is to be only provisional but it is through this temporary evil that a greater evil is to be made perpetual. If the guarantees of the Constitution [free speech, the right to vote, no soldiers in time of peace to be quartered in any house, without the consent of the owner, and persons protected against unreasonable searches] can be broken provisionally to serve a temporary purpose, and in a part only of the country, we can destroy them everywhere and for all time.[31]

The President continued to point out what he saw as the fallacy of the Congressional Act in planning to take voting privileges away from whites who knew something about decision-making processes and state government and give those voting privileges to illiterate Blacks without first educating the Blacks in the concept of self-government. He saw the Reconstruction Act as creating a situation that would not help the Blacks but instead would cause the whites of the South to hate the North and to retaliate in any way they could. While President Johnson may not have understood the psychological dynamics of what would happen, he could see that if even the right to express self through the vote were taken away from men who had been active in state governments, their anger toward such treatment would be turned somewhere. Stripped of their self-identity as contributing citizens, such individuals did one of two things: either they turned their anger back toward self or they projected it outward onto the Blacks as symbols of their own defeat. Those who internalized their anger were heading toward self-defeat—a form of fear of success which left many of these former white leaders dependent, passive, hostile, and withdrawn, living in the past and feeling they had been wronged. The anger of the majority was channeled toward defiance and hate of the North. As I examine the history of the South, especially the strong need to keep alive the events of the Civil War and the dreams of the Confederacy, I can see where the feelings, in rural areas in particular, had their beginnings in the Reconstruction Act. One way for those whites who had been the leaders of the South to tolerate the insults that they felt were imposed on them by the North through the Reconstruction Act was to deny the situation and to fantasize about the past—"the South would rise again; the Confederacy was not dead." Keeping the Confederacy alive and displaying visible reminders of its existence at every opportunity was a form of defiance in the beginning—a psychological means of fighting back, which has been used by all peoples in all parts of the world in every century who have felt themselves captives and felt the necessity to hold on to their identity through passive resistance. And to a large number of whites of the South in 1867, the Reconstruction Act was the beginning of a form of imposed captivity.

These were details that President Johnson could not know but which he seemed to sense would come to pass, and, therefore, in his 1867 message to Congress he made a plea that the Blacks of the South be educated for self-government and that the whites of the South as well as the Blacks be an important part of their new government. Like President Lincoln before him, he asked that the South not be considered merely a conquered province as New Mexico had been in 1848, to be disposed of according to the will of the conquerors. In his message Johnson gave his logic as to why he felt Blacks, if put in positions of state government, could not use their franchise wisely (unless they had help) and would be vulnerable to manipulation and easily duped by the unscrupulous men who were waiting for such opportunities. The president spoke of the privilege of franchise. He drew a comparison between the former Black slave of the South and the foreign immigrant of the North, reminding Congress that the immigrant was required to live five years in this country, "show a knowledge of our institutions," and pass an examination before being allowed to vote, although he may have been actively involved in the politics of his own country before he came to America. The president continued by pointing out that 4 million former slaves had been made citizens by the Fourteenth Amendment of 1866:

> Yesterday, as it were, four millions of persons were held in a condition of slavery that had existed for generations; today they are freemen, and are assumed by law to be citizens. . . . The plan of putting the Southern States wholly, and the General Government partially, into the hands of Negroes, is proposed at a time peculiarly unpropitious. The foundations of society have been broken up by civil war. Industry must be reorganized, justice reestablished, public credit maintained, and order brought out of confusion. To accomplish these ends would require all the wisdom and virtue of the great men who formed our institutions originally. I confidently believe that their descendants will be equal to the arduous task before them, but it is worse than madness to expect that Negroes [can at this time] perform it for us.[32]

For this stance and for opposing Congress and those who were in favor of bringing the South to "her knees," President Johnson was impeached for "high crimes and misdemeanors," but he was acquitted by one vote, and thus "the country was saved from the disgrace of using a clause of the Constitution as a weapon of personal and political vengeance against the highest office of the land."[33] Nevertheless, the president had failed, with the result that the Reconstruction Act became the law of the South. (Figure 8 is a cartoon from *Puck* depicting military rule in the South.) David Saville Muzzey describes how the South responded both to the act and to the iniquitous state governments set up under the act.

> Deprived of any legal means of defense . . . the South . . . resorted to intimidation. Secret organizations, chief of which was the Ku Klux Klan, took advantage of the Negroes' superstition and fear to force them back into a position of social and political obscurity. Bands of young men on horseback, robed in ghostly white sheets, spread terror through the Negro quarters at night and posted on trees and fences horrible warnings to carpetbaggers and scalawags to leave the country if they wished to live.[34]

In the spring of 1877, ten years after President Johnson's message to Congress, the last of the federal troops were withdrawn from the Southern states, and "home rule" was established in a

Fig. 8. Reconstruction, carpet bag, and bayonet rule—cartoon from *Puck* in the 1870s. (Courtesy of the General Research and Humanities Division of the New York Public Library, Astor, Lenox and Tildon Foundations.)

South whose economy was ruined, whose credit was gone, and whose time and psychic energy, which should have been devoted to economic recovery, were absorbed in the struggle to wrest political control from the exploitive Northern carpetbaggers and to define the role of Blacks in the new social order. And in the end it was the Blacks of the South who were to be victimized by both the South and the North.

Some of the more extreme forms of discrimination toward the Black in the South did not come about until twenty or more years after Southern whites had regained control of the South, so they could hardly have been a direct reaction to Reconstruction. Woodward believes the reason for this increased discrimination against Blacks was due largely to the need for a means to help reconcile the North and South and to solve class conflict among whites in the South.[35] Various ways were planned to keep Blacks under control. The sharecrop method was one way.

The Sharecropper System

The sharecropper concept continued to enslave millions of people for nearly a hundred years. The owner of the land supplied tools, machinery, and seed. In return the tenant gave him a stipulated share of the crop. This system of paternalistic control was often abused to the point of distorting records so that regardless of the size of the crop, the tenant was never out of debt.[36] Those who were too old to work the land were often turned out without any concern for their age or their care.[37] It was not only the Black tenant who was caught in this web but also the white tenant, in later years and in larger numbers. Where formerly the sharecropper system applied mostly to Blacks, by the mid-1940s 5.5 million white workers and their families were caught in the system, compared to slightly over 3 million Black workers and their families.[38]

While many of these plantation systems were small with only a few hands, others were run as big businesses and thus, because of good business management, they showed larger profits in good years and lost less when crops were poor. One of these large operations was Panther Burn Plantation, where 9,000 open acres were cultivated for cotton. The story of the management of this cotton plantation is given here in detail so the reader can get some feel for the many controls of the plantation system that still exist in some rural areas of the South.

Panther Burn Plantation

Harris Dickson describes the plantation with these words:

Panther Burn is not a mere plantation; it's a principality, wonderfully prolific, whose mellow miles lie along the banks of Deer Creek. Seven hundred black families live and labor here— 1700 "head" as the Negroes put it, counting men and women, big and little. And seven hundred mules. Stores, gins, blacksmith shops, a residence street for white employees, railroad station, post office and churches form a busy community, with its own school district where 350 black children are instructed.

Four white managers supervise all planting operations, each having his separate fields for which he's held responsible. New ground is annually being added, more and more cotton produced. In ten years production increased from 1426 bales to 5940.

Tenants are divided into two classes: the "renters," consisting of thrifty Negroes that own their mules and gear. To these will be assigned as many acres as their families and hired hands are able to cultivate, for which the "renter" pays a fixed rental—seventy pounds of lint cotton per acre. "Share hands" own no stock, nothing except their hides and legal clothes to cover them. They are given land, cabin, mules, gear, everything, then split fifty-fifty with the landlords.

While Panther Burn has perhaps a higher percentage of intelligent Negroes than most plantations, yet tenants and share hands alike need the daily direction of white men. In varying weather, on diverse soils and with different seed, nearly every Negro must be shown how and when to work his crop.

To show him is the job for a trained agriculturalist. The manager must know. He consults the boss, four managers confer with one another and see that things are properly done.

Any manager sufficiently competent to be retained year after year on Panther Burn must understand his business; and, furthermore, he must by some sort of instinct sense the Negro psychology. Many a planter fails because he cannot get results from his labor. Some are too hard, many more are too lenient. The Negro is a shrewd judge of white men and gives willing obedience to those who treat him fairly. But if any Panther Burn tenant or share hand refuses to cultivate his crop as directed, the landlord simply takes a loss and moves him off the property.

Frederick the Great once said, "An army goes on its belly," so does a plantation, and Panther Burn's service of supplies clicks like a clock. From early spring a regiment of human beings must eat, drink and wear clothes on credit, until cotton turns into money about September 1st. Seven hundred mules standing idly at the trough will eat themselves up in a year.

The pockets of a cotton-farming Negro may bulge with money at Christmas, yet before the first of February it has vanished for gasoline and gingersnaps so the boss begins issuing rations on credit. There's the rock where many a planter has been wrecked. If the season looks promising he allows his tenants too much latitude at the store. The crops fail and he loses all.

Heretofore Panther Burn tenants and share hands were supplied with actual commodities. To subsist a family of three, this standard ration was issued every two weeks:

```
16 pounds dry salt meat . . . . . . . . . . . $1.92
 8 pounds lard . . . . . . . . . . . . . . . . . . 1.20
24 pounds flour . . . . . . . . . . . . . . . . . . .75
24 pounds meal . . . . . . . . . . . . . . . . . . .60
 5 pounds rice . . . . . . . . . . . . . . . . . . . .30
 1 gallon molasses . . . . . . . . . . . . . . . . .80
 2 plugs tobacco . . . . . . . . . . . . . . . . . .30
   salt . . . . . . . . . . . . . . . . . . . . . . . . . .05
   coffee . . . . . . . . . . . . . . . . . . . . . . . .35
                              Total    $6.27
```

Epicures would consider it a skimpy menu, but the Negro may supplement his store rations by growing greens in the garden patch to cook with salt meat. He may [raise] . . . cabbages, potatoes, all sorts of truck which the soil produces most generously. Busy hens should supply omelets. Pasture lands, free of rent, encourage him to keep a cow. His hog pen too is free. . . . Store stuff is cut to the minimum, and Negroes are compelled to do what they should always have done from choice.

Here's one case: Steve Jackson, Senior, has five grown boys, a wife, daughter, and cousin to help him work. Fifty-five acres of cotton, and twenty-three acres are planted in corn with beans to grow upon the stalk, and give back to the land what the corn takes out.

```
  5 acres in soy beans for stock feed and hay
1/2 acre of cow peas for table use
3/4 acre sweet potatoes
```

1/4 acre tobacco for smokes and "twist"
  1 acre Louisiana sugar cane for molasses
1/2 acre sorgum cane
1/4 acre Irish potatoes
1/8 acre peanuts
  1 acre kitchen garden, cabbage, onions, peppers, collards,
    tomatoes, all sorts of green food
  2 cows, 13 head of hogs; plenty of chickens
12 or 15 acres of free pasture, fenced in

Steve Jackson and family, like most of Panther Burn Negroes, can live pretty well and owe very little at the end of the year.

It has long been a rule on Panther Burn never to buy stock feed. Fancy figures for cotton will seduce many a planter to increase his yield by devoting every acre to lint and raising no corn, on the theory that a successful cotton acre brings cash enough to purchase more grain than can be grown on two acres. Panther Burn, however, sticks to the live-at-home idea, one third of its acreage being planted in alternate hills of corn and soy beans. Added to green stretches of alfalfa, upward of two thousand five hundred are growing feedstuffs. Next year these lands will go back to cotton and the crops be rotated.

Partly because of the 1930's disaster and worse in 1931, the plantation has changed its service of supplies. Instead of doling out meat and meal and molasses, the bosses have adopted a "cash limit" system. Every other Saturday all tenants and share hands assemble at the store, where the head of each family is given a small envelope of cash. This is based upon seventy-five cents per acre per month, so that a Negro whose wife and children help to cultivate thirty acres will receive on "limit day" an advance of $11.25. He gets no further credit and pays cash at the store. The store is extremely well handled, wholly independent of the plantation. All plantation purchases are charged up and their merchandise must show a separate profit.

The store too is somewhat of a bank. Here and there a prudent Negro saves his money, which he leaves there on deposit, drawing four percent interest.[39]

White-Black Racial Prejudice

As has been shown, much of the present ill will in race relations and much of the earlier violence, such as lynchings, had their beginning in the dark days of the Reconstruction period following the Civil War. The poor whites of the South, many of whose ancestors came to America as indentured servants or who were pushed into the hills by the powerful landed whites, now turned the fury of their hate onto the freed Black. During slavery these whites had been able to eke out a livelihood in odd jobs of short duration when extra hands were needed in the harvest or when they were employed by a small plantation which had only a slave or two. Now they were competing for their daily living with those who had been slaves. Many times the Black exslave was more skilled, better trained, and had a higher education than the poor white worker and was, therefore, preferred by the white employer. The answer to the problem as seen by white men was to keep the Blacks subservient.

The Rise of Segregation and Lynchings

Keeping the Black subservient meant keeping him poor and uneducated. But at the same time, the Black's labor was necessary to the restoration of the South's economy. Ironically, the preservation of segregation became the special function of the poor white, who had traditionally been as victimized by the prevailing economic, social, and political conditions of the wealthy white as the Black.

It was not by accident that poor whites took over the control of Blacks through segregation, Jim Crow laws, and lynchings. It was an arrangement entered into by white men of the upper class and white men of the lower class. In a book that is both an autobiography of a Southerner and an analysis of the South, Lillian Smith tells the story of two men and the bargain they made:

> Once upon a time, down South, Mr. Rich White made a bargain with Mr. Poor White. . . . He called in Mr. Poor White and said, "I've been thinking a lot about you and me lately— how hard it is for us to make a living down here with no money and the rest of the country against us. To keep my farm and mill going the way I want them to go, making big profit off of little capital, I have to keep wages low, you can see that. It's the only way I can make as much as I want to make as quickly as I want to make it. And folks coming in from the North have to keep wages low too, for that's our southern tradition.
>
> "It's a good way for us rich folks and it's not bad for you either, for you're smart enough to see that any job's better than no job at all. And you know too that whatever's wrong with the

South isn't my fault or your fault but is bound to be the Yankee's fault or the fault of those freight rates. . . .

"For instance, the nigger. You don't need me to tell you that ever since the damyankee freed him, the nigger's been scourging you, pushing you off your land, out of your job, jostling you on the sidewalks, all time biggity. If he hadn't been freed, he'd never bothered you, for I could have kept him on the farm and bossed him like I bossed him for 200 years. But the damyankees always know better, don't they! Here I am busy at my mill with no time to boss him, and here he is pushing, causing lots of trouble. Thing I can't forget is your skin's the color of my skin and we're both made in God's image; we're white men and white men can't let a nigger push 'em.

"There's two jobs down here that need doing: Somebody's got to tend to the living, and somebody's got to tend to the nigger. Now, I've learned a few things about making a living you're too no-count to learn (else you'd be making money same way I make it): things about jobs and credit, prices, hours, wages, votes, and so on. But one thing you can learn easy, any white man can, is how to handle the black man. Suppose now you take over the thing you can do and let me take over the thing I can do. You boss the nigger, and I'll boss the money. How about it?

Anything you want to do to show folks you're boss you're free to do it. You can run the schools and the churches any way you want to. You can make the customs and set the manners and write the laws (long as you don't touch my business). You can throw books out of libraries if you don't like what's in them and you can decide pretty much what kind of learning, if any, you want southern children to have. If science scares you and you don't like the notion of messing around with it, remember you don't have to, this is God's country and a free one. Anyway it'll tell you things you can't believe and still believe what you believe now so it's better maybe not to take much stock in it.

"If you ever get restless when you don't have a job or your roof leaks, or the children look puny and shoulder blades stick out more than natural, all you need do is remember you're a sight better than the black man. And remember this to: There's nothing so good for folks as to go to church on Sunday. To show you I believe this, I'll build you all the churches down at the mill and on the farm you want—just say the word.

"But if you don't have much to do, and begin to get worried-up inside and mad with folks, and you think it'll make you feel a little better to lynch a nigger occasionally, that's OK by me too; and I'll fix it with the sheriff and the judge and the court and our newspapers so you don't have any trouble afterwards; but *don't expect me to come to the lynching, for I won't be there.*

"Now, if folks are fool enough to forget they're white men, if they forget that, I'm willing to put out plenty money to keep the politicians talking, and I don't mind supporting a real first-class demagogue or two, to say what you want him to say—just so he does what I want about my business. And I promise you: Long as you keep the nigger out of your unions, we'll keep him out of our mills. We'll give you the pick of what jobs there are, and if things get too tight you can take over his jobs also, for any job's better than no job at all. Now that's a bargain. Except of course, if you're ever crazy enough to strike or stir up labor legislation, or let the niggers into your unions, or mess around with the vote, then we'll have to use the black folks, every goddam one of them maybe, to teach you a lesson. We'll tell folks—or our politicians will—that you're mongrelizing the white race with your unions, we'll tell 'em you're so low-down you're begging the nigger to be your social equal, and if that won't work, we'll tell them the black man is after your women. We have ways and we'll use them.

"Best thing you can do, seems to me, is to Jim Crow everything. It'll be easier for us that way to keep the niggers out of the unions and down on the farm where they belong, and it ought to make you feel better for a lot of reasons. For one thing, you can ride with us in the front of the streetcar and bus and shove the colored folks plumb onto the back seat. You'll like that and we won't mind much either—though God knows you can stink as bad as any of 'em when you go round dirty. But we'll put up with it, for we don't ride the streetcars and buses much anyway, and we can see how it makes you feel a lot better to know you can sit up front and the black man can't sit there; even if he's a college professor, he can't sit there, re-member! So fix that up any way you say. And you can do the same about trains and waiting rooms and toilets and movies and schools and churches and so on. And you can make rules about restaurants and hotels too if it'll make you feel better. And I reckon it will, though you aren't likely ever to go into one of the hotels or restaurants you put your Jim Crow rule on. But even if you don't have money to go in one of the them, it'll make you feel good to know you're sort of bossing things there. . . . So go on and fix all the Jim Crow you want. When you don't have meat to eat and milk for the younguns, you can eat Jim Crow and if you don't think too much about it, you'll never know the difference, for you don't seem to have much sense, anyway."

And Mr. Rich White and Mr. Poor White thought they'd made a good bargain.[40]

So it was to be that segregation presented the poor white man with a psychological release so strong that he simply overlooked the common lot he shared with the Black. Awarded social certification as the Black's superior, the poor white flaunted the white supremacy code because it artifically raised his position in society. He passed and enforced the Jim Crow laws.[41]

Woodward feels that Blacks themselves were aware of class differences and that the so-called crackers or poor whites were the ones insisting upon Jim Crow laws. Woodward describes what happened when the whites of the North began to abandon the Blacks:

> When Northern liberals and radicals began to lose interest in the freedmen's cause and federal protection was withdrawn, it was natural that the Negro should turn to the conservatives among upper-class Southerners for allies. While there was a certain amount of fawning Uncle-Tomism among the Negroes, there is little doubt that the prouder of them secretly despised the patronizing pose and self-flattering paternalism of the whites with whom they found refuge. It was no sentimentality for "Ole Marster" that inspired the freedmen, but the hot breath of cracker fanaticism they felt on the back of their necks.[42]

Since it was in the rural area that Blacks had the greatest degree of contact with poor whites, it was in rural areas that the caste system imposed its strongest hold to keep Blacks out of any work experience wanted by whites. As Allison David and John Dollard point out, the caste taboos on the Blacks were more "numerous and the punishments for infractions more severe in the rural areas than in the city itself. The severity of the controls upon Negroes increased in direct proportion to the distance of the rural area from a large town or city."[43]

Many authors have described the insanity of gloating white mobs who took part in the beastiality of lynchings, their tortures and perversions, the whippings, the stabbings and cuttings, the branding, the disfigurement, the dragging of a man or even a young boy for miles over country roads tied behind a car, the burning alive, the hangings, and even further mutilation after death—all done in an attempt to terrorize a race, to frighten a people into anonymity so they would not take certain jobs or live in certain neighborhoods.[44] It worked, as David and Dollard point out:

> It is not necessary to have a large number of such demonstrations in order to intimidate the Negro population. To be able to understand this fact, we must remember that human beings learn to accept restrictions by means of identifying with other persons with the family or group who *have been punished* for not learning the required behavior.[45]

Another revolting aspect of this period of Black history was the popular belief that all of this was done to protect white women, while the fact that Black women at the same time were constant and easy prey of white men was ignored without any thought expressed that they needed protection.[46] The truth of the matter is that it was never even suggested that the reason for most of the lynchings of Blacks was rape or sex. *The Changing Character of Lynching*, published in 1942, reports that of the 3,811 Negroes lynched between 1899 and 1941, only 641 or less than 17 percent, were even accused of rape—either attempted, alleged, or committed.[47] And it has been proven that many of the accusations of rape had no basis in fact. Investigations showed that white men, determined to get rid of a Black, would accuse him of an attempted sex crime, and that law officers would condone the lynching which automatically followed such an accusation. This was the injustice that white women of the South fought to change. Smith describes their action in this fashion:

> The lady insurrectionists gathered together in one of our southern cities [Atlanta, Georgia]. They primly called themselves church women but churches were forgotten by everybody when they spoke their revolutionary words. They said calmly that they were not afraid of being raped; as for their sacredness, they could take care of it themselves; they did not need the chivalry of a lynching to protect them and did not want it. Not only that, they continued, but they would personally do everything in their power to keep any Negro from being lynched and furthermore, they squeaked bravely they had plenty of power.
> They had more than they knew. They had the power of spiritual blackmail over a large part of the white South. All they had to do was drop their little bucket into any one of numerous wells of guilt dotting the landscape and splash it around a bit.

No one, of thousands of white men, had any notion how much or how little each woman knew about his private goings on [his years of sexual relationship with black women]. Some who had never been guilty in act began to equate adolescent fantasies with reality, and there was confusion everywhere.

This was in 1930. These women organized an Association of Southern Women for the Prevention of Lynching. Their husbands, sons, brothers and uncles often worked by their sides; many of them with sincere concern for the state of affairs, others because they had to.[48]

Thus the caste system for Blacks was developed in the South. It served to remove the threat of Blacks taking jobs wanted by poor whites; it served also to determine that, regardless of how much the Black person accomplished, he or she would still be considered second class and below the least accomplished white. In rural areas of the South the caste system guaranteed the availability of Black sharecroppers and tenant farmers. And since Blacks were not employed in the textile mills, the system guaranteed that there would be Blacks to pick the cotton.

Some of these rural Black cotton pickers would be paid by either the hour or the day, the women who picked always receiving a lesser amount regardless of the dexterity of their fingers or the length of time they spent in the field. A Black woman in the Alabama Black Belt in the early 1930s told it this way:

> We jest work by the day and pay $1.50 a month for this house. It's jest a piece of house. I gits 50 cents a day and my husband and the boy gits 65 cents each [the boy was sixteen]. We have to feed ourselves and pay rent out of that. My husband is pretty scheming, but sometimes he can't git nothing to do. I don't know how much time we lose, but he works most of the time. Course the boy stops and goes to school in the winter sometimes, but if he can git work to do, he works too.[49]

Other Blacks worked for what is called a "hand's share." This amounted to just enough to keep them alive. One old woman, also in the Alabama study in the early 1930s, told the following story:

> I works for a hand's share in the crop with the folks cross dere. My husband been dead. I ain't never had but one child and dat's de son what's right down dere. . . . I been up north in Birmingham with my sister . . . but I come back here, 'cause

dese chillun kept worrying me to come on here to live wid
them. It's mighty tight on me to have to go working in dese
fields half starved, and I ain't had a bit of money to buy a piece
of cloth as big as my hand since I been back. I washed fer white
people in Birmingham, and dey was good to me. I am jest gitting
long by the hardest. I works for dese people for a hand's share
in the crop. Dey gives me a load of corn and a load of potatoes.
I gits some of all the other stuff what's made, and when selling
cotton dey give me a little money out of the seed. I don't see no
money on time. Dey gives me a little something to eat 'cause I
works wid dem and dey gives me a little groceries. I never was in
this fix before in my life. I had good money when I come from
Birmingham. I had two fives and five single dollahs. I sho' gonna
git what I works for dis year.[50]

Few of the Black men in the rural areas were able to find any
work except in the fields, in logging, or in the turpentine camps.
The women obtained more regular employment working as household maids or doing laundry. In most cases it was the Black woman
who earned more money consistently throughout the year. As we
will see in part 3, it was not unusual for the men of the Black
families to leave in search of work or simply because they felt their
families could get along better without one more mouth to feed.

At the same time, Black adults were and still are in rural areas of
the South, caught in this sort of destructive work cycle; the pattern
of limited kinds of work experience was being perpetuated for the
Black child through limiting school experiences.

Education of Blacks in the South

R. Freeman Butts reports that "after 1876, when the upper-
class whites came back into power in the South, many of the laws
which for a time had been liberal toward the education of Blacks
were either revoked or disregarded. The easiest way to discourage
Blacks from trying to get training for anything other than menial
labor was simply not to vote adequate funds for Negro schools,"[51]
thereby condemning large numbers of Blacks to practically no
education. By insisting upon a dual educational system for whites
and Blacks, which was much more expensive, a nearly bankrupt
South almost guaranteed that without enough money to go
around, the Black schools would obviously suffer most. The Black
schools would be taken care of after the major needs of the white

schools were met. This policy was designed after 1876 by revoking the laws of 1868, and it became a policy of the educational systems of that section of the country, especially in rural areas, for nearly ninety years.

Education in the South

Writing on the history of education in the United States, Butts identifies an early difference between the South and other parts of the country, which also affected the rural areas. "In the South . . . from the beginning, education was looked upon as a private affair to be provided by those parents who were capable of providing it."[52] He goes on to say that in this respect the South followed the pattern of England.

> In general . . . "free education" in the South meant charity education for the poor, and upper-class parents therefore naturally did not want free education for their children. Here was a considerable difference, even in the seventeenth century, between New England [whose educational pattern of public education would later influence the Midwest and far West] and the South that was to have lasting importance. New England built up a tradition of free education as perfectly proper for self-respecting members of the community, whereas a stigma was long connected with free education in the South because of its connection with charity. The only educational concern of the state in the South was for orphans or children of poor and indigent parents who could not take the responsibility of educating their children.[53]

This early divergence in philosophy toward public education would account for dissimilar qualities and standards of education as well as for the marked differences in appropriations for monies for public education between New England and the South even today. It would also mean that the poor Southern white, too proud to "be beholden to anyone" would rather see his children uneducated than to have them take charity, which was what the public school meant to him.

An internationally known newspaper columnist, when speaking of the place of education in the South, said,

> The South did not really undertake to provide universal public education until nearly the turn of the century . . . they

remained near the bottom in most aspects of education. We had fewer teachers to teach and more pupils on less money than is true elsewhere in the country. The South continues to be the only region in America with a rising birth rate. We have a greater share of the nation's children, less money for their education, and fewer jobs to offer them after leaving school . . . our school system . . . is still geared to the liberal arts program so that few of our people come to town with any skill.[54]

This emphasis on a liberal arts education in all public high schools, with stress on preparation for college and very few vocational or technical programs even in rural areas, is still primary, and it still creates an educational problem in the 1970s throughout the South. Rural students having backgrounds with no emphasis on college or from backgrounds where even a high school education is deemed unnecessary need special programs that the average public Southern school does not provide. Students whose elementary education was limited either because of poor school attendance or because of inadequate preparation are ill prepared for a liberal arts high school experience where the curriculum has little relevance to their way of life. The result is failure in school, and school dropouts are increasing in number. The too-rigid curriculum may be the major cause for school dropouts in Southern states like Georgia, which in 1972 had the highest school dropout rate of any state in the country. And it is in the rural areas where the school failure rates are the highest and where students are the least prepared by their school experiences, whether they stay in school or drop out, whether they are Black or white.

Sixteen years after Ralph E. McGill's 1951 comments on education in the South, a geography professor writing on the same subject said:

Education levels in the South are low, whether they be measured in terms of school expenditure per pupil, teachers' salaries, percentage of seventeen-year-olds enrolled in school, or years of school completed by those twenty-five and over. In 1960, almost half of all adults in the South had only an elementary education, as compared with a third of the adults in the rest of the nation. And the poor quarter of the nation (the Southeast) has almost exactly half of those adults who had not gone further than the fourth grade.[55]

Expenditures for Public Education

An examination of the expenditure of public educational funds in the South in the mid-1930s shows a direct relationship to the present educational situation in rural sections in that part of the country. The national average annual educational expenditure for the school year 1935-36 as reported by the President's Advisory Committee on Education was $74.50 per pupil in average daily attendance. In that period ten Northern states averaged $107.47 per child per school year, compared with $33.16 spent in ten Southern states. When the racial differentials within all Southern states at that time were taken into consideration, they were frequently found to be as great or sometimes greater than regional differences. In 1930 the annual expenditure in eleven Southern states was $44.31 for each white child enrolled in school, and $12.57 for each Black child.

> When the unenrolled children—more prevalent among Negroes—are taken into consideration, the racial differentials are even greater. Then, too, there is the fact that educational funds are finally distributed county-by-county in most Southern states, and the greatest racial differentials readily occur in these small administrative units. In hundreds of Southern counties, the white child of school age receives ten times as much as the Negro child; in scores of counties, more than twenty times as much.[56]

The limited budget for the Black schools is pointed out by Robert B. Eleazer in the pamphlet *Thy Neighbor as Thyself,*[57] in which he quotes annual expenditures in 1932 for Lowndes County, Alabama of $75.50 per white child and $1.82 per Black child; Macon County, Georgia, $52.26 per white child and $2.59 per Black child; and in DeSota County, Mississippi, $28.26 per white child and $1.10 per Black child. Breaking this down into the actual expenditure per enrolled child, Eleazer later, in an unpublished manuscript, computed $86.75 for the white child and $4.30 for the Black child in East Feliciana Parish, Louisiana; $69.87 and $4.25 in Lowndes County, Alabama; $32.13 and $1.16 in Elbert County, Georgia; and $26.63 for whites and $.85 for Blacks in DeSota County, Mississippi.

Charles S. Johnson and his associates in their research in mid-Alabama during that same period had this to say about the Black school-age child and his school experiences:

Although being registered in a school does not mean regular attendance, there were many children who could not go to school at all. Children in the family [in the study] over eight are considered full farm hands, and only in exceptional cases were they found attending school. Again, children do not begin school until they are six years old. . . . The usual period during which school is kept open is October to May. Attendance fluctuates by months to such an extent as to keep the school work seriously disorganized and render impossible very consistent learning on the part of the children. There is fullest attendance when children are not needed in the field. Other factors, however, enter in to affect school attendance. Lack of sufficient clothing, and in winter particularly the lack of shoes, keep children away. Distance is another and extremely important factor. They walk usually from one to five miles and back each school day, for there is no service of bus conveyance such as is provided for white children of the county. At one school two children from the same family walked fourteen miles a day. Again, the cost of books, the special fees to supplement the teachers' pay—"for teacher's board," the families explain—keep the numbers down. The teachers although practically dependent upon these fees, do not always feel disposed to insist on them, particularly when it means losing the child because his parents could not provide the sums required. There are other occasions bringing urgent demands for money which the ordinary tenant families do not have. The introduction of sanitation, for example, sometimes means payment by the families for the building of approved toilets. If the schools are fortunate enough to get a competent teacher with ideas and a program, the extra items, such as simple playground equipment, must be privately purchased by the community [i.e., the parents themselves].

Two of the schools attended by the children of these families were held in a small church. One of the teachers was a young woman of about ninth-grade standing; the other, an older woman, crude but resourceful, was passionately devoted to the education of these children, but handicapped both by her own deficient background and by the lack of physical equipment, including a schoolhouse. . . . In 1930 there were in the entire [Alabama county under study] 8,580 educables, 1,435 white and 7,156 Negroes. For the 1,435 white children there was expended $57,385 and for the 7,145 Negro children $27,813. Alabama is, of course, one of the states with least ability to support education, and the expenditure for white children is seriously below the standard for the country at large. Moreover, although the ratio of expenditure has remained about the same over the last fifteen years, the amounts spent had been somewhat increased. In 1915 the total amount spent for 9,136 children was $28,792 of which sum $19,247 went for teachers' salaries for 1,283 white children and $9,545 for teachers' salaries for 7,853 Negro children.[58]

These differences between the white and the Black schools could naturally be measured also in library facilities, lunchrooms, transportation, and school buildings. In the absence of publicly owned schoolrooms, thousands of one-room Black schools existed in Negro churches, lodge halls, and empty tenant houses. There was also racial discrimination in teachers' salaries. In many rural areas the white teacher received 75 percent more salary than a Black teacher with the same certificate and equal years of experience. Added to this was sexual discrimination, the women of both races receiving less money than the men, although they were usually better trained. The Black female teacher also was usually the only, or the major, breadwinner for a large family.

Racial discrimination in the area of equal school facilities has been noticeable in the early 1970s when community after community, faced with using what was formerly an all-Black school building for the new integrated programs, suddenly deemed that such buildings should be completely renovated. In one community I know well, the renovation of the once all-Black high school has consisted of replastering and painting walls; refinishing floors; building an addition to the library; remodeling the kitchen; replacing drinking fountains, toilets, sinks, and lockers; adding a teachers' lounge; and putting in, for the first time, air conditioning units as well as replacing the overhead globe light fixtures, which have lighted the building since it was built, and replacing them with modern fluorescent units.

And so it came to be that such were the educational backgrounds and the psychological conditioning experiences for those Blacks who today are the grandparents, parents, and young adults living and working in the rural areas. Their total life experiences from early childhood on have not been conducive to having a high regard for an education, to being motivated to work for personal accomplishments, or even to have much faith in the future. These are the things which must be recognized by those who hope to design programs to improve rural living if they really intend to reach those who need the programs.

NOTES

1. (New York: Oxford University Press, 1957), pp. vii-viii.

2. *Ibid.*, p. viii.

3. "The American Negro" in *One America,* ed. by Francis J. Brown and Joseph Slabey Roucek (New York: Prentice-Hall, Inc., 1945), pp. 29-30.

4. *Brown Americans: The Story of a Tenth of the Nation* (New York: Viking Press, 1945), pp. 22-23.

5. "The Negro and Racial Conflicts" in *One America*, ed. by Brown and Roucek, p. 452.

6. Embee, *Brown Americans,* p. 110.

7. *Ibid.*

8. To see how completely cotton ruled the lives of men, women, and children, Black and white, see Harris Dickson, *The Story of King Cotton* (New York: Funk and Wagnalls Co., 1937). See also Herman Clarence Nixon, *Possum Trot, Rural Community South* (Norman, Okla.: University of Oklahoma Press, 1941).

9. Frazier, "The Negro and Racial Conflicts," p. 450.

10. (Chicago: University of Chicago Press, 1934), pp. xxi-xxiii.

11. The myth of Southern laziness has been spelled out by several authors, including David Bertelson, who, in the preface of his book *The Lazy South* (New York: Oxford University Press, 1967), refers to an article written in the late 1940s by H. C. Brearly entitled, "Are Southerners Really Lazy?" that appeared in *The American Scholar,* XVIII (1948-49). Brearly speculated upon explanations for the association of laziness with the South, which goes back to early colonial times. He listed poverty, ill health, poor food, the degradation of work because of slavery, the type of agriculture followed in much of the South, and, finally, the Southerners' belief in simply enjoying themselves. A warm climate may have a psychological effect, he argued, but there is no evidence that it reduces efficiency.

In his preface, Bertelson says that while all these reasons are valid, they leave many unanswered questions. He goes on in his own words to say ". . . the problem of explaining laziness remains. To get at what lies behind poverty, slavery, staple crops, and stressing personal enjoyment one must consider historically the meaning of work in the South." Pp. vii-viii.   There were many Southern writers of that time who felt that slavery was destroying the character of slave owners and was leading to a nonproductive, noncreative, authoritative personality. Among them was William Byrd, who in a letter to Lord Egmont praised the decision to prohibit slavery in Georgia and spelled out what he thought slavery had done to the meaning of work in the South. He stated, "Slaves blow up the pride and ruin the industry of our white people, who seeing a rank of poor creatures below them detest work for fear it should make them look like slaves." *Virginian Magazine of History and Biography*, XXXVI (1928), 20, also quoted by Louis B. Wright, *The Prose Works of William Byrd of Westover: Narratives of a Colonial Virginian* (Cambridge, Mass.: Harvard University Press, 1966).

George Tucker was also an early Southern writer who felt that the Protestant ethic of work was disappearing in the South. In the first quarter of the nineteenth century he quoted Colonel Grayson as having told a friend from New York that easy living among Virginia gentlemen and the resulting plunge into debt meant that the best estates were "constantly passing from the hands of those who inherited them." Contempt for work carried with it an element of pointlessness and meaninglessness. In Grayson's words, as quoted by Tucker, "As our whites who can command the labor of slaves are not permitted to work by their prejudices and pride for want of other employment they are very much exposed to the seductions of gambling and drinking." Tucker, *The Valley of Shenandoah; or Memoirs of the Graysons*, Vol. 1 (New York: C. Wiley, 1824), p. 70. In an essay written a few years previously, Tucker had implored planters to become interested in literature so that "many of our fox-hunters and hunters of squirrels and gamesters and tipplers would be spared the sad necessity of flying from themselves." *Essays on Various Subjects of Taste, Morals and National Policy* (Georgetown, Washington, D.C.: C. Wiley, 1822), p.83.

The degrading and dehumanizing effect that marketing in slaves had for white men who brought Blacks from the Gold Coast of Africa to the shores of America and the almost complete destruction of the very moral fiber and productivity of those men involved in slave running are the themes of such novels as Marguerite Steen's *The Sun Is My Undoing* (Philadelphia, Pa.: Blakiston Co., 1941), pp. 240-474, and Hervey Allen's *Anthony Adverse* (New York: Farrer and Rinehart, Inc., 1933), pp. 542-699.

12. Dickson, *The Story of King Cotton*, pp. 47-50.

13. *Where Hannibal Led Us* (New York: Vantage Press, Inc., 1967), p. 84.

14. *Marriage and Family Among Negroes* (Englewood Cliffs, N.J.: Prentice-Hall, Inc., 1966), p. 36.

15. Among the many books on the subject of the slave trade, see Steen's novel *The Sun Is My Undoing*, pp. 240-41 and 243, for some of the cultural differences among African slaves. Edwin R. Embree spells out the cultural differences among Blacks according to the geography of Africa. He says, "They came from tribes as different as the several nations of Europe. They were captured from provinces covering large parts of Central and Western Africa. Among them were Moors from the northerly coasts, and highly cultured Dahomeans from the West Coast, Bantu tribesmen from the equatorial regions, the peoples of the Cameroons, the Congo, and the vast stretches of the Niger Valley, the tall Blacks from the region about the Gold Coast. The great commerce in slaves ranged over four thousand miles of African coast, from the Segegal River on the north to the southern limits of Angola, and reached hundreds of miles inland." *Brown Americans*, p. 5.

16. Reul, *Where Hannibal Led Us*, pp. 84-85.

17. *Ibid.*, pp. 85-86.

18. "Preface," in *Shadow of the Plantation*, ed. by Johnson, p. xxii.

19. Lerone Bennett, Jr., " 'Jubilee,' The Making of Black America," Part VIII, *Ebony*, February 1972.

20. *The Negro in Mississippi 1865-1890* (New York: Harper and Row, Publishers, 1965), p. 216.

21. Freedom, in the thinking of Blacks, was to be the year of "jubilee," an interpretation they took from the teachings of the Old Testament. In Jewish history, "jubilee" was a year-long celebration held every fifty years in which all bondmen were freed, mortgaged lands were restored to the original owners, and the land was left fallow and no one worked the fields. In the book of Leviticus, the laws of the people given by God to Moses, observance of the jubilee is spelled out as follows: "And ye shall hallow the fiftieth year, and proclaim liberty throughout *all* the land unto all the inhabitants thereof: it shall be a jubile unto you; and ye shall return every man unto his possession, and ye shall return every man unto his family. A jubile shall that fiftieth year be unto you: ye shall not sow, neither reap that which groweth of itself in it, nor gather the grapes in it of thy vine undressed. For it is the jubile; it shall be holy unto you: ye shall eat the increase thereof out of the field." *Bible, King James Version*, Leviticus 25:10-12.

22. "The Negro and Racial Conflicts," p. 452.

23. Although 4,441,830 individuals at the outbreak of the Civil War were said to be Black, it is documented that a large number of these persons were at least 75 percent white, and some had less than 12.5 percent Negro blood but still were counted as Black. Writing on the National Census count for Blacks, Edwin Embree says, "Up to 1910 the only classifications reported were 'Black' and 'mulatto.' The general custom was to record as mulatto any person of African descent with one grandparent either white or Indian. This, of course, ignored the mixtures of more than three generations ago when the greatest amount of interracial mingling was going on. Under this crude classification the Census of 1910 reported about twenty percent of the Negroes as 'mulattos.'" Embree goes on to say that "surveys of careful students of race report much greater mixture." No special disgrace was attached to the begetting of mulatto children in slave days, and it is thought that the majority of slave owners mingled their blood with that of Negro girls "chosen for their comeliness, intelligence, and attractive personalities." Embree continues, "While accurate records of ancestry are impossible to obtain, such facts as are available indicate that well above half of the Negroes in America have some white or Indian blood, the extreme estimates on either side being the twenty percent 'mulattoes' reported by the Census and the eighty percent of mixed blood found by students of race." *Brown Americans*, pp. 6-8.

24. Ruth Elgin Suddeth, Isa Lloyd Osterhout, and George Lewis Hutcheson, *Empire Builders of Georgia* (Austin, Tex.: Steck Co., 1962), p. 250.

25. *The Negro Pilgrimage in America* (New York: Bantam Books, Inc., 1967), pp. 71-72.

26. Frazier, "The Negro and Racial Conflicts," p. 452.

27. Woodward, *The Strange Career of Jim Crow*, pp. 63-64.

28. In the period of Reconstruction in Georgia, 169 delegates were elected to the legislative assembly, "thirty-seven were Negroes, twelve were conservative whites, and nine were northern men who had come to the state to become professional politicians." James C. Bonner, *The Georgia Story* (Oklahoma City, Okla.: Harlow Publishing Corp., 1961), p. 332.

29. In some cases those "expensive furnishings" in the state capitols on which the members of the new legislatures spent money lavishly included gold spittoons with inlaid jewels and pearls.

30. David Saville Muzzey, *A History of Our Country* (New York: Ginn and Co., 1943), p. 433.

31. Message of President Johnson to the two houses of Congress, at the commencement of the regular session of the fortieth Congress, December 2,

1867 as recorded in the *American Annual Cyclopaedia and Register of Important Events of the Year, 1867,* (New York: D. Appleton and Co., 1868), p. 635.

32. *Ibid.,* pp. 635-36.

33. Muzzey, *A History of Our Country,* p. 434.

34. *Ibid.,* pp. 433 34.

35. *The Strange Career of Jim Crow,* pp. 53-54.

36. Erskine Caldwell, in his short story "Daughter," portrays a sharecropper who was forced to give up all his shares to the landowner to pay for a mule which had died of natural causes. *The Pocket Book of Erskine Caldwell Stories,* Pocket Books (New York: Simon and Schuster, 1947), pp. 208-13. Forcing the sharecropper to pay for any loss of livestock or equipment and to give up his shares and work for rent, food, and a limited amount of clothing was not unusual. Holding the employee financially responsible for the equipment he used was not limited to sharecropping. A white woman recently shared with me an incident from her early childhood home in which a Black maid accidently dropped and broke an iron. The family took fifty cents a week out of the maid's pay until the cost of a new iron had been subtracted. My informant said her family had seen this as fair treatment of the maid and felt that it would teach the maid to be more careful in the future. There seemed to be no awareness of what the loss of the money would mean to the maid and her family or what percentage the payment was of her total wage. It was, in this case, 10 percent, and if the new iron cost ten dollars it would mean two full weeks of her pay.

37. The subject of an old Black couple being put off the land they had worked for forty years was used by Erskine Caldwell in "The People vs. Abe Lathan, Colored," *The Pocket Book of Erskine Caldwell Stories,* pp. 214-23.

38. Embree, *Brown Americans,* pp. 111-13.

39. *The Story of King Cotton,* pp. 72-77.

40. *Killers of the Dream,* Anchor Books (Garden City, N.J.: Doubleday and Co., 1963), pp. 154-57.

41. For a factual account of segregation as reflected in Jim Crow laws see Woodward, *The Strange Career of Jim Crow.*

42. *Ibid.,* pp. 32-33.

43. *Children of Bondage* (Washington, D.C.: American Council on Education, 1940), pp. 247-48.

44. See the Memphis *Press Scimitar,* Memphis, Tennessee, January 27, 1921 for a fairly typical newspaper account of the burning of a Black. The reporter was able to cover the story because plans for the lynching of the Arkansas Black man had been made well in advance and the newspapers were notified to be ready to run an extra issue. Also see Walter White's *Rope and Faggot* (New York: Arno Press, 1969) for recounts of the gruesome tale of lynchings in this country even as late as the early 1950s. Among the many authors of fiction who wrote about lynchings see Erskine Caldwell, "Saturday Afternoon," *The Pocketbook of Erskine Caldwell Stories,* pp. 256-63, and *Trouble in July,* Signet Books (New York: New American Library, Inc., 1949), pp. 132-39.

45. *Children of Bondage,* p. 247.

46. It is also significant that it was the white women of the South who formed The Association of Southern Women for the Prevention of Lynching, publicly scorning the claim that lynching is necessary to their protection. This was not the first position white women had taken on issues related to Blacks. Harriet Elizabeth Beecher Stowe, for her writings on slavery—

124 Forces That Shaped the Boundaries

especially *Uncle Tom's Cabin*—was acclaimed by President Lincoln as "t] e little woman who brought on the Civil War." Many of the leaders in t] e antislavery movement were women abolitionists, including Lucretia Mo\t, Susan Brownell Anthony, and Sarah and Angelina Grimke of South Carolina. The latter not only gave up their slaves, as so many other Southerners did, but came North to join in the crusade. See Mildred E. Danforth, *A Quaker Pioneer* (New York: Exposition Press, 1961), for some of the direct work of white women involved in the freeing of slaves and in particular for the work of Laura Smith Haviland, the woman acclaimed as "superintendent of the *Underground Railroad*," who almost single-handedly was responsible for many slaves escaping into Canada. No mention of the Underground Railroad can be made without including the name of a Black woman, Harriet Tubman, the "Moses of her people," who was responsible for the escape of over 300 slaves. At one time, the state of Maryland offered $40,000 for her arrest as she slipped into the South time after time and conducted her people northward across the Mason-Dixon line.

47. Jessie Daniel Ames, executive director, Association of Southern Women for the Prevention of Lynching, *The Changing Character of Lynching; Review of Lynching, 1931-1941 with a Discussion of Recent Developments in this Field* (Atlanta, Ga.: Commission on Interracial Cooperation, Inc., 1942).

48. *Killers of the Dream*, pp. 126-27.

49. Johnson, *Shadow of the Plantation*, pp. 112-13.

50. *Ibid.*, pp. 113-14.

51. *A Cultural History of Education* (New York: McGraw Hill Book Co., Inc., 1947), p. 485.

52. *Ibid.*, p. 296.

53. *Ibid.*, p. 297.

54. Ralph E. McGill, "Cultural Growth and Domestic Problems," *Cultural Groups and Human Relations*, ed. by Karl W. Bigelow (New York: Bureau of Publications, Teachers College, Columbia University, 1951), p. 61.

55. John Fraser Hart, *The Southeastern United States* (Princeton, N.J.: D. Van Nostrand Co., Inc., 1967), p. 6.

56. Arthur F. Raper and Ira De A. Reid, *Sharecroppers All* (Chapel Hill, N.C.: University of North Carolina Press, 1941), p. 11.

57. (Atlanta, Ga.: By the Author, 1953).

58. *Shadow of the Plantation*, pp. 133-36.

Man is the only being who makes promises.

Friedrich Wilhelm Nietzsche
19th century German philosopher

7

Spanish-Speaking Americans

The second largest minority in the United States is that which includes the Spanish-speaking people. There is a tendency to group all such individuals together because of their common language and similarities in cultures, although they came originally to this country from such widely separated geographical sections of the world as Spain, Mexico, South and Central America, and the West Indies. They also came to this part of the world for different reasons. The first Spanish conquistadors came to explore and search for gold; later, families crossed the Rio Grande to settle and develop the country. Mexican peons were brought north to work in the fields; Puerto Ricans came to the mainland looking for better jobs;[1] and Cubans fled to the United States to escape Fidel Castro's rise to power.[2] Still other Spanish-speaking individuals came as students to American colleges from South and Central American countries. So the Spanish-speaking immigrant is both the oldest and newest to this country.

The history of our Spanish-speaking minority goes back to the exploration of Francisco de Coronado in what would become the southwest section of the United States nearly a century before the landing of the Mayflower at Plymouth Rock. But another generation passed before any attempt was made to colonize the region traversed by Coronado.

> Then, in 1598, Juan de Onate led a royal expedition north from Mexico, and on the upper waters of the Rio Grande laid out the town of San Juan. . . . But San Juan failed to prosper, and in 1609 a new headquarters was laid out, Santa Fe, in the present New Mexico. This proved to be the first permanent European settlement in the Southwest above the Rio Grande.[3]

Many of the early Spanish conquistadors mated with Indian women of the area or in Mexico, and their descendants, half Spanish and half Indian, settled the region of the Southwest that later became New Mexico.[4] (Figure 9 shows the extensive Spanish holdings, including the Florida peninsula and all of the region west of the Mississippi River except for what would become Washington and part of Oregon.) By the end of the seventeenth century the Spanish had founded many villages using the peon-patrón pattern, where one man became the leader or manager of the village and kept the others (peons), who were usually agricultural workers, in bondage to him through a debt system.

Those who today are the descendants of these early settlers call themselves Spanish-American *manos* or *Manitos* and look with prejudice upon the newcomers from Mexico or the Texan descendants of Mexican ancestors—the Chicanos.[5] Although both the Manitos and the Chicanos are of Spanish and Indian blood, they do not see themselves as being the same, and they resent any such inference.

The Chicanos are the largest group among the Spanish-speaking. They are Americans often born to first-generation Americans. Like the American Indians, Blacks, poor whites, and Orientals, the Chicanos too are struggling for social justice, for equality in determining and sharing the allocations of resources in modern American society.[6]

Mexican Immigration

Although the history of the Spanish influence in America is older than the Anglo-Saxon influence, Mexican immigration is

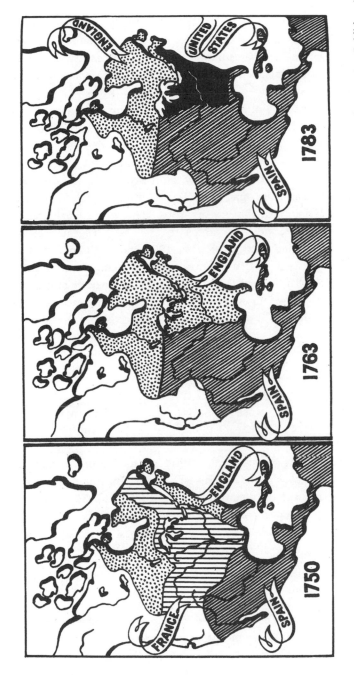

Fig. 9. Control of North America by Spain, France, England, and the United States, 1750-83. (Courtesy of Allyn and Bacon, Inc. Publishers.)

comparatively recent, beginning in 1848, shortly after the treaty of Guadalup Hidalgo. Most of the Mexican immigration has involved laborers who came in large numbers early in this century, especially into four states of the Southwest—Arizona, California, New Mexico, and Texas.

There is no way of knowing exactly how many Mexican immigrants entered the United States between 1900 and 1930 because not all states kept the same records as did the states of the Southwest, where most of the Mexican immigrants settled and where many crossed the border without permission. It is generally estimated that more than 2 million individuals crossed the Rio Grande during those thirty years, some going to the northern part of the United States and others to the East.[7] The numbers of emigrants leaving Mexico between 1900 and 1930 amounted to about 14 percent of that country's total population. In Table 3, Carey McWilliams shows the actual number of Mexican immigrants coming into the four aforementioned Southwest states between 1900 and 1930.[8]

TABLE 3
Mexican Immigrants into Four Southwestern States
between 1900 and 1930

	1900	1910	1920	1930
Arizona	14,171	29,987	61,590	114,173
California	8,086	33,694	88,881	368,013
New Mexico	6,649	11,918	20,272	59,340
Texas	17,062	125,016	251,827	683,681

Much of this Mexican immigration was used at first as labor for building railroads in the Southwest and for repairing railroad beds in other parts of the country. Between 1880 and 1930, 70 percent of all United States' railroad section crews were Mexican workers. Agriculture, however, soon became the largest employer of Mexican workers, especially in the cotton fields of Texas.

Mexican Immigrants Work in Agriculture

As cotton became big business in Texas, thousands of Mexican workmen and their families were imported to work the fields. As more and more Mexican workers were imported and larger areas were planted in cotton, white tenants and landlords moved out, leaving vast areas of Texas inhabited only by those of Mexican descent. A 1931 article in *Survey Graphic* tells that the white tenants were the first to leave rural Texas around 1900, but they were soon followed to the towns and cities by their former landlords. Since the Mexicans did not speak English and were not in the habit of sending their children to school, the rural schools in many areas of Texas vanished along with the white tenants and landlords.[9]

The author of *White Scourge,* himself very anti-Mexican, describes the situation this way:

> Before the incoming hosts of Mexicans three rural institutions—the home, the church, and the school—fell like a trio of staggering tenpins at the end of a bowling race. White tenants could not compete with cheap Mexican labor. Prosperous owners moved to town, leaving the menial work for Mexicans to do. Rural dwellings, orchards and yard fences went to wreck; deserted country churches made excellent hay barns and tool sheds for absentee landlords; and the large rural schools packed with happy white children dwindled into sickly institutions for a few indifferent Mexican *muchachos,* as a wilderness of ragweeds and cockleburs grew on the school grounds. . . . Mexicans did not hit the interior cotton lands with the impact of a hurricane, but seeped in silently and undermined the rural social structures like termites eating out the sills of a wooden house.[10]

The above is quoted at length to give the reader some understanding of the extent of anti-Mexican sentiment developing in Texas at that time—sentiment which laid the foundation for the attitudes found today toward Chicanos. An examination of what went on at that time in recruiting labor from Mexico and in treating laborers in Texas will illustrate also the lack of respect and concern for Mexican farm workers. As McWilliams points out,

> For a quarter of a century [prior to 1924] Texan growers had recruited labor in Mexico whenever they needed it. In large measure this traffic had been made possible by the activities of labor smugglers who developed a lucrative racket in Mexicans. The labor smuggler or "coyote" crossed the border, not only to round up crews, but to get workers across the line in violation of the immigration regulations. For a fee of ten or fifteen dollars, the coyote would arrange to get Mexicans across the line by having them "jump the fence" . . . or come across concealed in automobiles, carts, or trucks; or by fording the Rio Grande at

night. . . . Once across the line, the Mexican was turned over by
the coyote to a labor contractor (*enganchista*), who sold him for
a fee of fifty cents or one dollar a head to some agricultural,
railroad, or mining employer. Labor agents operating out of
Laredo and El Paso had forwarding agents elsewhere in
Texas. . . . Charging the employers a fee for supplying the labor,
the contractors charged the workers for transportation and
subsistence en route. The profits in this racket were really
enormous and the smugglers and coyotes and labor contractors
constituted an intimate and powerful alliance from Calexico to
Brownsville.

Another type of agent, the man-snatcher, also figured in this
dubious traffic. The man-snatchers made a business of stealing
Mexican labor and selling the same crew to several different
employers. Delivering a crew to an employer, they would steal
the crew at night and resell it to still another employer. In this
manner, the same crew would often be sold to four or five
employers in the course of a few days. Frequently the man-
snatchers raided crews imported by the labor contractors and
made off with them by force of arms. Shipments of workers en
route to employers were often kept locked up at night, in barns,
warehouses, and corrals, with armed guards posted to prevent
their theft. Crews of imported Mexicans were marched through
the streets of San Antonio under armed guard in broad daylight
and, in Gonzales County, workers who attempted to breach
their contracts were chained to posts and guarded by men with
shotguns.[11]

"Large planters," wrote James L. Slayden, "welcome the Mexican immigrant as they would welcome fresh arrivals from the
Congo, without a thought of the social and political embarrassment to their country."[12]

Continuing the portrayal of Chicano labor in agriculture,
Quincy Guy Burns says,

In California they settled thickly in agriculture and stock-raising
valleys, though some drifted to the cities. In both places their
life was lowly—mining, sheep herding, agriculture work, and
some mechanical work in the cities. In Arizona they followed a
similar pattern. In Texas they spread into all but sixteen counties, eking out an existence by picking cotton, shelling pecans,
and harvesting sugar beets. Their presence in Texas has made
one of the ugliest scenes in the theater of cheap labor.[13]

Chicano labor was also identified early with the sugar beet industry of this country. As the beet planting increased from 135,000 acres in 1899 to 376,000 by 1906 and 750,000 acres by 1940, the demand for Mexican labor kept pace, especially in the West and Southwest. The principal growing areas for sugar beets have always been California, Michigan, and Colorado. Mexican workers were used from the beginning in California; elsewhere the sugar beet companies experimented with other workers first. In Colorado, Japanese were used. Volga-Germans worked in the sugar beets in Nebraska and other areas, while Belgian and Polish workers were employed in Michigan. But it was soon found that non-Mexican groups showed a tendency to aspire toward farm owner-ship themselves, and in some areas, by dint of unbelievable hard effort, they succeeded in achieving their goal and did become farmers and growers. It was to curb this from happening that sugar companies everywhere began to shift more and more to Mexican labor in the belief that such workers would be willing to continue to work in the fields. This was particularly true after World War I and the passage of the Immigration Act of 1924 which limited immigration of cheap labor. In fact, it was at the insistence of the sugar beet companies that the contract-labor law was suspended from 1918 to 1920 to permit direct recruitment in Mexico. By 1927 it was estimated that, of 58,000 sugar beet workers, 30,000 were Mexicans. Today 66 percent of all workers in the industry are Chicanos. In states such as Ohio, Michigan, Minnesota, and North Dakota, Chicanos constitute from 75 to 90 percent of the present labor supply in sugar beets.

Braceros or Mexican Nationals[14]

The shortage of agricultural workers during World War II en-couraged a labor agreement between the United States and Mexico by which Mexican male workers were recruited and brought into the United States on contracts for work in the fields. On Septem-ber 29, 1942, the first shipment of 1,500 Mexican *braceros* arrived in Stockton, California with the slogan "Des Las Democracias Sera la Victoria" scribbled in chalk on their pullman cars. The labor agreement stipulated that imported workers were to be assured free transportation to and from their homes, that they were to be provided subsistence en route, that they were not to be used to displace other workers or to reduce wage rates, and that certain minimum guarantees governing wages and working conditions would be observed. The first group of braceros grew to 4,208 for the year 1942, and swelled to 120,000 in 1945.

The actual number of men who wanted to be part of the work force but who could not legally enter this country and who waded the Rio Grande or were (and still are) smuggled across the border is unknown. Workers who entered in this fashion are known as "wetbacks."[15] Since 1965, Mexican nationals who have permission to work in the United States are called "green card" workers.

Many of the workers who first came as braceros or wetbacks have stayed and are part of the increasing numbers of Spanish-speaking persons in this country. The numbers of new residents from Mexico increased very markedly in the years just before and at the beginning of World War II. Many combined factors— including the numbers of these newcomers and their reputation for hard work at low wages; the tension of the war; race and national-ity hatred; race riots between Blacks and whites in Detroit, Phila-delphia, and Harlem; and the terrorizing of Jews in Boston— created an atmosphere of tension and hate that brought about open hostilities in 1943 between Mexican-Americans and Anglo-Americans. In California especially, where large numbers of Mexi-can-Americans were living, and because the Japanese-Americans were being removed from the West Coast, Mexicans and Mexican-Americans became the target for new waves of prejudice.

Chicano-Anglo Tensions

The press began an all-out attack on the Spanish-speaking mi-nority. Headlines labeling all Mexican-American adolescents as "zoot suit hoodlums" fanned the feelings of discrimination, as did reports of assaults on young couples by gangs of Mexican-Americans. The result early in June 1943, was a riot in Los Angeles in which several thousand servicemen and other young men attacked every Mexican-American they could find. Mc-Williams, who was involved in taking testimony of that riot, de-scribes the scene:

On Monday evening, June seventh, thousands of Anglenos, in response to twelve hours' advance notice in the press, turned out for a mass lynching. Marching through the streets of downtown Los Angeles, a mob of several thousand soldiers, sailors, and civilians, proceeded to beat up every zoot-suiter they could find. Pushing its way into the important motion picture theaters, the mob ordered the management to turn on the house lights and then ranged up and down the aisles dragging Mexicans out of their seats. Street cars were halted while Mexicans and some Filipinos and Negroes were jerked out of their seats, pushed into the streets, and beaten with sadistic frenzy. If the victims wore zoot suits, they were stripped of their clothing and left naked or half-naked on the streets, bleeding and bruised. Proceeding down Main Street from First to Twelfth, the mob stopped on the edge of the Negro district. Learning that the Negroes planned a warm reception for them the mobsters turned back and marched through the Mexican east side spreading panic and terror. . . .

Throughout the night the Mexican communities were in the wildest possible turmoil. Scores of Mexican mothers were trying to locate their youngsters and several hundred Mexicans milled around each of the police substations and the Central Jail trying to get word of missing members of their families.[16]

Present Situation

Although today there is no such open hostility toward Chicanos as the riots of the 1940s, the position of the Chicano worker has not changed markedly. At the present time the Chicano minority in the United States is estimated in excess of 7,400,000.[17] The average Chicano is poor and is often underemployed or unemployed because of limited education or training. The majority are still employed as unskilled laborers or migrants in the harvests.

Color Prejudice toward Chicanos

The most difficult man-made forces against which the Chicanos have struggled are attitudes, values, and expectations based on prejudices against color and language. Wherever they go they are viewed as foreigners and are told they do not look or sound like Americans or have American names. Yet, ironically, their ancestors lived in the Western Hemisphere even before Columbus was born.

Over the years there have been many stereotypes of Americans of Mexican descent, including the picture of the Chicano "as a villainous character inclined to banditry in the old days and other forms of criminality in more recent years." He is also portrayed as "a strong peasant with a sweet disposition and the mind of a child."[18]

Even social scientists have been guilty of stereotyping. Miguel Montiel in a review of the literature has pointed out discrepancies in studies reporting cultural traits of Chicanos.[19] He feels that there has been a tendency to lump all Chicanos together and ascribe to them the same values, family patterns, and cultural traits while ignoring individual differences.

Prejudice based on color has been difficult for the Mexican immigrant to cope with, and it has been difficult also for the Puerto Rican immigrant. Discrimination based merely on color, as found in the United States, is unknown in either of those countries and, as a result, immigrants have no learned patterns of behavior to cope with the problem as they find it here. Manuel Gamio explains that in Mexico there has always been intermarriage between Indians, mestizos, and whites on the basis of social class. He says,

> Contact between these groups is the direct result of economic and cultural factors. Thus, the whites who are on a low cultural and economic level mix their blood with the Indians as naturally as with the whites. Similarly, the pure-blooded Indian who reaches a high economic and cultural level finds no barrier to intermarriage with the elements classed "pure white."[20]

As Gamio explains, "the darkest skinned Mexican [in the United States] experiences almost the same restrictions as the Negro."[21] Gamio goes on to compare Mexicans with other immigrants, such as the Irish, Italians, Germans, and Polish, who also experienced discrimination when they first arrived in this country. But, as he points out, by the second or third generation, Italians, Poles, Germans, and the Irish became Americans, while only a very few Chicanos have been able to do so.

NOTES

1. Probably the most knowledgeable person on Puerto Rican migration is Clarence Senior. See Clarence Senior, "The Puerto Rican in the United States," in *Understanding Minority Groups*, ed. by Joseph B. Gittler (New York: John Wiley and Sons, Inc., 1964), pp. 109-25; C. Wright Mills, Clarence Senior, and Rose Goldsen, *The Puerto Rican Journey* (New York: Harper and Bros., 1950); and Clarence Senior, "Movers, Migrants and the National Interest," in *Migration and Social Welfare*, ed. by Joseph W. Eaton (New York: National Association of Social Workers, Inc., 1971), pp. 23-54.

2. Richard Fagen, Richard A. Brody, and Thomas O'Leary, *Cubans in Exile* (Stanford, Calif.: Stanford University Press, 1968).

3. Mary Wilhelmine Williams, *The People and Politics of Latin America* (New York: Ginn and Co., 1945), p. 123.

4. For a study of values, concepts, and attitudes that have been maintained by the Spanish-speaking people of New Mexico, see Margaret Mead, ed., *Cultural Patterns and Technical Change* (New York: New American Library, Inc., 1955), pp. 151-77. See also John H. Burma, *Mexican-Americans in the United States* (Cambridge, Mass.: Schenkman Co., Inc., 1970).

5. Ronald B. Tayler explains that the word *Chicano* comes from a blend of Nahuatl, the tongue of the Aztec, with Spanish. In Nahuatl, *X* had the sound of *Ch*, and thus *Mexico* would be pronounced *Me-chi-cano*. The latter has been abbreviated by the descendants of Mexican culture to *Chicano*. *Sweatshops in the Sun: Child Labor on the Farm* (Boston, Mass.: Beacon Press, 1973), p. 146.

6. See Eliu Carranza, *Pensamientos on Los Chicanos: A Cultural Revolution* (Berkeley, Calif.: California Book Co., 1971), a collection of essays which deal with the Mexican-American's education and point up why there is the Chicano demand for equal opportunity and justice.

7. The works of Paul S. Taylor, along with those of Manuel Gamio, provide much of the original documentation on the Mexican immigration into the United States that occurred in the first quarter of this century. Taylor reports on the specific immigrant situation in three areas of the country: California, Texas, and the Midwest. The first in the series was *Mexican Labor in the United States: Imperial Valley* (1928), followed by *Mexican Labor in the United States: South Texas* (1930) and *Mexican Labor in the United States: Chicago and the Calumet Region* (1932). The fourth book is general statistical information on many aspects of the migration, *Mexican Labor in the United States: Migration Statistics* (1929-34). All are University of California Publications in Economics (Berkeley, Calif.: University of California Press).

8. *North from Mexico* (Philadelphia, Pa.: J. B. Lippincott Co., 1949), p. 163.

9. *Survey-Graphic*, May 1, 1931.

10. Edward Evert Davis, 1946, as quoted in McWilliams, *North from Mexico*, p. 178.

11. *Ibid.*, pp. 178-79.

12. See testimony of Emelio Flores before the Industrial Relations Commission, 1915.

13. "Latin Americans," in *One America*, ed. by Francis J. Brown and Joseph Slabey Roucek (New York: Prentice-Hall, Inc., 1945), pp. 347-48.

14. One of the best books on the subject of *braceros* is Ernesto Galarza, *Merchants of Labor: The Mexican Bracero History* (Santa Barbara, Calif.: McNally and Loftin, 1964).

15. See Julian Samora, *Los Mojados: The Wetback Story* (Notre Dame, Ind.: University of Notre Dame Press, 1971), for an up-to-date picture of the "wetback traffic."

16. *North from Mexico,* pp. 248-49.

17. "Mexican-Americans," *Business Week,* May 29, 1971, p. 48.

18. Leo Grebler, Joan W. Moore, and Ralph C. Guzman, *The Mexican-American People* (New York: Free Press, 1970), p. 6.

19. "The Chicano Family: A Review of the Research," *Social Work,* March 1973, p. 23.

20. Manuel Gamio, *Mexican Immigration to the United States* (Chicago: University of Chicago Press, 1930), p. 51.

21. *Ibid.,* p. 53.

Be ye lamps unto yourselves.
Be your own reliance.
Hold to the truth within yourselves
as to the only lamp.

Siddartha Gautama the Buddha,
the 5th century B.C. founder
of Buddhism

8

Japanese-Americans

Another race that, in the past, played an important role in rural America is the Oriental. That race has also experienced extreme discrimination, which has left Oriental youth of this generation feeling isolated and alienated from the dominant society. Many of the negative results of the treatment of Orientals can be seen in a few sections of the country where they are still part of the rural population; but it can be seen mainly in urban areas.

The most recent victims of widespread national prejudice toward the Oriental race are the Japanese. Although the psychological need of a country to use a minority as a scapegoat is frightening, it is, nevertheless, a pattern that has appeared several times in the history of the United States. Furthermore, it was often in rural areas that the most direct scapegoating took place or else it was the rural area that received the victims when the need for discrimination against that particular group had passed. The scope of this book is not wide enough to study the dynamics of this sort of situation, but I would like to present some of Stewart G. Cole's ideas on the subject.

Cole points out that during extreme crises when individuals are subjected to periods of acute social stress such as war, they suffer a sense of personal insecurity, frustration, and fear for their own well-being—even a fear for life itself—which often is expressed in prejudice against or scapegoating of some minority group.[1] He uses the treatment of Japanese-Americans during World War II as an example. He could also have mentioned the treatment of German-Americans and Austrian-Americans during World War I as examples.[2]

The passage of the Immigration Act of 1924, which prohibited Orientals from entering the United States as immigrants, brought bitterness, strife, and severe competition among Orientals already living in this country—especially the Japanese and segments of the white population. By 1940, through hard work, the children of Japanese immigrants (themselves American citizens) in California "controlled farm acreage valued at some $72,000,000. They played an important part in the operation of fisheries, hotels, laundries, restaurants, and produce markets. Moreover, discrimination against Japanese, for example in employment and in home and land ownership, forced them into communities made up almost entirely of Orientals."[3]

Directly related to the historical discussion of rural America in part 2 of this book is the relocation of Japanese-Americans in 1942—many of whom were farmers, farm workers, or were used as farm workers while in relocation centers (although very few have returned to agriculture).

The attack on Pearl Harbor at first brought a feeling of oneness to this country; we were all Americans regardless of ethnic heritage, and we had been attacked. For two months following Pearl Harbor the local Japanese on the West Coast were treated with more consideration by their non-Japanese neighbors than ever before. They too were Americans; they too were pained by what was happening. Then suddenly, for some unknown reason, Japanese-Americans were viewed as the *enemy*. The results were threats, vandalism to their homes and places of business, and attacks upon their persons. Japanese-American farmers along the West Coast did not know whether to plant their spring crops because they were unsure of the existence of a market for their vegetables. Japanese produce houses closed when fruit stalls were overturned.[4] Shops and stores were burned and robbed by non-

Japanese. Japanese-Americans were under attack in their country of birth.

Beginning in January of 1942, families were ordered by the government and the army to move out of certain areas or neighborhoods. Without warning the men of these selected families were interned; their wives and children were forced to move in with relatives or friends. Still, this did not affect large numbers of people. There were few if any complaints, as those most directly affected were not in a position to complain.

Then a major campaign against the Japanese was started. More and more influential persons expressed fear that Japanese-Americans were a danger to the coastal area. One of the most outspoken anti-Japanese was Congressman Leland Ford, who launched a personal campaign to remove all Japanese citizens and aliens and put them into concentration camps.

But when the orders came for the eviction of the people, the orders themselves were contradictory. The first orders came before President Roosevelt had stated his view of the situation. The Japanese-Americans were notified by the Department of Justice on February 10, 1942, to vacate their homes by the sixteenth of that month. But on February eleventh they were told that the Navy would handle the operation and that they had a month to prepare to leave. Within a week they were ordered to be out in twenty-four hours—an ultimatum which was finally changed to forty-eight hours through the intervention of Christian agencies. In the meantime, the president took some action. On February 19, 1942, he issued an executive order authorizing the Army to evacuate anyone of Japanese lineage, alien or citizen, from military areas. Later "military areas" were defined as the entire West Coast, and all Japanese and Japanese-Americans were to be moved eastward. The next step was to determine how many were to be evacuated and where they were to go.

> It was claimed in mid-March that the security of the Coast demanded removal of 110,000 Japanese. Yet of this number 70,000 were women and children, 13,000 men fifty-five or older. Of the 27,000 males remaining, 16,000 were American citizens, seventy-five percent of whom had never seen Japan. That left less than 11,000 alien males between the ages of twenty and fifty-five—most of whom were over forty.[5]

Nevertheless, the 110,000 individuals were notified, and mass movement began. People could take with them only what they could carry; even children's pets and toys had to be left behind. Junk wagons patrolled the streets buying for a few dollars the accumulated possessions of a lifetime. Evacuees, bewildered by conflicting statements about them in local press and radio reports, tried to dispose of their homes, cars, and furniture. Pressure was used to force the people to sell for almost nothing. Everyone—non-Japanese neighbors, former friends, and strangers—seemed intent upon taking advantage of their plight.[6] People left their personal property with those they thought were friends—or even with strangers, in the streets, in church basements, or in rented rooms—property that very few of them ever saw again.

They were moved first into assembly centers: race tracks, fairgrounds, abandoned CCC camps, and the grounds of the Pacific International Livestock Exposition. The largest group of 18,719 were housed in the stables at the race track at Santa Anita. From March until August of 1942, they stayed at the assembly centers. After consideration of several hundred locations and countless aerial surveys, ten camp sites were finally selected. The camps had to be some distance from strategic spots and had to have land capable of supplying some of the food requirements. When the camps were finally built, they were located on public lands—reclamation projects and Indian reservations in Arizona, Utah, Colorado, Wyoming, Arkansas, California, and Idaho.

Some of the people did work on projects outside the camps. Many were employed as farm workers in those areas or states where such workers were needed to save the crops when local help was not available. Bradford Smith describes the situation.

> Before the evacuated people would be shifted from assembly centers to relocation camps the need for their labor began to be felt in Western agriculture. Under the influence of the sugar beet interests a number of politicians who had been demanding internment of all Japanese changed their views and demanded the War Relocation Agency provide evacuees for thinning and harvesting. By the end of 1942 nine thousand workers had saved the beet crop and added 265,000,000 pounds of sugar to the arsenal of democracy. Meanwhile California, while steadfastly refusing the Japanese, had forced the federal government to import thirty thousand Mexican farm workers at public expense.[7]

The wage rate paid evacuees through the War Relocation Agency was twelve dollars a month for unskilled work, sixteen dollars for skilled, and nineteen for professional such as physicians or supervisory work. The resentment that the Japanese-Americans felt for being forced to abandon their farms to Caucasians after years of effort just when they were becoming profitable was expressed in their lack of enthusiasm toward farm work. They worked tirelessly in their little gardens planted before the camp barracks but took their time at War Relocation Agency work. When this was pointed out, many said, "What do you expect for twelve dollars a month?"

By December 1945 there were only ghost towns where the relocation centers had been, as the camps were abandoned almost overnight.

> Much as they had hated them, many of the last evacuees to leave felt a pain like that of homesickness as they looked back from the buses and saw the buildings drop behind a curtain of rising dust. To many it was the scene of their life's summit: first love, childbirth first experienced, the first relaxation after a lifetime of toil. Here 1,862 lives had ended, 2,210 couples had been joined and 39 separated. Many remembered no other life and many (5,981) would for the rest of their days carry birth certificates from places the dust had covered over and men forgotten.[8]

While the Japanese-Americans were now free to go, most of them were told they were not wanted in their old homes and in other places in the West.

> When the army first planned the evacuation of the Coast, it expected the people to find their own homes in states to the east. But even the few thousand who tried to make new homes for themselves were threatened with violence, refused in restaurants, turned away from filling stations, jailed, or forced to turn back.
> If the Japanese weren't good enough for California, they weren't good enough for Nevada, Arizona or Utah.[9]

Thus, they began to settle in the East, in rural areas and cities in the Northwest, and in urban areas like Chicago, Minneapolis, and Cleveland. Two-thirds of Seattle's prewar 7,000 returned—more of Nisei (American born) than Issei (Japanese born).

The total direct cost of the evacuation program to the American people was about $250 million. This, of course, takes no account of the millions of dollars lost by the evacuated,[10] nor does it erase the hurt and anger felt even today by those whose parents knew the lonely, forced isolation of exile within their native land. For the second time in American history the government evacuated all members of one racial group from their places of permanent settlement to designated, confined areas. Like the East Coast Indians, the Japanese-Americans suffered at the hands of their fellow Americans; they, too, were deprived of their rights and the land which once they had owned.[11]

As a result, they, too, have a strong feeling of having been wronged without justification. They, too, as do others of their race—the Chinese, the Filipinos, the Koreans—feel that at times they have had no control over their own destinies or even their own lives; rather they have been pawns in the hands of others. They were never seen as having made a contribution to the agricultural industry of this country, but instead they were seen as a threat (even when employed as stoop laborers in the fields) to be kept under control and exploited for fear someday they too might own the land.

NOTES

1. "Culture Patterns of Minority Groups," in *One America,* ed. by Francis J. Brown and Joseph Slabey Roucek (New York: Prentice-Hall, Inc., 1945), p. 335.

2. Under the Espionage Act of 1917 all German- or Austrian-born "enemy aliens," even naturalized American citizens, were forbidden to go up in airplanes or balloons, to come within a hundred yards of wharves or piers, or to be found in waters within three miles of the shore. An American household which had any German- or Austrian-born member was forced regularly to buy Liberty Bonds to prove loyalty to the United States government. While the whole country experienced wheatless, meatless, and heatless days, the German-American or Austrian-American households with a member born in Germany or Austria were more severely rationed in their sugar, flour, and meat. They were not allowed, even in their own homes, to speak German, play German records on the gramaphone, or sing German songs. It was made a penal offense for any man, whether a naturalized

citizen or native born, to refuse to do military duty or do anything that would be viewed as obstructing the draft.

3. Nelson L. Bassing and Robert R. Martin, *Solving Our Problems in a Democracy* (River Forest, Ill.: Laidlaw Bros., 1956), p. 590.

4. The greatest success of the Japanese-Americans in 1942 was in Los Angeles where, just before the outbreak of the war, they were said to be handling 60 percent of the volume of wholesale agricultural produce business, and they almost monopolized fruit and vegetable concessions in retail shops and markets. "Their success in this field of endeavor was due to the long hours they worked, to meticulous attention to detail and to constant care in eliminating wastage." For more on this subject see Dorothy Swaine Thomas, "The Japanese-American," in *Understanding Minority Groups,* ed. by Joseph B. Gittler (New York: John Wiley and Sons, Inc., 1964). For additional information about Japanese-Americans see William K. Hosokawa, *Nisei: The Quiet Americans* (New York: William Morrow and Co., Inc., 1969).

5. Bradford Smith, *Americans from Japan* (New York: J. P. Lippincott, 1948), p. 272.

6. For more on the treatment and feelings toward these Japanese, most of whom were Japanese-Americans, see "Issei, Nisei, and Kibei," *Fortune,* April 1944; Carey McWilliams, *Brothers Under the Skin* and *Prejudice: Japanese-Americans* (Boston, Mass.: Little, Brown and Co., 1943 and 1944 respectively); Leonard Broom, *The Japanese-American Family in World War II* (Berkeley, Calif.: University of California Press, 1956); Harry H. L. Kitano, *Japanese Americans: The Evolution of a Subculture* (Englewood Cliffs, N.J.: Prentice-Hall, Inc., 1969); and William Petersen, *Japanese Americans: Oppression and Success* (New York: Random House, Inc., 1971).

7. *Americans from Japan,* pp. 293-95.

8. *Ibid.,* pp. 317-18.

9. *Ibid.,* p. 329.

10. On November 10, 1958, when the Japanese Claims Section of the Justice Department closed its evacuation claims program, it was announced that $36,874,240.49 had been paid in awards out of some 26,522 claims considered. All but 3,000 of the settlements were made for $2,500 or less. The evacuees were hampered in their claims for compensation by loss of supporting documents. *New York Times,* June 25, 1962, p. 18.

11. For a very well-prepared discussion of the relocation of the Japanese-Americans and their experiences in exile, see Smith, *Americans from Japan,* pp. 261-361; U.S., Department of the Interior, *The Wartime Handling of Evacuee Property* (Washington, D.C.: Government Printing Office, n.d.); Toru Matsumoto, *Beyond Prejudice* (New York: Friendship Press, 1946); Dorothy S. Thomas and Richard Nishimoto, *The Spoilage* (Berkeley, Calif.: University of California Press, 1946); U.S., Department of the Interior, *Impounded People* (Washington, D.C.: Government Printing Office, n.d.); U.S., Department of the Interior, *The Relocation Program* (Washington, D.C.: Government Printing Office, n.d.); and Jobu Yasumura, "What Happens Next for Americans of Japanese Ancestry?" *Missions,* January 1946.

That I am a man, this I share with other men.
That I see and hear and that I eat and drink
is what all animals do likewise.
But that I am I is only mine and belongs to me
and to nobody else;
to no other man not to an angel not to God—
except inasmuch as I am one with Him.

Meister Eckhart, 13th century German author
Fragments

9

Farm Migrant Workers

Immigrants as Farm Laborers

The history of migratory farm labor is the history of immigration into the United States. For example, the early California farms, in acreage representing huge feudal estates compared to conventional farms in other parts of the country, made wide use of the same Chinese coolies who had helped to build the Union Pacific Railroad a few years before. These western land owners also encouraged coolie laborers to migrate from China, as well as gardeners and horticulturists from Japan, to work their fields. This same need for field workers brought Polish and Hungarian families to the sugar beets of the Midwest, Puerto Ricans to the blueberries of New Jersey, Barbadians and Cubans to the sugar cane of Florida, and Mexicans to the cotton of the Southwest.

The sugar planters of Hawaii, ever on the lookout for supplies of cheap labor, entered into arrangements with steamship companies to bring Filipino laborers to the Islands in slowly increasing numbers from 1906 to 1920. The 1930 census showed a total of

63,052 Filipinos in Hawaii, and a total of 45,208 on the United States mainland, the majority of whom were employed as agricultural laborers.[1] The poor and the oppressed of foreign countries have always been encouraged to come to America to work in the crops. The attitude toward them as human beings has been the same, regardless of their race or ethnic origin. As I have pointed out elsewhere,

> The pages of migrant farm labor history are dark with the exploitation of these suppressed racial minority groups imported to work in the fields. Always the procedure has been the same. The selection of workers has been a minority group which already knew poverty, deprivation and a standard of living lower than the average worker in the United States. These farm workers have generally been paid a lower wage than it would have been necessary to pay domestic farm help. They have been threatened with deportation if they complained about working conditions, wages, deductions taken from those wages, housing or discrimination.[2]

Influence on Immigration Policy

Along with factory owners and mine operators, the farming interests were also influential in pressuring Congress and national leaders to keep the gates of immigration open so that workers who could be used as unskilled labor might be brought into the country. In addition to the Orientals who provided much of the farm labor for the West Coast, blond, blue-eyed Scandinavians, who could barely speak English, as well as Russians, Germans, and Danes, worked as part of the threshing crews in the grain lands of the Great Plains states.

In the early years of this century, labor unions, which were becoming influential groups in national politics, saw the policy of *open-shop* immigration as a threat to their goal of raising wages and improving working conditions in the East. Under open-shop rules immigrants were expected to take any job under any condition at any wage. Thus, the American Federation of Labor and the Knights of Labor began to pressure Congress to exclude "all immigrants who could not read or write." The liberals and agricultural interests protested, pointing out the many contributions made to this country by immigrants. It was not until 1917 that the pressure of organized labor was strong enough to convince Congress to pass the Literacy Test Act, over President Wilson's second veto. As Samuel Steinberg points out,

> Critics of this law were of the belief that the restrictions were really aimed against southern and eastern Europeans, who had no elementary education back home and who had been coming into the country by the millions. Immigrants from northeastern Europe came from countries that had public elementary schools. They were not troubled by the literacy tests since they could read their own language.[3]

It was shortly after World War I that America went through a period of strong antiforeign feeling that resulted in isolationism. Immigration officials made a practice of deporting aliens who had broken the law or who were becoming public charges. Americans whose ancestors were among the early settlers in this country were hostile to the new foreign immigrants and blamed them for the rise of slums, crime, and child delinquency. Labor, including agricultural labor, continued to blame the foreign-born as a cause of unemployment. So great were the antiforeign feelings that Congress passed a Quota Act in 1924, which, until it was liberalized in 1965, was the Immigration and Nationality Act of this country. This act established a rigid and restrictive quota system, allowing for a total of 150,000 immigrants a year. It became in practice even more restrictive because the quota allowed larger numbers of immigrants from those European countries where the pressure to emigrate was slight, and fewer from those southern and eastern European countries whose people were eager to come. The result was that less than one-third of the total immigration quota was filled each year.

Continuing with his discussion of the restrictive features of the act, Steinberg points out that immigrants from Asia were excluded altogether—

> ...a fact which angered the Chinese and infuriated the Japanese ... the law was not to apply to the Western Hemisphere. Mexicans ... [therefore] were not placed under the quota system. This provision was welcomed by the fruit growers and ranchers.[4]

Mexican workers had been used widely for several years in agricultural stoop labor. California farm journals even spoke of the year 1920 as the "Mexican Harvest," but it was not until the passage of the Immigration and Nationality Act of 1924 that the door for Mexican workers in all areas of agricultural labor opened wide, assuring growers of a source of cheap labor.

Mobility of Farm Workers in the Past

The pattern of movement among farm workers started in the early years of this nation. Any present consideration of farm migrants must account for these years. At that time, migration consisted of workers moving from job to job within a small geographical area, or of hired hands moving from positions as tenants to owners of farms. The freedom, however, to shift in quest of richer land, a better climate, or a more congenial landlord has always been part of the American farming tradition, especially in the South where the percentage of movement among farm tenants always has been much higher than in any other section of the country (see Figure 10 for movement among farm tenants in 1935).

In his study of 612 Black rural families in Macon County, Alabama in the early 1930s, Charles S. Johnson found that

> There is great mobility among the tenants and share-croppers especially. In the group of 612 families there were 340, or 55.5 percent that had changed residence during the last five years. Many of these 340 families had moved several times during the five years. They gave various reasons for moving, such as "jest got tired of livin' down there," or they heard the soil was better in the present location, or in one case they wanted to move from the place because they saw so many of the family die. One tenant gave rather specific reasons for moving. He said: "I moved here 'cause I jest didn't like Jim____ and got tired of it. We made ten bales last year but look like we poorer than ever. We didn't get but twelve dollars 'vancement for five months from that cotton; course we owed him some from the year before. I don't know 'zactly how much it was he [former landlord] got for the cotton; but he tole me he got ten, seven, eight, nine cents for some of it. He was a fellow who wouldn't let you know his business and course you couldn't do a thing but take his word for it. He got all new people this year. All of them is pretty much from new communities. About six or seven families moved out, and I believe about twice that many moved in. He had to go over to Warriorstand to get the people 'cause

148

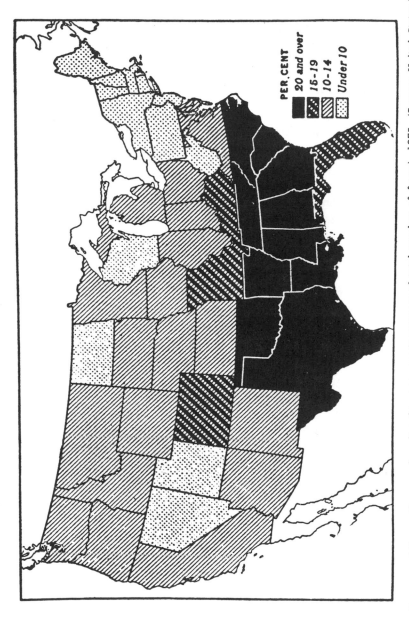

Fig. 10. Farmers residing on the same farm less than one year (percentage of total number of farms), 1935. (Source: United States Bureau of Agricultural Economics.)

nobody in this part would move in; so he got some new folks that didn't know him."[5]

Although movement from farm to farm in search of better soil or more favorable working conditions was always a part of the early patterns of agricultural workers, it was not until much later that regional migratory patterns of movement became common. The first migrant farm laborers in any numbers were disillusioned gold miners from the gold rush of 1849 and Eastern farm workers who wanted to see the newly opened West, especially the garden lands in the fertile valleys of California. Following the Civil War these earlier migrants were joined by former soldiers, both Union and Confederate, and homeless men from Eastern and Southern states. "In 1924 it was estimated that from 1,700,000 to 2,000,000 men and boys were moving about the country, living by begging, stealing, or irregular jobs [most of which were in the fields]."[6]

Although the transient farm worker was identified early, the needs and even the numbers of migratory families were not recognized until the operation of the transient relief program of the Federal Emergency Relief Administration. This Depression program gave care to a total of more than 200,000 families, or approximately 700,000 individuals, during two years of its operation from September 1933 to September 1935. John N. Webb and Malcolm Brown, early researchers on migrant families, point out why so little attention up to that time had been paid to families on the move:

> The underestimation of family distress migration during early years of the depression partly grew out of the fact that family mobility was less spectacular than the mobility of unattached persons. Needy families did not ride the freight trains or congregate at the yard limits where they would have attracted attention at every town along the mainline railroads. Instead they moved largely by automobile so that, except for the general state of disrepair of their cars and the frequent protrusion of personal belongings from the sides, they differed little in appearance from many nonmigrant travelers on the highways.[7]

The vast numbers of these families were trying to move from the East to the West, especially into California (see Figure 11 for the displacement movement of these families).

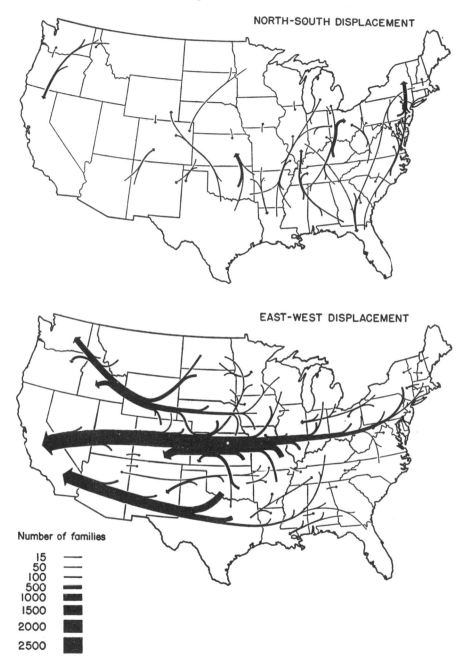

Fig. 11. Patterns of migration movement, United States, 1935. (Source: Federal Emergency Relief Administration.)

There never has been an accurate count of migrant workers at any one time. It was thought that the figure reached some 400,000 workers in the early years of the 1960s. According to a United States Department of Agriculture report,[8] that number decreased to 351,000 by 1966; a later report from the same office said that by 1968, the number was down to 279,000. It had dropped to 257,000 by 1970, 20 percent of whom were traveling a distance of a thousand miles or more in search of work each year. July is the work month that involves the largest number of workers covering the widest geographical area, whereas January is the month that involves the least amount of travel to the work areas. Figures 12 to 15 show labor demands in various parts of the country for January, April, July, and October. An examination of these maps will give the reader an appreciation of the amount of travel necessary to obtain work throughout the year.

Current Migrant Streams

The principal migration of agricultural migrant workers in the 1970s is still along five main streams. They follow the crops from the South to the North and then back to the South. Workers also move from low-wage areas to higher-wage areas seeking better working conditions. The streams of those looking for work constantly change; thus men and women who picked strawberries in California one year may go to New Jersey for peppers or blueberries the next season or to the cherries of the Midwest or the vegetables of south Florida.

The East Coast stream leads from the Everglades of Florida up the Atlantic seacoast with branches thrusting as far west as Lake Erie and northward into New England. This stream is made up mainly of southern-born Blacks with large numbers of Puerto Ricans and about 10,000 Black and white day-haul workers who come to the fields from Philadelphia and other northern cities. Each year is also finding more Chicanos from Texas entering this stream in Florida.

The central movement pattern, largest of all, originates in south Texas and sweeps northward on both sides of the Mississippi River. The western workers in this stream thin sugar beets from Nebraska to Idaho and Montana; the eastern workers pick fruit and harvest

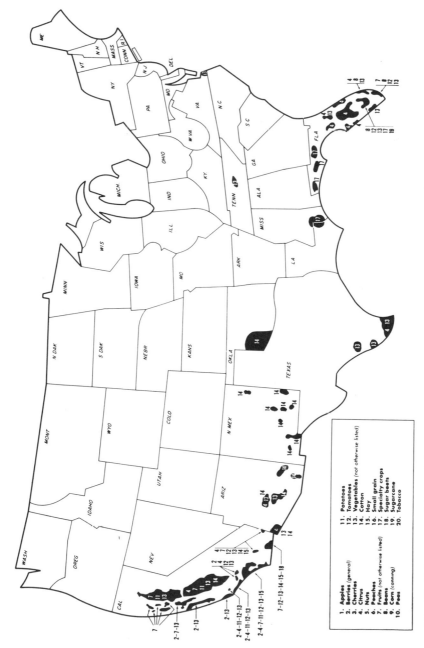

Fig. 12. Major areas of demand for agricultural migrant labor in January. (Source: United States Department of Labor.)

153

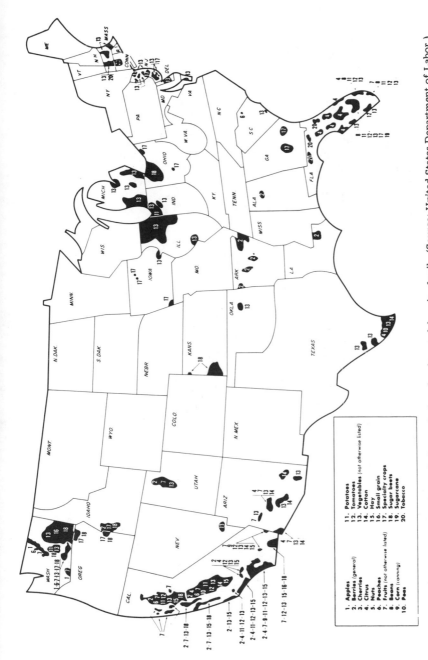

Fig. 13. Major areas of demand for agricultural migrant labor in April. (Source: United States Department of Labor.)

154

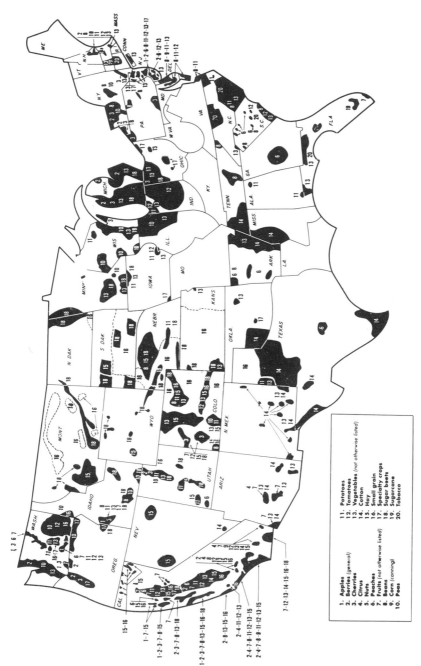

Fig. 14. Major areas of demand for agricultural migrant labor in July. (Source: United States Department of Labor.)

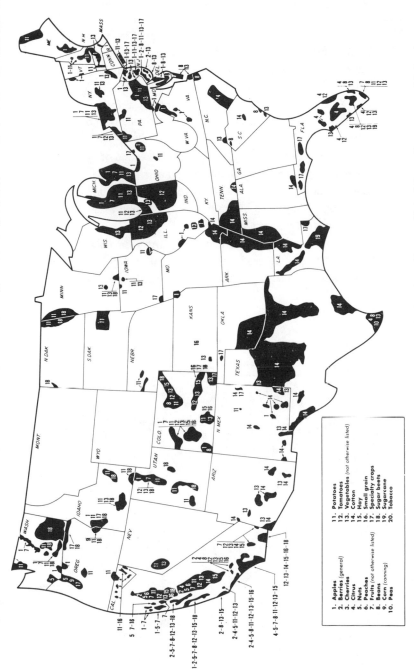

Fig. 15. Major areas of demand for agricultural migrant labor in October. (Source: United States Department of Labor.)

vegetables from Missouri to Wisconsin, Michigan, and Ohio. These migrants are mainly Chicanos, but some are Southern Blacks and Southern whites.

The third stream moves up and down the West Coast, staying mainly in California. These migrants are Chicanos, whites, Indians, Blacks, and a few Orientals (mainly Filipinos and Japanese). The fourth stream is found in the Southwest, where migrants work in the crops of Arizona, New Mexico, and southern California. The predominant culture here is Chicano, with some Mexicans, Indians, and a few Blacks and whites.

The fifth stream is concerned only with the harvesting of wheat, oats, rye, and barley. The workers, mainly Caucasian, come from Texas and Oklahoma. These are the aristocrats of the migrant workers, traveling mainly with house trailers or staying at motels. (See Fig. 16 for current migrant streams.)

On the surface, the movement of migratory farm workers would seem to be disorganized. Actually the movement is highly structured. It takes well-organized planning to move work crews in and

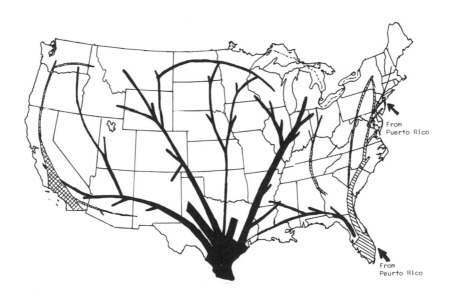

Fig. 16. Travel patterns of seasonal migratory agricultural workers, United States, 1970. (Source: United States Department of Health, Education and Welfare and United States Department of Labor.)

out of crops, to time the departure and the arrival from one section of the country to another in order to minimize the danger of being stranded. The exceptions in the organizational structure are the few individuals who are free wheeling and looking for work on their own, those who quit a job before it is completed and wander off in search of something new, or those who are dropped from a crew for one reason or another.

The pattern of mobility is determined, to a high degree, by whether the individual travels as part of a crew or is a free wheeler. Since the major reason for the crew structure is transportation and labor negotiations in transit, the crews disband when the terminal home base is reached. In most home-base areas where migrants are employed, the day-haul system is used. As most of this book deals with the life styles and experiences of farm workers, no attempt will be made at this time to discuss either crew composition or travel situations.

Historical events that impinge upon the present migrant farm labor situation are those primarily related to immigration and early migratory settlement patterns. Man-made forces include racial, cultural, and sexual prejudices as well as the low-status image of agricultural employment. This low status is an ascribed status which is not just related to the arduous nature of the work but is also reflected in the rapid mechanization of agriculture and the replacement of workers. The industrialization of agriculture and the ignoring of human factors in rural areas have resulted in a rapid substitution of mechanization for labor without any real provision being made to take care of the employment needs as represented in displaced manpower. The burden for finding new employment rests on agricultural employees themselves, in this case upon the migrant farm workers.

NOTES

1. The treatment of the Filipino farm workers has been described by Emory S. Borgardus, who says that "the Filipino competes chiefly with the white casual laborer. . . . Usually his services are arranged for through the Filipino labor contractor, who usually deducts a liberal percentage from his wages,

but who in turn furnishes him with rice and other cheap food and simple rooming quarters. . . . Through the Filipino contractor, he may be employed in small or large numbers, and for short periods or for whole seasons. He 'works far better' than does the white casual laborer, or most people of other racial groups." So say those who employ the Filipino workers. Emory S. Borgardus, "Filipino Americans," in *One America*, ed. by Francis J. Brown and Joseph Slabey Roucek (New York: Prentice-Hall, Inc., 1945, pp. 355-57.

2. *Where Hannibal Led Us* (New York: Vantage Press, Inc., 1967), p. 97. For details on the exploitation of minorities in American agriculture, see the following Carey McWilliams's books: *Factories in the Field* (Boston, Mass.: Little, Brown and Co., 1939); *Ill Fares the Land* (New York: Barnes and Noble, Inc., 1967); and *North from Mexico* (Philadelphia, Pa.: J.B. Lippincott Co., 1949).

3. *The United States Story of a Free People* (Boston, Mass.: Allyn and Bacon, Inc., 1954), p. 364.

4. *Ibid.*, p. 365.

5. *Shadow of the Plantation* (Chicago: University of Chicago Press, 1934), p. 117.

6. Paul H. Landis, *Our Changing Society* (New York: Ginn and Co., 1942), p. 189.

7. "Introduction," *Migrant Families*, Research Monograph XVIII (Washington, D.C.: Government Printing Office, 1938), p. xiv.

8. U.S., Department of Agriculture, Economic Research Service, *Domestic and Migratory Farm Workers: Personal and Economic Characteristics, and the Hired Farm Working Force of 1966: A Statistical Report* (Washington, D.C.: Government Printing Office, 1967).

*Neither heavenly nor earthly, neither
mortal nor immortal have we created thee,
so that thou mightest be free according to
thy own will and honor, to be thy own
creator and builder. To thee alone we gave
growth and development depending on thy
own free will. Thou bearest in thee the
germs of a universal life.*

Giovanni Pico Della Mirandola
  15th century Italian philosopher
Oratio de Hominis Dignitate

10

Psychological Effects of Rural Poverty

Years of frustration with dreams ending in disillusionment and
years that have spelled only disappointment and more debt or
dependence than before have left thousands of residents of all races
in rural areas unable to trust in themselves or others. To trust in
the future, to be able to dream of the future, requires a high degree
of fantasy and an ability to transcend the present. Many rural
Americans can turn only to the past and glorify what was; they
cannot face the present or think about the future. For many others
the problems of everyday living are so overwhelming, even in the
1970s, that the only way to cope is to deny the past, to say
nothing of the future. These individuals are fixated in the present.
They live by the pleasure principle which "indicates behavior on an
'I want what I want when I want it, and I don't want to postpone
my wants for anything or anyone' level . . . and are unwilling, and
to a degree unable, to postpone gratification of their instinctual
demands for any period of time."[1] There are a number of patterns
that many rural Americans (as well as nonrural Americans) have

used to gratify their instinctual demands; among these are mis-management of money, alcoholism, and accident proneness.

The Pleasure Principle

Individuals who live by the pleasure principle often use money to satisfy their impulsive desires. They use money as a form of self-indulgence to compensate for real or imagined lack of recognition and acceptance.

Much of the same self-indulgence exists in alcoholism, which currently is a very critical problem in many rural areas. Every alcoholic is an immature, insecure, oversensitive, and anxious person who is suffering from marked feelings of inferiority, who is unable to cope with responsibility, and who is unable to meet and enjoy people or to get on with personal responsibilities without the support of alcohol in fairly large quantities. Such a person reaches a point where he says, "nothing ordinarily seems worthwhile. It is only when I am drinking that life seems bearable."[2]

For years it has been a known fact that certain individuals act out their feelings of inadequacy through accidental injuries. When the accident itself is studied it is found to be a deliberate attempt on the part of the individual to injure himself, though of course he is unaware of his intentions.[3] Such persons usually have had to suppress their hostile feelings in deference to stern parents, fear of an external threat (such as loss of job or even life), or strict religious training. Thus, they have never learned to feel anger without it's being rage or to express differences without their coming out as an attack on others or on self.

The reality principle refers to a more mature type of adjustment, namely, the ability to form long-range goals and undergo temporary frustration and difficulties to attain these goals. To be unable to trust in the future is to live with an expectation of failure. For the individual who lives with this expectation consistently there is a sense of vast hopelessness. The psychological effect of this feeling of helplessness will be developed at more length later in this chapter after the concept of self-image is examined.

Development of Self-Esteem

Early in life individuals develop a wide variety of concepts and attitudes about themselves and their personal worlds. Some of these concepts are anchored to reality and form the basis for a healthy personal adjustment. Others deviate from reality. An individual's concepts—realistic as well as unrealistic—are drawn from his or her own experiences, from the attitudes and opinions communicated by others, and from own identifications. Among the concepts that are central are the individual's attitudes toward ownself, own environment, and own future.

The individual's self-concepts are clusters of attitudes about himself, some of which are favorable and some of which are unfavorable. These clusters consist of generalizations that he or she has made on the basis of interactions with his or her environment. People derive self-concepts from their personal experiences, from others' judgments of them, and from their identifications with key figures, such as parents, siblings, and friends.

Once a particular attitude or concept has been formed, it can influence subsequent judgments and become more firmly set. For instance, a child who gets the notion that he or she is inept, as a result of either a failure or being called inept by somebody else, may interpret subsequent experiences according to this notion. Each time thereafter that the child encounters difficulties, he or she tends to judge self as inept. Each negative judgment tends to reinforce the negative concept or self-image. Thus, a cycle is set up: each negative judgment fortifies the negative self-image, which in turn facilitates a negative interpretation of subsequent experiences, which further consolidates the negative self-concept. Unless this negative image is extinguished, it becomes a permanent formation in the cognitive organization. Once a concept is structuralized, it remains permanently with the individual even though it may be dormant; it becomes a cognitive structure, or scheme.

Among the positive or self-enhancing self-concepts are such attitudes as "I am capable," "I am attractive," "I can get what I want," "I can understand problems and solve them." Examples of negative or self-diminishing self-concepts are "I am weak," "I am inferior," "I am unloveable," and "I can't do anything right." The nuclei of positive and negative self-concepts determine the direction of an individual's self-esteem. When the positive self-concepts are activated, the individual regards self more favorably; in other words, he or she experiences an increase in self-esteem. Activation of the negative self-concepts lowers the self-esteem.

Self-blame is another concept in which the individual holds self responsible for his or her own defects and presumed deficiencies. This attitude is expressed as "it's my own fault I always make mistakes. I'm to blame for being so weak."[4]

Another group of attitudes revolves around the theme of negative expectations. The pessimistic view of the future is expressed in such attitudes as "things will never get any better for me," "I will always be weak and get pushed around," "I'm basically unlucky and always will be." When these attitudes are mobilized, they produce feelings of hopelessness.

When all the components are activated, a sequence such as the following occurs: The individual interprets an experience as representing a personal defeat or thwarting; he or she attributes this defeat to some defect in self and regards self as worthless for having this trait; he or she blames self for having acquired the trait and dislikes self for it; and, since the individual regards the trait as an intrinsic part of self, he or she sees no hope of changing and views the future as devoid of any satisfaction or filled with pain. Some of these attitudes have been reinforced in rural America through religious teachings.

The Influence of Calvinism

In many rural areas remnants of early religious dogma have been part of the poor self-esteem of individuals. The doctrines of Martin Luther and especially of John Calvin, both of whom emphasized the fundamental evilness and powerlessness of man, became the most influential on rural America of any religious teachings.

Religion for Calvin was rooted in the powerlessness of man, self-humiliation, and the destruction of human pride. Only if man despises this world can he devote himself to the preparation for a future world.[5] Through self-humiliation man comes to depend not on himself but on the strength of God. "For nothing arouses us to repose all confidence and assurance of mind on the Lord, so much as diffidence of ourselves, and anxiety arising from a consciousness of our own misery."[6] This doctrine preaches that the individual should not feel that he is his own master.

> We are not our own; therefore neither our reason nor our will should predominate in our deliberations and actions. . . . We are not our own; therefore, let us, as far as possible, forget ourselves and all things that are ours. . . . For, as it is the most devastating

pestilence which ruins people if they obey themselves, it is the only haven of salvation not to know or to want anything oneself but to be guided by God who walks before us.[7]

Therefore, man should not strive for virtue for its own sake since such would lead to nothing but vanity. The only solution is to deny self and to discard all selfish considerations and instead to pursue things pleasing to God, the result being that through complete submission and self-humiliation the individual hopes to find security. Calvin also assumed that salvation and damnation are not results of anything good or bad that a man does in his life, but are predetermined by God before man is born; thus the concept of being born *into* sin.[8]

Many helping professions have been concerned with the fatalism which results from this sort of religious doctrine and with the fact that the only way the individual can handle his or her own feelings of inadequacy is to maintain group identity. To do this, the individual surrounds his group with a halo and lends it a form of glory, such as "we are the true church of Christ." Writing on the character structure of modern man and the problems of the interaction between psychological and sociological factors, Eric Fromm sees a comparison between Calvin's theory of predestination and Nazi ideology, both of which emphasized the inequality of men. Fromm says,

> For Calvin there are two kinds of people—those who are saved and those who are destined to eternal damnation. Since this fate is determined before they are born and without their being able to change it by anything they do or do not do in their lives, the equality of mankind is denied in principle. Men are created unequal. This principle implies also that there is no solidarity between men, since the one factor which is the strongest basis for human solidarity is denied: the equality of man's fate. The Calvinists quite naively thought that they were the chosen ones and that all others were those whom God had condemned to damnation. It is obvious that this belief represented psychologically a deep contempt and hatred for other human beings—as a matter of fact, the same hatred with which they had endowed God.[9]

Fromm goes on to say:

> While modern thought has led to an increasing assertion of the equality of men, the Calvinists' principle has never been com-

pletely mute. The doctrine that men are basically unequal according to their racial background is confirmation of the same principle with a different rationalization. The psychological implications are the same.[10]

Sense of Being Wronged

Individual success may also be reduced within the Calvinistic doctrine by the belief that "salvation is not achieved through good deeds but rather by faith through the mercy of God." This also provides for denial of responsibility: "I am acted upon by others (others, in this case, may be another race, employers, or government) and forced into doing what I have done." This attitude may be expressed as "I am the instrument of God" or "I acted in self-defense." Out of the belief that responsibility and control lie outside of one's self comes a fatalistic attitude by which the efforts of the individual are seen as useless, and the safest approach is one of conformity without questioning.

Many of the present residents of rural America have a strong sense of having been wronged. For years their race, their sex, their ancestors, their families, or they themselves have known psychologically threatening stimuli and dehumanizing experiences. They are a minority whose total life experience has been one of exploitation by the dominant society. They have been treated like second-class citizens who have had no right to make decisions for themselves, or they have been paid less for their work. And many of them live in a region of the country where most residents feel they were and perhaps still are treated unfairly by the rest of the nation.

If the individual holds himself or herself responsible for what has happened, the degree of dissonance is overwhelming and the person's self-concept is destroyed. This is so emotionally painful that the individual's need is usually handled through secondary satisfaction, which comes from developing a sense of being treated unfairly. In other words, there is a *sense of emotional enjoyment* in being in the position of having been wronged; there is a high degree of satisfaction in indulging in the self-pity that goes with such a role. The individual, within his or her own thinking, achieves status, to which something is owed because he or she has been wronged. Such an emotional state—feeling wronged and psycho-logically enjoying that position—can be experienced by individuals, groups, and even sections of a country. In psychiatry this state is called "compensation neurotic." The gratification of martyrdom is a secondary gain. But it brings with it such a high degree of emotional gratification that it may be very difficult to overcome or even to work with.

The pleasure arising from the satisfaction of such a position can be, but is not necessarily, unconscious. Whether or not such pleasure is conscious or repressed depends on two factors: on the strength of those forces within a person opposing his irrational strivings—in this case, of martyrdom—and on the degree to which the mores of society sanction or outlaw the enjoyment of such pleasure. In the case where a whole section of the country, a race, or a sex feels oppressed unfairly, then pleasure in a suffering position is reinforced, and the individual who wishes to do some-thing about his situation will need to struggle against a community norm which says others are responsible for his plight.

In some cases, suffering and weakness are the aims of human striving. This phenomenon involves people who quite consciously want to suffer in one way or another. It is usually not the actual suffering of pain which is sought, but rather the excitement and satisfaction aroused by being physically bound and made helpless and weak. In other words, the need to suffer becomes more than that; it becomes a pleasure.

In extreme cases the need to suffer is so great that there can never be any compensation large enough to right the wrong this individual feels has been done to him, his people, or his section of the country. The sinner can never atone; the one "sinned against" can never forgive and forget but must always continue to feel wronged and, through his behavior, must show that he has been wronged.

The Need to Conform

When people have been pushed down and refused the right of self-expression, they learn to conform at an early age. If they are aggressive they will be punished or, under certain circumstances, even killed. The child under these conditions learns early that for self-preservation he must submit. Thus, he becomes a neurotic conformist.

> Success becomes dangerous. Any drive toward self-emancipation threatens the delicate balance. Any drive toward emancipation is attended by anxiety. The individual caught in this confusion maelstrom seldom recognizes the source of his anxiety. He does not know he is inwardly afraid that he will be killed or abandoned, should he dare to determine his own behavior, should he really assay his own decisions. To become a complete failure prescribes the safest course for living.[11]

The term *conformist* is sometimes used almost as a synonym for *compulsive personality* and *obsessive personality*, but it indicates persons who need to satisfy or placate the needs of others in order to feel secure. At the very time they are conforming to the wishes of others, they unconsciously resent the demands that they believe are placed upon them. In conformity the individual ceases to be himself but instead adopts the personality or role which his culture offers. He becomes like others and as they expect him to be. The conformist becomes an automaton and blends into others much the same as the chameleon changes its color to fade into the background of its environment. To conform means to lose spontaniety and creativity in order to follow the dictates or the teachings of others. Conformity and originality do not go hand in hand. The conformist does not think for himself because to do so carries with it the danger of offending others.

Double Bind

In situations where no one feels secure, where there is doubt of mutual love and fear of self-hostility, the straight-forward expression of emotion is stifled. This is the so-called double bind of communication. Words say one thing; tone of voice, facial expressions, or bodily gestures mean something else. The double bind is to convey two meanings at one time or to communicate in a way which comes across as no communication, either because of the words used or the irrelevant logic. From this sort of experience develops a sense of futility, a feeling of "what is the use?" Regardless of the effort the individual puts forth, there is always something to discredit or devaluate what he or she has tried to accomplish.

Fear of Success

Fear of success is a relatively common phenomenon that has been found in all cultures in various parts of the world. It is related to fear of the "evil eye" or fear of being enviable and to the danger of losing, which, in turn, carry the threat of being ostracized for having something (material objects, status, or prestige) unobtainable by others.

If a person does not want to succeed or if he expects to fail, he will do just that because he will behave in accordance with his expectations. This phenomenon of behavior has been labeled the self-fulfilling prophecy because the individual fulfills his prophecy of failure.

The unconscious fear of success develops in early childhood when there are strong pressures on the child to conform, to behave or believe only as others behave and believe. A child, especially a girl, from such an environment often feels loved as long as she is weak, helpless, or docile; but should the child show inclinations toward being strong, capable, or aggressive, the parents become anxious. It could be that the parents are afraid that the aggressiveness of the child will reflect on them and endanger their position.

Because there is fear that ill will result from success, there is a tendency to fail or to stop short of a successful accomplishment. Within some of the early cultures such a fear that the gods were envious of good health existed that the individual, when asked how he felt, would describe fantasized aches and pains. In other cultures children and horses were disfigured to protect them from the risks they would suffer if beautiful.[12] Fear of success in rural areas of America was reinforced through the fundamental religious doctrine in the literal interpretation of the Bible. Morris and Natalie Reader Haimowitz spell this out.

> The Holy Bible eloquently describes the Fall as the consequence of success. Adam and Eve discovered and ate the sweet fruit of the tree of knowledge. How were they rewarded for this example of initiative, curiosity, exploration (and disobedience)?

Their eyes were opened so they could see, learn, and be ashamed.[13]

Unto the woman, He [God] said, I will greatly multiply thy sorrow and thy conception; in sorrow thou shalt bring forth children; . . . And unto Adam He said, . . . cursed is the ground for thy sake; in sorrow shalt thou eat of it all the days of thy life. . . . In the sweat of thy face shalt thou eat bread, till thou return unto the ground; for out of it wast thou taken: for dust thou art, and unto dust shalt thou return.[14]

The Moral? If you discover something new, if you taste the good fruit of the tree of knowledge, or the sweet taste of freedom or success, you may be punished. If you violate the norms, if you disobey the rules, you will suffer severely. Be safe. Conform. A similar theme is repeated in the story of Eve's children. Cain, a poor farmer, was envious of his successful brother Abel, and killed him. The Moral? If you do too well, your brother may kill you.[15]

Fear of success may be ascribed to an ethnic group or to a certain sex. For example, it is a common experience of women within our society. The successful and productive woman frequently finds herself a suspect by both women and men. She is often viewed as a threat by other women who examine her critically for signs of aging or weakness. Her accomplishments, regardless of how outstanding, are reduced in importance by paying her less money for equal work and by stating that "for a woman she does quite well." There is always doubt that a woman can accomplish much, and the question of why a woman should want to achieve in the first place is often raised. The only explanation generally accepted is that such a woman is trying to defeat a man and therefore is denying her femininity. At an early age a girl is taught that if she accomplishes too much or is too intelligent, she will limit her possibilities of marriage, or, if she marries, she will reduce her husband's ability to function if she is too successful. From such attitudes arises her fear of success.

Success for either the man or the woman may also imply other dangers: "If I become too successful others will expect me to do more for them." Success then comes to mean "I am my brother's keeper." If one is successful, one must take care of those less successful, which may be something of a burden.[16]

The answer to such a paradox is not to try to achieve. In many rural areas there are also forces that act as the common leveler of the group. The individual must not achieve more than his ancestors achieved; if he does it will look as if "he thinks he is better than the rest of us" or "this style of living was good enough for his pappy, so it should be good enough for him." Among the American Indians, a person who desires individual success is looked upon with open contempt and must be ostracized because he is viewed as a danger to the tribe. His success is then reduced to a nothingness with the statement, "Only a man assisted by witchcraft, sorcery, or evil spirits could achieve so much." In all of these cases the incentive to succeed is diminished in comparison to the need to be accepted by the group. The individual can only feel wronged.

Results of Feeling Wronged

The danger in feeling wronged—whether for an individual, a community, a region of the country, or a race of people—is that psychic energy, which could be used for coping with everyday living problems such as rural poverty, is lost in the endless cycle of anger, blame, and self-pity. We cannot undo the mistakes of the past. We cannot undo the exploitation of the American Indians, the slavery of the Blacks, the incarceration of the Japanese, or the years of discrimination directed toward the Chicanos, poor whites, and other ethnic groups in rural areas. We cannot undo the historical events or the man-made forces that have helped create the rural poverty of today; but neither can we ignore the fact that a large part of those in rural poverty feel they have been so dehumanized that they have come to believe they do not count. Some of them unconsciously attempt to prove that fact; they try unconsciously to fail in everything they do. They have developed a fear of success that will take time and understanding to overcome. Some will not be able to transcend their own hurt and, regardless of what happens in the future, regardless of the number of programs or the millions of federal dollars spent to improve their situation, they will still feel that nothing has been done and that they still have no part in anything important.

*   *   *

Part 2 has attempted to identify some of the historical events and man-made forces that have a direct bearing on conditions in rural America today. Such problems as poverty, substandard housing, unemployment or limited employment, illiteracy, apathy or a sense of helplessness—all have their roots in the past. Most of these problems are the result of imposed forces which have denied people the freedom to develop to the fullest of their potential and have forced them to use all their psychic and emotional energies in coping with existence. Included among these man-made forces are prejudice, persecution, slavery, exploitation, the isolation of a race, seasonal work, and paternalism. Living under such conditions, individuals come to feel that the destiny of their lives is outside their control and, therefore, outside the sphere of their responsibility.

In analyzing the social needs of American Indians, rural whites, Blacks, Chicanos, and others, one must be aware of culturally oriented determinants of behavior. In the past there has been an effort to promote Anglo-American attitudes, values, and behavior without recognition for the contributions made by minorities to the history of this country. Likewise there has been no recognition of differences in culture as a base of self-identity.

In order to provide a firm sense of identity for those who make up the bulk of the rural poor, an historical perspective of the origin of their culture and its contributions to the growth and development of this country is needed, as well as a knowledge of characteristics of the culture today. Such will be the subject of the next part of this book, which is concerned with the meaning of cultural boundaries.

NOTES

1. O. Spurgeon English and Stuart M. Finch, *Introduction to Psychiatry* (New York: W. W. Norton and Co., Inc., 1954), p. 16.

2. O. Spurgeon English and Gerald H. J. Pearson, *Emotional Problems of Living* (New York: W. W. Norton and Co., Inc., 1955), p. 502.

3. For more on accident proneness see *ibid.*, pp. 256-57.

4. For a very complete discussion of the relationship between low self-esteem and self-blame (both of which are seen so often on the part of women as a result of their inferior status) as related to the predepressive constellation see Aaron T. Beck's *Depression: Clinical, Experimental, and Theoretical Aspects*, Part IV (New York: Harper and Row, Publishers, 1967), pp. 243-90.

5. John Calvin, *Institute of the Christian Religion*, trans. by John Allen (Philadelphia, Pa.: Presbyterian Board of Christian Education, 1928), Book III, chapter 9, p. 1.

6. *Ibid.*, Book III, chapter 2, p. 23.

7. *Ibid.*, Book III, chapter 7, p. 1.

8. *Ibid.*, Book III, chapter 14, p. 11.

9. *Escape from Freedom* (New York: Rinehart and Co., Inc., 1941), p. 89.

10. *Ibid.*, pp. 89-90.

11. James Clark Moloney, *The Magic Cloak* (Wakefield, Mass.: Montrose Press, 1949), p. 212.

12. William Graham Sumner, *Folkways* (New York: Ginn and Co., 1906), pp. 515-19.

13. "The Evil Eye: Fear of Success" in *Human Development*, ed. by Morris L. Haimowitz and Natalie Reader Haimowitz (New York: Thomas Y. Crowell Co., 1960), p. 744.

14. Gen. 3:16, 17, 19.

15. Haimowitz and Haimowitz, "The Evil Eye."

16. *Ibid.*, p. 746.

PART III

The Meaning of
Cultural Boundaries

*While traveling, having realized that all
those who have attitudes very different
from our own are not for that reason bar-
barians or savages but are as rational or
more so than ourselves, and having considered how greatly the self-same person
with the self-same mind who had grown up
from infancy among the French or Germans would become different from what
he would have been if he had always lived
among the Chinese or the cannibals . . . I
found myself forced to try myself to see
things from their point of view.*

René Descartes, 17th century philosopher
Discourse on Method

11

The Cultures of Rural Minorities

Culture Defined

Culture may be described as any behavior common to a group
of people and capable of being transmitted from generation to
generation or from one country to another and involving the
following six relationships of mankind: to God, to people, to living
things and material objects, to the earth, to time, and to space. A
specific culture arises out of the necessity of people to meet their
basic human needs, needs which are common to all mankind.
Needs include both (1) physical needs for survival, such as food,
shelter, procreation, and protection; and (2) emotional needs for
love, including both being loved and the opportunity to love;
acceptance, including a sense of belonging, which in turn contrib-
utes a feeling of self-worth; an opportunity to contribute to the
well-being of others as well as to self; and a feeling that life has
some meaning beyond the present, which comes with a sense of
relatedness to the universe.

175

Cultural Determinants

Physical and emotional needs are the basic human needs from which cultures develop. In turn, it is the culture that dictates the process through which individuals, who are part of that culture, relate to their supreme being, to other human beings, to their physical environment and material things, as well as to time and to space. It is also the culture that determines acceptable ways in which the individual's own instinctual drives may be expressed. Drives, in this sense, can be defined within the psychoanalytic framework to mean the two unconscious instincts which are psychic constituents of love (sexual) and aggression or, put another way, the two drives, creativity and destruction.[1] In short, a culture is the reality in which the individual lives and functions.

The means of meeting basic human needs through family roles, religion, friendship, work, use of time, and use of space are all determined by the culture and become the values and the customs of the culture. Although these means of meeting human necessities have a commonality in that they all arise from basic needs known to every human being, each culture handles these needs differently. Each culture is unique and appears strange to those in other cultures. But each culture is paramount to the people within its boundaries. In each culture are also social classes, castes, or levels determined by income, education, or inherited roles which account for a greater degree of individual differences within a culture than is usually found among individuals of the same social class in differing cultures. There is no culture of a particular social class such as poverty; instead poverty and all social classes are represented in every culture, although what is interpreted as poverty in one culture might be middle class in another.

Understanding Another Culture

In order to understand an individual, we must also know something about his culture, as well as where he and his family fit into his culture's social structure in comparison to the culture and social position of the person making the analysis. If the individual is part of a culture that is new to him or different from his own, this too must be examined in the overall analysis to see how he fits into the new environment and how his present experiences compare with those of his past.

Customs of the Culture

In determining the means through which basic human needs are met, we find that cultures also provide their own unique ritual structures which help protect objects or beliefs held as important. The basic human need to feel some relationship to the cosmos or to the universe is assigned, by the culture, to the role of religion, superstition, or a particular philosophic approach to life. Every culture has some form of religious belief as well as various rituals through which individuals relate to relatives and nonrelatives, to members of their own sex and to the opposite sex. The basic sex drive and the need for human survival force the culture to spell out the conditions under which procreation should occur and acceptable family roles, including the status of women and child-rearing practices. The culture determines the age for marriage, those who are eligible to marry, and what constitutes a legal marriage. The ritual of the wedding may be determined by the culture or left to individuals, but the value placed on marriage as the acceptable means for procreation is culturally determined and, for that culture, becomes a value which all should respect and follow. Those who do are rewarded and those who do not are punished.

The relationship of human beings to each other is also reflected in the basic need for food, which dictates the necessity to establish some form of acceptable work, the role of workers, how work will be rewarded and by whom. Because of the basic need for protection, the culture builds systems that will provide protection as well as some form of government for the people. The value of law and order arises from this basic need.

Geographical ties and the accumulation of material possessions are also reflected in a culture. An example of the latter is the value the culture places on giving away material wealth, a practice common among Indians, or keeping wealth for self-use, as is common in the dominant society.

The meaning of time and whether the culture is geared to the present or more to the past or the future also dictate behavior. For example, while the English clock "runs," it "walks" in Spanish;

hence, the English-speaking person must hurry to make use of time before it "runs" away, but the Spanish-speaking person may take a more leisurely attitude toward time. The English-speaking person who arrives late for work tends to say, "I missed the bus," making himself the active agent and accepting the responsibility for his tardiness. The Spanish-speaking person, however, is more apt to say that the bus left him.[2]

The meaning of privacy and the use of space are also influenced by the culture. Writing at some length on this subject, Edward T. Hall points out that in Japan the walls of houses are moveable, opening and closing as the day's activities change. In the United States people move from room to room or from one part of a room to another for each different activity, such as eating, sleeping, working, or socializing with relatives. In Japan it is quite common for the person to remain in one spot while the activities change.[3]

In addition to fixed space or informal space, intimate distance is also culturally determined. How close do people stand to each other when they talk in an intimate fashion? As Hall says,

> Much of the physical discomfort that Americans experience when foreigners are inappropriately inside the intimate sphere is expressed as a distortion of the visual system. One subject said, "These people get so close, you're cross-eyed. It really makes me nervous. They put their face so close it feels like they're *inside you.*" At the point where sharp focus is lost, one feels the uncomfortable muscular sensation of being cross-eyed from looking at something too close. The expressions "Get your face out of mine" and "He shook his fist in my face" apparently express how many Americans perceive their body boundaries.[4]

And yet such physical closeness would be considered proper within certain cultures. What would be considered intimate physical distance in the cultures of north Europe would be interpreted in south Europe as distance more appropriate for strangers or for those with whom one wishes little if any contact.

Value Systems

The process of meeting basic human needs evolves into a set of values for a culture which tend to be regarded as the natural and even the right way to do things. Values are so meaningful to those who hold them that they come to be accepted without question.

It is only natural, then, that culturally approved means of meeting basic needs are, as a rule, changed only slowly and reluctantly. Any attack on them is deeply resented. Others are expected to respect them, if not to accept them. In fact, one's values are usually regarded as desirable for other persons.[5]

These values and attitudes are kept as long as they bring satisfaction. Gratification, in turn, strengthens values.

The Individual's Value System

Culture provides the individual with his basic value system. These values are laid down as part of the personality development in two ways: (1) through the primary contact between the young child and his mother and other family members, and (2) through contacts with secondary groups as the child moves outside the family to play groups, school, and more formalized organizations involving children and/or adults. This process of adopting a value system and finding various means of coping with the environment is also called cognitive map making.

Cognitive map making is an essential aspect of learning for infants; and it is the basis of the value system that determines what is right or wrong for the individual and the society in which he lives. The baby uses the results of his active exploring, organizes these experiences, and holds onto them as an aid in orienting himself to the world, managing it, and getting around in it.

Among the many things related to values and cognitive map construction which are conditioned by these early experiences between child and mother are the following:

1. The development of curiosity: learning to want to learn. If encouraged, this desire later develops into a high regard for education.

2. Learning to evoke rewards: learning to love. When the individual feels he is loved he can develop a sense of acceptance of others and can value the lives and the rights of other human beings.

3. Learning by identification: learning to feel a part of the human race beyond one's own race. Being comfortable as a

person—male or female; white, black, brown, or yellow; rich or poor—this is the value of self-concept.

4. Learning to express emotions: learning to express anger, learning to cope with frustration, learning to be comforted, learning to fear, learning what to enjoy and how to express humor, love, tears, and laughter. All these become part of the individual's value of emotions and their control.

5. Learning to trust: the value of trusting others versus mistrust. Without trust there can be few, if any, meaningful relationships in life.

Through the ages human beings have tolerated change, even when it has altered their entire way of life. They have been able to tolerate it as long as their personal values were not questioned and they knew within themselves who they were. An individual could live in exile or could suffer discrimination as long as he could practice, even in secret, the relationship he needed with his God and the relationship to those he considered his family or his tribe and as long as he could communicate with nature and could locate himself and others in relationship to time and space.

Folk Culture

The popular term *folk culture* needs some exploration here because most of the content of this book could be said to refer to folk cultures. *Folk* refers to one's relatives or kin, but it also is used to mean the common man. When coupled, for example, with the word *dance,* it refers to a dance characteristic of the peasants or of the "common people." *Folklore* is that branch of ethnology concerned with the myths, traditions, and beliefs, together with the omens, charms, and customs of the common people. It is the study of a mental outlook toward nature and destiny and the customs which thence arise—the relations of the common people to their fellow human beings.

The difference between folk culture and general culture lies in the ways they are acquired. People learn a folk culture through contact with other individuals, by word of mouth and role models. Acquiring general culture goes beyond physical contact with people; here, information about the culture is learned through books, works of art, music, and mass media. In writing on the subject of folk culture, Charles S. Johnson said,

> ... that the "folk" is a people whose current history is recorded, if at all, by the ethnologist rather than by the historian or the newspaper.[6]

Robert Redfield expands on folk culture in his volume *Tepoztlan*, a study of one of the marginal people of Mexico, by saying,

> Such peoples enjoy a common stock of tradition; they are the carriers of a culture. This culture preserves its continuity from generation to generation without depending upon the printed page. Moreover, such a culture is local; the folk has a habitat. And finally, the folk peoples are country peoples. If folk lore is encountered in the cities it is never in a robust condition, but always diminishing, always a vestige.[7]

A very simple definition of a folk culture is a culture whose principal means of information dissemination is face to face, by word of mouth. History exists in the form of stories, legends, parables, and unrecorded ballads. Often the history and the culture are taught through artifacts in addition to the music, foods, and dances. As with the cultures of all people, the individual folk culture is regulated by customs and taboos which are taught often by gossip, teasing, and shaming the individual into conformity.

A rural folk culture is one based on a tie with the soil that goes beyond making a living from the soil. The land itself helps set the life style, the expectations, and it even influences the personality development of the people. This was evidenced by early Indian tribes among whom the raising of corn was not merely a means of securing food but was also a way of worshipping their gods. For those who work the soil there can be a strong sense of creativity and trust in the future. In cases of oppressed persons, such as the sharecroppers of the South, the tie with the soil can become one of bondage.

Folk Cultures in Rural America

In order to understand the rural poor of today, one must be aware that they do not represent one race[8] or one ethnic group, although for each section of the country there is a tendency to identify a single race with rural poverty. In the South, Blacks are thought of in relationship to rural poverty, although in actual numbers there are more poor whites than poor Blacks. In the West the Indians are identified as living in poverty, and in the Southwest it is the Chicanos. In the Appalachian area and the slash-pine regions of the Midwest many see only poor whites in rural areas, and people in the far North who are concerned with rural poverty speak only of Eskimos.

There are others among the rural poor: the Acadians of southwestern Louisiana; some of the Mennonites or Amish of Pennsylvania, Indiana, and Iowa and other areas; the peoples of mixed racial ancestry, such as the Spanish-Americans of New Mexico; the little, isolated communities of Indian, Negro, and Caucasian mixtures scattered through remote parts of Virginia, North Carolina, Alabama, and Louisiana; and large numbers of mobile poor who work as farm migrants. All are Americans; that is, they all live within the political boundaries of this country. But these rural residents live on the margins of what has become the American way of life. Most of these people of rural America are not only poor but also are representative of various folk cultures and races. In the following section, only those cultures that represent the largest number of today's rural poor will be examined.

A Perspective on the Culture of the Poor Whites

Although there is no one white culture per se, the whites who live in rural poverty are a minority in that they too are isolated from full participation in the dominant society. The poor whites of this country make up the largest number of people living in poverty, yet except for the poor of Appalachia and isolated areas in the upper Midwest, the whites who are poor have not been part of the discussion on poverty. Research, in particular, has ignored those poor whites who live in the rural deep South.[9] Studies have been made on the poor of Appalachia[10] and on whites who have migrated to Northern cities mainly from Appalachia,[11] but nothing has been done on the rural whites of the Piedmont, the Coastal Plain, or the Delta since the 1940s and even the 1930s. And much of the writings then were like *Tobacco Road,* playing up the "degenerate life of a backwoods Southern community," but making little if any attempt to see the people and their basic needs. It is understandable that poor whites today in rural areas are on the defensive when we recognize that these are the individuals who are currently being labeled as "poor white trash," "crackers," "pecker-wood," and "rednecks."

Because most of the rural poor white population of this country lives in the South, this section will emphasize whites of the South, and particularly of the deep South rather than of Appalachia (which is covered in chapter 12, "The Adult of the Appalachian Mountains") or any other section of the country.

The poor white person in the rural area, whether living in the South or not, is apt to have been born in the section where he lives. Generally, a poor person who has migrated from another state does not move into a rural area; he moves into a town or city instead.

Views on Religion

The majority of poor rural Southern whites are Baptist and subscribe to a fundamental doctrine, or else they have renounced a strongly fundamental religion altogether, saying that they had "too much of it" when they were children. Those who profess some religion stress the need to be "good Christians." Regular church attendance is also stressed, with the result that the church and its services are stabilizing factors in the life of people and are often used to put restraints on behavior. The fundamental doctrine of this kind of religion is apt to teach that most things man wants to do are sinful. Although such doctrine is changing rapidly today, there are still those in rural white America who believe that death is the final punishment followed by hell and the everlasting venge-fulness of a rejected and outraged God unless man prays for forgiveness and sanctification. Isolation is part of the reason this older religious doctrine is more apparent in Southern rural areas, but the age of the church-attending population is also a large factor. In rural areas there are more whites over fifty than of any other age other than children under twelve.

Peasantry

When work is done mainly by hands and feet, the advantages of division of labor are reduced. There are few tasks that both men and women and even children cannot do. Thus, the family in a peasant community is a sufficient unit, able to provide the necessary and minimum social cooperation. In short, the family is a self-sufficient and self-supporting group. It is the center from which the individual relates to other relationships. Individuals in such a social system are counted only as members of a certain family. In community organization the family, not the individual, is the unit. Therefore, in the rural America of the past the network of relationships was an extension of the family. Remnants of this structure still exist, especially among the rural poor whites in more isolated Southern areas of the country, and partly account for the reason that there is so little involvement of these individuals in the decision-making affairs of their local community. It also accounts for the reason that they are more apt to see the effect of the community on them as it "does things to us" than to see *their* relationship to the community, i.e., "we have something to say about what will happen." Southern rural poor whites have less of a tendency to take leadership roles than to follow and to do what they are told. They then handle their personal anger or resentment through gossip and slander and seldom carried-out threats which are never made directly to the person being slandered or gossiped about. Much of this will be explained when family patterns are examined.

Family Patterns

The region of the country seems to be a determinant in the division of executive authority in the rural home. The most democratic poor white families usually live in the far West and the Midwest or in those rural areas near a large metropolitan center like New York, Boston, or Baltimore. The traditional patriarchal pattern is found in various rural sections of the country among certain religious groups, such as the Amish, Hutterites, and the Mormons. However, the most traditional families are those living in the more remote areas of the South where the submissive role of the white woman has found its source for generations in the myth of *protected, sacred womanhood.* According to this myth, the white woman should be put on a pedestal to protect her from the rigors of life. Instead, this position keeps her from having any legal or emotional rights except at the whim of her husband, father, or brother. Therefore, even today it is not surprising to find the traditional, patriarchal, authoritative family structure to be the most common one among poor whites in rural areas of the South and the Southeast.

The Traditional Patriarchal Family Pattern

The traditional rural family is patriarchal and has clear-cut divisions of tasks for men and for women. In such a family structure the husband and wife do not show much affection for each other in front of the children or in public; affection, if any, is expressed only in private. The father is consciously feared, respected, and imitated, especially by his sons. Mother is the center of domestic life, and although she is not to work outside of the home for wages, she can work both in the house and fields and is expected to do so. The husband in this sort of home seems to be threatened by even a suggestion of his wife's being gainfully employed. Part of the threat is the guilt he feels when he is not the sole provider. The law, he says, expects him to feed his family; he expects to do so, and his relatives and friends have the same expectations; therefore, if his wife were to work it would look as if he were not man enough to take care of his responsibilities. He is not only afraid someone will question his manliness; he is also afraid that a job outside the home would give his wife freedom and that she might come in contact with other men, for he is not secure enough within himself to know he can trust her to remain sexually faithful.

There is a strong in-group solidarity in this type of family and many family celebrations. Dependence on the parents is encouraged and emancipation discouraged. The daughters-in-law are subservient to their husband's family. Sons are expected to go to their mother (or father, if alive) for advice and not to consult with their wives. Hostility of daughter-in-law toward mother-in-law is very common.

Large families are encouraged. Birth control methods are often felt by the man to be a detriment to the sexual act and to detract from his manliness, or else birth control is considered to be the total responsibility of the woman, and, therefore, it becomes her own fault if she gets pregnant. Adultery involving the woman is severely punished by the husband, who takes matters into his own hands, but sexual freedom for the husband is expected. Divorce is disapproved on religious grounds. Because desertion is rare, white rural families are more apt to include both husband and wife than are white urban families of the same income. Although this traditional patriarchal family pattern is rapidly decreasing in numbers, in the 1970s remnants of it remain, especially among whites in rural areas.

Family Roles

The man is considered the head of the rural white Southern household whether or not he is the wage earner. Thus, children are threatened with their father's authority. And although the woman is dependent upon the man, actually she makes many decisions, even though she will pretend to defer to the man. In the most traditional home the wife must consult the man if she is asked to do something, such as baby-sit for a neighbor or feed a dog when the owner is gone. The principle in back of this is that the man, as the boss, would be deprived of her services during the time she does something for someone else and, therefore, he should be part of the original agreement. On the other hand, he can promise the services of his wife without consulting her. In this type of home the man controls the money and asks for an accounting from his wife of what she spends. In other homes the woman is entrusted to "hold" the money but must give it to the man on demand for things he wants to buy, although the family may need groceries or the rent may not have been paid.

A major role for the woman is that of cook. Even in the poorest white homes in the deep South the woman bakes biscuits, corn bread, fixes grits, or "cooks up a mess" of blackeyed peas. Older children of the family look after younger siblings and may in some cases provide most of their care. They also take major responsibility for the homemaking. While on one hand an attempt is made to provide a carefree childhood, on the other hand children are pushed into assuming adult roles when the mother, in particular, is unable to cope with the many responsibilities of a large family.

Teaching of Sex Roles

Sex roles are taught in early childhood with an emphasis on what is proper behavior or proper toys for boys or girls. The father stresses, "no son of mine is going to play with dolls." Both the father and the mother use shame as a method of teaching sex roles. The mother may tell her son "not to be a calf" and cry at disappointments; little boys do not cry, only sissies cry.[12] It is improper for boys to wear women's clothes, even in a disguised form. Boys are not expected to be interested in cooking but should be interested in working outside, raising rabbits for example.

The instruction for the little girl is in learning to identify with household tasks. Her behavior, too, is controlled by shaming with such comments as "good girls, nice girls, decent girls do." There is a strong feeling in many homes that the girl can be protected from sexual attention by negative comments about her sex and threats of what she might become if she does not control her behavior, such as "no daughter of mine is going to be a tramp, so stop going around looking like one."

There is confusion in the sexual teachings in that children, both male and female, are often aware at an early age of extramarital relationships or common-law partnerships in the neighborhood, among the family friends, or even within the family, although such relationships are less frequently seen in the poor rural areas than among the urban lower-class whites. The child, on one hand, hears sex condemned and, on the other hand, sees sexual freedom. Becoming an adult may come to mean an opportunity for sexual gratification and a chance to act out what seemingly has been sanctioned through jokes, stories, and threats. One of the privileges of growing up, as seen by the child, is to be in a position to make decisions for one's self and others. For the boy from this background, who has been conditioned to believe that girls and women are inadequate for anything other than sexual relationships, child-bearing, child rearing, and cooking, growing up may mean sexual freedom. One white man in a poor rural area of south Alabama when interviewed for this book stated that he thought the "best reason for growing up was that he could really control a woman."

For the girl, growing up may mean marriage, which occurs at a young age for rural poor Southern whites and often entails living in the home of the parents for the first years of the marriage or in a trailer parked in the parents' yard.

Relationship of Siblings

Boys are told not to fight with their sisters and younger brothers, but at the same time they are expected to be able to defend themselves against male playmates or at school. Even when a child is told not to fight with siblings, his animosity toward his parents is often displaced on brothers and sisters who, in part, are seen as the real reason his parents are not free to give him the attention that he wants. The competition between children for parental approval is often handled through accepting the rights and privileges of various family roles, such as the "baby," the "clown," the "teaser," the "helper," the "bad boy," the "oldest girl," or the "only boy and therefore mother's favorite." A devious way to fight a younger sibling is name-calling, especially referring to another's immaturity.[13] Songs are made up to tease siblings and point out their weaknesses and to shame them into doing what is wanted. The competition may also be seen in rapid emotional mood swings, which at times explode from playful teasing into violent anger expressed in words, threats, or action. For the most part, however, siblings, both male and female, are taught to deny their anger and to express loyalty, if not love, for each other. Therefore, there are strong dependency ties among siblings and of adult children to parents. These ties among siblings tend to hold families together after the death of the parents, especially in emergencies.

Family Solidarity

Poor Southern whites, probably as a result of being on the defensive for generations, have a strong fear of being made fools of. Therefore, parents often discipline their children by saying they do not want to be made fools of by their own children or have the children make fools of themselves. In such cases, the child's behavior is seen by the parents as something that would reflect on the reputation of the family or the age or sex of the child. It is important to put up an appearance of family solidarity before the outside world. Children from the poor rural white culture are taught not to "tattle on" their parents. They are instead to emphasize "my father is right, my mother is virtuous." They are not to let outsiders know the family has problems or, in extreme cases, even needs. This has been interpreted as a "poor but proud" attitude by which a person would even deny that he was hungry, because to lose pride would be to have nothing.[14]

Because there is so much emphasis in the white Southern family on family relationships and family rituals—such as always serving applesauce and coconut cakes at Christmas, hot biscuits and gravy for breakfast, and assembling everyone for birthdays or anniversaries—there is little opportunity provided for outside relationships or for the introduction of new and different rituals. This type of self-isolation and preoccupation with kinship and narrow friendship systems is what gives the poor white rural family an appearance of provincialism, especially in the South. Migration, going away to school, or marrying someone from another section of the country, especially a Yankee, are viewed as rebellion and as threats to family solidarity and, therefore, are discouraged.

The white rural household is also apt to include on a permanent basis a grandparent or other relative, such as an unmarried aunt, an uncle, or adopted or raised children or grandchildren and, temporarily, other relatives who may be incapacitated by one cause or another. The household may be increased at any time also when relatives who live some distance away come for extended visits. All of this tends to increase the major focus on the family and the extended kinship system; at the same time it decreases interest in the wide community.

Family identity is also encouraged through facts and history about the family and visits to the family cemetery or to the site of the home where a grandparent was born. Even if the family were sharecroppers and did not own land, there are still ties to a certain county or a certain place where they lived. The family can also gain status through being identified with the history of the house in which they live, such as that it was once owned by a textile mill, was the first house built in the area, or was the scene of a battle between Confederate and Union soldiers.

Network of Friends and Acquaintances

The circle of friends and even acquaintances for the poor rural white family in the South tends to be relatively small or covers a small geographical area. An examination of those friends shows that they usually all know each other and are related to each other dynamically in important ways. Often they are blood relatives, or if not, they have other meaningful relationships. They belong to the same church, the same lodge; they lived in the same neighborhood as children and went to the same school. Parents know the friends of their children and also the parents of those children; often they will not let their children play with children whose parents they do not know. There is, in this sort of an interrelated friendship network, an informal policing of all children by parents who are friends of their children's parents and can, therefore, easily report on behavior.

Most of this rural neighborhood interaction involves close kin, distant kin, and early childhood acquaintances; the network does not necessarily include people who live next door to each other; in fact, the people next door may be excluded from all contacts. One white man in mid-Georgia, recently describing his family's friendship pattern, said he married the fourth cousin of his best male friend from grade school.[15] In turn, that friend married this man's sister. His children and the children of his best friend are now attending the same school. Most of the relatives of both families live in a two-square-mile area within a twenty-mile radius of where all sets of grandparents (except for one who came from South Carolina) were born. This entire family has no close friends that are not part of the early network. Playmates of their children tend to be the children of their own former playmates or cousins. This man hunts, fishes, plays poker, and drinks with his brothers-in-law, brothers, cousins, and men friends he has known since early childhood. His wife sews or exchanges tips for cooking game and fish with the wives of these men. Their children all play and go to bible school together.

People they have met who are not part of this early network are treated as newcomers or foreigners. These new acquaintances do not become friends; they are merely the people who live next door. They may have lived there for years but still not even be known by name to this family. [16]   They are usually not visited, and they are never called upon in case of illness or the breakdown of a car. They are not trusted with the children. Their children are merely class-mates, as others are classmates in the public school. They are not included in the family rituals of birthdays, fish fries, or the ex-change of Christmas gifts. This lack of real interaction with anyone outside of the network of friends fosters isolation both for this family and those who are not accepted into their network.

Summary

The culture of the poor white family of the deep South is not unlike the cultures of other poor white minorities, especially those who represent first-generation Americans from countries in middle and south Europe where the authority of the man was absolute and where women and children had positions of subservience. The harsh social environment and the degree of poverty in the South impinge upon the family there to produce little that resembles a comradeship between the parents. Their society has provided little opportunity for men and women to relate to each other on an intellectual basis with an equal exchange of ideas and, therefore, unmet human needs are channeled into a dependent tie between parents and children and a strong moral sense of responsibility for all kin, whether or not those kin are actually held in high regard.

A Perspective on Black Culture

Because very few Blacks live in any rural area outside of the South, this section looks at Blacks only in the South. The culture of Blacks on the Sea Islands along the coastal inland waterways of Georgia and South Carolina and Blacks in the Mississippi Delta or in the Black Belt of Alabama is slightly different, primarily in language dialects and in early myths and superstitions. Time and space, however, will not permit me to attempt to examine those differences, so I will point out only what I see as the commonali-ties of Blacks living in rural areas and will leave the differences for future writings.

The Role of the Black Church

The culture of the Black rural community revolves around the church, primarily the Southern or "primitive" Baptist church, which includes regular Sunday services, revivals, prayer meetings, baptisms, funerals, wakes, and special meetings oriented to community action rather than to religion as they were during the days of slavery.[17] If there is no church building, church may be held in a hall. If there is a church building, it may be used for lodge meetings, meetings of any secret fraternal order, or for meetings of the burial society.

The church service itself is an involvement rather than a mere receiving of instruction or doctrination and may be conducted by a deacon, a church mother, a church brother, or a church sister. The preaching part, sometimes done by a circuit preacher, is less important than the participation of the congregation. In some of the more remote rural areas this participation is still a form of "shouting and testifying" where several members may pray aloud at the same time. Fannie Jo Bishop describes this sort of congregation participation in chapter 20, "To Pick a Lug of Cherries," as that which occurred in her grandmother's church. Most of the congregation in rural Black churches today participate by singing, which is a major part of the Black religious service. Much time is spent on choir and solo practice to lead the congregation in the singing, which is accompanied by swaying and body movements that are in tempo with the music. If there is no music, the body movements themselves provide the beat and emphasize the words in a way that is similar to the "earliest forms of spirituals, in which prayers, possession, music and dance were linked in their ancient African affinity."[18] These early spirituals thus have been kept alive by today's church.

Services of the Black Community

The rural Black community still has remnants of the sick benefits and death benefits or burial societies which were once very common and which are a carry-over from the days before insurance when the Black community needed a way to provide for its own emergencies. The more remote the rural area, the more likely is this pattern of benefits and societies to exist. Each member of such a society pays dues depending upon his income. The society also provides social contact with regular meetings and opportunities for people to socialize and to be involved in a decision-making process. Such a society or a lodge may be the one and only uniting structure in the rural area outside of the church.

Cultural Controls That Influence Family and Individual Behavior

Notions of respectability vary slightly from area to area and seem to be tied to the customs of a particular Black neighborhood or section of a state. They seem to have their source in relationships with whites, especially wealthy white families with whom the poor Black of the rural area may have had a closer relationship through work as a maid or cook than with the poor white family who lived nearby. Notions of respectability affect attitudes toward marriage, illegitimacy, church attendance, burial rituals, and others. The Black community gossip exercises restraints on Black family behavior but not to as high a degree as such methods do in a white community, even when the two communities are within the same rural Southern area. The values and moral standards in the Black rural community come more from personal experiences and personal values of what is right and wrong than from a group standard. Therefore, gossip, in order to be effective, must be very personal and must hit at the ego-image or self-ideal of the individual. The approaches to gossip and slander which do control behavior mainly include such expressions as "he's making a fool of you; she's got everybody working for her while she just sits around looking pretty." Such comments make the pressure to change behavior strong because there seems to be a strong fear among rural Blacks of being made a fool of, and thus such a threat becomes a curbing factor in any relationship.

Family Patterns

All kinds of family patterns can be found in Black communities in rural areas. Contrary to the frequent claim that Black families are without a man in the household, from what I have seen in rural areas, I would say that between one-half to two-thirds of all Black families include both a husband and a wife who are either legitimately married to each other or have a marriage arrangement or common-law marriage that has existed for some time. If the family is receiving welfare or AFDC, the likelihood of the husband and father being in the home is certainly less. Most Southern states have not embraced the concept of the family being eligible for assistance if the father is in the home. Thus fewer men between the ages of eighteen and forty-five live with the rural Black family than men over forty-five. This, however, is not a cultural characteristic but rather a response to the external reality of the lack of available work for men in that age range in rural areas.

The Black rural family is usually an extended family, consisting of three generations and often relatives like aunts, uncles, or cousins and their children or married and unmarried women and their children living in the same household. Again this is not so much part of the culture as it is the Black culture's way of coping with the problem of providing food and shelter in the face of limited income or work opportunities for Blacks. Practically every rural family has some member—be it the father, the mother, or some of the children—who is not in the home but who lives at some other address. Sometimes children may be adopted into other families or raised by other relatives or friends who live some distance away.

Attitude toward Pregnancy and Children

In the rural Black family, pregnancy is treated as a fact of life. In the past, the coming of children was looked upon as the Lord's will. There has always been pride in large families, and Black women have been willing to endure miscarriages and still births in both a conscious and an unconscious effort to produce a large family. In a farm economy, especially one geared to cotton where all hands, large and small, were needed, a large family was felt to be essential. As a result, both men and women have developed a sense of guilt about admitting they, as adults, have never been a parent.

In the case of divorce and remarriage the children of a prior relationship, both legitimate and illegitimate, are accepted by the new spouse so that households in rural areas may have children fathered by different men or children born to different women who now are part of a household unit with a step-parent or even two step-parents. The Black culture feels that it is more important to accept the child on his own merit than to identify the child and his relationship with various members of the household unit.

The strongest emotional ties in the rural Black home are between the mother or grandmother and the children, especially the younger ones, regardless of sex. The mother may literally carry her children in close embrace wherever she goes. The greatest amount of attention is bestowed upon the baby, who is held and cuddled by all members of the family. Evidence of affection, such as holding close and kissing, is very common. The father or older brother will kiss a child without embarrassment. If the father lives in the home, a contradictory pattern may be established: he may attend and ignore, play with the child and then leave him to sleep or pursue personal interests. Some fathers who are in and out of the home try to assert themselves through disciplining the child, but most discipline is handled by the mother. It may be done through encouragement and rewards, such as "be mama's good boy," or she may spank or hit the child and afterwards hold the child close and try to comfort him. In her intense desire to love the child, the mother may keep him in infantile dependency unless there are younger children to demand her time. The older child is still encouraged to sit on his mother's or grandmother's lap, is stroked, held close, and crooned to and is encouraged to express his love the same way.

Household Tasks

Household tasks and sex roles seem to vary from family to family. It is not unusual for men, the husband or the son, to help with the household tasks, especially the cooking. In some homes, on the other hand, the man does not see this as his role. The rural Black woman has always worked both in the home and outside in the fields or through whatever employment system was available. Frequently she was the only one in the family able to get employment. She could also pick cotton or peaches during the harvest. Hers has always been a varied role. Her gainful employment, however, has not been because she preferred to work but because she had to work. Therefore, her concept of work is not necessarily one of emotional gratification.

Diet

The main diet of the rural Black is still that of his forefathers—
salt pork, rice, grits, cornmeal, collard or turnip greens, and syrup
or sorghum with an occasional catfish or rabbit. Since the diet is
also affected by the culture and one of the old wives' tales
common in many rural areas is that "greens are feverish," the diets
of Black families may contain very few vegetables.[19] There is, I
believe, another aspect to the avoidance of vegetables. Vegetables
are a very important part of Southern cookery. Much time is spent
on the preparation of vegetables in special Southern dishes. Since
Blacks do much of this Southern cooking in restaurants and private
homes, I wonder if vegetable cooking has not come to be associated with whites, which, coupled with the limited time, energy,
and food supplies in the Black home, might account for the lack of
use of vegetables, even when available.

The Role of the Black Woman as the Spokesperson

Because there are more favorable work markets for Black wom-
en than men, the role of the Black woman as the provider and the
spokesperson for the rural Black family has been more dominant.[20] Molly Washington and Laurabelle Webster, workers in
chapter 25, "Golden Grimes," are examples of dominant rural
Black women. Elsewhere I have also described the position in 1964
of a Black woman as the spokesperson for her family and her race.

> The room spoke of the personality of the woman. It was a
> simple room that served many functions. When, and as, her
> family grew it was all things because it was the largest room in
> the house. When her family was smaller this was the living room.
> Now, three of her married children and their families lived with
> her besides two small children of other relatives. The room
> doubled as a bedroom.
>   She was a strong willed woman in her sixtieth year and
> because she had lived fully she felt deeply and was not afraid to
> express her feelings. She spoke freely with the freedom tradi-
> tionally accorded Black grandmothers who are accustomed to
> express themselves as the official spokespersons for their fami-
> lies.
>   Her grandmother was born a slave six years before the
> outbreak of the Civil War on a large cotton plantation east of

Montgomery. As a child she heard stories of slavery from this grandmother who said Blacks had a harder time after they were freed than they had when slaves. The grandmother's master was kind to his slaves but determined no one, not even the President of the United States, should tell him to free slaves for whom he had paid "good hard cash." He ignored the Emancipation Proclamation issued by President Lincoln. It was not until four years after the Civil War that he finally freed his slaves. "That's when our real troubles commenced," her grandmother often said.

Her own parents were tenant farmers on part of the same plantation where her grandmother was a slave. She was born into the poverty and deprivation of tenant cotton farming. She remembered one year when her father raised only two bales of cotton on the thirty acres he farmed and both bales went to the white man to pay on a mule. They lived that winter on a little corn and some potatoes, eating once a day.

Even as a young child she hated the ugliness of their house. She hated its walls covered with newspapers to keep out the cold. She hated the odds and ends of cast-off furniture, the windows without glass shuttered tight against the darkness and strangers. She hated hearing her father say, "I ain't make nothin' on dis ole run down farm." She hated seeing the men of her race scrape and bow and answer, "yas, sir" or "no, sir" to white landlords who were there to get their share of the crops and who were quick to promise "to fix the house up" but who never brought them even a plank until the place was "rotting down." She hated everything about that type of living and she was determined to do better for herself.

Her life had not been easy. She married young. Before her first child was born she and her husband moved from the country into one of the long narrow unpainted wooden houses in a row of long narrow houses that are so common in Birmingham. Four rooms in a line from the front door to the back, built at a time when lumber was cheap, these houses offer the advantage of a yard, a front porch and the privacy of a single dwelling not found in the tenement housing of northern cities.

From the very beginning her husband, "sho 'nuf had a wanderin' foot." He sort of drifted in and out of her life and one day he "went 'long 'bout sumpin' else." Finally he went to Chicago and "forgot he had a wife and family in Alabama." She was pregnant with their fifth child.

The welfare "he'ped" and she "took in washin' for white folks." When the baby was older she went out to work as a maid. Over the years she built up steady employers. She had worked seventeen years for one family. She called them her "white folks" and said they depended upon her "to look after 'em."

She recognized the value of an education. Although her own education was limited she read widely, subscribing with money from her food budget to news magazines and the local paper. She had strong convictions about the issues of the times. She dominated the lives of her five children and insisted they get a high school education. She also forced them to think and talk about the future of their race. She encouraged them to be active in the various civil rights demonstrations. Had she been younger and able to hike she too would have marched to the Birmingham City Hall or down Constitution Avenue in Washington, D.C. She too would have sung "We Shall Overcome," and carried a placard bearing the slogan "Effective civil rights laws—Now!"

She felt Southern Blacks were on the threshold of opportunity and had to take positions of leadership. She felt even more strongly that leaders must be worthy of leading. Her race she thought lacked good decisive leadership not because her race was inferior but mainly because too many refused to take their place as Blacks. Likewise, she felt there were many white leaders who lacked good judgment and "common sense."

She had no desire to live any place other than Birmingham, Alabama. She had no desire to be something she was not. She taught her children to be proud of their race, proud they were Black. She told them to develop their talents as Blacks and not try to be carbon copies of whites.

She did want rights however for herself, her family and for her race. She wanted the same rights as other residents of her state. She wanted rights without discrimination and she would do everything she could to help her people stand up for those rights.[21]

Role of the Black Woman in Agriculture

The concept of Black women in agriculture is part of the tribal culture of various African groups who were represented among the Blacks brought to this country as slaves. From time immemorial many of these tribes considered agriculture as women's domain and hunting and cattle keeping as the work of men. So rigidly is this distinction maintained among the cattle-breeding Bantu tribes of Africa "that no man would think of using the hoe or digging stick."[22] Apart from the tending of the cattle, which is the men's province, the whole of the work of a Zulu community is performed by the women, including the cultivation of the crops.[23] The life of the average Congo woman vacillates between farms and babies, which form the two principal interests of her life.[24]

Throughout the period of slavery, women worked in the fields and only pregnancy and childbirth provided them with special foods and shorter work days or an acceptable reason for temporarily staying out of the harvest. Today, if the rural Black family has a garden, it usually is more the woman's responsibility than the man's.

Recreation

Both men and women engage in fishing if there is a stream, lake, or pond anywhere within commuting distance. It is a common sight in the South at any time of the day to see individuals or groups of people fishing along irrigation ditches or creeks. Children often accompany their mothers or their parents and play along the river bank, wait in the car, or engage in fishing too, if they have the patience to sit quietly. Fish fries as outings related to the church, lodge, the fraternal order, or more recently to action groups are very popular. Men in rural areas hunt for rabbits and squirrels, but hunting seems to be growing less popular for Black men than it is for rural whites.

Various forms of gambling are common, although gambling has always been condemned by the church. The dream of getting rich on a horse race or dog race or by breeding fighting cocks is part of the conversation that is often more fantasy than reality. However, games of chance, lottery tickets, and door prizes are popular items of discussion. The hope of having the winning number at the grocery store or in some other contest will cause all conversation in a house to cease suddenly if winning numbers or plays are being announced on television.

Historically the telling of stories has been part of the Black family culture. The stories seem to fall into three categories—those that relate history of the family, the community, or the Black race; those that convey superstitions and deal primarily with ghosts and spirits; and those that are humorous and may deal with actual individuals, jokes, riddles, or funny stories that have been passed from generation to generation as family jokes or as part of the local culture of the area.

The teller of the stories, the tone of his voice, and the place of the telling are also part of the family ritual and interaction. For example, most of the history stories are told by older members of the family who preface their comments with "my old parents told me" or "no one knows when he was born; it was so long ago they did not keep records." The ghost stories are often told at the time of a death in the neighborhood or at the time of a wake, and they encourage the belief that the spirit of the departed returns. Fannie Jo Bishop in the chapter "To Pick a Lug of Cherries" mentions this. The tone of the voice when one is telling a ghost story is very serious. If the story does not actually relate to a specific dead person it will be a tale of the "haunts" of a spirit, is usually told by older siblings to younger brothers and sisters, and may be part of an attempt to force them to stay in the house or to go to bed. Teasing and joking are part of the family culture for all ages, but especially for younger members.

Neighbors and Friends

The solidarity of the Black family is extended from kinship to neighbors, friends, and even strangers who are known through a mutual friend or acquaintance. A common bond is established among rural neighbors helping each other with food, clothing, and shelter when needed. The sharing of food supplies and the taking in of nonrelatives go back to the years following the Civil War when Blacks had to care for Blacks if they were to survive. Although there is a network of close friendship ties within the Black rural community, there is also a high degree of formality. For example, a middle-aged or older woman might address a life-long friend as Mrs. Moore and not as Mary, while she might address someone who is not a relative as Aunt Mary.

The chain of contacts that extends out from the rural area can be understood only when illustrated from personal experiences. The following is what one Black family told me about how members of their race traveled across the country at a time when most hotels and restaurants were not open to Blacks.[25]

> We made several trips between south Georgia and Washington, D.C. and places in the north, but always our travel patterns were the same. As everyone else did under those circumstances,

we shared with our friends and neighbors that we planned to make the trip, especially if it was the first time, and if we were taking children with us. Anyone who had a relative, friend or acquaintance along the route we hoped to travel (and we would change our route plans to fit the location of their relatives, friends or acquaintances) would supply us with names and addresses. It was common practice in those days to knock on the door of a stranger and say you had been sent by someone back home and that you and your family needed a meal and a place to sleep. It was expected that Blacks took Blacks in and in addition to food and a bed gave them information to help them travel through that area and to know where they could or could not stop. These strangers were an extension of family, and they packed lunches for their unexpected visitors as willingly as they would if they were blood relatives.[26]

This is what is meant by the cohesion of the Black race and why Blacks, even in remote rural areas today, know Blacks in various parts of the country where they themselves have never traveled, but because relatives and friends have had contacts there and have related these experiences to other family members, there is a feeling of family extension.

A Perspective on the Spanish-Speaking Minorities

Although the Spanish-speaking minorities of this country are very rapidly becoming urbanized—for example, only 20 percent of the Chicanos live in rural areas—they are still a very important part of the rural picture because of their continued ties to agriculture. The majority of Spanish-speaking individuals living in rural areas are employed in agriculture. And of those Chicanos living in towns and cities, 80 percent work in rural areas mainly as farm migrants. Therefore, this section is devoted to the Spanish-speaking culture.

Spanish-speaking Americans do not regulate their lives by the clock as Anglos do. Both rural and urban people, when asked when they plan to do something, give answers like "right now," "about two or four o'clock." Spanish culture (Chicano, Mexican, Puerto Rican, and Cuban) puts its major emphasis on the established present. To translate *mañana* into *tomorrow* leads to misunderstanding. The Spanish-speaking person does today what can be done only today; he does not put that off until tomorrow. But if it can wait he puts it off for *mañana*—for tomorrow—or any date in the future. Another way to explain this is to say that Spanish-speaking people view life differently. "The good things of life are to be savored fully unless overriding reasons require postpostment."[27]

To be Spanish-speaking is to belong to a *familia,* which entails not only loyalty to the family but also responsibility to all members. These kinds of kinship ties are the core of all the Spanish-speaking society, whether the families are from Mexico, Puerto Rico, Cuba, or one of the Latin countries of Central or South America. The pattern of family flows into other kinds of relationships and becomes the pattern for how other structures, such as work crews, are determined.

The Work System

Leadership in early Mexican villages was provided through the patron system whereby the leading man in the community, for some reason—whether it was financial status, knowledge of the outside world, or personal power—assumed a position of responsibility for the villagers much like a father's. The patron system was the reproduction of the family; thus often the patron was called *hermano major,* emphasizing that he had a brother-like relationship to the villagers, who, in effect, were his siblings. The Chicano farm migrant crew of the 1970s is also a reproduction of the patron system and, in turn, of the family. For example, the crew leader, responsible for the crew, has authority over the crew not unlike that of the patron of the Mexican villages and the father of the Spanish-speaking family.

Religion

The predominant religion among all Spanish-speaking people is Catholicism, a religion which has been a bulwark of the family system and preserver of the folk culture.[28] Religious festivals have become family celebrations. Sister Francis Jerome Woods describes this among the Mexicans and Chicanos:

> Religious festivals provide an occasion for recreation as well as for devotion, both in Mexico and in this country. The entire community or ethnic colony may celebrate such an occasion

with processions, dances, and prayers. In Southwestern centers, for example, streets in the Mexican quarter are blocked off for processions on such feasts as Our Lady of Guadalupe on December 12. Religious dances are performed around the image of Our Lady as she is carried in procession. On the feast of All Souls, November 2, the entire family usually goes to the cemetery where the day is spent at the graves of family members.[29]

Of all social institutions the family is most basic, for on it all others rest, and within the Spanish-speaking culture the family as a system is central to the individual's relationship to God, to his fellow man, to time and space, and to whatever geographical area the Spanish-speaking family deems home. Therefore, much of the religious ritual is related to the functions of the family.

The Family System

In the traditional family the father is the figure of authority whom the mother and the children are under strong obligation to support. The eldest brother, *hermano major,* is recognized apart from the other children and may at times have authority and obligations which are parental. For example, he has the authority to take over when the father is absent and to take the father's place in helping to raise the younger siblings should the father die. If there is no father the sister must have permission of her oldest brother to marry.

Male dominance is found throughout the culture, but the continuity of the household life depends upon the mother, whose functions are seen primarily as bearing and caring for children. Although speaking of the Puerto Rican culture, C. Wright Mills and his associates could well have been referring to Chicanos or to the Cuban refugees with this statement: "Ostensible power in the family resides in the male, although women are responsible for daily routine."[30]

Even within this male-dominated society there are exceptions in which family relationships are based on more give and take or where the home is woman-dominated, but by and large the man is considered to be the head of the Spanish-speaking household and the woman the heart of the home.[31] In many homes the mother is more like a sister to her children, siding with them passively against any stand taken by her husband. When she goes somewhere with her husband, the children usually go along too, so the Spanish-speaking woman is constantly playing two roles—those of wife and mother. Arthur J. Rubel describes the role of the Chicano woman as being

> ... submissive, unworldly, and chaste. She is interested primarily in the welfare of her husband and children and secondarily in her own requirements. Both the mother and father of the household are accorded extraordinary respect by their children, but the restraint shown in relation to each is derived from different sources. The father must be respected because of his authoritative position at the head of the household, whereas the mother is respected because she minimizes her own necessities in order to provide for her family better. Devoted to her family Mexican American mothers are consistently pictured and idealized as a suffering (*padeciendo*) woman.[32]

Boys within the Spanish-speaking culture have always known a high degree of freedom, including sexual freedom, whereas girls in the same family have been closely supervised and chaperoned. Although there is less close supervision among the lower class than the upper class, how traditional the individual family pattern is determines this factor rather than the social class. Even among farm migrant families there are some who supervise the activities of their daughters as carefully as do the richest families in Mexico City. Mills and his fellow writers spell out this pattern and other family patterns for the Puerto Rican culture.

> The male is supposed to be dominant, proof of his manhood being in direct relation to his sexual capacity. The woman is supposed to be submissive, and her submissiveness is guaranteed by a network of manners and politenesses which confines her major sphere of activities to the home, circumscribes her social contacts and places her under constant surveillance. As an incidental consequence, she is likely to overprotect her children.
>
> To the outside observer, the Puerto Rican pattern for women seems divided into two extreme types; either she seems to be dominated and repressed first by her family, later by her husband; or she seems to have apparent sexual freedom in an informal marriage relationship (common law marriage). Actually such patterns contain elements of the other: the supervised girl or wife has often managed to secure for herself much more psychological and physical freedom than is apparent; the seem-

ingly unsupervised lower-class woman is frequently much more restricted and dominated than appearances might indicate.[33]

Children are loved deeply in all Spanish cultures. Not separated from adults, they take part in whatever is happening to the rest of the family. Thus, they receive much attention from any and all family members whenever they cry. The primary family is also extended into a clan of relatives which includes godparents and often the families of the godparents. In addition, other relatives may help to meet the needs of the children.

> If a child is deprived of the care of his parents by death or illness or is abandoned by them, a relative usually takes over. Relatives help each other as a duty because they are "of the same blood"; a mother trusts the care of her child to relatives without misgivings.[34]

Along with loyalty and affection go obligations. The child is loved by his family, but in turn he is obligated to help support the family. Hence, children contribute to the family income from their earnings. Likewise, the obligation rests with the adult child, so aged parents are supported, and old people have a respected place in the culture.

The need to keep even adult children as close as possible is described by George M. Foster, who, researching the culture of a Mexican peasant village, says that newlyweds often reside in the home of either of their parents until the birth of a child, after which event the young couple establishes their own separate domicile. Although the site on which they construct their residence may be adjacent to that of the parents, each nuclear family household represents a "social isolate" which is considered to be independent from but nevertheless under the protective system of the larger family.[35]

A Perspective on the Culture of the American Indian

No greater extremes of cultural differences can be found than those between the primary Indian culture and that of the dominant culture. Looking at man's relationship to a supernatural being, to his fellow man, to the earth and things, to time and space quickly uncovers apparent cultural differences. The intention here is not to give an historical perspective on the dominant and Indian cultures, but rather to point out how, from the viewpoint of one, the behavior of the other would be interpreted as just the opposite of what was expected or intended and to show that an individual moving from one of these cultures to the other would need to completely reverse his personal value system.

Contrasts between the Dominant and Indian Cultures

The dominant culture's belief in the doctrine of a single supreme being, God, is in conflict with the Indians' original belief in many gods who lived in nature and with whom the Indians were in constant communication through prayer, songs, and dances.[36] Historically the Indian has prayed for material help and power to overcome an enemy; he does not pray for spiritual blessings and for forgiveness for his sins.

The dominant culture teaches individualism and individual ownership; the Indian culture teaches that individual identity comes from the tribe or larger group or council and that communal ownership is the only true ownership. The dominant culture stresses the accumulation of wealth and material things; the Indians feel the richest man is the one who has given everything away. The Indian culture teaches to share, not to hold back for self. The dominant culture teaches the individual that charity begins at home. The dominant culture teaches competition and aggression to prove self-worth; the Indian culture teaches cooperation and not taking the initiative. For the Indian to be competitive, aggressive, and take the initiative would be to separate himself from his social group. Instead of being congratulated, he would be censored by his kinsmen and neighbors who would believe that only a stingy man or one helped by witches would accumulate so much. Regardless of the nationality represented, Indian children are not taught to compete as white children are taught competition. When forced to do so in school, they feel guilty and usually withdraw rather than be ostracized by their classmates.

The dominant culture stresses land ownership and development through building, cutting trees, changing stream beds. The Indian culture maintains that man does not own the earth; he can use it only. Thus, trees and natural resources may be used but should not be destroyed. Their culture stresses that agriculture, for those Indians who engage in it, is an interrelationship between man and earth. Even in the arid Southwest where the raising of corn is part of the religion, the Indians do not think of themselves as wrestling a living from the soil, but rather as assisting the land to produce that of which it is capable. In such cases agriculture is not viewed as a means of making a living; instead it is a way of life tied to the religion of the people.

Many of today's feelings that Indians are "dirty" are carry-overs from the time when the two cultures first came in contact with each other and their cultural differences became focused on the burial of the dead and disposal of body wastes. The dominant culture even then taught that all waste and body refuse are repulsive and must be hidden from sight, destroyed, or buried in the ground. The Indian culture taught that all things related to the body must be returned to the elements by exposure to the sun, the wind, the rain, or snow. Thus the Indian's way of handling human waste was felt by the dominant culture to be dirty, whereas to the Indian it was a ritual necessary to ensure that bodily wastes were given over to the elements. Toward that end, even a human corpse was not buried, but was placed above the earth on a platform or in a tree.

Time in the dominant culture means starting a meeting at the appointed hour and ending by a certain specified time. But the Indians' culture places no stress on time limits; clocks are not part of their basic culture. Meetings, dances, and parties start when the people are ready, and they end when the purpose for being there is finished. The Indian culture also prescribes to certain rituals and forms of greeting that should proceed a meeting which have not been part of the dominant culture. Thus, the Indians think those of the dominant culture are rude and have no respect for manners; the dominant culture sees Indians as procrastinators and time wasters. The dominant culture says the Indian has no respect for time; the Indian says the white culture is controlled by time. An example of this difference in time emphasis may be seen in the Indian mother who has difficulty responding to the question typical of the dominant society about the ages of her children. Because her culture stresses the order of birth, she can easily recall who is the oldest, the older, or the younger, but she may have difficulty recalling their ages.

The territorial boundaries for the dominant culture are narrow; for the Indian they are without limits. The confine of small space is difficult for the Indian to tolerate unless he has the freedom to migrate. This freedom to migrate has always included moving the home itself, visiting friends and relatives, and, in the old days, searching for food and celebrating the holy days by traveling hundreds of miles to be together with other tribes. Along with need for open space and a sense of the freedom of movement is the Indian's comfort with aloneness and silence. The culture has historically provided many opportunities for the individual, especially the man, to be alone or to sit quietly without talking. Indians do not find silences awkward or embarrassing.

The Indian who takes what, in his culture, would be his to use, in the white culture would be stealing. The person who works and saves for himself and does not share with others in the white culture would be considered a self-sufficient individual; in the Indian culture he would be a miser who, in the old days, would have been driven from the tribe. The person who shares freely of everything he owns is said to be gullible by the dominant culture, but that same behavior is described as generous and noble-minded by the Indian culture.

An Example of Contrasts between Indian Nationalities —the Zuni and the Sioux

The name *Indian* is used to refer to a race of people who represent varied cultures and distinctly different nationalities whose value systems are as diverse as those of various Caucasian nationalities, for example, the English, Germans, Italians, or Greeks. Each Native American nationality or tribe, such as Navaho, Chippewa (*Ojibwa*), Pawnee, Comanche, or Apache, speaks its own language and has its own customs. An example of the great diversification among Indian nationalities is found if a comparison is made of the Zuni, who are matriarchal in their family role pattern, and the Sioux, who are patriarchal.

The Zuni, or, as they call themselves, the *Ashivi* of New Mexico, are one of several pueblo-dwelling tribes of the Southwest, but like the Hopis of Arizona, the Zuni are the most typical of the remaining Pueblo tribes. Descent among the Zuni is counted in the maternal line, and the women have an important place in the economic and household organization. Zuni life centers around cooperation and a rich ceremonial religion.

The name *Sioux* is derived from the French corruption of the Chippewa (*Algonquia*) word *Nadowesiwig*, signifying the "snake-like ones" or "enemies."[37] They called themselves *Dakota* and were once the largest of all Indian groups. Today the Sioux are found mostly in the Dakotas, Montana, and Nebraska. Sioux women hold a subservient position, although in recent years a few have risen to leadership roles, such as tribal judge.

The Zuni had no seemingly strong visible leaders as did those Indian nations with chiefs. Yet, they had and have today all kinds of leaders in their various religious cults. On the other hand, the history of the Sioux can be traced through chiefs or leaders like Red Cloud, Crazy Horse, Sitting Bull, Big Foot, and Crow King, to mention a few. Today among the Sioux the leadership lies with the tribal president and the tribal council.

Among the Zuni a man and wife can do most things together. He can help her around the house, and she can help him in the fields. It is more difficult for the man of the Sioux culture to help his wife around the house, for among the Sioux are very clearly defined roles of the sexes, which were part of their early culture. Agriculture, what little was done (the Zuni were the herdsmen and agriculturalists), was the work of women as was the cooking and the care of the home and, where the Sioux were nomads, erecting the teepees and taking care of the game. The men were hunters and were involved in the governmental affairs of the council and the religious rituals. Much of the man's time was spent evoking visions for directions from the gods to determine his occupation or his fate in battle or the hunt. The Sioux male was also responsible for teaching the boys the tricks of hunting, while the girls were taught by the women. Girls, like boys, were taught how to look for food, but for different things. The men would hunt for large game; the women would be responsible for gathering birds' eggs, roots, wild fruit, wild grains, and for fishing, which most years provided the major part of the food supply. Both males and females had to know what signs in nature indicated danger and how to do the religious dances, although the steps for the male and the female were, and still are, different—the male steps being more aggressive.

The Zuni demonstrate their affection for their children and grandchildren openly much longer than the white culture, whereas Sioux parents are more reserved. The Sioux are not at all demonstrative in their affection, especially when outside their homes. Thus, Sioux parents have been criticized by non-Indian school personnel for greeting their children at the end of the school year very matter of factly when they have not seen them for months.

The Zuni Culture

Economic Values. Among the Zuni, production is chiefly agricultural and wealth is in terms of sheep, with economic life organized around cooperation. Thus, the cultivated fields may belong to an individual or to a matriarchal household, but the work is done in common by the men of the household, and the produce is turned over to the women. There may be friendly rivalry about the performance of the common tasks in farming, but there is no individualism in ownership as the dominant culture knows it. This cooperation not only controls the family unit, but the existence of the whole tribe depends on a willingness to give mutual aid. Competition among individuals such as that in the dominant society has no tribal sanction. Herding and other work with sheep are also performed in common. The wool, lambs, and mutton are shared by the family and community, although the sheep may be owned by individuals.

Land tenure also reflects the cooperative character of life among the Zuni. Real estate is held by the tribe, and only those areas cultivated by a family are considered to be in the care of that social unit. Although the household is the central operating unit, relatives and friends join in various agricultural and sheep-raising endeavors, and the food for all those participating is furnished by the hosts who benefit from the aid of others. In fact, various seasonal feasts provide a form of distribution of food with reference to planting, harvesting, grinding corn, and so on. But the individual attains no personal prestige from such activities.

Religion and Government among the Zuni. Much of the community life of the Zuni revolves around the religious order. The basic controls are in the hands of a priestly hierarchy and a wide variety of religious cults. The basic cult is related to the ancestral group, but there are also six other major societies, including the cults of the sun, the rainmakers, the *katcinas,* the medicine cults, and the bow-priesthood. The head of the sun cult, the most powerful of the priests, is responsible for the welfare of the community. The rainmaking ceremonials are important for economic survival. Every adult male as well as a few women belong to the *katcina* society. The chief priest of this cult has great prestige as he embodies the characteristics of beauty, dignity, and kindliness—three basic virtues of the people. The medicine cults, to which both men and women belong, have to do with disease and its cure. If one is ill he must join, or, if one has been cured by a medicine man, he is obliged to join. At one time the bow-society dealt with war and with the overt executive needs of the community. In earlier times, when the Zuni occasionally indulged in warfare, the bow-priests were leaders in the battles. Now the cult serves as protection against the revenge of the ghost of an enemy.

Much of Zuni life revolves around the elaborate ceremonials of these cults. The priests must learn perfectly the extensive ritualistic formula and acts. But the ceremonies are carried on collectively for the good of the entire community. Within this larger framework individuals may make use of their own dances, prayers, and sacred formula. In some public ceremonies there are foot races, some of which are purely ritualistic with no announced winners. But one race, the twenty-five-mile stick-kicking contest, is highly exciting. Wagers are made and public interest runs high. Sides are chosen with two to six runners on a side, and the contest is on. Yet when one side has won, though the bets are paid, no great prestige accrues to the man who kicked the stick over the goal line. In fact, a man who consistently wins is prevented from participating in future contests so that others may have a chance.

Marriage among the Zuni. Tribal marriages are easily arranged and easily dissolved. They usually depend on personal sentimental choice and property considerations play little part. The men, as a rule, do the courting, and if a woman consents to marriage certain rituals of corn grinding, eating, and exchanging gifts that consummate the tribal marriage follow. The man then takes residence in the wife's household. If a marriage is not successful, a wife may divorce her husband by simply placing his few personal belongings outside the entrance to the house. This serves as a public announcement that she is through with him.

Zuni Sex and Family Roles. The family life revolves around matrilineal descent and maternal control of the household. The grandmother and her sisters, her daughters, and their daughters own the house and the corn that is stored in it. No matter what happens to the marriages, the women of the household remain with the house for life. Their husbands are outsiders. A man always goes for all important occasions to his mother's house, which, when she dies, becomes his sister's house. If his marriage breaks up, he returns to the same stronghold. The husband has little to say except to provide the economic necessities. The children are controlled and trained by the mother and her brothers. Their father is in many ways a stranger to them. He, in his turn, will be occupied with training his sister's children. Individual authority and responsibility, however, are largely absent in the household. Aside from necessary duties, the men spend much of their time in work outside the house or engaged in the religious activities.

The Culture of the Sioux

Governmental Structure of the Sioux. The early Sioux nations were divided into three major groups which spoke slightly different dialects—*Dakota, Nakota,* and *Lakota*—and which were able to communicate with each other through sign language. Each linguistic group, in turn, was divided into separate tribes with their own chiefs. Each tribe was further divided into related kinship families called bands. The relatives hunted and camped together under the direction of the oldest male member. This was their patriarch, the band chief. Within the linguistic groups were seven main divisions known as the *Oceti Sakwin,* or Seven Council Fires. When they came together in their national assemblies, the teepee of each division chief was placed in a designated spot. This was part of the protocol and ceremony of what in other countries would have been a royal court.[38]

Today each Sioux tribe is governed by a tribal council, usually consisting of thirty-two members headed by an elected president.

Historically, authority rested with the older members of the tribe and council; and young people, although better educated, were, and still are, expected to be silent when their more experienced elders were speaking. Today there is much disagreement and conflict over this tradition between the elders of the tribe and the new young leadership within the tribal councils.

Material Possessions of the Sioux. The Sioux were nomads for whom the accumulation of material objects, beyond what one could carry or what was essential for life, was not desirable. Therefore, the early Sioux culture taught the individual to give away, to share, and not to keep. In that culture the most hated person was the miser. Therefore, the young child learned generosity from the lack of value the adults placed on property and from their willingness to share their property with others. Teaching generosity is still common, although not as easy to achieve today. In the past, if a Sioux wanted something, he had the right to take it or to borrow it without permission and even to keep it if he needed it. If someone admired an object, it was to be given to him. This concept of sharing was applied especially to food.

The sharing of food was basic to the early Sioux culture. In the days of the nomad tribes, food was never hoarded by individuals or families. Food was shared and shared alike. It had to be shared for the preservation of the tribe. Those who dared withhold food for themselves rather than give to any member of the band who expressed a need, or a desire, were ostracized as not being worthy of being Sioux.

Today this tradition of sharing still holds true. No one, especially a relative, is ever refused food or is turned away at mealtime. Food is divided although there may not be enough for a division. There is no guilt about coming to be fed. It is not a form of begging or accepting charity. It is part of the tradition of the past. Those who have today must share willingly with those who do not have, so that tomorrow, they too will be eligible for the generosity of others. It is a cultural right for those who are hungry to expect to be fed. It is a cultural obligation for those who have food to share. In the world of the white man's culture where the Sioux lives, this sort of sharing reduces all to a degree of common poverty. Each year on the Reservation, this poverty becomes more evident.[39]

Traditional Sioux Family Roles. Historically the most important function of the Sioux mother was the care of her child, which took precedence over all other duties she was to perform. She gave constant care to her infant or any other infant that needed attention. An infant was not allowed to cry but was nursed by any woman who was present who had milk.

The affection between brothers and sisters of the Sioux was the model for all respect in the Sioux culture, while the loyalty between brothers was the model of all comradeship. In the traditional home, the Sioux man and his male relatives or male guests ate first and the women and girls last. In all decisions the father was the head of the home.

Sioux Taboos. The taboos of the culture had mainly to do with interpersonal relationships, taboos the child learned early. They were taught through shame and ridicule and by the establishment of channels of communication. The most elaborate system of communication existed between brothers and sisters who, after a certain age, could not speak directly to each other but only through a third person. Some have explained that this custom, which is still practiced by the older members of the tribe, was to prevent the possibility of incest, and others, including the son and the grandson of Chief Red Cloud, have told me that it grew out of respect for the brother-sister relationship. A brother and sister should never quarrel. Edgar Red Cloud chuckled when he said, "It is sort of hard to fight when it must be done through a third party." This taboo of direct conversation extended to parents-in-law and children-in-law of the opposite sex and between brothers-in-law and sisters-in-law.

One aspect of the early Sioux culture, which was also common to early white and Black cultures, is the attitude toward the menstruating woman. The Sioux culture, as did all primitive cultures, taught that the menstruating woman was unclean and that certain kinds of foods would spoil under her touch. The white rural culture, especially in the South, taught at one time that a menstruating woman should not can or process meat or make pickles or sauerkraut because such foods would spoil if she was involved in the process. This teaching was common in rural areas in the years before World War I and was still common among the older Sioux in the early 1950s. Thus they would caution the menstruating girl or woman not to touch the meat supply, regardless of what she might be taught in school about personal hygiene.

Parent-Child Relationships among the Sioux. The birth of a child among the Sioux, as among all Indians regardless of the tribe, is an occasion for great rejoicing. The young child is not separated from the activities of adults. Instead, younger children are always the center of attention. They are carried around on the hip, bounced, entertained, and played with by older siblings. Indian parents indulge their children. From the time of his birth until he can walk, the young child is constantly with the mother, nearly always within reach of her hand. It is also customary for the Indian baby to be nursed until he weans himself. As a result of this prolonged period of nursing, there is little thumbsucking, and pacifiers are seldom seen.

Children in the Sioux culture are never physically punished. They may be disciplined by scaring—by telling them that if they do not obey something will get them. In the old days they were told that the owl would come or the white man would steal them.[40] The teaching of the child, even the toilet training, is done by example. Thus, the concept of teaching by peers and through role models is an important part of the basic concept of the Sioux culture.

The extended family kinship pattern once made it possible for Sioux to handle a tense home situation by visiting relatives some distance away. The child today still has many homes away from home and may live with a mother who actually is a maternal aunt rather than with his own parents. A husband or wife may also leave his mate and go to stay with relatives for long periods of time. This is the culturally acceptable way for the individual to handle aggression.

*   *   *

Culture is based upon the study of behavior and behavioral products, but culture is neither behavior nor the investigation of behavior in all its concrete completeness. And yet in order to examine the problems of present-day rural America, one must see both the culture and the causes of behavior. In order to help the reader do this, the next chapters of this section will continue to look at the cultures of the rural area beginning with a more detailed examination of the Appalachian highlander.

NOTES

1. Charles Brenner, *An Elementary Textbook of Psychoanalysis,* Anchor Books (Garden City, N.J.: Doubleday and Co., Inc., 1955), pp. 16-32.

2. Lyle Saunders, *Cultural Differences and Medical Care* (New York: Russell Sage Foundation, 1954), pp. 116-17.

3. Edward T. Hall, "The Anthropology of Space: An Organizing Model," in *Environmental Psychology: Man and His Physical Setting,* ed. by Harold M. Proshansky, William H. Ittelson, and Leanne G. Rivlin (New York: Holt, Rinehart and Winston, Inc., 1970), p. 20.

4. *Ibid.,* p. 22.

5. Sister Frances Jerome Woods, *Cultural Values of American Ethnic Groups* (New York: Harper and Bros., Publishers, 1956), p. 8.

6. "Introduction," *Shadow of the Plantation* (Chicago: University of Chicago Press, 1934), pp. xii-xiii.

7. *Tepoztlan, A Mexican Village* (Chicago: University of Chicago Press, 1930), pp. 1-6.

8. *Race,* as used in this book, refers to a main biological division of the human species, the members of which have several traits in common. There are usually a number of subraces with somewhat distinctive physical characteristics within the larger categories. Skin color alone is not a reliable criterion for determining race, although it is usually used by the general public. The criteria that are used by sociologists include:

    1. head form
    2. nasal index
    3. facial projection
    4. skull capacity
    5. hair texture
    6. hairiness of body
    7. body build, height, and weight, which are of little use
    8. color of skin, eyes, and hair, which has not been too useful

Some writers give five major races—white, black, yellow, red, and brown. Most writers, however refer to three—white or Caucasian, yellow or yellow-brown or Mongoloid, and black or Negroid—and put all peoples of the world into these three races. If these categories are used, included in the Mongoloid race are the American Indians, among whom, even when full blooded, there are marked physical differences, as well as cultural differences.

9. Of the rural poor in the South, 81.8 percent are white, even though the proportion of poor people is higher for nonwhites than whites. U.S., Department of Commerce, Bureau of the Census, 1970 Census of Population,

General Population Characteristics (Washington, D.C.: Governmental Printing Office, 1971). By 1969, 6.7 million whites (of whom 65 percent lived in rural areas) and 5.2 million Blacks lived in poverty in the South. George Thomas, *Poverty in the Nonmetropolitan South* (Athens, Ga.: Regional Institute for Social Welfare Research, University of Georgia, 1971), pp. 9-10.

10. Thomas R. Ford, ed., *The Southern Appalachian Region: A Survey* (Lexington, Ky.: University of Kentucky Press, 1962).

11. Hal Bruno, "Chicago's Hillbilly Ghetto," *Reporter*, XXX (June 4, 1964), 28-31; John R. Hundley, "The Mountain Man in Northern Industry," *Mountain Life and Work*, XXXI (Spring 1955), 33-38; Richard Martin, "City 'Hillbillies,' " *Wall Street Journal*, September 30, 1965; E. Russell Porter, "From Mountain Folk to City Dweller," *Nursing Outlook*, II (June 1963), 418-20.

12. The dictionary defines *sissy* in this case as an effeminate boy or man.

13. Name-calling, shaming, and gossip are widespread methods used within the Southern white culture to control behavior.

14. This is the belief illustrated in *To Kill A Mockingbird*, when Scout Finch chided Miss Caroline Fisher, her first-grade teacher, for "shamin' " a member of the class by offering to loan him twenty-five cents to pay for his lunch. Harper Lee (New York: Popular Library, Inc., 1960), pp. 23-26.

15. From a personal interview for this book.

16. This accounts for why a stranger trying to locate someone may find that people who live next door or a short distance away have never heard of the individual. It is not unusual when inquiring in a remote rural area in the South to have people say, "Ask up the road, they may know" or "I don't neighbor with folks that live near here" or "somebody moved in last year on the Epp's place; they might be the ones." It is also interesting that Epps was the name of the original owner and that's how the place derives its identity, but the current tenant is without name and has little if any meaning to other poor whites who live in the same neighborhood.

17. Following the Civil War Blacks wanting to put their freedom to a test separated themselves from the churches of their former masters, which had been, for the most part, the Southern Presbyterian Church and the Methodist Church. The new churches for Blacks became the African Methodist Episcopal Zion Church and the Baptist. By 1926, out of 5 million Black church members, more than half were Baptist and the second largest number were Methodists. William Warren Sweet, *The Story of Religion in America* (New York: Harper and Bros., Publishers, 1939), pp. 470-76.

18. Guy Carawan, Candie Carawan, and Robert Yellin, eds., *Ain't You Got a Right to the Tree of Life?* (New York: Simon and Schuster, Inc., 1966).

19. Many babies in these rural Black homes today suffer from iron anemia as a result of being fed an almost entirely milk diet until nearly two years of age.

20. Women in this position, whether Black or non-Black, tend to see themselves in a hostile, demanding world in which they not only have to push and assert themselves in various ways if they are to get a job, but in which they also cannot rely on others, especially men, for protection or emotional encouragement. Such women discover early in life that they will be exploited in what they are paid for the work they do and in the lack of or limited recognition they will receive for any accomplishments. They all will also be objects of sexual aggression, if not sexual exploitation, which may come from an employer, a fellow worker, or even from a stranger. They discover early how to protect themselves or else they do not survive,

emotionally. Because they turn their psychic energy and hurt back toward self and it becomes their motivating drive, they may have a degree of success in spite of their environment but seldom because of it. Out of this kind of female assertion, which is mandatory if the lower-class woman, regardless of her race, is going to succeed, comes a kind of aggression that in turn is evaluated in negative, demeaning terms which say that this sort of a dominant woman has knowingly and willingly usurped the rights of men. She is guilty, the accusations say, of trying to *be* a man, when in actuality what she is trying to do is to put food in the mouths of her children and even of her husband. (Somehow it seems appropriate to point out here that the female animal in the wild will hunt for her young and will even bring game to her mate and that among many animal species the most active hunter is the female, not the male.) Because she has dared to be less than submissive, she becomes the target for hostility (she is described as a castrating, destructive female) from the men of her family, from her race, and from a society which forces all women, regardless of their social class or personal accomplishments, into a subservient position and claims that they are somehow less than women if they dare to try in any way to change their situation.

21. Myrtle R. Reul, *Where Hannibal Led Us* (New York: Vantage Press, 1967), pp. 73-75.

22. J. A. Hammerton, ed., *Manners and Customs of Mankind,* Vol. I (London: Amalgamated Press, Ltd., 1935), pp. 340 and 344.

23. *Ibid.,* Vol. II, p. 545.

24. *Ibid.*

25. Some of the feel for how the Black person needed to search for a place to get a drink of water or to rent a room is pointed out by John Howard Griffin in *Black Like Me* (New York: New American Library, Inc., 1960), pp. 24, 27-28, 63, 82, and 84.

26. Personal interview with a Black family in south Georgia.

27. Y. Arturo Cabrera, *Emerging Faces: The Mexican-Americans* (Dubuque, Iowa: William C. Brown Co., Publishers, 1971).

28. While the Catholic religion remains the principal religion in Puerto Rico, it has been adapted to the folklore of the island. Notes on the Puerto Rican culture prepared for case studies by the Council on Social Work Education point out the variety of religious patterns in Puerto Rico. "Although Catholicism has historically been the religion of Puerto Rico for much of the population, its form has been influenced by folk elements. Cults of the saints are strong in rural areas, and witchcraft beliefs may be tenacious. The official church stand on issues such as divorce and birth control has not received strict adherence. Spiritualistic movements and sects have a strong appeal to some parts of the population, and since the American occupation missionary activity has developed an active Protestant minority." *Socio-Cultural Elements in Casework* (New York: Council on Social Work Education, 1955), p. 38.

29. *Cultural Values of American Ethnic Groups,* p. 177.

30. C. Wright Mills, Clarence Senior, Rose Kohn Goldsen, *The Puerto Rican Journey* (New York: Harper and Bros., 1950), p. 8.

31. This is one reason Chicano women have been so hesitant to take a very active role in the Women's Liberation Movement. Another reason is that they, like Blacks, feel a strong responsibility to assist the men of their ethnic group to take leadership roles, and they hope that the liberation of women of their culture will follow.

32. *Across the Tracks: Mexican-Americans in a Texas City* (Austin, Tex.: University of Texas Press, 1966), pp. 67-68.

33. Mills, Senior, and Goldsen, *The Puerto Rican Journey*, p. 9.

34. *Ibid.*, p. 8.

35. "The Dyadic Contract: A Model for the Social Structure of a Mexican Peasant Village," *American Anthropologist*, LXIII (December 1961), 1173-93.

36. The Indian dance is a form of religious ritual, not personal recreation.

37. The Ojibwa (Chippewa), one of a tribe of Algonquian Indians living at that time in the vicinity of Lake Superior, were continuously having warlike encounters with the various tribes of the Dakotas, who lived farther west in what is now Minnesota. The Ojibwa became friendly with the French trappers who had come in large numbers to the Lake Superior area. Many of these Frenchmen married or mated with Indian women and became the fathers of their children, adding French influence to the Indian culture and giving a French pronunciation or mispronunciation to Indian names. It was in this way that *Ojibwa* was mispronounced as *Chippewa*, and Chippewa it became in the eyes of the United States government, although the Indian name for themselves was Ojibwa.

Name-calling was, and still is, a part of the method used by Indians to shame others. To liken an individual or group to something that is not respected is slander and is intended to reduce the importance of the other. Therefore, it was natural for the Ojibwa to call their enemies, the Dakotas, names that would carry the meaning of enemy. *Nadowesiwug* became important when it was picked up by the French and the English. The French mispronounced it *Nadaouesioux;* in turn the English, unable to pronounce the French word, called it *Sioux* and sometimes spelled it *Soo.* When placed on the reservations, the Dakotas were called Sioux by the United States government, and Sioux they have remained.

This disregard of the Indian name for their own people was only the beginning of a long list of things which made Indian identity very difficult to maintain. Today it is even difficult to get an accurate head count of Indians. The data on living Indians in the United States, according to the United States Census, usually show fewer Indians than are reported by the United States Indian Services. There are several reasons for this, the main one being the count of mixed bloods. The individual who is a mixture of Indian and white usually appears in the census as white because of his small degree of Indian blood; however, the rolls of Indian Service may count this person as Indian because he or she is entitled to shares in Indian tribal lands or income. Again, in states where there are mixtures of Indian and Negro the custom is to list all such individuals as Blacks. Further, the Indian Service registers all persons of Indian descent, whether or not they live on a reservation, whereas many mixed-blooded Indians scattered around the country are enumerated in the United States Census as white and Black.

All of this is a further blow to the Indian's self-identity when it is apparent to him that not even the United States Census can obtain an accurate head count of his race and, therefore, dumps him with Caucasians whom he may hate or with Negroes with whom he may not want to be confused. He is not white, he is not Black, and yet he has difficulty convincing his own government of his true identity.

38. Reul, *Where Hannibal Led Us*, p. 187.

39. *Ibid.*, p. 196.

40. Threatening children with stories of an animal like a wolf, a bear, or a large bird, or even threatening children with being carried away by or given to another race, is a common threat that is used, or it has been used, by every race and ethnic group in the United States. For example, Black mothers have disciplined their children with threats of the white man or of a

policeman. White mothers have threatened their children with stories of a Black man, a Japanese or a Chicano, an Indian or a gypsy, or even a migrant farm worker. Likewise, mothers of other races have done the same thing. Sometimes these stories are focused on age or sex and the person is said to be a witch or a monster who tortures small children. All of this, of course, builds up the prejudice of individuals and helps to keep racism alive.

I see these hills and fields at dawn and dark, in sunshine and in moonlight, in summer green and winter snow, and yet there is always a new view before my eyes.

Pearl S. Buck, 20th century American authoress
My Several Worlds

12

The Adult of the Appalachian Mountains

When one considers the culture of the Appalachian highlander, it is necessary to keep in mind an important fact: the geographical region termed Appalachia does not have a homogeneous culture. Appalachia is the mountainous land sweeping diagonally across thirteen states from southern New York to northern Mississippi, West Virginia being the only state completely within the area (see Figure 17). Although there are similarities in the geography of this mountainous area and similarities in the nature of the first settlements and the reasons the settlers came originally, differences and diversities also exist that have affected personal values and attitudes and have made the people view themselves not as a homogeneous group from the same section of the country, but as unique and different individuals.

This is a revised version of a paper which was presented at the Ohio Seminar for Administrators of Adult Basic Education held in Columbus, Ohio, September 19, 1968. The paper in its original form was published by the Ohio Department of Education in the Proceedings of the 1968 Conference.

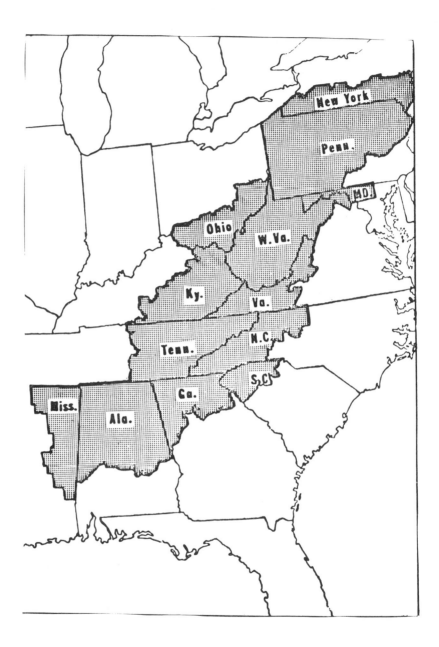

Fig. 17. The parts of thirteen states that constitute Appalachia.

Although there are similarities among the various mountainous communities, there are slight differences in dialects, customs, superstitions, and concepts of self-identity. These diversities have traditionally biased family against family, church denomination and religious group against church denomination and religious group, republicans against democrats, and even residents of one state against those who live across a neighboring state boundary. Terms such as *ridgerunner* or *hillbilly* or *redneck* or *snake* carry certain local connotations when applied by a native of the Blue Ridge Mountains of "Old Virginny" to a West Virginian, or to a native of the Smokies, or the Cumberlands, or to someone from the mountains of northern Georgia.

Descriptions of Appalachia

Speaking of the parts of the states which make up Appalachia, as early as 1921 John C. Campbell said,

It is difficult to write of a people who, while forming a definite geographical and racial group, were never socially homogeneous. Statements applicable to the remote rural folk are not true of their urban and valley kinfolk. Most so-called mountain traits are to be found in one form or another throughout the nation.[1]

Harry M. Caudill made the same observation in *Night Comes to the Cumberlands*.[2]

Also writing of the same area in 1962, W. D. Whetherford and Earl C. D. Brewer described it in these terms:

The region consists of one of the nation's last frontiers but it is a frontier in ferment, a country of contrast. There are isolation and invasion of tourists, rugged individualism and bulging welfare roles, pride and poverty, Elizabethan ballads and atomic bombs, the high altar and snake handlers, TVA and localistic Jefferson democracy, the mountain's sage and the modern scientist, rural traditionalism and urban technology, the Puritan ethic colliding with the power ethic of a mass society.[3]

The culture of Appalachia is Southern. A folk culture, it is found in the rural areas of eastern Carolina, southern Georgia, southern Alabama, in the Mississippi Delta, and the Louisiana bayous. It is closely related to the Ozark culture of Arkansas and

Missouri, and is found north of the Ohio River as part of the original culture of southern Illinois, Indiana, and Ohio. As a matter of fact, most of the earlier settlers in the Ozark mountains and in the hill-lands immediately north of the Ohio River migrated there from older settlements in the Appalachian highlands.

Geography of Appalachia

The southern highlands comprise a region of 112,000 square miles, one-half in the Allegheny-Cumberland belt, over one-fourth in the Blue Ridge Range, and less than one-fourth in the great Appalachian Valley.[4] From the standpoint of human geography the most important features of this whole region are its basins, gorges, and coves. "They vary in size from many small 'flats' gently rolling along small rivers, to such large basins as the site of Asheville. The distributions of these basins, valleys, and gorges have determined the location of population."[5]

The Appalachians are old mountains worn by the passage of time. The region referred to as Appalachia is bisected by the steep slopes, the plateaus, foothills, and valleys of the Cumberlands, the Great Smokies, the Black Mountains, and the Blue Ridge Mountains, which separate the broad Piedmont of the Atlantic coast from the basin of the Mississippi River Valley. It is a beautiful country of high, rocky crags, laurel thickets, and deep, narrow valleys with such steep walls that the valley floors seldom see direct sunlight.

The mountains are ever changing. In early spring, pale green ferns unfurl in deep rocky crevices, and the woods awake with the soft shades of rhododendron, dogwood, and redbud. In summer the hills are forest green. As summer moves toward autumn, the bittersweet berries turn orange and crimson, the poplar to pale yellow, the sassafras to shades of tangerine, and oaks to dull garnet. The snows of winter deepen the purple outlines of naked hickory, oak, ash, persimmon, and maple intermixed with pine, hemlock, and cedar.

Appalachia is a country of natural stone bridges, cold clear springs, heavy torrential rains, and thick impenetrable autumn fog. It is a rough terrain which for generations resisted the thrust of the farmer's plow and made difficult the cultivation of even small fields of corn, tobacco, buckwheat, or sorghum. Because of this, the Appalachian mountaineers depended mainly upon nonagricultural employment, such as the mining of coal or limestone or lumbering.

Effect of Geography

The walls of majestic mountains, the rocky soil, the inaccessibility of isolated valleys—all have influenced the personality development of the people who live in Appalachia. It affected the original settlement of this region and provided the reason why some of the early settlers came. It affected how they lived and how they viewed themselves in relationship to the world outside the southern Appalachian region.

It was a decade after the Revolutionary War before families moved in large numbers into the mountains, which up to that time had been a little-explored wilderness[6] (see Figure 18). For several decades following the initial settlement there were no social or cultural differences between the whites of Appalachia and whites in other areas of the then young United States. The mountains were not considered a disadvantaged area in which to live. All communities were frontier towns.

Early Settlement of Appalachia

The original immigrants to the mountains were the descendants of Anglo-Saxons who left England and Scotland because of religious persecution. A few of the early settlers in Appalachia were from landed English families, a handful of whom had been granted special charters by the king, in some cases giving them free title to thousands of acres of land westward from the coast into the foothills of the mountains. Still others among the early settlers wanted no part of slavery, which was becoming common along the gulf and seacoast. They showed their contempt and disagreement by making a break with family members who were slave owners. A few were small slave holders themselves who started westward to the bluegrass region of Kentucky but came to love the misty blue of mountains and decided to remain in the highlands and either keep their slaves as servants or grant them their earned freedom.

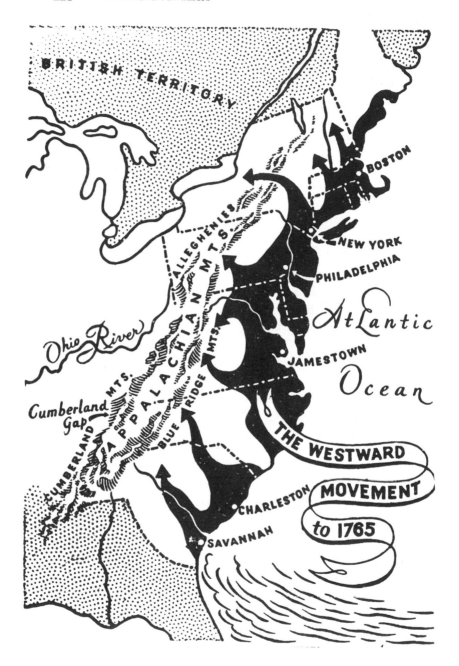

Fig. 18. Early movement westward into Appalachia. (Courtesy of Allyn and Bacon, Inc. Publishers.)

Years later the results of these early feelings toward slavery were reflected when Appalachia became the cleavage point between North and South, when families were pitted against families and brothers against brothers in the struggle of the Civil War. The effect of these relationships is still seen today in the strongly expressed anti-North and pro-South or anti-South and pro-North feelings.

The reason that the early settlers came to the New World and the social classes that they represented later affected their outlook on life. Writing on races and immigrants in America, J. R. Commons points out that the British immigrants "represented at least two grades of society that differed widely from each other." One was the yeoman, the merchants and the manufacturers skilled in industry. Beneath these individuals in rank were the indentured servants.[7] The majority of the indentured servants were brought to this country through the advertisement of shipowners and landowners, were forcibly captured and transported here for their crimes or pauperism, or were innocent citizens kidnapped off the streets of London or other towns.[8]

Francis J. Brown explains that this period "was a cruel, undemocratic, and intolerant one in England, and it was hardly better in the colonies. . . . There were differences in religion, language, and cultural traits, intensified by objections to the pauper and the criminal elements being introduced from England. The colonial assemblies were almost entirely in the hands of the English, and they were inclined to look down upon other ethnic and cultural groups as inferior."[9]

Brown, writing on the history, also has this to say: "There were two streams of Scottish immigrants. One came directly from the motherland, the other came through the province of Ulster in north Ireland and were referred to as 'Scotch-Irish.' . . . The war between Scotland and England resulted in large numbers of Scottish prisoners taken at Dunbar (1650) and at Worcester (1651) being sold into service in the colonies. . . . Two shiploads of Jacobites were sent over in 1717 and sold as servants."[10] They were bound out to work as unpaid laborers in the fields, the homes, and the craft shops to pay any debts they owed in Europe and their passage to the New World. When they had served their period of bondage, they were freed. Many moved into the wilds of the mountains where they carried with them a hatred for their former masters who represented wealth. They also carried with them a rebellious feeling toward all authority and a strong desire to be "beholden" to no man.[11]

In the cotton-producing states of the deep South impoverished and illiterate whites, often the descendants of those who were sent from prisons to the Georgia colony, "were driven" into the mountains in the years before the Revolutionary war by the "richer and stronger" slave-owning proprietors on the cotton plantations,[12] who, wanting to expand their acreage, found it easier to drive out the former owners or squatters than to buy their land.

Social Classes

There were social divisions even in the earliest Anglo-Saxon settlements of Appalachia. The "aristocrats," the slave holders, and the descendants of the more prominent Eastern families cleared the rich river bottoms in the wider valleys. 'They usually bought or claimed the right to use the summit of the surrounding mountains as grazing grounds for their sheep and cattle. At the mouth of small valleys, where a creek emptied into the river, lived farmers whose ancestors had fought with Washington's army. Further up the creek beds along the crest of the mountains and in back hollows and coves lived the "poor white trash."

These whites could trace their ancestry back to the slums of London and the prisons of Europe. For their livelihood they usually depended upon hunting, fishing, and doing odd jobs for farmers farther down the mountain. Their own farm land was poor—the so-called ridge farms that were scarred and cobblestoned with rocks around which a farmer "scratched in" a few rows of corn or pole beans and called it a crop. Seldom was this done according to any organized plan, and so these families were looked upon by the wealthy farmers and aristocrats as hand-to-mouth tenants and were called lazy and shiftless.

Many of these poor white families on the ridges of the mountains later learned to market their corn in the form of liquor. They became the first moonshine-still operators of the hills and developed a business whch, after 1920, gained national scope and which still, in the 1970s, is very active.[13]

The degree of social prestige in the early days of Appalachia was in direct proportion to the position of the ancestral family and the location of the family homeplace in relationship to the terrain. The farther up the hollow a family lived, the lower its social position.

Self-Imposed Alienation

The geographical isolation of Appalachia has solidified the tendency toward localization in government and suspicion of centralized authority. Although many of the early settlers were thrifty and perserverant and often built up a considerable fortune, they tended to be suspicious of those in positions of authority or wealth. They were passionately eager for freedom and were willing to work long and hard in order to achieve that freedom. They asked only to be left alone, especially by those outside of the mountains.

This attitude resulted in the fact that for more than a hundred years, until early in this century, the people of Appalachia existed apart from the main source of vitality and commitment to the wider society of our country. Even with the building of railroads and roads into the mountains, the people of Appalachia had limited contact with the rest of the nation, except as producers of coal, until the televised 1960 presidential campaign brought the people of Appalachia into the homes of viewers from coast to coast, and the rest of America began to consider the relationship of Appalachia to the economy of the nation as a whole. America had finally discovered its rural poor and found that in numbers they were mainly white.

Emile Durkheim, the nineteenth-century French sociologist, described a condition he called anomie—a state of individual rootlessness and detachment from society. This detachment, he pointed out, is not self-chosen but rather imposed. In that the majority of people in the mountains of Appalachia were detached for years from the society outside of the mountains, as well as detached from each other as an effect of their own social groupings, a form of anomie does exist in Appalachia.

Anomie is generally preceded by a structure of tightly organized groups that act in opposition to the dominant concerns. There are two constellations of ideas and beliefs that dominate the formation of these group structures. One exists around the fear of authority, a product of personal history that establishes bonds of relationship among individuals. The second is the fear of uncertainty growing out of a sense of helplessness in controlling the environment. How these two sets of fears came to dominate and color the culture of the Appalachian highlander is seen in an examination of the history of coal mining in the area.

Coal Mining

Coal mining became an important industry in the mountains following the Civil War. Although mining at first was not welcomed by the farmers, the coal mines prospered; and the sons, brothers, nephews, and cousins of many of the farmers went to work in the mines. Among the original settlers, coal mining was looked upon as honest work. It was an honorable occupation. It was no discredit for even an old aristocratic family, whose roots were deep in American history, to have among its kinfolk coal miners along with lawyers, doctors, and statesmen. Many of the lawyers, doctors, and statesmen worked in the mines to pay for their educations. Often coal mining was a part-time occupation for those who would someday represent their state in the federal government.

With the opening of more coal mines workmen were brought from Scotland, Wales, Italy, Poland, Rumania, Albania, Hungary, and Greece in large numbers by mine companies who found local men too independent to be good miners. The foreign miners, many of whom could not speak English, were often treated like slaves. They were recruited by those who promised them a life of wealth and freedom in America. The recruiting philosophy used with them became famous throughout the South, especially with tenant farmers: "promise them anything but give them nothing." The people came expecting high wages and a freedom they had never known in their native countries. They were taken off the ships in New York City and were loaded onto trains for the mountains of Appalachia. They were not allowed out of sight of the mine officials until they were in some tiny mining community in the mountains. There they found they were wanted by mine companies only for what they could produce. They were not wanted at all by those native to Appalachia. They were looked upon as outsiders and foreigners, and socially their families were never accepted by the families of the original settlers.[14]

They came from mining communities in Europe and were accustomed to the clouds of dust that rose from the loading docks as tons of coal poured into railroad cars. They were accustomed to refuse heaps of smoking slate dumps. Their wives were accustomed to seeing freshly laundered baby clothing streaked with flecks of coal dust or soot from coal-belching stoves. These foreign-born miners were excited by the production of coal. Their nostrils were not assaulted by sulphurous odors, their eyes by the bleakness and monotony of mining camps, their ears by the scream of machinery loading coal. They, like the Yankee officials of the coal camps, found little value in Appalachia except the coal inside the mountains and the mining timbers growing on the earth above.

These newcomers were skilled miners who knew how to mine coal, but they did not have the original highlander's philosophy of life or love of the mountains. They could despoil the highlander's beloved hills, seeing them not in their majestic beauty but as obstacles hindering the release of the coal. They could rejoice in the tearing open of another mountain and the building of another mining town.

From the establishment of the first mine the highlander viewed the coal officials as a threat to his self-identity. These officials exploited the land with which the highlander felt a oneness; they "stole" the coal and the lumber at a fraction of its real value from his ancestors, who had discovered the coal and once owned the timber; and now they brought foreigners from countries across the sea to take jobs in the mines that rightfully should have belonged to him and others who were descendants of those who discovered the coal. While the highlander had little contact with the mining officials, he came in daily contact with those who worked in the pits, and it was there he could make his real contempt and rejection felt. Therefore, he projected onto the foreign workers much of the anger he felt toward those who owned the mines and controlled the mining towns, exploiting the highlander and foreign miner alike. But those in control could not be touched, so the highlander vented his emotions on the newcomers who knew little of the English language and practically nothing of American customs and ideas.

The highlander rejected the foreigners not only because they were foreigners but because they came from the European working class, whom the descendents of the original settlers considered "uncouth peasants." Their early ancestors never received a citation from General George Washington, or received a land charter from the King of England, or brought the first wagon across the mountains, or had done anything to build the country which now provided them with work and a livelihood. These new workers were only tolerated. They were neither trusted nor liked, and in many cases they were ridiculed because their culture was different. They were ignored socially, and as a result they lived in isolation apart from their neighbors. Because of their loneliness and alienation they clung desperately to their languages and customs, a phenomenon which always occurs when migrants are forced to live as outsiders. Years later the same sort of a situation would be repeated, only this time it would be the highlander who was ridiculed for his differences when he left the mountains. He would live in isolation, neither part of the new community nor part of Appalachia, but holding to his mountain dialect and his Southern customs.

The newcomers to the coal fields of Appalachia were rejected not only because of their foreign status but also because of their religions. Most of them were Catholics who came to live among a strongly religious people whose Protestant ancestors suffered religious persecution at the hands of Catholics. Others were Jews— "crucifiers of Christ," "money changers," "extractors of the pound of flesh"—a religion even more hated and misunderstood by the followers of Calvinism than was Catholicism. So the newcomers were ignored and forced to have social contact only with others like themselves who were immigrants. Most of these families whose fathers, grandfathers, or great-grandfathers came as European miners have not really been accepted to this day, although they have lived in Appalachia for fifty years or more.

These early social divisions account for why two neighbor families, both currently on welfare, are viewed as representing different social classes depending upon the position of their "grandaddies." But should both families move to Akron and the two family heads be employed on the same assembly line, they would both be called "hillbillies" or "Southern white trash." If their families historically represented great social differences, either one might quit as soon as he learned with whom he would be expected to work, the one feeling or even saying he could not, even in the 1970s, have close association with such "riffraff and scum." On the other hand, the other worker would feel just as strongly that he could not bring himself to have a close association with the descendant of those who had treated his family so "poorly." Each would, in his own judgment, owe this to the memory of his grandfather, the one to a grandfather who "held himself to be superior to the likes of these people," the other to a grandfather who "held himself to be as good as those who seemed to think something of theirs did not stink."

Early Work History
and its Effect on Today's Workers

Even farming and hunting, in the days when they were the major occupations, were seasonal work with long periods of leisure after the crops were harvested. Between chores the individual, whether adult or child, could sit for hours on the front porch without feeling guilty or having an inner compulsiveness to be busy. He worked when he felt like it, completed a task, or left it uncompleted. Life was never so involved that it prohibited visiting friends, talking with kinfolk, or fishing, if that was what the individual wanted to do. Not to "sit for a spell" was a sign of "ill breeding" and a reason to be ostracized by the group. Nothing was so important that it could not be delayed in favor of personal interaction, especially with family members.

Sawmills and lumbering operations suited the mountaineer's work patterns. There was no issue about absenteeism in this type of work. If a man showed up, fine; if not, his work could be done later. If he were absent it was assumed that he had a good reason. It was his business, and no one asked him why. Under these circumstances there was no need for an employee to justify absenteeism.

Life in the coal mines helped foster this irregular work pattern. Most mines closed in May and did not reopen until late August or September. During the long days of summer the idle miner played cards or joined other miners to talk about politics, religion, or the weather. Besides these weeks of summer shut-down there were other layoffs resulting from strikes, broken machinery, or cave-ins.

In 1932 the bituminous mines in West Virginia and Virginia averaged 145 days of operation and 165 days of idleness.[15]

An article in the *West Virginia Review* describes the working philosophy of the coal miner:

> He works when he wishes and stops when he wishes. He toils as strenuously, or as lightly as he wishes. He leaves the working place when he chooses. In a mining community the mine whistle is only an alarm for the town. It is never a signal for the men to cease work.[16]

Generations of seasonal work or steady employment with long layoff periods conditioned workers to accept and even to expect times of unemployment. The fact that the company store or the employer extended credit during these times prevented the highlander from learning to plan for himself. It prevented his learning to control his impulses to buy or even to live within his income.[17]

The dependency fostered by being cared for with credit plans or welfare encourages an apathy about the future and a hopelessness that borders on lethargy. These attitudes are currently found in Appalachia. It is, in fact, a cycle: paternalism fosters dependency; dependence carries with it an expectation of being cared for.

Firsthand Knowledge of Appalachia

My first knowledge of Appalachia came vicariously through my parents as they related tales of their own early childhood and young adult years spent in the foothills and the mountains of the Appalachian range. Perhaps the scarcity of detail in the open sweep of Montana prairie land, my native state, made the hills, mountains, and valleys of their native state so precious that they spoke of them often. When summer winds made rippling lakes of the long western slough grasses or when the winter sky was a sheet of dull pewter and the prairie faded into snowy ghostlines, my parents told me stories of dew-drenched valleys in the Appalachian Mountains. They described rocks gray with lichen, giant trees, waterfalls, and cool, green banks of moss and fern. They told of their ancestors, the true highlanders of the south Appalachian region, a people whose heritage was richly entwined with the early development of our nation.

My actual experience in Appalachia came later, and it has continued more than thirty years as I have made numerous and lengthy visits to mountain homes, mining towns, and isolated farms, traveling into tiny coves and hidden valleys to attend church revivals, community sings, box socials, candy pulls, weddings, funerals, family reunions, and political rallies. It has spanned more than a generation. I have seen children grow to adulthood and establish homes of their own, fewer and fewer of these homes being in the area that was the domain of their family.

Psychological Tie to the Mountains

I found in many years of direct contact with Appalachia that the people of the highlands are proud of their Southern heritage and that they have deep psychological ties to the "home place" which defy distance, or time. Regardless of where they live outside the rim of their mountains, they feel like strangers in a temporary abode.

This love of mountains was described in an old ballad entitled "The West Virginia Hills":

> O, those hills, beautiful hills,
> How I love those West Virginia Hills.
> If o're sea, or land I roam,
> I will think of happy home and
> My friends among those West Virginia Hills.

This feeling of being an outsider often makes it difficult for the Appalachian highlander to put down permanent roots in communities like Cincinnati, Columbus, or Cleveland. Accustomed to a person-to-person culture in which a stranger is invited to "sit a spell" and to relate family history, the new community in the North with its rush of urban living seems cold and indifferent to the migrant highlander.

The psychological tie to the mountains is further enhanced by the "homeplace," the ancestral home or place where the grandparents lived and which is still owned by the family. It actually may never have been owned by the grandparents but merely viewed as their home.

The widowed mother of one Appalachian family lived for

thirty-nine years with a son and daughter-in-law who owned the house. She was the dominant person in the family. She managed their household, disciplined their children, and worked the garden. She was hailed as the family head by neighbors and kin alike. The son's property was referred to as her house. Now the house is owned by a granddaughter of the son who built it; it is often visited by other descendants of the grandmother, who thirty-five years after her death still refer to the house as "grandmother's homeplace."

Housing

The original homes of Appalachia were small log cabins; later slightly larger "Yankee frame" or clapboard houses were built. As in all parts of early America, houses were crowded. Rooms were few, small in size, and families were large. The same situation exists in Appalachia today. A house is still largely viewed as a shelter from the elements. Visitors to the mountains notice the unpainted, drab houses that do not reflect personal pride. Outside paint has never been important compared to inside paint and wall paper. The mountaineer looks from the inside out; when outside he lifts his eyes to his beloved mountains. For this he gives the Bible as his guide and quotes from the Psalms, "I will lift up mine eyes unto the hills, from whence cometh my help."[18]

In 1963-64 my husband and I stayed in eastern Kentucky with a family on the crest of a mountain. It was the spot that the man's grandfather had selected when he "came across" from South Carolina, "laid claim" to the level "pocket" of the mountain top, and built a log cabin against the lea of the rocks on the side where the mountain fell away in a sheer wall of lichen-covered rocks toward the valley far below.

When we left the settlement four miles from the cabin, the road toward the mountain crest was deceptive. At that point it led gradually upward past discarded coal tipples where former miners came to pick up their winter supply of coal from the old slag dumps. Suddenly the road became a track cut into the mountainside. It hung precariously above the treetops. It wound upward with numerous washouts and rock slides in places barely as wide as our car; another rock slide, a few more heavy rains, and the road would be a footpath. Two miles from the cabin the road ended in a neighbor's yard. It was there we would leave our car and proceed on foot.

To reach the four-room log cabin, we climbed a path so steep in places that we held onto bushes and were grateful for the walking sticks our host provided and which he said were sturdy enough to mash the head of even the biggest rattlesnake we might run across. He had killed three big ones coming down to meet us. He carried their rattles for luck. The wall of the mountain rose before us, and toward its summit wound the path. Part of the way the path followed a clearing cut by the Tennessee Valley Authority as a power line route. Prior to the power line construction this footpath had been less accessible. Supplies were brought in with a mule and a stoneboat. The family members rode the mule to the store four miles away, or they walked and toted things in a sack on their backs. In winter they seldom left the mountain, and in the spring they had to clear slides of rocks and dirt away before they could get down to see their neighbors.

Electricity had brought to this family many comforts they had never known previously. One item they referred to as a "comfort" was a small television set. As we watched programs that evening we were aware of the contrast between a telephone commercial showing a housewife in a chrome and copper kitchen and the surroundings of our hostess.

This mountain woman used a wood cookstove. She boiled grits in an iron pot once owned by her grandmother. She made her own laundry soap with lye from wood ashes. She had never lived in a house with a telephone. Yet from the front door of her cabin there was a twenty-mile view across the Cumberland Mountains, and as the sun faded into the purple mist of distant peaks, our host said, "Seems like the world's down there at our feet!" And indeed it was.

There is another cultural factor that affects attitudes toward housing in Appalachia: the fierce desire for personal independence. A man's home has always been his castle. It is his to build as he wants and to defend as he sees fit. If a man wishes to build a house, he can build it any size or shape, out of any material he chooses.

For generations houses of all types have been built in Appalachia next to each other, on the ridge a few feet above each other, or on the ledge a few feet below each other without any thought about effects on property valuation or zoning or building codes or whether or not the location of the house had anything to do with pollution of the water supply. There has always been one code in the mountain: not to block the view of a neighbor. And that code has been adhered to faithfully.

Throughout the Appalachian region almost every community is a contrast of houses. There are large and small houses, a shanty on stilts next to a brick ranch with a full basement, a mixture of inside plumbing and outside facilities, of hardwood floors and rough hewn pine boards. There are artistically furnished rooms and those crowded with unmatched odds and ends bought without thought as to existing furniture or colors.

Another cultural factor that affects the care of the home is the impulse to quit a task before it is completed. Home repairs are often postponed until major repairs are necessary. In a trip through Appalachia it is not unusual to see one side of a barn painted, a roof half shingled, or a partially finished room that was started years ago and left uncompleted even though the need for additional space grew more critical.

One family I have known since my first visit to the mountains has lived in the same four-room house for thirty-six years. They raised seven children there. Originally they rented the house from the coal company for whom the man worked. It was the coal company that built the house and later wired it for electricity. When the mine closed in 1950, the family bought the house for $200. It had no bath or inside water then; it has none now. Family members, usually the women, carry water three-hundred feet along the mountain ridge from a spring above the house. This spring is cleaned out and maintained by a neighbor. Twenty feet down a steep rock below their house is another spring from which water could be piped. Seventeen years ago the man measured the distance, bought the pipe, connections, and an electric pump—all that was needed to bring water into the house. Today, the pipe and connections are stored in the top of a shed, and the pump is still packed in its original shipping crate. The family still carries drinking water from the spring and keeps rain barrels under the eaves to collect rain water for laundry and baths. Each summer the man vows to "git the water in the house." The woman tells him, "it would be nice to have water in a sink," but she accepts carrying water as part of her household duties and does not really expect to have running water and therefore is not disappointed when nothing happens.

Family Roles

The concept of the family is one of extended relationships in which three or more generations often live together. There is little of the philosophy of the companionship marriage. The man is the head of the household. He is often overshadowed, however, by the woman, who actually makes many of the decisions he claims to make. According to one mountaineer, "The husband is the head, but the wife is the neck, and she turns the head in whatever direction she wants him to go."[19]

The culture of the region dictates that following the honeymoon a young couple will settle down in the same valley where their parents or siblings live and that they will enter a life of farm work, employment in the mines, or work in one of the glass or chemical factories where relatives have worked. It was not unusual for a young couple to live in the home of their parents or other relatives. After marriage a man continues to spend a good deal of time playing cards, drinking, fishing, or just talking with male friends. The woman has female friends with whom she talks, sews, or gardens. Outside of church and family reunions most parents and their children do very few things together as a family. The culture is segregated as to the sexes—men with men, women with women—and as to age—adults versus children.

Traditionally emancipation of adult children has been difficult. There was once a mountain saying that a child should never move further away "than you could see the smoke from his chimney."[20] Adult children refer to their fathers as daddy, and how daddy feels about something determines how the adult child behaves. It is not unusual for adult children, themselves parents or grandparents, to turn to their parents for continued advice and direction.

Role of Women

Family life in the early settlement of Appalachia was shaped in part by the older European tradition and in part by the challenge of the unexplored region. On the one hand, those who came from the early colonies along the coast were steeped in patriarchal tradition. It was only natural for them to look upon the husband as head of the household and to consider the wife and children as subordinates. Justification for the inferior status accorded women in the church as well as in the home stemmed from Biblical sources which the mountaineer still enjoys quoting. The first pertains to the woman's position in the church and is from I Corinthians:

> Let your women keep silence in the churches: for it is not permitted unto them to speak; but they are commanded to be under obedience, as also saith the law.

The other verses relate to the woman within the home, the first also being from I Corinthians, the other three from Ephesians:

> And if they will learn anything let them ask their husbands at home: for it is a shame for women to speak in the church.
>
> _____
>
> Wives submit yourselves unto your own husbands, as unto the Lord.
>
> For the husband is the head of the wife, even as Christ is head of the church: and he is the savior of the body.
>
> Therefore as the church is subject unto Christ, so let the wives be to their own husbands in everything.[21]

Writing on the position of the Puritan woman in early New England, Edmund S. Morgan describes the traditional position of the woman of Appalachia whose ancestors brought to the mountains the same Protestant ethic that their ancestors brought from England to New England and to the Virginia coast. "In seventeenth century New England, no respectable person questioned that woman's place was in the home. . . . The proper conduct of a wife was submission to her husband's instructions and commands."[22]

From the earliest period in Appalachia there has always been a clear division of labor in the highlander's home. An older brother or cousin, charged with seeing that a little girl got safely to a spring, would walk ahead of her and would let her carry the pail of water without assistance because to do anything else would not be proper behavior for a boy. Although he had a deep affection for his sister or cousin, he would not see any need to take over her work. Likewise, today an adult son can comfortably rock on the front porch and watch his aging mother hoe the garden and feel no compulsion to help her and no guilt about her obvious fatigue, because gardening has always been considered part of a woman's responsibility.

Although the general attitude on the part of mountain men, even now, is to permit women to do this sort of work, their attitude is largely offset by a very real and fundamental respect for womanhood. In general, it may be said that the average woman submits unquestionably to her lot of hard work, excessive child bearing, and the role of her husband. It is something of a paradox, however, that when she becomes an old woman with a large family of grownup children she comes into her own and assumes somewhat the role of a matriarch. She is often consulted, looked up to, loved, and respected. Usually she is the real head of the home and may dictate to her adult sons and overrule her daughters-in-law in making family decisions such as whether to move, to visit the homeplace, or to move to Detroit where the son has been offered a job. The source of this paradox may also be found in a Biblical quotation:

The aged women . . . be . . . teachers of good things:

That they may teach the young women to be sober, to love their husbands, to love their children.

To be discreet, chaste, keepers at home, good obedient to their own husbands. . . .[23]

Child-Rearing Practices

Other Puritan assumptions were also brought to the Appalachian areas by the early settlers. "Children were ignorant and children were evil. . . . The pious parent, therefore, was faced with two tasks, instruction and discipline."[24]

The harsh life of the frontier demanded an adult-centered culture.[25] The needs of parents came first, the wishes of children second. Even today, discipline usually is not handled as part of a long-range plan for the children, but rather children are told to stop something because father is watching television or mother does not like the noise.

Large families of eight or more are common. New babies are welcomed regardless of numbers by all family members. There is a good deal of dialogue between parents and the young infant who is encouraged in his beginning efforts to form sounds and words. This is not so much to meet the needs of the baby as it is to meet the needs of the adult. The baby or young child is often the chief means of entertainment for parents and older siblings who may spend long hours playing with the infant. This adoration may end abruptly with the advent of the next child who then becomes the center of attention. Jack E. Weller explains family relationships: "The mountain family is a closely knit one not because of shared activities but because of emotional dependence."[26]

Early childhood training and experience not only foster loyalty to the family but encourage emotional dependence upon the parents. Because most contacts are with relatives, many children have little or no opportunity to relate to nonrelatives before their school experience. They see themselves in relationship to grandparents, aunts, uncles, and cousins. Although they are expected to conform to the wishes of the parents, most children are overindulged. In the hills they are free to roam, to hunt for blackberries high on the mountain top, to explore a cave. Parents, aware of the "hard life" of adults, allow their children the happy, carefree days of summer with few, if any, restrictions.

There is very little vandalism or delinquency in the mountains, but many of these children and young people have difficulty when they move to metropolitan areas. In the city their roaming curiosity is viewed as "running away," and the parental permissiveness that allows this behavior is labeled "parental neglect." There is little in their early training that teaches the children self-discipline and self-control. The few rules and regulations that they may encounter in their homes are based more on family values than on whether or not the behavior would be antisocial, contrary to community values, or delinquent.

Children may be kept out of school to do things with the family or because the school program does not fit the pattern of family living. This attitude toward school attendance goes back to a time when children in farm areas were kept home to help plant, harvest crops, or to hunt and when little value was placed on education. Today, the "desirability of knowledge is generally conceded, but only so long as it does not interfere with the basic social and economic life of the family."[27]

A Culture Oriented to Self and Extensions of Self

The highlander's culture is centered around an extension of self. Each situation applies to an individual in a very personal sense. The individual views his community in relationship to himself, not himself in relationship to the community. Such an individual has difficulty accepting criticism. The northern employer who finds fault with a worker from this culture, in the thinking of that worker, is not criticizing the individual's work, but rather his worth. Not only is the worker in this situation insulted by what the employer has said, but all that he stands for is insulted.

A college graduate we met in Birmingham, Alabama is a good example. She had moved recently from the mountains of Tennessee where her family had lived for five generations. They were a well-known and highly respected family. No one in that section of Tennessee doubted their word on anything. Her grandfather and her father had often borrowed money from the local bank without signing a note because their word was enough.

While driving in Birmingham she was stopped a few doors from where she lived by a policeman who asked to see her driver's license. She explained that it was at home. The policeman insisted that he could not take her word that she was a licensed driver; he needed proof. He said he would be willing to cooperate because she "appeared honest." He drove behind her to her house where she produced the license.

Two and one-half days later this college-educated woman was still seething with anger. "She had never been so insulted in all her life," she said. Her family in Tennessee had been insulted. Someone had doubted the word of her family; someone had implied that she, a Pritchett,[28] could not be trusted to tell the truth and therefore had to prove her honesty.

Agencies, such as welfare agencies, that must seek proof of marriage or other facts of eligibility, should be aware that many mountain people view such questions as an insult. If a caseworker does not accept a couple's word that they were married, the couple assumes she must suspect that they are "living in sin" or that she is calling their children illegitimate. If she believed they were married she would not ask to see their certificate. Anyone asking for such proof needs to explain to the Appalachian highlander why such information is needed, being careful to point out that the client's statement of the marriage or birth date is not being questioned.

The alienation that the highlander feels outside of his mountains, the ridicule he fears and senses, may cause a self-imposed isolation. He may never really think of another community as home, although he may live and work there for years. It is very difficult for a person from this background to view one experience in the framework of another. He sees things only in relationship to self. He is opinionated and bases his concept of what is right or wrong on his own experiences. His total concept of the world is in relationship to self. As he depends upon his five senses for much of his perception, it is difficult for him to understand something he has not seen. He views life in concrete terms and has difficulty with abstractions.

On the job such a worker often misleads others by his silence or virtual silence or by withdrawing from the discussion. The supervisor asks, "Do you understand?" The mountaineer may nod or say "yeah" and then fall silent. What does the nod, the "yeah," or the silence mean? They could mean that he does not want to understand, that he does not understand and does not want to show his ignorance, that he was not listening and does not want to admit it, or that he understands but does not agree. There is no way of telling from his "yeah" or shoulder shrug what he understands, and he is not going to volunteer this information.

There is a tendency for these adults to think of themselves as surrounded by situations that are detrimental to their personal progress. They feel surrounded by others who are envious, jealous, or hostile. It is very difficult for such individuals to take responsibility for their own position in life. Their culture has provided few opportunities for their self-choice. They have been forced into situations because of others. It is the hand of fate. It is easy, under these circumstances, for them to think of themselves without fault, surrounded by those who continuously place obstacles in their way. Those who put "blocks in their pathway" are simply referred to as *they*. When defined, *they* become neighbors, employers, anyone in a position of authority, or the government. Many living in Appalachia blame their present financial situation on the farming methods of their neighbors, the Tennessee Valley Authority, or the federal government for taking the best land for parks and projects. If they do not blame the federal government, big business, the North, or their neighbors, they blame the supernatural; God is punishing the world for being wicked, and they as well as sinners must suffer. The highlander may use a Biblical basis for his conviction, such as this quotation from the Sermon on the Mount:

> But I say unto you, "Love your enemies, bless them that curse you, do good to them that hate you, and pray for them which despitefully use you, and persecute you:
>
> That ye may be the children of your Father which is in heaven: for he maketh his sun to rise on the evil and on the good, and sendeth rain on the just and on the unjust.[29]

They may also be members of another religion (Jews, Catholics), of a different political party, foreigners ("Wops," "Hunkies," "Poles"), a family of "inferior" or "superior" ancestral blood lines, or newcomers—those who have come to the mountains from outside, especially Yankees who have no ancestral ties to the region and must therefore always remain newcomers.

It may be very difficult to help many Appalachian highlanders take some responsibility for their own action. Usually they will hint that they have played a role in creating their own situation. It is, however, little more than a hint of insight and usually is immediately contradicted by a lengthy explanation or a description of themselves as victims who have been manipulated by others. There is reality in what they say. People in Appalachia have been exploited and manipulated by those from outside the mountains.

There is a good deal of jealousy and rivalry between neighbors or even relatives, and much envy is expressed in acts or spite or through gossip. Lawsuits are common and often are over disputed property lines, dissatisfaction with a will, or damage reportedly done by a dog, cow, or hog. In these cases the person being sued, informed on, or gossiped about is usually thought to be better off in some way, and the lawsuit is an attempt to even the score and remove the threat.

Gossip has always been a strong factor in this culture. It has been a method of both punishment and control. Among those on welfare there is considerable discussion about the various agencies and their workers, and jealousy is expressed if one family gets a larger AFDC or Old Age Assistance check than another. If a person's allotment check is cut, he usually feels that the cut was influenced by an informer.

Although there is no common culture in Appalachia, there is much in common among all mountain people that needs to be understood. Loyalty to the family is one of the major concepts. As the early pioneers moved into the deep forest they carried with them their Scottish and English ballads, their drive for independence and individuality, their sense of humor, and their clan loyalty which was transformed into loyalty for family. The code of the mountains was, and to some degree still is, never to desert a kinsman, right or wrong. Feuds, such as those between the Hatfields and McCoys in the late nineteenth century, grew out of family loyalty. "A man has a right to defend his family."[30]

Although loyalty to the family has been growing weaker in recent years because of out-migration, nevertheless, many of those who geographically leave Appalachia never psychologically separate from their kin. "Moving means establishing a home like the original one and carrying on the activities that preserve a sense of family and cultural continuity."[31]

Loyalty to family is more than affection for family members. It is a deep obligation to help each other and to share together, to provide care for the sick and a home for the aging. If kin are in need, there is an automatic impulse to help even if one is in debt, has no job, or is living on welfare. This is frequently seen in industrial centers of the North where various members of a family may move in with each other. When Jim's brother-in-law was out of work in Canton last winter, he and his family moved in with Jim. There were four adults and seven children living in a three-room apartment. Later a cousin arrived from Tennessee with her new-born, illegitimate child. She and the baby slept on a cot in the kitchen. As Jim explained to me, each of them would do as much for him; therefore, they were welcome to stay as long as he had anything to eat and a roof over his head, regardless of what the landlord said.

The extended family provides a cloak of protection. Members of the extended family help each other become established in the new community by sharing housing, providing food, or finding work. Likewise, those who remain in the mountains provide a haven of security for those who leave. It is not unusual for the Appalachian highlander to take his children out of school and travel half way across the country because a fourth cousin is being married. He may have learned not to tell his employer that he simply feels like going home. Instead he claims he is leaving because there is no work, because he can't make enough money, because he has back trouble, because he is sick or has had a death in the family. He is really saying that he is homesick for the mountains and for those who understand him—his kinfolk. Frequently a migrant's visits to Appalachia are due to his feeling that there is a lack of recognition for him in the new community, to problems he must face, or to a need to be surrounded by family and friends who are part of his value system. When he returns to the mountains he may not talk about his problems, but his deep needs for closeness with his kin have been satisfied in the coming, and the trip provides him with an opportunity to brag about his successes in Dayton, Detroit, or Chicago.

Unfortunately these frequent returns to the mountains do not fit the pattern of the life-styles in the new community. Schools object to absences of students while they visit a grandparent, uncle, or cousin in Tennessee, West Virginia, or North Carolina. Employers are alarmed by the high rate of absenteeism or the impulsive quitting of an assignment or even a job to go back to Kentucky or northern Georgia for a few weeks.

Migrants from the southern Appalachia region who have made an adequate adjustment to other communities are those who think of themselves as residents in the new community, rather than visitors or employees away from home.

Out-Migration

There has always been considerable out-migration from those areas of underemployment or places where the family farm has been so divided among descendants that there is no longer enough acreage to provide a livelihood. The out-migration pattern has been consistent over the years. Large numbers of people have gone to the industrial cities of north and central Ohio, to western Pennsylvania, and to Detroit and Chicago. The most important factor affecting the selection of a place to look for work is kinship ties. Migrants tend to go to those areas where family members are already established.[32]

Appalachia faces a combination of economic, social, and environmental problems rooted in the past and related to how the mountain people view themselves and how they are understood and accepted by other areas of the country. No one discipline has the answers to the many problems that are found in the region—not education, public health, medicine, religion, business, industry, or social work. What is needed is combined effort and a pooling of information and knowledge from all disciplines. But what is needed most is acceptance. Given a chance, the people of the southern Appalachian region have the potential to help themselves become more self-sufficient, productive citizens regardless of whether they elect to remain in the deep valleys of their beloved mountains, or whether they migrate to other parts of the nation.

NOTES

1. *The Southern Highlander and His Homeland* (New York: Russell Sage Foundation, 1921), p. 14.

2. (Boston, Mass.: Little, Brown and Co., 1962), pp. 3-10.

3. *Life and Religion in South Appalachia* (New York: Friendship Press, 1962), pp. 161-62.

4. Campbell, *The Southern Highlander*, pp. 10-11.

5. Rupert B. Vance, *Human Geography in the South* (Chapel Hill, N.C.: University of North Carolina Press, 1932), p. 241.

6. *West Virginia Review*, 1926, p. 355.

7. The subject of indentured servants is discussed more fully in chapter 4, "Early Immigrants and Indentured Servants."

8. J. R. Commons, *Races and Immigrants in America* (New York: Macmillan Co., 1920), pp. 26-44.

9. " 'Old' Immigration—British Americans," in *One America*, ed. by Francis J. Brown and Joseph S. Roucek (New York: Prentice-Hall, Inc., 1945), p. 34.

10. *Ibid.*, p. 30. The best summary of the Scottish influence in America is

found in D. MacDougall, ed., *Scots and Scots' Descendants in America* (New York: Caledonian Publishing Co., 1917).

11. The concept of "beholden" became part of the culture and has been identified by many writers. In several of his novels, William Faulkner has shown the extremes to which this concept may be carried; probably his best example of such an extreme is found in his novel *As I Lay Dying* (New York: Random House, Inc., 1930), pp. 109-11.

12. Charles S. Johnson, *Shadow of the Plantation* (Chicago: University of Chicago Press, 1943), p. 7.

13. For a complete description of moonshine activities in the mountains, see Caudill, *Night Comes to the Cumberlands,* pp. 151-64. For additional information on moonshining, see Loyal Durand, "Mountain Moonshining in East Tennessee," *Geographical Review,* XLVI (1956), 168-81; and Anne W. Armstrong, "The Southern Mountaineers," *Yale Review,* XXIV (1935), 539-54. This author along with others feels that prohibition with the opportunity to make money by moonshining speeded the demoralization of the mountaineers.

14. Myrtle R. Reul, *Where Hannibal Led Us* (New York: Vantage Press, 1967), pp. 30-32.

15. May Van Kleeck, *Mines and Management* (Charleston, W. Va.: West Virginia Mine Assoc., 1934), p. 185.

16. *West Virginia Review,* September 1930, p. 387.

17. An excellent detailed description of coal mine paternalism may be found in Caudill's *Night Comes to the Cumberlands,* pp. 110, 113-15, and 122.

18. Bible, King James version, Ps. 121:1.

19. From personal interviews.

20. From personal interviews.

21. Bible, King James version, I Cor. 14:34-35; Eph. 5:22-24.

22. *The Puritan Family* (New York: Harper and Row Publishers, 1944), p. 10.

23. Bible, King James version, Titus 2:3-5.

24. Morgan, *The Puritan Family,* p. 59.

25. For a more complete description of the adult-centered culture, see Jack E. Weller, *Yesterday's People* (Lexington, Ky.: University of Kentucky Press, 1966).

26. *Ibid.,* p. 59.

27. Marion Pearsall, *Little Smokey Ridge: The Natural History of a Southern Appalachian Neighborhood* (University, Ala.: University of Alabama Press, 1959), pp. 144-45.

28. Not her real name.

29. Bible, King James version, Matt. 5:44-45.

30. Jean Thomas, *The Blue Ridge Country* (New York: Duell, Sloan and Pearce, 1942), p. 49.

31. Pearsall, *Little Smokey Ridge,* pp. 169-70.

32. James H. Copp, "Family Backgrounds of Rural Youth," in *Rural Youth in Crisis: Facts, Myths, and Social Change,* ed. by Lee G. Burchinal (Washington, D.C.: U. S. Department of Health, Education and Welfare, 1964), p. 39.

So blue my hills, so misty blue,
So tender sweet the skies above,
So old my hills, so ever new,
So rich with life this land I love.

Ann Hark, 20th century American authoress
Blue Hills and Shoofly Pie

13

"I'm Glad Yo' Come"

We had decided to explore the side valley to see if I could remember the area and could find traces of the grape arbor where long ago the neighborhood children had a playhouse or the spot where we had dammed the sulfurated waters that flowed toward the creek from an abandoned mine shaft. We had tried, that summer I was eight, to make a swimming hole until our mothers dissuaded us from such adventures. But now as we drove to the end of the side valley, we were stunned by the changes around us. On a bridge built by strip miners we crossed a nearly dry creek bed where previously we had forded a stream, driving our car carefully around the huge boulders which the men of the area never removed although they expressed fear that one would someday break a car spring.

Surrounded by towering walls of green hills, these valleys had once been beautiful. They were still beautiful when I returned

This is a revised version of a chapter with the same title that first appeared in *Where Hannibal Led Us* (New York: Vantage Press, Inc., 1967). This book is now out of print.

eight years later. They now had gone suddenly ugly. On my first visit to this West Virginia community there had been three productive mines in the main valley whose coal supply was said to be inexhaustible. That was at the time when coal was king in West Virginia, and everything there was related to coal or coal mining. Work was so readily available that men came from other parts of the country to work in the mines. That was the time when a miner would shower after an eight-hour shift and dress in a white linen or seersucker suit and go up-town to the pool hall for an evening with the boys while his wife washed the dishes and put their children to bed.

Before coal was king, this had been a farming community, but with the opening of the third mine the farms had completely disappeared from the main valley. In place of farms all things were connected with coal mining. The stone and brick farm houses, the orchards, the barns were all destroyed and replaced by railroads, loading docks, ramps, tipples,[1] a recreation hall, a company store where the miners had to buy their groceries, clothing, and furniture, a medical and dental clinic, and rows and rows and tiers and tiers of identical or nearly identical company houses for the miners. Required to live there, they had their rent deducted from their wages.

Most of the houses in mining camps in West Virginia were built in the thirty years from 1895 to 1925. Built of oak, black walnut, or "yellar" poplar at a time when lumber was available, the houses of this coal camp were of two designs. They were either one-story, four-room single-family units with tiny front porches, or they were two-story duplexes with two rooms upstairs and two down for each family and a double porch on the front. The houses were painted and repaired by the mining companies who owned them. To encourage the upkeep, some coal companies held contests and awarded prizes for the best flower gardens, and a few even made monthly inspection tours to check on housekeeping techniques.

Like all mining camps, this town had a sameness created by everything being painted one color. Here the color was yellow. The store, the recreation building, the clinic, the school, the church, the houses, the tipples—all were the same shade of bright yellow which, in time, turned buff and finally peeled in ragged, ugly patches. But at the time of my first visit, everything was freshly painted a deep lemon yellow. It was still freshly painted when I came back as a teenager and only slightly dimmed when I came again as a young adult. At the time of our last visit in the early 1950s the houses were no longer bright with paint, for coal dust had spread a black scum over everything. Yet the beauty of the hills remained, and the sun rose in the morning out of a pale mist of fog that slid motionless through the high gaps of the hills, hanging for a time above a spring that fed the stream far below.

The last time we came to the valley there was talk of the three regular mines closing. They had always closed for a time every summer and opened again in the fall, and at first the men tried to believe such would always be the case. But this time it was different. The mining companies closed their offices and left the area. New mining officials came. They were strip miners. They explained the high expense of regular mining and said that strip and auger mining was the solution and that there would be a profit in it for everyone—the people who owned the land, the company, and the workmen. They said that with heavy earth-moving equipment they could tear deep into coal, with bulldozers they could push aside the trees and rocks and could lay bare the deposits. They would not have the overhead expense of a regular mine with men working underground. These new men who came talked about the money this would bring into the area and the work that would be available for the people. Some could sell coal rights that had never been developed; for others there would be work, lots of work. There were those who did not believe what they were told, who were afraid of this sort of mining and who raised questions. They wondered how many miners would be employed in a mining operation done with a bulldozer and a loading crane. They asked if the strip miners intended to move on after they had taken out the coal and left the ugly open scars. These people, few in number, pointed out that West Virginia is a country of heavy, torrential rains where decapitated hills and prolonged rain would result in great erosion. Their caution was ignored by those who felt that people who raised such questions stood in the way of progress; the community needed work and the strip mining operation would offer work.

Now, after eleven years, we had come home to find a valley and its enclosure of mountain-like hills despoiled beyond anything we could ever imagine from the annual letter John Henry sent us. Even the contour of the hilltops was changed. The hills themselves were denuded of trees, rocks, and topsoil, and what the bulldozers had not torn aside, the unusually torrential rains of that early spring (1963) had washed away.

The strip miners had come and attacked the hills; they had torn the coal from the ground and left. When a vein of coal lay near the top of the mountain, the strippers had blasted and carved at the stone and earth with bulldozers and cranes until they opened bare the vein of coal and flattened the top of the mountain. When they finished they had transformed the high, majestic sweep of hills into a table-top mesa, an open wound that when the rains came bled down into the valley, choking the springs of the hillside with slipping gobs of yellow clay, as bank after bank gave way and oozed downward, clinging for a time against the remains of a rail fence or a deserted springhouse. And when the pile of mud was deep enough, it would wipe out all traces of the fence and push the springhouse off its rock foundation, causing it to slip toward the valley.

When the strip miners came to sell the people on the idea, they promised many things, but, like most of the promises to the people of Appalachia, nothing was forthcoming. So, on a fall day in 1963, we drove in disbelief into the side valley past smoldering gob piles of coal refuse whose smoking masses ignited by spontaneous combustion added to the gloomy haze that lay in the valley and half hid the sun. The once silvery train tracks that had carried loaded coal cars were now ribbons of rust or had been removed as silent testimony that never again would this community know the active productivity of coal mining.

We came to the end of the valley to see before us the yellow, pock-marked hillside. There was no sign that there had ever been a grape arbor or a spring-fed stream in that area. We turned away; there was nothing there except savage waste. As we reached the main valley, John Henry Blake and his wife, Rebecca, came toward us riding in a pickup truck that showed need of body repairs. Having seen a strange car from the ridge road, they thought it was us and had come to meet us. We followed them up a steep, rocky roadway to the second tier of buildings past long rows of empty houses, some with boarded doors and windows, others open to the weather, all shabby and dirty and needing repairs. Like the others, their house had once been painted yellow; it too showed the need for a hammer and nails and new boards. The front porch sagged and half the steps were missing. All of these houses had been owned by the coal company and rented to the miners. When the mines closed they had been offered to their occupants. John Henry agreed to buy this four-room house, the company had kept his pay for his last two weeks of work, and the house was his "free and clear."

It was on the front porch of this same house, which John Henry and his first wife, Lucia, then rented, that I, when eight, stood enraptured as loaded cars glided from the mine across the valley, rounded the top of the tipple, and plunged to the railroad loading dock below. It was John Henry who had smuggled me through an abandoned mine shaft into one of those mines when I was sixteen. This he had done, although he, like all miners, held the superstition that a woman in the mine would cause a cave-in. John Henry had led me through the maze of black corridors through the "rooms" where the miners worked so that I could see where some thirty years before, his father had assisted my father, then a young photographer turned coalminer, to take pictures of the unsafe working conditions. The evidence of those pictures was violently denied by the coal company, but years later under union pressures the company gradually began to introduce safety measures. Thus, on my visit to the mine I saw ventilators and roof supports where in the early photographs there had been nothing but thin columns of brittle coal.[2]

I had known John Henry since my first visit to West Virginia. Even then he had worked in the mines as his father and older brother had worked in them, and as his twin sons would work in them before they closed. When the truck stopped before their door, he greeted us. His movements still showed a lithe, muscular grace which belied his more than sixty years and his serious cardiac condition. His heart was enlarged and weakened, the result of years of working in poorly ventilated mines.

We had never met his young second wife, Rebecca, or their three small children. While we stood talking with them she ignored us and busied herself taking their few groceries into the house. It was obvious that she was uncertain of the things we might talk about, things in a life outside the mountains of which she did not know. It was obvious that she was afraid of being left out of our conversation, and therefore she pretended to be busy, preoccupied with other things.

Her husband greeted us as his "kin-folk" saying, "It's about time you came home where you belong. This is where your Pappy would want you to be." We were welcome, he said, to stay as long as we wished. "The fare's poor; we're on welfare. The bed's hard." He winked. "But if you can put up with my ornery wife, you can stay all winter." He called her by name. She stood in the doorway watching us. Like most natives of the southern Appalachian mountain region, she was suspicious of outsiders, fearful they would either exploit or ridicule her or her loved ones. She moved slowly in her relationship with strangers. She would trust us as she saw her husband trusted us, but that would take time and must come on her terms. Meanwhile she would be polite and would show her "up bringing." She invited us into their home. She made coffee and brought a plate of cookies she had saved for our coming. I did not offer to help with her preparations. I would help her later, but to move too fast into her kitchen would cause her to resent me deeply.

Not only was Rebecca suspicious of outsiders, but she and her neighbors were also suspicious and jealous of each other. Feeling that no one can be completely trusted, they, like most poor families in Appalachia, had a limited number of people outside their own kin with whom they interacted. This resulted in the family being the main source, and in some cases the only source, of emotional support.

We drank coffee, and she brought out boxes of pictures, mostly pictures of her relatives. She told us about her brothers, sisters, and cousins, about their marriages, their children, and when, where, and how they had died. Of those living we must know where they lived, how they felt about her, and how she felt about them. She was beginning to accept us. She risked sharing of herself, telling us how she felt about something. She watched closely for our reactions and listened carefully to our words. She was much too intelligent to be fooled by mere words. She was perceptive of our attitude and in tune with our feelings. When we were able to convey our interest in her as a person, she was satisfied.

This was an unsophisticated mountain woman, simple in her beliefs. She was also firm in her convictions and honest in her assessments of people. She could care less about who we were, where we were from, or what we did. She did not care what others thought, even her husband, and this in a culture where the woman is subservient to the man. Instead she would assert her independence; she would arrive at her own conclusion, in her own way, in her own time. She would make her decision about whether to accept us or merely tolerate us for the sake of her husband. She was directed in this, as in all decisions, by her own intuitive sensitivity to people and what her parents and grandparents had taught her to perceive in a stranger. After we had looked at her pictures and had seen the dried flowers from her mother's funeral and a wooden rose her grandfather had carved for her grandmother's what-not shelf, we discerned she was more accepting of our coming. Suddenly she turned to me and said, with child-like simplicity, "I'm so glad yo' all come. Come on 'elp me, let's git somethin' to eat on the table. Yo' all must be plum near starved."

NOTES

1. A tipple was an apparatus for tipping coal cars to empty them into freight cars; it was also the place where the coal cars were emptied into the railroad cars.

2. In the boom years of World War II safety measures once again were ignored and many a cave-in resulted because coal support columns had been "shaved too thin" in an effort to get out more coal and thus to earn more money.

Perhaps it's true, that God is not responsible for everything.

Ulla Isaksson, 20th century Swedish authoress
The Blessed Ones

14

"They Say They Kant 'Ford Hit"

We walked the tracks through the railroad tunnel. It was a short tunnel lighted by the long shafts of late afternoon sun that followed us from the north side of the mountain. We were in semi-darkness for a few hundred feet, and then suddenly ahead of us was warm, yellow sunlight and in the distance children's voices. The train tracks came out of the darkness, ran across the narrow limestone ledge, and then spanned the river on a long trestle. The tiny, three-room house clung to a sliver of rock between the steep hillside and the bank of the river. The house and those behind it on the slender ridge had been there a long time. They were so close to the tracks that they were stained by train smoke from the days before diesels when the railroad had used steam engines.

Below was the yellow-green water of the river, its restless current moving, yet seeming not to move. The river curved here in a gigantic elbow and flowed along the base of another mountain to the east. It turned in a horseshoe bend and reversed its course toward the west into the more populated area of the town, a mining community deep in the coal fields of eastern Kentucky.

257

On the mountain to the east was the opening of the largest mine. Its entrance was almost at the summit. Two sets of tracks swept from near the crest to the tipple at a point across the river level with the house. When the mine was operating the loaded cars could be counted from the front porch as they dropped down the hillside, growing in size as they came ever closer, gaining in momentum until their wheels screamed against the rails.

When we came from the darkness of the tunnel into the warm September sunlight, Melissa Louise Cowper was sitting on the edge of the porch, her feet on the ground. She was a tall, gaunt woman, ageless. She was piecing another crazy quilt, feather-stitching along the seams of the irregular pieces with brightly colored embroidery floss. As she put it, she could never "just sit and do nothin'." She had to keep her hands busy.

Her husband, Robert Lee Cowper, sat behind her. His chair was tilted against the side of the house, the front legs free of the porch floor. His work-gnarled hands lay motionless across his lap. Sometimes he folded them together, always with the right one on top as if to hide the stub of the index finger and the malformed thumb on his left hand.

The two of them sat without talking, watching their grandchildren and their neighbors' children at play. Sometimes they glanced upward toward the mine, but now they looked toward us. We stepped across the rails, picking our way over the crushed limestone ballast, and came to the edge of their porch. They were expecting us. They knew we would come eventually, either across the railroad trestle or through the tunnel; there was no other way. They knew we would sit on their porch and talk with them and later with their children, their children's children, and with neighbors. They knew they would put us up in their only bedroom, the room in which their twelve children had been born and where one had died.

Although they were secretly pleased with our visit, they were not accustomed to expressing their feelings in words, and for that reason they were uncomfortably stiff in their greeting. They said "mam" and "sir" in a formal way and fell into long periods of silence that said they seldom had a visitor who was not a kin. They were mountain people from a long heritage of mountain people. Theirs was the language of the hills, the language of their Anglo-

Saxon ancestors. They could rub shoulders with a farm yeoman of Shakespeare's day and not be out of step. In the way of mountain people they were undemonstrative in their greetings. We were welcome to come, but they would reserve overtures of friendliness until they had known us longer. Then they would invite us into the house and take the double-ring wedding quilt, which was nearly a hundred years old, out of the trunk, where it was kept for special occasions, and spread it over the foot of the iron bed where we were to sleep. In their own way through actions they would tell us that they felt comfortable, and that we were welcome to stay as long as we wanted.

Robert Lee had worked in the main mine "nigh onto forty years." There he had continued to work until the mine closed four years before our visit. Six of his seven sons and three of his sons-in-law had worked there "some time or utter." His grandaddy had worked when the mine was first opened in the days when coal was slid down the mountainside on piles of brush interlaced together. When his pappy went to work there, mules had been used to draw the coal cars. A few little burros were used deep in the mine when he "fust commenst to work up thar." But in more recent years practically everything had become mechanized. The big machines did most of the work with less danger to the men, although accidents still occurred. With the digging and loading machines there was less need each year for men. The year the mine closed they took out more coal than ever before in a single year and used fewer men to do it. There was still coal in that mine, lots of coal! The mine closed because the owners wanted to close it, not because of a shortage of coal.

Part of the anger that Robert Lee felt toward the mine owners was a deep-seated resentment that the company had used the men, exploiting them but never appreciating the fact that the men risked their very lives to bring the coal out of the earth. He never felt that the company saw the men as human beings. Rather they were seen as human machines who went deep into the ground, dynamited the coal from the vein, and kept the product moving. Should they have an accident or become ill they were discarded as if they were an obsolete piece of machinery to be replaced by a new recruit. Evidence of this sort of treatment could be seen not only in this town but in communities throughout the coal-producing regions.

There were men crippled from accidents or wheezing and coughing from lungs damaged by coal dust who, unable to work, were asked to move out of the company housing but who did not have the wherewithall or the contacts to go elsewhere. They stayed on, existing as best they could in the community where they had helped to enrich the company that now ignored them completely.

Robert Lee held up his maimed hand, saying that he had been in two accidents the year he injured his hand. He had lost the finger when he and two other men were caught on the track and the loaded cars pulled by the electric locomotive came through. He and one of the other men flattened themselves against the wall on one side; the third man tried to do the same on the other. A rod from one of the cars struck Robert Lee and his companion. It gashed a hole in the other man's thigh and mashed Robert Lee's hand against a timber. The third man on the other side had tried to climb onto a ledge, but he lost his balance, falling onto the loaded car. He was carried forward and dragged against the horizontal collar poles supporting the roof of the tunnel. His agonizing cries of pain echoed back along the corridor above the rumble of the loaded cars and left the men gripped in fear. They felt they had heard the "cry of death," as they called it, and thus were not surprised when their fellow worker died the next day of internal injuries. According to the superstition of the miners, his death had been predicted in the echoed cry. Robert Lee said he would remember the man's screams to his own dying day.

The second accident involved a cave-in when six of the men were trapped for a day until their fellow workers could dig them out. Part of that time Robert Lee was pinned under a slide of coal. As he recalled, he expected never to walk again. He thought his back had been broken, and even when it was discovered that the weight of the slide had been held by a slab of limestone from the ceiling, he still could not move his legs for several days. Thinking about it now, he guessed he was "just too plum scared" to even try to walk and needed time to recover.

The accidents he could accept as part of the hazard of coal mining, but what upset him the most was the closing of the mine. As he talked his eyes changed in expression, hardening under his shaggy brows. He brought the front legs of his chair down hard against the porch floor in a gesture of quick anger. The owners and the mine management had said they could no longer afford "to keep hit open," he explained, disbelief written in every fiber of his being. The mine owners had said they could not afford to meet the demands of the union for another increase in wages. They had said that their profit was too slim and that the payments they were forced to make into the Miners' Health and Welfare Fund were too high—more than they made from the coal. They said they were forced to close. This he could neither accept nor understand.

How could this be the case, when the cost of coal had risen until coal miners could hardly afford to burn it? Most of the people across the river used gas. His own coal was brought through the railroad tunnel, and the man who delivered it charged an additional five dollars a ton just for pushing it through the tunnel in a wheelbarrow. When a coal company made that kind of money, how dare the owners talk about a competitive fuel market where oil, gas, and electricity were replacing coal? In fact, he did not blame industry; few people could afford coal these days. The mine owners also talked about depreciation on machinery and increases in freight costs. These problems were their problems, not the miners' problems. All he was concerned about was that now the mine was closed he was out of work. He was willing and able to work. In fact, he wanted to work, but the black coal remained deep within its seams; the coal cars remained idle at the top of the shaft; and the rails down the mountain to the loading dock were coated with a heavy color of rust. There was no answer to his feelings. All we could do was listen.

Melissa Louise had worked on her quilt without comment. At times she sewed furiously, her needle reflecting her response to her husband's feelings; at other times her needle was motionless. When Robert Lee finished, she sighed and stood up, folding her quilt top against her breast. "And hat's it," she said, her voice without emotional affect as if Robert Lee had expressed her own feelings.

It was dark, the mine entrance no longer distinguishable. Melissa Louise said that she would turn on a light and that we should come into the house as soon as we could see where we were going. We moved indoors into the light. Outside in the darkness hung the silence, the deathly silence of a mining community out of work.

15

"Keep 'Em Outta Hyeh"

We could see her coming as she made her way slowly down the steep, rocky path, walking as if attempting to balance the load she was carrying. When she was close she spoke with a dialect betraying that she was native to this remote mountain region. From her later comments and her physical appearance she would be classified by some as a red neck, a cracker, and by still others as "po' " white trash. She was obviously hungry for human contact and wanted to talk.

She wore a dress of two patterns of flowered material. It was covered by an apron with its own floral design. Her hair, brushed straight back, was pinned in a bun at the nape of her neck. She wore no makeup and probably never had. As she said later, she did not "hold much with those kinds of fixin' up."

The dark brown stain on the edge of her upper lip and at the corners of her mouth said she dipped snuff. She carried a pail of table scraps mixed with what looked like commercial chicken feed. She said she had trudged over to the other side of the mountain to her son's to get something to feed her laying hens as she was "plum out" of anything, and it was too early for her welfare check which would enable her to "go fetch some from town."

"Reckin' yo' all got car trouble!" She smiled a warm, friendly toothless smile that showed the brown pinch of snuff packed against her gums. "That's about all a little old car is fit fur, his trouble."

I explained that we had stopped to let the motor cool after the long haul across the mountain. When she sensed that we had time to talk she freed the pail and let it drop to the red clay dust of the roadway. She had carried it fastened to a wide piece of truck innertube worn like a shawl around her shoulders. She leaned an elbow against the side of our car and talked. Occasionally she would pause to spit a long stream of dark snuff juice aimed with uncanny accuracy at a stone, a bug, or a slight indentation in the roadway.

She wondered how we got there and if we had any "kinfolk in these parts." Her questions were direct and to the point. "Whar you' from, an' whar you' goin', an' what mought yo' name be?"

She "reckin'd as to how" we were not "feds" or with the welfare department; we looked too "down on our luck" to be either. It was a statement of fact, not a question. She needed to rest, and we were there and looked as if we had nothing better to do than to talk. She warned us not to go wandering off into the woods. This was a bad snake area, and since snakes started crawling out about this time of day to sun themselves on the warm rocks, it was easy to walk into a nest of rattlers before one knew they were around unless he knew how to travel in snake country. There were three kinds of rattle snakes here—Eastern diamondbacks, timber, and pigmy; but even worse were the copperheads, who didn't make a sound but were as poisonous as rattlers. She talked at length about what to do in case of snake bite and how many times she had found a snake in the chicken coop after the hens' eggs.

She then moved from snakes and chickens to religion, politics, home cures for various illnesses, the high cost of food, to marriage counseling, moonshining, how to raise "younguns," and how and when to plant a garden according to the phases of the moon. The moon, she thought, also had a strong supernatural influence on the everyday living experiences of people. The growth and decline of the moon determined planting, hoeing, and harvesting, whereas a new moon would spoil the meat even in the coldest weather. The curing of lumber and the building of houses should also be gauged according to the phases of the moon, or else the wood would shrink and warp in the sun, and the roof would leak.

She had lived all of her life in the mountains. Born a few miles to the east in northern Georgia, married before she was fifteen, she and her first husband "come hyeh" to a place "jist over thar in the next holler," near where her son was living. She was the mother of fourteen children and the step-mother of four. All of her "young-uns" were married and had "younguns" of their own "ceptin' " two teenage sons who were still at home and made her eligible for Aid to the Families of Dependent Children. She spoke with pride. She had forty-three grandchildren and three great-grandchildren, and none of " 'em've ever been carried to a doctor." She had cared for them through all illness, major and minor, recommending and preparing teas, poultices, and tonics made from wild herbs that she would gather and dry.

Somewhere from far away down toward the valley, probably in a grassy spot along a creek, came the bawl of cattle. A neck bell on an unseen cow tinkled faintly. From the direction of the woman's son's house back over the mountain came the angry sound of dogs. The woman straightened. She moved back from the car and stood for a moment, listening.

Satisfied, she turned to us and continued to talk. A few minutes later a ragged, mangy dog slinked into view. He was a combination of several breeds, mainly hound. The bare skin of his hips showed inflammed sores, scars from battle encounters with the teeth and claws of angry animals. He leaned into the air, putting his weight on three legs, poised to run. His rib cage rose and fell in bold relief above the hollows of his sides. He was, the woman said, a road "dawg." He belonged to no one, and no one belonged to him.

The half-starved animal stopped a few feet away and sniffed hungrily at a pile of fresh refuse dumped in the littered ditch. It was a trash dump like those found throughout the rural South where car bodies, bed springs, discarded mattresses, tin cans, bottles, and paper are heaved onto road shoulders and into rivers and creeks. The dog gingerly approached the waste pile. His movement disrupted the feeding of a pair of monstrous rats who measured him defiantly and returned to their eating. As if from experience, the dog kept his distance from the rats and came at the garbage from a slightly different angle.

The woman explained about the dog. A female bitch heavy with pups had been "dropped" in the area. She "an' the rest o' the litter must've bin killed when some ornery no good sicked an' whooped a pack of big old coon-huntin' dawgs on 'em. This on' learned to take good keer of hisself." He had lived up and down this part of the road for "nigh onto two years. It's a wonder somebody ain't shot 'em jist to show they could hit somethin'."

She talked on about the dog, saying that everyone around there always believed the mother dog was "dropped out by some nigger from down south. 'Cause hits jist like something a nigger up an' do to be mean, hoping the mother dawg'd kill chickens an' livestock 'round hyeh fur her pups.' "

She began to explain her feelings about Blacks. Her voice choked with the force of her emotions. Her prejudice was ingrained; she had no use for "any nigger." She thought the country would have been better off had all Blacks been shipped to Africa. "Tis hard 'nough," she said, "fur honest decent white folks to make a livin' without havin' good jobs goin' to niggers." She went on. "Hits 'nough to skeer yo' plum to death the way niggers air taken over things nowadays. It's gonna to be the ruin of this country."

She concentrated for a long moment on an orange and black caterpillar that moved through the dust at her feet. More to herself than to us, but still talking about Blacks she muttered, "All I kin say is, jist keep 'em out of hyeh or you'll have a funeral on your hands. The men folks 'round hyeh would jist as soon shoot one as look at 'em. They'd do hit an' never bother to ask, 'What mought yo' name be?' "

The sun had slid behind the rocky crag of the next mountain. Long, dark shadows lay across the road. A mule brayed, waited, and brayed again. Suddenly the woman seemed aware of time. "Now, yo' all come back," she said, "yo' hear? My boys air comin' soon an' I got to feed 'em." She picked up the pail of chicken feed and fastened it to the innertube around her shoulders. Slowly she crossed the road and disappeared as she had come, into the piney woods.

*The man who sat on the ground in his tipi
meditating on life and its meaning, accepting the kinship of all creatures and
acknowledging unity with the universe of
things was infusing into his being the true
essence of civilization. And when native
man left off this form of development, his
humanization was retarded in growth.*

Luther Standing Bear, 20th century chief
  of the Oglala Sioux
Land of the Spotted Eagle

16

The Ride South

The car had been new eleven years before. Exposure to sun,
rain, hail, and snow had faded its once deep-maroon color to
motley garnet. One front door had been replaced; it was yellow.
This combination of yellow and faded maroon provided an unusual
two-tone effect. The trunk lid was fastened with a piece of wire.
The lock was broken intentionally when the key was lost by a
former owner. The tires were two different sizes and were a
mixture of retreads, white sidewalls, and all black. The tailpipe was
loose, and a crack in the manifold channeled forth the muffler
sound. Each time the car moved away from a stop, there was a dull
roar.

By the standards of modern transportation, it was unreliable. It
was even unsafe. For the Sioux Indian family who owned this car,
however, it was all the transportation they had. It was all they
could afford. At times, when it needed new tires or repairs, as now
it needed a new muffler, it was more than they could afford.

It was five years old when they bought it. Before that time they
had traveled with a horse and wagon. In those days they made

mostly short trips to Pine Ridge or Wounded Knee. With the car they could travel from their home in a remote section of the South Dakota badlands to stores in Rapid City or Hot Springs. They could work in the peaches and potatoes of Colorado and the sugar beets of Nebraska and Montana and occasionally in the hay harvest of Wyoming. They could visit family and friends.

Now the car headed south, taking part of the family to visit relatives in Colorado and taking us to New Mexico. We had made arrangements to return in a truck with migrant workers from western Texas headed for the sugar beets of Montana; the migrants' trucks would pass near Oelrichs, South Dakota. We would ride that far as part of their crew.

Along the creeks the ground was yellow with dandelions. It was the time of color in every coulee and along the base of every butte. It was a time of greenness, of nesting songbirds, of wobbly-legged colts, of long-tailed lambs. And for us it was time to travel toward our rendezvous with the migrant trucks.

Only part of the Running Elk family made the trip. Andrew, the father, who worked on the ranch of a white neighbor, and five of the older children, who were in school, stayed home together with their aged grandfather. A married daughter, Janet, and her three children stayed with them and would make fried bread and cook for them while their mother was away.

Bessie, the mother, James, who was six, and four-year-old Helen, together with Joyce, the eighteen-year-old married daughter, her twenty-two-year-old husband, Keith, and their five-month-old baby, Tita, went with us.

Most Native American families, both on and off reservations, take their children out of school to visit relatives. They frequently take them out of school for other reasons as well. Bessie and Andrew were unusual in that they had a strong conviction that the future for their people depended upon young Indians getting good educations. Therefore, they encouraged their children to complete high school. This was not always easy. It was not always easy for the family to keep their focus on the goals of education when they had so little income and so many pressing needs.

There were times when there was not enough food, when they divided one potato among the entire family. Necessities that could be taken for granted by other Americans for this Indian family became a struggle. It was difficult, for example, to obtain a sufficient supply of water. They hauled their water from a creek a mile from where they lived. They hauled it in an old dented milk can which they wedged in the trunk of their car tying the deck lid down with a rope. Since the top for the milk can had been lost, if they drove fast or hit a rock the water splashed out, so they drove home slowly trying to save every drop; water was precious. Sometimes James sat in the trunk and held onto the can of water. In summer the stream nearly disappeared, and cattle waded among the rocks to drink. With the cattle using their only water supply, it was hard to get even a few gallons that were not muddy or foul smelling.

Beyond the daily struggling for food and water and maintaining a house that gave shelter from the elements, Andrew and Bessie had an unusual intuitive awareness of certain societal changes and their effect on Native American youth. These parents could see the contrast between the experiences of their own adolescence and the experiences of their children. They felt that it was more difficult to grow up an Indian today than it had been even in the days of the Depression. They could see that every young Sioux seemed caught between the traditional Indian culture and the role expectations of the dominant white race and that they lacked leadership models among their own people. This was even more pronounced than when they were adolescents and were less subject to contact with whites. They felt they had not been as aware in the early 1930s that Indians were the most deprived of all Americans as young people were in the mid-1960s because of mass media. In their youth they had not seen young people who felt so trapped, confused, and angry that they lashed out at the world in acts of hostility or self-destruction. Young people in their day had been more passive. They had not been as openly critical of life in general.

Andrew and Bessie understood that there were few adults in leadership positions among their people who could help adolescents find a goal in life. They sensed that changes in the traditional patterns of Indian living had caused many of the problems. In the traditional Sioux culture parents provided physical care and affection for their children. Discipline and controls were not responsibilities of parents, but, instead, came from the tribe or band. In former days children and teenagers were taught to behave according to the standards of the tribe. They were taught by the examples provided by their leaders, the chiefs. In the modern world there is no place for the model role of the chief, no leadership to serve as an example and set standards of conduct for the young, especially as almost every one of those in leadership positions are non-Indians.

When the Indian was the dominant race of the Great Plains, roles within the family were clearly defined among the Sioux. The father was the hunter and the warrior. The mother was the camp maker; she did the domestic work and all labor not related to hunting or war. The education and training of children were the concern of the whole tribe. No individual, young or old, was free to make a decision for himself. Every act and every decision had to be considered in light of its effect upon others. The preservation of the tribe demanded that all members work together. Each individual did his or her assigned tasks, in the assigned way, determined by the standards of the group. This was how it was in the beginning before the imposed controls from the white man's culture created what for the Sioux was an experience of bondage.

The years since the creation of the reservations have seen generations of Native Americans, young and old, caught in this struggle between two cultures, victims of federal paternalism and educational starvation. They have expressed their frustration through such emotional and social problems as apathy, drunkenness, hostility, quarreling, divorce, and poor work patterns. The assumed roles of the modern Indian family identify the husband as the provider and the wife as the homemaker, but in reality neither of these roles may be possible if the man is unable to find work, if the woman becomes the provider, or if the welfare department is their sole support. In the midst of such disorganization there are Native American parents who work hard to provide for their children physically as well as emotionally. There are parents who encourage their children to obtain the educational training necessary for jobs of the future, whatever they might be.

And so it was with Andrew and Bessie Running Elk. There was little drinking in their family and little quarreling. They worked together making and beading leggings and moccasins for sale to tourists, using designs and colors that have been part of their culture for hundreds of years. On winter nights the entire family gathered in the largest room of their three-room log house. This room was at once living room, dining room, kitchen, and bedroom. In the glow of a kerosene lamp they talked while they worked on the beading. Sometimes the parents related stories of their own youth. Other times the aged grandfather told of the days when the Sioux roamed the Plains. In summer they built a pine-brush shelter in which they sat and talked, and at twilight they sat around a mosquito "smudge" of twisted green grasses. They sang songs. When the stars appeared, they drove their old car across the prairie to visit relatives and close friends.

As was traditional among Sioux Indians, the ties of this family extended beyond the father, the mother, the children, and the aged grandfather. The family included both the relatives who lived near and those who lived away. The uncles and the aunts were like other sets of parents. The cousins were truly brothers and sisters, especially those near the same age. In fact, those were the titles they were assigned. As it was in the beginning with the Sioux, all of the mother's sisters and female cousins were called mother and all of the father's brothers and male cousins were called father, while the mother's brothers were uncle and the father's sisters were aunt. If a relative wanted or needed something, it was shared. This, in their language, was *teola* and implied more than giving food or shelter; it meant giving of one's home, sharing of one's self emotionally.

Now part of the family was going to see relatives whom they had not visited in months. It was time to take the baby Tita to be seen by the larger family. The mother, Joyce, and Keith sat in the front seat. The rest of us were in back. We took turns holding the baby, who slept most of the way.

We started when the east was a faint blush of color. We stopped only briefly. It was a long trip, something over 400 miles. Mile after mile the old car moved through the sun and shadow. It stopped and started with a dull roar from the cracked manifold and a banging of the loose tailpipe.

Bessie and her children were a happy family, and there was much good-natured teasing and laughter among them as we traveled. Sometimes they sang songs in English or in their native Sioux dialect, Lakota. Once Keith sang a solo, an old Indian ballad, and the others joined in the chant, clapping their hands. The notes were high, shrill, and penetrating. The occupants of a passing car shouted at us and turned to stare. Keith's voice was solemn. His eyes held a glint of laughter as they met mine in the rear-view mirror. "They probably think we have a carload of howling coyotes here," he said. "If we don't watch, the Humane Society for the Prevention of Cruelty to Dumb Animals will be checking on us."

Near dusk Keith turned into a narrow gravel road. "Here we are!" he called. The house was like others in that scatter of a neighborhood. It was small and lacked paint. It showed the many odds and ends of old lumber from which it had been constructed. Some boards showed previous nailholes and flakes of paint. The family was covering the exterior with gray asbestos shingles. It would be finished as they could afford to buy a few bundles of shingles at a time.

The neighborhood was a small subdivision made up entirely of Indian families. It blended into other sections which contained homes of various minority peoples—Chicanos and Black and white migrants who once lived in the deep South. Merely because they were neighbors did not bring them to a closer understanding of each other. Merely because they had common needs or the common bond of poverty did not help them accept each other. They were suspicious and prejudiced. Thus, they watched each other cautiously.

There are many non-Indians in such communities who are convinced that Native Americans live the way they do in substandard housing because there is something basically wrong with them. Such persons may be heard to say, "Perhaps only inferior Indians are left. If not, you've got to tell me why Indians are so far behind Blacks. Show me any Indians who contributed to art, science, or the professions of America."

Even in the ghetto-like neighborhoods, Indians live on the outer fringe in the least desirable parts. They live in an immediate neighborhood where they can relate only to each other. They have little contact with the larger part of the community. Indians, like most minorities, have a tendency to seek their own kind, their own relatives and former friends. Such self-restriction provides more emotional security than would a neighborhood of strangers or a neighborhood made up of other races. This style of living, however, is usually imposed as a result of racial discrimination on the part of a community that feels no desire to have any "truck" with Indians.

In such communities Indians have an unsavory reputation. They are accused of having no pride in their personal appearance or the appearance of their homes. It is said that Indians lack morals. In these accusations there has been no attempt to distinguish between individuals. Once again, a whole race is condemned.

The relatives ran to greet us as we turned into the driveway. Whatever affects one family of the neighborhood affects all families, so those who were not relatives also came to greet us. They asked about the family at home and about the trip. They joked about the old car, patting its fenders and saying it had done well to make the trip in one day.

These were Bessie's relatives. This was the home of her older sister. The family patriarch lived next door. He was the oldest living family member. He was an uncle, older than the aged grandfather in South Dakota. As the patriarch, he was the official spokesman for the entire family. It was he who kept the family's records and history. Whenever there was a marriage or the birth of a child, such information was sent to him so he might keep the record. He tried to strengthen kinship ties that were threatened by involvement in the complexities of a modern society.

The aged patriarch had not seen the baby Tita. He held the sleeping one close. He peered into the tiny face, trying to see the features of his father or his grandmother.

His sharp, old eyes peered at us. They were dark and penetrating. For a long, thoughtful moment he studied our features, much as he had looked at the sleeping babe. He commented that my cheek bones were high. He did not act as if he expected an explanation. I did not offer one. Then his gaunt face relaxed into a warm smile. He held up his hand making a sign of greeting that said we were welcome. Because of his acceptance, we would be accepted by the relatives of this family wherever they might live. Because we came with Bessie and the others, we were an extended part of the family. It was assumed that we would stay for the night, just as it was expected that Keith and Joyce would stay. The matter was settled. We would stay. The next day Keith and Joyce would drive us to the spot where we would meet the trucks.

The relatives had eaten, but it was assumed that we must be

hungry. There was soup, one piece of roast rabbit, some fried bread, and *wojapi*. We should make out! Neighbors and other relatives brought other gifts of food, an extra blanket, a quilt, a pillow, and a chair for our comfort. They came one by one through the evening, not only to see Bessie and her family but also to meet us because they were curious and they did not really trust our motive for being there.

Bessie's sister gave us for our use what originally had been a small porch enclosed now as a tiny room. It contained an old studio couch whose rusty hinges opened after much protest to make into a full-size bed. The ancient springs were so weak that they sagged until we could feel the hard, sharp imprint of wood beneath. The family had given us the best they had. They gave us the only room in the house with a door. The other doorways were hung with plastic curtains. It was also the only room with one bed. Even the kitchen floor provided a sleeping place for Keith, James, and two of the teenage boys. We were treated as kinfolk and still we were honored guests. They were careful to see that we had the softest pillows, the least patched sheet, a quilt. The next morning the coffee was hot and strong.

We said good-bye to the children the evening before, as we planned to leave near dawn. The next morning the entire family, including the aged patriarch and the children, except the baby Tita, gathered around the old car to see us drive away. Few understood what we were doing, why we were there. But for an evening and a night we had been one of them, and they wanted us to know. The old patriarch, their spokesman, told us in Lakota that they "would look for us until we came again." As he talked he moved his hands toward the sky, to the earth, and to the four points of the compass. In his manner and intonation were the unhurried ritual, tradition, and eloquence of speech of his ancestors when they had entreated the blessings of the Unseen and the Eternal upon the traveler until such time in the moons of the future that they would meet again, never as strangers. Suddenly there in the light of early morning we understood the true meaning of *teola*. We had found our home away from home.

World wrongly called the new! This clime was old
When first the Spaniard came, in search of gold,
Age after age its shadowy wings had spread,
And man was born, and gathered to the dead;
Cities arose, ruled, dwindled to decay,
Empires were formed, then darkly swept away:
Race followed race, like cloud-shades o're the field,
The stranger still to strangers doomed to yield.

Author unknown

17

From South of the Border

They came northward from south of the Rio Grande from the rural sections of Mexico. They came from the tiny hamlets and villages and from the cities. They came north, crossing the river into Texas to find work in the crops. Their fathers and their grandfathers before them had been peons, peasants who worked the soil. They were peasants who harvested the grapes for wineries or tended the flocks of sheep on the hillside for masters who owned the stone and adobe haciendas in the valleys. Their basic diet[1] was the same as their ancestors' centuries before—beans, stews highly seasoned with chili pepper, squash, and thin, unleavened cakes of maize meal, called *tlaxcallis* by the Aztecs[2] and *tortillas* by the Spaniards.[3]

Their skin was brown, a dusty shade that spoke of their Indian ancestry. They were descendants of Aztec and other ethnic and cultural groups of Indians who had developed in Mexico one of the

---

Adapted from a chapter of the same title which first appeared in *Where Hannibal Led Us* (New York: Vantage Press, Inc., 1967).

276

most advanced civilizations in the world before their conquest by Hernando Cortez in 1519.[4] Before the Spanish came, their distant Indian ancestors had not been peasants but skilled artisans, judges, merchants, priests, physicians and growers; they were land owners.[5]

'The Indians of that early civilization gave a great deal of attention to the raising and development of plants for food, for medication, and for pleasure.[6] They tapped mountain streams into aqueducts for irrigation and cultivated maize, beans, cacao, maguey, and cotton as standard crops. So great was their interest in plants that their cities had extensive botanical gardens and nurseries of a magnitude unknown in Europe or other parts of the world visited by Cortez and his soldiers.

The lust for gold, however, blinded Cortez and his followers to the agricultural and artistic contributions the Indians might make to the civilizations of the world. They saw only the possibility to conquer, to possess, and to exploit. They crushed the empire of Montezuma, enslaving the people and using their skills in building, mining, and agriculture for the glory of Spain.[7] Few of these Spanish conquering adventurers, better known as conquistadors, were educated men, but within twenty-five years and with the forced labor of their skilled captives they constructed great palaces and cathedrals in widely separated places in the jungle. They also put Indians to work extracting silver from their own mines and clearing thousands of acres of valley land for the planting of tobacco and sugar for shipment to Spain. When they had exploited fully the central section of the country, they pushed northward searching for rumored gold. They spread across the Rio Grande, but not before taking Indian women as their mistresses to bear their children, even as Cortez took the Tabascan Indian chieftain's daughter, Malinche, as his mistress.[8]

When the first Spanish explorers arrived in the Rio Grande basin about 1540, they found the Indians of that area irrigating and cultivating land along the Rio Grande and the Upper Pecos in what is now New Mexico.[9] Irrespective of how long the Indians had lived in the area or what legal and moral claims they might have, the Spanish explorers claimed the land and all that was upon it or in it for the king of Spain. As they had done earlier in Mexico, they also claimed the most beautiful of the Indian maidens as their mates. And thus it came to be that, a quarter of a century before the Mayflower landed at Plymouth Rock, the forefathers of those who someday would be known as Spanish-Americans and Mexican-Americans had already left the imprint of Spain on the history of that land which was destined to become the southwest region of the United States.[10] But even more, the imprint of Spain would be left in Mexico in the continued development of the Indo-Hispanic culture.[11] The descendants of the early conquistidors often inter-married with the Indians. Some of their offspring were pheno-typically more Spanish than Indian, others more Indian than Spanish.

As in any culture, economic classes had existed from the begin-nings of Mexican culture. But in the Indo-Hispanic culture a division developed between extreme wealth on one hand and extreme poverty on the other. There were those who held title to the land, and there were those who worked the land. The poor peasants, little more than serfs, labored on the land in the depth of deprivation. In their hearts was a desire to own their own land, to have the right to labor as they chose, to be paid for their services and not feel the oppression of those who were born into land ownership.

From their heritage of two cultures, these peasants made songs for everything. They sang for a new day, for the promise of the harvest. They sang when the green grapes on the hillside were the size of pin-cherries and when the moon hung like a copper plate above Popocatepetl. They sang with the dawn, with the darkness, and at fiesta time. They had songs about the pale wash of dawn, the beauty of a desert sunset, and of Popocatepetl sleeping under blankets of snow. They sang of people. They sang of man, of his worth and dignity, man as absolute ruler of his home and of woman—obedient, respectful, cheerful, and patient. They sang of Mamacita, "jewel of the home"; they sang of the beauty of woman.

Their songs told of children taught to grow in self-sufficiency and to honor the value of work. The songs told of growing old with the wisdom and knowledge that comes only with age. The songs told of the family—grandparents, parents, children, uncles, aunts, cousins, and godparents. The songs told much of the family. The people listened and made the songs part of each new generation, and thus the songs became part of their culture.

During those years of the middle-eighteenth century, before the outbreak of the American Revolution when the thirteen colonies along the Atlantic seaboard were chaffing under the tyranny of Great Britain, settlers from Mexico entered the valley of the Rio Grande. Given large grants of land by the king of Spain, who wished to bestow favors upon his loyal Mexican subjects, those favored ones became the landed aristocrats of the Rio Grande Valley and claimed land which was occupied and cultivated by Indians. Some of these Indians were killed or driven out; others intermarried with the new settlers from south of the river adding even more Indian blood to the Spanish. The landed aristocrats, in turn, encouraged peasants to come northward to help in the harvest and with the cattle and sheep.

And so the peons, the tillers of the soil, traveled northward. They came to work and to live in the great valley. They were a simple people, a sincere people, devout in the observation of their religion, steeped in the tradition of their culture, and held together by strong family ties that excluded contact with those who came from backgrounds different from their own. And because there were few outside contacts, their culture did not change. Their culture remained foremost in importance to them.

So the poor families, those who had long tilled the soil in the provinces of the south, crossed the Rio Grande and came to work in the early gardens of what later would be Texas. A few Mexican workmen crossed the river when its north bank was a republic flying the lone-star flag and recognized as an independent nation throughout the world. Farm workers came north from Mexico after Texas was admitted to the Union as the twenty-eighth state. Some worked for a time on the north bank of the Rio Grande and then returned to Mexico. Others stayed.

In the first decade of the twentieth century, Mexican workers entered the United States in a trickle, but beginning in 1910, for a period of twenty years, they poured back and forth across the border.[12] After 1930 Mexican immigration was slowed, but with Pearl Harbor, the Second World War, and the need for farm workers in the United States laborers were encouraged to move north and a mass exodus resulted.[13] In addition to the newcomers from Mexico there were thousands of other farm workers and unskilled laborers whose parents or grandparents had come from Mexico but who themselves were born in the United States. These were the Mexican-Americans, or, as they referred to themselves, the *tejanos* (Texans). They were American-born citizens with a Spanish and Indian heritage. Viewed as foreigners by other Americans, they were called "Mexicans" and sometimes given the face-slapping name "greaser."

These Spanish-Americans worked in the great crops of Texas— the cotton, the sorghum, and rice. They worked in the vegetables— the tomatoes, potatoes, and cabbage—living on the edge of the towns in the poorest housing.

Sometimes they locked the doors to their one- and two-room shanties and took their families northward. They came by the thousands to the vegetables of California, the sugar beets, beans, and cherries of Michigan and by the hundreds to the cucumbers of Wisconsin and the apples of Washington. Although their children were born in Colorado, in the broad Red River Valley of North Dakota, and in Ohio, they were still called "Mexicans." By the early 1940s, entire families of Texan-Americans followed the harvest. They crossed and recrossed the migrant streams and formed new streams, pouring northward looking for work. Most of them would return to Texas when the harvest was over.[14]

With automation in the cotton fields of Texas, thousands of the Mexican-American residents of that state were suddenly without work. Despite these problems, more and more Mexican agricultural workers came from south of the border, flowing across Texas and pouring into California. These were the *braceros* or Mexican Nationals who came under contract, an agreement involving the governments of Mexico and the United States.[15] Some entered the country without permission, without passports. They were the wetbacks who came by the thousands to work in the crops. When caught, they were deported.[16]

The braceros came only for the harvest. The men came alone, unable to bring their families. They were in the United States for months, sometimes for years. The treatment of braceros—poor housing, poor food, verbal abuse, threats of deportation as trouble-makers if they complained, low wages—constitutes one of the darkest chapters in the history of exploitation and abuse, of man's inhumanity to man, that belongs to migrant labor.

The availability to south Texas of the cheap labor of the braceros forced many more Mexican-American families in the late

1950s and early 1960s to join migratory labor crews headed northward. These American-born families who had depended for employment upon local growers were unable to live on the wages that were paid Mexican braceros, whose home-base cost of living was much lower than that necessary in the United States. They were unable to compete with foreign laborers in their own state. But although they left their homes in Texas and pushed into the north, the threat of braceros followed them. For Mexican labor was also brought northward, and because of the contractual agreement between the two federal governments, there was a minimum wage paid the braceros but there was no minimum wage for the services of American-born agricultural labor. In addition to the threat of the braceros and other cheap labor, the constant threat of the mechanical harvesters loomed. Traveling further from Texas, they penetrated deep mountain valleys and followed rivers with strange-sounding names into a world they had never suspected existed—only to find that the harvesting machines were there too, as well as the dominant culture which was very different from their own.

Long ago the peasants of Mexico sang of everything. Today the people still sing. But today they also listen to a tempo of new sounds which are part of the new life they see about them. They listen to the sounds of this new life which holds the hint of a promise, but which they know, which they can *see*, will destroy so much of the culture they still hold sacred. The new way of life says that a family is a unit consisting only of parents and children. It says there is no time for the uncles, aunts, and cousins, or the godparents. It is a new philosophy of life which says that the aged are not wiser and should not be allowed to dictate important decisions to the rest of the family. The old may even be senile. If so, they should be sent away to an institution or a home for the aged. This new way of life says that children have the right to question the knowledge of parents, especially the absolute authority of fathers. Adolescent girls are no longer to be accompanied by a chaperon. Instead they are to have freedom, even as their brothers have always had freedom, to learn the ways of a man. This new way of life seems to say that money and social prestige are more important than the dignity of the individual and the worth of man or the honor of the family. And so the people struggle emotionally. They are sorely troubled at the thought that parents are expected to grant freedom for children to come and to go without question to places where those children may be exposed to dangers that parents themselves do not understand because they have never had such experiences. They are troubled that anyone should think that allowing this sort of freedom can show more love for children than parents for generations have shown through their acceptance of every child they bore, regardless of the number, and through the deep respect they have for the true meaning of the family. They question that there could ever be greater love than this. Still the new friends and classmates of their children have so much freedom and so many material things. Is their culture wrong to be in conflict with the new world in which they find themselves?

The people struggle with these new concepts of family relationships, of the so-called right of the individual to know happiness at any cost. They wonder about the wisdom of much of what they see in modern America. And they approach change cautiously. Long ago their early Indian forefathers learned to listen patiently, to evaluate carefully, and to feel deeply before they acted. And the people know, regardless of what the dominant society may think, that their forefathers—the Indians of the plains, river valleys, and mountains and the soldiers of Spain—were brave and wise. So the Mexican-American people of today hesitate. They will consider and think a long time before they change their Chicano culture to that of the Anglo, an action that to them would negate their cultural consciousness as it is manifested in *el Movimiento de La Raza*.

NOTES

1. Michael D. Coe explains that while the Indians of Mexico ate some of the same foods as Indians in other areas, their "typical method of food preparation as a unified complex appears to be unique. The basis of the diet was the triad of maize, beans, and squash. Maize was, and still is, prepared by soaking it overnight with lime and grinding it with a hand stone (Spanish *mano*) on a trough or saddle-shaped quern (*metate*, from the Nahuatl *metatl*). The resulting dough is either toasted by the housewife as flat cakes known as *tortillas* or else steamed or boiled as *tamales*. Always and everywhere in

Mesoamerica, the hearth is comprised of three stones and is semisacred." *Mexico* (New York: Frederick A. Praeger, 1962), p. 18.

2. Jacques Soustelle, *The Daily Life of the Aztecs,* trans. from the French (London: Weidenfeld and Nicholson, 1961), pp. 147-49.

3. Coe, *Mexico,* p. 18.

4. "When the Spanish Conquerors arrived on the continent, the indigenous population of the territory which today constitutes the Mexican nation was found divided into numerous ethnic and cultural groups speaking in all about a hundred and twenty-five languages and dialects." Triyillo Carlos A. Echanove, *Mexico: A Sociological, Economical and Political Approach* (San Diego, Calif.: Division of Social Science, San Diego State College, 1966), p. 27.

For details on the conquest of the Aztec see William H. Prescott, *Conquest of Mexico* (New York: Book League of America, 1934). *Conquest of Mexico* was first published in 1834 and is the best known and most highly respected research on this period of Indian history.

5. For more on the various social classes of the Aztecs see, in addition to Prescott, Soustelle's *The Daily Life of the Aztecs,* pp. 36-94.

6. Herbert J. Spinden, in *Ancient Civilizations of Mexico and Central America* (New York: Anthropological Handbook Fund, American Museum of Natural History, 1928), pp. 249-50, points out that "the plants domesticated by the American Indians were developed far beyond the wild types, much farther, than the domestic plants of the Old World. This development must have extended over many centuries. The first horizon of agriculture was based on plants of an arid highland environment. The second horizon of agriculture was based on these same plants after they had been slowly modified to fit a humid lowland environment, as well as on certain new plants of humid lowland origin."

The French translation of Soustelle's material in *The Daily Life of the Aztecs,* pp. 194-98, gives a good description of the plants, herbs, and seeds used by the Aztecs in their pharmaceutical practice.

A number of writers have described the extent of the plants raised for pleasure which were found by the Spaniards on their arrival in Mexico. Among these is Prescott in *Conquest of Mexico,* pp. 174-210. The following is quoted from Soustelle's description of the 300-room palace of King Mexaualcoyotl at Texcoco, which was said to be surrounded by "gardens 'with many fountains, ponds and canals, many fish and birds, and the whole planted with more than two thousand pines . . . and farther on besides the temples, there was the bird-house, where the king kept all the kinds and varieties of birds, animals, reptiles and serpents that they brought him from every part of New Spain; and those which were not to be had were represented in gold and precious stones—which was also the case with the fish, both those of the sea and those that lived in the rivers and lakes. So no bird, fish or animal of the whole country was wanting here: they were there either alive or figured in gold and gems.'

"Besides his palace at Texcoco the same king had had gardens planted in other places, particularly at Tetzctzinco. 'These parks and gardens were adorned with rich and sumptuously ornamented *alcazars* [summer-houses] with their fountains, their irrigation channels, their canals, their lakes and their bathing-places and wonderful mazes, where he had a great variety of flowers planted and trees of all kinds, foreign and brought from distant parts.' " *The Daily Life of the Aztecs,* pp. 124-25.

7. See William H. Prescott, *Conquest of Mexico,* pp. 46-47.

8. Malinche was later baptized and christened Dona Maria. See Upton Close

and Merle Burke, *The Ladder of History* (New York: Macmillan Co., 1946), p. 198.

For more on the subject of Spanish exploitation, see Jose Vasoncelos and Manuel Gamio, *Aspects of Mexican Civilization* (Chicago: University of Chicago Press, 1926).

9. William Trout Chambers, *Texas—Its Land and People* (Austin, Tex.: Steck Co., 1952).

10. Y. Arturo Cabrera, *Emerging Faces: The Mexican-Americans* (Dubuque, Iowa: William C. Brown Co., Publishers, 1971), p. 2.

11. See Vasoncelos and Gamio, *Aspects of Mexican Civilization.*

12. For more information on Mexican workers in the first three decades of this century see Carl Frederick Wittke, *We Who Built America* (Cleveland, Ohio: Press of Case Western Reserve University, 1964), p. 466; or E. M. Alvarado, "Mexican Immigration to the United States," *National Conference on Social Work Proceedings* (New York, N.Y., 1920), pp. 479-80; or F. Calcott, "The Mexican Peon in Texas," *Survey*, June 26, 1920, p. 437; or Paul S. Taylor, *Mexican Labor in the United States: Imperial Valley* (1928), *Mexican Labor in the United States: South Texas* (1930), *Mexican Labor in the United States: Chicago and the Calumet Region* (1932), and *Mexican Labor in the United States: Migration Statistics* (1929-34), University of California Publications in Economics (Berkeley, Calif.: University of California Press).

13. The number of people who moved north at this time has been estimated to be at least 100,000 a year. Wittke, *We Who Built America*, p. 466.

14. For a discussion of migrant labor problems in Texas, see Carey Mc-Williams, *Ill Fares the Land* (New York: Barnes and Noble, Inc., 1967), pp. 230-56.

15. One of the best books on the subject of braceros is Ernesto Galarza, *Merchants of Labor: The Mexican Bracero History* (Santa Barbara, Calif.: McNally and Loftin, 1964).

16. For more information on this subject, see Sheldon L. Greene, "Wetbacks, Growers and Poverty," *The Nation*, October 20, 1969, pp. 403-6. Two excellent recent books on the subject are Julian Samora, *Los Majados: The Wetback Story* (Notre Dame, Ind.: University of Notre Dame Press, 1971) and Carrol Norquest, *Rio Grande Wetbacks* (Albuquerque, N.M.: University of New Mexico Press, 1972).

PART IV

The Meaning of Experiential Boundaries

We can say the brotherhood of man, and pretend that we include the sisterhood of women, but we know that we don't.

Germaine Greer, 20th century Australian authoress
The Female Eunuch

18

Generation Gap and Roles in the Chicano Family

The day was overcast with an occasional sliver of sunlight. The air was balmy and warm. Spring with a hint of summer had come to the Red River Valley. They sat wedged in the open doorway—the mother, Josefina Hernandez, and two of her children, Armando and Ramona. They were laughing and joking together, stretching their bare toes in the warm wind. Outside in the dirt of the yard, the younger children—Ileana, Santiago, and Alfredo—played. Inside was the sound of voices. The Hernandez family, like the other Chicanos in their crew, were in North Dakota to thin sugar beets.

Josefina smiled and replied to my greeting in Spanish. As I approached, she called her oldest daughter, Julia, seventeen, with whom I had talked previously. She sent Carmen Maria to bring me a chair from the house. She placed it for me, then returned to her seat on the doorsill. Through the open doorway I could see the two teenage boys, Garcia and Julio Cesar. They half listened to our conversation, half wrestled with each other. I knew their wrestling would continue as part of the nonverbal communication so apparent in the migrant subculture.[1] If Julia shared too much with

287

me, or if Garcia or Julio Cesar felt they were ignored too completely by us, they would break into our conversation with a
teasing comment, a contradiction, or they would interrupt by
moving their wrestling to the doorway or into the yard at our feet.

Julia and I talked about school. She had completed sixth grade.
She flushed with pride as she told me this; sixth grade was an
advanced education in her family, especially for a woman. She
wished she could have gone further, she said, perhaps to tenth
grade, although school had not always been a happy place, but her
father needed her to help support their family. He said she was old
enough to earn money and help buy food. There was no bitterness
in her voice as she told me this; it was an accepted fact in her
culture that education, and especially education for the women,
was less important than earning money. So Julia had dropped out
of school at the end of sixth grade. She did housework part of each
year in "El Valle"—an abbreviation migrants have given to the Rio
Grande Valley—for a teacher who helped her with her English. The
rest of the time she traveled with her family, working side by side
with her father in the fields.

Julia felt school now was more pleasant than when she had first
entered.[2] Schools then were frank to state that they did not want
Spanish-speaking students. Schools then made no provision for
children with special needs who could not speak, read, or write
English, nor did schools help such children make contributions
from their own culture to the learning experience of the classrooms. Some schools even punished children for speaking Spanish
on the playground, or else the attitudes of teachers and school
administrators made the Chicano children feel that everything
about their culture was bad, including their language and the
customs practiced in their own homes. Schools conveyed the idea
that Chicano children should deny or forget their backgrounds and
become "Americanized" like Anglos. Unfortunately, most of the
school personnel understood neither the Chicano culture they were
condemning nor one word of Spanish with which to communicate
with the students when they first entered school.

Julia related how, on her first day in school, she was confronted
with English and expected to understand it, although she had never
spoken or heard the language in her life. Spanish was the language
of her home; her mother, her grandparents, and her godparents

could speak nothing else. Her father, Octavio, had a limited knowledge of English but never spoke it in his own home. When the
teacher conveyed that it was bad for Julia to speak anything other
than English, she wondered if that made her parents, grandparents,
and godparents and younger brothers and sisters bad because they
did not speak English, or if it was only that her teacher thought
they were bad. If it were true that her family and her culture were
wrong about the language they used, were they not also wrong
about other things, such as family loyalty, family roles, discipline,
and views toward religion and folk beliefs? Julia said that in those
early days of her schooling she felt confused and alone and not
certain what was expected of her or even certain which of the
adults in her life she should believe, her parents or her teachers.

At seven Julia found English a foreign language. At seventeen
she still thought in Spanish. She felt uncomfortable with English as
a means of communication, although her English was very good.
She associated her discomfort with the many unpleasant experiences she had had with teachers who, by criticizing her English
pronunciation, her spelling, and her attempts at written essays, had
filled her with a deep sense of shame for being a Chicano.

Although Julia still wishes that her school experiences could
have been different and happier and that they had not tried to
alienate her from her own culture, she no longer is resentful,
because she sees that conditions are changing, that today there are
special programs for migrant children, and that younger children
are being given opportunities she never knew. She even worked on
one school project, and, although she wished that the Anglos
involved had better understood the Chicano culture and had seen
how often their teaching illustrations conflicted with Chicano
values, she saw many good things.

Her nine-year-old sister, Natacha, is in the first grade and has
been in a summer program. Julia described the program saying the
teacher used an aid who could speak Spanish and the children
played language games acting out words and pretending they were
letters of the alphabet. In this way they were beginning to read. As
Julia talked about Natacha and the summer school program, she
showed no embarrassment that Natacha was not at grade-age level.
There was only warm family pride in her sister's accomplishments.
In the culture of the Spanish-speaking family, whether it is Cuban,

Puerto Rican, or Mexican, no relationship is closer than the bond between sisters.[3] And so in this family the older sister showed pride as she talked about the school where Natacha was learning to read and write. She did everything she could to encourage and to help her sister, wishing the girl could some day graduate from high school. But Natacha very likely would need to drop out of school and help support the family. As Julia explained, if she were to marry and move out of the home, Natacha would need to take her place as a wage earner. Natacha would need to quit school to work, or at least to work more hours than she went to school. The Chicano culture does not consider a girl's education as important as that of her brothers, so Natacha would be asked to drop out of school and work full time before her brothers would be asked or told to do so.

Although education is viewed as more important for boys than for girls, all children, regardless of sex, are expected to have a sense of responsibility for the well-being of the family. Every child is part of the family and, therefore, is expected to work for the family and even to help support the family. As Julia explained, migrant farm work is so uncertain and the income so limited that the father alone is usually unable to support the family. This is why, Julia said, so many young couples in her culture live with their parents. They are needed to help provide extra income, or else they themselves need financial help. Members of the Spanish-speaking family are supposed to help each other and to share in many common activities as part of an extended family.

In the traditional Chicano family "a well-brought-up . . . girl knows enough not to behave either as a boy or a 'bad' girl. She does not press for competitive excellence in school. She does not display initiative outside the circumscribed pathways . . . reserved for girls. If she does, retribution is swift."[4]

Julia explained that this pattern of living is changing, as are many other things within her culture. Although there are changes in the female role, women who are too aggressive and independent are still looked upon with suspicion. Julia spoke of her cousin Cristina Gomez, whose marriage ended in divorce last winter because her husband could not tolerate the fact that she had more education than he and a better paying job. More significant even than her higher paying position was the fact that she had taken a training course through one of the agencies and got an office job in a place where men also worked. Santos Gomez could not accept the fact that a married woman should be working all day in a place where men worked, unless she was accompanied by her husband or brother as she was in the fields. He demanded that Cristina quit her new job, and when she would not he began to drink heavily and hang around her office building waiting for her. He even came up to the office where she worked, wearing his field clothes and accusing her of being too friendly with her male coworkers.

This new experience of having wives, daughters, and sisters in middle-class jobs or in leadership roles on Anglo committees is a difficult one for many Spanish-speaking male migrants to handle. Julia herself had a similar experience in which her new role was threatening to her father.

The previous summer Julia had worked as an interpreter in a migrant educational program. She was a teacher's aid and was paid more per hour than her father made in the fields. At first Octavio was pleased that she had a new job, but when Julia received her first paycheck, it was very difficult for him to accept the fact that a woman could make more money than a man and, more especially, that a daughter should make more money than her father. In their culture it was not thought to be good for a woman to have a higher education or to receive a higher salary than a man. Such a thing would be an attack on a man's self-esteem, on his manliness; it would make him feel inferior. It could make him less a man.

It was also difficult for Julia's father to accept the widening circle of her acquaintances that resulted from her job with the migrant education program. In the traditional Chicano culture the daughter's confidants are limited to her mother, her sisters, and her close female relatives. This is a traditional family culture in which the most meaningful relationships are found among relatives, including *compadres* (godparents). Initiating contacts beyond that narrow confine has always been discouraged, especially if the *amigo de confianza* (especially close friend) is Anglo, as was true in Julia's case.

Julia's dark eyes grew thoughtful. "These are difficult times for our people," she said, her voice a mere whisper. "They are hard times for fathers, and they are hard times for grown daughters. When we are little girls, our fathers play with us and talk with us;

but as we become adolescents, our fathers are more distant, more critical of our behavior, more fearful that we may bring disgrace on the family. A father will forgive his son or his daughter anything except an act that dishonors the family name. The father as the head of the house, or *jefe de la familia*, represents the family to the outer world. It is he who is held responsible for his family's reputation. The accomplishments or the failures of his children are a reflection on him as proof of how well he has fulfilled his place as *jefe de la casa* (boss of the house). Therefore, the behavior of each family member reflects on the *jefe de la familia*. A daughter could bring great disgrace to her father's name if she did not conduct herself as she should.

"In our culture it is not as important what sort of work a person does or the amount of money earned as it is important that behavior honor the father's name," Julia continued. "For the woman this means that she be virtuous, shy, and obedient to her father. It is hard to explain this to those who are not of our culture who come to talk with us about new migrant programs and wonderful opportunities for jobs and training. It is hard to try to explain that the opportunities they offer can cause greater problems among our family members than those created by poverty. We have always lived in poverty; we know how to react to it, but we do not always know how to react to change. Many of us are not certain we want to change or that we should. The marriage of Cristina and Santos was not destroyed by poverty; they worked eight years together in the fields, but their marriage was destroyed by Cristina's new job and the fact that Santos could not change with her."

Julia became philosophic. "It is hard today for a Chicano woman," she said. "It is hard to be a wife in the old way and still do the things that people in the training programs suggest. It is hard to be an obedient daughter, to do as the father commands, and still serve on planning committees with Anglo community people who do not understand a daughter who is obedient. It is also hard to be a husband accustomed to the old pattern and now faced with the new roles of women. It is very hard to be a father who sees his children grow up and become different from what he understands is the right way of life. It is indeed hard today to be a Chicano migrant worker who sees the old way of life changing but who still wonders how he fits into the new and what all of this will really mean to the culture of his people."

Apparently the point of tolerance of our conversation had been reached by Garcia and Julio Cesar. It was time, they felt, to break it up. They crawled over their mother who still sat in the doorway, telling her she was getting fatter every day and pretending to step on her bare toes. Amid gales of laughter from their mother and sisters, they pushed Julia as they ran past, challenging her to a race, daring her to catch them if she could. The race was on, the serious moment of our discussion was lost. Julia would show them that a girl could run as fast as any boy, regardless of what they said. She caught Garcia by his shirttail, dug her heels into the ground, and dragged him to a stop while her mother and the rest of her family laughed hysterically. They would all spend the rest of the day teasing Garcia, telling him he could not run as fast as a girl, while he would protest, saying Julia must have cheated in some way. She wore shoes, he pointed out, whereas he was barefoot and had just stubbed his toe and was slowing down naturally, so it really was not fair that she was given credit because in an honest race she could never have won. No girl could.

NOTES

1. For more on patterns of communication among migrants see Myrtle R. Reul, "Communication with the Migrant," *Child Welfare*, XLIX (March 1970), pp. 137-45. This article was reprinted in *Legal Aid Briefcase*, XXXVII (July 1970), pp. 245-52.

2. Thomas P. Carter in *Mexican-Americans in School: A History of Educational Neglect* (Princeton, N.J.: College Entrance Examination Board, 1970) identifies three interrelated factors that influence Chicano school children: their subcultures, the quality of available education, and the nature of the social system affecting them as a minority group. Carey McWilliams, *North from Mexico* (New York: Greenwood Press, 1968), pp. 79, 171-72, 216-17, and 219, gives a detailed report on how the educational needs of Chicano children were viewed from Texas to California. A third book by Herschel T. Manuel, *Spanish-Speaking Children of the Southwest: Their Education and Public Welfare* (Austin, Tex.: University of Texas Press, 1969), emphasizes the educational deprivation of the Chicano children taught according to an Anglo system and details how this often leads to a high drop-out rate.

3. A book that addresses this subject is Arthur J. Rubel, *Across the Tracks: Mexican-Americans in a Texas City* (Austin, Tex.: University of Texas Press, 1966).

4. Leo Grebler, Joan W. Moore, and Ralph C. Guzma, *The Mexican-American People* (New York: Free Press, 1970), pp. 366-67.

. . . most children need the safety of several parental substitutes to widen their world of choice and increase their sense of a world which is not so vulnerable as the individual home.

Margaret Mead, 20th century
  American anthropologist
Childhood in Contemporary Cultures

19

With the Salazar Family

The Family

We met the Salazars, Joseph and Maria, in 1948 in Michigan. Antonio, their first child, was a tiny baby then. They were one of four Chicano families from Laredo, Texas, who were picking strawberries for our former neighbors that year. Maria's uncle, Ricardo Alvarez, was their crew leader, and all four families were related either by blood or marriage.

Joseph Manuel Salazar, although only twenty, was highly respected by the others as a hard worker who was scrupulously honest in his dealings with everyone. He was also acclaimed by the others in the crew as a "handsome devil" who even at that time of shorter hair wore long sideburns and tilted his Stetson at an impish

Adapted from a chapter by this title in the manuscript *Families of the Open Road* being prepared by Myrtle R. and Paul A. Reul. Some of this material is also mentioned in "Sociocultural Patterns Among Michigan Migrant Farm Workers," Center for Rural Manpower and Public Affairs, Michigan State University, East Lansing, Mich., 1967 (mimeographed).

angle. Sometimes he tilted it far over his eyes and watched Maria from a crack under the brim as he teasingly made comments which brought a shy smile to her lips and occasionally a bright color to her cheeks. It was common knowledge that Joseph idealized his wife and had never had any interest in another woman after he met her. Although it was not uncommon for men of his culture to have considerable sexual freedom even when married, Joseph seemed content to spend his nights with Maria.

Maria Teresa Morales de Salazar was a slender beauty in those days; later she would put on weight which would belie her 115 pounds of 1948, but she would always be beautiful. Her skin was olive, showing her Indian blood; her hair appeared blue-black in the sunlight; but it was her eyes that were her most arresting feature. They were dark, almost black, with long, curling lashes which made them appear even darker and larger. There was a gentleness and yet a feeling of strength hidden within her. At seventeen she already had a certain air of maternalism which made it seem natural that children of the crew should crowd around her and compete with each other for the privilege of holding Antonio or helping her with various household tasks. The two years following that first summer in Michigan Joseph was in the army, but as soon as he was discharged, the Salazars and their relatives returned to the same grower and continued to drive from Texas to Michigan each year. We came to know them well.

In 1963 when we were preparing ourselves for a year of involvement as farm migrant workers, we wrote the Salazars asking if we could, on occasions, become part of their family. We wanted to travel with them, live in the same housing with them, and in this way see firsthand the experiences of Chicano agricultural workers. They said we could. We joined them first in January 1964 in southern Florida.

The Salazar Family in 1964

In 1964 the family consisted of Joseph and Maria and their eight children. As the oldest child, fifteen-and-one-half-year-old Antonio was third in command and was expected to look after and discipline his siblings any time his parents were not present. Antonio was frank in saying he wished his parents would stop reminding him he was the oldest. He did not mind bossing the others around, but somehow it took some of the joy out of his correcting them when he and they were reminded that such was his duty and responsibility because he was the firstborn.

In addition to Antonio, whose deep, masculine voice belied his shy, boyish grin, there was Nita, twelve. Her dark eyes were too large for her thin face. Tiny Elena, eight, was smaller than seven-year-old Contessa. As a result, Contessa took great delight in trying to convince everyone that she was the elder and that Elena was really much younger, even younger than plump, five-year-old Juana.

Four-year-old Delores was the dancer of the family. She made up steps, poised on her toes, and twirled around the room and up and down the roadway constantly imitating the *fandango*. She would snap her fingers, tap her heels, bringing them down hard, and click her tongue against her teeth to imitate the click of castanets. She had discovered watching a street dance that the *fandango* had moments of pause and recovery when the music stopped and started. Even without music she would stop suddenly, stand rigid, her left arm in the air, the fingers of her right hand snapping out the measure, and then suddenly as if on cue she would bound into movement, quickening the pace of her little feet to the tempo of her fantasy guitars.

Delores was the most sensitive of all the children. She would cry when she found a dead bird and when anyone in the family got hurt, whether or not they cried. She idealized her father, and he claimed that she was more beautiful than any of the winners in the local photographic contest and that she had more real talent than the lady bareback rider on the circus posters. Delores announced that she would someday be a circus lady, and her whole family would always have free tickets to come to her performances, a dream the others always encouraged.

Gay, three-year-old Angela laughed contagiously at everything, but it was eighteen-month-old Miguel who was the real monarch of the family. One toss of his mop of black ringlets, one pout on his full lips sent his devoted sisters to his defense, to supply him with anything and everything he wanted.

Family Activities

The family did simple things together and engaged in many family jokes with much teasing and laughter. In the late 1940s it was customary for American families to sit around the radio and listen to George Burns and Gracie Allen, to Ozzie and Harriet Nelson with David and Ricky, or to other serials, the stars of which became such a part of family ritual that they were like family members. Joseph and Maria and their relatives developed a pattern of listening to radio as a family, a habit which was easy to transfer to television when they could finally buy a second-hand set. Milton Berle, Jack Benny, Ed Sullivan, or the fights became as much a part of their family entertainment as had the earlier radio programs. After Joseph was out of the service they bought a small portable television set which they took with them in their travels. Along with Antonio's transistor radio and a friend's guitar, it was their main means of family recreation, although at times they became extravagant and spent their hard-earned money for a carnival or a show, usually a drive-in movie, if they had transportation.

One time after we had joined the family, Joseph returned from a nearby town with tickets for the circus. Holding Delores high above his head until her curls touched the ceiling of the migrant house, he asked her in a serious tone, "I wonder how word got out that you want to be a circus lady, and they sent the circus here so we can go?"

Delores squealed with delight and hugged her father so hard Joseph's Stetson fell off. "Honest, they knew?" she asked, big eyed.

He assured her *they knew* as the others came running, throwing themselves against Joseph, hugging and tugging at his legs.

"Is there really a bareback lady rider with this circus?" Contessa wanted to know.

"Yes," Joseph tousled her hair with his free hand, "and a midway with a Ferris wheel too!"

"Honest to goodness?" chimed in Elena.

"And rides like at the fair?" questioned Juana.

"And rides, and you can go on everything again and again," Joseph promised holding aloft a hand full of tickets.

"You must have spent almost every cent you had," Maria said, trying to sound cross.

"Just about," he admitted cheerfully, "just about."

Joseph opened his arms filled with children and enveloped his wife, hugging her close until she caught the children's enthusiasm and answered Angela's question, "Can we all go, every last one of us?"

"Every last one of us, baby," Maria said, "every last one of us." And she hid her face on Joseph's shoulder so the children would not see that her cheeks were wet with tears.

Joseph's Background

Joseph Salazar had come to south Texas from a northern Mexican village. His parents were recruited to pick cotton when he was an infant. They were promised good housing and good pay. Nothing for them in south Texas proved to be as it was described by those who came to their village to recruit them to work. Expecting to find a higher standard of living when they came to the United States, they found instead that their first housing in Texas was a floorless shack with the promised cookstove a pile of field stones. Joseph's mother arranged three of the stones so that fire could be burned in the center, and on them she placed pots in the way of their people who once had said that the mysterious power of the Old God, the god of fire, lived between the three stones of the hearth. Each morning it was Joseph's mother's duty to fan to life the smouldering coals in this hearth and to begin each day with the rhythmic slapping and flattening of the maize-dough between her hands into the pancake-like *tortillas* or *tlaxcalli* just as each day had been started by the women of their people for thousands of years.[1]

If Joseph's entire family worked, the pay they received then was barely enough to sustain them. Each of the children was in the cotton field full time by the age of eight. Even when the male members of the family became naturalized American citizens their standard of living was not improved. They were still as poor as they had been in Mexico.

Like many migrants of his generation who lived and worked

under these conditions, Joseph never attended school. He was
needed to help support his family, and compared to that need an
education was not important, or so he and his parents thought. He
could barely read or write at the time of his marriage. His induc-
tion two years later into the United States army provided his only
formal education. Although he spent most of the time in Korea, he
took a reading improvement course, and by the time he returned
home he could read near a seventh-grade level.

Maria's Background

Maria had had three years of formal schooling before she
dropped out to work with her parents, who also picked cotton. She
was fifteen when she and Joseph were married; he was eighteen.
Except for the two years that Joseph was in the army and Maria
stayed in Laredo with her parents, the entire seventeen years of
their marriage had been spent following the crops. Their eight
children were born in seven states. Maria worked steadily at her
husband's side, staying home only on the last days of her pregnancy or immediately following the birth of her baby. She took
each new baby to the field when it was a week old. She would put
the baby in a clothes basket covered with mosquito netting and
place it in the shade of a tree, car, or nearby bush where her baby
slept. If there was no natural shade, Maria would cover one corner
of the basket to make shade. Later when her baby was a toddler,
she would use a large cardboard box for a playpen. She would
move it with her from one side of the field to the other and check
it each time she emptied her basket, bucket, or hamper. As the
older daughter, Nita had the major task of giving physical care to
the younger children although Antonio was their disciplinarian. If
Nita too were helping in the fields, the responsibility for child care
was passed on to the next oldest sibling.

Parents' Attitudes toward Their Children's Future

Although the Salazar family would return to Laredo for part of
each winter, a truck box, a labor compound, or housing on some
grower's farm was more familiar to the children than the tiny,
three-room house they called home and which they shared with

Maria's parents. Like most migrant parents, Joseph and Maria did not want their children to become migrant farm laborers; they wanted them to have an easier life.

Although they saw education as a way to obtain that life, it was difficult for them with their limited income and their constant moving to keep their children in school. Furthermore, they often found it difficult to comprehend modern education and felt inadequate to offer encouragement to their children, even though they saw their own lack of an education as the major reason for their present living conditions. They were aware that teachers were impatient when Antonio, Nita, Elena, or Contessa interrupted the regular routine of classes by arriving in the middle of a semester. Joseph and Maria knew how difficult it was for their children to attend strange schools and sense that they were not wanted, either by children or adults.

Parents said that, although it was not true everywhere, rejection occurred so often that they understood why large numbers of Mexican-American teenagers became discouraged and dropped out of school. The young people did not feel the schools wanted them, but Joseph and Maria knew that by dropping out they only perpetuated the same pattern of limited education as their own parents had.

This was the Salazar family with whom we would travel. This was the Chicano family who allowed us to become part of them, and in turn they became our family in order that we might view the experiences of farm migrants from their vantage point.

In Florida

It was a Sunday afternoon in early January when the truck in which we rode pulled into a labor compound[2] in southern Florida. The camp was at the end of a narrow road lined with fields of tomatoes, beans, and sweet corn stretching a mile on each side in long, even rows. Trucks and cars loaded with migrants were arriving from Texas, Alabama, and points north.

The compound was enclosed by a barbwire fence. The driving speed, five miles an hour, was posted at the gate, but as an extra control measure ruts had been dug every few feet across the roadway. Thus the road itself became an obstacle course over which each driver guided his vehicle in and around the many children who used the narrow track for a baseball diamond or a sandbox.

The camp was rectangular in shape with two-room cabins arranged in long rows. Each building, approximately eight by sixteen feet, was covered on the outside with roll-brick type roofing. Each room had an outside door and two glassless screened windows. These window openings were closed by batten boards hinged at the top, which formed a shutter when propped open with a stick. Each room rented for five dollars a week.

There were nearly 200 families in the camp that Sunday afternoon who hoped to find work the next day in the tomatoes or beans and possibly later in the sweet corn and cabbage. They often paid their rent with money borrowed from their crew leaders or a friend. The larger families needed two rooms, and even then they were crowded. A very few rented a cabin and a half. After the first week if work was scarce, they would give up the extra room.

The camp provided cot frames, a table, two chairs, and a two-burner kerosene cookstove for each family. The bedding was furnished by the migrants themselves, including mattresses. Each room was illuminated by a single, naked bulb suspended from the ceiling. If the bulb burned out the migrant could buy a replacement at the camp commissary or go to bed in the dark.

At the center of the compound was a utility building with showers, toilets, and an automatic washer and dryer slotted for twenty cents. There were faucets from which drinking and wash water could be carried back to the individual cabins.

Our Housing

As the cultural head of our family, Joseph made arrangements for our housing. He rented three rooms of which he gave us one. The others used the two rooms. If they wished, Elena and Contessa could share our room. For fifteen dollars Joseph received four narrow folding cots and three chairs, one with a broken back. He gave us a cot; if Contessa and Elena joined us, two of us would sleep on the floor. We spread a blanket over the link springs as we did not have a mattress.

Since our living quarters needed cleaning, we bought supplies at

the camp store. A small box of detergent, a scrub brush, scouring powder, and a can of insect spray were nearly double the prices that they would have been in a supermarket. At the commissary we were told that a white family had just vacated our half of the cabin. Apparently they had left hurriedly. On the floor, as if dropped accidentally, were a woman's red shoe, a green plastic belt, a baby's bonnet—all practically new. In one corner was a pile of coffee grounds dumped over broken beer bottles, a new head for a sponge mop, a plate, and a bowl nearly full of rice and black beans.

Long ago a former occupant had attached a low shelf on the back wall as a niche for a wash pan. A piece of blue plastic shower curtain was thumbtacked around the shelf. The plastic was so brittle with brown streaks of age and dirt that as I tore it away it cracked along the folds. Behind the curtain were two rusty gallon pails whose ammonia odor and contents proclaimed them as urinals. Probably they were used at night, or rainy days, or for emergencies when the distance to the utility building seemed too great.

We borrowed a pail from Maria and poured hot, sudsy water across our floor. Little bublets of dust foamed along the cracks as the sudsy water disappeared in the dry wood. After several pails of water and much scrubbing, there remained only the fresh odor of soap and clean wood. Our one-room cabin was ready for occupancy.

Camp Atmosphere

Then we toured the camp. Only Angela, Delores, and Contessa went with us as Miguel was asleep and the others had duties to help Maria or Joseph. Delores danced just ahead as we walked along the road, but both Contessa and Angela felt a stronger need for close physical contact. Contessa was content to link her arm through mine while Angela wrapped her chubby little hand around my husband's forefinger and refused to let loose even for him to fill or light his pipe until we were back again at our quarters late in the afternoon.

Most of the women of the camp were washing clothes. Since few felt they could afford the laundromat, they were using their own galvanized sheet-metal washtubs and scrubboards. Because there were few clotheslines, they hung their laundry on the barbwire fence, using the barbs in lieu of clothespins. Some of the women or young girls were cleaning their living quarters as we had cleaned ours. They swept the soapy water through the open door.

Living Openly

Half hidden by a truck, two young lovers melted hungrily into each other's arms in a long embrace. There was no place in the camp to conceal their physical desire for each other; it was expressed openly, matter-of-factly, as a natural phenomenon of courtship. They might move in and live together in an open common-law marriage, or, if old enough to meet state requirements and if financially able to afford a license, they might be married by a justice of the peace or a minister.

After passing three rows of houses we came to the crap game. Six players and double that number of spectators sat on their haunches around an army blanket shooting crap. The old blanket spread in the dust of the roadway provided a surface for the rolling dice and the assorted piles of quarters, half dollars, and "green foldin' money" which changed hands. Each player cupped the dice lovingly, blew on them for luck, and rolled them between moist palms crying, "Come to pappy! Baby needs a new pair of shoes! Be there baby! Roll seven!" There was tense silence as the group watched for the facing of the dice. In the excitement of the game one man swore softly to himself, repeating one four-letter word over and over irrespective of who won.

The cries of the crap game were at times all but drowned by a public-address system broadcasting from an open spot near the utility building. A visiting evangelistic minister was preaching a sermon to a crowd composed mostly of Black women and children. The young minister tried enthusiastically to encourage his congregation to sing to the recorded hymns, but few were familiar with the words. Finally, someone suggested the public-address system be turned off and they sing the songs they knew, "real soul music." One Black woman began to sing: *Let's all gather at the river . . . the beautiful . . . the beautiful . . . river . . . that flows past the throne of God.* Others joined, clapping their hands to beat out the rhythm, swaying in union.

Suddenly an angry voice carried above all other sounds, a father denouncing his young son. "You lazy pup," he shouted, slapping at the boy. "Go fetch some water so your ma kin git supper. Now git goin' . . . 'cause I'm starving' and I'm plum' gonna take my belt ta ya if ya hang 'round hyeh another moment."

Interest in the crap game diminished. The betting continued, however, and the piles of money again changed hands. Two men started a contest with trained grass frogs to see whose frog would jump the farthest when it was nudged with a pointed stick. Since bets ran high, the gamblers borrowed money from each other to pay them. Some went back to the housing to get money their wives had tucked away to pay the rent or buy food. Usually they did not ask or tell their wives, they just took the money. As the male heads of the households, they felt that the money was theirs to spend in whatever way they wished. Some wives did not agree with this philosophy and openly expressed their anger; a few tried physically to prevent their husbands from taking the money; but most of the women, regardless of race, accepted this arrangement without question, seeing gambling as "a need of a man," like his need for sex and for food.

The voices of the minister and his singers had died down in prayer and then came again louder than ever, deep with emotional feeling. *There is power . . . power, Wonder working pow'r in the blood . . . of the Lamb . . . there is power, power, Wonder working pow'r, in the precious blood of the Lamb.*

Further down the road a group of male Chicano teenagers were playing softball. The younger children and their fathers stood watching, cheering and calling comments. A transistor radio propped against a stone, its volume turned to its highest, blared rock music. Two preadolescent Black girls walked by, stopping long enough to do their improvised interpretation of the latest dance steps. They were in a world of their own, unmindful of their male audience, not really caring what anyone thought as long as they were left alone to do "their own thing."

Delores stood and watched, enthralled with their movements. Once as they danced she spun around on her toe and dropped to one knee in a graceful curtsy such as she had seen the ballerina do on television. The Black girls ignored her, so she stood by until they left; then she did a few steps in a perfect mirrored imitation of what the older girls had done and walked on ahead of us as if she had no further interest in the music or the softball game.

Seated in the doorway of every occupied cabin were members of families, both young and old. There were some who kept strictly to themselves, who appeared almost unfriendly. Most, however, spoke and waved to acquaintances and strangers alike and were willing to talk about their experiences, assuming everyone who was in the camp on that day must be there for work tomorrow. They were almost eager to have someone who was willing to talk with them.

The camp occupants represented different nationalities and races. The occupants were different, and yet they had a common bond of employment. They were in the same farm labor camp and would harvest the same fields. They had arrived in various ways, some riding in trucks and buses, some in their own cars, others hitchhiking or even walking. Although the majority had come from south Texas or from other places in Florida, they had followed different routes and had arrived at different times. They unpacked and went to see if a neighbor had heard of a family with whom they worked last season or in some other state. Sometimes they explored the camp even before they had unpacked.

The security light by the utility building blazed in an arc that cast a diffused glow over the entire camp. Slowly the families went inside. From the open windows came murmured voices without words, the blare of a radio, a baby's cry, a hacking cough or a muffled laugh.

Slowly the sounds subsided. Weary, spent from long hours of travel, the workers sought oblivion—on narrow cots, on hard floors covered with a blanket or a coat. One by one the single, glaring light bulbs were turned off, the cabins were darkened, the radios were stilled, and only an occasional forced, hacking cough or the cry of a child broke the stillness. The camp slept.

In Texas

The second time we joined the Salazar family was in Texas. They had returned to the lower Rio Grande Valley after the tomatoes and sweet corn had frozen in Florida and there was no early spring work in Alabama or Georgia because of heavy cold rains. Joseph and Antonio got a few days' work potting trees in a nursery where they had worked previously. The family moved in with Maria's aunt and uncle, both of whom were now in their early sixties. This was the uncle who once had been their crew leader but who now was badly crippled with rheumatoid arthritis, although he worked odd jobs whenever he could find them. The aunt did housework for an Anglo family, and they lived frugally on her wages as their main income. But their home was still open to all relatives who needed a place to sleep or a meal, just as it would always be open to relatives and friends who had such a close relationship of obligation and trust (*de confianza*) that, although they were not blood or in-law relatives, they could act in the same familiar fashion and were as welcome as if they were family.

Urban Ghetto Living

The Salazars' relatives lived in a long, narrow apartment building squeezed between other long, narrow buildings, heavy with the sour odors of clogged plumbing, rotting wood, and garbage. The front room flush with the sidewalk was once a grocery store. It now housed a cousin and his nine children. The uncle's apartment was at the rear, two rooms and a windowless kitchen. The living room was only wide enough for two ragged over-stuffed chairs, a chest of drawers, and a television set.

There were two double beds and a cot in the bedroom. The aunt and uncle and twelve-year-old Nita slept in one bed. The four younger children—Juana, Delores, Angela, and Miguel—slept in the other, cross-wise, with the baby at the foot. As a rule Joseph and Maria slept on the narrow cot although some nights Joseph slept on the floor. Antonio curled across the two upholstered chairs in front of the television set. A bed was made on the floor at his feet for Elena and Contessa.

There was only one bath in the building. Originally there was only a toilet, but ten years ago the landlord installed a second-hand tub whose dripping faucets produced only cold water. The plugs for both the tub and the lavatory had long since disappeared and the only way to hold the water was to stuff the drain with a cloth or tissue, which in turn helped to plug the draining system even more. No one in the building except Maria's aunt felt any responsibility for scrubbing the bath; and as there were no cleaning people, the tub, bowl, and lavatory were usually scaled with water discoloration, rust, and dirt. Maria's family used their own galvanized washtub for bathing as it was easier to fill with hot water.

The children from families in adjacent buildings played in the open area where one apartment house was shorter than the others. They also played in the narrow space between the buildings, which on one side was barely wide enough for a nine-year-old to squirm through should a ball or a cat disappear into the passageway. The children were always afraid that the cat would be hurt by the rats, whose domains were the garbage cans and the gaping holes in the foundations of the building from which they sometimes gnawed their way into the apartments above.

We arrived after the family had eaten. Elena took me to the kitchen where some tortillas, beans, and hardboiled eggs had been saved for our coming. She pulled the string attached to the single bulb in the ceiling. The room was flooded with light which brought into bold relief the cockroaches swarming over the walls searching for an escape. Some of the insects dropped onto the table and hid under dishes; others dropped to the floor and scurried under the ragged linoleum. Their thin agile bodies vanished as if by magic. In the darkness they would reappear until the light was turned on; then they would scurry to hide again.

In Idaho

For a long moment I lay in the darkness wondering why I was awake. I recalled the events of the previous afternoon when we had arrived in the Snake River Valley of southern Idaho to work in the sugarbeets. Since this grower had no housing, he gave us bales of straw and a discarded innerspring mattress and told us to sleep in the barn.

Joseph gave the two of us the mattress and insisted that we sleep in the lean-to on the side of the barn while he and Maria shook out the straw to make beds for themselves and the children in one corner of the barn.

I lay in the dark wondering if I had been awakened by the

restless stirring of Miguel or by the bulge of an uncoiled spring in the mattress suddenly pressing into my side. Suddenly I was aware that my face, arms, neck, and back burned as if on fire. There was a moving sensation along my hairline and across my cheek. I brushed my face. My fingers crushed a sticky mass against my forehead. I smelled a foul, pungent odor.

I felt on the floor for the flashlight and turned the beam on the bed. Scurrying away in the floodlight were hundreds of newly hatched bedbugs, barely discernable against the dirty pinstriped ticking. I moved the shaft of light along the edges of the mattress. Large bedbugs were clustered in the corners, in the folds of the material, in rust-brown masses. I ran the arc of light up and down the walls. Here and there a broad, flat, rust-red insect disappeared between the cracks. Because the lean-to had once been a chicken coop, the odor of chickens still lingered and, although the grower had seen that the building was hosed out, some of the floor and wall boards were stained by slight remains of droppings where the chickens had roosted. Since bedbugs live as parasites on fowls, they are often found in bird and chicken nests. They may also exist for long periods of time without food. The day had been hot, perfect for hatching eggs, and thus the building was swarming with infestation.

Coping with the Environment

The only hope for rest that night was to find some repellent to drive away our unwelcome guests. An old barn lantern hung from a nail in a rafter. It had provided us with light for our evening meal, and now it would provide us with a solution to our problem. The base was half full of kerosene. We poured some over a handkerchief, saturating the cloth. We worked by flashlight, wiping along the edges of the mattress, pushing the cloth into the folds. We squeezed drops from the handkerchief onto the corners of the mattress. The bugs of all sizes welled up, running frantically away from the light and the spread of the kerosene. The odor of the lamp's oil on the dusty, mildewed mattress was nearly as repugnant as the odor of bedbugs.

We could hear the fitful cries of Miguel and the restless movements of Angela and Delores a few feet away in the main area of the barn where they slept on pallets of straw. The next morning Miguel's face was blotched, and one eyelid was swollen closed. The older children showed self-inflicted fingernail scratches where they had dug at their arms and legs to alleviate the burning, itching discomfort of insect bites.

That day Maria and I fumigated and cleaned to rid our quarters of the bedbugs while the men worked in the fields. We lugged the mattress out into the sunlight, but the task of cleaning and fumigating was almost impossible for the area of the old barn was huge. Everywhere there were deep cracks that provided natural hiding places for the insects, so our efforts seemed futile.

This was not to be our last encounter with bedbug-infested housing during our migrant experience. At one place the corrugated cardboard partitions used to separate a toolshed into stalls for individual families provided an ideal nesting place for bedbugs and cockroaches. Those walls of cardboard were almost as difficult to fumigate for insect infestation as were the wood walls of the barn in south Idaho.

After that experience we never traveled again without a can of insect repellent, and before we went to bed we saturated the bedding and the walls, especially in the area where the children would sleep.

The Truck in the Mountains

The sides of the truck were solid wood, as was the tailgate which dropped to form a step. When closed, this tailgate became a windowless door which locked the riders inside. The truck box was completely enclosed with a gray canvas tarpaulin whose loose ends hung over the tailgate or rolled up to allow for ventilation. Although most migrant truck boxes are provided with benches around the inside, this one had only foot lockers, crates, and boxes which contained the possessions of the riders and doubled as seats. Blankets and mattresses on the floor were the beds for children and the pregnant women.

Because the truck box was enclosed, there was no sensation of distance or nearness. There was only the sensation of sameness. It was a sameness with a rolling, jerking, bumping, bruising motion. There was no view of the countryside unless one stood on tiptoe

and peered out under the edges of the tarpaulin. It was impossible to have an orientation to direction. There was only the feeling of constant motion and the rush of the truck over the highway.

It was impossible to keep from bumping into a fellow passenger or the sharp edge or corner of a box when the driver braked to a quick stop. Being so long in motion made everything seem unreal. The only reality at all in that world of open highways, drive-ins, grocery stores, and service stations was the truck. The truck became an island of security. It was our home.

Our family had joined a crew of families traveling to the Yellowstone River Valley of eastern Montana to thin sugar beets. The crew leader rode in the cab with the driver. The other men and their families rode in the box. Since we were a few days late in finishing the job in Idaho, the crew leader was pushing to make the trip as fast as possible. We made few stops.

In Transit

The adults in our crew had learned to relax and rest through years of such travel. Most of them slept for hours. They eased their tired back muscles by leaning hard against the sides of the truck. They learned to let their arms hang limp, to give themselves completely to the motion. They knew that eventually they would reach their destination. The roads they took or the direction they traveled was the concern of the driver, not theirs. They asked few questions about where they were. They expressed little interest in what others did in the communities through which they passed.

School teachers and others who know the extensive travel of migrants assume school children will have a good grasp of geography. They are unaware that much of the travel is at night when the riders are asleep or that the children are often seated on the floor of a truck box which provides little opportunity for them to view the countryside or even to know the names of places they pass through.

Our meals were mostly hastily prepared sandwiches, a can of cold beans opened with a jackknife, or hot dogs from a drive-in washed down with pop and hot coffee. If the driver stopped at a spot where we could build a fire, we warmed the beans; otherwise we ate them cold from the can.

If the adults were not sleeping they talked about their experiences. Usually the men told of their exploits, how many fights they had won and how much money they had earned. All of this was a good-natured, grandiose kind of bragging which everyone recognized for what it was, but which men were allowed to indulge in because it was part of their culture and because they were men. When the young children and women were not present, the men were also expected to take part in grandiose bragging about their sexual exploits.

Sometimes the old people told stories of their childhoods in Old Mexico. Other times Gregorio, a friend of Antonio, would take his guitar from his case, tune the strings, and sing the songs of his people. Many were old songs that dealt with the misfortune of the migrant. One which the older people liked and to which they were always adding new verses was "*Los Betabeleros,*" a ballad that told the story of workers recruited in San Antonio in 1923 to work in the sugar beets of Michigan.

In the long hours of the afternoon the children played guessing games—whose fist held the pop bottle cap they passed back and forth or whose father would buy them candy or pop or both when the truck stopped for gasoline. Miguel's fat legs carried him in a wobbly uncertain gait across the blanket from his mother to Nita, to Contessa, and back to his mother. He flashed an impish grin as he teasingly approached each in turn and convulsed into hysterical laughter when he fell over his own feet and landed in Antonio's lap. His big brother tossed him across his shoulder, laughingly threatening to throw him out. Delores and Angela pounced on Antonio, and for a few minutes there was a tussling struggle of laughing shouting children until their father reminded them there was too little space in the truck for such rough play. His voice was stern, filled with the authority expected of a father in his culture; but he looked at them with loving approval. They understood him and respected him because he was their father. They obeyed and returned to a quiet game.

Calamity

It was near the Continental Divide, at a spot where a stream plunged into an abyss with a single leap, that the motor burned out. The attendant at the last service station who had changed the oil had only partially tightened the pan plug. The oil had slowly seeped away, draining out around the plug until it was dangerously low. On an upward grade the motor began to clatter. The truck vibrated, and before the driver could pull off on a level spot, a rod had gone through the cylinder wall. The extent of the damage could not be determined without the help of a mechanic, but first we had to find one.

The driver determined from a road map that the nearest town having a garage that could supply parts was fifty-seven miles away. He made the decision. He and Joseph would walk in that direction hoping they could get a ride. He stated he knew that there was a good possibility they would walk all the way. The traffic that time of year was heavy through the mountains—mostly tourists—but drivers, probably fearful of picking up any hitchhiker in that remote area, would be afraid to offer a ride to two migrant men.

Those of us who would stay with the truck gave the driver all the money we had. We had learned long ago, as all migrants learn, to be prepared to pay cash for anything. If migrants cannot pay cash or have their grower employer vouch for them, guaranteeing payment, there is no likelihood of their getting credit, especially in a part of the country where they are unknown.

Family Roles

Antonio was in charge while his father was away. He was responsible for seeing that his mother, his sisters, and Miguel were safe and warm. He was their protector. At dusk he ordered them all into the truck, reminding them that there were bears in the area. They obeyed him as they would have obeyed their father. True to her culture, Maria accepted the fact that her oldest son was the absolute head of her household while Joseph was absent. Accepting the subservient position of women in her culture, she knew that her son expected her to carry out his instruction even as he expected Contessa and Miguel to obey him. Therefore, she and the children crawled into the truck and huddled against each other for warmth.

Coping with the Situation

Other families joined them, mainly women, small children, and one or two old men. The other men sat by the fire over which we heated cans of black beans for our supper. The truck box was too small to provide a sleeping space for everyone. The mothers encouraged their children to stretch out, while they sat with their backs against the truck walls. They pulled their few blankets around their shivering shoulders and spread them tent-like over the children trying to sleep at their feet.

The sun had been warm during the day, but with darkness the temperature dropped. A recent ten-inch snowfall had closed the high passes in the Teton mountains further south, and the night wind was bitter cold. Near dawn the temperature dropped further. Frost settled through the canvas tarpaulin, forming a coating of ice a few inches above our heads. The cold penetrated our blankets. We were too uncomfortable to sleep. Our only solution was to crawl out of the truck and put more wood and pine cones on the fire. We huddled near the blaze until sunrise while the smoke blackened our faces. We were to repeat this experience several times until we burned all the branches we could find in the area, and still Joseph and the driver had not returned. We went further and further from the truck to scrounge for fallen limbs and pine cones as we had no way to cut trees.

Two days later the men arrived with a wrecker. Our truck was hauled to the garage, and the motor replaced.

In Wisconsin

The House

The ornate gingerbread along the facade of the porch and the peak of the roof proclaimed that the farmhouse had been built before the turn of the century. It was built by the grower's parents a few years after they had emigrated to Wisconsin from Germany. When the house was new, the room at the front had been the parlor where, according to the grower, the now ragged blinds were raised only when company was entertained; otherwise the room was kept dark so that the carpet and wallpaper would not fade. The house had once been the showplace of the farming neighborhood. Now aged, part of the floorboards of the front porch were missing, making it necessary for those who used the house to enter through the kitchen door. The parlor, the living room, and the dining room each housed a separate migrant family, and two more lived in the five bedrooms on the second floor. These five unrelated families used the common kitchen with its wood-burning cookstove and the privy in the back yard.

A clematis vine clung to a rusty trellis and framed the dining room window with purple petals. Below that same window were the remains of a flower garden. A few weed-choked roses, delphiniums, and day lilies showed behind an untrimmed hedge. The ten members of the Salazar family and their two adopted family members were housed in what originally was the dining room which had a bay window looking out upon the flower garden.

Working Conditions

The winds stirred the cucumber vines with a breath that was hot. All day twelve-year-old Nita worked with the rest of us, leaning, picking, filling the five-gallon paint pails with which the grower had provided us for picking containers. All day she dragged the half-filled pails through the heat. Wet with sweat, her blouse clung to her thin body. It was hard work, but in order to get through the winter her father needed the money that he would get from his share of the cucumbers.[3] So Nita and all members of the family older than Juana worked, picking cucumbers. Five-year-old Juana cared for Delores, Angela, and Miguel when they were not in the day-care program held at one of the nearby schools, and even there she was the older sister in charge.

The Dream of a Twelve-Year-Old

In the evening when Nita returned to the house after being in the field all day, she dug the weeds away from the roses in the flowerbed under the dining room window. When I asked why, she said simply, "I pretend this is my house, and if so I want my rose garden to be as beautiful as one I once saw in a park."

On another day she stood in front of an ornate, built-in china closet which covered most of one wall in the dining room. She ran her hands lovingly over the oak paneling, opening the once-glassed doors and pulling at the ornamented brass knobs of the heavy drawers that formed the base. Her face was a study of emotion. There was longing in her being, deep longing in her sensitive dark eyes and the lonely movements of her body. She brushed her cheek along the door leaving the imprint of her lips on the one remaining pane of glass. I spoke to her softly from the doorway, "Nita, you look thoughtful," I said; "tell me what you are thinking." She answered, "Oh, this is the most beautiful house I have ever seen." Her voice choked. Her eyes seemed a darker shade of brown, and, although they were free of tears, I had the impression standing there that this slender, young girl who dreamed of someday becoming a nurse was weeping internally. She ran the tip of her tongue along her upper lip. Her tearless weeping subsided. She spoke slowly. "It is the most beautiful place I have ever seen. I wish our family could have it all to ourselves and that we could stay here forever." She hesitated, swallowing hard. Her voice was strong, full, and vibrant like a crescendo on a violin. "I wish," she said, "we didn't always have to go away. I wish we too could just belong somewhere."

NOTES

1. For a very beautiful description of the role of the Mexican peasant woman as she begins her day, see John Steinbeck, *The Pearl* (New York: Viking Press, 1947). See also Oscar Lewis, *The Children of Sanchez: Autobiography of a Mexican Family,* Vintage Books (New York: Random House, Inc., 1961). For an interpretation of the psychological meaning of the sound of the preparation of food as well as the place food plays in the emotional needs of people see Myrtle R. Reul, "What It Is Like To Be Hungry," *School Foodservice Journal,* May 1973, pp. 22-23.

2. This is my term.

3. A rather common practice in cucumber harvest is to share the proceeds from the sale of the first picking between the grower and those who harvest the crop. This is used as an incentive to encourage workers to pick the fields clean, which is most important in the first picking as it prepares the fields for the actual harvest, which begins with the second picking. Usually the division between grower and picker is half and half. The first picking always produces fruit that is inconsistent in size, shape, and volume. Often the first cucumbers will not bring top market. In addition to making a clean "sweep" of the field for their share, the workmen are expected to weed the cucumbers and to arrange the vines so they will be easier to handle in future pickings.

20

To Pick a Lug of Cherries

To the cherry grower faced with the harvest of his 1964 bumper
crop, we represented four more hands to separate juicy, ripe fruit
from untouched trees. We were in the Grand Traverse region, the
center of Michigan's cherry belt, where more cherries are harvested
than any other spot in the world and where the 1964 tart cherry
crop would be a record-breaking 611 million pounds on top of 266
million pounds of sweet cherries. For the first time packers and
processors in the area had established daily quotas on the number
of lugs of fruit they would accept. Because growers were feeling
the pinch on the amount they could sell, migrants were limited in
the number of pounds they could pick. Pickers were allowed to
work four hours a day. They could not pay their living and travel
expenses. Thousands left for other parts of the country, for other
crops.

It was August. Normally the cherry season in northern Michigan
is over, but this year vast sections of most orchards were still
untouched. Close to the shores of Lake Michigan, on hillsides,
along peninsulas jutting into the blueness of the water were the

319

fruit plantings. Trees were a mass of red with branches touching the ground. Fearful that limbs would break under the weight of the fruit, growers asked pickers to strip lower branches and leave the tops. The cherries were smaller than usual and overripe. Picking a lug was slow work.

Then suddenly the quota was lifted. Processing plants wanted more cherries. Growers were crying for additional pickers. There were few migrants in the area. Farmers advertised radio appeals in English and Spanish, hoping to attract harvesters from other sections. Orchard foremen became systematic. Rows were assigned, and workers were told to "pick clean." Many workers resented working on trees that had fruit left only in the top or situations in which certain pickers or crews got better rows than they. There was much dissatisfaction among the laborers.

We Arrive in Grand Traverse County

A few days earlier we had left Joseph, Marie, and the children in the Wisconsin cucumbers. We planned to join a Florida crew in New Jersey. We drove eastward. As we neared the border where Wisconsin touches Michigan's Upper Peninsula, we bought the sixth new tire of our trip. The cost cut deeply into our funds. We needed to find work, and soon.

We had been plagued with car repairs in state after state throughout the entire eleven and one-half months. Besides six new tires, we had replaced a fuel pump, a muffler and tail pipe, a battery, a carburetor, and two gasoline tanks. These replacements were in addition to a complete transmission overhaul, motor tune-ups, and replacement of brake linings and light bulbs. Our garage bills were unbelievably high, and much of the workmanship was less than dependable. By the time we arrived in the Michigan cherries it had become apparent that we could have traveled for less money by public conveyance than we spent in the garages. Our transportation expenses were no different from those of our fellow migrants who are frequently overcharged for car, bus, or truck repairs that barely last until they can reach the next community or garage. We, as they, tried under those circumstances to cut food costs, putting car up-keep first on our priority list. It became more important to buy gasoline and oil than to have a doctor's prescrip-

tion filled, go to a dentist, or buy meat, fruit, or vegetables or a
newspaper.

As we entered Grand Traverse County our funds were nearly
depleted. We would need more money if we were to continue to
the east coast. Hearing the appeal for cherry pickers, we decided to
stop and work. Cherry picking for us would not be an entirely new
experience, and we should be able to earn enough money in a week
or ten days to take us on to the cabbage of New Jersey without the
danger of being stranded in an area that might not provide work.

We were neither strangers to cherry picking nor strangers to
Grand Traverse County. We knew people there. We thought we
knew the working and living conditions for migrant workers in the
area. Had we been asked on that August day, we would have said
that we knew the area well. We would have said that, as the then
third largest user of migrant labor,[1] Michigan rated well on the
national scale and that the western section of the state, from Grand
Traverse County to Berrien County, included communities whose
attitudes and awareness of the needs of migrant workers were more
progressive than those found elsewhere. We thought we knew
Grand Traverse County and we did—as tourists, visiting friends, as
professionals teaching there, as a liaison between the Michigan
State University School of Social Work and certain social work
agencies, and as an insurance salesman—but what we did not know
was Grand Traverse County from the perspective of migrant
workers. For years we had driven past migrant housing in the area.
We had seen migrants in the stores of the communities. We had
spoken to them and asked about their working experiences. They
had told us the area was a "wonderful place," that they always
made "good money" in cherries, and that that was why they
returned year after year.

We had attended several cherry festivals. We thought our eyes
had been open, but we were soon to discover that we had been
only superficial observers, seeing selectively what we wanted to see.
We had not seen the migrant housing from the viewpoint of the
large families who stayed there, from the viewpoint of migrant
women and children, from the viewpoint of various ethnic backgrounds and racial feelings. We had not seen the area from the
point of view of the migrant who had such limited income and who
had to contend with the cost of food sky-rocketing. Independent

storekeepers maintained two price lists, one for year-round residents, the other for tourists and migrants. We had not noticed that seldom, if ever, were migrant workers directly involved in cherry festivals except as observers lining the sidewalks. They were not part of any community decision-making process.[2]

We found in our short experience as migrant cherry pickers in the region that what we saw was quite different from what we had seen over many years of professional contacts. We were to discover that we had not seen certain aspects of the area until we had seen them through the eyes of a migrant at the top of a cherry tree.[3]

Before we began our travels, we had known that an individual's perception is conditioned by his or her experiences. We had also known that each human being sees and hears selectively. It was in the Michigan cherries, however, that we saw familiar things take on a strange dimension, even a different meaning, when experienced from a new vantage point. And so it was to be that we returned to a section of the country, beautiful beyond description, a section of the country we had loved since first we had seen it, but this time we came in a role different from any we had experienced there before.

Our faces and hands were browned from weeks of sun. Our diet for months had consisted of bare necessities. We were thin to the point of looking emaciated. Our muscles were firm. We moved up and down ladders in a way that said we were accustomed to such a life. We looked like what we were, itinerant farm workers.

We selected a road in a section of Grand Traverse County where we had no previous contacts. A grower, a Mr. Carl Smith,[4] was advertising for pickers. We asked for work. He gave us buckets and a picking harness and assigned us a row across his orchard. The orchard manager supplied us with lugs. Later our filled lugs were loaded onto a tractor-wagon, and we were credited the amount we had picked.

When we were not working in this orchard, we filled our car with gasoline and drove up and down familiar roads; we crossed and criss-crossed the county. We covered other counties from Charlevoix to Kalkaska and communities from Northport to Hart, Shelby, and Muskegon. We talked with migrants—whites, Blacks, and Spanish-speaking. We saw their housing and its contradicting extremes—housing that was excellent, housing that was deplorable, housing that gave privacy, housing that was overcrowded. We went back to the orchard where we worked and talked with those who picked nearby about their feelings and impression of their experiences.

Remembering our previous superficial contacts with migrants in the area who had told us all was well in their worlds, we could appreciate Sister Woods's comment that "Mexican-Americans are hesitant to express negative feelings to Anglo-Americans."[5] We would add that they are more willing to express their feelings to Anglo fellow migrants, whom they see as having many of their same experiences, than they are to Anglo nonmigrants. We also soon became aware of how almost impossible it is for a community or an employer to find out how Black migrants feel. John Fraser Hart described this difficulty when writing about the Southern Black employee and his relationship with his white employer with whom he maintained his job over the years "only by practicing the most abject subservience." "It is a truism that nobody's cook [in the South] believes in integration."[6] Jack E. Weller found among the peoples of Appalachia that subjects which "might engender conflict are not discussed."[7] Certainly feelings about race and crowded housing, the end of the harvest bonus, and fair employment practices are subjects that "might engender conflict" and therefore may be denied or ignored by the white migrant from the mountains of Kentucky, Tennessee, or northern Georgia.

In other words, we very quickly came to realize why residents in the cherry area of Michigan, even professionals, had never heard a migrant, regardless of race or ethnic background, really describe how he honestly felt about the conditions under which he grew up or under which he now lived and worked.

We Begin Work

On our first day in the cherries, the sky was overcast, a pleasant relief from the recent torrid heat. We worked quietly, not talking even to each other, absorbing the "feel" of the orchard, sensing the presence of those who worked on the rows next to ours but being careful not to speak to them until we had some indication that they wished to acknowledge our existence. We were the newcomers, the outsiders, those who were the most suspect until some sense of relationship could be established. The other workers would watch us, even as we watched them, to see if we were novices or professional pickers, to decide if we were locals or migrants, to observe if we picked fast and clean or if we cheated and sneaked from our row to steal the best fruit on some other picker's tree. In some cases we would never be trusted; we would always be ignored and avoided.

The cherries were soft to the touch. Their juice stained our skin. It dripped across our wrists, forming an adhesive. Soon our hands and arms were covered with a gummy dirt that smelled of crushed cherry leaves and would take scrubbing to remove. But scrubbing would not remove the black color on the cuticles around our nails.

One of the first things we noticed was the lack of toilets in the orchard. We inquired and found there was one privy located near the barn. This toilet was half a mile from where we worked. It was used by men, women, and children. It was used by workers who lived in the grower's housing as well as by those who were day help. Several times workers who had diarrhea from eating fruit were unable to get to the toilet and they crawled under the protection of a tree. This sort of behavior was accepted as an everyday human occurrence. If fellow migrants saw such behavior, they ignored it and turned away, giving as much privacy to each other as an orchard can provide. The lack of toilets or a place to wash before handling fruit and vegetables was not unique to this orchard. We found similar conditions all over the country. Only a few places provided a sufficient number of portable toilets or separate facilities for sexes.

Next to strawberries, for us, cherries were the easiest crop to harvest. We had no difficulty setting a production rhythm that resulted in our picking more lugs that first day than most of the other couples in the orchard. Later in the week we would have days with a higher production rate. We would also sense that our picking ability created animosity in the man of a husband-and-wife team who, up to that point, had picked the most cherries. It was obvious that Hank Beal needed to feel superior in some way. He and his wife, Betty, had picked for this grower for fifteen years, and each summer their daily average was higher than any other couple. He acted crushed and pouted like a small child when, on the second day, the orchard foreman teased him about our score and said he was "losing his touch." On the fourth day when the orchard foreman said our lugs once again were piling up faster than anyone else's, we asked him to total our lugs as two lugs less than Betty and Hank's, regardless of how many cherries they had picked. The orchard foreman said he was in favor of competition because it increased productivity. As far as he could see, "lowering the total was a hellava note." It made more sense to him to raise our total than to lower it. The foreman obviously did not like Hank Beal because he felt he was a "bragging little peacock with a hooked nose," but at least he did not tell Hank how many lugs we actually picked.

Hank came over "to talk with us," biting on the end of a freshly lit cigar. He explained as he blew out smoke rings, that he had gotten back to his old stride. He had been "off" for the past couple of days he said, and that was why it looked so good for us. He had slacked off, but now he would really show us some "fancy picking." He'd run us a "race for our money if we wanted to stay in there and fight."

The Williamsons

Although picking cherries is not difficult, back muscles do tire from the constant motion of reaching, stretching, bending, leaning, and finally kneeling to empty filled buckets into the lugs. In the late afternoon of the first day, we took several short rest breaks, and during one we started a conversation with a white family on the next row.

We had noticed them earlier, a man and woman and their thirteen-year-old daughter. A four-door sedan, about nine years old, with cardboard replacing one back window, was parked at the end of their row. We noted a Florida license plate and started our conversation by asking where in Florida they were from. The woman, who said her name was Ida Mae, answered, "You probably ain't never he'rd of the place. Most folks up here never he'rd of anything in Florida 'cept Miami. 'Tis way down by Lake Okeechobee. We're from Belle Glade." Roger Williamson, her husband, worked in the Clewiston sugar mill. She was "on at a packin' shed." We said we knew Pahokee, Belle Glade, and Clewiston, that we had been there during the February freeze looking for work. It was enough that we knew the area, that we too had been there, that we too had been out of work. It was as if they needed to believe we were Floridians, that they needed to deny our Midwestern accents and our Michigan license plates.

It was as if they accepted us wholeheartedly and felt they could trust us and talk honestly and freely. They began to warn us how to keep out of trouble and get along with the people in that area. They did not like Michigan. They found people there to be too distant or too busy to show any interest in them. They missed the person-to-person contacts of the rural South. They were lonely and homesick. They had not done well in the cherries of Michigan. They needed someone to talk with, and we were there, and we would understand what they meant because we "knew Belle Glade."

The Williamsons were "born, bred, and married in south Alabama."[8] They had been "tractored out" when the cotton plantation on which they had worked was bought by a corporation. They never had worked at anything except agriculture, and suddenly in their neighborhood there was a surplus of unemployed farmers. All seven of their children had been in school. Barbara Jean, the baby, had been in first grade. They had been destitute. They had no place to live. The new owners were tearing down the share-cropper shacks to plant more cotton. They had told the Williamsons that there would be less property tax on fields without buildings, so they were getting rid of all houses. One by one their neighbors had moved out of Alabama. Some "went down to Pahokee and got on in the packin' sheds." The Williamsons had decided to go too. They quoted themselves as having said, "If others can make it down there, we can." They had piled everything they owned into an old car, filled the gas tank and started. They had had twenty dollars; they arrived with less than eight. It was the winter of 1957-58, the year that became known as "the winter of the great freeze." There were thousands of stranded migrants all over Florida who had lived that year in cars, cardboard boxes, and shacks or whatever they could find. Many were without food, adequate clothing or heat. Hundreds had been in Pahokee and Belle Glade looking for work when the Williamsons arrived. There would be no work until the frozen crops could be replanted and reach maturity. A former neighbor had taken them in, but this neighbor was nearly as destitute as they. And so they had lived on cull potatoes for five weeks until Roger earned some money unloading a case of machinery and bought a "few groceries. Never before had sausage patties smelled or tasted so good." As Ida Mae recalled, "for us it was a terrible winter," but there was nothing to do except stay in Pahokee and hope things would get better. There was nowhere for them to go. There was nothing for them in Alabama.

That spring they joined a migrant crew and headed north. They stayed in a variety of housing: at one place it was a tent, in another a chicken coop, and in still another they and several other white families lived in the basement of a barn where sleeping areas were partitioned by cardboard stalls. They decided after one season with a crew that in the future they would travel by themselves.

The second winter, Roger "got on" in the sugar mill and Ida Mae was "taken on at the packin' shed." It was good work, but only from November until mid-April. There was no work during the summer, so each spring they would follow the crops north, working as freewheelers, and each summer they would return to Florida late in August so the children could start school.

The summer of 1964 was their first experience picking cherries. They never quite seemed to get the knack of it. Roger worked nights in one of the Traverse City packing plants. He liked that work better, although it meant that he was tired in the morning before he started in the cherries. As he put it, he was not "much 'count to Ida Mae as a cherry picker." Sometimes he slept under a tree until noon.

One morning Ida Mae and Barbara Jean came to the orchard alone. We had heard Roger coughing the day before and wondered if he were ill. Ida Mae said that he did have a sore throat and should be in bed, but that he was at work. He had been transferred from the night to the day shift.

That was the first of several days of cold rain. Three times we had to seek shelter in our cars. Ida Mae held her empty picking bucket over her head as she ran. The water squashed from her shoes. As soon as the rain stopped, she would trudge back to the tree she was picking. After the rain the wind turned colder. Ida Mae was drenched when she left the orchard near five-thirty. She looked tired, discouraged, and miserable. Although she had worked steadily between the rain showers since seven that morning, she and Barbara Jean had picked only eight lugs. They had earned four dollars. If they stayed until the end of the harvest, they would be paid an additional eighty-cent bonus.

The hourly average for the two of them that day was .5053 cents; for each it was .25266 cents per hour. The next day the rain was more frequent and their hourly rate was thus less.

Other Crews in the Orchard

Picking the row next to ours and six rows beyond was a group of Blacks from western Tennessee and eastern Arkansas. Across the orchard road were a crew from Florida and one from Georgia. They were all part of the Eastern migrant stream. This year their crew leaders changed the travel pattern and, instead of going up the east coast, came to Michigan.

The group from Georgia was anxious for the cherry season to end. They wanted to be eligible for their bonus, but they had promised to pick tomatoes in Ohio, and the tomatoes were already ripening. They had picked cherries for six weeks. They had made about as much as they usually made picking beans or cutting asparagus. In July the weather for them was pleasantly hot, but no one had told them how cold Michigan nights can be in August. They had brought few blankets. There was no heat in the tool shed where they stayed. When it suddenly turned cold, they made a stove from two discarded oil drums and a length of stovepipe. It was a strange looking contraption, but it kept them warm. As one said, "Des places, dey giv'd yuh all to lib in whens yuh all is pickin," ain't much. . . . It sho' ain't 'zackly home. . . . . But whens yuh dis far frum home . . . 'nd yuh po' . . . Yuh got ta puts ups with whats ever yuh kin gits, 'nd shuts yuh mouf', and makes yuh self comfort'ble as yuh kins."

The Second Day

Most of the morning of the second day we stood on ladders stripping the upper branches. From that high perch the orchard sloped downward. Far up to the west was a glimmer of open lake. It was the first time since we had come to the orchard that we were aware of water, the sky, or the movement of branches heavy with blood-red fruit. It was only a fleeting awareness. The immediate task of picking demanded our attention and our energy. It was not a task that could be dismissed lightly if wind-whipped cherries, stems, leaves, and "dotter" were to be removed. It was a job that required concentration. It required a constant rolling motion of fingers against thumbs, a motion that "milks" the fruit off trees. As our pile of lugs mounted, our wrists ached. We were more conscious of ladder steps cutting into our legs when there was a need to lean forward to reach a branch than we were of the distant view of lake or clouds.

When poets write of the nomad's life, the beauty of open spaces, the feel of the solid earth beneath the picker's feet, the odor of ripe fruit, they fail to recognize that for the nomadic gatherer of the harvest there are more immediate tasks which dim and distract from the beauty of nature. For the nomadic harvester there are long, unfinished rows of cherry trees, each tree like the last, heavy with overripe fruit. There is the ache of muscles. And when the picker leans against his ladder to ease his tiredness, if his eyes rest for a moment on a cloud bank to the east, his first thought is to find shade from the glare of the sun or protection from the rain; and automatically, almost machine-like, his fingers reach again for unpicked cherries to fill one more lug. If he is aware of the spectacular beauty of a castle-like cumulus cloud, it is a secondary part of his unconscious reaction. He feels it is a good day. There will be many filled lugs when he leaves the orchard.

The Third Day

The rain started in the night, heavy gusts of cold rain. It continued in the early hours of morning. In the orchard the trees were wet, but the picking went on. We worked along the outer edge, waiting for the wind to dry the trees so we could crawl under and harvest the handfuls of fruit that hung in the shadows of the leaves.

Slowly our pails filled, were emptied, and were filled again. Slowly the wet red cherries sprawled across the bottom of the lug, covered the bottom, reached the midpoint, and then formed a level surface across the top of the wooden box. We started another lug. Always we started one more lug.

We lived in a world of cherries, of ladders, of filled pails, empty pails. It was a world of driving to the orchard, stopping at the store to get something that "would fix" quickly, of driving home to our trailer. It was a world of early breakfasts and late, late suppers of sandwiches in the field. It was a world of working, eating, sleeping, and getting to work early again. It was a world of falling into bed too tired at night to care that arm, leg, and back muscles ached and would be stiff and unyielding in the morning. There was a sameness about each day. It was a pattern that made it difficult to tell one day from another. Was it Thursday or Saturday? Had we been standing on ladders for four days or five? Who really cared? The cherries went on and on. And the cherries were all-demanding. They had become our world; we talked of nothing else, we thought of nothing else. The world outside the orchard seemed distant and unreal. It did not, at that period of time, touch our lives.

The third day continued to be one of cold, continuous rain, a slow drizzle. The pickers worked steadily, silently. In the afternoon the rain came hard; the pickers left the orchard. The filled lugs were few.

Death reached into the orchard that day and touched the Valecillos family. Arthur Valecillos's brother and daughter-in-law were killed in a car-truck collision in another county.

Arthur and Antoinette left to make funeral arrangements. Their children picked cherries, fearful they would lose the family bonus should the picking end. The orchard owner was not unhuman. Had he been asked, he probably would have made arrangements for the entire family to leave and still be eligible for their bonus. He was not asked. He probably did not know of their loss. Arthur was afraid to approach the grower with the request that his family be allowed to attend the funeral. His fear was born out of his ever-present insecurity that a job was truly his, of being promised a bonus and finding he had forfeited it in a way he could not comprehend. This time he would not run the risk. While he and Antoinette were gone, their children would stay and pick cherries. Hector, their oldest son, would be in charge; the others would take orders from him as if he were the father.

Two days later Arthur and Antoinette returned, knowing there was no time for grieving. Death for them had to be set aside; bereavement had to be postponed or denied entirely; they had to return to their cherry picking as if death had never occurred. Although there was no time for the Valecillos family to grieve, other pickers were forced to certain realizations through this family's loss. Other migrants were reminded that someday, in some way, death would come to those they loved. Because they too were afraid of death, they either ignored the loss of the Valecillos family, pretending it had never happened, or else conveyed their compassion in some way. With some it was a hand grasp on Arthur's shoulder, a pat on Antoinette's arm. Others expressed their feelings in words. Still others contributed to a collection or put part of their cherries into the lugs of one of the children.

The Fourth Day

There was a hard rain the morning of the fourth day followed by a north wind that was cold, almost snow-like. Our fingers were numb from the chilled cherries. Our arms ached to our shoulders. We finished one side of the orchard and moved to a new spot. There was no laughter or singing. There was little talking. Everyone was wet, miserable, and cold.

The Fifth Day

The fifth day we spent on ladders in the warm sunshine. A hint of summer had suddenly returned. Snatches of conversation and sounds drifted to us. There was a dull rattle of cherries striking an otherwise empty bucket and the sound of cherries being poured into wooden lugs. There was the distant noise of the tractor. There was a knocking, banging sound of empty lugs being dumped and stockpiled for the filling. There was the thud of lugs heavy with fruit being placed on the wagon. Far to the west two young brothers quarreled. There was the sound of hard slaps along with quick, angry sobs and shouted accusations that one had taken the other's cherries. There was the exasperated voice of their mother trying to make peace.

In the row next to us someone told a story of being stopped by the police for turning the wrong way on a one-way street. A friend helped calculate how many lugs of cherries it would take to pay the fine and court costs. The friend counseled that the next time it would be cheaper to go to jail than to pay such an unreasonable fine. At least in jail, he reasoned, the traffic violator would be fed. Even if he lost thirty days of picking time, it would be better than giving most of what he had earned to a judge who, knowing he was a migrant fruit picker, "just socked it to him."

Almost daily the local paper carried long lists of arrests and fines of migrant workers. The newspaper report of municipal court action during the picking season seemed to bear out the migrant's accusation that migrants paid higher court costs, fines, or served more days in jail than local residents arraigned on more serious charges.

In some communities the police are the only source of help available to migrants. Sometimes their help is in the form of transportation, other times food, and in at least two communities we found that the police department provided a fund out of their own pockets for helping stranded families. We also saw the opposite. We were warned by fellow workers in several areas to avoid being involved in even a minor violation because of the danger of being jailed.[9]

Nearby in the cherry orchard a newlywed Chicano couple planned for the future and home they hoped to own. A local white picker who had retired from a sales job complained to another white picker about the federal government's regulation as applied to Social Security. His Social Security, he said, was not enough to live on; if he supplemented it with more than "Uncle Sam said he should," he was penalized and "had to pay the government." He and his wife picked cherries, prunes, peaches, and apples. They lived as frugally as they could. If they were merely existing now, what would happen when they were too old to pick fruit and had to live entirely on their Social Security?

Suddenly from across the orchard sounded one voice, a chanting, lilting, musical call for a "bid" on cherries, "on cherrios." The lyrics were original. They were a wailing bit of Basin Street Blues transplanted from the old French Quarter to the shores of Grand Traverse Bay. The song ended with a chorus of "Oh, cherrios, oh cherrios, nothin' here but cherrios." The solo was followed by running comments accompanied by a tempo beat pounded out on a picking bucket. It was a moment of nonsense. It was a moment of relaxation. The Black entertainer ended his act by proclaiming that each and every picker here present would someday "have his own cherry orchard." By that time "there will be only growers. There will be no pickers." Everyone would have to pick his own trees, "so we can have cherries, cherrios, sweet cherrios to eat."

Before we left the orchard that day near sundown, we had finished our twenty-ninth lug. Again, we had the largest number picked by any couple. For over ten hours we had swung up and down our ladders. We had dragged ladders around trees, lugged ladders into place, and crawled into the top branches. We had stretched, balancing on tiptoes on the very top of the ladder to tear away more fruit. All day we had been slapped by branches, scratched by rough bark, jabbed by sharp stick-like twigs. We were now ready for hot showers, for the soothing creaminess of hand lotion, for a hot meal, and for the cool cleanliness of laundered sheets.

That night we were unusually tired. We both commented that whenever we closed our eyes we saw cherries, branches heavy with cherries, cherries in lugs, lugs and lugs of cherries. "Nothing nowhere but cherrios, cherrios, red, ripe cherrios."

Fannie Jo and Her Crew

Saturday as we turned into the orchard lane, we saw workers milling around their housing. They called to us, saying there was no cherry picking that day. They had been told there would be no more picking until Monday. Their crew leaders were at the house. The grower was "payin' off." From him we got the story. The packing plant had all the cherries it could use until Monday. As carload after carload of commuting pickers were turned away, there were mixed reactions expressed about the two days' "vacation." Some seemed pleased and said they were going fishing. Others were upset, especially by the inconvenience of driving to the orchard for nothing. Still others were angered at the loss of picking time, knowing that the now-rotting fruit on the trees would require more careful sorting on Monday. A few threatened to quit; some actually did, saying they had had their fill of cherries. They would find something else.

Morale among the Black group from Mississippi had reached an all-time low. They wanted to leave for home. Cotton picking in the mid-South would start soon, and cotton was their major livelihood. Now the cherry grower was saying that there would be another week of cherry picking, and he was trying to convince their crew leader that they should stay. There was confusion about the bonus and their rate of pay. On one of the days of cold rain the grower had tried to encourage their efforts by telling some of them, "with every lug you pick, think of it as being another sixty cents." They understood that he was promising to pay them sixty cents a lug, plus a ten-cent bonus. Their disappointment, when they found they were still being paid fifty cents a lug,[10] was expressed in sullen anger and grumbled threats to leave immediately.

The crew felt that they had every right to be upset. The previous week they had been told the cherry picking would be finished by Saturday. Now it was Saturday, and they were being told they would need to stay one more week to be eligible for their bonus. Morale for the ten remaining crew members had been low all week. Their individual production dropped steadily until it was only a third of what it had been the first week.

When they arrived, their crew had numbered twenty-three. From the very beginning there had been dissension; some were dissatisfied with the poor housing and left immediately. They said they could get housing elsewhere that provided more privacy than six-foot high cardboard partitions in a milkhouse. They could find housing with running hot and cold water and a place to take a bath. The only water here was from an outside spigot. The only cooking facility was a two-burner electric plate. One by one the crew members had left to find work on their own or to return to Mississippi. Their crew leader, a woman, Fannie Jo Bishop, tried desperately to encourage the few who had remained to stay out the season so that she could fulfill her contract with the grower.

Fannie Joe held her crew with an iron hand. She checked each tree they picked. She looked over their cherries so that every lug that passed her inspection was in perfect condition. She disciplined her workers. She "rode hard" on anyone who spent too much time talking and not enough time working, including her own eighteen-year-old son, Lonnie.

Like the typical crew leader of migrant workers, Fannie Jo came up from the ranks. She had saved enough money to buy a bus. Like all crew leaders she was the nearest thing to a labor representative who listened to the grievances of her workers. Under federal law as their crew leader she was responsible for collecting and paying their Social Security taxes unless she was "named as an employee in a written agreement entered into with the person for whom the agricultural services are performed."[11]

Fannie Jo had traveled every migrant stream in the country. Her pattern in recent years had been to go from the cherries in Michigan to the cotton in Mississippi, the winter vegetables in Florida, and the strawberries in Louisiana. In years past her long slender brown fingers had "worked vegetables" from Florida up the east coast until cotton was ready in Mississippi. For five years she had gone from Mississippi cotton to the west coast. She knew the harvests of California, and knew them well. Everywhere she had found a sameness in attitudes toward migrant laborers whether she was in the Everglades of Florida, the truck gardens of New Jersey, or in one of the many valleys of California. Most of her life she had worked cotton, hoeing in the spring and early summer, picking through the late summer and fall into the cold rain of winter. She was a perfectionist. Every lug of cherries she piled on top of another was free from leaves, dried or spoiled fruit, or bits of twigs.

Fannie Joe was born at the edge of the Delta in Mississippi, the Delta which she said stretched all the way from the "Peabody Hotel in Memphis clear down to Catfish Row in Vicksburg."[12] She had never known anything about her father except that he was a big man who laughed a lot and who caught a train north before she was born and was never heard from again. She was raised by her grandmother when her mother "run off to Memphis to be a prostitute in one of the cheap hotels." Two white men had talked her mother into going, and she left, sitting up front between them in their shiny black car, not even looking back to wave at Fannie Jo and Granny standing in the doorway. She came back down the Delta only a few times that Fannie Jo could remember. She seemed more like a big sister than a mother, showing off her high-heeled shoes, her jewelry and perfume which, according to Fannie Jo's grandmother, smelled like "the very breath of the devil." She tossed her head and dressed in a too-tight skirt and thin blouse through which the brownness of her dusty skin looked like cream. For a time, Fannie Jo's mother sent money for her daughter's support, but this stopped after a few months, with the result that Fannie Jo and her grandmother lived on what they could make.

The grandmother "worked" cotton, and when Fannie Jo was seven, she too was "pickin' cotton in the fields." She was a better "chopper" than a cotton picker. She worked before school and after school, and when she was eleven she quit school and went to work full time in the cotton.

One year Fannie Jo and her grandmother raised some sweet potatoes to sell. She told us the story:

> We carried 'em to the white man's store; he done promised us one-half penny a tater. He counted 'em over an' figgered what we had comin' and gave Granny a dollar. I started to figurin' myself 'cause it didn't seem like nuf for eight crocker sacks of big sweet taters that had made half a wagon load when a neighbor carried us to the store. Granny, when she saw what I was doin', said fer me not to do that cause white folks don't like fer colored folks to do their own figgerin'.
>
> While Granny went back to the store to get a sack of grits, some rice, and a dime's worth of fat-back, and a gallon of coal oil for our lamp—all of which came to mor'n the dollar the white man paid us, I checked over those sweet taters and foun' sho' nuf I was right, there was near six hundred taters in that pile.
>
> Granny was mad at me for countin' em; when I told her she got cheated, she cuffed me long side the head an' said she'd whulp me good an' hard when she got me home if I didn't stay 'way from those sweet taters and not go 'bout remarkin' that white folks made 'stakes. She told me I'd get myself in a heap of trouble if I didn't make my mends with the Lord an' watch my tongue 'cause I sure nuf was turnin' into a uppity nigger; an' 'sides, she said des white folks, theys knows best.

According to Fannie Jo, her grandmother always tied her head up in a scarf handkerchief which she wore all day and slept in at night. She had a white one she wore to prayer meeting and on Sunday to church. She also insisted that Fannie Jo keep a handkerchief around her head. She said it was to keep the sweat out of her eyes, but when Fannie Jo was older, she told her it was to keep her "naughty" or "nappy" hair out of sight of the white folks " 'cause somethin' bout nappy nigger hair makes 'em mad.' " All the women and girls who came to their little church wore handkerchiefs on their heads or hats pulled down over their hair. The men and boys kept their heads shaved, apparently for the same reason. Many of the men wore their caps wherever they went.

Fannie Jo's mother was the only Black woman Fannie Jo knew who left her head uncovered. Fannie Jo's mother's hair looked different from the hair of other Black women Fannie Jo saw. It was straight and looped around her head, and sometimes it hung down her back. Each time she came to visit, it was a different color. When Fannie Jo asked her mother about it, she explained that she used a "straighten' iron" and "creams to take the kinks out" of her hair[13] and that she sometimes bleached and dyed it.

Fannie Jo's mother tried to impress upon Fannie Jo that the only way she would ever get anywhere in this life was to begin to take notice of her appearance. Finally, her mother seemed to lose interest, saying that Fannie Jo was "the ugliest and scrawniest youngun she had ever seen and there was nothing about Fannie Jo that would appeal to a man. That ugly scar on her cheek did not help with her appearance," her mother stated.

Fannie Jo was eight the day the truck drove into their yard. Her grandmother had gone to the store, and Fannie Jo was alone. There were two white men in the cab and a gun rack in the rear window. When Fannie Jo saw them, she was afraid. They may have only intended to tease her in a sadistic way, but when they lunged at her with threats of what they would both do if they caught her, Fannie Jo ran screaming toward the cabins of the other Black farmers who worked on the same plantation. Years later she was able to recall the panic she felt as she ran, fearful every step that she would feel strong hands grabbing her, throwing her to the ground, and tearing at her clothing.

She understood the intended meaning of what the men said to her. Fannie Jo could not remember a time when she had not known about sexual relationships between men and women. She had seen sexual intercourse. She had taken part in sexual exploration with other Black children, although she knew it was something her grandmother would severely punish her for if she were caught in the act of exposing herself.

When Fannie Jo was four, she went looking for the "stolen nest" of one of her grandmother's hens. The grandmother had more need for eggs than for baby chicks and when the hen stopped laying in a box in the shed, she instructed Fannie Jo to look for the

nest and get the eggs. It was in an old hay pile that Fannie Jo
found the nest and she gathered the eggs in the apron she wore
over her Sunday dress and started through the edge of the woods
to the house. As she came around a bush, the fifteen-year-old son
of a white tenant farmer was standing there unbuttoned, urinating.
He held "his thing" out for her to see. She stared, unable to move.
She wanted to run, but she trembled instead, and her legs would
not "work." It was the first time Fannie Jo could recall having seen
the maleness of a man, although she sensed sexual differences and
was not surprised at what she saw. The boy grabbed her arm. He
bruised her skin as he pulled her under a bush. She wanted to
scream but she could not. She tried to protect the eggs and felt
them crush within the folds of her apron.

"Do you know what a rooster does to a hen?" the boy asked.
She did not answer, but she knew what roosters did to hens. She
also knew what a boar did to a sow pig and what male dogs did to
female dogs. She did not answer the boy. He hurt her and she
cried. He threatened "to slit her throat" if she told anyone. Then
suddenly he was gone. She ran home crying and tried to share the
whole "horrible thing" with her grandmother, but her grandmother
spanked her for being so clumsy as to break the eggs. Fannie Jo was
never certain whether her grandmother believed her story about
the white boy, whether the spanking was the old woman's way of
expressing frustration and fear, or if she actually thought the little
girl had lied.

Four years later, on the day when Fannie Jo was being chased
by the two men, she remembered the white boy and the bush in
the woods, and she ran faster, jumping over a junk pile of cans and
broken jars. She fell. A jagged piece of glass gashed her skin open in
a line below her eye from the edge of her nose to near her ear.

When they saw Black faces peeking from behind cabins the
white men got back in their truck and drove away, leaving her on
the ground. As soon as the truck pulled away, the others came and
someone ran to fetch her grandmother. Everyone was gathered
around, saying it was wrong; those men had no right to chase
Fannie Jo and make her fall. They said that the two men were the
same ones who drove up and down the roads, looking for Black
men. If they saw one alone, they would beat him up if they could
catch him. They might shoot at him or try to run him down with

the truck, although they did not know him and the man had not even spoken to them.[14]

While Fannie Jo's grandmother worked on her face, the people talked in low tones about the white men in the truck. They were angry that this had happened to a little girl, but they were more frightened because they felt so helpless. If they reported the episode to the sheriff, it would be worse. The white men would not be punished, and the Blacks would be hunted and more terrorized than they were already. There was nothing they could do except stay off the roads, cut across the fields to the store, and stay close to each other when they were not working. Perhaps in numbers there would be protection, and perhaps in time these white men would lose interest in their game and leave them alone.

Fannie Jo's grandmother said, "For to git a cut to stop from bleedin', the best thin' was to get some spider webs that grow up in the corner of the house and put 'em in the cut and tie 'em on. The spider web would jist grow right in there and stop the bleedin'."

The cut healed, leaving a raised, red welt that convinced Fannie Jo that she really was an ugly, repulsive female whom no man would find attractive enough to want to marry. She felt guilty and somehow responsible for all that had happened. She felt that she had failed her mother by not being dainty and graceful. She felt she had failed her grandmother by not accepting her attitude toward life for Blacks. Her grandmother was resigned to their fate. She was skeptical of any white person "if he showed as if he wanted friendship with her or to help her; the only kina' white folks she knowed 'bout was those to go out an' work for and to get back home out of their way as soon as she could. She's never been in any white folks' house and never et at the same table with no white folks an' if she ever did, she thinks she'd choke 'cause she couldn't swollow her food."

Fannie Jo's grandmother saw her church as a source of help. There was prayer service the first Sunday night in the month; the second Sunday, the brothers preached; the third Sunday night, the sisters testified; the fourth Sunday, the brothers preached again. As soon as one had finished preaching, anyone could sing. Everyone could shout with the spirit of the Lord anytime, even during the preaching.

Her grandmother said, "I don't care what pain you got, you

forget all 'bout it when you shout. Some of us colored folks, we just got to shout or 'bout bust." Sometimes her grandmother would stop still in the middle of the cotton field and would look up at the sky and start singing "Nobody Knows the Trouble I've Seen, Nobody Knows but Jesus," and then she would go back to picking cotton faster than ever. She did not talk much about her religion; that is, she did not try to convince others that they too should have her convictions that the Lord would someday claim His own, would even catch His children up into the sky right out of the cotton fields. She just went along living her faith, singing and praising the Lord, and "testifying for Him each third Sunday."

Fannie Jo used to watch her grandmother shout, clap her hands, and then jump up and sway back and forth, going into a sort of dance as she shouted and sang out her praises to the Lord and her hopes for a better day for herself and her people. Somehow Fannie Jo felt that any better day that the future held for her would have to be of her own doing. Singing and shouting would not get it. She would need to work, and work hard. She would need to get away from the Delta area of Mississippi; it was a violent, cruel place where no Black person could ever get out from under the heavy foot of the white man.[15] Fannie Jo promised herself she would get away, but not like her mother. Someday she would amount to something; she would be her own boss; someday she would even boss others.

She quit school in the fourth grade, so she could work full time in the fields and earn money. She was eleven years old and in the fourth grade because she got "left down a year 'cause I didn't have no shoes." At that time education didn't seem important. At the age of eleven, she could handle a hoe as well as a man and could work almost as many hours without tiring. Then, too, the school that she attended had around fifty students and one teacher in a one-room building with a leaky roof and four books. There was neither blackboard nor paper on which to write. Sometimes the children found scraps of paper, and they had one pencil they passed around, but usually they learned their "figgerin" out in the school yard with a sharp stick, scratching the ground. That was how Fannie Jo learned to add and subtract. The crashing blow for her education came, however, when the white school board covered the Negro school building with black tar paper and painted the white school "a pretty white" so children would know where they belonged." It made Fannie Jo hate the color black more than ever, and hate for the color was transferred to dislike for school. She would never wear black if she had a choice. Fannie Jo's antagonism toward the word *black* was so intense that she preferred to be called nigger than to be called Black. Her feelings did not change over the years, and in 1964, when "Black is beautiful" was becoming the slogan of freedom for many members of her race, Fannie Jo referred to herself and her race as Negro. Her son, Lonnie, who was with her in the Michigan orchard, wanted to be called Black and was just as angered if anyone referred to him as being either colored or Negro as if they had called him nigra or nigger.

The house in which Fannie Jo and her grandmother lived was elevated on wooden blocks, and when it rained, water stood around the door for days. In dry weather the children crawled under the porch to play, where the half-dozen multicolored hound dogs her grandmother somehow managed to feed slept in the coolness throughout most of the year. There was no glass in the windows and at night her grandmother closed the wooden shutters to keep out the "poison" night air. As long as Fannie Jo could remember, there had been a leak somewhere in the roof. It was mended many times by one of their neighbors, yet when it rained they went to sleep to the sound of water dripping into a pan or pail. The walls were covered with several thicknesses of newspapers to keep out the wind, and her grandmother let her pick out colored pictures from an old magazine they found to paper the wall around her bed. Her grandmother instilled in her a pride in neatness, and although their house contained only meager articles, the place was always clean—except for sweeping down the spider webs, which the grandmother felt should be left in the ceiling corners in case there was an emergency in which the web would be needed to stop blood or to be used as part of a charm to ward off a curse.

Fannie Jo's grandmother believed in ghosts and haunts, and whenever there was a death in the area, her grandmother took her to the wake as well as to the funeral. "Sitting up with the corpse" at a wake was very " 'portant." It was also a time for eating with the church members near her grandmother's age, and sometimes putting a dish of food out on the porch for the spirit of the dead person.[16] Whenever there was a death in the neighborhood, her grandmother would spend a good deal of time talking about the spirit of the departed and would expect to be haunted by the ghost. She felt it was very important to observe certain rituals, such as putting the broom across the door to prevent the ghost from coming inside and "riding 'em" in their sleep.

Fannie Jo never married legally. She wanted to make certain we understood the differences between a legal marriage for which "you have papers from the cote-house" and common law marriages, "shacking up," living with someone, and other unions of arrangement. A marriage of agreement may be one to which both parties are faithful and which both feel is a good marriage, but which does not have the sanction of the law.[17]

Fannie Jo had two consent marriages or consensual unions. To these two unions three children were born. They became Fannie Jo's financial responsibility when their fathers walked off with "new" women. Fannie Jo had also lived with other men for short periods of time, but never with any thought of marriage. In all cases it was the men who walked out on her, usually because of an argument about money. They expected her to do most of the providing, sometimes complaining that she paid her insurance and the rent before she brought home beer and cigarettes for them.[18]

Fannie Jo found that the best means of self-expression was work. She worked hard, traveling as part of a migrant farm crew, saving as much money as she could until she was able to own her own bus. Going back to the Mississippi Delta to make up her crew, she treated her people so fairly that they had a devotion to her that was unusual among farm labor crews. For years she traveled with most of the same workers from Mississippi to Florida and up the east coast to upper New York. She spent part of each year in Mississippi cotton. Although her grandmother had been dead many years, it seemed only right that she think of Mississippi as home.

She had never before had as much trouble with a crew as she was having the summer of 1964 in Michigan. She had employed someone she had known in the Delta area as a driver that summer, and she had the feeling that he was antagonizing other crew members, trying to encourage them to leave her crew and make up a crew under his direction. She also suspected that the grower was negotiating with him "to bring up a crew from Mississippi the following summer." She sensed the grower did not like dealing with her, a woman, mainly because she was hard-nosed and demanded rights for her workers, even as she demanded that they do a full day's work and that she personally inspect every lug of cherries they picked.

Fannie Jo was not paranoid in her analysis of what was going on within her crew. Her driver, Benjamin Grant, talked with us about the "wonderful offer" the grower had made, encouraging him to get together a crew of his own, pointing out that a crew should be headed by a man and that a man like Benjamin should not take directions from a bossy woman like Fannie Jo.

This was Benjamin's first trip out of the Mississippi Delta. He had worked all of his life between the cotton fields and a garage in a small community. He was a good mechanic and the garage owner let him and his family live upstairs above the garage, rent-free. The grower said there was nothing about a motor that Benjamin did not know; "he could sweet talk a sick motor into purring like a contented kitten."

Benjamin had known Fannie Jo most of his life, and when she approached him and asked if he would be her driver, he decided to do just that in order to find out what life was like north of Mississippi. Benjamin had known a way of life that was so competitive and that granted so little recognition in terms of financial or personal gains that an individual who wanted to get out had to think only about himself and not be concerned with loyalty to family or members of his own race.[19] Under these circumstances an individual might steal money his own mother had earned scrubbing floors and, without any sense of guilt, use that money to leave the area for a new life with no intentions of ever coming back or even of writing to his mother. Should the mother die, he might return for the funeral with an outpouring of tears and grief expressed through costly flowers and loud lamentations over his loss. Under the same circumstances a "friend" might "inform on a friend" to have him arrested so that he could take over his job or even move in with his friend's wife.[20]

It was a jungle kind of competitive existence that Benjamin had known and that he wanted to escape. Thus he tended to focus on his own personal needs, having little concern for the effect of his actions on others. To him Fannie Jo represented success. She owned her own bus, or at least she was buying her own bus. She could afford to hire a driver and was paying him as much as he could make in the garage. She had a crew of men and women she could "boss around." She traveled. She got to go into the office or the house of the white man, the grower, and dicker with him about working conditions. She was the one the white man from the United States labor department office talked with and the only one in the crew he called by name. She was a somebody, the "boss lady."

While Benjamin admired Fannie Jo, he also was envious of her successes and wished he could be in her position. He did not see Fannie Jo's many problems of labor management, the expenses of owning her own bus, or the fact that she was held responsible by both the grower and the members of her crew. He did not see any of the disadvantages. He saw only her power, and he was envious.

To Benjamin, Fannie Jo may also have represented a woman to be exploited. Elliot Liebow found in his research that sometimes a lower-class Black man views himself as a "ruthless Exploiter of Women ... the result is that man-woman relationships tend to ... come to an abrupt and frequently violent end. . . ."[21] Benjamin began to see himself in Fannie Jo's position, and he began to look for flaws in her leadership that he could point up to the other members of the crew. He encouraged their dissatisfaction, especially in the confusion about the pay rate and the bonus. He hinted that perhaps the grower was actually paying her sixty cents a lug plus the ten-cent bonus and that she was "pocketing the extra dime for herself." He stated she should have taken a firmer stand with the grower; she "sold her workers out." A male crew leader would get more for crew members. If he, Benjamin, had been in Fannie Jo's position, he would have done more. He talked on, saying what he would do if he were their crew leader without any realization of the restrictions that would be placed on him if he truly were a crew leader.

The position of crew leader sounded glamorous to Benjamin. He did not see beyond the glamour. He had no awareness of his own limitations. His comments excited the more discontented members of the crew who may have seen any crew leader as an exploiter, an oppressor, one other person with a foot on the backs of workers.

On Saturday morning the crew milled around waiting to be paid while Fannie Jo talked to the grower about the rate of payment. We could see Benjamin moving from one individual to another, sharing his opinions. Sometimes he merely listened, nodding his head and saying "that's the truth"; other times he reminded them "they was just po' folks tryin' to get ahead."

Fannie Jo returned to an angry crew. It had polarized in her absence around Benjamin. The workers expressed their anger toward her, threatening to quit, threatening to get drunk, threatening to stay in their quarters and not show up again in the orchard. She retaliated with anger, threatening not to pay them their wages until they were safely back in Mississippi. She yelled at them, "If yo'r lookin' for a gravy train, ya awreddy got it. I ain't tryna chisel nobody. Now I done tole ya'. Now ya c'mon an' get busy cleanin' up 'em livin' quarters or get yo'self as best ya kin downs to the bus station an' get permanent-like outta my sight."

The grower, out of his own need and probably to assure himself of future workers, encouraged Benjamin to agitate discontent in Fannie Jo's crew. From what we could observe, it appeared that the grower felt Benjamin would be less demanding than Fannie Jo. He began to take Benjamin aside to talk with him about becoming a crew leader. One day when he had assigned Benjamin to work on one of his tractors, he promised him a job working with farm equipment the next summer when Benjamin brought his crew up from Mississippi. Benjamin derived the impression from the grower that he needed only to bring a crew north and have them pick cherries and he, Benjamin, would be able to repair some machinery and have the rest of his time free to go fishing; and still he would make as much money as Fannie Jo made this year. He did not think he would need to spend his time in the orchard. He thought his crew would work better without so much "checkin' on." The grower agreed.

One day the grower had Benjamin look over the living quarters in the milkhouse and explained how he "planned to fix them up before Benjamin's crew arrived next year."[22] It was at this point that Fannie Jo began to talk about her suspicions. There was a "stink somewhere," and she knew where it was. She knew her major problem was Benjamin. She also realized that she needed him to get the bus back to Mississippi. There was no one else she could trust to drive. She could not fire Benjamin; she could only mistrust him. She could only hope to hold enough of her workers to complete her contract with the grower. The more discontented her crew became, the more she held them in line with rigid discipline, refusing to allow them to go into town or to sleep late, even when they were "sick."

Never again will we see a piece of cherry pie without recalling Fannie Jo hiking toward us through the orchard, her straw hat at a rakish tilt above the bright piece of cloth that covered her hair. The worried lines of her face would break into a warm, friendly smile when she saw us and her eyes would narrow in thoughtful concentration over some question we asked. "Sho nuf . . . ," she would say, "Yo'all done picked yo'self a heap o'cherries this afternoon . . . Sho nuf . . . we all done worked hard . . . What do ya'll say we just forgit this workin' stuff and go fishing?"

We never went fishing with Fannie Jo. She had too many things to do, too many worries, too many responsibilities to handle. She used to say she never quite understood how she got herself "tangled up" in a crew-leader job in the first place " 'cause it sho' nuf be my death." Yet she never allowed a lug to go out with her crew number on it that had not been carefully scrutinized. Instead of going fishing or to town, she sat on a box with her old straw hat across her forehead and picked over and discarded cherries and disciplined her dwindling crew.

It was the beginning of the third week in August, and cotton picking was starting in Mississippi. It was time to leave, but the cherry crop of Michigan said, "tarry a little longer." So Fannie Jo and her crew worked on as did some of the Spanish-speaking families. Those families were part of the Texas-Michigan migrant stream. One family would go from the cherries of Old Mission to the potatoes of the Saginaw River Valley. After potatoes they would return to the cotton of Texas. They would work there until the cotton season was over, and then they would be unemployed until it was time to come north again for cherries and potatoes in Michigan. Still another family would pick tomatoes in Illinois on their way to the cotton of Texas. A third would go from cherries to Michigan prunes, peaches, and apples and then would head for the vegetables of the lower Rio Grande Valley. In each of these many places there was a farmer or grower awaiting their arrival, but the Michigan cherry growers tried to hold them until the cherries were harvested.

To the grower faced with the spoilage of his crop, the lack of pickers at such a time is a major "headache." He may lose everything he has invested, including his own labor. To the worker threatened with the loss of his job, it is a fickle dilemma that is often solved by a whimsical change in the weather. If he stays and helps one grower through the entire season, he may lose an opportunity to work someplace else. The next year the first grower may not have a crop. If a worker does not come about the time he is expected, he may find other workers or mechanical harvesters in the field when he does arrive. Even if he comes faithfully, whenever and wherever he is needed, he can find other pickers or mechanical harvesters in the field. There is no assurance of how long the work will last, if there is work. There is only the need to make a living and to stretch money earned in one crop somehow until there is money earned in another.

The workers continuously face such questions as these: How many lugs of cherries does it take to fill the gasoline tank? How many does it take to get to that spot "down the road apiece" where the cotton or apples are waiting to be picked or where celery cutters move across the fields? How many lugs of cherries has it already taken to buy an extra blanket, warmer clothing, food and gasoline so more cherries can be picked?

The Williamsons' Problems

On Monday when the pickers returned, there were rain showers intermittently between periods of sunshine. We were in a different section of the orchard and again had a row next to Ida Mae and Barbara Jean Williamson. Roger still worked days in the packing plant. It was while we waited for the trees to dry after a sudden downpour that we asked about their housing. Had they found a place in Traverse City or did they drive some distance as we did? Ida Mae's blue eyes filled with tears. Her voice tightened with hurt. There was about her an air of embarrassment, of shame, and at the same time a fierce pride. We felt her need to talk. We sensed she could be frightened by questions; we sensed her need to maintain dignity and self-respect, and yet she had a need to tell us that the three of them were living in their car. They had no housing.

When they arrived in early July, they had tried to rent a room, an apartment, a house trailer, or a furnished house. There was nothing available for the forty to fifty dollars a month they could pay. It was the season of tourists, and weekly rents for cottages and apartments were that much or more. They had driven the length of the county in a heavy rain and electric storm that first night, looking for a place to stay. Not even a motel or hotel room had been available. What sleep they had was in their car.

The next day Roger got a job in a packing plant at a dollar twenty-five an hour. They found a grower where Ida Mae and Barbara Jean could pick cherries. The farmer used day help. He had no housing. He put three cots in the barn for their use.

When Roger was "changed to nights," he helped with the picking. He moved and placed the ladders. Although it was good to have Roger's help during the days, when he was away at night Barbara Jean and Ida Mae were afraid alone in the barn. They "lay awake, shivering and listening to the sounds of mice in the grain loft, watching stars through the cracks in the siding, and imagining the worst and wondering how to get the police should they need protectin'."

When the weather turned cold, the barn became intolerably drafty. They moved into their car, and after a few nights they decided to find an orchard closer to Traverse City where the grower had housing. There was still nothing they could afford to rent.

They found most of the grower housing was already filled with pickers who were either Chicano, Mexican, or Black. Ida Mae was afraid of all three; admittedly she was prejudiced. She had no use for anyone of a race or culture other than her own. She was afraid that if they moved into migrant housing she or Barbara Jean would be molested or exposed to possible infections.

Ida Mae had been conditioned from early childhood to view those with darker skin as inferior, immoral, ignorant, as dirty, having a bad smell, and carrying disease. She believed, as did the majority of poor whites who grew up in the Southern United States, that "decent" people could only be protected from disease and germ-carrying nonwhites by having separate drinking fountains, toilets, waiting rooms, sections of buses, trains, theatres and segregated schools, restaurants, and housing. She had heard her father and other men say many times that there was a "darkie" after every white man's position and that Black men would work longer hours for less pay and would bring down work standards for everyone if they got "into self-respectin' jobs." The only solution was to keep Black men out of choice jobs and let them have those white men did not want. After all, coming originally from Africa, they could stand the hot sun and therefore should work in the fields all day, whereas too much Alabama sun on a white man would "cook his head and cause softenin' of his brain," and therefore he should do field work only in the early morning and toward evening.

Ida Mae also had been taught to fear the sexual potency of the "nigra man." She believed that any white woman was a potential rape victim if she so much as found herself alone with a Black man.[23] White women who were taught to view Blacks as having strong, uncontrollable sexual impulses directed toward them as white women also projected these same dangerous impulses onto others; thus they feared Chicanos and Indians as well. This was how Ida Mae felt. She had never in her life spoken to a Mexican or a Chicano, but in her mind she classified them as she did "niggers."[24] Anyone whose skin was darker than hers was "all right as long as he kept his place," which meant that he was not to use the same facilities she or her family used or to come in close contact with her or her family.

The Williamsons had come to this orchard the day before we arrived. Their car continued to be "home" because the grower's housing was filled. When Roger worked nights, Ida Mae and Barbara Jean parked in the packing plant parking lot as if waiting for him. They were afraid to park along highways or streets because the police would make them move. They were afraid to stop in too isolated an area for fear they might be molested. Although they locked the car doors, they were afraid even in the lighted parking lot that someone might break in, and they lay awake recounting news stories of murder and rape, listening for the footsteps of the attacker they were positive would come some night. Nights when the weather was cold, they ran the car motor. When Roger worked days, the three of them searched for a spot where they could park unnoticed until morning. The operator of a service station allowed them to use his restrooms to change clothing, although it was against company policy. They found a laundromat with a rental iron, and each morning they looked neat and clean and not at all as if they were living in their car.

Ida Mae said their biggest problem was preparing hot food. They had no way to prepare anything, not even coffee. Although they went to the cheapest restaurants and ordered daily specials or to drive-ins for hamburgers their food expense some days was more than they earned. They tried making sandwiches but found it no more economical than going to restaurants.

The Williamsons also had car expenses which cut deeply into the ten dollars a day Roger earned at the packing plant. Discouraged, they wondered if they should have gone to some other area or even stayed in Florida and depended on odd jobs. Every year it was more difficult to find enough work to warrant their travels. Each year it was more expensive. Still this was the only work they could do, and there was small chance at their ages of getting into anything else.

We returned to our cherry picking, deeply troubled. We talked quietly, almost in whispers. My husband felt concern for this family who was ill prepared even to pick cherries and, therefore, earned little, although they tried hard. He was impatient with a system that caught both grower and worker in a vicious cycle. Here, he pointed out, was a family working long hours at hard labor, unable to make enough money to rent a room or bed in which to sleep. Here, he said, was a grower whose income was limited by the amount of fruit he could sell, who had more money tied up in sprays, fertilizers, taxes, ground cover, equipment, and wages that year than he would make from his entire crop of cherries. While this dilemma existed for both grower and worker, my husband continued, there were fruit and vegetables rotting, unpicked in the fields of our country; meanwhile there were hundreds of American counties with thousands of hungry and malnourished individuals. At the same time, he pointed out, spiraling food costs clearly indicated that profits were being made by someone from the exploitation of others; yet profits, he was certain, would not be made this year by the cherry growers of Michigan or by the migrant workers who picked their fruit.

As a woman professionally trained to understand the problems of individuals and families, I struggled between myself as a social worker and myself as a migrant worker. I struggled between anger and empathy, between being objective and being subjective to the point of over-identification. My professional self said we must contact an agency or the local authorities or even a friend in the area and find help for this family. Somehow, we must tell Ida Mae and Roger about the services they were entitled to as human beings. On the other hand, if I were to maintain my role as a migrant worker, I should betray no knowledge of community resources or service delivery despite my deep sense of anger that housing conditions such as those provided by Mr. Smith and others for women and children should go unnoticed by a state with the reputation and wealth that Michigan has. My professional self said we must try in whatever way we could to make the public aware of the needs of migrants. My migrant self said, in the meantime, that we must try to think of immediate ways to help the Williamsons within our migrant roles. The hard fact was that it was not realistic for fellow cherry pickers to produce housing as if by magic. If we found living quarters for them Ida Mae would know we were something other than what she thought, and she would be afraid that she had disclosed too much to those who "might make trouble for her and hers." She would feel betrayed and would be less likely ever to trust anyone again.

We could offer to share the bathing and cooking facilities of our own quarters, a trailer. We could offer to loan them an extra blanket. Ida Mae declined our offers, saying, "I thank you. We can make out. We ain't never been beholden to no one; as my Pappy always said, 'us Carters'—that's my maiden name—'always pay our own way.' I'm still obliged to both of you though." Knowing the Southern rural culture of poor whites, we knew she was saying more than merely that she did not want to impose on anyone. [25] She did not want anyone to push in and take over her life. We could sense her appreciation for our offer, and we had to respect her desire to take care of her own needs.

There were a few ways in which we could help. As the fruit got worse and more wind-whipped, the grower told us to pick wherever we could find good fruit. Thus we could watch for trees extra heavy with fruit and call them to Ida Mae's attention. My husband could help with heavy ladders. Beyond that we could not intrude. They had to take care of themselves. They scorned the services of any social work agency. All they needed, all they asked, was the right to have a place to live, the right to work, the right to make their own way.

That night the weather was colder and there was more rain. We sat for a long time talking about Roger, Ida Mae, and Barbara Jean, listening to the beat of the water against the side of our trailer. We knew they were at that moment trying to find a spot to park and sleep in their car. For us it was distressing, not just because it involved our fellow workers, but because the Williamsons were symbolic of all families of the open road. They asked for little, they expected little, and, in turn, they received little.

As a professionally trained social worker, I knew I was "over involved." I also knew that many migrants felt the same anger and frustration that I was experiencing, and that this accounted for why they often appeared too self-involved to even discuss the problems of fellow workers. When someone tried to talk about his bad luck, others could match his story with one of their own—like one child saying to another, "That's nothing, you should see my cut." Migrants discussing problems interrupt each other. They talk past each other. They do not listen to each other. They do not want to hear what has happened to others when nothing can be done. It hurts too much to know the problems of others. It is much easier to feel "those people" suffer as punishment for their sins. It is easier to accept such feelings than to be torn by anger and righteous indignation because a fellow human being is denied the opportunity to help himself, or even to express himself.

Toward daylight, I fell asleep.

Martha Campbell

Barbara Jean and Ida Mae were in the orchard when we arrived. It was another day of quick showers and wet, slippery ladders. The ladders had no safety catches. They were wooden and had aged from exposure to the weather. Some had been broken and repaired. It was noon when Martha Campbell, a white picker, had an accident. She slipped on the top step, caught her foot in a branch, lost her balance, and fell backward. She landed hard. Her picking bucket, still fastened to her harness, was crushed against her side. Martha and her husband, Spike, had followed the cherry, peach, and apple harvests for nearly twenty years. On a ladder, Martha was agile. She had never had an accident. She was positive now that she was not hurt. She had only slipped. She waved away the hands that reached to lift her. She pulled herself into a sitting position. She leaned against the tree as if forcing air into her lungs. Her face was pasty white. Huge drops of sweat stood on her forehead. She was not hurt, she kept saying, more to assure herself than those who knelt close by. She would sit there a moment, she said, until she got her breath and then she would go back to picking. She took hold of the ladder and pulled herself to her feet. She was unable to stand upright. She was taken to a doctor over her protests and later to the hospital. An examination disclosed three broken ribs, a cracked vertebrae, and an umbilical hernia. Surgery would be necessary. The grower's crop insurance, a short-term policy, would cover $500 of her hospital and doctor expenses.[26]

There were some in the orchard who said Martha should not settle for medical expenses, that she should sue Mr. Smith. They pointed out that with the amount of land he owned and the size of his cherry crop, he could certainly afford to pay her "a little something." Besides, his ladders were unsafe, he had been negligent. They felt it only right that she be paid for her pain and suffering.

The orchard foreman thought that Martha would probably put on a "real show," pretending to be hurt more than she was. He was certain that she would "play the whole accident to the hilt, would claim she was paralyzed, or else would wear a brace, or would walk with crutches, and would get herself a shyster lawyer and try to take the Smiths to the dry cleaners." He talked on, to no one in particular, but to anyone who would listen. "The awful part of this thing is that Carl Smith worked hard for everything he's got. He started out here with nothing, as poor as any migrant would ever hope to be and worked himself up. Now he stands a good chance of losing everything he's got on the say-so of some hysterical female cherry picker." The foreman identified with the grower, with the so-called establishment. Most of the workers identified with Martha. Some were indifferent. They did not want to get involved even to the point of talking about it or in some cases even to admitting it had happened.

Spike returned to the orchard the next morning. It was the day of Martha's surgery. He came, he explained, "to protect our bonus," hinting that the grower was waiting for an opportunity to cheat him out of what he had coming. He reminded his fellow workers that he and Martha had picked both sweet and tart cherries and had averaged close to twenty lugs a day, in spite of inclement weather. They had more than $100 coming in bonus which they could not afford to lose. Spike returned to the orchard, although he said frankly that he was "in no mood for picking cherries." He was instead in the mood for a "good fight" if someone "looked at him the wrong way." He would work part of the day and then go to the hospital. It might be said, from his behavior, that Spike was psychologically defended against the fear of loss which he did not dare to face honestly and that he was acting out his anxiety by using various defenses such as denial, projection, and undoing.[27]

Concerned about Martha, Spike wanted to talk about the accident. It was difficult to get a comprehensive picture of her injury from him. He tended to change her symptoms each time he told the story and to exaggerate the doctor's report, although on being questioned he admitted that he had never actually talked with the doctor or seen her x-rays. There was almost an element of hysteria in his mannerisms. His mood swung from depression to over-optimism. One moment he said all would be well; he smiled and even laughed. The next moment he expected the worst; he knew she would never get well; she would be permanently crippled; she would never be able to work again. He would shift again and deny that she might be permanently crippled—she would be able to work again but maybe not this year. Then he softened this threat by saying, "Maybe she'll work later this fall." A few minutes later he related Martha's injury again, this time saying he was afraid she would not be able to pick plums and apples. The next crop for them that year would be peaches. He could manage that alone. But Martha was "an extra good apple picker." Last year she had averaged 115 bushels a day for five days. She had been paid twenty cents a bushel. They had saved enough from apples and from what Spike earned cutting pulpwood "to see them through" until strawberries were ripe the following summer. After strawberries they had picked sweet cherries and then tarts. They had hoped to do better this year than last. The trees were loaded with green apples and it looked as if this would be a productive year. But now with

Martha hurt, he was not certain how they would manage until spring. He did not think he could make enough money cutting pulpwood to support them until strawberry time. He was quite certain that he alone could not pick enough apples to cover their expenses. "Maybe it will ha' ta be welfare," he said. The muscles of his unshaved cheeks suddenly became taut. "We've never asked welfare fur help. We've never thought we would, but with this thing with Martha, it may ha' ta come to it." He wanted to sue the Smiths, and yet he wanted no part of any lawsuit. He was ambivalent. He handled his feelings by saying that others told him he should sue the Smiths, but that he had no intention of doing so. Once he said, "I'll have their farm fur this," but the mood passed, and later he said, "I'm not the kind of monster waitin' 'round like a vulture 'to cash in' on this kind of sicha-ashm. All I want is fur Martha to get well and fur the medical bills to be paid. What that insurance policy don't cover, I'll ha' to." He began to talk about extra jobs he would get to earn money to pay the bills, but the amount he claimed he would earn reflected a grandiose impression of his own worth as a worker. Seeming to be consciously aware of that fact he would return to his discussion of welfare.

Other Problems in the Orchard

It was a day of bright sun. Far to the west Lake Michigan was like polished turquoise. In our Garden of Eden, the cherry orchard, there suddenly was a new problem. An old man, a local white picker, left his ladder between the rows while he went after lugs. When he returned, the ladder was gone. No one knew where it was. One white worker volunteered that some of the Black workers "snitched" it, going on to comment that Blacks were always taking what they called a short cut across this corner of the orchard but that they were actually "out scouting for whatever they could find," especially filled lugs, new pails, and good ladders. He went on, "After all, everybody knows Negroes have sticky fingers and will steal anything that ain't nailed down and then lie about it." We did not bother to tell him that yesterday one of the Black crews had lost "a pile of seven buckets" which they were positive had been stolen by "those damn Mexicans." Later, the buckets were found where they had been left, under a tree. The crew had been looking in the wrong row.

Other pickers joined the old man in his search for the ladder. They found nothing. They could not take more time from their own picking, so they returned to their trees. He looked alone, encouraged by the shouted comments of his friend, Spike. Finally he found his ladder. Barbara Jean was using it. To her a ladder was a ladder. Because this one was light and extra long, she could reach to the very top of her tree. She did not realize she had taken a ladder someone had already claimed. She found it between the rows and carried it to her tree.

The older man talked the situation over with Spike. Spike promised the return of the ladder. He climbed down from his own tree, and together they walked purposefully toward Barbara Jean and Ida Mae. They demanded the return of the ladder and threatened to call the grower or orchard foreman if they did not get it.

They were unnecessarily harsh. Had they asked, the ladder would have been returned. It was a harshness born out of exasperation from time lost looking for the ladder. Spike's severeness was born out of his anxiety about a wife who faced surgery in a few hours, born out of feelings of guilt about what he should do about her accident. The ladder was recovered, but the episode brought tears to the eyes of a sensitive young girl and anger to the heart of her tired mother. It was one more unpleasant thing in a long chain of unpleasant events.

Later when we passed their tree and asked how they were doing, Ida Mae said, "Not so good." She explained that good cherries were scarce. There were so many wind-whipped, dried, and rotten ones, it took "a lot of pickin' to get a salable lug." If she had her way, they would be back in Belle Glade. They had all they ever wanted of the harvest of cherries. They would never come to Michigan again.

The day before there had been a more serious accusation. Joe Roy, one of the Black pickers from Georgia, said forty dollars had been stolen from his suitcase while he was in the orchard. Joe wanted the police called and the entire camp searched. Most of his crew did not believe he had lost the money as he claimed. They were not even certain he had that much money. Most of the other workers thought if he had had the money he lost it in a crap game. Some said he had spent it on a couple of women. Still others thought he was only trying to make trouble because he had been told to either "shape up and work" or else "catch a Greyhound for home," and that if he had forty dollars, he must have stolen it from someone, "cause he sho' ain't worked 'nough to make 'at much."

The workers stood in groups talking, leaving the cherries to hang. One of Joe's fellow crew members said he had brought "disgrace to the entire camp." There was fear Joe's behavior would reflect on the entire crew. If the police were called, everyone would be questioned; yet if Joe had lost the money as he claimed, his loss should be investigated. The crew leader talked to Joe, other crew members, and the grower. He told us that this was part of the "headache of being a crew leader." This part of his job, he added, had nothing to do with cherries; "worker problems" were also his responsibility. He had to keep his people working, for if they stood gossiping about the money and changing the amount every time they told the story, then they did not pick cherries and that "was skin off his nose." He therefore had better "talk with 'em."

Later the money mysteriously reappeared. Some of the other pickers who knew about the situation thought a collection had been taken among the crew so that the police would not be called. They thought that if the money had been stolen "it never got out of the crew" or at least "members of the crew knew what happened." Those who thought that a collection had been taken among crew members said this must have been done at the grower's suggestion. They thought Mr. Smith might not be overly anxious about having the "police snoop around" and draw attention to his housing. This would be especially true if he were afraid Martha Campbell would sue him as a result of her accident. He might, under those circumstances, "kick in five dollars" himself toward replacing the forty Joe Roy said he lost.

Regardless of the source of the money, Joe Roy decided it was best not to say anything more about the situation, and the matter was dropped. He said he gave the money to the grower to keep until he was ready "to get on the bus." The crew went back to work.

This crew stayed in the basement of the barn. There was no way to lock the sliding door to prevent strangers from entering while the pickers were in the orchard. There was no place to keep money except on one's person, under the mattress, or in a suitcase. Some workers asked the grower to keep their money until they were ready to leave. A few sent money home as postal money orders. Others, like Joe Roy, hid their money or carried it around.

We saw one member of this crew the following summer, and he told us he started for home with his cherry money in his pocket. He fell asleep on the bus, and someone "stole all of it."

The End of the Harvest

The fruit "ran worse." It took a lug and three-quarters to make one lug that the packing house would accept. The grower, Carl Smith, spent most of the afternoon sorting before he allowed the fruit to leave the orchard. Although he complained bitterly and loudly about the quality of some lugs and the time spent "doing the pickers' work," he did not compliment those whose work was done well. The picker who was careless, who overlooked leaves, stems, and rotten fruit, was paid fifty cents a lug, the same as the picker who carefully sorted and cleaned his fruit. There was nothing in Carl Smith's attitude that encouraged workers to be more conscientious or even to want to return another year.

Suddenly it was over. The grower and his farm manager came through the orchard, telling us that when we finished the lug on which we were working the picking was through. There were still tons of unpicked cherries, but the harvest season was over. Aimlessly the pickers wandered through the orchard, saying good-bye and wishing each other good luck. Here and there people exclaimed, "I never saw this tree before. Look at those cherries, man! And I thought I was pickin' big ones!"

We were through with the harvest, but when we got to the house we found we would need to return for our money. Carl Smith had not gone to the bank and would not "pay off until the next day." The closing of the picking season had not caught him unaware. He had told us on Saturday that the cherries would not "run beyond Wednesday." It was now Wednesday, two o'clock in the afternoon, but yet he was not prepared to pay his workers. He offered no explanation for his behavior. The workers could make a special trip to the orchard if they wanted their money. For those who were on their way to the tomatoes of Ohio, the cotton of Louisiana, the potatoes of Saginaw, it meant a delay of several hours, but they desperately needed their money, and for that reason they would wait. They would complain among themselves, but they would do nothing that would attract Carl Smith's attention to their anger, although they harbored a deep sense of rage that he could treat them in this subservient way.

We returned to the orchard the next morning. When we arrived, most of the others were there. Roger, Ida Mae, and Barbara Jean had been waiting since seven. They were anxious to get started for Belle Glade. Fannie Jo's bus was parked, waiting to be loaded. Cars, other buses, and trucks to carry pickers to the tomatoes of Ohio, the tomatoes of Illinois, the peaches of Benton Harbor—all were waiting. Workers milled around. They "cleaned camp." They burned trash. They performed aimless tasks, but mostly they waited to be paid and grumbled about the treatment. Carl Smith had gone to town. He would be back "presently."

We drove to the orchard. We waited through the morning. There were others who joined us. We sat under a tree. The orchard foreman drove past with the tractor, picking up the empty lugs from between the rows. He said we should go to the house. The owner had returned. It was two o'clock in the afternoon, exactly twenty-four hours since the official halt to cherry picking. It would have taken less than twenty-four hours for the pickers to drive to their next job; instead they had had to wait here for their money. Roger, Ida Mae, and Barbara Jean had spent an extra night sleeping in their car. The day workers had had to make an extra trip to the orchard. There was neither an explanation for the delay nor an apology for the inconvenience.

When we were paid, we were charged for a picking harness. We had turned it in the day before with the buckets, but it had disappeared before we were credited. The charge was one dollar and twenty-five cents—two and one-half lugs of cherries. We had no Social Security deductions. There had never been an inquiry about Social Security numbers. We were not members of a migrant crew, so therefore the responsibility for deductions and reporting Social Security rested with the grower. In our case, however, although we needed to declare the money as income, the grower did not have to report our Social Security. An agricultural employee earns Social Security credit only on work for each farm operator who pays him "one hundred and fifty dollars or more cash wages in the year" or who employs him "on twenty or more days."[28] Neither of us qualified. Neither of us had earned $100 and we had not worked twenty days. We did, however, even with the cost of the picking harness, have more to show for our days in the orchard than most of our fellow harvesters. We also fared better than some in that we were told we had a job should we return next year.

The real wealth of our experience was not the payment or the promise of future work; it was the days of interaction with fellow migrants. For a short time we had laughed together and worked together. We had shared each other's problems, and now we would scatter, never to be together again. But because we had been there and because for a short time we had related to each other, occasionally our thoughts would turn backward to a bay of blue water, to trees blood-red against the hillsides, to the odor of cherries, lugs and lugs of cherries—"cherrios, everywhere, just cherrios."

NOTES

1. Only California and Texas at that time used more migrant labor. In 1973, Michigan was exceeded only by California.

2. I am describing the situation as we saw it existing in 1964 in Grand Traverse County. I am pleased to report that conditions at the time of this writing are much improved. In 1965 Michigan passed a law requiring that migrant housing be inspected and licensed. Working conditions, health facilities, educational programs for children, day-care services, and social-welfare services for migrants have all been upgraded, not only in Grand Traverse County but throughout the state. These changes have been the result of concerted and combined efforts on the part of grower groups and state and local agencies—both public and private, civic and church groups, and concerned citizens as well as the efforts on the part of migrants and former migrants.

3. I do not wish to imply that we found conditions in the cherry area more shocking than those we saw in other states where migrants were employed. I do mean to say, however, that conditions varied greatly from grower to grower, and that the range of shocking conditions was much wider than we ever would have suspected from a casual observation or even from asking the migrants themselves.

4. Not his real name.

5. Sister Frances Jerome Woods, "Cultural Conditioning in Mental Health," *Social Casework*, **XXXIX**, (1958), 3-7.

6. *The Southeastern United States* (Princeton, N.J.: D. Van Nostrand Co., Inc., 1967), p. 94.

7. *Yesterday's People* (Lexington, Ky.: University of Kentucky Press, 1966), p. 79.

8. The expression "born and bred" is English and is common in the mountains of Appalachia and rural sections of the South. It means born and raised or trained—for example, "born and bred a farmer."

9. Many of these traffic violations result from poor driving skills, lack of driver-education requirements, or driver examinations in the migrant's home-base state. Many violations are also the result of lack of uniformity in state laws pertaining to speed limits, turns, or law enforcement. From prior experience, the migrant may be only prepared to avoid speed traps in certain areas and unprepared for the general enforcement of state laws on side roads. In his own state he may seldom, if ever, see the policing of roads other than main highways, and even then there may be very few police cars on main highways. There may be so few police in certain areas of the state where he lives and so many willful violations, such as improper parking, not coming to a stop, or turning without a signal, that the police ignore such violations. In the rural areas of Southern states many cars are driven without license tags or may be given a state inspection sticker although mechanically defective. In the Northern states, a driver could be ticketed for not having a tail light, windshield wiper, or a horn, but a migrant may have driven in his home community for several months without any one or all three of these items while the police paid no attention. A migrant often is not prepared for law enforcement or for handling the situation if he is stopped for a violation. He may have been conditioned to expect that by slipping a five-dollar bill into the arresting officer's hand he could avoid a ticket and the possibility of a much larger fine. He is not prepared for this to be viewed as a bribe.

10. This was the same rate paid eleven years earlier in 1953, for harvesting tart cherries in the Grand Traverse region. It was still the rate being paid in the area in 1964.

11. U.S., Department of the Treasury, Internal Revenue Service, "1970 Internal Revenue Service Tax Guide," Circular A.

12. It is interesting that this is exactly the same definition of the Mississippi Delta as that given by David L. Cohn in his book *God Shakes Creation* (New York: Harper and Bros., 1935).

13. William H. Grier and Price M. Cobbs have this to say on the practice of straightening hair: "One aspect of the Black woman's life which attracts little attention from outsiders has to do with her hair. From the time of her birth, the little girl must submit to efforts aimed at changing the appearance of her hair. . . .

"At the time of this writing, the overwhelming majority of Negro women have had their hair fixed by some method, including the use of a hot comb. The hair is oiled and the heated comb is applied. Usually there is some incidental burning of the scalp. The ordeal itself is long and tiresome involving hours spent waiting while the overworked beautician moves from customer to customer. To look 'presentable' the woman must have her hair pressed every week, or at least every two weeks. Plus, the Black woman is never free of the painful reminder that she must be transformed from her natural state to some other state in order to appear presentable to her fellow man." *Black Rage* (New York: Bantam Books, Inc., 1968), pp. 34-36. See also David L. Lorens, "Natural Hair: New Symbol of Race Pride," *Ebony*, December 1967.

The Afro hair style, which has become increasingly popular for Blacks of all ages in the 1970s, reveals the natural hair texture. It means a release for the Black woman from hot irons, pressing combs, and oils, and she can allow her hair to grow in its natural way, which was denied to previous generations of her race.

14. This sort of terrorism of Blacks has been described by many authors, some of whom are Guy Carawan, Candie Carawan, and Robert Yellin, eds.,

"Here's A Man Being Shot for a Dog," *Ain't You Got a Right to the Tree of Life?* (New York: Simon and Schuster, Inc., 1966), p. 163; Ann Fairburn, *Five Smooth Stones* (New York: Bantam Books, Inc., 1966), pp. 796-800; Harper Lee, *To Kill a Mockingbird* (New York: J. B. Lippincott Co., 1960), pp. 153-54, 190, and 238; Richard Wright, *Black Boy* (New York: Harper and Row, Publishers, 1966), pp. 63-64, 138-39, 198-201.

15. Describing the life in the Mississippi Delta in *God Shakes Creation*, David L. Cohn points out that crimes there are primarily those of violence. The whole area is "an armed camp." Almost every person carries arms of some sort; "nowhere are crimes of violence committed with less hesitation than in the Delta," and "nowhere do criminals escape with lighter punishment."

16. See more on this subject in Georgia Writers' Project, *Drums and Shadows: Survival Studies among the Georgia Coastal Negroes* (Athens, Ga.: University of Georgia Press, 1940), pp. 58, 59, 114, 160, 192, and 194.

17. Elliot Liebow makes a careful distinction between these relationships in *Tally's Corner* (Boston, Mass.: Little, Brown and Co., 1967), pp. 103-16.

18. *Ibid.*, see more on this in the chapter "Lovers and Exploiters," pp. 137-60.

19. Liebow states it this way: "Friendship is at its romantic flamboyant best when things are going well for the persons involved. But friendship does not often stand up well to the stress of crisis or conflict of interest when demands tend to be heaviest and most insistent. Everyone knows this. Extravagant pledges of aid and comfort between friends are, at one level, made and received in good faith. But at another level, fully aware of his friends' limited resources and the demands of their self-interest, each person is ultimately prepared to look to himself alone.

"The recognition that, at bottom, friendship is not a bigger-than-life relationship is sometimes expressed as a repudiation of all would-be friends or as a cynical denial that friendship as a system of mutual aid and support exists at all. When Tally threatened to withdraw his friendship from Richard, Richard dismissed this as no real loss. 'Richard is the only one who ever looked out for Richard,' he said.

"A similar attitude tends to the assessment of friendship as a 'fair weather' phenomena. . . .

"Attitudes toward friends and friendships are thus always shifting, frequently ambivalent, and sometimes contradictory. One moment, friendship is an almost sacred covenent; the next it is the locus of cynical exploitation: 'Friends are (good only) for money.'

"These shifts and apparent contradictions arise directly out of the structure and character of the individual's network of personal relationships. They arise from the fact that, at any given moment, the different relationships that comprise the individual's network of personal relationships may be at widely different stages of development or degeneration. They arise too from the equal ease with which a casual encounter can ripen into an intense man-man, man-woman relationship and the equal ease with which these relationships break down under stress." *Ibid.*, pp. 180-82.

20. This characteristic of exploiting others for personal gains is not a racial characteristic, but it is a characteristic of people of a certain class or certain background of experience. It is found among whites as well as nonwhites who feel that the only way they can get ahead is to grasp things for themselves. In some cases these individuals have been so damaged in their psychosocial development that they do not have the capacity for empathy, pity, or concern for others. They can think only of themselves and the guilt or remorse they express in their tears and gifts is motivated by self-pity.

21. *Tally's Corner*, pp. 215-16. I believe that this attitude toward women is

more a lower-class phenomenon than it is a racial characteristic and that it is found among all races and all ethnic groups.

22. The next year we returned to work in the same orchard. Benjamin brought a crew from Mississippi. The housing and the working conditions were the same as they had been the summer of 1964. The grower had not improved the milkhouse quarters. Benjamin's crew was also disillusioned. As the head of a crew, he did not have Fannie Jo's leadership qualities or firmness. He tried playing one member against another with promises which he could not keep. Most of the time he did not know he could not keep the promise until it was too late to back out. All he could do then was make more promises. The pattern of authority he used with his workers was much the same as the pattern that had been used with him by his white employers. The philosophy was "promise them anything, but deliver very little."

23. This subject has been analyzed by various authors. Lillian Smith states, "In the name of sacred womanhood, of purity, of preserving the home, lecherous old men and young ones, reeking with impurities, who had violated the home since they were sixteen years old, whipped up lynchings, organized Klans, burned crosses, aroused the poor and ignorant to wild excitement by an obscene, perverse imagery describing the 'menace' of the Negro men hiding behind every cypress waiting to rape 'our' women. In the name of such holiness, they did these things to keep the affairs of their own heart and conscience and home, as well as the community, 'under control.' And not once did they dream their women did not believe their lies." *Killers of the Dream,* Anchor Books (Garden City, N.J.: Doubleday and Co., Inc., 1963), p. 26. Smith goes on to say, "Southern culture has such few words in the mind to make the difference between human and animal. The words of the white mind are words that turn the Negro into animal, words deliberately fed to people to place the Negro beneath the level of human, to make him not only animal, but a 'menace.' " Pp. 140-41.

24. Manuel Gamio describes the prejudice in Texas toward Mexican-Americans: "The darkest skinned Mexican experiences almost the same restrictions as the Negro. . . . As an extension or reflection of racial prejudice, individuals of Mexican origin but of white skin are also socially discriminated against. The stigma of indigenous blood is so deep that the word 'Mexican' which implies a little or great deal of Indian blood and the corresponding pigmentation has acquired in the South a derogatory character. In general, to distinguish between white and brown Mexicans, the whites are euphemistically called 'Spanish' and they themselves adhere to the distinction. . . ." *Mexican Immigration to the United States* (Chicago: University of Chicago Press, 1930), pp. 53-54.

25. The extremes to which the concept of avoiding being "beholden" may be carried out are described in two novels: William Faulkner, *As I Lay Dying* (New York: Random House, Inc., 1930), pp. 109-11 and Lee, *To Kill a Mockingbird,* pp. 24-25.

26. Some policies protect property owners from liability but pay nothing toward hospitalization or medical care unless there is a liable suit. In some states an employee is not covered under the property owner's insurance. Any injury sustained on the job is an occupational hazard covered under the worker's own insurance. Unfortunately for the farm migrant he is in a hazardous occupation which usually is not covered under the grower's insurance, and he seldom can afford health and accident insurance on himself. His injury may need to be paid for out of his own earnings or else by some type of public welfare agency or public health fund. Because of his transient situation, the migrant is seldom in a position to bring a liable suit, even should there be a liable situation.

27. Psychological processes that defend against anxiety and provide tempo-rary security were first called defense mechanisms by Sigmund Freud. Generally speaking, an individual is unconscious or dimly conscious of the defense and of what he defends against. The basic defense maneuver is repression. Repression is a mental device evoked especially when internal danger (which is inherently difficult to perceive, grasp, and identify) threatens, and it is closely related to primitive flight mechanisms; unpleasant-ness is thereby avoided, not perceived, or forgotten. For more on this subject see Sigmund Freud, "Inhibitions, Symptoms and Anxiety" (1926) and "Introductory Lectures on Psychoanalysis, I and II" (1916-17), in *Complete Works* (standard ed.; London: Hogarth Press, 1961), pp. 20 and 15-16 respectively.

28. U.S., Department of the Treasury, Internal Revenue Service, "1970 Internal Revenue Service Tax Guide." Circular A.

> *. . . not to laugh at the actions of men*
> *nor yet to deplore or detest them,*
> *but simply to understand them.*

> Baruch Spinoza, 17th century
> Dutch philosopher

21

The Cuban and the Barbadian

They fired the cane field. A gentle wind moved through the long, green tops with the music of a whisper. Two men watched in silence the thin spirals of smoke drift upward while waiting for the field to burst into a raging flame. They could hardly speak each other's language. Seeming to have nothing in common, they made no efforts toward verbal communication.

The middle-aged Cuban, obviously there in the role of overseer, stood on a raised point of ground. He wore a wide-brimmed straw hat, whipcord riding breeches, and knee boots, and, although he worked along the muddy canal that ran through the sugar cane, his clothing showed little soil. The few spots of dirt on his white jacket came from airborne flecks of soot and bits of charred cane stocks.

This is a revision of a chapter of the same title that first appeared in *Where Hannibal Led Us* (New York: Vantage Press, 1967). The race relations in this chapter are described as they existed in the winter of 1964 before the Supreme Court order against racial segregation. Attitudes and feelings of, and toward, foreign workers, however, have not changed, and the interpersonal relationship between the Cuban and the Barbadian would be the same today as it was then.

His stance expressed arrogance and near disgust for his sweaty companion.

The dusky-skinned Barbadian stood in the ditch. A young man hardly out of his teens, he wore the soot- and sweat-stained garb of the cane cutters: dark shirt, black cap, dungarees, and heavy boots coated with muck. His shirt clung to the wetness of his body and his face and hands were streaked with dirt. A gunny sack soaked in the canal and ready for fighting the flames lay at his feet. While his eyes searched the cane field, he ate his lunch—some form of yellow rice and pinto beans on a paper plate—with his fingers. The sugar company delivered the food, which had been prepared by West Indian cooks, to the fields in metal containers to keep it hot. It was dipped out in portions for the workers who continued their tasks while they ate or stopped, if they could, for a brief period and sat on the ground at the end of the cane rows.

We spoke to the Cuban, as he seemed to be in charge. I wanted to photograph the men at work burning the field and wondered if I could have permission. He answered in Spanish, saying that if I would wait a few minutes the field would be ablaze and I could get the picture. The fire sputtered, sizzled, and in places died out. The men stood with their backs toward us—the Cuban intent upon the field, the Barbadian intent upon his food. The Cuban appeared aloof. It might be said that he appeared unfriendly, that he felt superior, standing so straight and tall and looking down from the raised point of ground. The distance between the men was more than a physical distance created by the ditch and its upper bank; it was a psychological distance, conditioned by culture, class, status, and well-established attitudes communicated nonverbally through body language. Each saw the other from the viewpoint of his own culture, and each represented to the other a different social class which strongly predetermined that they had nothing in common and that they would resent each other.

I asked the Cuban, who had turned toward us, the reason for firing the cane. He looked puzzled. I knew that his English, like my Spanish, was limited. I asked him if the other man spoke English. He thought so, and, although he had never attempted to talk to this man and had never seen him before this morning, he in his role as field overseer would ask for us. He spoke to the Barbadian in Spanish, pointing to us and at the smoking field in an attempt to convey that we had questions to ask.

For the first time since we had approached the field the Barbadian looked toward us. Quickly emptying his mouth, apologizing as he did so, he smiled—a warm, friendly smile. He folded his paper plate and buried it in the soft muck with his heel. He spoke excellent English with a British accent. He was from Barbados, the "little England" of the Lesser Antilles, 166-square miles of tropical paradise. He would be happy to tell us about the firing and harvesting of sugar cane. We sensed his eagerness to talk.

We explained that we were from sugar-beet country and had never before seen the harvest of sugar cane. He smiled widely. He knew of our state. Many from his island had worked in the orchards there. This was his first trip to the United States and he wished he could see more of the country. We wondered about his experiences thus far. At first he said they had been wonderful. I commented that cutting sugar cane was hard work, which he must have realized since he had obviously done it in Barbados or he would not have been recruited, and I wondered in what way his experience in America was wonderful. After a long moment of silence while he looked at me, he said very softly, "Honestly it is not wonderful at all."

He then began to talk, at first quietly without emotion. He said that all of his life he had wanted to visit the United States. As a child in school he had read most often those parts of his books that related information about this country. He knew the history and the geography of every state and dreamed some day he would see Niagara Falls, the Grand Canyon of the Colorado River, the great redwood forests, and the giant sequoia of the Sierra Nevada mountains in California. All of these places he knew and had visited in his fantasy. When he found he could come to the United States as a cane cutter, he had looked forward to the trip as an adventure. It would probably be his only opportunity to come, because Barbados was so far away and transportation so expensive. We asked if he had seen any other part of America since he had arrived. He answered "no" with wistfulness in his voice. In the American cane fields he found that life was a cycle of work, sleep, and work. Did we understand?

The workers are brought from the sugar plantation camps to the fields in trucks and returned to the camps in the same trucks. The camps are some distance from town. Everywhere there are cane fields—vast, stretching cane fields. There is no place for the workers to go and no opportunity to go any place. There is nothing to do but work and sit around camp playing cards or talk with other cane cutters from the West Indies. There is no more interaction with Americans here than in the cane fields of Barbados. There is no transportation for the workers to go places other than to work, and the town's people do not come to the camps, at least not as far as the workers are concerned. In fact, strangers are discouraged from coming into the camps unless they have business with the sugar company. Workers are free to walk into town, but when they do they have no real contact with Americans. They feel neither wanted nor welcomed.

They find that American Blacks hate them, although both are Black, because they are better educated, speak better English, and do not usually squander their money. They are also more aggressive than American Blacks. As Ira De Augustine Reid points out, although the Caribbean islands were the clearing house or a midway point for African Negro slaves on their way to America, the

Caribbean Negro has "developed into a spirited aggressive culture-type . . . singularly different from that of the American Negro."[1] To American Black men these more aggressive Black cane cutters from the islands are a threat and might want to date their women. To some women and to the con-men who are looking for victims, the cane cutters are an easy mark: they are lonely and they can be encouraged to part with their money.

The Caribbean Blacks also face the stone wall of racial and regional prejudice in the white community. To the whites, the cane cutters are Black foreigners and therefore should know and keep "their place," which means that they should stay in the camps and keep out of town except to spend their money.

All of these things the young Barbadian in the Florida sugar cane understood, but understanding did not keep him from being disappointed on this, his first trip, to America. He felt shut away from everything except work. Working in the cane, he said, was "like being in the army": there was no freedom. The three of us laughed at his comparison. From the corner of my eye I caught a meaningful sideward glance from the Cuban. It was a mixture of aloneness, of being shut off from our conversation, and at the time it was filled with reproachful scorn that we so willingly conversed and laughed with this common cutter of the cane.

We continued our talk with the Barbadian. Had he been prepared for work in a country with this much racial prejudice? He hesitated and smiled apologetically. He had had some awareness but not really enough; no one from a Caribbean island could be truly prepared for the racial prejudice of this country, because it is not the prejudice to which they are accustomed.

In Barbados and Cuba and the other Caribbean islands class barriers and class distinctions are observed rather than racial differences as in the United States. Reid points out that "the Black . . . populations of Barbados . . . look down upon the poor whites of the island, known as 'Red Legs' or 'Scotland Johnnies.' "

Reid identifies many of the problems that face a Black who comes to the United States from one of the Caribbean islands, where the whole concept of Blackness is different from that found here. Although he is talking about the Black immigrant who comes here to live permanently, many of the same situations he found in his research exist for the migrant worker who comes to Florida for a season. Reid says,

> The Negro immigrant to the United States is faced with grave problems of social adjustment. Not only is he an alien by law and fact, but he suffers a complete change in status by emerging from a group setting where he was the racial majority into one where he becomes part of a racial minority. He brings a cultural heritage that is vastly different from that of the American Negro. . . . His mode of living, his relationship with government, his idea of "liberty," even his traditions, are vastly different. Briefly, then, the immigrant who becomes Negro upon arrival brings to the United States Negro population a different set of mores, with a different life experience. The problem he faces is distinctly one of cultural adjustment.
>
> Though he has been advised as to working conditions, and the possibilities for employment, he is not versed in the ways of job-seeking. . . . Being a stranger, he is ignorant of the law, the modes of life and the prejudices he is about to face. As a result, he becomes the unwitting victim of a direct and indirect type of exploitation. . . . The Negro immigrant finds that he must adjust in a three-fold way—from the point of view of nationality, mores, and the social role played by his racial group. He experiences a complete change in his environment.[2]

These factors in environmental change have been classified by Henry Pratt Fairchild as both physical and human.[3] The many objects, places, events, and people that make up a physical setting are interdependent. Humans do not exist except in relationship to all the other components of a given environmental situation. The Black immigrant from the Caribbean islands comes from a semi-tropical area where mild temperatures, heavy rainfall, lush plant growth, and earthquakes are all part of his environmental experience, and all have been part of his personality development.

In Barbados, where the majority of the population is Black, the instructors in an orientation program pointed out to the cane cutters who would work in Florida that they would be expected to use separate drinking fountains and toilets and that the places where they could sit and eat would be separated from those of the whites, regardless of the whites' social class or lack of status position. All of this was a new experience for them. Blacks in Barbados were accustomed to going any place they had money to pay their way. They had never known racial restrictions, and so they were told to be very careful about what they did—to keep to themselves and speak only if spoken to; to pretend not to hear or even to understand English if anything unpleasant were said; to remain aloof from any situation which would cause trouble, for if they didn't, they would be without jobs. They were told to be ambassadors of good will for Barbados. In that capacity they were given recent information about their island and asked to share it with Americans in the hopes of attracting more tourists to Barbados.

In spite of all the warnings, this young cane cutter came with high expectations of seeing America and Americans, but he found things to be very different from what he had expected. He found he had almost no contact with any American. It was easy, he said, for him and the other workers to feel isolated, to feel that they were being exploited, and to become bitter in this strange "Godforsaken, lonely place" where the workers were so much at the mercy of the sugar company. And no one here seemed to care what was happening to them. If there was the slightest hint of trouble with a worker, he was immediately threatened with deportation and no attempt would be made to find out why he felt the way he did or what had happened to him since his arrival in this country. In fact, if the worker talking to us had been overheard, even though all he said was true, he could be sent back to Barbados as a "rabble rouser." He would thus be blackballed as far as any future job as a cane cutter in this country was concerned. In fact, he could be labeled as a communist, which was what usually happened when workers dared to say the sugar company treated their foreign employees as prisoners.

The fire rose for a moment, then it died back. Still they waited. I asked the Barbadian about his island home. He said it was the first time since he arrived that anyone had asked him about Barbados. He seemed so overcome with the question that he had to struggle for words. I had the feeling, standing there before him, that he had left us psychologically; for a moment he was transported from that smoking south Florida cane field to a bit of sun- and sea-washed island—to Barbados. The statistics of his orientation were forgotten. He was no longer recruiting tourists. He was a lonely, homesick adolescent. "It is beautiful, beautiful beyond description," he said sadly, "just beautiful."

The two men agreed to let me take their picture while we waited for the fire. The Cuban posed with the Barbadian and then asked that I take a picture of him alone. He wanted to tell us about himself, he said, and what had happened to force him to leave Cuba.[4] He asked if we could understand him, as he knew so little English. We nodded, indicating that gestures, common words, and body language could help us grasp his meaning. And it was in this way that he told us of himself.

Once, before Castro, he had been a land proprietor in Cuba and had owned a large sugar plantation. With Castro in power there was no future for Cuba, and he had dared to speak out and say so.[5] He was finally arrested and questioned for three days without sleep, food, or water. Four times he had been told that he was to be shot, and a gun was put to his head. He was finally released, but his sugar plantation, his home in Havana, his bank account, and all of his holdings were seized by the Castro government. He was reduced to the level of a laborer, and he was afraid for his life and that of his family. He could never accept Castro, and eventually he would be shot for treason, as were some of his friends. He arranged to escape from Cuba with his wife and son in a small fishing boat. Although they traveled in a storm and nearly lost their lives, they finally reached the Florida coast. Forgetting our limited knowledge of Spanish, he ended his story in his own language, but his feelings were clear and his fears and hatred were apparent. His anger hung around us almost like a physical thing.

Suddenly much of the Cuban's earlier attitude was clear both to the Barbadian and to us. This man was the victim of a dictator's scheme. Once in his homeland this Cuban had commanded respect by his very name and position; now he too labored for a foreign sugar company. Being a common laborer was far more difficult for him than it was for the Barbadian, who had never known material wealth, because he had owned much and lost. For a few seconds we looked deeply into the soul of this man and saw fear struggling with dignity. We could see the aloneness of this man in an alien culture, who had no identity ties because the Cuba he had known no longer existed, and who was not yet part of any American culture. Like the Barbadian, he was a farm laborer in a foreign land, but he was more afraid; he could no longer turn his eyes southward to Cuba, the "pearl of the Greater Antilles," and think of it as his home. Under the guise of aloofness, arrogance, and pride there was a lonely, frightened man who hungered for human relationships and understanding.

Further south other cane fields showed bright lines of flame. They were ready to be photographed. We had much to do, and we could no longer wait for this field to burst into flames. We moved toward the road as the men turned their attention to the problem of relighting the fires, which by now had completely gone out. The Cuban still stood on the little ridge of black muck with his back toward the Barbadian. The Barbadian still stood in the ditch. They were silent, each man in his own world, but between them there seemed to be a sense of something which had not been there previously. As we reached the road we stopped and looked back. They turned, saw us, and waved simultaneously.

NOTES

1. *The Negro Immigrant* (New York: Ams Press, 1968), p. 49.
2. Ibid., p. 35.
3. *Immigrant Backgrounds* (New York: Wiley and Sons, 1927), pp. 1-6.
4. For more information on why Cubans left their country in exodus primarily to the United States, see Richard Fagen, Richard A. Brody, and Thomas O'Leary, *Cubans in Exile* (Stanford, Calif.: Stanford University Press, 1968).
5. See Mario Lazo, *Dagger in the Heart* (New York: Twin Circle Publishing Co., 1968), for a startling report of Castro's rise to power, why Cuba was lost to Communism, and the role played in all of this by the United States State Department.

But the young, young children, O my brothers,
 They are weeping bitterly!—
They are weeping in the playtime of the others.
 In the country of the free.

Elizabeth Barrett Browning, 19th century
 British poetess
 The Cry of the Children

22

The Pecking Order

It was early afternoon. I had returned to our living quarters to change into a long-sleeved shirt for protection from the mosquitoes which hung in clouds above the strawberries. The housing in which we were lodged resembled a motel—single rooms in a long row, each with an outside door, each room assigned to a family. I could hear the knocking, loud and persistent, on the door next to ours. No one was inside. The young white man and his pregnant wife who lived there were both in the fields. From other sections of the camp came sounds of voices and shouts of children; at this end I was alone.

The knocker moved to our sleasily constructed door, which rattled under the force of the blows. It was an insistent knock, a plea that someone be inside. I opened the door and found a boy of about eight with blonde hair caked into the film of sweat and dirt on his forehead. His face looked as if it had been pushed into the earth. His blue eyes were anxious, frightened, and yet angered. "Is your daddy home?" he asked, childlike, giving my husband a title more familiar to his own experiences.

"No," I answered. He moved back, his eyes fervently moving beyond me in a quick search of the empty room behind my back to see if I had told the truth. His eyes darted toward the next door, but I knew that no one was home there either. "Is something wrong?" I asked, detaining him as he tried to turn away. "Do you need help?"

"Yes," he sobbed, moving toward the other door even as he spoke. "Those bastards[1] hav' taken my bike, 'n' they're bustin' it all up ta hell 'n' gone, 'n' they won't giv' it back. They won't even stan' up 'n' fight . . . fight fair like gouge fer gouge. There ain't no chance with 'em, they've got sticks, 'n' an iron pipe." He clenched his teeth. "Those damn, black stinkin', filthy, dirty niggers. Those sons-o'-bitches, those scum . . . those scum . . . those filth. . . ." He choked against his own flow of words.

They were coming to find him, a taunting, jeering group of older Black boys,[2] yelling obscenities that matched the vocabulary of the younger boy. The leader, a thin boy about eleven, was on a bicycle. As he rode past, the other boys poked at the wheels with

their sticks and piece of iron pipe as they shouted, "Ride it, man, jist don't let this liver white son-o'-a-bitch ever git his hands on it. Ride the wheels off, screw it into the groun' . . . giv' it ta me, don't give it ta him . . . god-damn. . . ."

As soon as he saw them, without waiting for my comment or even asking if I would help, the owner of the bicycle dashed after them screaming, "You sons-o'-bitches, you black sons-o'-bitches, give me back my bike or I'll kill you; I'll gouge your eyes out; I'll kill you dead. . . ." His final threats were lost in the shouts of the others.

The harder the younger boy ran, the faster the bigger boy rode, and the louder the others laughed and shouted. When they tired of baiting him, they let him have his bicycle—after they had let the air out of both tires and held him face down in the dirt until he promised never again to ride it in that camp. The gang leader told him he was "lucky"; they did not make him give them all the money he had earned picking strawberries for one full week to buy back his bicycle.

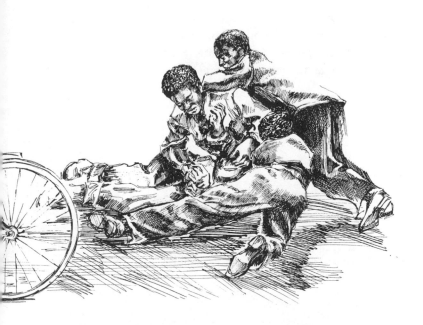

As he pushed the deflated bicycle toward the other end of the housing, he swore at them, putting together every combination of obscenity he had ever heard. They pelted him with tin cans and garbage and swore back until they saw the grower's son coming. Then they scattered in all directions.

The little boy's family was new to camp that day, which meant he was fair game for all the other boys. I do not know if he did anything to provoke the attack. Some children "promote aggression, to prove the world is hostile and 'mean.' "[3] Perhaps this new boy, an outsider, felt that he needed to prove himself before he would be accepted by the others. Or the attack could have been unprovoked and brought about merely because of his status symbol, the bicycle—something no other boy in the camp owned.

Some children would hate him simply because he had something they did not have. Others would be his friend in order to have a ride. Those who were part of a group prowling through the camp looking for someone, or something, on whom to vent their pent-up frustrations found a scapegoat in this newcomer.[4] Each member of the gang was retaliating against him for all the times each had found himself ostracized. Like a flock of chickens who will peck a strange chicken to death, they would torment this boy until he either left or retaliated in such a way they would respect his physical strength. He could fight their leader and show he was not afraid, or he could take his bicycle inside the housing and keep it there, riding it outside only if an adult was nearby to offer him protection. He chose the latter course of action and kept his bicycle and himself hidden. A week later his father decided to move to another camp where his son would feel safer.

NOTES

1. This type of language is not unique to a migrant child. It is not unusual for any child, especially a boy in the so-called latency period between the ages of five and twelve to add profanity and various four-letter words to his vocabulary. As Irene M. Josselyn points out, the use of such words gives the child "a fuller sense of emancipation. He, backed by his group, dares defy authority." *The Happy Child* (New York: Random House, 1955), p. 101.

2. Irene Josselyn also discusses the gratification children experience within their play group and how they channel their aggression. She says, "At times the children may play together as a group attacking an imaginary enemy. They find strength in numbers and in a common danger or goal, even though the enemy exists only in a fantasy. At other times, the real group or individual may attack another actual group or individual cloaked in the fantasy of enmity. In the latter instance, the wish to strike out aggressively is becoming loosely linked to competitive urges that are being redirected into play." *Ibid.*, p. 94.

3. Hertha Riese, *Heal the Hurt Child* (Chicago: University of Chicago Press, 1966), p. 462.

4. A scapegoat is a symbolic target at which hostile-aggressive impulses are aimed. Hostile-aggressive impulses are natural for all children in the stressful process of socialization. In the process of interacting in the peer group or the family, conflicts occur. Many of these conflicts cannot be resolved in their original aggressive form. Unresolved conflicts produce tension which becomes so unpleasant that it must be discharged in a way that will not create additional threats to the individual or the group. If an opportunity is not provided for the individual to work out these feelings, he may choose an object to symbolize his conflict. This symbol becomes the scapegoat on whom he can project his feelings of hostility and thus drain off his own tension.

Scapegoat theory in this type of situation is described by Gordon W. Allport as having three stages:

1. Frustration generates aggression.
2. Aggression becomes displaced upon relatively defenseless "goats."
3. This displaced hostility is rationalized and justified by blaming, projecting, stereotyping. *The Nature of Prejudice,* Anchor Books (Garden City, N.J.: Doubleday and Co., Inc., 1958), p. 331.

The person as a symbolic target may be a family member or a member of the peer group, but it is more apt to be an outsider, a stranger, someone of a different race, religion, or ethnic background. It is usually someone who is different, looks different, acts different, and is weaker (physically or in position) or someone who has something that is envied or who may be a threat. The threat is often expressed by children as, "He will get the attention and love that I now have." In the adult it comes out as, "He may get my job or something else I value, or he will marry my daughter; therefore, it is only fair that I protect myself and my loved ones from this individual who is less than a human person."

Riese points out that parents who scapegoat their child may see the child as the problem but may not see that they themselves have a problem in their marriage or in their relationships. *Heal the Hurt Child,* pp. 169-72. Norman W. Bell and Ezra F. Vogel, also looking at the family who scapegoats its child, discuss the emotionally disturbed child being used as a scapegoat for family tensions. *A Modern Introduction to the Family* (New York: Free Press, 1968), pp. 412-27.

PART V

Isolation: The Boundary of a Migrant's Occupation

We are all in the gutter,
but some of us are looking at the stars.

Oscar Fingall O'Flahertie Wilde, 19th century
Irish author and poet

23

Isolation of Farm Workers

If one word were used to describe the farm worker's relationship to the community where he works, that word would be *isolation*. This is even truer for the migratory farm worker and his family than it is for year-round farm workers. This separateness of worker from community arises partly from the nature of farm work—the rural setting, the acreage, the crop, the limited number of other employees or type of work.

Farm Workers' Limited Involvement in the Mainstream of Culture

The principal factor of isolation for the farm worker, however, is his limited role in the farm community. It is the farmer, grower, or rancher who is part of the in-group. The hired man or seasonal worker is the outsider. Characteristically the in-group has a sense of

---

This is a revised version of an article with the same title originally published in the *Michigan State Economic Record,* IX (June 1967), 3, 6, 7.

solidarity, mutual goals, a sense of belonging. On the other hand, the out-group, here represented by farm workers, is always on the fringe of things.

One reason that farm workers are on the fringe of things is that they are thought to have little to offer the community. The average farm laborer has a limited formal education: either he is a school dropout or he may never have gone to school at all. He generally has limited experience or no experience or training other than that for agricultural work. He may select farm employment because he has a shy, withdrawing personality that makes it difficult for him to work in close proximity with others. Or he may have difficulty adjusting to a monotonous daily routine, such as an assembly-line job, and thus chooses agricultural work because of its variety.

The farm worker, whether migrant or year-round, is usually a member of a minority group—a Black, an Indian, a Chicano, or of some ethnic group represented among poor whites. As such, he may be caught between two cultures, that of his employer and his employer's community and that of his birth. Because of his employment he must hold two divergent sets of ideas, attitudes, and habits. Living in such a dual world is not emotionally gratifying for the individual. Under such circumstances, a person becomes more fiercely entrenched in his own heritage. His cultural differences suddenly become more apparent and this results in even more isolation.

The psychological effect of attempting to hold on to one's own heritage is seen among immigrants. An extreme example are the Swiss immigrants in New Glarus, Wisconsin, a village that is "more Swiss in decor and architecture than a village in Bernese Oberland" and where the residents have maintained a group identity that is traditional Swiss in its culture. Herbert Kubly describes the creation of this island of Swiss culture by people who felt isolated from the mainstream of the dominant society that surrounded them.

> The difference between New Glarus and Switzerland's Kanton Glarus, for which it was named by its founders in 1845, is a trick in time. Switzerland, a 20th century industrialized country, keeps abreast of modern developments, while in New Glarus the nostalgic descendents of the pioneers have preserved mid-19th century Switzerland. Even the language we speak, a Swiss-German patois, is an archaic one little spoken in Switzerland,

including words and phrases no longer understood in the old country. . . .[1]

Farm Workers' Temporary Employment

Another reason for the isolation of the seasonal worker is an aloneness created by the temporary status of his employment. The two greatest factors which motivated his becoming a migrant worker in the first place were (1) limited work near his own home, and (2) the promise of work or better opportunities in some other section of the country. The average migrant worker is highly motivated to support himself and his family. He does not join the migrant streams so much out of dissatisfaction with his home area as out of necessity. His stay in a community can be terminated when a freeze, a windstorm, or hail wipes out an entire crop, forcing him and his family to move on in search of another job. There is never the security of a permanent job; every work situation is temporary.

Community Relations

Many communities subtly isolate the worker. Very few places make seasonal workers feel they are accepted or welcomed or that the community would be glad for them to become permanent residents. The migrant may not realize how isolated he is unless he tries to become involved. He may find many places closed to him. Let him try to get involved in a decision-making process, and he will soon discover that he is not part of the in-group; he is always an outsider who has very limited rights, and those rights become even hazier if he pushes too much to be part of the community. If he threatens the status quo, he will probably find himself more isolated than ever before.

Too often the migrant worker and his family are made aware that they are not wanted other than for the work they do or the money they spend. Migrants leave most of the money they receive in the very community in which it is earned. Although they work hard to harvest the crops and spend money freely, migrant workers still frequently feel that local citizens have contempt for them. They know they are called "fruit tramps." They know people are often afraid of them and expect them to be dishonest. They are the first to be suspected or blamed should something go wrong while they are working in an area. They are often arrested on the slightest provocation and fined heavily. They are housed in everything from comfortable, clean motel-type quarters to unrenovated chicken coops and barns. They may be cheated, overcharged, and underpaid. Employers may take advantage of them because they have trouble speaking English and because competition for non-agricultural, nonskilled jobs has forced them into the migrant streams and, therefore, they dare not question their rate of pay. It is difficult under these circumstances for any individual to feel that he is an important part of a community. It is difficult for him to maintain a sense of self-worth unless he can create it for himself and his relatives within his own family. Although the kinship family plays an important role among migratory farm workers because it gives them a feeling of belonging and worth, at the same time it may create what appears to be a clannishness that helps to isolate migrant workers even more.

Our Experience with Workers' Isolation

Working and traveling as migrant farm laborers, my husband and I had a chance to see rejection and isolation imposed by both communities and employers. In one place migrants needed to prove that they had the cash to pay for medical services before they could see a physician or dentist, regardless of their need. We ourselves were called filthy Mexicans and dirty Indians, depending upon the race of our fellow workers or travelers. We slept on a discarded mattress in a lean-to attached to a barn, while other workers in our immediate crew, including small children, slept inside the barn on the ground on piles of straw. We were charged for equipment even though we turned it in at the end of a harvest. Our Social Security numbers were completely ignored as if there were no federal program to cover farm workers.

In one remote rural area I was very ill for several days before we were able to find a physician. He barely glanced my way as I walked into his office, indicating with a nod of his head where he expected me to sit. He felt the swollen glands in my neck and with a slight pressure on my chin indicated I was to open my mouth. During the examination he kept up a running commentary with his nurse regarding the moral character of migrants.

Suddenly he called to his nurse. "Would you believe it?" he cried, pointing into my mouth. "Would you believe it? Here's *one* who has actually been to a dentist—look!"

He went on, "This one has a bad throat and ear, but otherwise she seems healthy enough; she has none of that flabby welfare fat so many of these people have, but just give her time."

The physician was eventually informed of our identity, and a week later, when I returned for a second office visit wearing the same attire I had worn seven days before, there had been a transformation. I was suddenly "Dr. Reul." He held his office door open for me to enter and shook my hand in greeting. Despite his deference to my position in academia, one to which he himself had once aspired when a younger man, his first question was, "What are you and your husband doing living and working with *those peo-ple?*" He seemed utterly unaware of the fact that only a week before in that very room he had identified us with "those people" when he spoke of me to his nurse as if I were an object and had called me "this one." I did not feel at that moment the need to remind him that I was same individual I was the week before.

Although I have never had a medical examination in which I felt quite so dehumanized, this doctor at least was providing excellent medical care at a very reasonable cost for "those people." I have never had better treatment for an ear and throat infection than I received from that physician in that very remote rural area.

Months later, after we had left the migrant stream, we returned to one grower for whom we had worked, asking to talk with him about his experience employing migrants. Naturally he did not recognize us as his former employees. He had had only a most superficial contact with us in his role as our employer, and now we looked different. He had no way of knowing we were ever migrants. He spent the afternoon describing the "riff-raff and scum" with whom he had to contend as he could no longer have braceros, Jamaicans, and Barbadians harvest his crops. The foreign workers were the only ones who truly "knew how to work." His total attitude was one of contempt for American farm migrants. He kept saying such things as,

You know what that race is like. [He was not referring to a race; he was referring to farm migrants.] You can't expect them to be like us; they're not as intelligent. Otherwise they'd try to amount to something and get better jobs. They're just looking for handouts. They don't want work. They just use the migrant streams to get to a state that has higher welfare grants than where they have been living and that has migrant medical programs which pick up the tab when their babies are born or they're sick.

This grower is not alone in his feelings. There are more people in this country who persistently discriminate against the poor than there are those who discriminate against race or religion. In our country, poverty is considered punitive: people would not be poor if they were not inferior or lazy. As Stewart G. Cole says,

> ... [such a] practice of discrimination rests upon the enlistment of prejudiced attitudes. It is not uncommon for members of socially privileged groups to consider those who are economically poor as morally inferior stock. . . . The language of prejudice can only be understood as it is regarded semantically. Verbal symbols may be used to vilify a people. Innuendo, smear words, or plain uncomplimentary remarks are commanded to lower the level of acceptance of certain groups. Now and then organized propaganda is circulated by the press . . . or whispering methods [this has been especially true of propaganda against religious groups] to keep a minority group in its place. The purveyors of prejudice may resort to nonverbal means of indicating their disapprobation of racial, religious, or culture groups. Their gestures indicate prejudice. The way they look at the out-group [whose identity may be determined on the basis of sex or occupation], their tone of voice, the discourtesy, the emotive words, shrug and swagger: these devices for communicating attitudes and wishes are powerful forces which divide peoples and categorize them in terms of a variety of upper, middle and lower social classes.[2]

Such attitudes also tend to isolate those who are discriminated against and to deny their existence through avoidance. The out-group or out-individual is ignored as if he were not there. Members of the out-group are excluded not only from personal contacts but also from channels of leadership, status, and respect.

Employers' Isolation of Workers

The farm worker may be isolated by the employer for whom he works. This is both a conscious and an unconscious attempt on the part of the employer to keep workers from being tempted by other offers of employment. Such an employer views his workers not only as his employees, but also as his personal property. Thus, he may control their visitors, their trips to town, even their free time.

The farmer or grower has not developed this frame of mind without some provocation. Because of the shortage of harvesters, growers are increasingly suspicious of anyone who wants to visit migrant housing for fear they are other growers pirating workers. A grower may suspect that the visitor on his property is there to stir up or organize his migrant workers or to snoop into the housing he is providing—in short, to make trouble for him. The grower may encourage the crew leader, who transported the migrant workers, to do most of the crew's shopping and thus keep the workers isolated in or near the labor camp until the harvest is completed. The grower may say he is doing this for their protection or convenience, but the migrants feel that they are prisoners under such conditions.

A farmer may keep his hired man isolated in the same way. The farmer's attitude is, "As long as he works for me, I do not want him wasting my time going into town or talking with people whose identity I do not know." The farmer would rather do errands, such as pick up tobacco, than run the risk of having his worker exposed to the wider community.

Cultural Factors that Effect Isolation

Whites from Appalachia, the Ozarks, and the deep South are conditioned by what they know is often the attitude of those who do not understand their culture. Many feel that they are viewed as poor white Southern trash. Feeling inadequate and afraid of being hurt, they remain aloof. The alienation they feel outside their own geographical area—the ridicule they fear and sense—may cause a form of self-imposed isolation. They may never really think of another community as home, although they may live and work there for years.

Blacks in the migrant streams usually have lived most of their lives in the deep South. They learned at an early age to respond in one way toward a white employer and another way toward members of their own race. As they move into an open, competitive society, some Southern Blacks find that they are unable to cope with the anxiety of expectations outside of the caste system in which they grew up, and so they withdraw into their own racial group or family. They sense that whites expect Black migrants to gamble, to be promiscuous, to fight, to cut each other, to lie, to steal, to be dirty; and although they feel much hostility toward those who have these attitudes and expectations, they may find it easier to handle their anger within their own racial group than to express it openly toward a white employer.

Lower-class Blacks, Southern whites, Indians, and Chicanos have difficulty identifying with the problems of the middle-class growers and management. Each ethnic group has been taught by its culture that employers, the federal government, and big business are not to be trusted. The poor of these groups have always been exploited by those for whom they worked. They have learned to protect themselves by teaching their children to be on guard, to see things only from the viewpoint of the worker. To do otherwise would be traitorous to their own kind. Distrust of any employer outside of their own ethnic group has become part of the culture.

While growers and farmers often view these workers as lazy, dishonest, and destructive, the workers, in turn, see their employers as exploiters. Farm workers often view the farmer as being extremely wealthy, financially secure, and having connections at the state or federal capital through which to defeat any bill introduced for the benefit of the common man. It is difficult for the farm worker from this background and with these experiences to believe that his employer or the agencies from his employer's community are really interested in his well-being.

Effects of Isolation

Research on the psychological effects of isolation indicates that the more people are isolated, the more they withdraw from human contact altogether and become even more separated within their own group. Observing groups in isolation and the individual's behavior within those groups, Irwin Altman and William W. Haythorn found that each person selected a territorial area, such as a bed or chair, which seemingly gave him a sense of belonging or of owning something that exemplified his identity.

> Territoriality for specific chairs and areas (positions around the table) was low at first but steadily grew as days in isolation progressed. This might tend to happen on the basis of habit alone, but the interesting aspect of the problem is the degree to which it happened.[3]

Those who were not able to tolerate the experimental tests in isolation for long periods of time showed a slightly different pattern of behavior in selecting territorial boundaries than did those who could stand isolation. Altman and Haythorn continue:

> For isolates, developmental patterns were different, with bed territoriality established first, followed by side-of-table and finally chair territoriality. Perhaps two factors associated with beds led to this rapid and persistent jurisdictional behavior. First, beds possess a high degree of personal character associated with olfactory cues, body contact, amount of time spent there, and general cultural practices regarding the inviolability and sanctity of a person's bed, bedding, and pillow. Second, beds were located in a fixed geographical region, an extremely critical aspect of animal territoriality. The next order of territoriality occurred for areas around the table . . . chair preferences became strong next and reached their peak during the final days of isolation. Side-of-table territoriality may have developed more rapidly because it entailed a fixed geographical area, while chair territoriality involved movable objects. . . .
>
> Isolates also exhibited gradual withdrawal and increased "cocooning" behavior in social activities. While amount of time asleep remained constant, they spent more and more time alone through days and less time together—phenomena often qualitatively described in reports of groups in naturalistic isolated situations such as the Antarctic.[4]

Applying this psychological ecology of isolation to the farm migrant situation, we find that for the migrant in transit it may be quite difficult to establish constant territorial boundaries. For this reason the car, bus, or truck in which the migrant travels becomes an extension of self.

> The only reality in all that world of open highways, of small grocery stores, or service stations, the only reality in all that world was the familiar outlines of the trucks. The trucks became an island of security. The trucks became a figure that was familiar in the world of strangeness and indifference.[5]

The transient individual's conscious and unconscious feeling that his mode of transportation is an extension of self, namely of his ego boundaries, also accounts for his reluctance to dispose of his much used car or truck when it can no longer be used for transportation. To others it is a junked car cluttering up the yard; to the former migrant it was a means of escaping from a sense of frustrated helplessness into action (moving *away from* or *toward*), and at the same time its outlines provided him with territorial boundaries of security. It was his cradle of comfort; it was his bed, his table, and his chair.

When people live under conditions of alienation, they have a greater need to establish territorial boundaries within which a stranger or nonsignificant other may not intrude. Isolation sharpens the territorial boundaries and makes the individual more hostile to the idea of intrusion. The territorial boundary in such a case may be the work area—"my row" or "my tree" or "my assignment"—and it will include the tools of the work, such as "my ladder" or "my hoe" or "my picking basket." It can be a seat on the bus, a position in line or in the truck, a place to leave personal items, or a spot to sleep. It may include small personal items that have become a part of the identity of self. In limited surroundings these items become even more important, and their arrangement or display is part of the territorial area that this person feels belongs to him. Margaret Bourke-White illustrates this in describing an experience she had while working with Erskine Caldwell in 1937 on material for their book on rural poverty, *You Have Seen Their Faces*.

> I remember one occasion when we went into a cabin to photograph a Negro woman who lived there. She had thick, glossy hair and I had decided to take her picture as she combed it. She had a bureau made of a wooden box with a curtain tacked to it

and lots of little homemade things. I rearranged everything.
After we left, Erskine spoke to me about it. How neat her
bureau had been. How she must have valued all her little
possessions and how she had them tidily arranged her way,
which was not my way. This was a new point of view for me. I
felt I had done violence.[6]

In his studies of isolation John C. Lilly found that the experience of isolation itself acts as a stress. He collected autobiographi-
cal cases from literature on polar and sea-faring experiences. He
also interviewed persons having such experiences who had never
published the details. From all of this he concluded "that isolation
per se acts on most persons as a powerful stress. The effects
observed [in isolation] are similar to those of any extreme stress,
... [which means that] other stressful factors [encountered, for
example, in everyday living] add their effects to those of isolation ... [with the result that] mental symptoms [tend] to appear
more rapidly and more intensely"[7] among individuals experiencing
isolation. In other words, we could well expect that psychosomatic, neurotic, and even psychotic symptoms would appear
more often among those individuals and families who are isolated
not from choice but, instead, by a community or by neighbors who
have determined that, because they are representatives of a
minority group, foreigners, or newcomers, they therefore are inferior and must be kept in their place. And migrant farm workers
can be categorized under all of these labels.

There is a new restlessness among migrant farm workers today
that will increase in the future. Their new aggression is the result of
national change, social action, and the civil rights movement.
Workers of all races are more outspoken about their dissatisfac-
tions. They may refuse to work in an area where housing is poor or
working conditions are bad. They are less easily intimidated than
they were five years ago. They are also going to be less accepting of
community isolation. They feel they have a right to be included
and to become personally involved.

In general, isolation and withdrawal will vary inversely with the
degree of acceptance of the workmen, both seasonal and year-
round, into the mainstream of the community. Farm communities
and areas dependent upon farm workers are going to find that
unless they reach out to the people who work in the crops, there

will be a marked decline in the numbers of those willing to remain isolated on the fringe of the American scene. As a result, fewer individuals will wish to be identified with agriculture as an occupation.

NOTES

1. "Where is Tell?" *Holiday Magazine*, July-August 1971, pp. 49, 70.

2. "Culture Patterns of Minority Groups," in *One America*, ed. by Francis J. Brown and Joseph Slabey Roucek (New York: Prentice-Hall, Inc., 1945), pp. 466-67.

3. "The Ecology of Isolated Groups," in *Environmental Psychology: Man and His Physical Setting*, ed. by Harold M. Proshansky, William H. Ittleson, and Leanne G. Rivlin (New York: Holt, Rinehart and Winston, Inc., 1970), p. 235.

4. *Ibid.*, pp. 235-36.

5. Myrtle R. Reul, *Where Hannibal Led Us* (New York: Vantage Press, 1967), p. 218.

6. Bourke-White, *Portrait of Myself* (New York: Simon and Shuster, Inc., 1963), pp. 126-27.

7. "Mental Effects of Reduction of Ordinary Levels of Physical Stimuli on Intact, Healthy Persons," in *Environmental Psychology: Man and His Physical Setting*, p. 221.

The beautiful truth burst upon my mind—I felt that there were invisible lines stretched between my spirit and the spirits of others.

Helen Keller, 20th century American authoress
The Story of My Life

24

A Whisper of Work

There had been another freeze sometime before daylight, and a thin line of ice showed at the water's edge. This was the second night we had slept in our car parked next to one containing a stranded migrant family. Both nights had been cold, but this morning our windows were covered with heavy white frost caused by our own breath. The coats we used as blankets were cold and clammy. Gingerly we stepped onto the icy ground, picking our way carefully between the sharp, white coral rocks and shells that formed the footing of the levee. We ran toward the lake to wash for breakfast. Through the fog we could see the public pier, empty of fishermen; then the wind changed, and the pier faded into the mist.

Sara, the mother from the other car, was already at the water's edge. She wore a man's sweater buttoned hoodlike over her head. It made her fat body appear even more shapeless and large. Her teeth chattered as she dipped the corner of her ragged towel into the shallow lake. She glanced at us and smiled shyly. It was cold, we said; she nodded. She squeezed the towel with one hand and with the other passed the wet cloth over her face; then she spoke. "It smells rot'n, 'n it taste rot'n," she stated emphatically, tossing her head in the direction of Lake Okeechobee. We could not help but agree with her. The lake that morning did smell like decaying vegetation.

Sara continued her observation of the lake, the weather, and how good it would be to have one night of sleep in a soft bed. She dipped the towel up and down in the lake. Mechanically she wrung it out and handed it to Nancy, who had joined us. "Go an' give it to the boys to wash," she stated, "so's we can eat. See that your Pa's got the fire goin' good so as I can cook mush." Her tone was almost harsh, although neither her face nor her body expressed anger, and her voice sounded angry as if she were defying Nancy to disagree. Nancy nodded, turned without a word, and ran toward the fire, her tiny legs and arms looking more like those of a six-year-old child than those of a ten-year-old.

Nancy was like her father: quiet, withdrawn. It was hard for either to express themselves in words. Sara told us earlier that sometimes Jake barely spoke to anyone for days and rarely, if ever, to a stranger. She was surprised that he had talked with us. It had always been difficult for him to ask for a job. It was as if he expected to be turned down or felt that he had no right to apply for work; for that matter, it was as if he had no right to ask for any kind of help.

Sara stood with me a moment, not talking, watching Jake put more wood on the fire. We could see him through the smoke. He coughed, and his body sagged with the motion. He had not shaved for nearly a week, and the stubble of his dark whiskers made his face appear gaunt and old. He looked, Sara told me, as tired and stiff as she felt.

This was the third night that the seven McConnells had slept in the park, huddled together in their car. The Pahokee policemen had been "real nice" when they arrived. They showed Jake where Boy Scouts had piled firewood, and they said it would be all right for him to keep a small, open bonfire burning as long as it was so cold. The policemen even suggested that Jake park his car close to the long-needled Australian pines at the base of the levee where there would be some protection from the cold wind that swept across the lake. Beyond the levee, Pahokee was completely shut from their view by the steep bank of the rock and earth-filled dyke. Although they could not see the town without climbing the levee or driving up the steep road, its sounds drifted to them—the screech of car brakes, the slam of a door, voices without words, the bark of a dog, or the low of cattle. But on this side of the dyke were only stillness, the dark stretch of evergreens, and the never-ceasing movement of the wind across the surface of the lake.

To keep warm, the family sat so close to the flames of their open fire that the smoke blackened their faces even as it blackened the bottom of the enameled saucepan in which they reboiled coffee grounds. Their clothes, smelly with wood smoke, were soiled from charcoal. Sara said she was not as concerned about their need for a place to bathe or even to wash clothes as she was to have a better place to cook. She was a good "Southern cook," she said, when she had "somethin' fittin' to cook on." She commented that it was hard to fix anything decent over a green wood fire, and then she spoke wistfully of the two-burner kerosene stove they had sold in Sebring. Almost as if she were chiding herself for remembering, she concluded by saying that there was no use thinking about the things they had sold or traded this winter or other winters in order to get food and gasoline. She broke off talking about the stove and divided the cornmeal in what she said would be a "taste of fried mush to go 'round." She called to Jake that if they did not get something to do pretty soon they would be "plumb out of vittles" and they would have to "boil grass."

The day before we met them, Jake had hiked north of town to one of the packing sheds. It was shut down because of the freeze, but he found some potatoes that had rolled from a truck along the side of the road. Sara wrapped the potatoes in wet paper and baked them in the hot wood ashes, and, although she had no seasoning, not even salt, the children each had three. According to Sara, they could have probably "et more 'cause not even the burned parts of the skins was left when they got done."

This was not the first time these parents and their five children had been stranded, nor the first time they had picked up vegetables from the side of the road or brought home discards from the fields and packing sheds. There had also been times when they had searched through garbage dumpsters in back of produce markets to pick out half-spoiled oranges and tomatoes. They would cut away the rotten parts to have the luxury of food which they could not afford to buy, although sometimes the odor of the decayed produce made the good parts they salvaged seem less attractive. Something about obtaining food in such a way filled them with a sense of shame, as if they had stolen something, and although they ate the food with a physical hunger, it did not satisfy their emotional need; no satisfaction came with being filled. They could not say that they enjoyed this food as they had enjoyed the food they had raised in their garden in Kentucky.

Although this was not the first time the McConnells had known what it was like to be out of work, there was an ominous foreboding that morning in the park at Pahokee which depressed Sara and made Jake feel helpless in the face of his family's destiny. Thus they were both willing to tell us some of the experiences of their lives.

Jake and Sara were born in the mountains of Kentucky. She was fifteen and he was nineteen when they had married and bought a little "place up there at the end of the holler." The land was too steep and rocky to raise much of anything " 'cept a little corn an' some 'tatters"; but with a cow or two, a few chickens, a hog, and a "patch of salad greens" they had managed to "git by." Indeed they managed quite well, they said, until their family got so large that they could not raise enough food for their needs and still make payments on the "place." Each year there was a new baby. Each year they were further and further in debt. They had "kin folks" who lived in the same holler, and although these relatives shared hunted game and canned goods, they were as poor as the McConnells and could not be relied upon for any kind of "hard cash," which was what the family really needed.

When Sara was pregnant with Dosie, their tenth baby, a public health nurse talked with her about having so many babies. It sounded to Sara as if this woman, who came from the capital, was saying that it was wrong for her and Jake to express their love by having children. Sara did not understand why the nurse would imply that she had already had too many children, that it was wrong to bring so many babies into the world. Every woman within Sara's circle of acquaintances had as many children as she could. Every woman felt that a large family was a blessing[1] and that a woman who was barren, like Sarai[2] in the Bible, should be pitied. She and Jake had heard many a mountain preacher refer to God's commandment to Noah and his sons to "be fruitful and multiply."[3] Sara said that she and Jake had never done anything to prevent her from becoming pregnant, but that Dosie, for some reason, was their last baby, and the public health nurse never came to see her again.

The year Dosie was born, Jake and Sara lost their Kentucky farm. They could no longer make even a semblance of a payment, and the man who held their mortgage foreclosed. He said that he hated to do so because he had known their "people" for years and he knew they were honest folks, but he had to have some money or let the place go for taxes. The only solution for Jake and Sara was to let him have the farm and to try to find a way to support their family. The only work they knew was farm work, but there was no demand for farm workers in their area of Kentucky. Those who needed help could not afford to employ workers, or else the pay was such that Jake could not feed and clothe his ten children on what he could earn as a hired man. After talking with relatives, they made a kinship-family decision. Jake and Sara and the children would become "free wheelin' migrant fruit pickers" and follow the crops. They would go to Florida or Texas and work together as a family. They would not join a crew; crew leaders could not be trusted.

With promises to write relatives when they found work, they headed south. They provided their own transportation—an old, black Dodge sedan of ancient vintage that Jake kept running, often making minor mechanical repairs along the highway. They contacted growers and lived in whatever housing was available. Everything they owned they carried with them; wherever their car stopped was home.

The baby, Dosie, died with what later was proven to be epidemic gastroenteritis, diarrhea of infancy. The infant died on one of their trips when medical attention was unavailable. They had tried to find help, but they could not locate a doctor who would treat a sick baby without payment. No one seemed concerned about the seriousness of their situation until they walked into a hospital in a strange community with Dosie's body. Then suddenly everyone was interested.

There were many questions from the hospital authorities, the police, and various community agencies. Did the infant die a natural death? What had they given Dosie to eat? Had there been parental neglect? Was there evidence of abuse? The questions flowed around the McConnells, but no one seemed aware of their grief or seemed to understand the depth of their emotions and their confusion. Sara tried to explain to us how she had felt: "I just felt sort of numb all over." It was as if her body moved without her. She could not cry; she could hardly speak; she could only stare at the people who asked questions, seemingly without feelings. Jake was his usual noncommital self. He gave the appearance of wanting to evade questions. His attitude brought forth more questions. Jake refused to answer. The authorities became suspicious. Jake just stood there, defiant and guilty looking, staring at the floor or the ceiling. Sara said she could see that he looked guilty, although she felt that he had no reason to act, look, or feel guilty. Jake always looked guilty whenever he was "upsot." The police said an autopsy would be required to determine the cause of Dosie's death.

Jake and Sara shied from the thought of an autopsy. They wanted to refuse. They wanted to scream at the doctor that they could never allow Dosie's body to be cut into, that such a thing was "wicked." They had heard of medical experimentation on bodies, but in their mountain culture such a thing as cutting into a dead body was mutilation of the image of God. They believed that, because man was created by God in His image,[4] to add anything to or take anything out of the human body was wicked—was a sort of blasphemy.

They knew, however, that any protest on their part would never be understood by the medical authorities. Such an outcry would only reinforce the suspicion that somehow they, the parents, were guilty of Dosie's death.[5] They nodded their consent; the cause of death had to be determined. The medical report proved there had been no abuse. Dosie had died from epidemic gastroenteritis.

Those who know the depth of poverty are sometimes labeled as being devoid of such human feelings as love, tenderness, and affection. It has even been asked, "How can a migrant family who lives in a car and 'gypsies' who travel from one part of the country to another suffer any deep loss when death means there is one less mouth to feed or one less body to clothe?" Sara sensed this attitude on the part of those who asked the questions that awful night and those who made the final decisions the next day.

After much discussion of legal residency, the local welfare agency finally agreed to assume the burial expenses. They thus took over and made all burial arrangements. Jake and Sara felt that they had no part in the decision making; things were as they had to be. The funeral was a graveside prayer. The minister was late for another appointment, and it seemed to Sara that his prayer was hardly long enough even to "be respectable." For Jake and Sara there was a lack of realness in these people who moved through their lives with such efficiency, who got things done and made decisions quickly, and yet from whom there radiated so little warmth and human understanding. Although the seeming indifference of the minister and agency representative helped them sustain their composure and contain their tears, the cold, businesslike atmosphere did not sanction their expressions of grief.

Within a few hours Jake and Sara were free to leave; the funeral was over; Dosie had been buried in an unmarked grave. Fear, from what cause they did not know, was still the strongest emotion they experienced. They were afraid, and of what they were afraid they were unable to determine. Their fear was almost a panic. They could shed no tears. Their grieving process for Dosie was postponed.[6] They left the community as they had entered that community, feeling empty, feeling very much alone, and unable to believe that Dosie could be dead and that never again would they hear her laughter.

The haste of their leaving was due to what seemed to them to be a veiled threat that their other children might be removed from them unless they could prove that they would provide more adequately for their needs than they had for the needs of Dosie. The family drove away from that awful place in silence. There were no words to express the empty hurt conveyed by the sight of Dosie's last bottle still on the front seat where it had been dropped, half-filled with catnip tea. They drove all day without eating and spoke only to the gasoline station attendants. They did not even talk among themselves. Nothing they could say about the people they had met seemed right under the circumstances, so they drove mile after mile in silence, seeming to find relief only in putting distance between themselves and that place.

A year later Jake and Sara returned to that same community. They tried to find Dosie's grave, but the cemetery had been enlarged, and they were never certain that they had found the exact location of the little unmarked spot where they had stood huddled together on that sad day. They did not know whom to ask for this sort of information. In Kentucky there was always a cousin who knew where each new grave was made, but in the place where Dosie was buried there were no cousins.

Someday they hoped to "git enough money ahead" for a decent marker, one with a lamb on top or perhaps a little angel. Then they would go back to that place and find her grave. If they had a marker, they would certainly be able to find someone who would help them. They would have a reason for asking directions. Surely no one would refuse to help them find a grave that needed a marker. In the Appalachian mountain culture of which Jake and Sara were products, a marker for a grave, a "proper" funeral, and a well-kept cemetery are part of the value system, not only of the family but also the community. To have kin buried in an unmarked grave is proof of irresponsibility; it is a circumstance that should create guilt because it illustrates a lack of respect or even love for the departed.

For generations members of the McConnell family had been buried in a tiny cemetery high against the steep hillside not far from the farm where Jake and Sara had lived in the early years of their marriage. The cemetery was looked after by relatives who came twice a year to "cut the filth" and plant flowers.[7] The cemetery was where they felt all "departed relatives should be placed." The day the arrangements were being made for the funeral, Sara had asked if Dosie could by any chance be buried in the McConnell cemetery.[8] The welfare department said they had no funds to return Dosie's body to the Kentucky mountains. The welfare worker seemed to have little understanding or patience with an unemployed migrant farm worker who would make "such a request." Jake and Sara were reminded that they were not in a position to choose where their child was buried. They were not even residents of that state, and they should be grateful to the local taxpayers who were willing to bury their dead child. They could hardly expect those taxpayers to assume the unnecessary expenses of shipping a body to another state.

Sara said it was on Dosie's birthday anniversary, something over three months later, that she cried for the first time. She said she sobbed and thought she would never stop. Her tears seemed to come from deep within her, like hiccups, until she gasped against the pain. On that day she walked away from where their car was parked; she walked along a narrow dirt road with her unchecked tears wetting the front of her dress. On a grassy spot under a large tree she laid on the ground and wept until her body was finally drained of all emotional pain. After a long time she said she became aware of the patterns that the sunlight, coming through the branches above her head, made on the ground. She laid still without moving, recalling the words of the twenty-third Psalm she had learned when a child in the Kentucky mountains. Much later, when it was nearly dark, she went back to the car, to Jake and her children.

She sensed that Jake understood what she had done, that he understood her need to be alone, that he had not followed her or come to look for her for that very reason. He did not ask her where she had been, but he did put an arm across her shoulders in a self-conscious, awkward way and for a moment tightened his fingers against her skin until she nearly winced with pain.

Sara said that, to her knowledge, Jake had never "shed one tear over Dosie." He did not talk about Dosie, even to her. When the other children mentioned Dosie's name Jake became even quieter than usual. Finally she asked the other children not to talk about Dosie when their father was around. Sara said she knew Jake grieved. While Jake was never one to talk much about love, he had always shown a good deal of affection for their babies. When Dosie was alive, he would rock her in his arms and sing some of the old mountain ballads to her. Even as a tiny baby she would drop the "sugar tit"[9] out of her mouth to smile and coo at "her daddy." According to Sara, "Dosie was her daddy's girl." He would sing as they drove to the fields, and whenever they camped he would hold Dosie and sing a special song for her as he had always sung a special song for each of their babies. Jake had a good voice, and the words of these old songs had been taught to him as a child by his own grandmother. Since Dosie's death Sara said she had never heard Jake sing or whistle or even hum one note. She had asked him once to sing when they were driving late at night and there was a full moon, but Jake said his heart did not feel like singing. So Sara never asked him again.[10]

Jake and Sara had been gone from Kentucky too long to be residents of that state. In the more than seven years that they had worked as migrants, they had never stayed one place long enough to meet legal requirements for a new residence. Most jobs lasted only a few weeks, some a few days; occasionally one would continue for two or three months. The longest they had stayed in one spot was nine months. Jake had then worked in a turpentine camp in southern Georgia where he chipped the bark of the slash pines and sprayed the wounds with sulfuric acid to stimulate the flow of pine sap. The work was hard, but Jake liked it; he enjoyed working in the woods. They had hoped to stay on that job longer than nine months, but the low wage scale for workers who bleed the crude gum from the pines and the poor housing conditions they encountered forced them back onto the highway to work in the vegetables. The boss in the turpentine camp had promised them housing, and even without furniture they thought they could camp in a house and sleep on the floor and be more comfortable than they would be sleeping in their car. They had stayed in all kinds of migrant housing, but the deserted tenant shack that the turpentine boss told them they could use was as bad as any they had seen.

The old building leaned at an angle and looked as if it would collapse in the slightest wind. It had no window sash or screens, and the roof leaked, not in one spot but everywhere. In cold weather snakes slithered through the rotten timbers of the floor. A black snake or king snake was bad enough, Sara said, but when they killed a copperhead, they figured they had better sleep in their car. They were afraid the next one would be a rattlesnake. As soon as the first bean crop was ready to harvest, they went "back down the road."

Their son Marshall signed up with the Navy three years after they left their Kentucky home. Their three oldest daughters married, each before she was seventeen. The girls and their husbands traveled for a time with the McConnells, but finally they dropped out of the migrant stream to raise their own families. Their husbands, being younger, were able to "git on" in a thread mill and a garage where a man of Jake's age did not have "a ghost of a chance gittin' in." They too had no special training or education, which meant that they received less than the minimum wage and were in no position to help support the McConnells.

When the old Dodge gave out, their son-in-law helped them get a "deal" on a newer one through the garage where he worked. Sara said it sounded silly, but they all gathered around for one last look at the old car before they left. That old Dodge was more than just a car, she said; it was a piece of Kentucky, and it was sad to leave it behind. She and the children cried silently, and even Jake bit his lip.

In the early morning, at the edge of Lake Okeechobee, five of the McConnell children—Brian, fourteen; Morgan, thirteen; Rachael, twelve; Arthur, eleven; and ten-year-old Nancy—dipped into the blackened pan for their share of the fried mush. They were all of school age, and yet they had not attended school one day of that school year. They had gone only a few weeks the year before and the year before that. The children usually did not have shoes good enough for school, and they seldom were in one place long enough to make it seem worthwhile to go through the experience of registering at a strange school. In the orchards the children could all go barefoot. Occasionally a grower would say something about not wanting them in the fields on a school day because he would get into trouble. Once a truant officer threatened to arrest Sara and Jake unless the children were in school, but usually no one seemed concerned that five blue-eyed, tow-headed children, whose ancestors were among the early settlers in this country, were growing up without receiving a formal education.

It was early February 1964 when we met the McConnell family. We came often to the little park in Pahokee when we were not in the fields. It was on such an occasion that we accidentally parked our car next to theirs. When we sensed that they were stranded, we stayed, sleeping in our car as they slept in theirs, washing in the lake as they did, sharing with them our meager supply of groceries, and talking about mutual experiences searching for work. Although they assumed that we too were stranded and that it had been a bad year for us, even as it had been a hard year for them, they were suspicious and distrustful when we first arrived.

It is almost an inevitable characteristic of people of the mountain culture to approach strangers with caution, not to trust them. Close kinship and friendship ties with one's own sex are also a characteristic of the mountain culture. These aspects of their culture forced the McConnells into a dilemma. On one hand, they did not want to trust anyone they did not know. On the other hand, the kinship network, which normally would have provided strong emotional supports, was not available to them. In this strange spot, without kin or friends, they were also denied the opportunity to talk with other adults of their own sex, and that too was an important part of their mountain experience. Having lived in a folk culture where others had been concerned for their well-being, the McConnells felt almost intolerable isolation as stranded migrants. They felt alone, cut off from human beings, starved for an opportunity to "jist gab."

They were lonely. We were there. We too seemed to be alone in the midst of isolation. Intuitively, but warily, still on guard, they reached out, testing our reactions and trying to sense our motives, our attitudes, and our prejudices. We knew that if they could sense that we honestly accepted them as human beings they might be comfortable enough to trust us. We knew also that if their prior experiences with strangers, even fellow migrants, had been too dehumanizing they would remain distant and suspicious; or they might become more distrustful, antagonistic, even hostile, or withdraw completely. We could only wait, respecting their privacy by keeping near our own car and talking with them about safe, nonthreatening subjects, such as the weather and the lack of work in Pahokee and Belle Glade.

Their hunger for human contacts proved stronger than the protective reserve they used with strangers. Their need to be near other adults was stronger than their fears of self-exposure. Sara approached our car to ask if we had some salt. She sat down on a park bench with us, gratefully accepting our offer of a cup of coffee. Gradually she began to talk first about the coffee, the lake, the trees, and then about herself and her family. She talked first with me and then with both of us.[11] Suddenly, it was as if a dam of emotions gave way within her. Her need for human contact was so great that she talked compulsively, on and on, seemingly unable to stop. Jake joined us. Nonverbally he involved himself and took part in the conversation through body language. Through his movements and facial expressions he encouraged Sara to be the family spokesperson.

Later we all sat around their fire, and Brian told us about his exploits, sometimes fantasizing in a way which seemed to indicate he was a braggart, trying hard to impress us with his physical strength, his work achievements, his good luck, and his intellectual capability in that he could always guess the answers to a quiz or puzzle long before anyone else in his family had the answer. We sensed that behind Brian's self-confidence, and at times superior attitude, there was an uncertain, young fourteen-year-old adolescent struggling for self-identity and asking to be accepted as a person in his own right.

Sometimes Brian contradicted his mother about dates and events and asked his father to confirm his accuracy. At those times Jake nodded or added a few words, never a complete sentence. Sara did not seem to mind Brian's interruption; it was almost as if she understood the dynamics of his emotional needs. When he became too critical, she half-laughingly rebuked him with, "Okay, dumb-dumb, you've had your say."

"Dumb-dumb" seemed to be a family expression used by the parents with each other and between the children and their parents. The expression was used as a form of behavior control, as a means of telling the other person that he had gone " 'bout far 'nough." It was said in a teasing tone without anger, but it resulted in a change of action every time it was used.[12] It was the only disciplinary technique we observed within this family.

Although Rachael, Arthur, and Morgan were friendly toward us, they never had much to say. They spent most of their time in the backseat of their car wrapped in old quilts reading and rereading a pile of comic books they had picked out of a trash can in the park. Rachael, like her mother, was overweight to the point of being obese. Her two younger brothers were thin and pale and seemed rather tired and listless. We suspected that their limited diet might well be a major cause.[13]

Ten-year-old Nancy had a stronger need for human contact than any other member of her family. Her need could have been related to her age at the time of Dosie's death—she was three—and to how the different family members had suppressed Dosie's death. Their psychic energy could have been so drained by their own loss that they did not have enough emotional energy to gratify Nancy's needs for affection or even to recognize or understand the fear and anxiety she must have felt when her "baby sissie went home to live with God." Did she somehow feel responsible for Dosie's death? Was she afraid that she too might die, that she was bad and should not live? What were the feelings and the fears of a three-year-old? For that matter, what were the feelings and the fears of a total family who had to deny any emotional reaction to the most important crisis of their lives? There was no way to measure how much of that experience was built into Nancy's present need for physical contact, a need to be held close.[14]

On the second day of our acquaintance Nancy sat next to me by the fire. Slowly she inched closer until she could lay her head against my shoulder. Suddenly her thin arms reached upward around my neck in a strangling hug. She "guessed" she would call me "Aunt Myrtle," she said, " 'cause your eyes are blue, like my favorite aunt's in 'tucky." She went on to explain that I was here and her aunt was a long way away, so far away they never saw her anymore.

I agreed to be Nancy's "pretend Aunt Myrtle." Sara watched with a half smile, and Jake nodded approvingly; his glance seemed to express gratitude that anyone would show interest in his little girl. When Nancy mentioned Kentucky, Jake for the first time began to talk.

In a low monotone he talked of the Kentucky mountains. A wistful homesickness colored his description. He questioned aloud why they had ever left, why they had not gone back; even if there were no work it would not be as bad as waiting by the side of the road in some strange place. At least in the mountains people cared if you lived or died; here no one knew or cared that you existed. His tone was flat, without affect; the words were bitter, but they came from Jake without bitterness, almost as if constant isolation had destroyed his capacity to express feelings of anger.

The harvest year of 1963-64 had been one of extreme weather and few days of employment for Jake and Sara. They had worked two and one-half weeks in southern Texas late in the fall. In January they had driven from Texas to Homestead, Florida, to pick tomatoes. They had worked two days before the tomatoes froze. Then they had followed a whisper of work to the orange groves of Sebring, but cold rains had slowed the orange harvest, and no workers were needed. Jake heard that the packing sheds at Pahokee were hiring, so they sold their two-burner kerosene cookstove at a secondhand store and traded their spare tire, a jack, and a few odds and ends of old tools for gasoline. They circled Lake Okeechobee to Pahokee. They arrived with two gallons of gasoline, thirty cents in cash, and enough corn meal for three days of fried mush. But the cold freeze that had blackened the tomatoes of Homestead froze the sweetcorn in the Glades. The packing sheds in Pahokee and Belle Glade were closed.

Each morning Jake and Paul walked out to one of the packing sheds or to the vegetable icing station, and once they went to the Labor Department Employment Service office to register for work—anything. Each day they joined other workers, men and women, who stood in groups on street corners, who talked to strangers, who asked for jobs doing any kind of "honest work." Each night that they came back to the cars tired and hungry Jake looked more and more discouraged and more and more as if he should apologize for asking for work or even for being alive. If he could only find some way to get out of Pahokee, he said, maybe his luck would change; maybe he could pick up a few days of odd jobs.

On the fourth day of our stay in the park a tourist stopped on his way to Miami. Having heard the story of Sara and the children from the police, this man gave Jake ten dollars to help him get to someplace where there might be work. Although Jake impulsively wanted to show his pride and refuse the money, he accepted it, he said, to get Sara and the children out of this "sorry mess." Somehow his aversion to help for himself could be redirected when help for the children was at hand. So Jake took the money and got caught up in the excitement of leaving. He had heard of a rumor of work further north; they would "try their luck." They would leave at once. They were "movin' up the road," Nancy told me, "maybe someday all the way back to 'tucky and her favorite aunt with blue eyes."

Sara's good-bye hug was nearly as revealing as Nancy's; it was almost as tight, betraying almost as much fear of the unknown. A whisper of work had called them; they headed for the filling station near the closed icing station that handled the cheapest gas in town. They filled the tank for the first time in weeks. Gasoline was more important than food, if they could not have both. We gave them a loaf of bread and some store cheese as a farewell gift and waved good-bye as they pulled away. They were following another whisper of work, this time toward Alabama. Maybe the pot of gold would be there at the end of the rainbow in the form of work and good housing; maybe it would not. The first major crop in Alabama would be early potatoes, and the harvest of potatoes was several months away.

NOTES

1. Speaking of the South Appalachian area, Jack E. Weller said, "Large families are considered a blessing; for many years past, the more children there were, the more help there was in making a living. Eight or more children are not at all uncommon." *Yesterday's People* (Lexington, Ky.: University of Kentucky Press, 1966), p. 62.

2. "But Sarai was barren; she had no child." Bible, King James version, Gen. 12:30. "Now Sarai Abram's wife bore him no children." Gen. 16:1.

3. "And God blessed Noah and his sons and said unto them be fruitful and multiply and replenish the earth." Gen. 9:1.

4. Gen. 1:27.

5. This is how it seemed to Jake and Sara. This is not necessarily what the agencies involved intended to imply.

6. Many authors, including Helene Deutsch in "Absence of Grief," *Psychoanalytic Quarterly*, VI, No. 12 (1937), 12-22, have written on the subjects of delayed reaction to death and the postponement of the normal grieving process.

In his paper "Mourning and Melancholia" (1917) Sigmund Freud defines mourning as a reaction to the loss of a loved object, characterized by ". . . a profoundly painful dejection; loss of capacity to adopt new love objects; turning away from any activity not connected with thoughts of the lost person; and loss of interest in the outside world—insofar as it does not recall the lost loved one." *Complete Works* (standard ed.; London: Hogarth Press, 1957), pp. 243-44. Freud states a paradoxical position which existed at that time, i.e., grief is a normal reaction characterized by symptoms of abnormal behavior.

In psychoanalytic theory, mourning is that painful process during which the capacity for love (libido) becomes liberated from the lost object of love. Otto Fenichel describes mourning as a gradual "working through" of a wild and self-destructive kind of affect which, if it were released in its full strength, would overwhelm the ego. *Affect* used in this sense means feelings or emotions. The most basic affects are pleasure and displeasure. Affects are both felt and exposed usually, as in the case of grief, by facial expressions, tone of voice, or body language. Therefore, affects are said to carry information not only about the internal feelings of an individual but also about the readiness of that person to do something about the situation. Thus mourning that takes place for a period of time is considered to be a defense against being overwhelmed by the primitive affect of self-destruction. There is, for the individual in mourning, such an overwhelming sense of loss and displeasure that life would not be worth living if he were unable to mourn during the needed period of time. Mourning is considered a normal reaction when it is a predictable response to the loss of a valued object and when it is used in the defense of the ego. When mourning has been successfully completed, the ego becomes once again free and uninhibited. *The Psychoanalytic Theory of Neurosis,* quoted in Lorraine D. Siggins, "Mourning: A Critical Survey of the Literature," *International Journal of Psychiatry,* III (May 1967), 420.

Erich Lindemann describes the duration of the grief process as dependent upon the success with which a person does grief work, i.e., emancipates himself from the ties of the deceased, readjusts to the environment in which the deceased is no longer present, and becomes able to move out and form new relationships. Lindemann observed that unless this process evolves completely and satisfactorily, other expression in more serious forms of psychiatric or physical illness may take place. "Symtomatology and Management of Acute Grief," in *Crisis Intervention: Selected Readings,* ed. by Howard Parad (New York: Family Service Assoc. of America, 1965), pp. 10-11.

Harry Milt says that the syndrome of acute grief generally lasts from about one to two months before beginning to lessen in intensity. On an average, the grief has passed in about six months, although it may be reactivated in stressful situations related to the anniversary of the death or to other memories of the deceased. "Grief," *Trends in Psychiatry,* Vol. III (Rahway, N.J.: Merck and Co., 1966), p. 9.

George L. Engel points out that the grief process will be modified by the abruptness of the loss, the degree of preparation already made, and the emotional significance of the loved one. (I would also add that unusual circumstances of death and lack of sympathy in the environment for the person's grief would delay or hinder the normal grieving process, would affect its duration, and would even account for physical illness or fatigue rather than seeming grief on the part of the mourner.) The initial phase of grief is generally shock and disbelief. The next phase is characterized by a developing awareness of the loss, marked by the painful effects of sadness, guilt, shame, helplessness or hopelessness, feelings of loss and emptiness, crying, anorexia, sleep disturbance, somatic symptoms of pain or other discomfort, loss of interest in usual activities, and generalized impairment of functioning. Following this period of disorganization, there is a prolonged phase of recovery and restitution during which grief work is taking place that will eventually lead to a reestablishment of a feeling of well being. *Psychological Development in Health and Disease* (Philadelphia, Pa.: W.B. Saunders Co., 1962), p. 279.

In a chapter entitled "Generic Features of Families Under Stress," Reuben Hill describes the course of adjustment in crisis including the crisis of death of a family member. In *Crisis Intervention,* ed. by Parad, pp. 32-52.

7. For additional information on the care of family plots, see Weller, *Yesterday's People,* p. 60.

8. This desire to be buried in the family cemetery, which is expressed often in the Appalachian area, is also part of the culture of whites and Blacks of the rural deep South, and apparently it was also part of the cultural patterns found in various parts of Africa by both Thomas Basden and William Bosman. In his writings on the Ibos of Nigeria, Basden said, "The desire of every Ibo man and woman is to die in their own town, or at least to be buried within its precincts. For a long time it was very difficult to persuade a man to travel any distance from his native place, and if he were in need of medical assistance seldom would an Ibo agree to go from home in spite of assurance that he would be able to have better treatment elsewhere. In case of death occuring at a distance, if it can be done at all the breathern will bring the body home for burial." *Ibos of Nigeria*, (Philadelphia, Pa.: J. P. Lippincott Co., 1931), pp. 115-16. Describing the coast of Guinea, Bosman said, "The Negroes are strongly fond of being buried in their own country; so that if any person dies out of it, they frequently bring his corpse home to be buried, unless it would be too far a distance." *Description of the Coast of Guinea* (London: Printed for Knapton, *et al.*, 1705), p. 232.

Missionaries who worked in West Africa also have reported that only relatives could be buried in the same piece of ground. Interview with John Pearce of Hinesville, Georgia, an exmissionary in West Africa, as reported on page 196 in the appendix of the Georgia Writers' Project, *Drums and Shadows: Survival Studies among the Georgia Coastal Negroes* (Athens, Ga.: University of Georgia Press, 1940).

The custom of returning the body to its native town for burial was found to be prevalent among the coastal Blacks of Georgia. Georgia Writers' Project, *Drums and Shadows*, p. 113.

9. A sugar teat, or sugar tit, as it was called, was once used extensively throughout America, especially in rural areas, as a pacifier for babies. Occasionally it is still used. It was made in a number of ways depending upon whether the person making it was using granulated sugar, brown sugar, maple sugar, or raw sugar, honey or molasses, or sorghum syrup or corn syrup. The principle was to give the baby something sweet to suck on knotted up in a piece of cloth. Usually it was prepared by tying a small amount of sugar into a corner of an old sheet or a piece of union underwear. Sometimes it was prepared from a lump of honey knotted in a rag and moistened with milk. Other times bread was saturated in syrup and tied in the rag if the infant was too young to suck on bread without choking. Some times a "fretful" baby was lulled to sleep with a sugar teat moistened in cat-nip tea, brandy, or paregoric. In sections of Appalachia and the deep South children sometimes sucked on a sugar teat long after they had been weaned and toilet trained.

10. The interpersonal relationships, especially within the family, are so important in the folk culture that nothing must be done or said that in any way will threaten that relationship. Jack Weller states it this way: "Subjects that might engender conflict are not discussed." *Yesterday's People*, p. 79.

11. After years of observing and talking with relatives, friends, and acquaintances whose family roots are deep in Appalachia, I would say that a woman of the traditional mountain culture would be thought of as "forward" and even sexually seductive if she engaged a married man in direct conversation without using his wife as a mediator. The culture teaches that women should relate to women and men to men, and a woman should be very careful about doing or saying anything that would reflect upon her morals or her reputation.

In order to teach the "proper" sex roles, the early code of the mountains required that girls and boys be seated on different sides of the school room, and at noon and recess they played in separate sections of the playground. This type of sexual segregation is described in the novel by John Fox, Jr., *The Little Shepherd of Kingdom Come* (New York: Charles Scribner's Sons, 1903), p. 40.

Sexual segregation was also found in mountain churches where men were seated on one side and women on the other. Rather than engaging in common activities, men would hunt, fish, or play poker together and women would sew, garden, or just talk together. This characteristic has been noted by every author who has written on the Appalachian culture. I would like to point out, however, that this characteristic is not unique to that part of the country. It is a characteristic that has become related more to social class than to ethnic group. In her survey of selected facts pertaining to lower-class families, Suzanne Keller states, "The lives of the sexes are sharply segregated and their interaction is defined almost exclusively in sexual and familial terms." *The American Lower Class Family* (Albany, N. Y.: New York State Division for Youth, 1968), pp. 73-74.

12. Joking and teasing to test interpersonal relationships both with family members and with friends are also characteristic of the Appalachian culture. Sara and other members of the family could laughingly tease or say something as a joke and have it accepted by members of their culture, or those who understand their culture, without any danger of damage to interpersonal relationships. Humor, in this case, becomes a defense against emotions that may be anxiety-creating if they are expressed. "Humor and the related techniques of wit and comic devices . . . can reduce anxiety, turn grim reality into something more acceptable, and gratify forbidden impulses." Fredrick C. Redlich and Daniel X. Freedman, *The Theory and Practice of Psychiatry* (New York: Basic Books, Inc., 1966), p. 130.

13. Nutritional deficiencies, the result of a diet deficient in vitamins and/or minerals or a diet consisting of only starchy foods, are common among migrant workers and their families. Such deficiencies are reflected in night blindness, infantile scurvy, failure to gain weight, gaining too much weight, rickets, pallor, anemia, physical weakness or fatigue, poor teeth, and a lowered resistence to infections.

14. This craving to be held close and to be cuddled has not always been recognized by helping professions. Unwed motherhood could well stem from this basic emotional need. A woman's need to be embraced may be interpreted as sexual surrender by a man. The girl or woman in this situation may engage in sexual intercourse as a secondary means of satisfying her primary need to be held and comforted like a small child. When she becomes pregnant as a result, neither her needs nor those of her child can be met without help.

This physical-contact-need syndrome may be expressed in other behavior as well. For example, it may appear as mental illness. Joining a ritual group in which open expressions of affection are accepted is another outlet for this need.

25

Golden Grimes

I met Laurabelle Webster at the edge of the apple orchard. Her game leg had given out. She sat resting on a discarded apple crate, while her young great-grandson, Franklin, whose almost adult-size pants were tied to his middle with a piece of clothesline, aimlessly picked the lower branches above her head. Laurabelle, nearly sixty-five, had worked in the cotton since she was "knee high to a grasshopper." Her home was outside Atlanta, Georgia. Years past she had been part of the migrant stream which traveled from southern Florida to central New York; now she usually went only to Florida to work celery. Sometimes she found enough work as a maid in white homes in Atlanta to "get by" for the winter. If it were only herself, she could have managed, but she had this eight-year-old great-grandson to look after. So, for the second year in a row, she came "back up the road" when the pickers pulled out of Pahokee in April. She had taken care of Franklin since his mother had died when he was a few months old, and he had come to look to her for direction more than to anyone else in the family. He preferred to come with Laurabelle on her trips than stay with

414

his grandmother. Laurabelle said she had " 'dopted" Franklin and thought of him as her own.

Nine years ago she had worked here in central Virginia for an apple grower. He was a good man. He paid what he had promised when the work was finished so his workers could leave. She thought it was better to go to a grower she knew, even if he paid less, than to run the risk of trying someone new. Maybe, she mused, as one grows older one gets more cautious about trying new things and going to strange places. Time was, she said, when this migrant life was an exciting adventure for her. She had looked upon it as an opportunity to meet new people and to see how things were done in different parts of the country. If she did not like one place, she could always move on. Now she was not as certain of herself. It was good to go back where she was known. Besides, there was Franklin to be considered. She could get plenty of work in a lot of places, but some of the camps or crews were so rough that they were "not a fit place for a youngun, what with the language and carryin's on." Last year she was in a farm labor camp in New Jersey with a "bunch so rough" she put the boy on a bus and sent him back to Atlanta to her daughter-in-law until she could return in the fall. She was "not gonna have that boy see and hear such things." She felt sorry for parents who had no place to send their "chilluns," and so they were exposed to experiences "far beyond their years."

Laurabelle worried about what the world was coming to, "what with the way people carry on with no respect for themselves or others." Her dark face was serious. "Dere's so much cuttin' and killin' goin' on and hard feelings 'tween white and colored." Young children "sass their elders" and are allowed to run free and wild and do as they please. "Even worse is the way older folks behave, drinkin', swearin', and gamblin', lazy, lyin' and runnin' 'round with 'nother man's woman or 'nother woman's husband."

I had not seen a toilet in the orchard, so I asked Laurabelle if there was one. She answered my question with another question, "Does you jest have to make water or do somethin's else? 'Cause they ain't no toilet out here. If you jest wants to make water, git behind a tree over there; but if you has to do somethin's else, you'all goes behind that brush pile over yonder." She smiled a broad grin. "I fixed myself up a box with a hole in it, and no one knows whether I'se jest sittin' here restin' or jest sittin' here doin' my job. Besides, taint none of their business so long as I don't make a spectacle of myself. 'Pears to me they'd provide us po' folk with some kind of toilets if they want us to work for 'em. Some places I'se been they has toilets in the field made from tin or burlap fixed 'round frames so they don't blow open in the wind. But lots of places I'se been they don't has nothin', jest like they don't has nothin' here 'cept some brush or a patch o' woods."

That was how I met Laurabelle. Two years later my husband and I visited her home in Georgia. She did not work in the crops that summer; her leg was giving her "real miseries," and she was baby sitting.

This was not the first time we had visited migrants in their own homes, nor was it the first time we were struck by the lack of evidence to back up such common statements as, "All these people are accustomed to living in hovels; they don't know any better. They don't want good housing. They wouldn't take care of good housing. They don't know how to take care of things like flush toilets because they have never had any."

It is true that some migrants do live in shacks, but not all migrants. Some migrants are not accustomed to electricity or electrical appliances, to flush toilets, to screened windows and doors or even glass panes in the windows; but the majority of migrants do not live that way if they have a choice. And some migrants have provided well for their own needs as Laurabelle had provided for hers. She and her husband had bought the small plot of land in 1912 and built their house themselves. Her husband had worked in nearby cotton fields until his death in the mid-1950s. He was "a good man," according to Laurabelle. She said he "never was in jail, never was handcuffed nor had a knife or fist fight like lots o' men do."

Laurabell's home was more luxurious than we expected. She explained that she and her husband had worked very hard and put every penny they could get their hands on into their house and furniture. They wanted their "chillun" and their "grandchillun" to have more than they had.

They encouraged their children to get an education. "I didn't git far in school," Laurabelle once told me; "I had to work all my life, but no one could ever cheat me none figurin'. I could tell 'em how much I had comin' for pickin' cotton or apples. I kept my chillun in school 'cause I could see it's your brains now-a-days what carries you through this world, not how much cotton you kin pick. Although I didn't get the chance to go to school very much, my chillun dey all fine scholars and my granchillun have bin even better." Four of Laurabelle's six children had completed high school. The son who made his home with her was a carpenter. She was proud he was a member of the union and that he made more money some days than his father had made in a week picking cotton. Thirteen of Laurabelle's grandchildren had completed high school. Two had gone to college; one was a teacher, the other a nurse.

Laurabelle thought it was " 'portant for parents to have nice things in their homes so their chillun would know how to act when they git out in the world with cultured folks." She said she thought this was " 'specially" true for members of her race if they ever " 'spected to git ahead." She pointed with pride to her own color television saying it cost nearly $400. She used all she made during two years of picking apples to buy it and a red davenport for her living room. She said she bought both of them for her grand-children, especially for her great-grandson, Franklin. As long as she was physically "able to work and keep things up, none of them need ever be 'shamed of their home. They'd never need to feel other common folk were better than they were 'cause they had a nicer home and furniture." Laurabelle said she did not want Franklin "actin' like an ignorant country boy all his life." She " 'spected him to really 'mount to sum'pun' "; perhaps he would even go to the University of Georgia where her cousin worked as a maid. She intended to do everything she could to provide him with opportunities, even when it meant spending hard-earned money on things that some people might think were nonessentials and that prompt such comments as: "Just like one of those lazy, stupid migrants to throw her money away on a red davenport and a color television instead of saving it for her own old age. She will be around one of these days asking taxpayers to support her on Old Age Assistance."

If Laurabelle recognized such criticism, she ignored it, and it was with much pride that she showed us through her five-room house. Two things she said she missed most when "on the road" were her bathroom and her good well water. Lots of growers did not provide a place for their workers to take a bath, she said, and no place could she get good cold water like she had at home. As she talked she took a water bottle from her refrigerator and poured us each a glass. "Ain't no water anywhere compared with that, " she said simply. "As they say, 'there's no place like home' and when I'se been up the road workin' I'se more than ever 'preciate what I'se got right here in Georgia, and I'se wouldn't trade this house and land for all the apple orchards in Virginnie."

After a few days in the orchard I was shifted from picking to the sorting shed. I saw Laurabelle occasionally if the weather was bad and she came inside to get warm or if she brought Franklin in to eat lunch with Josephine, Tom and Molly's daughter. The children always ate lunch together, nice days in the orchard and on rainy and cold days in one corner of the shed.

Outside was a slow, cold drizzle. Inside was the odor of new apples mingled with tobacco smoke from Lewis Noyes's pipe. Noyes was the process superintendent. His sense of humor more than his mechanical know-how kept the plant running. As the grower put it, "If Noyes can't get a person to work, that person ain't worth his salt, and no one can get him to work."

Noyes moved constantly. He walked up and down the room keeping an eye on the machinery and an eye on the workers. He made a teasing comment here or gave a word of praise there. Most of the time he just walked, saying little; occasionally he would look at his watch. Sometimes he left the building to check the orchard to see how the fruit was holding up. When he came in out of the wind, his clean-shaven face looked like a carrot, his eyebrows a straight line of dark above his blue eyes. His mouth slid sidewise in a crooked grin as he smiled, which he did often. The general feeling was that Lewis Noyes was an "all right Joe to work for."

Several of the workers in the grading plant were local residents. The grower's wife filled in when there was a shortage or if one of the regular women had to leave early. She worked hard, and the others respected her because they sensed she expected nothing from them that she herself was not willing to do or was capable of doing.

A pale amber flow of apples bounced and skidded over the slotted rollers that moved on the sorting rack in front of us. We were working Golden Grimes that morning, and it was my responsibility, together with Sally, Tess, and Ruby—the other three sorters, to pick out and discard the rotten, bruised, and imperfect fruit. In an eight-hour day we took two fifteen-minute coffee breaks and an hour for lunch. The women sorters were paid one dollar an hour. Unless the equipment was stopped for repair, it ran as long as there were apples to be sorted, and every person remained at his station as long as the conveyor belt carried the fruit.

From the moment Lewis Noyes flipped open the switch, which plunged the machinery into motion, until he touched the off switch, Tom Washington hoisted each full crate of apples to the level of the conveyor belt and gently poured them out. Pushing the apples forward with one hand until there was a single layer of movement, he quickly picked out what twigs and leaves he could reach with the other hand. Then he struggled to hoist another crate into place. Filled crates were moved forward by one of the stackers, and the empty crates were piled for return to the orchard.

The stream of yellow apples moved to the end of the belt and dropped onto the rotating polishing brushes. The apples danced and quivered as they were rubbed to a high wax-like polish and pushed onto the rolling slats of the sorting table where we waited. Nimble fingers darted up and down cleaning out and discarding the trash. Beyond us the apples moved across the sizing mesh. There they dropped through the holes. Polished, sorted, and sized, they rolled down the separate chutes toward the packers who gave them a final inspection and packaged them for storage or shipment.

The work at the sorting table was tedious, although not difficult. It required standing in the same position with little relief for hours. It was not long before the tips of my fingers, in contact with the cold, moving apples, felt a tingling cold sensation which spread to my hands. The discomfort of icy hands was later lost in the greater discomfort of aching feet. We stood two on each side on the top step of an elevated platform. There was little opportunity to change positions until time for the coffee break. My feet hurt, my legs ached. I found myself spreading my toes. I arched my feet and stretched up on tip toes and then rocked back on my heels. I stood first on one foot and then on the other, trying to convince myself that I had in this way rested rebelling muscles that wanted nothing so much as to sit down or get off the confines of those steps and walk rapidly up and down the room.

Just before three o'clock my feet had an unexpected rest. One of the stackers handed Tom a crate of Golden Delicious, and he poured them onto the conveyor with the Golden Grimes. The conveyor was stopped so that the Delicious apples could be sorted out.

It was the only time I saw Noyes impatient. He spoke to no one in particular but everyone in general. "Those kids out there stacking crates, those high-school dropouts, don't know one apple from another and couldn't care less, but God after five years working apples you'd think Tom would know a Delicious from a Grimes."

This was the fifth season Tom had worked for this grower. He and his wife Molly and their four children drove up for the season from South Carolina in their ten-year-old Plymouth. Most of the year they worked cotton around home. Occasionally Tom cut a little tobacco in eastern Tennessee, but they found apples in Virginia to be the most profitable work for them. So each year the grower notified them when the early apples were ready, and they packed their belongings in their Plymouth and headed toward the Shenandoah Valley. The older children, Carter and Sapphire, worked with their mother in the orchard. Nice days the baby spent in a playpen under the trees. On rainy days the playpen sat in one corner of the packing shed. On those days seven-year-old Josephine watched him while their parents worked.

Josephine, her hair in tiny braids each tied with a red or blue piece of yarn, sat by the playpen, her back towards the sorting table. Molly had taught her to be "respective" to her elders, yet by her very actions Josephine showed her hostility toward whites. Her Black culture taught her always to be on guard, always to be suspicious. The only time she could relax and be a little girl was when she and Franklin were together; she would giggle and whisper and seemed to forget that she was surrounded by whites.

Molly, like every Negro mother since the days of slavery, had to teach her children how to grow up Black and survive in a white society. Many authors have described the role of the Black mother in this type of teaching.[1] Molly followed the same pattern as her mother and grandmother had before her, punishing her children severely if they verbally expressed their dislike for whites, and yet conveying her own fears and mistrust of whites through her harsh discipline. As children Molly and Tom had learned to conform to this pattern, to express their hostility subtly. Molly's younger sister, Dorothy, a maid for several white families, had openly told the children that when her employers "treated her like dirt" she retaliated by spitting in the pies she was baking or other food she was preparing. Subtly expressed rage has been part of Black behavior for years, but anger has been expressed openly only recently, with the generation of Tom and Molly's children.

The three children expressed their mistrust of whites in various ways. Fifteen-year-old Carter looked straight ahead, his features mask-like and frozen, refusing to recognize or answer any white person. He followed orders, picked the apples where he was told, but no one was going to make him carry on a conversation with anyone other than a member of his own race. Although willing to talk with whites, Sapphire had dropped all pretense of being "polite and keeping her place." She no longer said, "Yes, ma'am." She was bold in stating her likes and dislikes and what she felt were her rights. At times she was almost supersensitive in her interpretation of slights or affronts toward her race.

All three of the Washington children expressed their impatience with the more passive roles of their parents. They exceeded the normal adolescent critical analysis of parental behavior. Their generation gap was complicated by Black-white relationships.

The generation of Tom and Molly had learned to tolerate whites and, in some cases, to relate warmly to them. The generation of Carter, Sapphire, and Josephine rebelled against such tolerance, their intense commitment being to expose the hypocrisy of race relations for what it really was. Many of that generation, including the three Washington children, would probably always be uncomfortable with whites or else go around picking arguments or accusing every white person with whom they had contact of being a racist.

Eight years later in 1973 Carter stated openly that he would "starve first" before he would take another job working in the fields or orchards, regardless of how much pay a grower offered. At the age of twenty-three Carter associated work in agriculture with slavery, sharecropping, and the history of work for his race. Carter classified farm work of any kind with other nonprestigious jobs, such as cleaning streets or collecting garbage, which once had been the only work available to men of his race. Carter felt that if he continued to follow the farm-work pattern of his father and grandfather he would be a failure and a discredit to his race.

The year we met the Washington family in the apples of Virginia Molly was a faster picker than Tom. Her legs did not seem to tire from the rungs of the ladder, and her dark fingers darted among the leaves grasping two or more apples in each hand with only enough pressure to separate the stems from the trees and not enough pressure to bruise. She knelt down when she unfastened the canvas bottom of her picking bucket and let the apples carefully spill into the crates. The orchard supervisor prized Molly as what he called his "number-one picker."

The supervisor watched Tom and decided that Tom's legs would not hold up on ladder work. He would be more useful in the grading shed dumping the incoming apples onto the conveyor belt. For this Tom would be paid one dollar and fifteen cents an hour, and there was work in the grading plant as long as there were apples, regardless of the weather.

Whereas Molly was quick to learn and had to be told something only once, Lewis Noyes had to "keep an eye on Tom." Tom's behavior may have been a way of expressing anger at his position, because unless he was "spoken to" two or three times daily, he would dump the apples too fast, allowing them to bunch up on the conveyor belt so that there was danger of them being bruised or punctured by stems.

For awhile, after being reminded, Tom would carefully feed in the apples. Then suddenly he would get careless and spill more apples on the conveyor than it could handle, and Noyes would have to "chew him out." But for all that Tom was "exasperating," he was dependable. He would show up for work every day. He did not smoke or drink or waste time "shooting off his mouth" with the other workers. These were facts which stood in Tom's favor. Other workers might be more intelligent and might try to remember something they were told, but other workers were not always so dependable, and, besides, Tom was married to Molly. So each year when it was time to harvest apples the grower contacted them, and two or three times a day Lewis Noyes showed Tom how to spread apples on a conveyor belt. With the first heavy frost early in

November, Tom and Molly and the children packed their Plymouth and headed back to the cotton of South Carolina and the five months of schooling that Carter, Sapphire, and Josephine averaged each year.

Across the table from me Sally's fingers darted among the apples turning, inspecting, and discarding. Throughout the process she engaged in a running conversation that echoed up and down the room from the time she arrived in the morning until she left at night.

Sally was a plump woman in her late twenties. When she smiled her pretty features were marred by a wide, gaping hole where two front teeth had been. She was self-conscious about those teeth and tried to cover the opening with her upper lip. The result was a twisted expression which drew more attention to her mouth.

Sally's husband had taken "French leave" about three years before. He claimed he was going to Baltimore to look for work. Sally heard he had "taken off with another man's wife" and gone across the mountains to Knoxville. She tried for a time to locate him and then gave up, figuring she and her two children were better off without him. At first, after his leaving, she worked as a waitress. After her teeth were extracted, she was laid off. "Who wants a toothless waitress?" she asked, as a matter of fact. "I can't cook and they have dishwashers, and I don't want any part to do with welfare, so I got myself a job here in the apples. It pays better than housework, and it's more steady. Besides you don't have someone checkin' to see if you dusted the top of the doors, orderin' you 'round like a dog, and 'pectin' you to do a lot of extra things like ironin' and tellin' you to use the back door and eat in the kitchen and stay out of sight when company comes. True, your legs ache from standin' on this platform, but my legs ached from runnin' back and forth waitin' on tables, and my back ached from scrubbin' dirty floors. So it all adds up to 'bout the same thing. Here I can wear whatever I want, no cost for uniforms, no worryin' about keepin' my hair done nor my fingernails polished." She laughed ruefully. "The apples sure don't care what I look like, and I go home at night ready for a hot bath and tired enough to sleep without wantin' to run around. I get all the spotted apples I want for nothin', and my aunt, who lives with me and takes care of my two kids, cans a lot of that stuff. She's got boxes of it stuck back under the bed or the sink. Certainly helps out on the grocery bills, which is more than my husband has ever done for me and his two kids."

"Luck is like a wheel," Sally went on philosophically, "always turning, and sometimes those who ain't got nothin' gets on top, and those who has today ends up with nothin' tomorrow. So maybe there's still hope for me 'cause I sure ain't got nothin' except achin' feet from standing here on this old platform."

Tess was the wife of the local shoemaker. She described her husband as a steady worker, but shoe repairing was irregular, so she helped out whenever she could with work in the apples. She liked the work in the apples because she could set her own hours. She had been working for this same grower off and on for six years. He was a good man to work for. He had a good packing shed boss in Noyes, who tried to give the workers "a decent shake."

Tess was born just before the First World War on a small rented farm a few miles to the southeast in Culpepper County. She laughingly described her father as "not much of a farmer." He finally "wore the ground out plantin' tobacco all the time." Because of her farm background Tess could identify with problems of growers better than most workers could. She explained that the apples we sorted had been "sprayed at least twelve times" and that there was a lot of money spent on fertilizer. As she put it, "Apples are just like wheat or tobacco; you gotta build up the soil and keep down the weeds, and all that adds to the cost."

Ruby's family had been "reared for generations along Pleasant Creek in West Virginia." She was born in the early years of the Depression. Her family moved from Pleasant Creek shortly after her birth when construction began on the Tygart River Dam. Farmers whose land would be flooded left their farms at that time to find work in the coal mines, the glass factories, or on farms in other valleys. Ruby "got on" at a glass factory as soon as she turned sixteen and could quit school. After she was married, she lived a few months in Pittsburgh where her husband worked in the steel mills. He had some sort of respiratory infection which was irritated by work at the mill, so they drifted into harvest work after their first baby was born. Now, with all six of the children big enough to pick, they "did all right" following the fruit, especially if Hank did odd jobs between crops. Once he worked at a garage.

The owner wanted him to stay, but when the strawberries were ripe, Hank "got an itchy foot to see the country. He just couldn't take working for one boss." So every few months they "headed up the road."

Sometimes they returned to a grower for whom they had worked other seasons. Other times they went a few miles down the road to a new grower. Still other times they checked with the employment office to see what was available. Hank could give no reason for moving constantly except he "could not stand living in one place too long." Sometimes he would stay until the end of the season. Other times he would pack up and leave early, forfeiting any bonus he had coming, if a bonus was paid. Like many migrants Hank did not think much of the bonus system. "It's just a gimmick to hold the pickers," he said. "They really don't pay nothing extra. They just knock it off the regular pay and hold it out. They're not giving you nothing! You earn every red cent you get! Yep, the bonus is a gimmick to line the pockets of the grower. If you stay through, he says you get a bonus, but I say you just get paid what he should have paid you in the first place. If you leave early and don't collect your bonus, it's that much more in the grower's pocket. He gets the work done for less. In the long run it all comes out of the picker's hide."

Ruby was a tall, thin woman in her early thirties whose once deep red hair was prematurely gray. Sometime recently she had attempted to recapture the original coppery tones with a red dye, and the ends were a firey paint-red, the color of bright wool, but the hair two inches from her head was her drab natural color.

Ruby's dark eyes smoldered with a sullen hostility whenever the grower's wife took her turn on the apple-grading platform. Although Ruby respected the ability of the grower's wife to work, there was at the same time about her a blind and instinctive resentment. As she said, "It hardly seems fair that any one person could be able to do so many different things and do them all well and at the same time be her own boss." Ruby's hostile attitude was not resentment springing from a sense of poverty. It was not the seething, silent anger of the impoverished against the rich or the feeling of injustice that decent people like herself should have to fetch and carry all of their lives for idle, lazy wasters. Ruby did not feel sorry for herself because she had to drudge in the crops with roughened hands all day in order for this fine lady to spend her time in idleness. Ruby knew how hard the grower's wife worked. She knew the grower's wife took care of her house and her children and that she waited on customers at the roadside stand in front of the house. Ruby knew she ordered all of the supplies, did the bookkeeping for the business, and was an officer for one of the state fruit commissions.

Nor was the resentment she felt for the material wealth of the other woman. Ruby did not feel that the other woman knew how to relax and enjoy her wealth. Yes, if anything, she—Ruby—had the better of it in that regard, for she would not drive herself from early morning to late in the night, she told me with contemptuous bitterness, the way the grower's wife drove herself. What Ruby resented was the grower's wife's security, the security of never having to travel with the seasons, of having the businessmen of the community tip their hats and call her by name. These were the things Ruby envied in the other woman. These were the things Ruby had never experienced.

The grower's wife viewed Ruby as a steady worker, but not as an ambitious worker. There were days when she thought Ruby was paid more than she was worth. She also thought Ruby was careless with her personal appearance. A few times when she came close to Ruby she got a whiff of rank body odor, of sweaty feet and unwashed socks. She was repulsed. She had all she could do to be "even civil." "How can migrants be so dirty," she asked me, forgetting we too were migrants, "when we give them a good place to work and provide them with running water? Why don't they take a bath? You'd think these people would be so glad to be in a nice place like this, they'd show a little appreciation. You have to be a certain kind of person to be a fruit tramp, and that sort of person don't want no truck with things like soap and water."

Without realizing what she had said, the grower's wife, like countless others, had allowed her reactions to one person to color her feelings toward migrants in general. Ruby was careless. Ruby did not take a bath or change her socks. Ruby's old tennis shoes smelled of sweaty feet, so disgust toward Ruby was projected to all workers who followed the harvest. Migrants were dirty, lazy. Migrants were unappreciative of things a grower might try to do to make their life more comfortable.

On other occasions the grower's wife expressed resentment of the freedom from responsibility which she assumed migrants knew. Intellectually she was aware that her way of life held more material and emotional security, but she did envy the migrants' impulsive buying, their self-indulgence, their freedom to take time off from work if they wished. Her personal life was different; it was more controlled. The cost of operating the orchard was always with her; there was the need for a new tractor or repairs for a truck that took priority over a new car, new bedroom curtains, or a vacation. She too was weary of the harvest of apples and the long hours she spent in the packing shed, but she was not free to take a day and just loaf in the sun. Every hour must count; every hour was related to the business.

Her fatigue and unconscious envy was often expressed in unduly harsh criticism of the "irresponsibility" of migrants who spent money on new cars they could not afford. Although she resented so many migrants' driving comparatively new cars, she would have been equally as critical of apple pickers who were late or did not arrive at all because their old "rattle-trap car" had burned out a clutch or needed a new transmission fifty miles up the road. It was hard for her to believe that the migrant placed the same value on his new car that she and her husband placed on a new tractor or orchard sprayer. For the migrant the new automobile was not merely a prestige symbol, it was a necessity, even as the sprayer was a necessity. Without dependable transportation the migrant would have no work; without a tractor and sprayer the grower would have no marketable apples. For each there was a necessity; for each there was a value. But they were not the same, even as their lives and their experiences were not the same.

NOTES

1. Robert Coles, *Children of Crisis* (New York: Dell Publishing Co., 1967), pp. 66-67; William H. Grier and Price M. Cobbs, *Black Rage* (New York: Bantam Books, Inc., 1968), pp. 46-53; Charles S. Johnson, *Growing Up in the Black Belt* (New York: Schocken Books, 1967), pp. 297-99; Richard Wright, *Black Boy* (New York: Harper and Row, Publishers, 1966), pp. 30-31, 55-58, 67-68.

Beyond plants are animals,
Beyond animals is man.
Beyond man is the universe

Jean Toomer, 20th century
American poet
Brown River, Smile

26

Mozart in the Tomatoes

It was a tiny community, much like hundreds of other communities scattered throughout the Midwest. Once it had been a mecca for farm families who came there to shop. Now an express route bypassed the town and gave direct access to the markets of Toledo, Detroit, and Cleveland. There were few farms left in the area. Those remaining were large and specialized operations whose owners contracted to grow one main crop for either a seed company or a cannery. For most farmers that main crop was tomatoes.

The little community with its large, old houses and neatly clipped lawns was a link to the past in the midst of a highly mechanized area. Farming here, as elsewhere across the nation, was big business, which required a knowledge not only of soil, plants, and fertilizer, diseases, blights, weather, planting, and harvesting but also of packaging and transporting, world markets, labor relations, taxes, and politics.

Here, as elsewhere in the mid-1960s, family farms were facing the beginning days of reckoning. Owners of small farms, unable to balance the high cost of production, publicity, and advertising found their only choice was to sell or lease their land to larger farmers. In the midst of this, life in the little town was virtually unchanged. It still circled around the lodge, the church, and the school, as it had for the past 100 years.

The Sunday school superintendent was the deputy sheriff and also the town barber. Herman Wilkins was born in the little community, graduated from its high school, and, except when he took his barber training in Toledo, had never lived elsewhere. Once he made a trip to Colorado, after which he became an authority on the West. He was, in fact, prone to be an authority on all other subjects.

Deputy Sheriff Wilkins took his duties seriously. The town was a "quiet, peaceful, law-abiding place," and that, he said, was how it was going to remain. Between customers at the barbershop he patrolled the streets in his car, flashing its blinker at teenagers and reminding residents of various town ordinances which pertained to parking, garbage pickup, or leaf burning. He questioned every stranger who came into his barbershop wanting to know where they were from, who they knew in town, how long they planned to stay, and why they were there. There were many of the town's people who resented what they called Wilkins's "nosiness." More than anything they resented his inability to keep information to himself. Nothing was confidential, and details of domestic quarrels shared with him were soon public knowledge. Although he was labeled behind his back as "a nosy gossip, worse than any old woman," he was tolerated in his role because he was the only man in town who really wanted to be deputy sheriff. "So, if he is happy and feels important, why not let him be happy" was the general attitude.

At the break between Sunday school and church several people clustered around to tell us they were pleased we had come to worship with them. Suddenly Herman Wilkins began to describe his experience apprehending three migrant workers from a nearby labor camp. He held the rapt attention of the group who encouraged his narration with their questions and comments. The arrest had occurred the night before on the main street of the town. The charge was drunk and disorderly conduct. "One of those migrants was obviously dangerous," Deputy Sheriff Wilkins began his story. "He had a knife, and while it was not a very large knife and one he claimed he used to trim fingernails and pick out briars, he looked like the kind of character who would stab you if he had half a chance and could get hold of a knife big enough to do the job. That migrant really was drunk, and yet he kept spieling off about his Constitutional rights to legal representation and a fair trial. He could sure talk! Even more than that, he could sing, although most of it was in some kind of gibberish, not English—probably Hungarian . . . maybe Russian. He looked like a communist. You can't tell what will come out of one of those farm-labor camps. They're all a tough bunch, and lots of them are communists. . . ."

"What was he doing first, Herman, that attracted your attention?" someone interrupted.

"He was standing there in the middle of Main Street. It was after midnight, and here this guy was singing up a storm." Sheriff Wilkins looked indignant. "Two other fellows were sitting on the curb egging him on. You could hear them all over town. That guy bellows when he sings."

"What did they do when you drove up?" another person asked.

"The guy who was singing just stood there with a silly, drunken grin on his face and said, 'Hi, officer.' At least he knew I was a representative of the law. I asked what he thought he was doing."

" 'I'm giving a concert for my friends,' he said. 'This town lacks cultural entertainment. Officer, you're welcome to stay if you like.' "

"I'd heard about all I wanted to hear from that riffraff and scum when he made the crack about our town not having culture. I told him our town was a clean, decent place that didn't cater to his kind of entertainment."

"Good for you, Herman," chimed in the town grocer. "What we have to do with those tomato pickers is let them know we won't stand for any carousing and loose morals around here. There won't be any more problems like this if we just let them know from the beginning that we won't take this kind of nonsense. Culture, indeed. . . ."

His irritated mumbling was cut off by a middle-age woman. "You know, we live out near one of the Price's camps. The Prices raise more tomatoes than anyone else around here, so they have hundreds of those pickers," she explained to us. Then she hurried on. "Frankly, I don't sleep good as long as those people are here.

They can walk into town from out there, so they go up and down past our place anytime of the day or night. We can hear them laughing and shouting back and forth to each other, and Sandy just goes wild. They are all scared to death of dogs, especially the colored ones, so we keep the gate locked and just turn Sandy loose. Those pickers keep on the other side of the road and don't come near the gate, especially when Sandy jumps against it and snarls."

"Sandy is a big German shepherd," someone informed us.

The woman continued, "Sandy looks mean, but he would not hurt a flea. He's gun-shy and afraid of thunder, but he does know how to bark and show his teeth. One day I just told Mr. Price I didn't like the looks of his tomato pickers. He laughed and tried to tell me they were all okay. He says they're all checked good before he takes them. Those who come from Puerto Rico, he said, are checked even more than those who come up from Florida. He can say what he pleases, but I don't trust any of them. After all, they're here for only a few days or weeks, and then they're gone—where, nobody knows. There would be nothing to keep them from doing most anything while they're here."

"Beth, it might not be quite that bad," her husband chided thoughtfully. "Besides, you know we could be giving our guests a picture that we're not a very friendly church and we are. What we should do is go out to one of those camps and invite some of those migrants here to Sunday school." He was half jesting, half in earnest, but it obviously annoyed the Sunday school teacher.

"I doubt if any of them would have an interest in church," he replied emphatically, "except perhaps for the Mexicans, and they would go simply because they are Catholic and the Pope tells them to go to church, if you can call Catholic doctrine religion and that so-called Mass a real church service. Besides, what would we do if some of those tomato pickers did walk in here on a Sunday morning? What would you say to them? Would you say, 'Here, sit next to me, and after church come over to my house for dinner'?"

The others agreed it would be an impossible situation and also a most unlikely one. I wondered what their reaction would be if we disclosed at that moment that we, the guests they had welcomed so warmly, were in their community for the sole purpose of picking tomatoes for their Mr. Price and that he had not "checked us out carefully." He had just put us to work picking tomatoes. Only a few hours before we had soaked the green plant stains from our hands with full-strength chlorine bleach, and even now hanging in our trailer were the work clothes we had worn yesterday, which would need to be washed before they could be worn tomorrow. I speculated on the type of reaction such information would bring from Deputy Sheriff Herman Wilkins, the Sunday school teacher, or the couple who owned the dog Sandy.

Suddenly I was aware of the voice of the petite, white-haired woman who had first welcomed us at the door, who later invited us to come and sit with her and who had asked that after church we stop by her house for a bouquet of fall flowers. She was speaking to me. "You know, my dear," she said, "that trailer park where you folks are staying is not very far from one of those labor camps. You want to keep your door locked. You really can't tell what might happen in a place like that with those kinds of people. If you run into anything that doesn't look right, you just let Deputy Wilkins know. That's Herman's job. The trailer park is outside the town limits, but Herman knows a lot of people in the county sheriff's office, and they let him take care of things out there because they know how this town feels.

"We have an ordinance here about people living in trailers, and we had quite a to-do with a lot of town meetings when the Whites decided to put a trailer park on their place. We found there really wasn't anything we could do about it if they wanted to put in the park because their property was just outside of the village proper. But we did tell the Whites that we expected things out there to be quiet, and I will say this for them, they have kept the place up, and the people who live there seem real nice and respectable. We have never had any trouble with people from the trailer park, and we have even had a few come here to church like you folks."

"Have you ever had any trouble with migrants from the farm-labor camps?" I asked.

"No," she said, looking at me rather startled, "but we don't aim to have any either."

Tuesday night was unseasonably hot for mid-September, and we sat outside long after midnight drinking coffee. Earlier we had been joined by one of our neighbors, but now the trailer park seemed to be asleep. Suddenly we could hear a man coming. Obviously he was taking the shortcut from the main highway to the side road that passed the trailer park and that would lead into another road, a seldom-used back entrance to the farm-labor camp. Intermittently he sang, and between songs he gave what sounded like an oration or speech. When he was closer, we could make out the words. His syllables were slightly slurred. He sounded intoxicated.

"Ladies and gentlemen of this lovely community," he shouted, "lock your doors! Hide under your beds! Call your deputy sheriff to defend you! Call your deputy sheriff to come with his little paddy wagon and take me back to the county seat with its filthy jail. Certainly your deputy sheriff would say you must be protected from me at all costs. He would say that, and yet not for anything would I harm one hair of your heads. You're not in danger from me, citizens of this lovely community, but you are in danger! In the words of Socrates spoken just before his death in his famous discourse. . . ." The man stopped speaking. He laughed a low, rather mirthless laugh. "You know, your precious Sheriff Wilkins never heard of a discourse; when I tried to tell him about Socrates and his discourse, he thought I was using a dirty word. Poor Sheriff Wilkins, pipsqueak of a little man, trying so hard to feel important and yet hung up on sex so that he thinks discourse and intercourse are one and the same and that everyone has the same kind of filthy, dirty mind he has. . . ." He again was silent for a long minute. "But so much for Deputy Sheriff Wilkins," he said. "Now back to Socrates. In case you don't know his discourse, I'll quote from it for you. 'It is not difficult, oh Athenians, to escape death, but it is much more difficult to avoid depravity, for it runs swifter than death.' So hear me, citizens of this lovely community, and beware of the words of Socrates. Take warning—the conditions in your town are no different from those referred to by Socrates. So it is in your town as it was once in Athens of old. Here in this sleepy, little Midwest town there is a satisfied complacency; there is a smugness, a rejection of anything or anyone that is different, and in that there is danger! Wake up, you who are asleep! Wake up, lest you die without ever having lived!"

He was singing again. His deep baritone voice was clear and full. Each note was perfect. He was singing something from Mozart's opera *Don Giovanni*. The "foreign gibberish" to which Herman Wilkins referred was Italian.

In the direction of the farm-labor camp a dog barked. Lights appeared in several trailers. We decided to talk with this man to see if we could quiet him. A return to jail for disturbing the peace did not seem justifiable. We walked toward where he stood. His light shirt was a blur against the darkness. When we were within a few feet, we spoke, talking quietly. It was a nice evening, we said. It was, he agreed. He stood without moving, muscles alert, as if attempting to sniff out our intentions. What did we want?

How would he like to come into our trailer for a cup of hot coffee? He stared with disbelief. We . . . were asking him . . . to have a cup of coffee . . . with us? Did we know he had just gotten out of jail that afternoon? The other two fellows who had been picked up with him had been released the next day, but he had to shoot off his mouth as usual. He rocked on his feet, grinning foolishly. The county sheriff had made an example of him and had kept him three days. Did we know he was a jailbird? Yes, we knew all that, but we had nearly a full pot of hot, strong, black coffee that was waiting, and he was welcome.

Without further words we turned toward our trailer. He stood as if undecided. From the direction of the town came the headlights of a car. He mumbled something about being told to keep moving and not get into any more trouble around here. He said he had no intentions of leaving town. His things were still at the labor camp, and, besides, the tomato season was not over and he needed work. But he would not press his luck with the deputy sheriff at this time of night. He would keep quiet and take us up on our offer of coffee. He paused for a moment and then bowed low. His arm moved in an exaggerated sweep as he lifted an imaginary hat from his head and trailed it in the dust at our feet. We were to be his hosts. He straightened up and walked between us toward the trailer.

We went ahead to turn on the light so that we could drink our coffee inside. He followed us to the open doorway where he paused, blinking as if the sudden light hurt his eyes. He was of medium height, spare and slight and lean. His thin, eager face was brown from sun and wind. His dark, straight hair, with a touch of gray at the temples, was long and unkempt. The finer lines of his chin were blurred under the growth of a four-day beard; the decayed stub of a tobacco-stained front tooth showed that the fillings or crown which had once been there sadly needed replacement. His eyes were bright and quick. His glance was restless and comprehensive. He was older than we had assumed from his voice. Years of working with railroad section gangs, cutting trees for pulpwood, doing heavy physical work in all kinds of weather, plus hard drinking, had taken their toll. He stood in the doorway, looking disheaveled and dirty. He smelled of sweaty, unchanged clothes. He did not enter; instead he held up his hands embarrassedly and asked if he could wash before he had coffee. Was there a public bathroom in that trailer park? There was. Did we have a towel and soap we would let him use? We did.

His hair and beard were damp when he returned. There were still ingrained, grimy stains of work around his fingernails, but his hands and arms were clean. He asked for a newspaper so his pants would not stain our chair. "Do not tell me your last name," he began. "It is enough to know your first names and that you too pick tomatoes for a living. I do not want the burden of knowing who you really are, but never again will I see a cup of coffee without remembering this night and what the two of you have done. And what you have really done, you can never know." For a moment his voice was full, husky.

"But enough," he said, "enough of such nonsense. We are friends and we are having a party. I am called Perrie. It sounds French. At least that's what poodle owners think. Wherever I go I can always start a conversation with a poodle. 'Perrie, old boy,' I say, 'that's my name, too. Are you my namesake or am I yours?' Sometimes I even try to start a conversation with the poodle's owner, but usually I don't get beyond *'Parlez-vous francais.'* Maybe it's my pronunciation. She thinks she has been insulted, and all I have tried to do is convince her that I am French and to ask if she speaks French." He laughed uproariously. We sensed his laughter was a cover, a defense for deeper emotions. "Maybe I should say instead *'Je parle mal le francais,'* but that's a lie." His voice was grave. "I don't speak French badly." He began to talk about himself, seemingly unaware we were present. "I spoke French before I spoke English," he explained. "My father was French Canadian. He never learned English. He wandered across the border into upper New York State, and my mother always said he couldn't find his way back to Canada because he couldn't read directions in English. He never said why he left Canada nor why he didn't go back."

After the third cup of coffee our guest became philosophical. "One thing I like about working the crops," he said. "No one really cares who you are, where you are from, or where you are going. Today I am a picker in the tomatoes. Tomorrow I may work in the apples. Nobody in the apples will care what I did yesterday in the tomatoes. They will care only what I do in the apples. Each picker is like a ship without an anchor. There are some who would like to anchor in a safe harbor. They're the ones who want to get out of the migrant racket. There are others who are afraid to be scrutinized, afraid to come close to people, and there are those who are restless and cannot settle down and will keep going 'til they die."

"Which are you, Perrie?" my husband asked.

"This may sound strange to you," he answered, "but I am going to say it anyhow. I know what I am really doing. I am seeking; I am hunting, not for something but for someone. I am searching to really find myself," he said. "For seven years I have looked, always trying to find myself, trying to understand what I have become or even what I was before I became what I am now. But most of all I am trying to see where I am going. Oh hell," he broke off abruptly, "this is a lousy way to be talking when we are supposed to be having a party."

I asked about his singing, saying I had enjoyed what I had heard of *Don Giovanni*. He was surprised it had been recognized. He said he sang it poorly; he had become careless. His old teachers would have been critical of such a performance. He had been a music major in college, graduating with honors. He had taught voice at a private school in the East and had married. His wife had died shortly after the birth of their daughter, a musical genius. She became his life. She studied piano and ballet and showed great promise in both. For eight years he had lived for her. Seven years ago she and a young classmate had been killed when the car Perrie was driving skidded through a stop sign. Driving too fast, he had not seen the stop sign until it was too late, and they struck a truck loaded with steel. He, and he alone, was responsible for their deaths, he said. He had murdered them. As long as guilt gnawed at his guts, he felt that he had become somehow different from his fellow man. He shrank from close contacts, preferring to be alone. He drank to forget, drank constantly; in fact, seldom was he sober. Finally he was discharged from his teaching position and began to drift.

The pangs of an empty stomach and the desire for sleep from exhaustion drove him to physical labor. He joined a farm migrant crew. He earned the reputation of working like a "madman" or one "possessed" from "can see to can't see," that is, from dawn to dark. No one in the crew cared if he was moody, if he did not speak, or if he drank to handle his depression. Although he felt no need for close friendships, out of his own suffering and loneliness had come an empathy for others. He was angered and incensed at man's inhumanity to man. He saw members of the American middle class as the greatest hypocrites of all. He rejected them, although once he too had been a member of the middle class and had been as "blind as they." He tried with his words and his songs to shock them out of their apathy. In return they would jail him for disturbing the peace. He had been jailed many times, always for the same reason. He had said too much; he got too close to the truth; he asked people to see themselves as they really were, and this they could not tolerate. So he must be sent away; he must be punished.

It was late, and he stood to leave. He would return to the farm labor camp. He said good-bye. Outside he hesitated as if there were something else, and then finally he turned away. I had stacked the coffee cups in the sink when there was a light knock at the door. Perrie had returned.

Would we mind if he made himself a bed on the lawn chairs in the back of our trailer. He promised he would be gone by daylight. He did not mind telling us that he was afraid to go into the camp at that time of night. There were a few characters there who could be faced all right in daylight but who might be nasty with someone a little unsteady on his feet. Perrie had been gone three nights, and he did not know where the others might be sleeping. One could even be in his bunk. If he made a mistake and bumped into them in the dark, and if they too had been drinking, trouble could arise. One of the fellows was pretty handy with a knife—he hoped we would understand his caution, and he would appreciate sleeping in back of our trailer. There was an old blanket in the trunk of our car which we gave to him. He stretched between the chairs.

When we awoke the day was already bright with sunlight. The blanket was folded across the empty chairs. Monsieur Perrie was gone.

Days later the truck on which he was riding stopped to dump empty hampers in the end of the field where we were working. He waved, indicating he recognized us. He did not speak, but he stood watching us as the truck pulled away. We never saw Perrie again.

Perrie was not the only unattached individual with whom we had contact during our migrant experience. Another was Jim Parker, a potato worker from Aroostook County, Maine, who lived most of the time in self-styled isolation in order to keep "off the bottle and on the wagon." Once a year he went on a "real binge." He lived it up, went to the city, saw the sights, and convinced himself he could still hold as much liquor as the next guy. His yearly fling lasted from a week to a month, after which "somehow or other" he got himself back to his cabin. Until the end of the next potato harvest he would ask his neighbors to shop for his food and his supplies. He never left the area between binges, and, except once a year, he never trusted himself with even a drop of any type of alcoholic beverage.

"Before I finally got up here," he told us, "I hit the bottle pretty hard for three years. In fact, I hit skid row. It was down in Portland that I drank 'til I began to see things. You know you hear 'bout people seein' snakes and elephants, and it sounds funny, but it's really hell. One day when I was crossing Commercial Street the light changed, and the cars started to move toward me. I stood there with great drops of sweat running down my ribs. The cars grew 'til they were like ten-story buildings moving down the street. I ran and ran and screamed. The street got narrower and the racing cars larger. Finally I fell in front of one of them. They told me later that several days had passed before I came to in a strait jacket . . . I was blind. The doctor told me there was nothin' wrong with my eyes. I just didn't want to see. He said it was hysterical paralysis of the optic nerves and would clear up in a few days. It did! Then he told me I'd really go blind permanently if I kept drinkin' like a fish. It was scary when he put it that way, so I decided then and there I better take myself away from wine, women and song.

"Before I settled in Portland, Maine and worked in a second-hand store, I had spent twenty years roamin' 'round the country workin' in the crops. I had worked in potatoes up here in northern Maine. It was dirty work but no worse than any other kind of farm work. Now I decided I needed hard work if I was goin' to squeeze myself dry, and I had to be as far away from any source of liquor as I could get. More than anything else I had liked the open spaces of northern Maine, and I liked the people I had worked for here. So with the clothes on my back and my fiddle case, I hitchhiked out of Portland. I was such a mess I didn't get many rides. I walked most of the way to Caribau and lost the fat flabbiness around my middle."

It was hard to imagine this man as "flabby around the middle." At fifty-four he had the lithe grace of a cat with powerful muscles that could toss a filled barrel of potatoes weighing 165 pounds on a tractor trailer with as much ease as if it were a peck bag. He was Irish. His mother was a devout Catholic and his father a "traveling salesman who stayed long enough to win the farmer's daughter, marry her, and leave her pregnant."

Jim was born on his grandfather's farm in northern Maryland. As a teenager he had worked as a hired hand for a neighboring farmer. Then he discovered he could make more money picking fruit, so he joined a crew headed for the Hudson River Valley. He found there were all kinds of growers. Some were decent and paid well; some treated their workers like fellow human beings. There were others, however, who were always "ridin' a worker or who cheated when it came to payin' up." He found crews were made up of all kinds of people. "Some you took a likin' to, and others you learned to stay away from."

There were other kinds of people in Jim's experience— prostitutes, gamblers, and bartenders who had their hands out and who, if they got half a chance, had their hands in the migrant's pockets. There were those who would "slit your throat as soon as look at you."

According to Jim, life as a migrant farm worker was "like knowin' whether or not a woman has the 'clap,' whether she is safe to play around with or whether it is best to run the other way. You pick up a sixth sense; you tune in. Your sixth sense tells you whether you can trust someone. And it helps you out-think the other guy before he out-thinks you."

This former migrant who now works only the potatoes in Maine lives a simple life. His home is a one-room tarpaper shack at the edge of a woods. He leases enough land for a tiny garden. His food varies little from meal to meal—pork 'n beans, fried sausage or fish, plain, boiled potatoes, sometimes a vegetable eaten from the single kettle or pan in which they are cooked and washed down with cups of strong, black coffee. When the pots are empty they are washed. Each evening when he finishes his few tasks of housekeeping, he takes his violin from its case, turns the pegs, and tunes the strings.

He plays by ear. He cannot read a note, but he feels music and plays half the night tilted back on a stool with his shoulders resting against the wall, the violin cradled on his chest. He tightens the bow, rubs it soundly over rosin, and draws it with a light, careful touch across the strings until the sound is full and perfect. He recalls songs his mother sang, music he heard in the dives of Portland, and more recent tunes he has picked up from radio and television.

Jim made his first violin from the wood of cigar boxes. He shaped the parts with a jackknife and sandpaper. He bought the strings with money he had earned doing chores for neighboring farmers. He got the idea for a violin when a band of gypsies camped near his grandfather's farm and one night he crept close to their campfire, attracted by the sound of music. One of the gypsies saw him and invited him to sit with them. It was there he saw a violin for the first time. When they noticed how fascinated he was with it, the gypsies let him hold the instrument and move the bow across the strings. They said he had a "real bowing arm. He would become a master of the violin." From that moment the violin for Jim Parker became a thing alive. Its tones were deep and vibrant and echoed in his being long after the sound had melted into silence and he had returned to his own bed. He would have a violin. He too would play, as the gypsy had played, with complete abandonment.

His grandfather forbade him to go back to the gypsy camp or to waste his money on such nonsense as a violin. So he made his own and taught himself to play. Years later when he was cutting tobacco in Connecticut he saw a violin in a pawn shop. He paid $125 for it at a time when wages for a general farm hand were a dollar and a half a day and the "going rate for pickin' strawberries was a cent and a half a quart." Jim laughed. "I could have bought a pretty good car for $125 thirty-one years ago," he mused, "but the car would have been worn out by now, and this old violin of mine is still goin' strong. In fact, this violin was the best buy I ever made. It's the only thing to show for my entire life.

"I married once. We had two kids—two girls. My wife couldn't take my drinkin'. I didn't blame her, although at times she got a little tipsy herself. Don't know what's become of her. She got pretty sweet on a fellow we met in upper New York. One day they left, went down to New Jersey, and took the kids with 'em. I figured it was better for the girls to be raised by their mother, even if she lived with another man. I couldn't offer 'em much. Saw 'em for awhile whenever I went through Patterson but haven't heard from 'em in twelve years. Those kids must be young women by now."

He stroked his violin thoughtfully; then he went on, "My grandfather and mother both are dead. An uncle inherited grandfather's farm. I heard once he mortgaged the place and lost it. I've never gone back. I wrote for a few years and then stopped. There wasn't anything to write about. We just didn't know each other anymore. I'd seen and done things they'd never heard of. I used to ask migrants who'd worked in Maryland if they'd heard of my grandfather, but news is hard to come by that way, and after awhile I stopped askin' and even stopped thinkin' I'd ever been anywhere but here in Aroostook County. Yes, you'd say I'm kind'a an off-the-road migrant, but crew migrants would say I'm not one of 'em, and to people here I'm not one of 'em either. I'm just a fiddlin' fool potato picker, who is here to help 'em when there's work to be done and who stays out of their way the rest of the time."

The earth responded to him. When he and the soil were not interfered with, . . .

Marjorie Kinnan Rawlings, 20th century
American authoress
When the Whippoorwill

27

By Their Own Choice

Three days before we came to work for the grower, the six Jessops had moved into this double corn crib which was still partly filled with corn. This housing was worse than any Hester Pearl Jessop had seen since the place where they had lived in the Red River Delta of north Louisiana when she was a child. They lived now in the storage section between the two cribs where a tractor was housed in winter. Loose boards had been laid on the earth for a floor, and a canvas tarpaulin had been nailed across the end for a door. A sudden gust of wind carried an eddy of dust under the canvas and swirled it along the rough boards of the floor. A single electric bulb hung from an extension cord, looped around a nail in the wall, bringing current from the barn. Here there were none of the conveniences provided at the other camp. There were no cupboards, closets, or boxes in which to store things. There was an old wood-burning cookstove in the yard where they could cook and heat water. The Jessops had their own galvanized tub for washing clothes and bathing. The parents and their four preschool-age children slept on three army cots provided by the grower. Still they had come here on their own.

We asked them why they had suddenly left housing that we personally knew was excellent. It was motel-type, with showers, flush toilets, laundry facilities, and buildings that were neatly painted. There was a play yard for the children. The housing and the yard were clean, and still there had been unrest among the workers, a muttered anger that finally caused the Jessops and most of the others to move.

We asked, "Wasn't there work?"

"Yes," they answered, "there was plenty of work."

"Wasn't the housing comfortable?"

"Yes," they said, "it was the best in which we had ever lived." It was much better than what they had lived in in the red hills of northern Louisiana when they were at home. For the first time in their lives they had had all the hot water they wanted to wash clothes and take baths. That was really a nice place, and they were sorry to leave the hot water and the good beds.

Why had they come here? Here they felt free. Here nobody was telling them what to do, how to behave, how they should arrange their things in the house, or how to raise their children. Here, if they wanted to make some *cafe noir*—the universal drink of Louisiana made of chicory and coffee laced with brandy or bourbon—or if they wanted a bottle of wine or a fish fry or a barbecue (if they could ever find a goat or a lamb) they could do it. If they wanted to have a dance all night, nobody cared. All this grower wanted was to have his fruit picked and picked clean and carefully; but how they did it—whether they stood on a ladder or a box, whether they picked the underside of the tree first or the top, whether they filled one crate before they started another or whether they partly filled two or three, whether they got out early in the morning or slept until noon and worked until dark—was up to the pickers. They liked this sort of freedom. They could not stand having someone "lean as hard" as the first grower had. This was not a new story to us; we had heard it many times in many parts of the country. White and Black workers were more inclined to resent being constantly reminded of how to do their jobs than were the Chicano workers. As they put it, they did not like being "rode" or having someone "breathin' down" their necks or "chewin' 'em out."

James Jessop, who three days before had moved into the corn crib, explained it to us this way: "Once I knowed what they want done and how they 'spect it done, I want 'em to leave me alone and let me do it. I gess I've picked enough fruit to know a little sumpin' 'bout how to do the job. Ever since I was ten I've picked strawberries to the north 'n' east of New Orleans where those parishes ship 'em out by the railroad car load so I gess I know a little sumpin' 'bout strawberries; 'n' cherries' 'n' apples ain't no different.

"Now, why'd that last guy ever put up swings fur the kids if he didn't want 'em used? He was always 'round yellin' 'bout sumpin'. Somebody, 'cordin' to him, was out bangin' his things or knockin' off paint. He was always findin' fault an' gripin' 'til ever' one was jist tempted to get even with him. If he'd tell you nice-like why he didn't want sumpin' done, it would not be so bad; but he'd say, 'Any damn fool should have more sense than to do it that way.' I don't have to take that kind of crap from nobody. I may be po'. I may not have much schoolin', but I'm not a goddamned fool for any man, and I don't aim to be treated like one. So I said under my breath, 'You go to hell, and pick your own fruit,' and we jist moved out without givin' him any reason."

*That the education [of the poor to trust]
comes slowly need excite no surprise. The
forces on the other side [that create mis-
trust] are ever active.*

Jacob A. Riis, American writer and reformer of
the 19th century
How the Other Half Lives

28

Man's Inhumanity to Man

The migrant may be taken advantage of when he comes in daily contact with those who make their livelihood from the openly acknowledged exploitation of their fellow man. In fact, the migrant may spend his entire life within a maze-like jungle of individuals whose main purpose in life is to con others, or to make a profit from their misfortunes. For example, should the migrant die, his widow might be charged an exorbitant fee by a mortician of the same race or ethnic background for an expensive casket that is far more luxuriant than any bed the migrant had ever known in his lifetime.

Often the exploiter is a businessman who supposedly is in business to offer a service to the migrant. One such individual is Edgar King, the owner of a bar frequented by migrant crew leaders and their workers. In talking even a few minutes with this man one gets the impression that his capacity to relate to people is limited, as his eyes seldom seem to focus on anybody or any one thing. There is an air of superior contempt about him, except when he is trying to convince someone to change his mind, and then he is cunningly conniving. He is a large man, gregarious in his obesity. The folds of his jaws under his drooping, half-open eyes disappear into rolls of fat exposed above the open neck of his shirt.

Edgar King knows that his bar is a favorite meeting spot for crew leaders shanghaiing workers with promises of ample work, ample pay, and excellent living conditions—workers who too often find that ample conditions really mean ample profits for the crew leaders. Edgar King knows these things; in fact, he encourages them. Crew leaders and male migrant farm workers are those he caters to; they are his most important customers. They can do anything short of murder on his premises. He would not care if they did kill each other, except for the fact that murder would bring the police around for more than a casual survey. His customers can do anything they want as long as they drink his whiskey and wine and leave behind in his cash register most of their earnings of the week; as long as they drop a few dollars at poker and dice in his back room, that is all that really matters. He knows that many of those who visit his establishment cheat, "roll," and rob less experienced fellow workers, using every dirty trick in the book. But as long as they drink deeply and spend freely, from his point of view it is not his concern how the money that changes hands is obtained any more than it is how the drinks he serves might affect the brains or stomachs of his clientele. If an officer of the law questions him about any of his patrons, he simply shrugs his fat shoulders, shakes his round head, and disowns knowledge of anything that is not above board. If there are too many questions, he slips the officer a "twenty spot." So far, this seemed to be the solution to any problem Edgar King had to face.

We got him to talk to us one morning when his establishment was empty. We told him we were making a study of migrant farm workers, and we were interested in knowing how he, as a business-man, saw the people who frequented his establishment. How did he perceive the conditions that migrants lived under? What did he see as the solution to their many problems? He rubbed fingerprints from the top of the bar with a clean towel, staring at me with his little eyes. "Sister," he said, "you can't stand over here on this side of the bar and look at that stupid mass of humanity and have any respect for 'em. They're all animals. It's just some of them are bigger animals than others, and in that jungle out there"—he gestured with a fat hand, on the third finger of which a two-carat diamond flashed—"out there in that jungle," he went on, "those that have any guts are goin' to be able to claw their way to the top and get out, and the rest of the scum—those that can't—ain't worth helpin'. You and your kind would probably say I am a sort of a vulture, picking the flesh off the dead. Maybe so, but in this racket, sister, everyone 'spects to be taken, so they're not grieved. They just think 'easy come, easy go.' And if I don't get there first someone else will. These slobs are just no damn good, I tell you; so if I fleece them a little and put the money from my cash register back in circulation in this community, that's probably the only real decent contribution these no-goods will ever make."

Edgar King was frank in discussing the activities of his business with us. He described himself as a "civic-minded businessman." We did not represent a threat to him. He could tell us the truth—about what went on in that building and the one next door in the hours between dark and daylight. He spoke without compassion for the experiences of people. He saw himself as a shrewd businessman, conniving to make a living and endeavoring to "turn a buck."

His best customers were young men. For them, and others who were interested, he provided prostitutes. Edgar King explained that when he first opened his bar he put one prostitute in the back room where she was available for the groups of men who played poker and craps. Then the demand for craps, poker, and prostitutes grew until he bought the building next door where five or six prostitutes could be available any time of night. For him it was a very profitable business, he said. He charged each man ten dollars, he paid the "girls" five, and pocketed the difference. He was not interested in employing "high class prostitutes" or concerned about veneral disease.[1] He was interested only in obtaining women who were willing to entertain large numbers of men and who, if they received five dollars per man, would not complain about the treatment they received, even when on occasion they were "slapped around, received a black eye, a cut lip, or a bruised hip." Most of the women were "hooked on some drug" and would do "anything for money"; "if freaked out" enough they would not even remember how they got the bruise.

Along with poker, Edgar King said he kept some craps going and brought in a player, Alex Folsom, whom he described as a "real expert" who could spin the dice horizontally so that they stopped exactly as they were thrown. He could also throw them end over end so that the side numbers never came up. Edgar King laughed and said he did not need "crooked or loaded dice"[2] when he had a "dice hustler" like Alex.

Edgar King did try to keep minors out of the bar section so he would not lose his license; but if a fourteen-year-old boy wanted access to a prostitute and had ten dollars, his money, according to the bar owner, would "spend" as well as ten dollars from a man of thirty. Edgar King had no qualms about a boy's age. As long as the crew leader brought him in and he had the money, nothing else mattered.

In addition to cheap whiskey, which Edgar King keeps in bottles marked "Bonded Scotch," he at one point made contact with a drug pusher and invited him to see if some of the drugs being tried on college campuses would "take" with the migrants. But so-called "soft" or "head" drugs like marijuana and LSD ("acid") or even the amphetamines (speed, Dexedrine, Benzedrine, or Methedrine) did not appeal as an escape route. Some of the crew leaders and truck drivers who stopped at the bar used barbiturates and pep pills, but the farm workers who came to King's place of business were more interested in oblivion, which alcohol and body drugs, like heroin, provide. Very few, however, were interested in even talking about heroin; it was too expensive, and those who did get hooked on it dropped out of farm work because it didn't pay enough to support such a habit. Furthermore, the cramps, convulsions, nausea, or chills they experienced if they "needed a fix" were not conducive to farm labor. So the drug pusher whom Edgar King recruited decided that any drugs he might supply could not be fitted to the migrant life style. He told King to forget the whole idea; he was not interested in wasting his time with farm migrants when he could do much better with middle-class students at the local high school. Therefore, alcohol continued to be in high demand; it was the drug which kept Edgar King busy at his cash register. Alcohol was the drug his business was licensed to sell, and anyway he would be less apt to have trouble with the police if he stayed away from other kinds of drugs in his place.

Moreover, he found other ways to encourage the workers to part with their money. Reflected in the mirror behind the cash

register were glittering pieces of cheap, gaudy jewelry that Edgar King attempted to pawn off at a fantastic profit on half-intoxicated men. He would encourage them to buy their wives, sweethearts, sisters, or mothers "a lovely genuine diamond, ruby, or emerald as an expression of their love." Although untutored in psychology, Edgar King is a past master at making an intoxicated male feel guilty and want to atone for his behavior with a gift to the woman in his life. Every Saturday night Edgar King sells dozens of these gifts to men to bring back to the migrant camps instead of the groceries their families need and for which they supposedly went to town with the crew leader. Edgar King does not care that the truck never went near a grocery store or that the migrant is dropped off at the door of his housing in a semiconscious state without money or groceries. What makes Edgar King happy is that the migrant takes home a rhinestone necklace, a plaster-of-Paris statue of the blessed virgin, a silk shirt, or a bottle of rank perfume representing all the money he earned working in the crops that week.

The crew leader is also happy because now this migrant will need to borrow money to feed his family, and by this time next

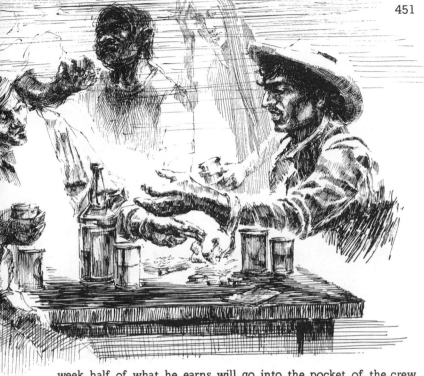

week half of what he earns will go into the pocket of the crew leader. Much of what is left the crew leader may win at a craps or poker game before the workers leave camp the following Saturday for their weekly visit to King's bar and multifaceted business establishment. Commenting on the interest rate charged by crew leaders, Edgar King said that, although it was high, the migrant was further ahead borrowing from a crew leader than trying to raise money from a pawnbroker. A pawnbroker seldom gave more than 10 percent of the value of the item being pawned, and the migrant's chances of getting enough money ahead to reclaim what was pawned were remote. At least with the crew leader he had a "running chance."

The migrant who finds himself on this sort of treadmill is truly in the midst of the jungle described by Edgar King, and if he is unable to "claw himself out," he may seek oblivion in alcohol or he may act out his rage on a fellow migrant and be jailed or even imprisoned. Even prison may be an escape from the hopelessness of this type of situation, where one human being exploits another until he has drained off everything, sometimes even the will to live.

Migrant farm workers are not the only rural residents who

experience exploitation and fraud. Sales crews selling inferior materials or repairmen offering inferior workmanship cover rural areas as well as urban areas practicing their tricks, such as "tearing down" a furnance or even breaking a part and then announcing that it cannot be repaired, it can only be replaced. Such con artists are frequently able to fast talk rural people into buying their items because poor rural people often display an astounding faith in what a salesman says, forgetting that his job is to sell and that he may even be ignorant about the product he is pushing and usually will not be around to explain why the product is deficient.

In rural areas where housing is a major problem the selling of mobile homes is another means of exploiting large numbers of poor people. Purely on the basis of numbers, the real victims of trailer selling in rural areas are the aged whites more than the nonwhites. In recent years in this country house trailers have become a way to get around building codes and obtain cheap semi-mass-produced housing, which, while it is not too expensive to produce, is not really inexpensive to buy, especially in view of the fact that it deteriorates quickly and loses its economic value long before it is paid for. Many mobile homes are so poorly constructed that they cannot withstand the move from the factory to the place of permanent location. They have cupboard doors that do not close, ceilings that sag, loose wall paneling, and many other so-called minor defects before they are even occupied.

Once a family has bought a mobile home, parking it is a whole new problem. Parking a trailer in the country is not allowed in some counties even if the individual owns the land. In most places mobile homes must be kept in a trailer park, a situation that brings the rural resident into new kinds of experiences, many of which he is not prepared for, such as the crowded spacing of trailers, the location of trailer parks, or the rules and regulations, which seem in many cases to limit personal freedom. A good illustration is an aged couple we met in Florida who were ill prepared for the new situation in which they found themselves and were taken advantage of before they even realized what was happening.

The Randalls, Burton and Eleanor, were past their midseventies. We first met them at a shuffleboard contest in the trailer park where they lived. They were active, alert, and had a joy of living unrelated to chronological years. They were unsuspecting in their complete trust of people, even strangers, for they had never known a way of life that did not involve trusting others. In their part of the country neighbors had to rely upon each other; they had to borrow and loan; they had to accept strangers because they were all dependent upon each other. But the day before we met them the Randalls had had a new kind of an experience; they had had what they called an "unpleasant adventure," one they wanted to talk with me about. They felt talking would help, but they did not want their children, friends, or neighbors to know for fear they would think they were "old fools" who, not having enough sense to take care of themselves, should be in an institution.

They would tell me their story in their own way. First, I should know something of their background to understand why their emotional shock and financial loss seemed so great to them. Until three years ago they had owned a small dairy farm in north central Minnesota. Severe winters in that section of the country, the heavy demands of operating a business, and their advancing age caused them to sell the farm and retire to the orange groves of Florida with the feeling that they could take care of themselves for the rest of their lives if they lived frugally, which they always had. They bought a trailer and leased a lot in a trailer park near Lake Wales. There were things about the trailer park they did not like: the trailers were close to each other, and they did not feel the privacy they had known on their farm. But even more they were bothered by the regulations that there could be no children in the park. This meant that their great-granddaughter could not come and spend the summer as their grandchildren had always spent summers on the Minnesota farm, and they did not have the money to make frequent trips to Chicago where she lived. But they felt that they had no choice but to "do the best we could under the circumstances and put up with seeing her occasionally." This was the same attitude as that of all the others who made up this "community of golden agers" who did not have the money to live where they had more freedom to determine how long their guests could visit them.

In their long years together the Randalls had never known "very much actual cash." They had developed a productive farm out of a quarter-section of cut-over land, which once was said to be worthless. They bought the land cheap, but it took all their money.

Being young, newly married, and eager to work together, they had cleared the fields, picked up stones, and planted crops. Money they earned from the land they put into seed and fertilizer, fences, and pure-breed stock. They were building for their family and their retirement. Burton reached across and patted Eleanor's arm. Then he directed his comment to me. "Mother, here—I always call Eleanor Mother—was my right hand; without her help I would have given up. She worked right there in the field by my side and even helped with the milking before we got a milking machine." His voice choked. He cleared his throat and moved quickly into their experience of the day before.

It had been a warm day in early January when they had driven toward Miami for a holiday. It was their Christmas present to each other, and they had planned it for months. They would not make a reservation; instead they would stop at a motel in the late afternoon. Not wanting to feel pushed, they would take their time. They had left their trailer when the eastern sky was streaked for the sunrise. They had driven slowly, stopping often to enjoy sights along the highway. First, they paused and admired the citrus groves. Then they stopped at the vast ranchlands near Lake Okeechobee and compared the strange hump-on-the-shoulder breed of Brahma cattle with the cows they had raised in Minnesota. They stopped to exclaim over an enormous flame-red poinsettia growing in a doorway. They tried to count white egrets in a newly plowed field. The stopped to stretch under a row of tall, slender Sabal palms and watched while sugar cane fell before the wide knives of the West Indian cutters.

At a spot where smoke could be seen from a fire in the Everglades they had stopped to eat and fill their tank with gasoline. The proprietress of the restaurant, with a piece of meat on a short stick, lured a small alligator up from an Everglade canal. They had never been this close to a wild alligator. They wished that their six-year-old great-granddaughter could be there; when they traveled they spoke often of their children, grandchildren, and especially their little great-granddaughter, Jody.

They were now south of the cane fields deep in the endless, flat, grassy lands of the Everglades that reminded them of the prairie lands of North Dakota. White ibis paced through shallow waters, and occasionally a blue heron fluttered up from one of the canals.

The sky was an immense blue dome, like a "northern Minnesota sky."

Since the signs advertising fresh orange juice were appealing, they stopped at a small stand located on a filled area, surrounded on three sides by the tall grasses of the Everglades. The juice was delicious. The attendant, a man, said it was freshly made from navel oranges. He explained that every customer who stopped there that day to buy orange juice got a free chance on a lady's alligator handbag. While they sipped their juice, he asked them to take their chances. They had nothing to lose; the chance was free; it was a show of appreciation for their business. But how nice it would be for such a lovely lady to win one of those beautiful bags! If she won he would even take her picture and put it up right there in the stand so that others could see the happy expression he knew would be on her face when he put one of those lovely bags in her arms. The man said he could tell that Burton would really want the honor of winning her the bag, but first she should have a turn. "Ladies first, bless their hearts, always is my motto," he smiled and handed Eleanor a cup.

The whole experience started innocently. Eleanor needed only to pour little red balls out of the cup onto a board with numbered holes. It was easy. The man tallied her score. He seemed surprised it was so high. She had rolled those balls like an expert; he flattered her by saying he had never known a woman to have had such a score. He handed the cup of red balls to Burton. Burton's score was lower than Eleanor's. It was Burton's turn again, the man explained, because his score was lower. In that game all turns belonged to Burton. Eleanor thought it strange, but the man said it was the way the game was played; the person who started with the lowest score got all the turns. The man called it a game for the loser and said the highest possible score was 100 points. It was like nothing the two of them had seen before. The red balls rolled across the board. The score remained the same. The man said they had won fifty cents. They laughed and said they would take it in orange juice. The man explained that in order to get the fifty cents they must put a dollar on the counter. The red balls rolled again, and the man said they would need to put out two dollars, and then it was five, and then ten, and then it suddenly somehow or other got to be twenty-five. The man said it was something to do with a special number that Burton had put one ball through. The man kept saying how lucky Burton was; he had the hands of a winner. There was no question that as soon as he got a feel for tipping the cup he would roll the winning numbers. He must not even think about getting discouraged because he definitely was going to win one of those bags "for this lovely little lady." The man explained to Burton that he had only a few points to go to win not only the alligator bag but also $50 even $100 which would give them a free vacation trip.

At one point Burton turned away from the game as if he might be thinking of leaving, but the man detained him by pulling down some of the handbags from the shelf. He opened them so that Burton and Eleanor could see the inside compartments, how roomy they were, how well the bags were made. He wanted them to see the many assorted sizes and styles and to know that Eleanor would have her choice of any bag in the place. There were also boxes of jams and jellies under the counter. These too were prizes. The man said he could cash travelers' checks. He said it would be a pity to stop when they had only a few points to go. He knew they would win and would get back every penny they had played. He seemed like a nice man.

They had only one travelers' check. That morning they had thought it would be more than enough to take care of their needs for the two days they planned to be gone. The man cashed the check. The red balls rolled back and forth from the cup to the board, from the board to the cup, and back to the board. Each time they were asked to put money on the counter the amount doubled. Their score added slowly. When they had $50 left they had "earned ninety-five points." The man said that they would get the five points or even more easily; all they had to do was put up the $50. They put all the money they had on the counter. The little red balls rolled. The tally was three.

Certainly they had another travelers' check? The man half stated, half asked. They needed only to put a $100 bill on that counter to win the bag and everything they had played. No more checks? No cash? Such a pity when they were so close to winning so much. The man shrugged. "That's the way the ball rolls." He folded the money into a fat wallet. "Some days you win and some days you lose."

They seemed like such a nice couple; they reminded him of his own grandparents. He had been certain they would win, or he would never have encouraged them otherwise. He did not want them "to go away empty handed." To show them his heart "was in the right place," he would let them have their choice of a small box of the jellies or five dollars. Eleanor took the five dollars.

The road to Miami stretched straight south through the Everglades. The road toward Lake Wales stretched to the north. The wind moved through the long needles of the Australian pines along the canal and gently parted the marsh grasses. A young rabbit scurried across the road, as they turned their car northward.

Even the next day the unexpectedness of the encounter in the Everglades dazed Burton. He could still recall the rabbit, the trees, and the wind. He shook his old head, unable to grasp what had happened, what had gone wrong. He had never in his life thrown money away like that. The only place he had ever seen such a game was once when he went to the state fair. But there he just walked up and down the midway and looked, because everyone said the games were dishonest and he could see the prizes people got did not amount to much. But here the prize was different: the bags were lovely, and they were well made. "I wanted so badly to get her that alligator handbag," he confided, his old voice quivering; "she never had an alligator bag."

Sensitive to his motivation, Eleanor would not criticize for anything. She had never been a wife who "found fault" or "harped" on his mistakes. She was aware, however, as he was aware, of what the loss of $105 did to their budget. That near trip to Miami would have to be their "big extravaganza" for the season. In the future they would never accept the offer of a chance on anything. It had been an unfortunate experience, one they could not afford, but they would know better next time. "Besides," she said, and she lowered her voice to a whisper so he would not hear, "I never did like alligator bags; it never seemed right to me that alligators were killed just to make purses."

NOTES

1. Veneral disease is one of the health problems often found under these conditions. I do not mean to imply that the percentage of veneral disease is higher for migrant camps than it would be for army camps or the general population of the city; however, veneral disease, especially gonorrhea, does need to be recognized as a health problem of some migrants. Even when the symptoms of syphilis and gonorrhea are recognized by the migrant, he may not have the money to go to a doctor. He may hesitate to describe his symptoms should he go to a doctor. He may refer to it as a problem pertaining to his "privates" and have difficulty talking about it to either the doctor or the nurse because such a discussion is not part of his background. Under these circumstances it is not unusual for such a migrant to confide in a fellow migrant worker or his crew leader. Sometimes the latter sells him a salve or some other preparation which supposedly will cure the disease but which instead is merely a gimmick to get additional monies from the migrant.

2. Crooked dice are loaded, beveled, or shaved so that one side comes up more often than any other.

*If you would know the value of money,
go and try to borrow some.*

Benjamin Franklin, 18th century
American journalist and statesman
Poor Richard's Almanac

The Squeeze

The year 1970 was only ten days old when Enrique Castillo contacted us and asked to talk about a new situation with which he was faced. It was only ten days into the new year, and already Enrique had problems that he found overwhelming. Work was scarce in his area; heavy frost had done much damage to tomatoes both in Texas and Florida. Enrique knew he would have trouble getting a job this winter, and yet in comparison to getting work this new experience was more complicated for him. He had lived through heavy frosts and lack of work before. But never had Enrique felt the need to talk to someone as much as now. He needed someone he could trust, who might understand these new and complicated problems with which migrants were faced.

This need to talk with someone was a new experience for Enrique who, until now, had always felt free to express himself; and, as a result, others had looked to him as a sort of leader or spokesman. He had always been able to solve his own problems, except financial ones, and had never needed to turn to others outside of his family for advice.

459

Enrique Castillo was Joseph Salazar's cousin, his first cousin, which in this Chicano family represented a relationship closer than a brother. Joseph encouraged Enrique to contact us, and he did. He was going to Immokalee, Florida in mid-January. Perhaps we could meet him. We could be in New Orleans the third Saturday in the month and ride as far as Perry, Florida, where we could take a Greyhound bus home. And thus it was arranged.

Enrique, Isabella, and their children, four-year-old Manolito and the twins Carlos and Carlitos, two and one-half, were waiting at the bus station when we arrived in New Orleans. They had had tire trouble and were afraid that we would be waiting for them or, worse still, that we would be gone. There is so little basic trust in the life experience of the migrant that he expects disappointment and is surprised when his suspicions do not materialize.

Enrique explained that he was going to a place near Immokalee where they had worked last year because there was no work around Corpus Christi. They had promised the Florida grower that they would return, but last year they had had trouble with a dishonest crew leader who had cheated them, so this year they decided to drive their own car. However, they needed to borrow money for the trip.

Enrique had borrowed money before from an Anglo who owned a store and gave Chicanos credit for their groceries and supplies. This store owner charged a flat sum for interest, much higher than banks, but banks required collateral, which most Chicanos, including Enrique, did not have. This man got away with charging the high rate of interest because most Chicanos did not know how much they actually paid; and even when they did, as Enrique did, there was nothing they could do about the situation when they needed money.

This time Enrique had asked the storekeeper for $75. The man insisted that he take $100, saying that the larger amount was easier for his bookkeeping system because it could be repaid in four monthly payments of $30 each, including the interest. An even amount like that, he explained, would be easier for Enrique to remember. It was agreed.

Enrique said he was glad he had taken the $100 instead of $75. Before he reached New Orleans he had had two flat tires. Apparently he had picked up some spike-like nails, and although one tire was merely punctured and could be repaired with a "boot," the other had to be replaced, all of which took a deep toll in the money he had borrowed. Something had also gone wrong with the speedometer cable: it made funny buzzing noises and the needle went "crazy." A replacement would have meant another repair bill, but for the time being the speedometer could wait until he earned some money. Besides, this was no time to worry about the car. We were here and could tell him what to do about the big problem— the one with the men who had made him the offer.

Sometime just before New Year's, Enrique had been contacted by two Anglos. They told him they were part of a community action group trying to help migrant farm workers organize into a union so that they could fight for their rights. They were looking for men like Enrique who were trusted by their own people. The men talked about higher pay, better housing, education for children—all the things Enrique had talked about so many times; all the things he had wanted for his family and his people. The two men talked fast, reminded Enrique that he was a poor migrant, but that he was as good as anyone else. They told him that others had told them of his pretty wife and good children. They seemed to be trying to appeal to the concept of the male role in Enrique's culture. They said others had told them that Enrique was a good man, an honest man. He could help his people if he would only talk with his people and get them to listen just as he was listening. The men kept making sensible statements, such as "you want a better life for your kids than the one that you've got now, don't you? You want a better house and a newer car, and you want your children to go to college and be somebody."

When the men first talked to Enrique, they said nothing of a union. They told him they wanted him to know that migrant workers had friends. He was suspicious, wondering what they really wanted. When they left, he never expected to see them again. But they returned a few days later and again talked about how hard Enrique worked, how little he made, and how much the world owed him. He continued to be suspicious of their motives.

Enrique had never thought of anyone owing him a living. All he wanted was a job, a chance to work. Yet it could be true that he had something better coming. Perhaps he had been cheated more than he recognized. He would listen to what they had to say as he had nothing to lose. The men told him he was a fool to work so hard. He could have a job as a union organizer. They appealed to his male vanity, saying he could quit work in the fields altogether if he would get his people organized so that they had decision-making power.

They explained that he could have a job behind a desk with a secretary and be paid a good salary. He could make more money as spokesman for his people than he had ever made in the fields. Enrique had mixed reactions as he listened. He felt it was a dream. They painted a word picture and put him in it. He felt himself listening at the feeling level, almost believing. He wanted to believe, yet he tried to see what they were doing to him in the light of his own world experience. What they promised could not be true, not happening to him, not Enrique Castillo, who was being singled out and told that he could make $8,000 to $12,000 or more a year without getting his hands dirty.

Enrique told us, as he measured off with his hands two or three feet, that sometimes the men used big words, and he did not follow everything they said. But their promises for his people were clear. Chicanos would get what they had coming—things that had been denied them by growers, process-shed foremen, or other employers. Enrique asked how he was to earn the money they promised. They said merely by talking to his own people, because they would listen if he told them that he trusted labor organizations and that he trusted these new "friends" who were here to help them unionize. Where would all this money come from which they promised? They said from dues. All migrants would be glad to pay dues, the men explained, when they saw how much they would get. It would mean more pay for fewer hours of work, insurance, vacations, and sick leave like factory workers had. The promises sounded good. Enrique agreed to get some friends together to hear more details. He figured they had nothing to lose. The men said they would bring others to the meeting.

Enrique's best friend was Humberto Diaz. Humberto and his family lived in a partitioned corner of a vacant store in which there was space for a meeting in the back room if the men sat on boxes or on the floor. One of the men who had first approached Enrique returned, accompanied by four strangers. They entered the room shouting *"La Huelga,"* and told the group they too were migrants.

Three men were Black and one was white. Enrique felt uneasy from the beginning. The men moved with an assertiveness; they used words he did not understand. The white man talked as if he were well educated. He said he was an attorney, a "migrant attorney." He said he was there to fight for legal rights of farm workers. "We'll show them what a good fight is really like," he said. Enrique did not understand who was going to court or why. He was suspicious of lawyers and courts. His prior experience with even the police was not good; furthermore, his culture taught him to stay clear of any such entanglements. He did not trust the police, lawyers, or courts. The disheveled appearance of the white attorney also bothered him. Why would an educated man look so dirty? The man wore ragged levis and was barefoot; his hair hung to his shoulders and, like his matted beard, needed washing. Enrique did not think he was a "hippie"; the hippies Enrique had known were gentle; this man seemed hostile and demanding. He was an angry person. Enrique began to question the motives of all the men. He did not trust them, and yet he was not certain why. They claimed to be his friends, his soul brothers. They said they were there to help poor people like himself, but yet they did not sound like they really knew his world.

All three of the Blacks had "Afro" haircuts and wore necklaces made of the teeth of some large animal. One wore a black beret. He kept raising a clenched fist in a gesture that Enrique had seen on television in connection with the Black Panther movement. All three Blacks said that they had been active in the Newark, New Jersey riots. They told about the burning and destruction and the way they got national television to focus on the plight of the poor. They said the only way to point out needs of the downtrodden in this country was to do something that would shock people into paying attention. These men said they had no patience nor time for talk. Poor people were tired of talking. No one listened to words anyway; no one had ever really listened to words. People only "listened" to action. The four men shouted at Enrique and his friends, yelling for them to take action, pushing everyone to "get with it, man" while there was still a chance for migrants.

All four of the new visitors admitted that they had never worked in the crops. They said, however, that they were well acquainted with the problems of farm workers because the prob-

lems of Enrique and his friends were no different from thousands of poor Blacks and Puerto Ricans in the ghettos of the cities. They said many things Enrique agreed with and other things which bothered him. He agreed that poor people, especially farm migrants, were exploited. He had been exploited. But he was afraid of all this talk about riots, strikes, burning or destroying crops which these men suggested. His hesitation brought contempt from the visitors. They shouted at him, "Man, what's wrong with you? Don't you know you've got to fight for it? Where is your sense of machismo?

"They've been crappin' all over you all your life, man, same as they've been crappin' all over us and then rubbin' our noses in it. You're tired, man, tired! You're fed up! Man, you're fed up! The only problem is a lot of people in this country don't seem to know that you are fed up; they haven't heard what you and other poor people have been saying; but in 1970, they're gonna hear. They're gonna do more than hear! They're gonna see! You're gonna tell them to give you your rights or else they can harvest their own crops! You're through! And if they don't listen, there won't be any crops for nobody to harvest! If the poor people in America can't have a real stake in America, then it's time they destroyed this country." Enrique felt a sense of shock at the degree of hate he sensed in these men. All his experiences of being exploited and all his mistrust had never made him hate with the inner rage these men showed. He wondered what had happened to make them that way. He did not know that the strength of his family culture may have been the buffer between himself and the hostile world which made his attitude so different from that of these men.

Humberto did not agree with Enrique. He thought the men made sense, good sense. He supplied them with examples of exploitation that he had seen—exploitation that came from crew leaders, from growers, and from attitudes of community residents toward migrant farm workers. He, too, turned on Enrique and tried to persuade him to throw off the yoke of oppression and free himself.

Humberto was someone Enrique could ignore. He had known Humberto many years and knew that he was up and down, for or against something all of the time, and that he could change his mind easily, so it was hard to say how he stood on something. But these men were different. They were skilled in knowing what to say to allay doubts or to needle one into an aggressive attitude. He did not understand the psychology they used or even that they used psychology, but he did recognize them as skillful operators. He saw they had studied the group of men before them. They seemed to understand individual behavior, the way to appeal to different individuals, and how to make use of certain members of the group to inflame them all to action. Although Enrique admired the skills of these visitors, many of their statements troubled him. He knew that many of the things they claimed to be the truth were false. He also sensed that they were intent upon destroying what they called the "establishment of the status quo"; they felt this was the only way poor people could solve their problems with the organizations that currently dealt with poor people.

While Enrique was in their presence, he was almost persuaded to pledge his assistance. What the men said made a lot of sense. Still, they knew nothing about farm work. They said a lot of things that Enrique knew were not true. They said no grower or crew leader could be trusted. They said all growers and crew leaders should be viewed as enemies of migrants. They said no grower or crew leader had ever really worked a day of their lives but made every cent they had by cheating poor workers like Enrique and Humberto. This Enrique knew was not always true; some growers had been migrants themselves, and he had seen many farmers work as hard as any migrant, often longer hours. He also knew some crew leaders who were honest and treated their workers well. At the same time, the men, with Humberto's help, kept giving examples of migrants who were held down, treated unfairly, or cheated; and this Enrique also knew was true.

The most upsetting thing for Enrique was when one of the men turned everything he said around and used each argument against him. When Enrique said he was thankful to have work, he was told that he was a good worker and deserved more consideration than he got. It was not his fault that he was poor. It was no disgrace to be poor. It was pathetic the way he was victimized. Because he was trying to support himself and not live on welfare, the country owed him at least a living wage if not more. Certainly if he sat down on welfare, it would cost the country to support him and his family; therefore, the public should be willing to help him keep off welfare. When it came to the grower, he was merely lining his pocket with profits Enrique had made for him and should be forced to share those profits by paying Enrique the same wages factory workers made. If the grower were to pay him that much, Enrique would still get only what he had earned. "Look," they said, "why should your kids starve so that some grower's kids can have a Thunderbird or go skiing in Switzerland?"

The men brought with them federal publications, material on the Fair Labor Standards Act, housing standards for agricultural workers, registration of crew leaders, insurance, and social security benefits. They pointed out the discriminatory exclusion of agricultural employees under the National Labor Relations Act, the unfair coverage of migrant farm workers under the federal minimum wage, the inadequate policing of the crew leader registration, the limited application of the workmen's compensation to migrants. They even showed Enrique the printed passage in which it is stated that "all agricultural workers except those performing agricultural labor" are covered by workmen's compensation. They reminded Enrique that one of the main concerns of Caesar Chavez was that migrants have no protection from pesticide accidents and that many have died and others have been hospitalized as a result of poisoning from chemicals.

The men showed Enrique a recent report prepared by a Subcommittee on Migratory Labor of the Labor and Public Welfare Committee of the United States Senate that identified these kinds of hazards. Migrants are exposed, the report stated, to DDT; they may inhale fumes or absorb it through their skin or even swallow sprayed food and, as a result, may die. Another pamphlet described the benefits of Social Security. The men reminded Enrique of the inadequate coverage for migrants because their earnings are not usually reported. After the men had shown Enrique what he was "entitled to have by law," they asked him how many places he had worked in the last two years where he did receive the minimum wage or where he had housing with running hot and cold water or where his children were not allowed to work in the fields or where he and his family were provided with protection when chemicals and pesticides were being used. They also wanted to know how many crew leaders Enrique knew who had cheated him or others and how many migrants past the age of sixty-five he knew who drew Social Security. The men seemed interested only in bad situations. They did not want to hear anything that was good in any work experience. The attorney brushed aside one comment Enrique made with, "One rotten apple ruins a barrel. The best way to get rid of rotten apples is to dump the barrel."

They told Enrique they were looking for men like him who were hard to convince and not like Humberto, easily swayed. He, Enrique, would do great things for himself and his people because he was a thinker. Once he came to think the right way—their way—he would be a real leader, a true man.

Later, when Enrique told Isabella about the men, his doubts returned. Isabella expressed fear of what might happen if he continued to talk to them. Although a Chicano usually does not consider the advice of a woman, Enrique did heed Isabella's suggestion that he talk to his cousin, Joseph Salazar.

His doubts became stronger when Joseph said he did not like the sound of the story. Joseph said Caesar Chavez stressed non-violence. Joseph said migrant farm workers would eventually unionize, but he was not certain that threatening to burn down packing or storage sheds or to destroy crops would get the changes migrants needed. He was afraid violence or threats of violence would drive more and more farmers to stop using migrant labor. He reminded Enrique of the tomato harvesters he had seen in California. There a machine using fourteen workers picked fifteen tons of tomatoes an hour, replacing more than 100 pickers. Joseph said he heard that Michigan would use very few migrants in sugar beets in 1970 as a direct result of "trouble with workers in 1969" when "outsiders" encouraged migrants to strike.

Joseph knew a worker in Colorado who could not get a job. The sugar beet growers were afraid he was a trouble maker because he had tried to organize some of their people at the suggestion of men like those who came to see Enrique. Joseph said the beet growers called these men communists and said anyone who had anything to do with the likes of them should be sent to Russia or Red China. Joseph said it was all well and good for outsiders to talk about organization and migrant force, but when all was over, they were not in any danger of losing their jobs; they were not really farm migrants. Nor were they in a position to support Isabella and the three children if Enrique could not get work. Joseph also questioned their suggested tactics. He was worried that their approach would do more harm than good for migrants.

Later Enrique told the men what Joseph said, but they pushed it aside, saying Joseph was too cautious for this day and age. Migrants could not afford to be that cautious. Enrique's doubts increased. If he held back and did not do what the men wanted, they would find someone who would. He would lose out, both with his friends and with his employers, if the organization was successful. Yet if he went ahead and organized a demonstration and it failed, what would happen to him? He came to the conclusion that 1970 would be a difficult year, even a frightening one. Enrique needed to talk, to think the proposition through carefully. He told Isabella he would wait as long as possible. He would stall the men, go to Florida, and on the way would talk with us.

South of Tallahassee we turned on Route 98. The speedometer once again was "acting up." It continued to make buzzing noises. The needle made one last zig-zag across the dial and finally stopped moving altogether. It was a bright, sunny morning, and the road stretched away empty as far as we could see. It had recently been resurfaced. It was an excellent track. Enrique said the car handled well, and he felt good since he had had a chance to talk with us.

We were seven miles from Perry, where we were to take the bus. Enrique glanced back to speak to the twins when he caught sight of the state police car in the rear view mirror. He saw it pull out of a side road. Instinctively he slowed his speed, but already there was the blue flash of a blinker. Enrique stopped. He rolled down the window and waited for the policeman to approach. There were two; one remained in the cruiser.

The officer questioned Enrique routinely. He was courteous, but he had the ticket partly written even before he left the patrol car. He asked for Enrique's driver's license. Was Corpus Christi Enrique's present address? It was. The policeman held the license in his hand and explained he was giving Enrique a ticket for speeding. Enrique tried to tell him about the speedometer cable, but the policeman was firm. There was no excuse for speeding. He finished writing the summons, which stated that Enrique had unlawfully committed the offense of speeding in violation of Section 317-221 of the Florida State Statutes. He showed it to

Enrique, saying he wanted Enrique to know his rights. As long as Enrique was from out of state, he would have to post a $30 bond. He could pay the officer in cash, or he could go to the sheriff's office and pay it there. If he did not have the $30, he could call from the sheriff's office and get the money. When the fine was paid he could continue, but not before.

Enrique's jaw set in a stubborn line; he said he wanted to see the sheriff. The officer looked surprised. He hesitated. Then, as if an afterthought, he said he had better have a look at what was in the trunk. He told Enrique to open it and take everything out. Enrique did. The officer found nothing of interest. He again explained about paying the $30 and not going into town. Enrique repeated his desire to see the sheriff. The officer said he wanted Enrique to talk to the other policeman in the cruiser. Enrique got into the police car.

Carlos and Carlitos started to cry, asking where their father was going. Isabella did not explain. They cried at her, hitting the back of her seat with their fists. She screamed at them in Spanish, telling them they were driving her to an early grave. It was obvious Isabella was afraid; the children sensed her fear and cried harder. She ignored them. "What will happen," she asked us, her lips trembling. After a few minutes Enrique returned and slid under the wheel. He was silent except to say that the policemen had kept his driver's license and had ordered him to follow them.

At the sheriff's office Enrique and the policemen went inside. We asked Isabella if she wanted to go too; she said no. She was afraid to go in and yet afraid to stay away. She wanted to do both. Would Enrique be jailed if he lost his temper and said too much? She recalled Enrique's temper before they were married. He could always take care of himself, but no one—Chicano or gringo—pushed him around. Isabella said Enrique had had some unpleasant experiences with policemen when he was a teenager. He had been stopped, questioned, and even searched without provocation, other than the fact that he had brown skin and was Spanish-speaking. Because of these early experiences he was suspicious of anything concerning policemen or the law. She was afraid of what might happen now.

Later Enrique told us what did happen. Inside, the state policeman who arrested him stepped behind the counter and got some forms from a clerk. Enrique asked about the sheriff. He was told the sheriff was out of town and that the state policeman who wrote the ticket would take care of what needed to be done. If Enrique wanted the deputy sheriff to witness his signature, that could be arranged. The bond was $30. His case would be heard in thirty days, but he need not appear. The $30 would be forfeited and would apply as a fine. Traffic cases were heard once a month, but January cases had been heard. Enrique could appear in February court if he wished; if so, there would be court costs in addition to the fine. The fine for speeding was at least $30, if not more. Enrique could not tell if he was being told this because he was from out of state or whether it was because he was a Chicano. One thing, however, was clear: he could pay the $30 today or go to jail. His driver's license would not be returned until he settled the charge for speeding. Enrique again attempted to explain about the speedometer. Mechanical failure was no excuse. The fact that the speedometer was not working meant his car was defective; his car could be impounded as being unsafe until repaired.

Enrique counted his money. He had less than $50; he gave the deputy $30, putting the rest in his pocket. It was barely enough to get to Immokalee. If there was no work they would be stranded. Even with good work he would need to be paid soon. Growers do not like migrants to ask for payment each day or to ask for an advance on what they have earned. In this year of indecision Enrique was not certain how the grower he had worked for last year would feel if, the day he arrived, he needed to borrow money so Isabella and the children could eat.

The deputy sheriff filled out the Cash Appearance Bond. He wrote in the date, the name of the sheriff, the name of the county, stated that the location where the money was taken was the sheriff's office, and signed his name as deputy sheriff of the county and handed Enrique a copy. The piece of blue paper stated:

The sum of $30 is security for the appearance of the defendent upon the conditions hereinafter set forth. If the said defendent shall appear before the county justice court, in and for Taylor County, Perry, Florida, at 10 a.m. on the 17th of February, A.D., 1970, to answer the charge of speeding, bond thirty dollars, and shall not depart the same without leave, said money so deposited shall be returned to the undersigned depositor, both to be forfeited or estreated by order of the above court.

Enrique attempted to read it, but the words were without meaning. He knew only that he had less than $20 to get to Immokalee and to live until he could earn some more. How he would be able to get back to Corpus Christi and pay back the $100 he owed he did not know.

Slowly he walked toward the car. He was able to tell us that the day seemed dark and overcast although the sun was still shining. The twins and Manolito ran toward him and buried their tear-stained faces against his thigh. He had come back; he had not gone to jail. He held the children close against his body, leaning down to press his face into their hair. He swore softly at first to himself, partly at himself, but mostly at a system that made children afraid their father would be jailed; that made it necessary for a migrant to borrow in order to travel; that made it possible for migrants to be exploited by crew leaders; that made it necessary for workers to think of strikes, boycotts, and other radical measures in order to force attention to their submarginal existence with the hope that something could be done to enable them to support their families more adequately. He swore aloud, half in English, half in Spanish. His mouth was set in a determined, hard look we had never seen before on the face of Enrique Castillo. We knew he had made his decision. It would be easier for him now to believe those who encouraged him "to take what he had coming." It would be more difficult for him to hope that the "establishment," made up of agencies, institutions like the police department, the courts, and employers, was really concerned with the "likes of him" and honestly intended to see that improvements were made. Things were not that changed from when he was thirteen and had worked in the brick yard to help support his grandmother; he still had to fight for everything he got. Perhaps the way a Chicano farm worker of the 1970s needed to fight was through organizing a type of union. He would get back home as quickly as he could and take that job the men offered.

PART VI

Services:
Their Role Within the
Territorial Boundaries
of Rural Poverty

When I was young I felt so small
And frightened, for the world was tall

Anne Spencer Morrow Lindbergh
    20th century American authoress
    Bring Me a Unicorn

30

Implications for
Education of the Migrant Child

Concern for the Education of Migrants

Since the mid-1960s one community after another has become
concerned enough about the educational needs of migrant children
that summer schools, extended classes, and enrichment programs
are now offered in areas where migrants come to work. There is
also a growing awareness that illiterate children as well as illiterate
adults, regardless of their state of residency, are detrimental to the
economic well-being of our total country.

This concern for the education of all children received real
impetus in the late 1960s when a number of major education
programs and projects for migrants were funded throughout the
country through the United States Office of Education under titles
I, III, and V of the Elementary and Secondary Educational Act of
1965. In addition to the Office of Education's contribution, the
Office of Economic Opportunity (OEO) has spent large sums of
money under title-B of the Economic Opportunity Act of 1964.
Although the Department of Labor is not directly involved with

475

education in the traditional sense, it is nevertheless a participant in migrant education through its Manpower Administration and more specifically through its Rural Manpower Service.

Large amounts of federal monies have been made available through these channels to local districts for staff, supplies, and consultation. Added to the availability of money is the growing awareness that migrant farm workers are leaving the streams in large numbers and settling in local communities where they might have a relative or friend—a pattern of settling that will continue. Automation, chemical weed and harvest control, reduction in the number of farms, and the phasing out of crops requiring large numbers of stoop laborers are all part of the reason that fewer people are finding work in agriculture. The high cost of travel, the limited amount of available work, the low wages compared with those of industry are also factors that influence the yearly decrease in the number of such workers.

It is almost ironic that professionals and helping service agencies have only recently become aware of migrants and that this should be occurring at the very time when migrant farm labor is decreasing rapidly and will probably almost disappear entirely from the labor market scene within the next decade. Certainly the long-distance type of crew migration of entire families will disappear.

The problems of farm migrant workers and the educational needs of their children have long been part of the unmet social issues in every state where fruit, grain, and vegetables have been harvested. One county with which I worked recently in developing its first summer school program for migrant children had had thousands of migrants and their families working in the area since the early 1920s. And yet, the educational needs of such children were not recognized as a local responsibility for more than fifty years and probably would not have been recognized then had it not been for the promise of federal monies and the assurance that the migrant program could be expanded to include local nonmigrant children and even nonpoverty children. This plan was interpreted as adding to the educational experience of the migrant child. The plan, however, failed to admit that the migrant child had something to offer to the educational experience of the nonmigrant child, if nothing more than that the migrant child's existence was, in effect, the reason that federal funds were available for the program and were adding to the income of the community. And this example is not unique; it is repeated in all parts of the country.

Although the employment of migrants is not new, year after year in all parts of the country their needs and problems have been viewed as temporary situations which somehow would go away if they were ignored; but they have not gone away. This has been especially true of the educational needs of the migrant child and his parent. Those educational needs have been clearly identified for more than twenty years.

In 1951 the President's Commission on Migratory Labor said:

> This Commission wishes to reiterate its conviction that the education of the children of migratory farmworkers (and their parents also) is one of the most urgent and most essential of many steps which the Nation can and should take to improve the lot of migrants who have for so long been deprived of what the rest of us take for granted.

In 1954 the United States Department of Agriculture estimated that the number of migrant children under eighteen years old ranged between 175,000 and 225,000. The number of these children in 1962 was estimated in the hearings before the Senate subcommittee on migratory labor to be 150,000, and the 1969 report from the Senate subcommittee estimated that the figure was between 150,000 and 250,000.

A 1959 study by the Colorado State Department of Education found that 16 percent of all migrant parents surveyed had no formal education and that less than 25 percent had completed the fourth grade.[1] A 1960 survey by the United States Department of Agriculture, as reported in the *Monthly Labor Review*,[2] found that migratory farm workers twenty years old and older had completed a median of 6.9 years of school compared with ten years for all Americans in the same age group. A survey paper prepared for the 1960 White House Conference on Children and Youth says that migrant children are far below grade level and that their average achievement in school generally is under fourth grade—the minimum standard for literacy.[3] More recently, a national report from New Jersey has said,

> Though complete data are not available, school reports from several states show that possibly as few as one migrant child in

fifty enters high school and fewer than this graduate. Consequently, vocation-training courses and school-guidance services usually offered in the high school are virtually out of reach of these youngsters.[4]

Although the needs of the migrant schoolchild may be similar to those of the disadvantaged schoolchild in the urban ghetto, there are certain differences. The migrant child's parent is preoccupied not only with economic problems and with the care and protection of a large family, but also with travel from one part of the country to another, with the physical energy of harvesting a crop, as well as with meeting the demands of a crew leader and/or a grower. There may be little time or physical and psychic energy left for the migrant parent to be concerned with the emotional welfare of his child. Therefore, the child's feelings may be ignored or resisted, depending upon the culture and experience of the parent. The parent may have been so emotionally deprived in his own childhood that his own needs must be met first without too much consideration for the needs of others, even his own child.

It is impossible to understand the educational needs of migrant children without some appreciation for the perspective of their various cultures and an awareness of the role that events in American history have played in molding these cultures. Certainly the influence of slavery, Reconstruction following the Civil War, sharecropping, the isolation of rural and mountain areas, discrimination, and the value placed on education have all been major influences in determining how present migrant children feel about themselves and their education.

The problems related to migrant education have not gone away, even if the facts and research on the subject have been ignored. Today no community which employs migrant farm workers can afford any longer to ignore them because migrants are settling out and becoming permanent residents in those very communities, and they are bringing their unmet educational needs with them.

Family Experiences of the Migrant Child

The migrant child—whether Chicano, Black, white, Indian, or Puerto Rican—for the most part comes from a family with more than five children and has lived all or most of his life under crowded conditions in a household that undergoes constant changes with movement of relatives in and out. The migrant child frequently has aunts and uncles younger than he is, who may be a permanent part of the household. Even in the home-base community the family may have moved continuously in search of lower rents, more adequate accommodations, or work. So the migrant child has been accustomed to many changes in residence.

The Spanish-speaking child will usually know a home in which both father and mother are present. The family—in addition to parents and siblings—will consist of grandparents, uncles, aunts, cousins, and godparents and their children. Since, in the Spanish culture, the strongest feelings of belonging are in the family, a child may never have played with a nonrelative prior to going to school. Among the Chicano migrants the work crews are often made up entirely of family members.

In the traditional Spanish-American home—whether Mexican, Puerto Rican, or Cuban—the man is the head of the household. He is the one who makes most decisions and is always the spokesman for his family.

> The woman in the Spanish-speaking home also has a clearly defined role. In addition to being the mother, the homemaker, the center or heart of the home, it is her duty to help her husband fulfill his role as head of the family, to help him work in the fields if that is his work. Her mission in life is to give her husband respect, from herself and her children, which in turn enhances his manliness. . . .
>
> The reason for Chicano parents taking their children into the fields is to keep the family together. They feel it is important for every member to work toward something for the family. The children are part of the family and therefore they contribute to its income. . . .
>
> At an early age a child learns respect for his elders. Above all else, he is taught to honor and defend his family. He is also taught to defend himself in a hostile world so he can maintain his dignity as an adult.[5]

In white migrant homes the kinship ties are also recognized. Thus a married uncle and his family or grandparents or a fourth or fifth cousin may move in and stay for various lengths of time. There is very little common-law marriage or divorce among white migrants. "Family membership is along extended family lines with the grandmother playing a dominant part. While the man is the head of the household, the woman is often the one who actually makes decisions."[6]

> This is an adult-centered culture. The needs of the father come first, the needs of the children second. Children are expected to consider the needs of the parents for quiet or rest. . . . Babies are played with by both parents. Infants are over indulged while very young but later must conform to the wishes of the parents.[7]

> Among the Black migrants, the woman, especially the grand-mother, still plays the more dominant family role. Divorce, separation, common-law marriages, or unwed parenthood are the usual reasons for the female family head; although there are some migrant families where the legal husband is present, and the woman still makes all of the major decisions. There are also many "adopted" children, or relatives being raised by other family members, or children being raised by non-family members.[8]

Most households, furthermore, include extended families, consisting of nuclear families, boarders, lodgers, and impecunious relatives, living in overcrowded quarters.[9] As a result, migrant children, regardless of race, may be bewildered about the characterological identity of their parents and all of these other family members. There may have been a series of legitimate or illegitimate "daddys" who have come and gone. Some may have stayed on when the child wished they would leave; others may have suddenly disappeared just as the child was forming a relationship with them. Under these circumstances it is not unusual for children of the same family to provide the school with different facts when asked for ages or names of parents and siblings. Even very intelligent children become confused about who all these people are, whether they are related or not, and, if they are related, to whom they belong.

Effect of Crowded Living

The pattern of moving in with relatives, friends, or acquaintances when the family head is out of work or faced with a crisis is common to Chicano, Indian, Southern Black, and Appalachian and Southern white cultures. In the Black migrant family it is not unusual for several daughters and their offspring to move back into the home of the mother. A grown son, whether a married man or a bachelor, may also live in the home and be an active part of the family interaction. Children living under these conditions are often alternately overprotected and neglected.

In her work with extremely deprived Black children Hertha Riese found "that the overstimulation of crowding and the ever-repeated deprivation inherent in changing residence lead, in final analysis, to mental and emotional impoverishment." She goes on,

> Development of a self, well-defined against an equally well-defined objective world, is impeded; hence . . . there emerges . . . an aimless search, an obsession to touch and resourcelessly release everything; or the child is under compulsion to handle and "experiment" with everything promiscuously in the most inappropriate and dangerous manner. . . .
>
> Obsession to touch, however, may lead to obsession to take. Gratification of unsatiated tactile needs has to be secured. A sense of mastery has to be gained by the freedom to touch, to do what is wanted, whenever it is vitally wanted. The child who has reason to doubt that he owns that freedom, needs to verify it, and to ascertain it continuously. . . .
>
> The legal concept of ownership is not easily imparted to a child who because of absence of material things has not been confronted with the privilege of owning objects at home. He is faced with the necessity for collective or consecutive use of the very few objects in the family, even clothing.[10]

In an overcrowded environment the child may have few things, if any, he can call his own. Riese comments on this sort of an experience as it relates to respect for the property of others. This may account for why many children from such home environments are so destructive in the school setting.

> If a child has been raised with the idea that he possesses nothing and owns an object only as long as he holds it, he has difficulties in developing respect for other people's property. Permanently, under the stress of anxiety, he cannot even conceive the idea of property; therefore the idea of sharing cannot take proper shape. . . . [11]

Female-Headed Black Family

There has been a tendency to label the female-headed Black family as disorganized, lacking strength, and as not providing a male model. It might be well to recognize that such a universal negative assumption may stem from the threat that the female-headed home represents to the traditional paternalistic family pattern rather than from reality. As Black history is reviewed it should be recognized that in order for any semblance of family life to exist at all during and immediately after slavery there had to be a new family pattern, and one did evolve to meet environmental threats. This family pattern was the female-based, extended family in which the mother, grandmother, aunts, and other members of the larger family banded together to share the responsibilities of earning a living, providing a home, and rearing children.

When this woman-headed family is truly examined, it does have structure, interdependence, and stability. Ironically it is this so-called disorganized family that gave strength to both Black men and women to cope with years of discrimination, segregation, physical violence, and open exploitation. It was the grandmothers, mothers, and aunts from such homes who eked out a livelihood as maids in white households and who, at night, returned to their own families and prepared food, sewed clothing, and ministered to the needs of their children, husbands, or lovers. It was these women who took their children to church and spoke out to their neighbors and others about the real needs of their people. It was these so-called weak, disorganized women who dried their tears after a lynching or who claimed the body of a son or who took their meager earnings to pay the fine of a jailed Black person. These same women were also the ones who gave permission for their children to integrate the schools and who walked beside them through the jeering mobs of whites. In more than one situation it was a gray-headed grandmother, the female head of the household, who threw her apron over her grandchild's head to protect him or her from the spittle of those who screamed, "Nigger, keep your place." It is hard, in the face of such facts and researched evidence, to understand the rationale behind statements that such homes of poverty have no stability, structure, or strength.

Nikki Giovanni, a Black female poet, captures some of the depth of feeling that spells out the strength of the Black family. The following excerpt is from her "Nikki Rosa":

. . . and though they fought a lot
it isn't your father's drinking that makes any difference

but only that everybody is together and you
and your sister have happy birthdays and very good Christmases
and I really hope no white person ever has cause to write about
   me
because they never understood Black love is Black wealth and
   they'll
probably talk about my hard childhood and never understand
   that
all the while I was quite happy.[12]

Pseudomaturity

Psychologically much of what is seen in the migrant child's family relationship, regardless of race, exemplifies reaction formation. Often the strength of the family is a reverse side of weakness. Children, especially older siblings, must assume responsibility for younger family members. This means that children from such an environment are most accustomed to assuming responsibility and following through on that responsibility. They are ordered by the parent to look after the baby, cook the meals, or clean the living quarters. On one hand, this type of experience helps to develop a sense of responsibility; on the other hand, if there is no opportunity for play and involvement in the interest of peers, a child, catapulted into adult responsibility, develops a form of pseudomaturity which breaks down later.

The individual who has been forced to grow up too fast will usually later seek the childhood or adolescence he missed. He may seek a vicarious experience through his own children; he may seek it through an "adolescent fling"; or he may turn into an adult with an immature, childlike personality who demands his own gratification ahead of that of his spouse or children.

Strengths of the Migrant Home

The strength which the migrant child has been exposed to has arisen out of the efforts of the adults around him to cope with the many negative aspects of their constantly changing environments. Although some of the coping efforts used by adults lead to new difficulties, the migrant child at least sees an attempt at self-improvement, even when it entails only moving on in the hope of finding another less conflicting situation.

Those trying to work with the migrant child and his family should focus more on what migrants are trying to accomplish with their behavior rather than on what they actually do accomplish, which may be failure.

Another strength which the migrant child brings to a school is the particular culture that he represents. There is a greater ethnic tradition among migrants than among the urban representatives of the same culture, although the rural family who has not migrated is apt to be more orthodox or less changed from the original culture than is the migrant. What the migrant child brings from his culture to the classroom can be used in teaching his peers. There are many experiences of migration he can share, although he may not necessarily have a grasp of geography. He can, for example, provide information about crops and the harvest of crops. Instead of trips to zoos and museums, a class would profit much from a visit to the migrant work situation where the migrant classmate could act as a guide and where the children could see how food is gathered and processed, how people travel, and even perhaps where and how they live.

Migrant Parents' View of Education

> Migrant parents are not interested in their children's education. They never come to school to register them; they just send them, usually without previous school records. They take them out of school unannounced. They do not attend PTA. Seldom do we ever meet these parents.[13]

Such is the belief of many educators and residents in communities where migrant farm laborers are employed. Some say that if the parents were truly interested in their children's education they would stop migrating. One county superintendent in an area that employs large numbers of migrants said, "They are not hostile toward the school or education, but I can't say they have a burning desire to have their children learn."

Rarely can farm migrant parents be found who want their children to continue as farm laborers; so, although it may not be widely known, most migrant parents are more truly concerned about their children's achievement, or lack of achievement, in school than are many middle-class parents who may be actively involved in school programs. Some middle-class parents unconsciously use the school to enhance their own social position or to receive community recognition for themselves. PTA leadership may become a power play to enhance the ego of the parents rather than a real commitment to the education of their own children or, in some cases, to the value of education in general.

If these visible community leaders had to endure the living and working conditions similar to those of migrant parents, if all community recognition for their stance on education were removed, they too could probably be evaluated as apathetic toward education. Seldom would a middle-class family be willing to give up a job and use most of their savings for travel to return to an area where they know there is no work and will be no work for several weeks or months in order for their child to attend school. Seldom is a middle-class family called upon to separate, to leave their children with relatives or neighbors, and not see those children for months in order for the children to go to school. Seldom is an affluent parent required, as the reservation Indian parent is, to send his child to a government-operated boarding school. The Indian parent, in many cases, has no contact with either the school or his child for the entire school year.

Sacrifices and attempts to encourage or guarantee education differ from family to family. Some examples may help the reader understand the degree to which some migrant parents have gone to see that their children get an education.

George and Martha Covington are white parents originally from a remote rural section in southern Georgia and now part of the north-south migration between the fruit belt of upper New York and vegetable processing of southern Florida. They have been labeled "red necks" who have no regard for education because they have never attended a school conference or even "set foot" in a school building since their three children started school. George and Martha work in the winter months on the "platform" of a packing shed in Pahokee and in summer come to the Lake Ontario area in northwestern New York to pick cherries and apples. They leave the lakes of New York at the peak of employment in late August or early September and return to Pahokee, although there will be no work in the packing sheds until mid-November. The reason these parents leave work in the north and return to Florida for weeks of no work, or limited employment, is so that their three children may start school at the beginning of the fall semester. These parents are vigorous in stating that they want their children to have the educational opportunities that they missed. Within the realism of their experience and their life style, the Covingtons are coping with the problems of education for their children in the only way they know. They do not see the necessity of talking with the school authorities or attending school and teacher conferences.

As the head of a Puerto Rican farm migrant family Gilberto Gomez laments the emphasis on material things and lack of real concern for interpersonal relationships and recognition of the value and honor of the family which he sees throughout the continental United States. He feels children on the mainland have too much freedom. He is worried about what happens when his children from the Puerto Rican culture come in contact with the middle-class values of the school and the behavior of non-Puerto Rican children. He said, "Children here have no respect for their elders or the property or rights of others." Gilberto believes that the only future for his five children in a changing world lies in their getting good educations, but he will try to protect them and preserve as much as he can for them from his own culture. Therefore, wherever the Gomez family works, the five children attend school. Ana Victoria, their mother, takes them to school and goes to meet them each night or walks them to the bus if there is such transportation. She walks with them partly to see that they cross the road or railroad safely, but mainly she is there to keep them from being beaten up by other children and "to protect" her teenage daughter, Hilda Maria, from the feared attentions of men and boys, which in reality might consist of nothing more than their talking with the teenage daughter or asking her for a date. Protection in the form of a mother or grandmother chaperone is common among recent immigrants from Mexico, Puerto Rico, and Cuba and will be practiced to various degrees in any migrant camp where there are more traditional Spanish-speaking families, although the custom of chaperoning the unmarried daughter is rapidly dying out.

Another example of parental encouragement for education is seen in the behavior of six-year-old Rebecca's father, Toby Barlett. Toby himself was a seventh-grade school dropout in a West Virginia coal-mining community. Although his Anglo-Saxon ancestors had lived in this country even before the Declaration of Independence, no one in his family had more than a fifth-grade education, so they were not concerned when he quit school midway through his seventh year. After he dropped out of school, Toby drifted around the country from one temporary job to another before he found that he could fare better in agricultural jobs where there was less educational competition. He found he could make a living harvesting crops, and the farmer did not ask if he had a high school diploma as did the factory personnel manager.

But Rebecca's father is determined she will finish high school. He will see, he says, that she has encouragement to get a "good" education because he knows what the lack of an education can mean to an adult who wants work. Whenever he buys groceries he checks the racks of children's books, and although it sometimes means less food, he buys her a new book. The cardboard box that contains her collection of books, and that he calls "Becky's library," is the last thing he loads into the truck and the first thing he takes out. Each night, regardless of where they are, he reads to her and hears her "say her letters." He sums up all his feelings by saying, "Becky has to 'mount to somethin' and not jist be a fruit tramp like her old Dad."

Vance Moore, a Black in his midforties, is a former cotton picker from northwest Mississippi. He is the father of nine, six of whom are in school. Until the early 1960s Vance never knew an experience other than working in the cotton of Mississippi. But when mechanical harvesters were introduced in the area he was no longer able to support his family with work near home. Now he and his three oldest sons go to Michigan each summer to pick strawberries, cherries, and apples. From Michigan they go to Florida to cut celery in the winter. Vance leaves his wife and younger children in Mississippi so they can stay in school. While months of separation are hard, it is better than "disruptin' the chillun's education." Vance hopes his six children will complete high school because he sees the need for his race to be well educated.

Silvester Lopez and his eighteen-year-old son, Joaquin, leave Michigan each fall for San Antonio, Texas, their former home, where they work during the winter months planting trees for a nursery. Silvester, a Chicano, is the father of eight children. Seven stay with their mother and aunt and uncle in Michigan where they can attend school without interruption. Silvester stays in Texas until May before returning to Michigan. It is hard to be away from his family from seven to eight months each year, he says, but he feels that it will be worth the sacrifice because someday he, Silvester Lopez, an almost illiterate farm worker, may be the father or the grandfather of a priest or a doctor.

The extent of the educational sacrifice parents like Silvester Lopez make when they leave their children with relatives, friends, or neighbors so that their education will not be interrupted can be understood only if viewed within the parents' own culture. In the Spanish-speaking cultures the strongest feelings of belonging are centered in the home and parents and children; even married children stay as near each other as possible. Therefore, the hardest thing the parents must face is to put the educational needs of their children ahead of all that the family symbolizes. The parents must even take part in helping to create a situation that may weaken the bonds of the family and speed the breakdown of their own culture. Although they see this happening, education for their children is a must.

Another extreme sacrifice facing migrant parents is the financial expense of buying school clothing, books, and supplies. Such expenditures represent a high percentage of total family income, and in some cases the family does not have the money to meet these expenses. In one family a pattern of every-other-day attendance on the part of twins was traced to a single pair of shoes. Migrant children have dropped out of their senior year in high school because of their inability to cope with the expenses of graduation—class ring, pictures, cap and gown, invitations, or proper clothing for the junior banquet or the senior ball. Under the migrant's travel and living conditions it may be difficult to provide freshly washed or ironed clothing; yet most migrant parents make extreme efforts to dress their school children in clothing that is clean, even if it means going without food to buy new clothing.

To enroll a child in a strange school, the farm migrant parent needs a great deal more basic trust in education as a process than does a nonmigrant, middle-class parent in that same community. The middle-class parent is usually already part of the community and, as such, has some control over the decision-making process and curriculum of the school or at least can wield the threat of a voting control over the school system. The farm migrant parent, on the other hand, has no knowledge of the school's educational philosophy or its expectations of parental involvement and level of grade achievement for students. Nor does the migrant parent have voting privileges in that community or probably in any other community. All the migrant parent knows is that there is a school in his work community and that he, as a parent, is expected to send his child there.

Many farm migrant parents knew a very irregular pattern of education themselves. They were, as school-age children, geared to a cotton economy where school vacations coincided with the harvest. In such a farming community, as was once true in all of rural America, education was secondary to farm work. All of the children had the same pattern of irregular attendance and, therefore, were not forced to compete with classmates who had the advantage of an uninterrupted school experience.

It is difficult for any parent, regardless of educational background, to understand the degree of competition in the average elementary classroom today or the amount of pressure that faces children struggling with new math, new reading methods, or new social science—learning concepts and facts which, five years ago, were taught only in high school. The differences of the educational experience of the parent from the educational experiences of the child are difficult enough for the middle-class parent to grasp. It is almost impossible for migrant parents, who themselves completed less than six years of formal schooling, to have an idea of how much can be lost when a child misses a few days of school. Irregular attendance may not be proof of lack of interest in education; it can be that the parent is not aware of the accelerated pace of present education and the large amount of content that is covered in one day.

Although migrant parents may not understand these things, they do not need to be told that there is no future in stoop labor. They have seen the coming of automation in the fields. They know their children must have a skilled trade or profession to live decently. They do not need a lecture on the value of education. They are not apathetic toward the concept of education being their children's one and only avenue out of poverty. Migrant parents do, however, need encouragement and understanding from educators and the general public in order to make the educational dreams which they have for their children a reality.

Developmental Theory

Erik H. Erikson's psychosocial theory of child development will be used in this section as a framework for analyzing the child growing up in rural poverty, especially the migrant child. Five of Erikson's eight stages of man will be reviewed as they relate to the rural child. These five stages are selected because they cover the child's development from infancy through adolescence; the last three stages pertain to the adult. Not only does successful accomplishment of any task at the appropriate time in a child's process of physical growth facilitate mastery of other tasks which are being worked upon simultaneously, but such success creates readiness for succeeding tasks. Failure in dealing with the developmental task predisposes the individual to further failure. All eight of the stages of man and their resolutions, both desirable and undesirable, are illustrated in the following table.

TABLE 4
Erikson's Eight Stages of Psychosocial Development*

Stages	Age	Resolution or Outcome†		
		"Healthy"		"Unhealthy"
1st	First year	Basic trust	vs	Distrust
2nd	Second-third year	Autonomy	vs	Shame and doubt
3rd	Fourth-fifth year	Initiative	vs	Guilt
4th	Sixth-twelfth year	Industry	vs	Inferiority
5th	Adolescence	Identity	vs	Role-diffusion
6th	Young adult	Intimacy	vs	Isolation
7th	Middle-age adult	Generativity	vs	Stagnation
8th	Aged adult	Ego integrity	vs	Despair

*This table is adapted from Erik H. Erikson, "Growth and Crisis of the Healthy Personality," in *Symposium on the Healthy Personality*, ed. by Milton J. E. Senn (New York: Josiah Macy, Jr. Foundation, 1950), pp. 26, 99.

†Definitions of the following terms are taken from Erik H. Erikson, *Childhood and Society* (New York: W. W. Norton and Co., Inc., 1950), chapter 7, pp. 219-33.

Trust—Implies not only that one has learned to rely on the sameness and continuity of the outer providers, but also that one may trust oneself and the capacity of one's own ego to cope with urges and that one is

(Table 4 continued)

able to consider oneself trustworthy enough so that the providers will not need to be on guard lest they be nipped.

Distrust—Lack of trust and a feeling of inner badness.

Autonomy—Ability to make a choice, to hang onto or let go, to risk, to experiment.

Shame and *doubt* *Shame* refers to negative feelings about the self, often experienced as a feeling of being completely exposed, i.e., painful self-consciousness and a sense of being small. *Doubt* is closely related to shame and refers to feelings of uncertainty about one's self and one's capacities.

Initiative—Pleasure in attack and conquest, taking responsibility for beginning or originating, ability to think and act without being urged.

Guilt—A sense of having done a wrong or committed an offense.

Industry—Ability to bring a productive situation to completion.

Inferiority—A sense of inadequacy in which the individual despairs of his capability and considers himself doomed to mediocrity.

Identity—A sense of ego identity is an accured confidence that the inner sameness and continuity are matched by the sameness and continuity of one's meaning for others.

Role diffusion—A need to fight a lack of sense of identity by temporarily overidentifying with groups, ideas, causes, cliques to the point of complete loss of self-identity and a lack of really knowing what one stands for or who one is.

Intimacy—Situations which call for self-abandonment in close friendships, marriage, and in physical contacts.

Isolation—Avoidance of intimate experiences because of a fear of ego loss.

Generativity—Interest in establishing and guiding the next generation or whatever in a given case may become the absorbing object of a parental kind of responsibility.

Stagnation—A regression from generativity to an obsessive need for pseudo intimacy, punctuated by moments of mutual repulsion with a pervading sense of individual stagnation and interpersonal impoverishment.

Ego Integrity—An acceptance of one's one-and-only life cycle as something that had to be and that, by necessity, permitted no substitutions; it thus means a different love of one's parents.

Despair—The lack or loss of accrued ego integration signified by fear of death: the one-and-only life cycle is not accepted as the ultimate of life. Despair is the feeling that the time is short, too short for the attempt to start another life and to try out alternate roads to integrity. Disgust hides despair.

Basic Trust versus Distrust

The child who develops a feeling of trust in others will also later develop a sense of trust in himself, which is paramount to a healthy self-concept. Likewise, the child who senses he cannot trust others fails to develop a sense of self-trust. The sense of self-trust develops also when the child feels he is trusted by others. It enhances his own self-confidence when he knows others have confidence in him. This sense of trust in others and in self is the undergirding of interpersonal relationships. The individual who can trust is willing to risk and can relate emotionally to others. The child who has not developed a sense of trust will have a need to be suspicious of others, to withdraw from interpersonal relationships, to employ defenses to keep a psychological distance from others, and, in extreme cases, to withdraw into schizophrenia and paranoia.

There is a tendency to think of the child in rural poverty as being maternally deprived or experiencing a limited amount of mothering because of the many demands that are made upon his mother to cope with the reality of their poverty. Although some rural children are deprived as some research has shown, maternal deprivation should not be viewed as a general phenomenon in poor rural areas. The mother living in rural poverty may not be using the same child-rearing practices as those approved by the middle-class researcher, but she may still be giving her child a good deal of emotional affection. Frequently the culture of the rural family has certain built-in features that provide the child with additional emotional support. For example, the extended family provides a number of mother figures—grandmothers, aunts, and older siblings who can help give the child a feeling of belonging.

There is a general basic distrust, however, in these rural areas that is reinforced for the child: a distrust for those who are not of the child's own ethnic culture, neighborhood, or family. Outsiders are to be suspected, they are not to be trusted. They are to be looked upon with disfavor. While it is true that the suspicion of others is one of the characteristics of maternal deprivation, in this case distrust may have developed from cultural teachings rather than from emotional deprivation. The child may have received maternal affection and still be very selective as to whom he relates, although he has the capacity to relate.

This first stage of developmental patterns coincides with Freud's psychosexual oral phase, in which the basic need gratification is for dependency. The child needs to feel wanted and cared for.

Autonomy versus Shame and Doubt

The alternate outcomes of Erikson's second stage of psycho-social development, autonomy, are shame and doubt, which, in the adult, may be expressed in paranoiac fears. This stage coincides with the Freudian psychosexual anal stage involving the toilet training experience. It is during this stage that the young child begins to explore his environment, to examine things, and to ask questions. The child also begins to assert his own feelings, his likes and dislikes. If, during this stage, the child is given permission to learn, he begins to do things for himself. He expresses his needs through negativism and through asserting his own right to do something, or at least his own desire to do something. This is the positive side of the experience. If the child is encouraged and given direction by the parent or other adults, a sense of accomplishment, a growing confidence in self, and a feeling of permission to do new things develops. If the child is too restricted or discouraged, creativity is hampered. The child begins to feel shame for even thinking about things that are not highly esteemed by the adults he knows. The child doubts his capability because he feels small in the face of large obstacles (the adults). If the oppression of the child's activity is too great, the desire to learn can be stifled. The child will withdraw into his own guilt and shame rather than run the risk of losing the adults' love.

All children in this second stage need an opportunity for self-expression through exploration. The development of autonomy will be more difficult for children in rural poverty than for middle-class children of the same age; however, it will also vary for children living under similar circumstances. The child in rural poverty has advantages over the child in the ghetto in that the environment of the house in rural sections extends to the outdoors, and in the country even a small baby may sit on the grass or on the bare ground examining a leaf or tearing apart the petals of a flower or feeling a stone—exploring, inquiring, and learning.

In Appalachia, the Ozarks, and rural areas of the deep South the geographical boundary of the yard, trees, and hills is a recognized part of the culture and expands the world for the child. In the culture of these areas, rural families, regardless of race, own dogs (usually large numbers of hound dogs), so the young rural child is aware of the birth of animals (if not the actual birth process, at least the care of the young). The out-of-doors for the young rural child, migrant or otherwise, provides experiences to the senses and provides opportunity to smell, touch, see, hear, and put in the mouth to taste. Such experiences are provided by the wind, rain, snow, and the light and dark patterns of shadow and sunbeam movements which are part of the everyday experiences.

In his novel *Anthony Adverse* Hervey Allen tells how a young infant strapped to a backboard suspended from the peg in the wall entertained himself for hours by watching the sunlight through the leaves of the trees, by watching the pigeons as they came to eat in the courtyard, and by watching the movement of people in and out of his line of vision.[14]

In overcrowded rooms the exploration of the child may be hampered or the parent may discourage exploration in a way that is limiting for the child. The child of poverty, especially the nonwhite child, may also have other restrictions that are far more devastating because they cause him to have deep feelings of shame and doubt for being black, brown, or yellow, Indian, Negro, or Oriental and therefore somehow inferior. The child in the early stages of development may come to feel that if one is from a particular background or family or race or is a girl[15] one is not expected to explore or want to learn. Such experiences or impressions destroy creativity and encourage shame and doubt and prevent the third step of development which comes as the child has more contacts with the wider community just prior to the school experience.

Initiative versus Guilt

This third period of development Freud called the Oedipal phase. It is at this stage that the child imitates sex roles and explores what it is like to be an adult. As Erikson points out,

> ... the danger of this stage is the sense of guilt over the goals contemplated and the acts initiated in one's exuberant enjoyment of new locomotor and mental power: acts of aggressive manipulation and coercion which go far beyond the executive capacity of organism and mind and therefore call for an energetic halt on one's contemplative initiative.[16]

Pathologically the conflict over initiative is expressed either in hysterical denial, which causes the repression of the wish or the abrogation of its executive order by paralysis or impotency, or in overcompensatory showing off in which the scared individual, so eager to "duck," instead "sticks his neck out."

It is more difficult for the child in the lower-class rural area or migrant home to develop a strong feeling of initiative. It is not unusual in such a home for the child's plans or ideas to be viewed with contempt, the general attitude being "he is too young to know or to understand." This attitude may result because it is extremely threatening to parents with authoritative personalities to accept the initiative of their child, especially an intelligent child. On the other hand, because of the parents' limited education or limited understanding or use of English, the child may be asked to interpret or help make adult decisions. The result is inconsistency in the child's problem-solving experience.

In lower-class rural homes boys more than girls may be discouraged from taking the initiative. Boys may see little future in initiative if they see men unemployed or not involved in any decision-making process. The child may come to accept the fact that it is because the adult male is Black, Indian, Chicano, Puerto Rican, or poor white that this occurs. If the child represents one of these minorities, he may not develop any self-confidence. He may feel that he is in a hopeless situation from which he cannot break out and wonders why he should fight it. Why try when the gain is not worth all the effort?

On the other hand, girls from a minority background, whether poor white or poor nonwhite, by this stage of their development conclude that the female adult role is one of work which may even involve supporting a husband or being the sole breadwinner for the household which she heads. J. W. Lawrie spells out what happens to the child when he gets the double message concerning work and what that double message does to his concept of self. Lawrie is writing about the Black child but his material also applies to the non-Black child.

> Increasingly it becomes clear, I think, that there is a subculture in our society that doesn't want to work, at least in the way the white culture defines work. The Black child (and maybe the white child) of unemployed parents learns in school, in church, from television and other institutionalized culture-carriers that work and striving are for "good people." People who work hard, save their money and plan for tomorrow are good people. But he also learns that he and his father do not work and probably will never work.
>
> He is therefore in a state of psychological unrest. He can

conclude either that he and his father (if indeed one is present) are not "good," or that work is not good. Given this semiconscious and unspoken choice, the outcome is predictable: work is not good and people who tell him it is are liars.

The anti-work ethic is solidified by creatively practiced teenage rituals: hanging around the candy store, cutting school, dropping out, stealing, playing the numbers, etc. The teenager who does these things is known to his friends as a "player," the exact opposite of "worker," which is the white man's culture's name for a "good" boy.

This process is accompanied by heavy psychological pain. Although the player comes to a logical decision (given that work is not an alternative for him), he is often tempted unconsciously to accept the other horn of the dilemma: he may come to feel that he and his father are indeed "no good." There is good evidence that this happens in many cases. Kenneth Clark has shown that one of the most debilitating effects of racial prejudice is that the victims come to believe in and even cherish their "inferiority," thereby becoming true Uncle Toms.

The cultural outcome, then, is the defeated group, psychologically riddled with self-hatred and anger, or a group of players . . . ill-equipped candidates for jobs in almost any white business that values cooperative, striving, middle class work behavior.

At the level of depth psychologically one might try to understand Black failure in work programs. First, the Black son comes to understand that in the white culture the father works. He may unconsciously learn that working is good when, and only when, the father is doing it [and this is easily seen within a society that discredits and downgrades the efforts of women by allowing a lower pay scale and less recognition for their accomplishment]. "Working is being a man," says his unconscious. The equivalence between being a man and working is reinforced again in his contacts with white culture. He also comes to understand that in his family, typically, his father doesn't work. But, crucially, his mother does.

He might go through the following unconscious process:
1) men work
2) my father does not work
3) my mother works
4) therefore, my father is not a man and it's my mother's fault. From what we know of unconscious thought, the last statement flows directly from the first three—not logically, but psychologically.

At the same time, he is unconsciously moving through the major question of the Oedipal conflict [Freud's third stage of psychosexual development]. The boy's unconscious wish to possess his mother, according to classical thought, is met with a severe fear of the consequences, i.e. being castrated by the father. Faced with this threat, the boy identifies with his father—takes on his values, loves him, and thereby stops competing with him. He marries "a girl just like the girl that married dear ole' dad," and life moves along. But for the Black son, this would mean identifying with someone who is already "castrated."

Thus, the young Black may be faced with the unconscious choice of identifying with a castrated father or living in fear of castration if he does not. *In either case, he can develop without a sense of manhood, power potency or dominance.*

As a result one of the white culture's favorite stereotypes may become fulfilled in the Black's behavior. Defensively, the Black man may act lazy, childlike and funloving. He is an unemployable, alienated, cut-off "boy" as a result of trying to avoid an insolvable unconscious conflict. *Working is being a woman, and not working is being a castrated man.*

The Black man does not "work and support a family like the rest of us." His son goes through the same unconscious problem with the same "boy" outcome. It is no accident that militant Blacks hate the name "boy" with a fury. It cuts to deep layers of conflict.[17]

Industry versus Inferiority

The fourth developmental stage corresponds to Freud's fourth period of latency. The concern of the schoolage child is to develop a sense of usefulness, a sense of acknowledgment and recognition through work or personal effort. This is an extremely difficult period for the child from rural poverty, especially as he approaches puberty and begins to make a self-appraisal in comparison with his peers. In order for the child to make a positive adjustment to the developmental tasks of this period, he must be able to have a positive identification with those who know things and know how to do things. This may bring the subsystem of his family into conflict with the larger system of education.

For the child who is becoming increasingly aware of how his culture and family-life system differ from that of others and who is becoming increasingly aware also that others, even those in professional roles, consider his culture or social class inferior, it is extremely difficult to form a positive self-identity. The classroom too often is the scene of innumerable failures for this child. His language deficiency, his mispronunciations, his misspellings, his lack of sophistication in those areas which seem important to educators add to his feelings of worthlessness. He senses that he has nothing to contribute to the learning situation, and he defends against the emotional pain of acknowledging this. Instead, he comes to view the educational experience as having nothing to offer him. He withdraws and may even drop out of school, claiming he is "getting nothing" out of his educational experience and can no longer afford to waste his time.

Others from this same educationally limited background have an insatiable appetite for learning, which may lead them to use educational degrees to overcompensate for what they believe consciously and unconsciously to be their inferior position that is due to race, social class, or sex. Such overcompensation may be motivated by a strong feeling of anger and a desire to "show them." In the long run this child is usually doomed also to failure or to isolation because there is not enough satisfaction for his need for recognition of his accomplishments. As a group, the Japanese-Americans have come to use educational attainments as a way of trying to gain acceptance for themselves in an alien, hostile, non-Oriental world, as well as to prove they are not inferior, as they have been so labeled. Outside of the Jewish subculture (which has had much the same type of motivation) there is no ethnic group in America today with as high an educational attainment.

Identity versus Role Diffusion

The resolution of the fifth state is either identity or role diffusion. A firm sense of identity develops as the individual comes to grips with who he is and who he is not, where he is going, and with whom. Thus, he has a purpose in life and a means of relating to that purpose. As Erikson puts it, this is the stage of development where "puberty rites 'confirm' the inner design for life."[18]

The danger in this phase of development is role diffusion that is caused when the individual is confronted with self-doubt and lack of confidence. When that happens there is a lack of self-identity;

there is no feeling of relatedness of self to the cosmos. Life under these conditions may have little purpose.

It is difficult for the adolescent from a minority culture (and white rural poverty is a minority culture as well as the Indian, Chicano, Puerto Rican, Cuban, and Black cultures) to develop a sense of identity when the dominant society has predetermined that the minority is inferior and has never given, nor will give, anything that is positive to the development of the country.

What the Migrant Child Brings to School

Writing about the Black child in the eastern migrant stream, Robert Coles points out what the child brings to the school by way of interpersonal relationships. He says,

> By the time a migrant child goes to school he has been taught his do's and don't's, to fear certain others, to get along with people in certain ways. Impulsiveness, self-assertion, rivalrous expressions, and envious feelings tend to be strongly discouraged at home, but allowed of children as groups, that is, in conjunction with brothers and sisters. Thus, groups of children can fight other groups, or envy one another openly as long as they act collectively.
>
> Mothers show great warmth and open affection, kissing and fondling their children but also show quick anger toward them and severe punishment of them, most often slapping accompanied by shouting. Rarely is one child punished alone. Often the mother will remind the others that they, too, have done similar wrongs in the past, and will in the future. There is an absence of grudges in parents. A punished child will likely as not be embraced seconds or minutes after being punished. . . .
>
> This may explain what many observers of migrants notice, their capacity to change moods and behavior so rapidly; they can be fearfully, grimly silent especially before non-migrants and then quickly joyful and talkative with one another. . . . I suspect that their early training sets the stage for what they will later need, a highly developed sense of flexibility in their personality, an ability to manage the constant restrictions of the external world, but still not succumb to the apathy and despair that would fatigue and immobilize them. In a sense there is a "bounce" to the way these children are punished that teaches them fast recovery from a slap as well as specific responsive obedience to it.

Much of the hardest punishment goes into confirming the child's sense of submission to the non-migrant world, or passivity before it. There is a striking difference in the relationship between the child and his family "at home" or in travel, and the child at school, in the fields, even on the street. At home the children play together easily and warmly. They are free with their parents, and their parents with them. Open expressions of love and demonstrations of it are seen. . . . Yet in contrast to such openness of feeling and of anger, closeness of relationship between children, when migrant children meet many people on the "outside" they often appear isolated, guarded, withdrawn, suspicious and apathetic or dull.

Thus, in many respects migrant children are brought up to have two rather explicit ways of responding to the two worlds of their family and "others." Though of course, all children learn a version of that kind of distinction, there is a sharpness of contrast to the two-fold behavior in migrant children that is as if they have two sets of attitudes, two personalities, one for their family, one for the rest of the world.[19]

As a result of these and other kinds of experiences the migrant child arrives at the school with many cognitive and precognitive deficits in addition to his limited ability in English. Harry Beilin and Lassar G. Gotkin have identified some of these limitations.

He is less capable, for example, of making perceptional discriminations among physical objects in his environment, less able to deal with the pictorial representations of objects and actions, and more limited in the ability to conceptualize in even primitive ways.[20]

Although Beilin and Gotkin were speaking of the urban slum child, some of their observations are valid when applied to the migrant child from a poor rural background. Their observations on the school's role in meeting the needs of disadvantaged children are especially pertinent.

Those who prepare curricula for disadvantaged children need to recognize that these children arrive in the classroom with other characteristics which inhibit learning. The disordered life in which the slum child grows does not, in general, foster the development of those internalized controls that keep a child attending to a task for protracted periods of time or enable him to attend to what the teacher is saying and doing. These children are much more easily distracted than their peers and much more likely to act out their wants in physical ways. Their requests are more often transmitted through action than words, and are therefore often perceived as hostile and aggressive. Such children characteristically nudge or touch the teacher to get her attention. They take the ruler another child is using rather than ask for it. The ruler is just as likely to be used as an extension of the arm in a fencing match as an extension of the arm for measurement. The order and self-discipline required of the learner in school settings are alien to the experience of many of the children we are describing. This kind of self-discipline, however, is as necessary to learning as are cognitive skills since teaching may be delayed until some semblance of personal and group order is achieved.

One is likely to find, too, that materials, devices and language which are new and different hold little attraction. The child may be intrigued and stimulated by the initial novelty of the school but interest will progressively wane, even more than with other children, unless something more sustaining than novelty is introduced. If novelty is not followed by some success with the newly encountered materials, the frustrations resulting from unsuccessful attempts at mastery will result in a retreat from the potentially interesting school environment.[21]

The migrant child can be easily overwhelmed with the total learning experience. There is need for repetition of material in smaller units since the child may have difficulty remembering or retaining information even very recently acquired. In the language of information theory, these children have rather limited channel capacity, and overloading the channels will only break down the communication system between teacher and learner. The average teaching and learning pace of any classroom is an overload for the migrant child until he has had a chance to adjust to his new experience. In many cases by the time the migrant child has adjusted to the classroom as a system and has learned his way around and is finally ready to view course content and the conceptual approaches to the subject matter as taught in his grade, the crops are harvested; and the child leaves for a new overload experience in a new school, in a new community with new expectations. If this child is evaluated in terms of socialization and ability to cope with various systems, much has been accomplished by his brief stay in the school. However, if this child is evaluated in terms of scholastic achievement, which he usually is, nothing has been accomplished by his having been in school, and, in fact, time has been lost, for this child is further behind for his grade level.

Psychologically this child was not in a position to learn when he entered the school—at least not to learn what is measured favorably by achievement test scores. In other words, the migrant child uses his psychic energy that is necessary for learning to preceive his new environment, to test his prior experiences against the reality of what he finds in the present, and to control his own inner anxiety. The new, incoming migrant child or the anxious, frightened child does not free his psychic energy for classroom learning. The migrant child is both the newcomer who is uncertain of what will be expected and, therefore, the anxious child, worried, hoping to be accepted by the teacher and fellow students, but at the same time afraid of rejection. Such a frame of mind and channeling of psychic energy are not conducive to classroom learning for anyone, regardless of their intellectual capabilities. Therefore, it should not be too surprising that school records show migrant students are, on the average, about one and one-half months behind in mathematics and two and one-half months behind in reading compared to the regular students in the same classroom, and that by the time they reach sixth grade they are on the average about one grade level behind the regular students in mathematics and about 1.6 grade levels behind in reading. For individuals this grade level retardation may be as high as three or more years, especially in reading. Because reading is such a key skill and becomes increasingly important in junior and senior high school where all subjects depend on the ability to read and comprehend, the dropout rate for migrant students reaches its peak between the seventh and ninth grades. Another psychological aspect of school failure is that the migrant child at this age is in a psychosocial developmental stage that requires an assessment of self in relationship to peers, and the migrant child, as does every minority child (and the migrant child is both), becomes increasingly aware that he does not measure up very well.

The work of Lloyd S. Tireman (1948),[22] Harlan Sininger (1931),[23] George I. Sanchez (1932),[24] Madison L. Coombs (1958),[25] and George Boyce (1960)[26] has shown a general tendency for pupils to become more and more educationally retarded as they progress through the schools and for many from financially disadvantaged homes to either drop out or become hopelessly lost in high school. Educational retardation may be defined as the extent to which students fail to achieve academically according to their capacity for such achievement. Children of normal intelligence are expected to move through the public-school grades on an extremely homogeneous age-in-grade scale. Academic performance at grade-placement for children in the normal range of intelligence indicates achievement that is neither retarded nor accelerated.

The results of current testing programs reinforce the previous findings that as minority, ethnic-group children (especially the poor of all races) progress through the school grades, their achievement falls further and further behind. Not only are these students from one to two years overage for their grades on the average, but they are also educationally retarded an additional one to two years in achievement on standardized tests. Miles V. Zintz points out:

> The testing program showed that groups of Anglo children scored from approximate grade placement to one-half year of retardation in achievement. Spanish-American students were, on the average, one year educationally retarded in fifth and sixth grade, but they were an additional year over-age in grade. Indian children tended to be two to three years retarded in reading ability in sixth grade and were one to two years over-age in grade.[27]

In the *Navajo Yearbook* Robert Young has also emphasized that one of the major problems in the field of Navajo education is educational retardation. This educational retardation was strongly felt when the Indian children were transferred to public schools. Public school personnel were concerned that Navajo children accepted for enrollment be "up to grade." Of 9,751 children whose records were analyzed in December 1957, only 6 percent were "up to grade"; 40 percent were retarded at least one year, and 54 percent were retarded two or more years.[28]

The low quality of segregated Black education is well documented. Making a study in 1957 for the National Scholarship Service and Fund for Negro Students, R. L. Plaut states:

> Negroes, furthermore, have long been aware that most of their schools in the South, and often the *de facto* segregated

schools in the North, are rundown, poorly staffed, and short-handed. Second- and third-rate schooling for Negroes leaves them without the ability to compete with white students and robs them of the initiative to compete. Even the 1955 Speaker of the Georgia House of Representatives admitted recently that "Negro education in Georgia is a disgrace. What the Negro child gets in the sixth grade, the white child gets in the third."[29]

In his "Review of Evidence Relating to Effects of Desegregation on the Intellectual Performance of Negroes," Irwin Katz gives a few specific instances of educational disparity at the grade school level. He said that Findley, in 1956,

> . . . found in testing for achievement in the Atlanta schools that from forty percent to sixty percent of white pupils met the standards set by the top fifty percent of a national sample on the different tests; but only two percent to ten percent of Negro pupils met this standard on the various tests. In Tennessee, according to Wyatt in 1962, Negro students averaged one and a half to two years behind grade level when transferred to biracial schools in the upper grades. In earlier grades, transfers performed satisfactorily. The same report described the status of Negro and white teachers in a Tennessee urban area. Only forty-nine percent of 901 academically qualified Negro teachers passed the National Teachers Examination; among white teachers, more than ninety-seven percent of 783 qualified teachers passed the test. The Tennessee survey showed that the academic retardation of the segregated Negro elementary-school pupil is progressive.[30]

Other data indicate that the racial gap in achievement continues to widen through high school and college. In 1963 S. O. Roberts pointed out that less than 3 percent of Negro graduates of segregated high schools would meet the standards of admission of nonsegregated colleges.[31] Even in the urban North, where schools have always been legally integrated, the education afforded Negroes tends to be inadequate. Martin Deutsch found that in time samples of classroom activity, from 50 to 80 percent of all classroom time in New York City elementary schools with predominantly Black, lower-class children was "devoted to disciplining and various essentially non-academic tasks." By comparison, only 30 percent of classroom time was given over to such activities in elementary schools attended mainly by white children of roughly similar economic status.[32] All of these factors add to the lack of achievement of the nonwhite child.

Zintz continues,

> It is apparent from data obtained in 1960 that there continues to be one full year of over-ageness for all minority ethnic groups. This is not as significant, however, as the indication that even though the sample children were over-age in grade, they were an additional one and one-half to two years retarded in achievement as measured by a survey reading test. Over-ageness and retardation must be combined to determine the full extent of educational retardation.[33]

The frightening aspect of all of this is that the severity of educational retardation found in migrant education and among minority ethnic groups, especially in rural areas, in the 1970s follows the same pattern recognized and identified more than forty years ago by Sininger and Sanchez and repeated in every decade since, and yet apparently nothing has been done to rectify the situation.

Even in the highly publicized federally financed programs currently in operation, an appraisal of the end results is continuing to show that (1) in reading, mathematics, and language skills migrant children are below other students in the same class; (2) educational deficiencies become more serious the higher the migrant children move in grade levels; (3) grade retention rates for migrant children are higher than those for other students. In other words, regardless of the amount of monies spent or effort put forth, the end results of the situation have not changed markedly in the past twenty-five years. It could well be that our entire approach is wrong or that we are expecting academic results too quickly. We must begin to find ways of helping children achieve a high level of education without having to destroy the child's own culture in the process.

The question that must be answered by our nation is this: How long will we go on allowing another generation of children to grow up uneducated, unable to cope with the problems of making a livelihood in an increasingly complex society where even the best educated individuals find it difficult to comprehend the current issues?

NOTES

1. U.S. Department of Health, Education and Welfare, Office of Education, *Selected State Programs in Migrant Education,* by George E. Haney (Washington, D.C.: The Department, 1963).

2. LXXXVI, iii.

3. *Children and Youth in the 1960's* (Washington, D.C.: White House Conference on Children and Youth, 1960).

4. *Selected State Programs in Migrant Education.*

5. Myrtle R. Reul, "Sociocultural Patterns among Michigan Migrant Farm Workers," Center for Rural Manpower and Public Affairs, Michigan State University, East Lansing, Mich., 1967, pp. 3-9. (Mimeographed.)

6. *Ibid.,* p. 19.

7. Myrtle R. Reul, "A Preview of the Migrant as a Rehab Client," *Rehabilitation Record,* November and December 1969, pp. 1-7, also reprinted in Frank M. Loewenberg and Ralph Dolgoff, eds., *The Practice of Social Intervention: Roles, Goals and Strategies* (Etasca, Ill.: F. E. Peacock Publishers, Inc., 1972), pp. 430-37.

8. Reul, "Sociocultural Patterns," p. 19.

9. Suzanne Keller, *The American Lower Class Family* (Albany, N.Y.: New York State Division for Youth, 1968).

10. *Heal the Hurt Child* (Chicago: University of Chicago Press, 1966), pp. 71-72.

11. *Ibid.,* p. 74.

12. Toni Cede, ed., *The Black Woman: An Anthology*, Signet Classics (New York: New American Library, Inc., 1970), pp. 15-16.

13. Direct quote of a school official whom I interviewed.

14. (New York: Farrar and Rinehart, Inc., 1933), pp. 115-25.

15. The contradictory message which the girl in our society receives from her family, her teachers, and the general public is that if she is too smart, too independent, and, above all, too serious about her work, she is unfeminine and will, therefore, never get married. This has conditioned very intelligent women to be "anxiety ridden over the prospects of success. . . . They seem to be in a state of anxious conflict over what would happen if they succeeded.

"It is almost as though this conflict is inhibiting their capacity for achievement. The fear of success manifests itself mainly in women of demonstrably high intelligence coming from homes where high achievement is much valued. . . . The negative attitudes we find expressed toward successful women have increased to a disproportionately greater extent than have the positive ones. . . . Our culture has made a deep split in the souls of its women, and the result is insupportable anxiety which can bear up only by transforming itself into the malevolence of what is known as passive-aggressive behavior. Behind the passive exterior of many women there lies a growing anger over lost energies and confused lives, an anger so sharp in its fury but so diffused in its focus that one can only describe it as the price society must pay for creating a patriarchal system in the first place, and for now refusing to let it go." Vivian Gornick, "Why Women Fear Success," *Ms,* Spring 1972, pp. 51-52.

16. *Childhood and Society* (New York: W.W. Norton and Co., Inc., 1950), p. 224.

17. "Making It the Hardest Way," *Psychology Today,* III (November 1969), 30-31.

18. *Childhood and Society*, p. 228.

19. *The Migrant Farmer: A Psychiatric Study* (Atlanta, Ga.: Southern Regional Council, 1965), pp. 17-18.

20. "Psychological Issues in the Development of Mathematics Curricula for Socially Disadvantaged Children," in *Education of the Disadvantaged*, ed. by A. Harry Passow, Miriam Goldberg, and Abraham J. Tannenbaum (New York: Holt, Rinehart and Winston, Inc., 1967), p. 290.

21. *Ibid.*, pp. 290-91.

22. *Teaching Spanish-Speaking Children* (Albuquerque, N.M.: University of New Mexico Press, 1948).

23. "An Age-grade Study of the San Jose Training School and Its Two Control Schools," *University of New Mexico Bulletin School Series*, I, No. 2 (Albuquerque, N.M.: University of New Mexico, 1931).

24. "The Age-grade Status of the Rural Child in New Mexico Public Elementary Schools, 1931-1932," *Education Research Bulletin* (Sante Fe, N.M.: New Mexico Department of Education, November 1932).

25. U.S., Department of Interior, *The Indian Child Goes to School*, by L. Madison Coombs, *et al.* (Washington, D.C.: The Department, 1958).

26. "Why Do Indians Quit School?" *Indian Education*, May 1, 1960.

27. "Problems of Classroom Adjustment of Indian Children in Public Elementary Schools in the Southwest," in *Education of the Disadvantaged*, ed. by Passow, Goldberg, and Tannenbaum, p. 95.

28. "The Navajo Yearbook," Report No. VII, Arizona Navajo Agency, Window Rock, Ariz., 1958.

29. *Blueprint for Talent Searching* (New York: National Scholarship Service and Fund for Negro Students, 1957), p. 5.

30. In *Education of the Disadvantaged*, ed. by Passow, Goldberg, and Tannenbaum, p. 135.

31. "Test Performance in Relation to Ethnic Group and Social Class," A report, Fisk University, Nashville, Tenn., 1963.

32. Deutsch, *Minority Group and Class Status as Related to Social and Personality Factors in Scholastic Achievement*, Monogram No. 2 (Ithaca, N.Y.: Society for Applied Anthropology, 1960).

33. "Problems of Classroom Adjustment," p. 95.

31

Why It Is Hard to Trust: Implications for Health Services

It seemed to Sylvia Williams that the schools were always picking on her children. She explained to us why she felt that way. Teachers, she said, were constantly sending notes to her, asking one time that she provide her children with cleaner or nicer clothing or another that she see that her children bathed more often or that she take them to the public health nurse for a rash check. She remembered one teacher sending seven-year-old Linda back to the migrant housing when she showed up at school wearing only a dress. The teacher felt Linda's behavior was indecent and told the little girl to go home and not return until she was "properly dressed." Linda had not been able to find a pair of panties that morning that were not "in rags," nor had she been able to find a pair when her teacher sent her back to camp. The only whole undergarments owned by the Williams girls were the two pair being worn at that moment by Linda's older sisters, Irene and Jackie. They, as the older, had laid first claim to the best items of clothing. Linda stayed out of school the rest of the week until her mother got paid and could go to Woolworth's to buy some panties.

508

Sometimes it seemed more than one woman could do, Sylvia told us, to have enough money to buy a change of outer garments—a dress, a shirt, a pair of dungarees—to say nothing of anything more. Things like pajamas, slips, and panties, even for herself, were a luxury they could seldom afford; certainly, they could never afford more than two pairs of panties apiece and usually only one.

The school authorities had criticized Sylvia for keeping Linda out of class and said she should have told them Linda did not have any panties and they would have got her some. Sylvia said she told them she would remember to do that next time. She wanted us to know, however, that after the way the teacher had talked to Linda, implying that she was a filthy, bad, naughty girl to come to school without panties, she, as their mother, would always try to provide clothing for her children and not have to be "beholden" to the teacher or school people for anything.

Sylvia had almost a fanatic reaction to even the suggestion of donated clothing or food. She said, "Once when I was a little girl, one of the churches took it upon themselves to bring us a basket of food an' some of their castoffs." Sylvia said she would rather go naked than ever be so humiliated again. She remembered her mother took the basket and box into the house "an' put it up on a cheer" while the children gathered around to see. Their "pappy" wanted to know what "that church bunch was adoin' on his place, what with their pra'ers an' sangin' an' lookin' down on the po' folks an' all." He would not even look at the contents of the box. Sylvia said that she could remember when it was time to eat Christmas dinner her father was so drunk he was asleep on the floor with his head under the table and refused to touch any of the dressing and fancy salad the basket contained. Somehow, in her childlike thinking, it was conveyed to her that her father's heavy drinking on that day was related to the church basket. She was puzzled and hurt when her father "kept faultin' us 'bout ever-thang."

But the real humiliation for Sylvia came later, after the Christmas vacation, when she wore the red dress from the box to school. Her mother thought the dress was too short and lengthened it with a belt of contrasting material. Sylvia had danced on her toes on the road toward school, but her warm pride of ownership was short-lived. The original owner pointed out to the whole school that the red dress had been hers until she got tired of the "old thing"; but if she had known Sylvia would ruin it with that awful-looking white belt, she would never have consented for her mother to put the pretty red dress in the church box. Sylvia said that never again, in the twenty-nine years of her life, had she allowed herself to take charity from anyone, and she certainly would never submit her children to the humiliation of wearing clothing provided by someone else, especially by people in the school.

Sylvia is tiny and thin with a wiry strength that is often amazing. Her brown hair is straight, her nose turned up a little, her skin of almost leatherlike texture from sun and wind. She might be described as a rather commonplace, plain, or even unattractive woman except that her eyes, a pale china blue, are anything but commonplace. They seem to flash blue lightning when she talks about the emotional aspects of her life. She enunciates her contempt for a situation or her anger toward an individual by spitting between phrases.

In her teen years Sylvia "dipped a little snuff." Her spitting, however, is not related to tobacco; it is a habit of her social class, indulged in at one time by both men and women. John Andrew Rice describes this habit by saying,

> I was born into a spitting world. Everybody except ladies and aspirants to that title spit. No public place was without a receptacle. . . . Most homes had them also—"bring paw his spittoon" was a familiar command—and in any case, it was a wise precaution to have one handy for the use of a spitting guest. Out of doors, there was greater freedom for the sport and it was here that spitters liked to prove themselves expert in placing shots and the traditional target was a knothole in a fence. To recall the distance and accuracy of the skill of legendary heroes would put a strain upon credulity. . . . Spitting was no indication of social status; only the elegance with which it was done marked a gentleman, who wiped his mouth with a handkerchief instead of the back of his hand.[1]

Sylvia's fifth cousin, who came up from Jacksonville "to show off his city ways, pappy said," got her in the "family way for Jackie" when she was fifteen. This cousin got out before her pappy found out what had happened and used "the seat of his pants as a target for his squirrel raffle." The cousin took her for a ride in his new car; the first time she had ever ridden in a convertible. When he got her "nigh on to fifty miles from home," he pulled off on a side road and told her she could let him do what he wanted or she could try to walk back. Sylvia said, "I scratched 'em so bad, he brung me back to the road that turned up on our holler, dropped me off an' told me to keep my mouth shet about what he'd done. We never seen that cousin agin and never heerd from 'im. I don' know whur 'e is."

When Sylvia's father found out about the pregnancy, he told her that she would have to marry so there would be no "wood-colt" to disgrace the family. A wood-colt is a mountain expression for an illegitimate child whose parentage is unknown or cannot be identified. In the early history of the mountains children were sometimes lost or, during an epidemic, were orphaned. They were raised by whoever found them, needed them, or wanted them.

The need to find Sylvia a husband, and therefore, a legal father for her child was very real. Jack Morgan, a hired hand on one of the farms a few miles down the river, had been looking Sylvia's way on more than one occasion, so her father encouraged him to ask Sylvia to get married. Jack was then forty-five, two years older than Sylvia's father. As her father said, "Jack ain't much on sweetartin', but he'll make ya' a good man; 'sides, you'uns ain't much of a doney-gal[2] yourself, knocked-up as ya' air."

Jack was willing to marry Sylvia, although she was four and one-half months pregnant. He would claim Jackie when she was born, and they would make the "best of things." Sylvia was fifteen and a half at the time. Later she and Jack had four children of their own. Linda, the baby, was six months old when Jack was killed. He was sawing a tree when it "twisted in the wind," and he was pinned against a rock. At twenty-two Sylvia was suddenly widowed with five children under the age of six to raise.

She could have gone on AFDC, but she chose to do farm work. She would not take charity. She felt she had done quite well supporting her children and herself, despite the irritation of those who had never had to work the way she did always offering her "helpful criticism." Sylvia said, "Why 'ont they leave me 'lone? I hain't never don nary a thing to contrary 'em." Sylvia went on to say she did not think that the teacher's notes and comments showed any real interest in her children; they were merely an attempt on the part of the school and the community to make life difficult for her, so she would move on to the next crop and not stay permanently in their school district.

Sylvia wanted us to know she was "havin' trouble with the schools again." This time it was over head lice. The twins, Howard and Hayward, had been sent home when "nits" were discovered on their heads. Nits are tiny, pearshaped, white eggs laid by female lice on the scalp of a human host. Nits adhere to hair roots as if glued and usually are not visible unless seen in the hair part.

On this occasion the teacher was suspicious of head lice and was "checkin' heads," starting first with Howard and Hayward. When she found the tattletale white flecks, she notified the principal. The three other Williams children, along with all other migrant children from their camp, were called into the principal's office to have their heads checked. Although no nits were found, the school-bus driver was contacted, and the children were taken back to the migrant housing with messages for their parents that they stay out of school until all danger was removed of infecting the school with lice. They would each need a slip from the school doctor before they would be readmitted to their classrooms.

Sylvia had dealt with lice before. It was not too difficult for her to "clean up" infected heads. She merely used kerosene, usually keeping a small bottle for just such a purpose; if she were out, she could get some rather easily. Cleaning up head lice was not hard, but she did resent the attitude of the school. She resented the implication that somehow it was her fault that her children had head lice. She resented the implication that she and her children were dirty and that that was the reason for head lice. What could a school expect when she and her family were constantly on the move, living in all kinds of places, under conditions where it was easy "to pick up" head lice, bedbugs, or cockroaches but not easy to take a bath.

Sylvia also resented that everyone in the migrant camp knew that her children were the only ones who actually had head lice and that all the other school-age children in camp were being inconvenienced because of Hayward and Howard. She knew the other children would retaliate by teasing the twins, by calling them names and picking fights with them. She knew there would be this sort of retaliation even on the part of children who were glad to be out of school.

Sylvia could understand that the school thought it was doing the right thing to protect the nonmigrant children in the classes. She could accept this fact as the way life was. But at the same time she was resentful toward a school and community that did not seem interested in protecting her and her children. She was resentful because a community could care less about the living conditions of farm migrant families, and yet they were always making trouble for her with their criticism and their questionnaires. She could take care of her part of the problem—the lice; that was simple. But how long, she wondered aloud to us, would it be before communities really did something about the living and working conditions of farm migrants?

Syliva also told us she resented the "pryin' questions schools asked." She did not think that many of the things they said they needed to know were any of "their business nor had one thing to do with school." She could understand the need for them to want information about the children, such as where they had gone to school in other places; but she resented questions about whether she had ever been married, where the children's father was, and why he was not with them. She considered such questions an infringement on her personal privacy.

The questions, however, that made her the angriest were those which, to her, implied she was not a good mother and did not give proper care to her children. She was "downright mad" when the schools asked her children to tell what they had to eat, how their mother fixed their food, and how many of them slept in the same bed, or how many did not sleep in a bed at all. Once she told Jackie to tell her teacher that her mother fed her things to make "shit come." After she had "simmered down a little," she told Jackie not to say that to her teacher; it would only get her into trouble. But that night Sylvia bought a *Good Housekeeping* magazine and she and Jackie went through the pages picking out the best sounding dishes and what the magazine said were the most nutritious meals. Jackie copied the information and made it up as a planned week of meals which she took to her teacher the next day, claiming it was what she and her family had eaten the week before.

The teacher was amazed and told the entire class that Jackie's project showed she had eaten the best balanced diet of anyone in her grade. Sylvia said she laughed until she cried when Jackie reported to her what had happened. She said the whole "trick" made her feel "downright good an' wicked, but it helped her pride a leetle to git the better of 'at she-devil" to offset the times when the teacher had acted "like as if she was lookin' down her nose at migrant kids."

Sylvia wanted to tell us her feelings in her own way. "You know," she said, "if 'at teacher 'ver pounded a hoe up an' down all day 'til her lower back felt it'd break in two, or 'at she'd knocked a kidney loose, she'd not be gettin' down on her hands an' knees at night to scrub no floor, 'specially when if she got her housin' all sweet smellin' clean it don't look a speck better 'n 'fore she started, 'cause what it needs mor'n soap an' water is paint an' new floorin'. If 'at teacher was so tired at night she'd hardly drag one foot 'fore the utter, she wouldn't be fixin' no fancy meals with salad greens, soda biscuits, gravy an' apple cobbler for her kids; she jist open a can of pork'n beans an' tell 'em to go 'head an' eat it otter the can while she'd sit ther an' rest, same as me."

Sylvia stopped for a moment and gave a low laugh before she continued. "If 'at teacher worked in the fields like us in the sun 'til she was hot an' sweaty, her armpits won't smell any better'n mine, so I don't know where she get off feelin' so high an' mighty an' thinkin' jest 'cause she has a good education an' holds down an easy job those of us who bend our backs to make a livin' ain't no better'n dirt. When people come 'round askin' me questions or doin' what they calls 'research on migrants,' I jest blurt out the first darn thing that pops in my head, whether it's true or not. In fact, I get a real kick out of pullin' the wool over the eyes of some of these people who acts as if they think 'cause I'm a migrant I'm stupid.

"My pappy was the same way; he'd give anybody an honest answer if he thought they showed him respect, but I've h'rd him tell some whoppers with a straight face when what he thought they wanted to know weren't none o' their affairs. After they'd leave he'd pound his leg and double up laughin' an' braggin' 'bout how he'd 'put it over on that damn fool yankee.' Everone to pappy was a 'damn fool yankee' if he hadn't heard of their pappy or gran-pappy an' what county in North Carolina they was from, or if he didn't trust 'em, and pappy didn't trust a lot of people, 'specially strangers who come 'round askin' personal questions.''

When Sylvia came in from the fields on the day that the nits were discovered by the teacher, she got out her kerosene bottle and an old pair of rusty scissors. She cropped the twins' dark hair close until their scalps showed plainly. She soaked rags in the kerosene and wrapped each head, covering the rags with a towel. She tucked the towel ends under, forming a neat turban. This, she reminded them, they were to leave on all night. In the early morning before she left for the fields, she repeated the kerosene application and scrubbed each head with soap and water and rinsed with vinegar. The children were now ready to return to school. Their heads were clean and free from even the slightest suggestion of head lice. The school doctor gave them permission to return to their classrooms.

Because Sylvia did not realize that combs and caps could be a source of reinfection, she made no attempt to sterilize these items. Within a short time, one or the other of the children would begin to show the symptoms of an itching scalp and the tattletale specks of white nits. Another note would be sent to her by an irritated teacher, principal, or recreation director. And Sylvia would respond with anger to the irritation produced by the note, seeing it as the "trouble those people were causing," and would reach for her kerosene bottle.

Along with keeping her children in school, Sylvia said her biggest problem was keeping her family well. Because of the high cost of doctors and medicines, Sylvia had learned to rely on various home remedies she had learned from her mother and grandmother. If the illness was too complicated for her to handle, she would try to get "home" to her grandmother, a seventy-seven-year-old "herb-doctor midwife" who still "prescribed" for many of her neighbors in the North Carolina mountains.

In her younger years this aged woman had developed a wide reputation in the mountain area for her ability to treat scabies and other skin diseases. Scabies, commonly called itch, caused by mites that burrow into the tenderest portion of the human skin between the fingers or toes or in the folds of the armpits, was very common in that area of the mountains at one time. It was highly contagious and had a tendency to spread rapidly wherever people lived in crowded households. Sylvia's grandmother developed a very simple and yet a very effective treatment—a salve made of equal parts of sulphur and lard. The treatment took four days to cure the worst cases of itch and established her reputation as being the best "doctor" in the mountains, better even than those with medical degrees.

This grandmother was Sylvia's preferred source of medical treatment, although at times circumstances forced her into consulting with a local doctor in whom she had "no faith." One of the times she was "forced into going to a doctor" was when a teacher found scalp ringworm on Irene's head when she was checking the little girl for head lice. The ringworm was a small, pink patch high above Irene's ear, almost on the top of her head, and was covered by dry, grayish scales studded over with broken hairs. When the main lock of Irene's hair was pushed back, the spot was very noticeable, although it had not been seen earlier by either the teacher or Sylvia. The school nurse said that ringworm was extremely contagious and every child in school must be checked. No other case was found. The school doctor shaved the immediate area and prescribed an ointment.

Sylvia had to make a special trip to town to have the prescription filled. She had to pay the crew leader for taking her, and after she paid for Irene's medication and added in the time she lost from work, the whole experience had cost her three-quarters of a day of pay. It also rained that week, so she lost two additional days. When she mentioned this to the school nurse, she was told she should have more concern about the health needs of her children and less concern about how much time she missed from the fields. As Sylvia explained to us, she did not resent the cost of the prescription, but the fact that there seemed to be no results. If she spent that much money on medicine, it should provide an immediate cure.

Sylvia tried the ointment on Irene's head about a week, and when the spot looked more inflamed and larger than ever, she paid a fellow migrant to drive her and her children across the mountains to North Carolina. Her grandmother looked at Irene's head for a few minutes, tested the spot for fever with her forefinger, and recommended that it be rubbed daily with equal parts of vasoline and table salt. They threw the half-used prescription ointment into the trash and applied the vasoline and salt. Irene's hair dropped out of the infected area, but the spread of the fungus was checked and gradually disappeared as new, healthy hairs returned.

Another time it was Sylvia herself who needed medical treatment from her grandmother. She was thinning parsnips when she developed a severe dermatitis, or parsnip poisoning, from the leaves. At first, the welts were only on her hands and arms, but a few hours later the rash appeared on her forehead and eyelids caused when she pushed her hair back from her eyes. Within a few hours her eyelids were so inflamed they would not open. Two days later her fingers were so swollen she could not close her hands, and her face and arms were a mass of blisters that bled. She tried everything that was recommended by the local druggist. None of the lotions he sold her helped. She went to a dermatologist who insisted that he be paid before he would give her an examination. His prescription proved to be as ineffective as the earlier lotions had been.

Sylvia paid someone to drive her from New Jersey to North Carolina, using up the last of the money she had made that season. Her grandmother powdered some alum and mixed it in sweet milk and spread the paste-like substance over the infected area. She kept a bottle of quinine water, she said, for just such emergencies and had Sylvia bath her blistered hands, arms, and face repeatedly to give relief from the itching. Twenty-four hours after Sylvia had begun the alum, sweet milk, and quinine water treatment, her dermatitis improved enough so that she could start out with another work crew.

Her grandmother's parting remarks to her were to stay away from all work in parsnips unless she was willing to spend a number of weeks in North Carolina drinking a secret tea the grandmother would brew for her. This tea would make her immune to parsnip poisoning and even to snake bites, but it would take a good deal of time to gather the many herbs that would be needed in its preparation as some of them grew only along the highest reaches of the mountains.

Sylvia believed her grandmother did know how to mix just such a potion. She knew there was a whole religious group in the mountains who made themselves immune to snake bites in some way. She thought it might be by drinking some kind of tea. She also believed that her grandmother and certain other old women of her grandmother's generation who, like her grandmother, were born with a caul across their faces had the power to foretell the future and to mix other kinds of potions, such as love potions and the kind that would get rid of a spiteful hex.

In our travels we met many migrants besides Sylvia Williams who had little faith in medical doctors and who depended upon home remedies or cures. We also met many besides Sylvia's grandmother who used herbs and drank teas made from plants growing along the road or from dried supplies they brought with them from their own section of the country. Usually it was the older migrant who prepared his own tonic, cold preventive, or cure for the chills and agonies. White migrants from Kentucky and West Virginia brewed a tea from boneset as a preventive for colds. Indian migrants made a tea steeped from sage leaves for the same purpose. Both teas are very bitter to the taste but are guaranteed by their makers to ease the discomfort of aching muscles when a patient is suffering from the influenza.

In Montana we saw an Indian migrant effectively stop the flow of bleeding by packing a deep cut with powder from inside a puff ball. He explained that this method for stopping bleeding had been used by his people for generations. They also dug up, cleaned, and pulverized wild rose roots and used the powder in small dosages for diarrhea. They chewed calomel roots for indigestion and nausea. These were their natural medications, the preparation of which was handed down from parents to children, and they were still believed in above any doctor's prescription filled at a drug store.

There seem to be many barriers between the migrant and the professional services he needs so badly. Sometimes the barrier is the migrant's own lack of trust; other times the barrier is the professional person's inability to communicate.

"You can't trust those migrants," an irritated welfare worker once told us; "they will lie to you every chance they get. I had one lie to me the other day, saying he did not have a cent of money and yet he sat there in front of me with forty dollars in his pocket."

Later this migrant told us his understanding of what had happened. He said that the social worker had asked if he had any money back at the migrant camp, and he told her "no." She next asked if he had any money at home. Home to him was Mississippi, and he had no money there and no way of getting any money from his relatives who lived there, so he told her "no." She also asked if he had any money he could use to pay the doctor, and he said "no." The money he had he was saving to make an overdue payment at a finance company, so he did not feel he had any money he could use for a doctor. ""Sides," he told us, "she never asked if I had money in my pants, an' so I didn't think she cared 'bout that. I would hav' told her 'bout the forty dollars I was savin' back for the Household Finance Company if she'd only asked."

The social worker thought she had asked. The migrant farm worker thought he had answered.

Sometimes the lack of communication is caused by the use of professional terms which the uneducated migrant does not understand. On one occasion we met a family whose five-year-old son had his arm in a sling. I asked his mother what had happened. "The doc," she explained, "said 'twas a broken clavical.' " She went on to tell me that she hoped that "doc knew what he was doing and set the right bone, 'cause once when my brother was a little shaffer, he fell outta an apple tree and broke his collar bone, and his whole shoulder sort of hung down kinda limp jist like Jimmy's does. In fact, I would say with my brother's arm hit appeared to act jist the same way as my boy's arm does." She added, "My hope is that when that clinic doc set the clavical, he also set the collar bone, 'cause I'd sure hate to need to take my Jimmy to another doc and have that bone taken care of when we git this here cast off. You know, if a bone ain't set right, it grows crooked and has ta be rebroken and then set."

Accustomed to using medical terms, the physician had never thought to explain to this mother that a clavical may also be called a collar bone because they are one and the same.

Other barriers to medical service are the migrant's lack of faith in medical treatment or the feeling that he will receive more personal attention if he goes to an herb doctor or a midwife.[3]

Alice Frazier, a Black fruit picker, told us that one of the little neighbor children she was raising developed such a case of worms that she was "thin and sickly looking." Intestinal worms are common among migrants, both adults and children. Alice, who had "raised up eleven children," only five of whom were her own (the other six had been motherless children she "adopted") had had experience making use of the knowledge of a Black midwife granny. This woman always knew how to treat even the most stubborn cases of worms in children which would not respond to any of the "patent medicines" Alice could obtain at the drug store.

This time Alice said she bought some vermifuge, and the little girl "passed a whole mess of pin worms," but she still appeared sickly. Alice took the child to a local clinic where they had to wait all day until everyone with an appointment had been seen and then they waited longer until all the local residents who came, as Alice and the child had, without an appointment, were seen. When finally they were called from the empty waiting room, it was too late in the day for the child to have an examination as the clinic's lab staff had left. The doctor offered Alice an appointment in three weeks, but Alice explained that the crops would be finished in that area in two more weeks, and they would be gone. The doctor said he was sorry because the child did look sick. He said he would try to do something for her even without the examination. He would write her a prescription based on the information Alice gave. Alice had the prescription filled and saw that the child took it according to directions.

The little girl still "acted puny." So, the first opportunity Alice got, she took her to the old granny who had treated some of the other children for complicated cases of worms. The old woman said it sounded to her like a combination of round worms and a tape worm. She would start treatment for the round worms first, using juice squeezed from jimsey weed by crushing it between stones. She mixed the juice with turpentine and gave it to the child on a little sugar and had her drink a large dose of castor oil disguised in orange juice.

When the midwife was satisfied that the round-worm situation had been handled, she gave the child a large dose of "physic salts" and had her go two days without eating. This, she explained, was so the tape worm would be "good and hungry," and the treatment would be successful. She had the child drink a pint of water in which slippery elm bark had soaked several hours. She next gave the little girl two heaping tablespoons of finely pulverized pumpkin seeds mixed with sugar. The child swallowed this with a glass of milk. Two hours later the granny gave her another large dose of caster oil.

The child truly had been infected with numerous worms of all kinds. The treatment was effective. As Alice told us of the experience, she pointed to a healthy-looking little girl at her side, saying that if she had not gotten help from the granny when she did that child would not be alive today.

There were other migrants we worked with besides Sylvia Williams who believed that illness or bad luck could be caused by a hex. Pedro Ordaz, a Chicano working in the cucumbers of Wisconsin, tried to diagnose his illness in a social sense rather than in a medical sense. Pedro believed his ailments were caused by the curse of someone who envied him his success in life. He and his family spent hours trying to identify certain individuals they knew outside their extended family who might wish Pedro ill. If they could identify the person responsible, they believed, it would then be possible to get something to break the curse so Pedro would recover.

That physical illness may be caused by envy or a curse and can be cured only by a charm is not only believed by most Chicanos and Puerto Rican farm workers but also by many American Indian farm migrants and, to a lesser degree, by Black and white migrants from the deep South and white migrants from the Appalachian and Ozark Mountains. According to Elena Padilla, a person in the Puerto Rican culture protects himself against possible envy of his good health or from being struck ill by fate for bragging about his good health by pretending to have aches and pains.[4] Should he actually become ill, he may resort to a healer, a druggist, the health advice of friends, or he may go to a physician. Should the medical treatment he receives from a physician fail, it is assumed that either the physician is experimenting with the patient and does not know what is wrong or else that the illness is caused by spirits and ghosts and, in that case, must be treated with hot baths and aromatic herbs that can be prescribed only by a spiritualist—an *espiritista*.

Pedro Ordaz and his family drove straight through from Texas to Wisconsin with Pedro doing all of the driving. He bought a bus in Texas from an Anglo who said the wheels had had a recent alignment and the motor was in good repair. The man made him what Pedro considered to be a good offer, one he could not afford to turn down, with payments extended over thirty months. Going into debt in that way over a long period of time was the only way Pedro could ever own a bus and get somewhere in the world. Pedro later told us that when the bus was delivered, he was so proud he drove it all over the Chicano section of his hometown blowing the horn and offering everyone a ride, whether he knew them ot not. He wanted everyone to see him in his big black bus. "See," he kept laughing and shouting as he opened the door for more riders to pack in, "see, I told you someday Pedro would own his own bus, but you didn't believe that day would come. Someday Pedro will even have his own crew, you just wait and see. Someday all of you are going to say, 'that Pedro, what a man.' "

Pedro spent money on several cans of car wax, a buffer pad, and a case of cold beer and had his friends and neighbors come that night to help him polish the old bus to a high gloss except for those places where the rust had crusted over the paint. While the men took turns rubbing the fenders and the body and drinking the beer, Pedro described the performance of his bus in glowing terms. Weeks later he wondered if he had been wise to brag so much or if it might not have been better had he slipped out of town in the middle of the night when everyone was asleep so that no one could put the "evil eye" on him and his bus.

Pedro and his family had barely started on the trip north when the bus began to act as if it were "cursed." There was too much play in the steering wheel, and vehicle "wandered" all over the road unless Pedro fought hard against the steering wheel. A mechanic at a service station where they stopped said it sounded like a worn steering column, but Pedro could not afford to have him check to see if the front spindles needed replacing. Pedro knew the bus should be repaired, that it was not safe to drive, but he did not dare have the mechanic start any work for which he was not prepared to pay. The bus used more oil and gasoline than he had expected, and he would have barely enough money to reach central Wisconsin without paying a major garage bill. When the cucumbers were harvested, then perhaps Pedro would have money for a garage, but first he had to get to Wisconsin; so he struggled on, pulling hard on the steering wheel to hold the bus on the road and praying to his saint that he could avoid any safety check points where the bus would need to be inspected by the police.

Later he told us about the long, hard trip and how his back had ached between the shoulder blades every mile of the way. He said he kept shrugging his shoulders to relieve the tension, but he could do nothing about the pain in his foot and leg. Not even his backache could distract him from the hurt of that foot. There was a new raw spot near his ankle, an open sore that seeped a bloody ooze. The first sore had started a year ago when the razor blade slipped as he was trimming a corn on his middle toe. He had always used an old razor blade to trim his toe nails and cut his corns. That time he had cut too deeply and the spot never healed, although he tried everything suggested.

Once he went to a chiropractor and had a "spinal adjustment" but had received no relief from the pain in his leg. The chiropractor told him one side of his spinal column was "out of line" and thus certain nerves were being pinched, which in turn caused his foot and leg to ache. The chiropractor wanted Pedro to come to his office for a series of eight treatments while he used a new electrical device that, together with the usual spinal manipulation, would "even up" Pedro's spinal column and take the tension off the one side. The series of eight treatments were offered at a special price in a package deal, but when Pedro paid for the first treatment, he decided he could not afford the others, although the chiropractor was very friendly and expressed a good deal of interest in Pedro as a person.

He never went back, although he had a number of notices reminding him of broken appointments and inviting him to return. Once the chiropractor sent him some literature translated into Spanish which showed various organs of the body adversely affected by pinched nerves. Pedro felt proud to have letters from a doctor who spoke Spanish and who took such a personal interest in him and his medical problems. He had never had this sort of attention before from any doctor, and had his work continued in that area he would have gone back to the chiropractor, regardless of the cost of treatment.

He got no further medical attention, however, and the sore spread from his middle toe to his other toes until a mass of open ulcers appeared, and his foot and leg were so swollen and inflamed he could not wear a shoe. While his leg had ached before when he was tired, never in the past year had it bothered him as much as it did on this trip from Texas to Wisconsin. He kept wishing his son, Manuel, could drive, but Manuel was only twelve and even small for his age. Although Manuel was too young to help with the driving, he was at least wiry and strong and could work long hours in the cucumbers, and he could help Marina care for the younger children while Pedro drove.

Marina was pregnant with their eighth child. She was late in her pregnancy, but she, too, was strong; she never had any trouble having babies. She would be able to pick cucumbers by squatting to get near the ground when she was too big and awkward to lean over. She would be able to work a full day right up to the very time the baby was due. She had always worked up to the day of delivery.

One of their children had been born in a wooded area at the edge of the field where they were working. Both Marina and Pedro remembered from the folklore of their childhood village that a woman in labor must keep in motion during the progress of labor and that she must give birth to the baby in a kneeling position supporting herself by holding onto whatever was available. Pedro held her under the arms until it was time to catch the baby so he did not touch the ground. Marina held onto a small tree and lowered herself until the placenta was delivered while Pedro tied the umbilical cord with a lace from his shoe and cut it with his jackknife which he cleaned by jabbing the blade into the hard earth and wiping it on his shirttail. Later, he burned the placenta, as was the custom of his people, and when the fire had died down, he sprinkled dried alhucema (lavender) on the ashes, and Marina stood in the smoke to remove any danger of postpartum hemorrhage. Pedro had carried the dried herbs in the back of his billfold for weeks for that very purpose.

When they got back to the housing and the grower's wife heard what had happened, she insisted that Marina and the baby be taken to the hospital. The doctor in the emergency ward examined them. He said Pedro had done as good a job with the umbilical cord as could be done. He replaced the shoe lace with a sterilized string, trimmed the end of the cord, put a drop of silver nitrate in each eye, weighed the baby and sent him home with Marina saying the hospital would admit only those infants to the nursery who were born in the hospital, and, in this case, neither the baby nor his mother needed to be hospitalized.

Two days later Marina was back working in the fields. She took the baby with her and nursed him under the very tree where he was born and where Manuel kept an eye on him while Marina worked. The grower's wife was aghast at such behavior and insisted that Marina should be in bed and not in the field; she was ruining her health, working so hard this soon after the birth of a baby. Neither Pedro nor Marina could understand why she was so upset. For them it was normal and natural for a woman to have a baby, even to have several babies, and return to work in this way. Women in their peasant culture had for generations been having their babies attended by a sister, a friend, their husband, or at most, attended by a midwife. Women in their culture had always had their babies at home and sometimes in the fields or even in the trucks while they were traveling. It was natural for a woman to have a baby and immedietely go back to work. If the woman had her baby in the field, she might wrap him in her undergarments or her shawl and put him in a shady spot while she continued the harvest. In the evening she would carry him home where she would separate him from the placenta, give him a bath, and burn the placenta.

It was natural for a woman of their culture to have a baby without undue fanfare; it did not seem natural to go to a hospital and to be attended by a staff of doctors and nurses, to be semiconscious from medication, and then to stay in bed for a long period of time and see the baby or hold the baby or feed the baby only when a nurse gave permission. Pedro liked to carry his newborn infant around and show his friends and brag, especially if it were a boy, and in the hospital he could only look at his own child through a glass window, and then the nurse had to point out which baby was his. Somehow all of this did not seem the way things should be with such a normal process as having a baby.

But Pedro would wonder about Marina and the birth of their eighth child when that time came. Now he was more worried about the bus and how it handled than anything else. Without the bus he and his family could not find work. They had worked for the Clarks in Wisconsin for three years and had promised to return this summer and pick cucumbers. Perhaps, Pedro told himself, he had been foolish to buy the bus and try to make the trip on his own. Maybe he was trying to do too much too fast and, therefore, had tempted fate and had aroused the envy of someone not as successful.

Other years Pedro and his family had gone to Wisconsin as part of a crew; maybe he should have gone the same way this year. Yet when the man talked with him about buying the bus, it had sounded like such a good idea. It sounded like a way for him to have something, to save money on transportation, and perhaps someday to have his own crew. Now he wondered if it were the wise thing to do, because apparently he had been beset with the curse of evil wishes which had resulted in a leg that hurt so he could hardly walk.

We worked in the Wisconsin cucumbers with Pedro and his family. Part of the first day he hobbled up and down the rows, bending in the torrid heat to strip even the tiny gherkins from the scratchy vines. But his leg became increasingly swollen, and the flies pestered him unmercifully. Pedro covered the open sores with cigarette papers to keep the flies away. He fanned his leg with his hands, he slapped at the air, but still the flies bothered, buzzing around his head, creeping up his shirt sleeves, biting him wherever they could find an exposed area of skin. Finally Pedro crawled into his bus and closed the door. He elevated his leg on one of the seats and sat in the heat with a folded newspaper to swat any fly that got inside. He sat there musing, trying to figure who it was who could be wishing him such ill fortune. If he could only identify that person, he could find a way to have the hex broken. He was more interested in trying to break the "curse of the evil eye" than he was in trying to find medical treatment for his leg because he was certain that no treatment would be effective unless the curse were broken, and then no treatment would be necessary. He would, however, try suggestions made by fellow migrants.

Someone who had contact with a public health nurse and who did not believe in the curse of the evil eye told Pedro to soak his foot in a strong, almost paste-like solution of Epsom's salts. Pedro understood him to say to soak his foot in strong salt water. He got two pounds of rock salt used for pickling cucumbers and made himself a brine. He submerged his sore foot and then spread the rest of the salt over the top, making a heavy, damp application. The salt burned in the open sores until he screamed with pain. He yelled for Marina and Manuel, shouting he was dying and ordering them to get him a pail of plain water for his foot. He fanned his leg with his fly-swatter newspaper. Still it burned, he said, like fire. The skin looked more inflamed than ever; it was near the point of bleeding. After this painful experience, Pedro was more than ever convinced that he was under the evil power of a witch, and no amount of reasonable persuasion could change his convictions or make him do anything other than try to find out the identity of the witch.

In our close contact with migrant workers we found that Pedro's situation is not unique. Many migrants are in need of medical care but do not trust physicians, nor do they know how to use medical services or even that medical services are available to them. They do not understand the seriousness of their own symptoms or the symptoms of their children or their friends.

We were working in the strawberries in Washington when a child fell off a truck and broke his leg. A routine examination at the local hospital in preparation for administering the anesthetic showed this child to have a malformed heart, rickets, a serious respiratory infection, and impetigo, and yet he had not been viewed as ill by his family. When he coughed and complained of chest pains, his mother diagnosed his problem as a bad cold brought on by the rains and damp fog. She gave him a bottle of cough medicine and dismissed the chest pains as no more serious than normal growing pains for a boy his age. She had had chest pains, she told him, when she was a little girl that her grandmother called growing pains, and she thought her grandmother was right because she did outgrow them.

When we were working in the apples of Virginia, one of the young adolescent pickers was hospitalized with a ruptured appendix from which he later died. He was part of a crew of unattached, nonfamily members that had been put together along the Alabama-Georgia border. His crew leader did not view him as a very ambitious worker and had planned to let him go unless he "got on the ball and spent more time on the ladder." For three days the young picker had been doubling up in the orchard, moaning with pain; but after stretching out on the ground for awhile, he would return to his picking. His friends thought he had cramps from eating too many apples and needed a purgative "to clean him out." On the third day one of the crew members gave him a strong laxative. Five hours later he was dead.

One of the greatest barriers, if not the greatest barrier, to professional services from the viewpoint of the migrant is the lack of respect often conveyed to him through the attitude of the professional person. The migrant is intuitively sensitive to the attitudes of nonmigrants and accurately senses contempt that may be expressed toward him as a person. Sometimes this contempt is expressed unintentionally by the professional person when he questions the judgment or the knowledge of the migrant. The migrant needs to feel that he has some sense of worth. He needs to feel that his culture or his background has equipped him with some means of coping with his everyday problems. He needs "to save face" when he comes to the professional person for help. Too often when he asks for services, he is made to feel like a fool.

One older migrant with whom we worked was angry with a doctor at a public health clinic who had stated emphatically and repeatedly that the migrant could not possibly have the type of affliction he claimed to have. The migrant said he had "catarrh of the head." The doctor said, "There is no such thing as catarrh of the head." The migrant resented the young doctor's attitude, and he expressed his disgust more verbally than most migrants might under the same circumstances. "What kind of doc air you?" he asked. What kind of book larnin' did you git that you kin call yourself a doc when you don't even know about somethin' so common as catarrh of the head?"

The migrant became "so riled" that finally an older staff physician was called to talk with him. This older doctor knew that "catarrh of the head" is a sinus condition caused by repeated colds. In his early practice in West Virginia he had seen many patients with chronic inflammation of the nasal sinuses irritated by coal dust from the mines, dust in the glass factories, or vapors in the chemical plants who had called their condition "catarrh of the head." This physician also understood the Appalachian and Southern rural cultures and the importance for the individual to be right. He could talk to this migrant in words the migrant would understand and would not resent.

He asked the migrant to describe his symptoms and to give his family history. The migrant said there was a lot of "catarrh of the head" in his family. As far back as he could remember, his father had "hacking spells." The physician examined the migrant's ears, nose, and throat and told him he was right in his diagnosis; he did have a severe sinus infection, or as he would call it, "a bad case of catarrh of the head." He hastened to add that modern medical schools do not use the term "catarrh of the head," but that they do teach young doctors to treat it under a new name, "sinus infection." The young doctor here in the clinic was well trained in that specialization; he was one of the best.

"You mean that young whipper-snapper of a doctor knows what to do for it?" the migrant asked, not bothering to veil the irritation he felt toward the younger doctor. "You say he knows what to do for it, but not what to call it?" The migrant shook his head with mock disbelief.

The old doctor winked and patted the farm worker on his shoulder. "We might say it is something like that," he laughed. The migrant smiled for the first time since entering the clinic. He looked more confident, as if he thought perhaps he could get some help in that place for the "ringin' in his head."

This migrant had been allowed to save face by the doctor. He had not been stripped of his dignity. He still felt as if he "knew something." There had in this case been positive communication between a professional and a migrant.

NOTES

1. *I Came Out of the Eighteenth Century* (New York: Harper and Bros., 1942), pp. 63-65. A report on spitting is made in B.A. Botkin, ed., *A Treasure of Southern Folklore* (New York: Crown Publishers, 1949), pp. 591-92. For the story of a "Champeen Terbaccer Chawer" and a tobacco spitting contest, see "Hillbilly Champeen," in *Bundle of Trouble and Other Tarheel Tales*, ed. by W. C. Hendricks (Durham, N.C.: Duke University Press, 1943), pp. 149-55. See also the novel by John Fox, Jr., *The Little Shepherd of Kingdom Come* (New York: Charles Scribner's Sons, 1903), p. 107 for a description of the spitting habits of both children and adults representing

varied social classes in the Cumberland Mountains and in the Blue Grass Region of Kentucky.

2. *Doney-gal* is an expression used by the older Carolina mountaineers. It means a sweetheart. According to Botkin, the term was brought to England from Spain and Italy by British sailors. It later was brought to the New World. "Doney is simply dona or donna, a trifle anglicized in pronunciation." Botkin, *ibid.*, p. 687.

3. Charles S. Johnson comments on this lack of faith in medical doctors which he found in the early 1930s among 600 Black families he studied in central Alabama. He felt that the air of resignation toward sickness and death seen in those families accounted for this lack of faith. *Shadow of the Plantation* (Chicago: University of Chicago Press, 1934), p. 198.

4. *Up From Puerto Rico* (New York: Columbia University Press, 1958), pp. 275-300.

Everything that gets done within a society is done by individuals.

Aldous Huxley, 20th century British author
Brave New World

32

Worker-Employer Relationships: Implications for Labor

Introduction

The problem of farm manpower and worker supervision must be viewed in the overall context of present needs and future trends in American agriculture. Agriculture and farm-labor management came into being as this country was settled. Farm-labor management developed at a time when we were an agrarian society, when the farm owner was also the farm operator and worked in his own fields. The relationship between the farmer and his hired man in those days was a "we" relationship. For the privilege of receiving a few dollars a month and his room and board, the farm worker felt a certain obligation and loyalty to his employer. It was this loyalty to the farm operator that made for a common relationship around mutual tasks.

Most farmers worked side by side with their hired help, supervising them through example and spoken suggestions. When the farmer said "today we'll plow the back field," the hired man knew it was his assignment to take responsibility for the actual plowing.

Although his employer might plow part of the field, it would be the hired man who would work through the afternoon if the owner needed to go to town for a new plow point. Regardless of who spent the greater actual number of hours in the field, the owner and the employee both spoke of their work as a joint enterprise: "our wheat is sprouting" or "our corn will be knee high by the Fourth of July." Because so much of the work was a joint effort, the hired man took a personal interest in everything that happened on the farm, and in turn he held a position of status as the hired man of his employer.

Modern Agriculture

Today fewer than 3 million farmers provide food for nearly 203 million Americans and the overflow goes to the destitute people of undeveloped countries. Although in recent years there has been a trend to fewer farms and workers in the agricultural fields, American farmers produce more and better products each year because of changing technology.[1] Figure 19 shows that although the num-

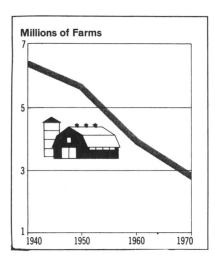
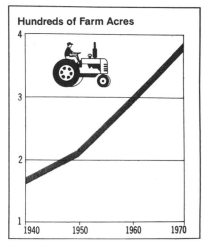

Fig. 19. Number of farms and average size of farms in the United States, 1940-70. (Source: United States Bureau of Agricultural Economics.)

ber of farms in the United States has dropped in recent decades the average size of farms has increased. Agriculture is still big business in almost every state in the United States.

Labor Situation

The greatest lag in agriculture has not been in technological advancement, where the breakthroughs are equal to those in medicine and industry. Rather, the lag has been in the use of manpower. The farm-labor picture today is confused by forcing the traditional hired man, who was adequate for the farm of the 1920s, onto the assembly line of the modern farm.

An additional aspect which must be recognized is the present background, training, and capabilities of available workers today and the kind of supervision they need. It has been recognized by industry that transforming a cotton chopper into an industrial worker involves a good deal more than merely enrolling him in a vocational course. The same is true in agriculture. With continued automation there will be less and less demand for the cotton chopper of the past, but it must be recognized that it takes a good deal of training to equip him to operate or repair the machinery now used to harvest cotton or any other crop. Although in the past agriculture could provide employment for almost anyone, regardless of his educational or intellectual capability, the highly mechanized farms of the future, like industry, will be able to use only those individuals who have specialized training or skill or who have the ability to be trained quickly. Thus, in order to meet the needs of both farmers and workers, a widespread program for training farm workers must be carefully planned and implemented.

Existing Employer-Employee Relationships

Probably there is no other employer-employee relationship that is as complex and temporary as that between the migrant farm laborer and the grower for whom he works. In any one season, even in one week, a migrant can have several employers. Because the employment arrangement is usually made by a crew leader, the worker may not even see the grower for whom he works and thus have no identification with him. If there is a good relationship between the workers and their crew leader there will be the pride of workmanship in what the crew does. If the crew leader is exploitive, there is nothing with which the individual worker can identify, and there may be little if any pride in personal workmanship. There may even be an unconscious anger expressed as hostility toward the grower.

The worker may direct hostility toward the grower because he is white, because he represents the dominant society, or because he is part of the decision-making establishment. Regardless of a worker's feelings toward the employer, the grower, he will have little sympathy for the problems inherent in producing agricultural produce. Even migrants who come from a farm background themselves and who intellectually understand the cost of fertilizer, spray, seed, and the care necessary to produce a crop do not, in their role as farm workers, identify with the problems of management or the problems of producing agricultural products. This is a much different attitude from that of the hired man of the past, whose prestige in the community was related to the prestige position of his employer. He was someone because he was the hired man of the most successful farmer in the valley. His own name might not be remembered, but when he walked into a store and the owner said to him, "Oh, yes, you are Mattson's hired man," he had a sense of personal worth. His identity was tied with the name of his employer, and he received a high degree of emotional satisfaction in the success of that employer. Thus he did everything he could to make his employer more successful and thereby enhance his own position. The hired man of the past invested emotionally of himself to the point where he lost himself in his work and took almost a pride of ownership in the fields and the livestock.

Occasionally a remnant of this sort of identification exists today. But the majority of factory workers, mill workers, and agricultural workers are not interested in the problems of management. It is not realistic to expect them to be interested in management problems. It is not realistic to expect them to understand problems of ownership when the end result, as far as they are concerned, is their paycheck. They see work as a means to an end, as a means of earning money.

To think of work in a creative sense, as the owner of the fields may view his work, is not part of the personal concept of the farm migrant worker. Likewise, it is not realistic to expect the farm worker to give ownership care to tools and supplies; he is not the owner. He is not identified with the problems of replacement or the cost of supplies.

It is very difficult to identify with the needs or wishes of any one employer when there are so many, especially in the case of day-haul workers. It is also difficult for workers to identify with employers whose very way of life is so different from their own. Often the worker envies the grower whom he sees as being extremely wealthy and having the opportunity to make a profit from his crops and to receive thousands of dollars each year in direct payment for cotton, wheat, and feed grain allotments or for the reduction of certain crops under federal price-support programs.[2]

Some farm workers, especially Blacks, have a feeling of injustice because they and their ancestors have had to fetch and carry for those who owned the land. Theirs may be a silent anger, or they may express it in words and actions. They may refuse to take part in what they consider to be demeaning tasks, although these tasks always have been part of what was expected in farming. The Black person may see such tasks as demeaning because they were the only kind of work members of his race were considered to be fitted to do for generations. For him to continue to do these same tasks makes him in his eyes a slave, even as they were slaves.

Other workers envy the security of the grower in never having to travel with the seasons, or they envy his standing in the community. Ruby, one of the workers in the Virginia apple sorting shed who is described in the chapter "Golden Grimes," felt and acted out resentment toward her employer because of her envy for the security of the employer's position of power in the community and active role in the decision-making process. As a migrant worker, Ruby had never felt she was part of any community. Permanent residents had never looked up to her for anything, and that experience she envied in others.

Still other farm workers come from backgrounds where their parents never trusted or identified with employers, and so from early childhood they have been taught to be suspicious of anyone in a position of authority or anyone who employs others. They have been conditioned to believe that all employers "stand on the necks" of their workers.

Needs and Supervision of Workers

One of the best examples of good supervision that we saw in our migrant experiences was that of Lewis Noyes, the sorting-shed superintendent in the orchard where Ruby worked. His ability to relate to individuals, his sense of humor, and his fairness were the assets he brought to the job. Even when he corrected a worker, which he needed to do daily, he did it without stripping the worker of his dignity.

We observed another example of good supervision, also in an apple orchard. We were in upper New York State during the pruning season. A young worker was being taught to trim trees. The supervisor worked on one tree while the young worker worked on another. The novice worker left more than he trimmed. Later he and the supervisor made an inspection tour. The supervisor pointed out a badly trimmed spot on the tree where the young migrant had worked and said, "One of us left a lot of water sprouts on that tree; we'll have to get 'em off closer than that." Later the worker told us how he felt about the orchard foreman: "He knew, and I knew he knew who did the lousy pruning job. He did not have to tell me to redo it. I wanted to do it right to please him." The worker had saved face, yet his mistake had been pointed out.

We saw other examples of foremen who understood workers and knew ways to help them to do the best job possible. We saw supervisors who could give encouragement with a deep sense of respect for people and, at the same time, give direction and make corrections. We also saw the opposite—supervisors who were condescending, who were contemptuous of the workers, who were unfair, and who were even sadistic in their demands.

In one packing shed I was instructed in how to pack fruit by the shed boss. He showed me how to put liners in his baskets. "Do you think you've sense enough to follow orders on these slips?" he asked. "You're on fancy pack," he said, "so only pack the best ones. Good color! Good fruit! Got sixty orders here for half and half, half pink grapefruit, half temples, or half kings. Now watch it, and don't mess up and mix these oranges. One of a kind to an order. Now this is a temple orange, and this is a king orange. Think you've got enough sense to tell the difference? Now get to it! I'll keep an eye on you an' if you mess 'em up, out you go and faster than you came in." I had not been singled out because I was a woman or because of the color of my eyes. He used the same approach with all of the workers. They were stupid, senseless, useless rifraff.

But if the workers were Black he had even greater contempt. It was the afternoon of my second day in the shed; the Black workers, young and old, dumped boxes from the tractors. Each box held nearly two bushels. Earlier an orange dropped on the concrete walkway and was mashed underfoot. One old man slipped on the wet floor and lost his balance. He struggled to stay upright. The box on his shoulder swayed in a wide arc. Some oranges slid from his box, dropped onto the conveyor belt, and were carried into a different variety. It was an accident, but it was all the packing-shed boss needed. He announced in a loud voice for all to hear, "Just like a nigger to do something like that. Just like a filthy, dirty, black nigger to mess things up. Niggers are all stupid. They're animals. They're mules. You can't teach a nigger anything."

The smile on the old man's face was fixed. His eyes were expressionless. There was an atmosphere of discomfort in the building, a sense of controlled hatred that welled out toward the platform boss from both the Black workers and many of the white workers who sensed that this supervisor had no more respect for them than he had for the Black man he was addressing and who now stood before him with quiet dignity. The shed boss seemed oblivious to the feelings of his workers. As far as he was concerned that was how a boss spoke to those who worked in the harvest. It was how a person in authority should act.

Another grower for whom we worked in a different state had the vilest tongue I have ever heard. He personally inspected the harvested fruit, and when he found some not to his liking because it was bruised or mashed, he used profanity and four-letter words to describe his opinion of everyone who worked in his orchard. He never approached an individual worker to criticize workmanship, but he aired his feelings openly, and his opinion of those who worked for him could be described only in the filthiest and the vilest of language.

None of us had control over our race, our nationality, or the place where we were born. Any of us resent criticism when it becomes a personal attack; and yet this sort of an approach is often used with farm workers. It is not unusual for a farm operator, grower, or field foreman, when criticizing workmanship or when disciplining a worker, to depart from the subject of the work itself, which often should be criticized and corrected, and instead to attack the person as worthless, lazy, and stupid or else to use the situation as an opportunity to voice racial, sexual, or ethnic prejudice. "Only a stupid hillbilly would do a thing like that. . . . You dirty Mexicans don't know how to live in decent housing. . . . Only a weak-minded woman would come up with that idea. . . ."

Training

Most followers of the harvest have not been trained to harvest crops efficiently. They often destroy vines, bruise fruit, and leave unpicked large amounts of fruits and vegetables simply because they do not know how to pick rapidly. A thorough training session would be profitable in which the workers would be shown how to harvest more thoroughly and told why it is necessary to harvest a certain crop in a certain way. As in any training program, instructions would need to be redemonstrated and repeated, but in the long run it would be profitable for the grower.

Automation has frequently created special problems for individuals who were proficient in one crop but not in any other. One cotton picker, who was part of a large labor force that was phased out in his state by mechanical pickers, found that he was unable to make enough to cover traveling expenses in the cucumbers of New Jersey and did even worse in the potatoes of New York. He had thirty years of experience picking cotton, but that was not too helpful in potatoes or cucumbers. A whole new set of muscle movements was necessary; a whole new concept of harvesting was mandatory if he was to make a livelihood in a crop he had never harvested before. Cotton harvesting in his area of the South was always prolonged over weeks and months. Once ripe, the cotton ball would hang until it was picked. Cucumbers had to be picked immediately or they would be too large to be harvested. There was much about the harvest of cucumbers that was different from picking cotton, and there was much the worker was not able to learn by himself; but no one gave him instructions. So he continued to make a poor showing. His work day became expensive for him as well as for his crew leader and for the grower.

At the opposite extreme from no instruction at all, we saw a number of growers or field foremen who insisted that everything be done exactly as they would have done it had they themselves been harvesting the crop. If they were right handed they thought everyone else should be right handed. Either of these two extremes leaves workers confused and angry.

Problems Identified by the Workers Themselves

The working environment itself rather than the hard physical labor is seen as a problem by farm employees. In the past there has been very little effort to consider the comfort or even the health and well-being of farm workers, whether in terms of their working, living, or traveling conditions. Investing a few extra dollars in portable toilets and supplying fresh drinking water to workers in the field have always increased production. Yet such basic "innovations" as these have been a long time in coming. The well-being of the workers must also be protected in other ways.

Safety

The farm employer must develop greater safety measures for workers in agriculture. Many accidents could be prevented if protective chain guards were used on conveyors, if orchard ladders were kept in top-notch condition, if picking containers were regulated as to size for men and women and children, if poisonous insecticides and weed killers were used or stored more carefully, if workers were more carefully instructed in the use of moving equipment, and if rules and regulations on the use of such equipment were established and enforced by the growers or by the field foremen.

Many packing sheds and grading plants in use at this time on farms and in farm communities all over the country would not pass inspection by a safety engineer. In some cases the grading platform is a makeshift construction set up for temporary use. There are few guardrails. Steps are often weak, slanted at the wrong angle; the risers are uneven so that a person going up and down cannot gauge the length of his or her step, especially if carrying an object. Steps are used in many places where a ramp would be safer, especially a concrete ramp that would not rot or be weakened by termites or pushed out of line by a truck. Some grading platforms do not have either steps or a ramp; instead, workers must jump up and down dangerous heights.

Housing

Unsafe conditions can also be found in the living quarters of farm migrant workers and farm tenants as well as in that generally available to low-income families in rural areas. Providing good housing, however, is more than providing adequate physical surroundings. The attitude of those who provide the housing is also important according to the farm workers themselves. Two years ago my husband and I visited one of the best labor camps we had seen anywhere in the United States. It had a play area for children. It had privacy for families. It had hot and cold running water and bathing facilities. The grower, an immigrant from Austria, was a perfectionist who had the reputation of being impossible to please. He had lost two crews at the peak of the harvest a few days before our visit. One crew had gone to a grower a few miles away who had one of the worst housing camps in the state and, we might add, one of the worst we have seen in the country. A description of this poor housing and the reasons one family gave for leaving the good camp are in the chapter, "By Their Own Choice." It gets into the real crux of the matter—that of employer-employee relationships—which will be explored later in this chapter.

Payments as Promised

In all parts of the country workers have expressed concern to us about their wages. Confusion over payments and/or bonuses is a critical issue. Chapter 20, "To Pick a Lug of Cherries," gives an example of a situation where workers thought they were being paid more than they actually received. Of the more than 1,000 migrant couples we interviewed on this subject, 6 percent said they did not even know the rate of payment they were supposed to receive for their work. In many cases where they had some prior understanding, they said the payment was much less than what they had been led to expect at the time they were recruited.

Improving Worker-Employer Relationships

Although housing, wages, and working conditions are vitally important, the most important ingredient of all is the worker-employer relationship, just as it is in industry or among professional workers. In fact, the real motivation for a job change among professionals and other workers is not so much better salary as it is what the authors of *The Motivation to Work* have called "job attitude factors"—the real reasons that cause someone to stay on a job or move to something else.[3] For example, the worker might move because he thinks the new job will enhance his work experience through greater recognition from new superiors or peers. The individual worker needs to feel that he is an important or valued part of the work experience. How his employer views his worth is expressed in the wages paid, working conditions, and the attitudes expressed. Worker-employer relationships start with recruitment and the honesty of the recruiter in spelling out the new working conditions and benefits. There is a tendency to oversell working conditions and the benefits of the new job—a job which, for the farm worker, may not even exist because too many other workers have been recruited.

Recruitment

The problem of pirating or stealing workers from other growers and high-pressuring them into coming into a certain area has been detrimental to worker-employer relationships. Many workmen feel that they were promised one thing only to find another when they arrived on the job—working conditions or payments were not as they had been described. Sometimes the misrepresentation came from a crew leader who obviously was exploiting his own people. In other cases, the people felt that the recruiting contractor who had come to them had misrepresented the job or had not prepared them for weather changes, for expenses, or for the lack of acceptance they would experience.

Further mechanization, increased opportunities for nonfarm

employment, and new social and legislative policies and laws affecting conditions under which agricultural laborers may be employed will influence the structure of the agricultural force of the future. Although the number of migrant workers needed in hand labor will decrease, those who continue to be employed on farms will demand better supervision and working conditions. They will demand and they will receive wages in line with those provided in industry for comparable skilled, semiskilled, and unskilled positions. In order to make the best use of workers, the employers' actual need for workers on certain kinds of jobs must be assessed more critically. Too often 100 farm workers are recruited to an area when only fifty workers are needed.

Systems Analysis

How many workers are really needed to handle a harvest? What skills do they need? How long will the harvest take? What are the variables, such as weather? A simple form of systems analysis in recruitment of seasonal workers would answer these questions and help in solving the following problems:

1. Where is the supply of workers? How far will they have to travel to the next job? Where and when is the demand for their service? What could a community do to provide year-round work in order to hold agricultural workers in the area of greatest needs?
2. Agriculture will need to develop better job descriptions by making more time studies and identifying actual skills wanted in workers.
3. There needs to be an educational or training system to show workers how to do the job that is expected of them.
4. The labor market will become more competitive. It is going to be increasingly difficult to find good workers for agriculture. Automation will help with the harvest, but automation alone is not the answer. There will continue to be jobs that need people. There will also continue to be rural people who need jobs. The problem is how to recruit and train workers. Agriculture can take a lesson from business. It takes more than wages to attract and hold workers.

Working conditions, worker-employer relationships, fringe benefits, and the public image of the employer—these are factors of real importance. The present image of the farmer or the grower as an employer is not a positive one, and that is part of the present recruitment problem. The public image of agriculture as the occupation of choice is also not a positive one, and that needs to be recognized. If people are going to be attracted to agriculture as a lifetime career, then the image of agriculture must be improved. Agriculture must be seen as an industry, and as a very important one in the economy of the country. But what must be seen even more clearly is that worker-employer relationships are the very core of that industry, even as such relationships are the core of all other kinds of employment. Therefore, the needs of farm workers for adequate working conditions, supervision, and fringe benefits are no different from workers in any other business or industry in this country.

NOTES

1. Since World War II American farms have each year been fewer in number, larger in size, more specialized, and have had higher capital investments with fewer persons involved in actual farm work. In the twenty-five year period from 1945 to 1970 the percentage of labor force involved in agriculture decreased from 25 to 5, and the figure has dropped even more in the 1970s with fewer migrant workers being used. Farms decreased in number from 5.6 million in 1950 to 3.2 million in 1967 and, by 1971, to 2,876,000, which is 1.5 percent less than in 1970 and 25 percent less than a decade ago. An article in the November 6, 1971 issue of the *Michigan Farmer* says that the number of farms in operation in the early 1970s is the smallest number since the 1870s. The size of farms has also changed with new advances in technology, new machinery, new plant breeding, chemical control of weeds and pestilence, new planting methods so that fewer workers can operate more acreage and can produce more products from the acreage. The average-size farm in 1950 was 213 acres; by 1961 this size had increased to 306 acres and by 1971 had grown to 383. According to the United States Chamber of Commerce, in mid-1971 each farmer was supplying forty-three people with food and fiber, whereas twenty-five years previously each farmer supplied only fourteen persons and in 1900 supplied seven.

The United States Department of Agriculture reports that one farm worker in 1972 is producing food, fiber, and other commodities for forty-seven persons. The United States Department of Agriculture also says that, despite the continuing decline in farm population, farming remains the nation's biggest industry. Farming employs some 4.5 million workers, as many as the combined employment in transportation and public utilities. And one out of every five jobs in private industry is related to agriculture.

Agriculture's assets in 1972 totaled $319 billion, equal to about two-thirds of the value of the capital assets of all United States corporations, or about half the market value of all corporation stocks listed on the New York Stock Exchange. Some 2.9 million United States farms realized a gross farm income of over $56.6 billion in 1969; while 1,840,000 farms sold less than $2,500 worth of products, another 260,000 had sales of $2,550 to $4,999; these farm families with incomes of $5,000 or less are the farmers who are listed among the poor in the rural areas.

2. A 1972 Comptroller General's Report to the U.S. Congress states: "From 1966 to 1970 the Department of Agriculture paid between $2.5 *billion* and $3.3 *billion* annually to growers of upland cotton, wheat, and feed grain under three commodity price-support programs. Late in 1970, because of concern about the cost of the farm programs and about the number of large individual payments [in 1970 17 producers received between $500,000 and $3.5 million dollars each and 300 producers received more than $100,000 each], the Congress enacted legislation limiting to $55,000 the total of direct federal payments a person could receive annually under each of these programs." Even in the face of this type of legislation, through the combination of farms and the establishment of new partnerships, the Comptroller's report shows that several individuals in 1971 were still able to collect considerably more than $55,000 in commodity price-support programs. U.S., Comptroller General, *Report to the Congress: Payment Limitation under 1971 Cotton, Wheat, and Feed Grain Programs Had Limited Effect on Reducing Expenditures,* April 12, 1972, p. 1.

3. The factors identified by Frederick Herzberg, *et al.,* that cause a worker to move because he thinks they will enhance his work experiences are greater

1. Recognition from superiors or peers
2. Possibility for personal growth with opportunities for additional education or a chance to work with a recognized authority in a certain field
3. Interpersonal relations with superiors, subordinates, and/or peers
4. Advancement through a change in status, rank, or position
5. Delegated responsibility
6. Variety in work assignments (more creative or less difficult work)
7. Job security as represented by tenure or company stability
8. Status position with a private secretary, private office, or a company car

Herzberg and his colleagues also feel that "one of the tragedies of modern industries is that many workers do not have the sense of making a genuine contribution . . . many jobs have been broken down into small parts . . . the result is that many people have little idea of what they are doing from the standpoint of real relation to the finished product, or to the social order as a whole." *The Motivation to Work* (New York: John Wiley and Sons, Inc., 1959), pp. 44-54 and p. 27.

Migration in this case may be a fight against being controlled by a job. The move can give the individual a feeling that he *does* have self-determination, that he has *some* authority to direct his own affairs. Even migrant agricultural workers may at times use migration as a means of escaping from a situation that to them is intolerable.

*—it's all adding up and one of these days
we're going to pay the bill for it.*

Harper Lee, 20th century
American authoress
To Kill a Mockingbird

33

Deprivation Amid Abundance:
Implications for Social Welfare

There has been a tendency in recent years not only to equate poverty with deprivation but also to classify all those who are poor as culturally or socially deprived and, conversely, all those whose income places them in the affluent category as nondeprived. Such classifications both deny different levels of deprivation and provide an inadequate and even an inaccurate measure of both deprivation and individual needs. To classify all poor as being culturally or socially deprived is incomprehensible and only creates myths and barriers to the use of services.

In any standard dictionary *deprivation* means the state of (1) being deprived of; (2) having been taken away from; (3) being kept from having. It is in this broader sense—beyond financial circumstances—that I will examine deprivation.

This chapter is an adaptation of two previous works: *Changing Services for Changing Clients* (New York: Columbia University Press, 1969), pp. 55-80, and a paper presented at the National Association of Social Workers Regional Institute in Norfolk, Virginia, October 8, 1968. A condensation of the latter paper was published as "Communicating with the Migrant," *Child Welfare*, XLIX (March 1970), 137-45.

There are many ways to be deprived—socially, physically, economically, spiritually, culturally, emotionally, and intellectually.

> ... the conditions of disadvantage can often be characterized just as significantly by the excess of certain kinds of stimulation or environmental attributes as by the absence or limitations of others. To be disadvantaged or deprived is to be exposed for example, to an excess of stigmatizing experiences, an excess of failure in school, etc. In short, the nature or disadvantage requires a conceptualization not only of what is limited or lacking, but also of what can be interpreted as excessive. Both conditions may, in addition, be present simultaneously in a given situation.[1]

Both may also be causative factors of behavior.

Examples of Deprivation Other Than Financial Deprivation

Mankind consists of social beings who need interaction with other human beings. If opportunities for such interaction are limited or nonexistent, if socialization is impaired, then a person is *socially* disadvantaged or *deprived*. He feels isolated. He experiences alienation. If an individual is mentally or physically handicapped, he is disadvantaged in that his physical or mental impairment keeps him from having the same experiences as the non-handicapped. He is, in that case, *physically* or *mentally deprived.*

The illegitimate child is *deprived of his legal right* to a name and to a social and legal heritage. There is always *deprivation in the four Ds* of the broken home: (1) death , (2) divorce, (3) desertion, and (4) disorganization. Anything that prevents a child from having a meaningful relationship with both parents is a form of deprivation, although physically the child may have adequate care.

The word *deprivation* is often used *medically* to describe an agent of disease. Prolonged deprivation of food brings about tissue malnutrition and eventually death by starvation. *Deprivation of specific foods* can be clinically diagnosed and labeled. Scurvy, resulting from lack of vitamin C, is a classic example. Certain kinds of psychological deprivation can also create irreversible physical stress. Deprivation, stress, and infections are not usually separate agents in the causes of disease. They are all part of one cycle—the breakdown in the defenses of the body that overcomes its tolerances, beats down its resistance, and in short, dangerously and perhaps fatally upsets the consistency of its internal environment. No matter which one of the three phases of the cycle—deprivation, stress, or infection—irritates a disease process or appears most plainly in it, the other two are always present.

Next to *economic deprivation*, so-called *maternal deprivation* is seen most often by social workers. Maternal deprivation was first discussed by Rene A. Spitz in a study that aroused much debate. Spitz said that when the mother is not emotionally present during a child's early infancy, and no adequate substitute takes her place, there is a pattern of retarded development, listlessness, and dwindling energy that often ends in mental illness or even death.[2] This is a phenomenon not dependent on income or on social class, but on the failure of the child to get emotional mothering.

> To speak, for example, of maternal deprivation as an explanation is to attempt to account for certain characteristics of infant development by the absence of the mother rather than by the presence of some specifiable set of environmental conditions. While mother absence may be a useful and convenient way to summarize or symbolize the conditions which will likely be present, the important point is that development is likely to be invariant with or related to the conditions which are present, not with those which are absent.[3]

The deprived, affectionless child presents as his major symptoms (1) reduced capacity to establish deep relationships; (2) inadequate social awareness and identification; (3) inability to control impulses adequately; and (4) limited capacity for insight. In the child's thought process there is marked concreteness with poor conceptualization, which limits fantasy life and creativity. Basic and rote learning are less affected.

Disturbances in any of a child's multiple aspects of functioning may lead to symptoms of learning retardation or *educational deprivation*. Ralph B. Rabinovitch, psychiatrist and director at Hawthorne Center in Northville, Michigan, says that the most common single and immediate cause for referral to his clinic is academic or social difficulty experienced by children in school.[4] He feels that this suggests the need for intensive study of the meaning of the school experience and ways in which that experience affects the child, as well as the influence of the child's capabilities and personality on the learning process. The most important aspects of functioning, Rabinovitch says, are (1) general intelligence, (2) specific capabilities, (3) developmental readiness, (4) emotional freedom to learn, (5) motivation, and (6) opportunity.[5]

The problem of primary retardation in reading apparently reflects a basically disturbed pattern of neurological organization. The cause is biological. Although definite statistics are not available, it is likely that the majority of children totally or severely retarded in reading have a primary problem, that is, their reading retardation is a symptom of disturbance in some other area. Often reading retardation is an indication that the child does not have emotional freedom to learn. The learning disability itself could be a form of counteraggression, anxiety, depression, self-denial, self-punishment, or symbolic association affecting learning areas—any one of which would be an outward expression of emotional deprivation.

An individual may also know extreme *emotional deprivation,* resulting in a lack of basic trust in others or in a poor self-concept. Financially, this person may be part of the affluent society, yet he or she is deprived. There are many individuals with great material wealth who have no personal philosophy, no purpose in life. They are bored. They feel that life has no meaning for them. They may experience anomie. They are *deprived spiritually.*

In their book *Toward Understanding Human Personalities,* Robert Leeper and Peter Madison give much food for thought when they point out that a vast majority of those in the affluent part of American society today are experiencing emotional deprivation or emotional "poverty." They say:

> Ultimately this [type of deprivation] may be what lies back of many of our difficulties of modern life. If so, it may explain, to a considerable degree, the selfishness and competitiveness that creep into so many situations. People may be seeking big incomes . . . not because they enjoy great wealth as such, but because they have been badly frustrated in their hunger for a meaningful life and they know that a large income has been one means of securing such a measure of emotional vividness. . . .[6]

These two authors call attention to what they have identified as some *indirect expressions of the feeling of emotional poverty:*

(1) *Pseudohungers for food as an expression of emotional poverty.* Craving for food that the individual does not really need and would not eat were it not for his emotional hunger. (2) *An exhorbitantly increased demand for closer human relationships as one effect of emotional poverty.* Dependency upon and the demand for more satisfaction from close human relationships than reasonably can be expected in a marriage or a friendship. Some people want others almost to revere them. (3) *Overdependence on sexual satisfaction as a compensation for emotional poverty.* (4) *The powerful and insistent demands of material comforts may be an expression of emotional deprivation in other respects.* Many persons who study our society come to feel that our interest in material products of our technology far exceeds their value as a means to a fuller life. (5) *Much interest in violence (directly or through fantasy) may be an expression of emotional poverty.* A survey of radio and television programs reported that killings and attempted murders were the two most popular topics on seven stations which were watched for a period of one week. A total of five hundred and eighty-eight killings and/or other crimes were counted, that is, eighty-four a day, or one every seventeen minutes day and night.[7]

Leeper and Madison think there are certain factors conducive to emotional poverty in our society.

(1) *Conformity Pressures* in a country founded in part on a belief in rugged individualism . . . each year it seems to become more difficult to be one's own individual self. . . .

(2) *Blue-Ribbon Motivation:* The individual is asked to be on top in his field, regardless of what it is. Even hobbies often become competitive. "One difficulty about blue-ribbon motivation is that it guarantees that most of the group will be losers. . . ."

(3) *Oversaturation of Major Interests:* [There is] an extensive concentration on one single activity.

(4) *The Neglect and Belittling of Concrete Perceptual Experiences:* Our culture has laid stress upon abstract knowledge and standardization. . . . [It has been forgotten that] some of our emotional experiences spring from things around us that impinge directly . . . upon us, that are perceived as having color, warmth, vitality and are likely to be as down to earth as the play of color in the fireplace, the feel of wind and rain. . . .

There is even a lot of tacit disapproval of living in the present in our middleclass culture. It is as if we had some leftovers from past religions [which prohibit] investing too heavily in present earthly pleasures. . . .[8]

Who Are the Disadvantaged?

There are currently three major kinds of financial poverty in the United States: (1) insular poverty—a depressed area such as Appalachia, where work patterns have changed; (2) case poverty—chronic, long-term, intergenerational poverty; and (3) functional poverty—those individuals and families who do not live in the usual pockets of poverty or who are not chronically disabled but who may function emotionally, socially, and economically at the poverty level.

Deprivation among Those in Rural Areas

Too often social workers have been concerned only with the poverty of urban areas, and yet close to one-third of America's youth live in a great diversity of areas described as "rural." Youths from such communities are less fitted for successful competition in our modern, urbanized society than their urban counterparts. They assign less importance to education. Dropout rates are high, reflecting the low educational level of parents or the attitude of parents toward education. School failure may, therefore, reflect low verbal skill, low self-esteem, or hostility toward parents or school personnel. With the decreasing number of unskilled and semiskilled jobs, all youths from low-income backgrounds are handicapped in competing for higher status occupations, and rural youths are severely handicapped in occupational achievement if they are not prepared for nonagricultural employment and if such nonagricultural employment is not made more readily available in rural areas.

Deprivation among Spanish-Americans

Poverty and deprivation are widespread among the Spanish speaking, both the 3,500,000 Chicanos (Spanish-speaking Texans) and Manitos (Spanish-speaking New Mexicans) and the 750,000 Puerto Rican American citizens. Even in similar urban areas, the

Spanish speaking more frequently live in poorer housing, are more overcrowded, and have less adequate sanitary facilities than their non-Spanish-speaking neighbors. Educational levels among Spanish-American adults are between three to six years below those of the total white population. One-fourth to one-half of the Spanish-American adults are functionally illiterate and school dropout rates remain high among Spanish-American youths. Because of lower levels of education and lack of skill, the unemployment rates among Spanish-American males are three to four times higher than among other white workers.

Deprivation among Blacks

Displacement of workers from agriculture combined with technological changes have made farm tenants expendable and have forced large numbers of Blacks into urban centers, both within and outside the South. The personal and social adjustment of these families has been greatly complicated because they are less educated and trained for job competition in their new surroundings. In many cases the adjustments to urban living are so difficult that families are more deprived than they were before their migration.

Deprivation among Whites

With so much national focus on minorities in recent years, poor whites in rural areas are feeling more neglected and rejected than any other racial group. Rural poor whites have always tended to mistrust anyone who was not part of their immediate communication network on the supposition that strangers or people outside of their direct experience would reject them. This traditional mistrust, coupled with current national emphasis on minorities, has led them to expect further rejection. They, therefore, endeavor to avoid the repetition of the painful experience of rejection by rejecting others first. Their mistrust also derives from lack of confidence in their ability to carry social responsibilities. Because of limited opportunity to acquire vocational, homemaking, or child-rearing skills, they develop a deep sense of inadequacy. They realize their inadequacies precipitate disapproval and criticism, and in an attempt to protect themselves, they tend to avoid close contact with people outside their family or they tend to deny they have problems.

They may even deny they are hungry, fearing they will be thought of as "worthless trash." For the same reason, they are often reluctant to discuss their situation frankly with persons who endeavor to help them. Their fear of criticism leads them to deny the existence of problems and to evade helping efforts.

Deprivation among American Indians

Of all racial and ethnic groups in the United States, the most deprived are the American Indians. Their housing is the poorest. Many live in earthen hogans, floorless log cabins, or year-round in tents in the Dakotas. Many have never known the luxury of electricity. They carry their water from a river or stock-watering pond. Indians are the least educated of any group in America today and have the highest rate of unemployment—in Alaska it is 80 percent and over. Their health needs are also the greatest, and their death rate is the highest.

The combination of the American Indian's present deprivation and the historical exploitation of his race causes many of his current problems. The effects of poverty long experienced by the Indian are compounded by the indifference and apathy of the general public and by his own inability to articulate his needs through the press or the ballot box. Among the more than half-million Indians, more than half are under twenty years of age.

Characteristics of the Disadvantaged

Poor Self-Esteem

There is abundant evidence that low self-esteem has destructive effects upon human behavior. There is also considerable evidence that persons who live under conditions involving family disorganization, financial instability, and social, sexual, or racial discrimination are likely to have low self-esteem. The destructive consequences of a poor opinion of self could be considered at length, but even a brief listing of the most evident consequences indicates that pervasive social, personal, and vocational harm results from such negative attitudes toward self. Thus we find that persons of low self-esteem tend to fear success; they tend to be socially withdrawn and apprehensive; they are inclined to reject their own perceptions and judgments and accept those of others; and often they tend to lack the social skills and ease which make for friendships and social participation. They are likely to be self-conscious and preoccupied with their own deficiencies, or they are preoccupied with their own anger at being perceived to have such deficiencies. In either case, they run the danger of being overwhelmed with feelings of helplessness and hopelessness. Such feelings are expressed in higher levels of anxiety, higher levels of (psychosomatic) symptoms, and reduced effectiveness in performing academic and vocational tasks. A sense of hopelessness may be the cause of the so-called lack of productivity on the part of employed women.[9] Lacking trust in their capacities and anticipating failure, which may be represented by lower salaries, lack of promotions, and lack of equal job opportunities, individuals with low self-esteem are inclined to be cautious in their exploration and limited in the risks they will assume. They are usually quick to cease their efforts. Convinced their powers are too limited to have favorable influence upon their future lives, they tend to lose hope and adopt a pessimistic and fatalistic view toward the failures and unhappiness that presumably await them.[10]

Studies report that many effects of low self-esteem occur among disadvantaged youths, particularly those likely to suffer from prejudice and social repudiation. J.S. Coleman's study of school children revealed that feelings of helplessness and inferiority, e.g., inability to affect one's future, were pronounced among Black youth.[11] Other studies point to feelings of passivity and defeatism among the poor regardless of race and underline the effects of self-image on the expectations of failure.[12] Helen H. Davidson and Gerhard Lang report that lower-class children believe that teachers reject them and expect them to fail, and they acquire their teachers' (negative) perceptions of themselves.[13]

Women, likewise, have been conditioned to accept the fact that they will receive lower salaries, fewer and slower promotions, and less recognition for their contributions and accomplishments.[14] In many instances where self-esteem has not been examined directly, observations of other attitudes, interests, and motives provide indirect indications of defeatism, anxiety, and withdrawal. Individuals who are known to be very capable seem to give up or not risk trying, and the only explanation is that they do not feel they have the right to succeed.[15]

Mistrust of Others

Deprived persons and/or their relatives usually have known some form of discrimination and are often subjected to rejection by the community in which they live. As a result they tend to isolate themselves from their neighbors.

One of the chief characteristics of both adults and children who come from deprived backgrounds is their lack of trust in others. The relationship with the parent, especially the mother, grants permission to the young child to reach out and trust others and to achieve the first developmental task—developing trust as opposed to mistrust.[16] If the parent does not trust the outside world or strangers, the child, too, will lack trust. The individual who is always suspicious of the motivation of others is a deprived person, although historically there may have been a valid basis for his parents' mistrust.

Fear of Authority

Because of their extreme mistrust, deprived persons have an exaggerated fear of authority. Everyone may have some fear of authoritative agencies, particularly of the courts, but individuals from deprived experiences have greater fears. Such persons feel threatened even by those who may have limited legal authority and whose approach is nonauthoritative. They are often afraid of their social worker regardless of the agency represented. They have a distorted view of the relationship to community institutions and endow them with greater powers than they actually have.

Socially deprived individuals often have strong feelings of anger, aggression, and hostility intermingled with their mistrust and fear. These hostile feelings, which may be natural reactions to their deprived social status, vary considerably both in intensity and form of expression. Some persons are openly hostile and aggressive, while others attempt to hide their negative feelings behind a facade of friendliness and extreme politeness. Another way to mask anger, hate, or hostility is with humor, to play the clown. This is the role of the comedian who amuses his audience at the same time he insults them, or others. Some comedians are very caustic or sadistic in the name of humor, and if anyone dares to question them that person has "no sense of humor" or cannot take a "joke." A joke, story, or pun thus becomes the defense to release personal hostility and anger. The anger stems not so much from current dissatisfaction, but from the painful and unhappy experiences suffered throughout life. Often these resentments go back to early childhood when such individuals themselves were exposed to neglect, abuse, or abandonment, or to a time when their parents or grandparents experienced discrimination.

Hopelessness

Deprived persons have a sense of hopelessness that underlies all other feelings. Many of the parents of today's deprived children suffer from a deep feeling of depression, under which is extreme anger, and their acting-out behavior is an attempt to ward off such depression. They find temporary escape by going on a drinking or spending spree, by sexual promiscuity, by fighting, or by engaging in delinquent acts. The acting-out behavior is not always expressed toward the actual source of the frustration; it may instead be projected onto others who in turn become victims.

Projected Anger

An example of this comes to mind from our migrant farm worker experience. It involved a Chicano father we met in a western state. He promised his wife and six children that when they were paid at the end of the week he would take them to a certain little restaurant for a meal. From the street they could see that the tables were prettily decorated with bright tablecloths and artificial flowers like the restaurants in old Mexico. It did not look too expensive. They could afford it, once. On Saturday the family "dressed" for their party. When they arrived at the restaurant they were turned away at the door although they could see many empty tables inside. The owner said they were "too large a party" to be served on such a busy day. To the family it was as if he said, "the likes of you are not allowed here."

How, under these circumstances, does a man save face in the eyes of his wife and children? How especially does he save face when, as a Chicano, he is the undisputed head of his household? How does he answer his children's question "why?" He could not express his anger to the restaurant owner. He would be jailed. He masked his true feelings as he walked away, but his anger was there, a sullen deep anger that multiplied. Each time he recalled the experience he was reinsulted. He remembered himself standing in the doorway surrounded by his children, asking permission to be seated and to order food. He saw himself as a begger being turned away. His anger welled inside; it had to be expressed or he felt he would burst. He bought two bottles of wine and drank them both on an empty stomach before returning to the migrant housing. Intoxicated, he became violent, kicking out screens, breaking furniture and windows, swearing. He was not angry with the grower who provided the housing. He had found the grower very humane; but he was angry with what the grower represented. The grower was symbolic of people who could go to any restaurant and not be turned away. So the migrant vented his rage. He felt it was the only redress he had except for employing a form of *brujeria* (witchcraft) to put the curse of the evil eye on the restaurant owner.

Social workers may be on the receiving end of projected hostility, as was this grower. Sometimes the social worker is the first individual in the life of a migrant who is interested enough to express concern for his well-being. If so, how well can he handle the migrant's projected anger? How well can he take a verbal attack which seems to be directed more toward him as an individual than toward the agency he represents? Especially, how well can he handle this situation when it involves a client whose position he has defended? In this day and age it is mandatory for social workers who work with the deprived to understand anger and how to handle anger—their own anger and that of others.

Many other concepts are also necessary for effective work with those whose cultures are different. For example, superstition in folk culture, such as the concept of the evil eye, should be understood by social workers.[17]

Superstition

Superstition is rooted in an unconscious fear of succeeding. The individual has a strong need to fail because he believes that if he is too successful others will be envious of him. If they are envious of him, they will wish him "bad luck." He believes not only that they have the power to make the wish, but that theirs is a "magical wish" and will cause him misfortune. Under these circumstances it is far better for him to be poor because he knows that those who are very poor envy those who have. Those who do not succeed envy those who do. It is believed by his culture that it is safer to be envious than it is to be envied. Not only is it dangerous to be in a position of being envied, it is lonely. One is set apart from one's family, neighbors, friends, or associates. It is felt that one must be vain and endowed with self-importance, a virtual strutting peacock, even to want to be different. An individual who wants to be different must think himself superior. This concept is expressed as: "He thinks he is too good for the rest of us. It was good enough for his pappy, and it should be good enough for him."

How the individual accepts his position and his sex role in life indicates what he is willing to do about his situation. Some people fight against poverty and try to rise above it; others seem to accept it as their lot in life, and some, usually middle aged or older, even go so far as to indicate that poverty is all they have a right to expect. They accept their present circumstances with a sort of passivity.

Passivity

Sometimes a person's apparent meekness and acceptance of his place are based on his religious convictions. "The poor will inherit the earth, blessed are the poor." Although the Biblical quotation is usually interpreted to mean the poor in spirit, it can also apply to the financially poor. If the social worker is not aware of these basic concepts, which are part of the frame of reference of the client, he may describe an attitude as apathetic when it is anything but apathetic.

There is apathy among the deprived, but not all that appears to be apathy should be defined as such. It could be that individuals are conserving their physical and psychic energy for things they consider to be more important.

Kinship Family Ties

Although deprived families form a closely knit circle chiefly for the purpose of protecting each other from outside interference, Chicanos, Appalachian highlanders, Indians, rural Blacks, and Southern whites form strong extended family ties as part of their folk culture. It is important for social workers to know whether the self-containment of families is an indication of deprivation or whether it represents the culture.

Inadequate Communication System

The emotionally deprived person retains many infantile attitudes and ways of behaving. His responses are often more appropriate to the preschool-age child than to the adult. He has difficulty deferring gratification or making judgments about money and other practical matters. Selfish and self-centered, he tends to get into trouble. Clinically one would say that this person has poor ego development and, therefore, is at the mercy of his impulses. The nature of his problem implies the need for experiences and guidance that will foster new ego development.

In his "Social Class, Speech Systems and Psychotherapy" concerning his research with the lower working class in England, Basil Bernstein reminds us that a deprived client's communication system may seem to be inadequate.[18] Bernstein warns the therapist that such a client has a low level of insight. He may seem to be negative and passive, thereby forcing the therapist or caseworker to take a more dominant role. Above all, the therapist will meet an unwillingness on the part of the client to talk about personal feelings. Such a client has difficulty verbalizing his personal experiences and understanding or accepting communications which refer to the source of his motivation. Bernstein points out graphically that language is not perceived by such an individual as an important media for describing feelings. Thus a special group of defense mechanisms are employed, including denial, disassociation, and displacement rather than the more elaborate defenses which rely upon verbal procedures, such as rationalization.

Communication—Its Role in Overcoming Deprivation

In casework settings all over the country, social workers have recently found that many low-income families who make application to their agencies fail to follow through in a continued relationship. Some terminate contact following the initial intake; still others lose interest after one or two visits to the agency. It seems virtually impossible to motivate them to return, even though their present problems have not changed. An examination of this seeming lack of interest indicates that several obstacles stand between the low-income client and the social worker.

The first obstacle is expectation. A major part of the problem is the discrepancy between what the client thinks he will get from the agency and what the agency sees as its function. The low-income client expects the therapist to take a generally active, although permissive role; he expects the worker to give answers, and he expects to get results. In short, he expects to have direct service, not words.

The low-income client knows he has a problem. He does not come to a social work agency expecting to be told this fact. Instead he comes seeking a solution to a problem he has already identified. He comes expecting the worker to take over his problem, to solve it by telling him what to do or by doing it for him or to him. For example, there is nothing in the prior experience of a farm migrant to prepare him for a relationship with a worker who asks how he feels about his problems or how he feels about various members of his family. Such a client can see no relationship between his problem and this sort of an approach to help; therefore, he is frustrated in what may have been his one and only attempt to reach out for assistance.

Another obstacle is communication. The whole therapeutic relationship, which is the foundation of social work treatment, is based on the belief that the condition which brings a client to an agency can be helped by "talking it through." Insight can be gained through talking; in fact the very "talk through" of feelings can provide a catharsis for anxiety. This is, therefore, the frame of

reference for the therapist and/or the agency. However, it is not
the frame of reference for lower-class clients, especially farm migrants, most of whom have much difficulty expressing themselves
verbally.

A Frame of Reference

By examining communication with the migrant worker in particular, many conclusions about communication with low-income
clients in general can be drawn. But first, two questions must be
answered: (1) In what context is communication being considered? (2) Who are the migrants?

For years social work has accepted the basic concept that in
order "to understand individuals in another culture it is necessary
to have some appreciation of their culture."[19] This same principle
applies to farm migrants. In order for a social worker to be able to
communicate meaningfully with migrants, that worker must know
something of how they live and work, how they travel, how they
view their world, and how their world is viewed by nonmigrants.
This sort of knowledge is essential before a worker in any agency
can begin to assess whether a migrant is in touch with reality. From
such knowledge the social worker will need to put together the
answers to further questions. What is the reality of the migrant's
experience against the background of his racial or ethnic culture?
What is the pattern of his learned communication, both verbal and
nonverbal, with those of his own culture as well as with those in
positions of authority, such as social workers?

Some barriers to communication with farm migrants are cultural
determinants. One example is the verbal expression of anger. Most
social workers are used to hearing clients who are angry raise their
voices. White, Black, and Chicano migrants will usually raise their
voices when angry; they may shout profanities, speak rapidly in
Spanish, or even scream threats. But an Apache Indian will lower
his voice until it is "a scarcely audible whisper" at a time when he
is angry enough to commit physical violence.[20] These and other
cultural characteristics must be understood and taken into consideration if the farm migrant is to be helped by social work
agencies.

The question of who the migrants are is more difficult to answer. Farm migrants in this country represent a cross section of all races and many ethnic groups. Lacking a common culture, migrants are bound together by the task they perform and the crops they harvest. Thus, it is through this common bond that they communicate with each other and with the outer world.

> Their lives, no matter where they work, are measured by the crops they harvest. They talk of personal events and relate them to a part of the harvest. The baby was born in the tomatoes of Ohio. The truck tires were new in the spinach of Texas. The older son broke his arm in the sugar beets of Wyoming. They do not mean these things happened in the fields of tomatoes, spinach, or sugar beets. They are saying these were the crops in which they labored at that time, and therefore these are the crops that control their lives and become a calendar to record all significant events.[21]

The migrant is part of a distinct subculture in the American society. The most obvious feature of this subculture is poverty, but poverty more extreme, more secret, more insidious than that found in any ghetto in the country—a fact which was noted more than twenty years ago.

> Migrant farm laborers move restlessly over the face of the land, but they neither belong to the land nor does the land belong to them. They pass through community after community, but they neither claim the community as home nor does the community claim them. . . . As crops ripen, farmers await their coming; as the harvest closes, the community with equal anxiety awaits their going.[22]

Not only are migrants rejected because of their occupation and the fact that they migrate, but they are also discriminated against because they are members of racial or ethnic minorities. Sometimes they are discriminated against because of sex, many women being paid a lower wage for the same amount and type of work as that done by men or being denied a higher paying job because they are women. There are also unique aspects of the migrant subculture which will be looked at after the process of communication is examined.

The Art and Theory of Communication

The experience of communicating with another human being is fraught with complexities even for a fully trained social worker. It is more complex for someone in the position of a migrant. A review of the theory and levels of communication can help us understand better the dynamics involved and the manner in which someone in the migrant's position uses communication.

Webster's dictionary defines communication as a two-way process of transmitting and receiving. This implies that before communication of any sort can take place there must be a sender and a receiver and that each must understand the language of the message to be conveyed, whether verbal or nonverbal. Even more important, especially as it relates to communication with migrants, is the unspoken intent behind the message; that too must be understood.

In her article "Communication: Client, Community, and Agency," Edith Varon describes communication as "a process in which, when it is truly effective, the senders and recipients of messages give them the same interpretation. Words—concepts—symbols—mean the same thing to different individuals when they have the same frame of reference."[23]

Rose Spiegel further identifies the process:

> When communication is consummated between persons, the experience is of an almost incommunicable, buoyant sense of openness, at-homeness, and acceptance—a sense of the flow of thought and feeling in a shared rhythm—Meanings are understood. Verbal and non-verbal communication fuse. There is a sense of "being on the same wave length," "in tune with each other," "in touch."[24]

In their book on nonverbal communication, Jurgen Ruesch and Weldon Kees identify functions of communication and the need for codification.[25] In later articles Ruesch spells this out in more detail. He says,

> In order to be understood, signals must be phrased in terms which are understandable to others. The technical aspects of this process are referred to as codification. When the receiver understands the code, the signal to him becomes a sign. Language is a sign system by which people have agreed to abide. . . . The accumulation of signs and their orderly arrangement is

referred to as knowledge if it exists inside of a person and as information if it is accessible to others.[26]

Regardless of what code or language is used and what kind of information is transmitted, specific instructions have to accompany any message if it is to be interpreted properly. These instructions are often referred to as "metalanguage," and the exchange as "metacommunication." In verbal speech the metalanguage is couched in the tonal qualities of the voice, expressed through gestures and contained in patterning of speech. In written language it is conveyed through interpunction and spacing of the sentence and through the context within which it is written.[27]

Nonverbal codification falls into three distinct categories: (1) sign language which is implied by gestures (migrants, especially Chicanos, make extensive use of gestures); (2) action language— body movements, such as the gait of walk; (3) object language— clothing or material possessions.

One reason communication becomes so complicated is that even though an individual defines his relationship by whatever he communicates he can invalidate this definition by using qualifications that deny his communication. Jay Haley gives an example of this simultaneous denial where the individual communicates on at least two levels.

"I think you should do that, but it's not my place to tell you so," in this way he defines the relationship as one in which he tells the other person what to do but simultaneously denies that he is defining the relationship in this way.[28]

Communication, as we are discussing it here, is the sum total of things that go on within the intrapsychic, self-contained system within the individual and that go on in the interpersonal system that constitutes communication between persons. Between an individual's intrapsychic system and his interpersonal system there are four levels of response that affect how the communication will be perceived: (1) the individual's level of feeling, both conscious and unconscious—what is felt about the issue being communicated; (2) his level of thinking—what is thought about the issue being communicated; (3) his level of speaking—what is said about the issue being communicated; and (4) his level of behavior or body language—the emotional affect that expresses how he is coping with his present situation. In other words, the fourth level indicates what the individual at this point in time is able to do about the situation. In the daily process of communication these four levels are always interacting and at times are in conflict with each other. The result frequently is a paradox. It is not unusual for an individual to behave or to speak in a way which belies his thinking and/or his feelings. This is often the situation that the migrant encounters. Because the migrant must be intuitively aware of his surroundings, he senses the prejudice, the distrust, or the dislike toward him which may not be expressed in words but which is betrayed in action or intonation or through body language.

Elsewhere I have described various ways such feelings are transmitted to migrants.

> There is an unspoken contempt for pickers. This contempt is expressed in many ways. It is there in making them wait for wages until it is convenient for the grower to pay. It is there in the way they are addressed. . . . Contempt is there when a picker asks for directions. There is contempt in the expressions. . . .
>
> The contempt is like an invisible wall. It is an aloofness which gives one the sensation of being unwanted. . . . We sensed others were on guard because they did not trust having migrant farm workers so near. There were some who were afraid [of us]. That emotion, too, was transmitted.[29]

If human communication took place only on the speaking or verbal level, the working out or defining of the relationship would be relatively simple. However, human beings not only communicate; they also communicate about their communications. They not only say something, but they also qualify what they have said.

Messages are qualified by (1) facial expression, (2) body movement, (3) intonation—an upward inflection can change a statement to a question, a slight smile may classify a statement as ironic rather than serious, a hesitation or pause or silence when an answer is expected can change the entire meaning of any statement. The communication must be appraised as being sincere or deceitful, serious or joking. In addition, a person of a different ethnic group must understand communication within his own group and the way that type of communication differs from the expectation of the dominant society.

When one person communicates a message to another, he is, by that act, making a maneuver to define the relationship. Maneuvers to define a relationship consist essentially of (1) requests, commands, or suggestions that another person does say, think, or feel something and (2) comments on the other person's communicative behavior.

The migrant faces a life of experiences in which he is maneuvered by others. He is told by a crew leader or a driver when and how to travel and is taken to an employer selected for him by that crew leader. He is ordered to work in a certain spot, in a certain way, until a certain time. He is told where to live and how he should feel about his job and working conditions.

In his discussion of maneuver, Haley says that if

> Mr. A asks Mr. B to do something the problem is immediately posed whether this is the type of relationship where A has the right to make that request. B is also affected by whether the request was made tentatively or apologetically, or whether it was a rude command.[30]

If Mr. B is a migrant worker, Mr. A might be the young teenage son of a grower, or Mr. A might be the orchard supervisor or packing shed foreman and, even more ego deflating, might be of a race or culture toward which Mr. B has much hostility. A forty-year-old male migrant may feel indignant at having a fifteen-year-old boy or a woman tell him what to do, but it is more difficult for him to take orders from someone of a race or nationality toward which he has a deep sense of prejudice. We saw many illustrations of such hatred: between the Barbadian sugar cane cutters and their Cuban supervisor, between Chicanos and Blacks, and on the part of Southern whites who resented having to take orders from dark skinned Puerto Ricans.

Conditions Affecting Communication between the Migrant and the Social Worker

There are many reality factors which deter effective communication, some of which come from the experience of the migrant and some of which are present in the interview, or attempted conversation, between the migrant and the nonmigrant. Hertha Riese identifies a common barrier to communication when she says,

> Between any two people who try to reach each other by the spoken word stands the history and experience of their whole lives. The imagery, the atmosphere, the meaning associated with each word is tinged with the reminiscences of the past. Every spoken word has a very different connotation for each partner to a conversation who can understand the other only by means of his own associations, thoughts, and feelings.[31]

Distrust of the Spoken Word. Regardless of their race or ethnic background migrants have known too few situations where words alone could be trusted. They are surrounded by constant experiences that take on almost a carnival "con man" atmosphere. Missing are the lights, the music, the good-humored acceptance of the carnival "sucker"; but the barkers, the promises, the "come-ons"—these are all there, part of the migrant's daily experience.

Migrants are promised jobs which often do not materialize because a grower, protective of his own interests, advertises for 100 workers when he needs only fifty. Migrants are victimized by loan sharks, high-pressure salesmen, and sometimes even by their own crew leaders or fellow migrant workers. In communities where the tourist season coincides with the harvest, migrants find food and other essentials increasing in price when they arrive, although such items still are advertised as being on sale or as cheaper when bought in quantity lots. But if the migrant multiplies the single item by the quantity number he finds there is no bargain; he has been misled by words again. With some simple arithmetic he finds he would pay more per can for the beans if he bought the so-called "bargain package of three," than if he bought the same number a can at a time.

The conceptual construct of an individual under these circumstances is one of basic distrust. The migrant is conditioned to be deceived by words, so he attempts to understand the intent in back of the words. In our months of travel we saw evidence of this intuitive sensitivity that migrants had developed to the feeling level of others. Their alert sensitivity is a "tuning in" to what another person is thinking, rather than to what he is saying. The migrant who does this is often confused by what he may sense as a paradox. The spoken word he hears does not ring true to what he senses is going on. What the migrant senses that the speaker feels he does not hear the speaker say, and yet the speaker claims his spoken word is how he really feels or thinks. The only answer for the migrant is not to trust.

Leisurely Tempo of Speaking. Some of the ethnic cultures represented among the migrant subculture encourage a leisurely tempo in their conversations or a prescribed dialogue of discussion before the main points of a question can be answered. This slow pace of speaking is found among the Appalachian mountain culture and the rural Southern whites and "does not reflect pathology but rather cultural patterns of speech and contemplation."[32]

Sol W. Ginsburg goes on to say that when one of these clients is conversing with a case worker, his long silence "does not mean rejection of advice but more likely a careful pondering of it. It can also be the comfortable silence of a deeply felt friendship for the worker. Indians also size up strangers during a prolonged silence since they do not find silence awkward or embarrassing as do most white people."[33] In the migrant's culture it is rude to plunge immediately into serious topics without a "warm-up" period in which the two individuals evaluate each other and decide what sort of a relationship there should be. This is a form of establishing rapport, which in some ways is related to establishing a relationship with a schizophrenic client. The migrant, like the schizophrenic client, may fear any close relationship and may erect all kinds of obstacles because he has been injured by past interpersonal contacts.

In this sort of a situation the migrant must come to regard the worker as a less threatening force than he regards other people; therefore, any relationship must be established slowly at the pace determined by the migrant.

There are other obstacles in communications with migrants which are related to those found among other low-income clients, although they are usually more complex for the migrant. Some of these obstacles to communication patterns may be found within the interpersonal relationships of the family. The child may hear the conflict of the adults and may view spoken words as a means of expressing aggression and hate but not of expressing tenderness or love. Working in Virginia with low-income families, Riese saw speech as a barrier or a weapon. She says,

> Due to the intellectual, emotional, and social-economic status of the parents, the children referred to us have known language not as a bridge between people but as a moat in a shouting war.

She goes on to say that "faulty articulation reveals the child's despair; he cannot believe that anyone will listen to what he has to say."[34]

Isolation. There have been in recent years a number of studies on the effect of isolation on human beings—both the physical and psychological effects. Although there are differences among these studies of perceptual and motor changes in isolation, disorganizing effects have been demonstrated in all cases.

George R. Ruff, in his article "Isolation and Sensory Deprivation," describes the effects of physical and psychological distance on communication.[35] If there is too high a degree of alienation or isolation the individual may become nonverbal. In experiments conducted at McGill University, isolation produced "generalized impairment of perception, which showed deficits are most striking in tests of visual motor coordination, apparent movement, constancy by shape, color saturation, figural after-effects, accuracy of tactual perception, and spatial orientation. These effects appear to result from a loss of an internal frame of reference used in structuring perceptual experience."[36]

Ruff continues, "Although it is difficult to generalize about the effect of isolation on cognitive skills, subjects consistently refer to the inability to maintain goal-directed thought"[37] which in turn affects the verbal skill in communication.

Major questions which need answering are: Does the migrant's type of isolation resulting from work and travel affect his perceptive ability? Does a client, migrant or nonmigrant, who is cut off from meaningful contacts with others perceive his world as it really is?

Delimited Environment. Much as a schizophrenic patient must, the migrant must fit his perception of events into a delimited environment. The migrant's conceptualization of his surroundings is neither instrumental in affording consistent understanding and mastery of events or feelings nor in line with what the migrant sees happening to nonmigrants. On one hand, according to the "great American dream," the migrant, if he works hard, does not become a public charge, and is ambitious, honest, and self-reliant, will be able to rise to any height. On the other hand, the migrant knows from experience that others are contemptuous of his type of labor. He knows also that the travel required for his job removes his rights as a citizen and denies him the fruits of the Puritan ethic of hard work and self-reliance. The acceptance of such "mutually contradictory experiences requires paralogical thinking."[38] Such an environment can afford training only in irrationality. The world which the migrant perceives for others needs to be denied for himself. All of this has a negative effect upon the individual's concept of self and even his expectations of self. In turn, his lack of self-confidence is communicated to nonmigrants as insecurity or perhaps as racial, sexual, or ethnic instability.[39]

Sleep Deprivation. In an article on sleep deprivation, Elliot D. Luby and Jacques S. Gottlieb describe behavior which is often observed in the migrant. These workers do experience sleep deprivation and it affects their ability to communicate. With loss of sleep,

> . . . cognitive disorganization begins with a general slowing of thought processes, accompanied by word searching. Subjects . . . stray from topic to topic. . . . Speech tends to become incoherent with confused mumbling which fades into dozing silence. Dream thoughts are interspersed with secondary process thinking as though there were a failure in repression. New learning is interfered with because the attentional or set impairment will not allow for the acquisition of new memories. Regulation and control of effect are frequently disturbed. Loud explosive laughter, sometimes inappropriate or at least overreactive can be heard.[40]

Luby and Gottlieb continue with a description of some of their subjects.

A number of men become easily annoyed and irritable, a state which may escalate to outbursts of seemingly unprovoked rage. Such hostile outbursts may be part of a paranoid resolution. For example, a subject suddenly threw down his cue while playing pool and began to choke his partner. After forceable disengagement he bitterly complained the assault was necessary because the partner was making a fool of him.

At one hundred hours or beyond, the sleep-deprived person appears utterly weary, grim and slowed. At this time the real psychosis appears. West *et al.* described their subjects in these terms: "Faces become elongated and immobile; the brow is furrowed with the effort to hold open drooping lids during drowsy periods of growing intensity. . . . During periods of great alertness there is a hollow-eyed suspicious stare. . . ."[41]

It is the exception rather than the rule for the migrant to have a comfortable, undisturbed night of sleep. He may doze in a bus, car, or truck in transit. He may curl up on a narrow cot, in a bed already crowded with other family members, on two chairs pulled together, on the ground on a pile of straw, or on the floor. His room may be infested with bedbugs or mosquitoes or "kant sees," and the wall above his head may drip with humidity or be white with frost. He may share a room with strangers or sleep in a barn surrounded by the sounds and odors of cows and horses. His rest may be disturbed by the quarrels of his neighbors, the cries of his children, his own hunger, or his anxiety. He may be so physically exhausted from his day of work he cannot relax into sleep.

Repeated Loss of Job. In a study of employment, Sol Ginsburg came to the conclusion that the emotional implication of losing one's job was so great that the only counterpart he could cite was the "loss of love a child suffers from a rejecting parent, especially a child who has done nothing to deserve it." There are some whose first reaction to loss of work is "fear and bewilderment, combined with optimism, born out of wishful thinking," but with repeated experiences of loss of work even these individuals become traumatized until they are afraid to tackle a new job or even to talk about the need for work.[42]

This is what one would expect of anyone in the migrant's position. The migrant is usually not in his employment situation by choice but because he has been tractored out, because the type of work he did previously is no longer available, or because he is not trained to handle any job which is available in his home community. He has lost jobs repeatedly. He will continue to know such experiences. He must not think too much about it, or he will be traumatized by his own anxiety and by the fear that he will not find work where he is going. In turn, he will convey a less positive image than he needs to present if he is to get work.

Depersonalization. There is much in the experience of the migrant that can lead him into what is known as depersonalization phenomena. James P. Cattell describes these phenomena as "feelings of unreality in reference to the self, the body, the external world, or the passage of time; feelings of unreality or detachment associated with states of elation; an 'as if' quality and loss of affective response."[43] This sense of unrealness is communicated as a detachment, as not quite "being with" the situation—all of which is viewed in a negative way by those who are assessing the ability of the migrant.

Since the migrant's total experience is one of constant change, beginning with his travel from one job to the next, a sense of orientation is difficult for him to maintain. Migrants frequently travel in a truck covered by a canvas tarpaulin which closes out any view of passing countryside. In a semishadow the riders sit on benches, boxes, and the floor, and they have a sensation of movement through space without knowing their destination, which in turn adds to their feelings of depersonalization.

Masking Denial. Denial in various ways confuses communication both within the migrant family and between it and the nonmigrant world. Some of this denial takes the form of "masking," which is both a conscious and an unconscious form of deception. It is behaving as if a situation did not exist. Theodore Lidz, Stephen Fleck, and Alice R. Cornelison describe masking as involving a "large degree of self-deception as well as an effort to conceal from others; but it involves a conscious negation, as well as an effort to unconsciously deny." The migrant, unable either to accept or to alter his situation, ignores it and proceeds as if it does not exist.[44]

It is only by reinforcing such a defense that the migrant is able to function. He has to conserve his psychic and physical energy for the task at hand and let tomorrow take care of itself. But it does mean that the migrant may have difficulty understanding the need to discuss something he has consciously denied.

One Chicano migrant told us about his fears and how he handled them.

> He shrugged his shoulders and smiled wanly. Here in this farm labor camp there was no time for such thoughts. Here a man could forget the taste of fear that seemed to tie his guts in knots. Here there was a house for his family, water to drink, and water for washing. Most important of all there was work tomorrow in the strawberries. Here in the warmth of the Washington sunshine his fears seemed such foolish fears, like the fears of an old man. He knew the fears would return when the crops were harvested and it was time to load his family into the trucks. Sometimes he wondered what would happen to them when he was too old to pick the long rows of tomatoes or to toss the filled crates of sweet corn onto the conveyors. Sometimes he wondered what would happen to his family if he admitted to himself that he had a dull ache low in one side and that he had a hard lump there that would not go away. Someday he would go to a doctor, but that took money which today he did not have. He would take care of those things, someday. Here and now there was warm sunshine. There was plenty of work. He could provide well for his family. "Someday, maybe tomorrow," he said. "Si, manana. I'll think about the future."[45]

Communicating with the Migrant

Much of the communication with the migrant needs to be on the feeling or nonverbal level. Basic to communication is the necessity to listen, whether the client speaks or not. When the client does not speak, the worker needs to tune in with *every sense of empathy* to receive the message which the client may make every effort to conceal. The migrant's effort to shut himself away will be lessened as he senses the quiet acceptance of his worker.

It may be very difficult for a migrant to take part in a conventional interview, to describe a situation and say how he feels about something. On the other hand, he can role-play or act out a situation and show the worker what transpired as well as what he did about it. In this sort of a situation, insight should not be the caseworker's major goal. He should, rather, assist the migrant in reorganizing old cognitive patterns in such a manner that new and adequate responses are facilitated so that the worker can better grasp the migrant's position.

The migrant can feel ill at ease in an office setting in the usual client-worker situation. Accustomed to action, to using his hands for tasks as well as for gestures, a migrant will be better able to talk about his concerns in his own settings, in his housing or the field rather than in the agency. In such settings there will be distractions—competition with television, noise, and confusion. There will be others, relatives and friends, who will come and go throughout the interview. The migrant knows little, if any, privacy; he lives his life openly.

The experiences of four researchers who were interviewing Chicanos on details of their marriages are not unusual and should be expected by any social worker conducting an interview in a migrant camp. They wrote: "Often there were small children in and out. On at least six occasions there were other females 'sitting in' on either part or all of the interview. In some of these cases, the respondent insisted that 'she had no secrets' from that person and responses were not inhibited by their presence."[46] It helps the worker to realize that the discomfort which he feels in this sort of situation is in direct proportion to what the migrant experiences in the agency office.

Any interview that is held with a migrant should more closely resemble a "visit" than the traditional office interview, because that is how it will be viewed by the migrant himself. Relating is the first step in casework, but to be able to relate, a person must belong to himself and be basically himself. Therefore, a prerequisite to relating is finding out what is expected. This is especially true for the migrant who, fearful of human interaction, is immediately on guard with any stranger.

The purpose of the initial interview, or visit, must be understood. What does the social worker hope to accomplish in his contact with the migrant? Is the purpose of the interview to establish a relationship in order to involve the migrant in some type of educational program, such as Head Start for his children or job training for himself? Is this contact to acquaint the migrant with community resources, such as health and welfare agencies? Is the contact to establish an on-going, supportive relationship for those migrants who "settle out" and who need help in establishing themselves in the community? Is this a situation where the migrant himself is faced with a crisis and needs immediate help? Or is this to be the first visit in a long-range treatment aimed at changing the migrant's life style or his personality structure?

Fear of being changed or molded by someone else and losing self-identity is very real for the migrant and is in back of much of his reluctance to become involved with social workers. Strangers in a migrant camp create other fears. There are some migrants who have reasons for wanting to keep their true identity or their whereabouts unknown. They may fear that any stranger is a policeman or a bill collector. Migrants accustomed to pressure salesmen and confidence men may wonder what the social worker *really* wants and will suspect that this person is no different from all the others who said that they too were interested in what happened to the poor migrant.

A few migrants are afraid that the stranger is a spy who will report to the grower or the employment agency and may affect their work in the future. Some employers in recent years have overreacted to attempts to organize migrants, to involve migrants in educational programs, or to recruit migrants for other jobs, seeing these attempts as threats to their source of employees. It is not all one-sided. Workers have frequently been pirated at the peak of the harvest or encouraged to display discontent by outsiders. Outsiders have also trespassed into camps or fields without the knowledge of the owner to photograph conditions for release in a newspaper. Many of the OEO (Office of Economic Opportunity) and Vista programs are in bad repute with growers. These attitudes and fears of employers have been transmitted to the migrants themselves and have, in some cases, been in turn projected by the migrants to social work agencies. The migrants usually do not know the difference between OEO, welfare, family service, and mental health clinics. There are many new programs under the direction of educational, public health, social work, or religious organizations that are trying to reach out to migrants, each with a slightly different approach. Some of this is also causing confusion for the migrants.

I have heard complaints from migrants themselves that in some places in the last two years so many well-meaning individuals are in the fields doing research or trying to involve the migrant in some sort of educational program that they are having trouble getting the harvest finished. Prompted by such circumstances, some migrants side with their employers in saying they want to be left alone.

We found our greatest success in relating to migrants came when they had an opportunity to become accustomed to seeing us around the camps, riding in the trucks, or physically working with them in the crops before we began to ask questions. We had no pressure of time. We could sit quietly and enter into the migrant's isolation, conveying by our presence that we were willing to talk but that we were not forcing ourselves into their private world. The struggle to maintain privacy is a very real part of a migrant's experiences, and anyone who respects his privacy will have less difficulty establishing a relationship with him. We were also careful not to begin a conversation with a personal question. Even the question "how many children do you have" can appear as a criticism of family size to a woman who has a family of eight or twelve children.

When we asked personal questions, we did not ask one immediately after another. The migrant often experiences rapid-fire questions which can painfully traumatize him to the point where he feels as if he is being "peeled like an onion, layer by layer until nothing is left." We found, generally, that it was easier for migrants to talk about personal things if they could be busy with their hands or when they were not seated in a face-to-face position. Riding in a bus, hanging clothes on a line, picking strawberries, or sorting apples from a conveyor belt—these were the times when the migrants talked most freely of their fears, hopes, and dreams. They seemed more ill at ease when they had nothing physical to hold onto.

Insistence upon verbal communication in an interview only empowers the migrant with ways to deny, such as near muteness, lack of spontaneity, or reducing answers to a minimum. He may tell the social worker a known untruth or may consider the social worker naive and attempt to shock him. The migrant may show impatience with questions or may be bitter or sarcastic or make accusations. He may show his need for power over an unconquerable world by being shrewd and deceptive in his communication. There is much bragging about drinking, sexual experience, gambling success, and even money earned in other crops.

This sort of behavior is certainly not unique to a migrant.

Almost all functional disturbances of communication can be traced historically to the fact that one person impinges upon another and produces frustration by illtimed, badly qualified, or inappropriate messages. . . . When communication becomes too frustrating, man finds ways to protect himself by withdrawing, screening, or otherwise controlling the exchange. But through this control, the feedback characteristics frequently are lost, so that the purpose of communication—correction of information and performance—is defeated.[47]

In an attempt to shield his identity from a threatening world, the migrant may pretend he has forgotten names and facts, may hesitate even to speak, or may mask his concern as to what the interview is all about by engaging in a flurry of unrelated activities. He may approach these activities as if they were the most important tasks in the world and may consciously attempt to show the visitor that he has middle-class values, such as cleanliness, or that he has material possessions, such as a transistor radio or television. A mother may search frantically for a comb and begin to smooth a toddler's hair or grab a broom and give an older daughter the job of sweeping the floor or the yard. There is often loud laughter or wrestling on the part of teenagers who may half stand, half lean in a corner or suddenly turn on a radio to full volume when an interview is taking place. All those present, even when not taking a direct part in the interview, are communicating by how they observe what is going on. They watch the social worker for his reaction to everything, and they watch the member of their group who is the most vocal to see that he does not betray too much too fast. If there seems to be danger of this happening, another person breaks in with a contradiction or changes the subject to a less threatening issue. Conversation at any point may be interrupted with what, to the social worker, could seem like much to-do about something else. This may be a form of rivalry for the worker's attention, an indication that certain members of the group feel neglected and left out.

Whenever a stranger is present, there is a good deal of spontaneous interaction between the migrant family or group members comparable to "in-joking" in a middle-class family—the sort of thing that is understood only by the in-group and has no direct meaning to the observer. Whereas a middle-class family might be more discreet in front of a stranger, the migrant family may use rowdiness as a means of relieving their anxiety. Among Chicanos, Indians, or other bilingual migrants there are frequent lapses into the native language. Even those who are bilingual may pretend they are not or that they do not even understand English. This may be a form of control, but even more important, it is a way of maintaining identity.

Most migrants are the sons and daughters of migrants, share-croppers, or parents who worked at other low-income jobs. Large numbers of the adult migrants were forced as young children into pseudomaturity through having to help support their family by working in the fields or taking over the responsibility for siblings or the home so that their parents could work. The result is an immature, infantile personality.

The social work approach, which seemingly is the most successful in working with immature personalities, is (1) to reach out, to go *to* the client with sustaining procedures of reassurance and with suggestions; (2) to directly influence the client through educational programs, of which group procedures and role-playing have been the most effective; (3) to provide opportunities for emotional catharsis and desensitization through ventilation of fears, hopes, ambitions, and anger. The immature personality must be helped to establish and maintain an identity.

The migrant is highly motivated to take care of his own needs but does not have the educational or emotional equipment to face the problems of adjusting in a society where his role will no longer be that of migrant. He needs help in making the transition from migrant to nonmigrant.

The migrant represents a cross section of all the clients known to any social work agency. His problems of communication are more complex because of his experience, his culture, and his own awareness of nonverbal interaction. But, if listened to carefully, he, like any low-income client, can communicate. He will express his needs and his feelings, but not always in words.

Before communication can take place, there must be a sender and a receiver. The low-income client is the sender; his message is coded with meaning. The question that remains to be answered is this: Can social workers listen to the incoming messages before they begin to send their own?

Successful Social Work Methods for Dealing with the Disadvantaged

Social work treatment, which seemingly has been the most successful in working with deprived individuals, regardless of race or circumstances, has featured programs that include (1) reaching-out procedures, (2) group procedures, and (3) cooperative endeavors.

Reaching-out Procedures

The social worker reaches out to the client geographically as well as emotionally. In his early contacts the worker attempts to gain an understanding of the family's deprivation. At this stage it is necessary to *demonstrate* interest and concern. Such demonstrations can consist of arranging for medical care or straightening out misunderstandings with school, employer, or with a public welfare agency. Often it is desirable to accompany the client to an agency or an institution. This helps to demonstrate real concern and to reduce the client's fear of authority. During the early period of contact deprived clients continue to expect disapproval, criticism, and rejection. They may engage in many maneuvers, such as breaking appointments or expressing a wish to end the contact in order to test the social worker's interest. In this relationship, as in others, the deprived client tends to reject quickly in order not to be rejected. He needs considerable time in which to overcome his mistrust and to accept the social worker's support and help. Some will never learn to trust.

The worker's aim in treatment is to help such clients learn to handle their affairs and their personal relationships with greater responsibility. As indicated earlier, many such clients were deprived in their early years, and, as a result, are fixated in their emotional development. Some are able to reach a higher level of maturity through a helping relationship that provides both acceptance and stimulus for further growth.

Group Procedures

Group procedures have been found to be especially effective with persons from deprived backgrounds. Individuals with similar problems and attitudes are brought together for educational, recreational, or counseling experiences where they gain confidence from each other. Supported by fellow members of their group, they feel freer to express negative feelings and to expose their own weaknesses. They are often able to complain about things they would never be able to talk about with a caseworker in the one-to-one relationship.

Through the exchange of ideas, opinions, and experiences, group members lose some of their sense of being different from everyone else. The discussions often serve to correct some of their distorted views.

Cooperative Endeavors

The number and severity of problems faced by deprived individuals require a battery of community services and resources. Although in the past five years there has been an increasing trend for agencies to join efforts to reach deprived families, each community, especially in rural areas, must be even more imaginative in introducing new and different combinations of agency services. Volunteer workers as well as staff members in all agencies can make a more significant contribution in their preventive and rehabilitative efforts if the usual traditional lines of service can be broken and if more of the comprehensive community service plan can be introduced. Nearly every deprived family needs such diversified community services and resources as (1) individual counseling, (2) health services, (3) financial assistance, (4) housing, (5) recreational opportunities, (6) vocational guidance, (7) training in homemaking and skills in parental education, (8) legal consultation, and (9) spiritual guidance. Within this pattern of need there is a place for churches, schools, libraries, employers, union and civic groups, private agencies, and public agencies to play an important role in providing positive experiences and in reducing negative attitudes.

The Role of Community Planning in Dealing with the Disadvantaged

Regardless of the agency that spearheads the effort, community planning should be broad and deep, with all segments of the citizenry represented. A successful citizens' advisory group for any planning must represent citizens' interests. The major role of such an advisory committee is to gather facts in order to forge a common community goal. After a committee has found the facts, all related public and private agencies must be included to carry out the program. Goals need to be set and priorities determined. Agencies may need to change the emphases of their programs, assume new roles, transfer functions, and together alter their activities to achieve a common goal.

If planning is to be effective, change and adaptation will have to take place—in welfare and employment services, in educational institutions, and in political structures. Undergirding every comprehensive project must be constant evaluation.

There has been a tendency in the past for communities to view most situations of deprivation as temporary. There is still, for example, a tendency to view the needs of the migrant worker and his family in this way. Year after year the same needs are seen in communities that viewed them as temporary the previous year and so did not make long-range plans beyond the immediacy of the present problem. Communities can no longer afford this sort of attitude. Every community must look at the problem in its entirety and within its proper scope. A broad, interdisciplinary approach is needed that calls for new patterns of community planning.

Along with community planning there needs to be a more sensitive awareness of the cultural values of America's various racial and ethnic groups and the contributions of their differences. Social workers, counselors, educators, physicians, psychiatrists, psychologists, lawyers, religious leaders, personnel officials, and all other helping persons will continue to be faced with the dilemma of conflict and tension created between the personality structure of their clients and the expectations of the dominant middle-class values. The adaptation that members of an ethnic group make depends to a large extent on the manner in which they resolve their cultural conflicts and meet their new situation. This means that the community, as well as the individual social worker, will need to have more respect for individual differences.

NOTES

1. U.S., Department of Health, Education, and Welfare, *Perspectives on Human Deprivation: Biological, Psychological, and Sociological* (Washington, D.C.: The Department, 1968), p. 2.

2. "Hospitalism," *Psychoanalytic Study of the Child*, Vol. I (New York: International Universities Press, 1945), pp. 53-74.

3. *Perspectives on Human Deprivation*, p. 3.

4. Personal interview.

5. "Reading and Learning Disabilities," in *American Handbook of Psychiatry*, Vol. I, ed. by Silvane Arieti (New York: Basic Books, Inc., 1959), pp. 857-69.

6. (New York: Appleton-Century-Crofts, 1959), pp. 250-51.

7. *Ibid.*, pp. 251-58.

8. *Ibid.*, pp. 258-65.

9. Vivian Gornick, "Why Women Fear Success," *Ms*, Spring 1972, pp. 51-52.

10. Stanley Coopersmith, *The Antecedents of Self-Esteem* (San Francisco, Calif.: W.H. Freeman, 1967); J. Diggory, *Self-Evaluation* (New York: John Wiley and Sons, Inc., 1966); M. Rosenberg, *Society and the Adolescent Self-Image* (Princeton, N.J.: Princeton University Press, 1965).

11. U.S., Department of Health, Education and Welfare, *Equality of Educational Opportunity*, by J.S. Coleman, *et al.* (Washington, D.C.: Government Printing Office, 1966).

12. S. Bloom, A. Davis, and R. Hess, *Contemporary Education for Cultural Deprivation* (New York: Holt, Rinehart and Winston, Inc., 1965).

13. "Children's Perceptions of Their Teacher's Feelings Toward Them Related to Self-Perception, School Achievement and Behavior," *Journal of Exceptional Education*, December 1960. See also David M. Gray, "Effect of Self-Esteem on Drawings of the Human Figure," *Journal of Consulting Psychology*, October 1962; Frances Degen Horowitz, "The Relationship of Anxiety, Self-Concept and Sociometric Status Among Fourth, Fifth, and Sixth Grade Children," *Journal of Abnormal and Social Psychology*, LXV (September 1962), 212-14; Irwin Silverman, "Self-Esteem and Differential Responsiveness to Success and Failure," *Journal of Abnormal and Social Psychology*, LXIX (July 1964), 115-19; and J.W. Staines, "The Self-Picture as a Factor in the Classroom," *British Journal of Educational Psychology*, XXVIII (June 1958), 97-111.

14. Helen S. Astin, Nancy Suniewick, and Susan Dweck, *Women: A Bibliography on Their Education and Careers* (Washington, D.C.: Human Service Press, 1971).

15. Max Bruck and R. F. Bodwin, "The Relationship Between Self-Concept and the Presence and Absence of Scholastic Underachievement," *Journal of Clinical Psychology*, XVIII (April 1962), 181-82; Max Bruck, "The Relationships Between Student Anxiety, Self-Awareness, and Self-Concept and the Student Competence in Casework," *Social Casework*, XLIV (March 1963), 125-31; O. J. Harvey, H. H. Kelly, and M. M. Shapiro, "Reactions to Unfavorable Evaluations of the Self Made by Other Persons," *Journal of Personality*, XXV (December 1957), 398-411; R. M. Suin, "The Relationship Between Self-Acceptance and Acceptance of Others: A Learning Theory Analysis," *Journal of Abnormal and Social Psychology*, LXIII (July 1961), 37-42.

16. Erik Erikson, *Childhood and Society* (New York: W. W. Norton and Co., Inc., 1950), pp. 219-33.

17. Myrtle R. Reul, "Level of Expectation Among Minority Groups," mimeographed colloquium presented for the Michigan State University School of Social Work, East Lansing, Mich., April 13, 1965, pp. 13-15.

18. In *Mental Health of the Poor*, ed. by Frank Riessman, Jerome Cohen, and Arthur Pearl (New York: Free Press of Glencoe, 1964), pp. 194-204.

19. Anne F. Fenalson, *Essentials in Interviewing* (New York: Harper and Bros., 1952), p. 49.

20. Marvin K. Opler, *Culture and Social Psychiatry* (New York: Atherton Press, 1967), pp. 175-76.

21. Myrtle R. Reul, *Where Hannibal Led Us* (New York: Vantage Press, 1967), p. 102.

22. U.S., President's Commission on Migratory Labor, 1951, "Migratory Labor in American Agriculture," in *Children in Migrant Families* (Washington, D.C.: U.S. Children's Bureau, 1960), p. 2. For more recent material on the experiences of farm migrants see William H. Friedland and Dorothy Nelkin, *Migrant: Agricultural Workers in America's Northeast* (New York: Holt, Rinehart and Winston, 1971), and Ronald B. Taylor, *Sweatshops in the Sun: Child Labor on the Farm* (Boston, Mass.: Beacon Press, 1973).

23. *Social Work,* April 1954, pp. 91-97.

24. "Specific Problems of Communication in Psychiatric Conditions," in *American Handbook of Psychiatry,* Vol. I, pp. 914-15.

25. *Nonverbal Communication* (Berkeley, Calif.: University of California Press, 1956), p. 6.

26. "General Theory of Communication in Psychiatry," in *American Handbook of Psychiatry,* Vol. I, p. 898.

27. Jurgen Ruesch and G. Bateson, *Communication: The Social Matrix of Psychiatry* (New York: W. W. Norton and Co., Inc., 1951), p. 314.

28. *Strategies of Psychotherapy* (New York: Grune and Stratton, 1963), p. 88.

29. Reul, *Where Hannibal Led Us,* pp. 268-69.

30. *Strategies of Psychotherapy,* p. 88.

31. *Heal the Hurt Child* (Chicago: University of Chicago Press, 1962), pp. 329-30.

32. Sol W. Ginsburg, *A Psychiatrist's Views on Social Issues* (New York: Columbia University Press, 1963), p. 112.

33. *Ibid.*

34. *Heal the Hurt Child,* pp. 312-13.

35. *American Handbook of Psychiatry,* Vol. III, pp. 362-72.

36. R. B. Voas, "A Description of the Astronauts' Task in Project Mercury," *Human Factors* III (1961), 149-65.

37. "Isolation and Sensory Deprivation," p. 369.

38. Theodore Lidz, Stephen Fleck, and Alice R. Cornelison, *Schizophrenia and the Family* (New York: International Universities Press, Inc., 1965), p. 180.

39. The most widespread examples of delimiting experiences are the effects of the discrimination against women in our society. Motivation and creativity have been adversely affected among women because of limited opportunities. Such delimitation is verbally expressed in comments such as "I am only a housewife."

40. "Sleep Deprivation," *American Handbook of Psychiatry*, Vol. III, pp. 406-18.

41. *Ibid.*, p. 409.

42. *A Psychiatrist's Views on Social Issues*, pp. 152-53.

43. "Depersonalization Phenomena," *American Handbook of Psychiatry*, Vol. III, pp. 88-100.

44. *Schizophrenia and the Family*, p. 181.

45. Reul, *Where Hannibal Led Us*, p. 219.

46. Roland G. Tharp, Arnold Meadow, Susan G. Lennhoff, and Donna Satterfield, "Changes in Marriage Roles Accompanying the Acculturation of the Mexican-American Wife," *Journal of Marriage and the Family*, August 1968, p. 408.

47. Ruesch, "General Theory of Communication," p. 903.

I have yet to see any problem, however complicated, which when you looked at it the right way did not become still more complicated.

Paul Y. Anderson, 20th century
American journalist
St. Louis Post-Dispatch

34

Barriers to Service for the Farm Migrant

Introduction

Agencies that form the service network in such areas as mental and physical health, education, welfare, and job placement should be the undergirding of a community, county, or region. Such agencies are the vehicles through which direct services are provided for individuals, families, groups, and neighborhoods. They exist for the purpose of providing service, and yet those who need help the most, the poor and especially those who are the rural poor, may be unable to use these services because of their restrictive policies, programs, or limited accessibility.

Originally some of this material was presented at the 15th Annual Workshop, "Barriers to Client Service Delivery," Veterans' Administration Hospital, Fayetteville, Ark., October 7-8, 1971. Parts of this chapter were also presented at a Veterans' Administration Hospital Workshop on Service Delivery in Alexandria, La., May 13, 1971. Much of this chapter also appeared as "Farm Migrants: Why Can't We Help Them Help Themselves?" and was the featured article in the Travelers Aid Association of America publication *Shifting Scenes*, Summer 1971.

584

One of the major problems in the delivery of service is that agencies and institutions, set up to provide service to the public, are usually middle class in their approach. Most workers in such agencies, whether professionals or otherwise, come from the middle class or are middle-class oriented from their educational experience. The literature and educational techniques they are taught are middle class. And even more far reaching, the value system they use to assess client behavior, patient behavior, student behavior, or employee behavior is middle class. The result is that those who should understand the needs and motives of individuals seeking help use a standard for interpreting behavior that does not always apply to the needs of the lower class. The standard of behavior they use was tested against a different experience reference and a different value system than those known to the individuals they are working with. Therefore, the person in need and the helping person communicate past each other—they do not send and receive the same messages.

I am using the term *middle class* in its broad sense to refer to middle income, fairly high living standards, and relatively high educational status. There is a tendency to view marriage and the family almost wholly from this middle-class perspective. Even in professional literature the "happy family" is the middle-class family, whereas families of the lower class are apt to be viewed as disorganized, "hard core," "multiproblem," "hard to reach," "broken," or they are said to be "without a decision-making process, structure, or strength." In its discussion of marital accommodation, the popular literature

> ... points up the necessity for the husband to help with the chores like closing up the house and putting the cat out but fails to take into account that not everybody in this country has a house to close up, even if we all can have cats, or even might want to have a cat, to put out.[1]

Popular literature and social science research become even less meaningful for the professional worker when applied to cultural differences, especially when it is used, as it is now, to apply to Black, Chicano, or American Indian families, and even to many poor white families in rural areas.

Barriers to the Use of Social Service

Migrant farm workers encounter more barriers to using services than those usually met by the less mobile poor in rural areas and those who live in the ghettos of our cities. Mobility makes farm migrants less visible as users of services. Their work and travel patterns, their isolation, their family roles, their cultures, and their superstitions all create conditions of need and hindrances to conventional assistance.

Additional problems are created for farm migrants by the general tendency of the helping services to mold people to fit their philosophy. Most agencies operate with a distinct bias toward the middle class and against the migrant farm population which is mobile and poor and, by occupation, is lower class. The result: farm migrants may go through the motions of doing whatever they feel they are expected to do in order to get the services they need. They may answer questions in ways they think employers, physicians, social workers, or educators expect them to, at the same time trying to hold onto their self-respect. They may deny their true feelings. They may pretend to have feelings they do not actually experience. One church mission used by a Travelers Aid Society to house stranded migrants reported a high degree of religious conversion. A closer assessment revealed that many of these "religious conversions were temporary. As one migrant told me and my husband, 'If it takes a few hallelujahs and praise the Lords to get a hot meal and a bed, then I can 'commodate 'em.' "[2]

Barriers Created by the Agency

Barriers to Use of Health Services

Barriers are created by the migrant's inability to describe his illness or accept its cause. Whether Spanish-speaking, Black, white, or Indian, he may believe his illness was caused by a "spell" cast by an envious person or was an act of God for his sinfulness. He has difficulty distinguishing symptoms seen on television, which he thinks the physician expects to hear, from those he actually has. His culture determines how he expresses pain—he may cry out he is "going to die" or be stoic and deny discomfort. His terms or the expressions he uses to tell of his illness may be confusing to the professional worker, educator, or physician.

A comparison of hospital attitudes toward middle-class and lower-class patients will help the reader identify several barriers to service for the poor in general and for farm migrants in particular. Family cohesiveness is usually welcomed by hospital staffs when it involves middle-class families. Physicians are pleased with a college-trained parent, spouse, or sibling who asks well-articulated questions about symptoms, causes, and the course of treatment or postoperative care. On the other hand, the hospital staff may not be as enthusiastic with expressed concern when it involves a large "immediate family," such as American Indian, Chicano, or Puerto Rican. This immediate family may include parents, siblings, parents- and siblings-in-law; cousins, aunts, uncles, grandparents; or god-parents and the children of god-parents. When this immediate family, several of whom may not speak English or may not have completed the third grade, visits the patient, they are confused by medical terms of etiology or pathology and by hospital policy regarding visiting rights and patient privacy.

Under such circumstances, the middle-class kinship family often feels restricted by hospital policy, feels stripped of dignity and worth. But the migrant farm kinship family sees this kind of treatment as personal, racial, or occupational discrimination. Hospital policy and medical jargon *build up* their suspicion of doctors and fear of hospitals. They cannot see the need for so many questions and forms. It seems to them that the hospital is more interested in obtaining information and in filling out forms than in providing even emergency services.

To the hospital staff the farm migrant worker and his family are distrustful of medical procedures, resent the authority of the hospital or doctor, and misinterpret or even misrepresent information they are given. They also ask blunt questions about illness or progress as if they were holding the doctor, nurse, social worker, or clerical staff accountable for the progress of their loved one.

To the farm migrant who does not understand his illness, injury, or treatment, the answer to his problem and his family's problem seems to be one of getting released from the hospital as soon as possible. In order to do this, he may deny his need for the very services he is in the hospital to receive. He may say he is well enough to leave regardless of how badly he feels.

Barriers to Use of Employment Services

The United States Department of Labor Employment Security Agency might be thought of as the one agency that farm migrants would be comfortable in using, but the truth of the matter is that the service of the federal employment agency is one which farm migrants need help in understanding how or why to use. They see the labor department as backing the employer. Their prior work experiences make it difficult for them to use any type of an employment service. Most migrants come from a background of paternalistic employment relationships—an employment caste system.

Whether they worked in coal mines, textile mills, as share-croppers on a Delta plantation, or as part of the peon system of Mexico and the Southwest, they had common experiences that helped to produce feelings of helplessness. Regardless of their ethnic backgrounds, they were told what to do, when to do it, and how; but their personal opinions, concerns, feelings, or rights were of no interest to their employers. The psychological result of (the response to) this sort of constant stimulus was a belief that there was no need for the individual to take responsibility for his personal success or failure or, in some cases, for him to plan for the future. After all, the individual worker had no control over his own destiny. Persons from this background do not know how to become part of a policy-making group or how to approach the power structure, except to ask for help.

After years of working in a paternalistic employment system, farm migrants may never have applied for a job through an employment agency. They may still go to a loading dock or stand on a street corner waiting for an employer to come to them as they always have. They may not know how to look for work on their own or may lack self-confidence to do any more than stand in a group on the corner to be picked up by a crew leader or a farm foreman. They may be screened out of a job outside of agriculture because they cannot read application forms.

Most middle-aged migrant farm workers have difficulty responding to complicated questionnaires or paper and pencil tests because of their limited education. Just how limited their education is I am finding in the analysis of data from an unpublished study I made in the late 1960s in Michigan. Out of 433 Texas farm migrant families employed in Michigan at that time, 17.26 percent of the men and 5.40 percent of the women had never been to school in their lives, and 55.32 percent of the men and 42.61 percent of the women had less than fifth-grade educations.[3]

Farm workers may have found that advertised jobs are not always available even when they make proper application. Growers sometimes ask for more workers than they need in order to be assured of help. From the grower's viewpoint this technique is good protection; from the workers' it makes their future less certain and destroys their confidence in applying for jobs, especially for jobs outside agriculture. It also makes them less likely to use an employment agency.

Application Procedures as a Barrier to Use of Services

Applications are usually taken in what the migrants see as an impersonal way. The data required on application forms as proof of eligibility for service often create problems for migrants. They see the questions as an infringement on their privacy. Because they do not understand the need for the information, they are guarded and do not volunteer facts for which they are not asked. Sometimes they are confused about what they are asked and what they should volunteer. As in the case of the welfare worker who thought the migrant had "lied" about not having money to pay his medical expenses while the migrant thought he had answered her questions truthfully,[4] the entire application process in any agency or institution may produce an environment in which individuals communicate *past* each other but never *with* each other.

Eligibility as a Barrier to Use of Services

Agency policy is often a point of great confusion for the migrant worker. He may not understand why he is eligible for one service but not for another, and sometimes the service he sees as the one he needs the most is the one which he is refused.

A fifty-seven year old former migrant now supported by his cousin and family obtains medical treatment at a local clinic. Were it not for his cousin he would have no food, no place to sleep, and no clothing to wear. The former migrant is severely crippled with arthritis and cannot work in the fields. While eligible for medical aid, he is not eligible for categorical relief under Aid to the Totally Disabled (ATD), Aid to the Families of Dependent Children (AFDC), Aid to the Aged (AA), or Aid to the Blind (AB). He is not totally disabled. He is not blind. He has no dependent children. He is under sixty-five. Unless a crew leader or grower has paid Agricultural Social Security Taxes for him, he will not even be eligible for Social Security when he is sixty-five, although he worked in agriculture more than forty years.[5]

One of the most confusing eligibilities of all for farm migrants to understand is that applying to their Social Security benefits. Agricultural employers' Social Security Taxes apply to migrants only if the following conditions are met:

1. An employer pays an employee $150 or more in cash wages in the year for agricultural labor [or]
2. An employee performs agricultural labor for an employer on twenty or more days during the year for any amount of cash wages computed on a time basis (day, week, etc.)[6]

If the agricultural worker is a member of an agricultural crew, the crew leader is "treated as employer" by the federal government, not the individual farmer or grower for whom the employee works, regardless of how long he may be employed. Frequently crew leaders neglect this responsibility and may even withhold amounts from the migrant's wages but never report them to the government. There is additional contradiction to the law which adds to the confusion of the migrant worker. The crew leader is only "treated as an employer" by the federal government and held responsible for reporting Social Security Taxes for his workmen if he himself "is not named as an employee in a written agreement entered into with the person for whom the agricultural services are performed."[7] In that case the responsibility for seeing that the migrant builds up benefits rests with the individual farmer or grower for whom he works twenty or more days and earns $150 or more in a year. Often neither the farmer nor the crew leader takes care of the reporting and payment and the migrant's Social Security may be glossed over; at age sixty-five he may find himself without benefits.

Agency Procedure as a Barrier to Use of Services

The migrant assumes he will continue to see the person with whom he made application when he first contacted the agency. He finds the agency deems otherwise. He first saw an intake worker, but later he is assigned a caseworker. In public welfare, with its high rate of staff turnover, he may have a series of caseworkers, each asking the same questions he answered for the intake worker. He does not understand the assignment of case loads. It appears to him that the agency is trying to catch him "in a lie." Why else would he be asked the same questions about his relatives and their income over and over by each new worker he sees? If his relatives could help, he would never apply for welfare because, in his culture, kin is responsible for kin and destitute relatives take care of each other although they may jeopardize their own livelihood. He does not understand or accept agency policy that forbids him to "take in" relatives and support them while he himself is on relief. Kin are his responsibility to feed regardless of the fact that the food was supplied by a welfare department.

Agency policy may compound a problem. The Ramoses were born in Mexico. Five years ago, they settled in a Midwestern state. At the time of this interview, Mr. Ramos was fifty-six, his wife was forty-four, and their eleven children ranged from eight to twenty-seven. Their source of income was a "Mexican products route." Mr. Ramos bought Mexican breads, tortillas, chilies, enchilada sauce, candies, spices, mojo criollo, and canned goods from a city warehouse and sold them to Spanish-speaking families in his area. With help from his older children, he made regular house payments and bought food and some clothing.

There were two expenses he was unable to handle and one for which he applied for help at the welfare department. A fifteen-year-old daughter was missing school because of chronic tonsilitis. Mr. Ramos wanted the agency to pay for a tonsillotomy. The welfare department explained that they could not as long as he owned a car.[8] The other concerned a contractual agreement. A seventeen-year-old son signed up for an art course through a correspondence school. When he could not make payments, he "dropped the course." The school threatened legal action unless Mr. Ramos paid the full tuition.[9]

Contractual problems and threats of lawsuits are common experiences for migrant farm workers. In addition to contracts for cars, furniture, clothing, or jewelry, much of which is overpriced to the migrant, contracts that cause him the most difficulty because of lack of interpretation are those involving services, such as roofing or siding for a house (sometimes a house he does not even own), correspondence courses, or dancing lessons. It is difficult for the migrant to resist sales pressure or the psychological appeal of material things, but it is even more difficult for him to make payments on time and to live up to the agreement of the contract. He needs legal advice and this is generally not available to him within the migrant stream.

Casework Approach as a Barrier to Use of Services

A service as intangible as casework is difficult to explain to a nonsocial worker. It does not make too much sense to say, "We help the client help himself to mobilize whatever resources he has (within self or environment) so he may take responsibility for bringing about a real change in his situation." Such an explanation of service is not even a rational discussion for a farm migrant. If he could *help himself,* he would never have asked for help in the first place; if his environment—the bean field, a truck, or a crowded migrant camp—had the resources, he could find them on his own.

He has trouble seeing how "just talking" will help. He needs and expects action. He is geared to a here-and-now situation. He lives from one emergency to another. He has a problem; he wants an immediate answer. How does he get to the tomatoes of Ohio? He sees no relationship between his early developmental stages and the present. He cannot understand why the social worker asks questions about his family relationships or about how he feels about various things that have happened. He is puzzled why anyone should think that because others have similar experiences, he should learn from them. He sees himself as an individual, unique and different.

Barriers Created by Lack of Awareness on the Part of the Professional Person

When a migrant is accepted for service, the agency—whether health, education, welfare, or employment—often is ill-prepared to understand his value system, his decision-making process, his family relationships, or even his language. His family is usually viewed as a nuclear family; however, such a family pattern seldom exists for the migrant. The migrant family most often seen by the agency consists of three or four generations of relatives, nonrelatives, or individuals adopted, raised, or accepted through marriage. The family may be headed by a man—not necessarily the father, by a woman, or by both. The female head of the family may be the grandmother, although both parents and their children make up the household.

The family decision maker may be a grandmother in Arkansas, an uncle on an Indian reservation in South Dakota, or the spokesman talking with the agency. It is the family decision maker who decides that the family stays in a community or goes somewhere else in search of work, travels in a crew or freewheels, leaving the children with a relative so they can stay in school or allowing the children to drop out of school and go to work in the fields.

The parents may be legally married, live in a consensual arrangement,[10] or be involved in a series of brief affairs.[11] The meaning of the family to children and the children to the family is constantly changing.[12] Under these circumstances, children in the same family may provide the public school with different facts when asked for ages or names of relatives.

Many schools blame migrant parents for their children's poor attendance, frequent tardiness, or slowness in academic subjects.[13] This is an unfair burden when the parents' stay in a community depends upon availability of work or a change in the weather. The parents and their children may arrive with a week left in the school year; they may depart a week after school starts. The parents may want a "good" education for their children and still not enroll them in the local school because their children learn so little when they are in a new and lonely situation. Many of the parents themselves attended schools when education was only necessary for a job outside agriculture. The pressing problems of earning money may loom more important than future earnings as a result of education.

School personnel attempting to schedule conferences often label migrant parents as disinterested in their children's education. Parents may not have adequate clothing to wear to a conference at the school. They may be uncomfortable with teachers, principals, or superintendents because of experiences in their own childhoods. They may be afraid the school wants merely to report problems. They are often confused by education or social work jargon and wonder afterward what the conference was all about. Parents may be ashamed of their own limited education and afraid they will say something to embarrass their children. For them it may seem safer to stay away than to run the risk of hurting their children in the eyes of a teacher or school principal. There is also the reality factor—to attend a teacher-parent conference means loss of work, loss of pay, and the expense of transportation.

Horocio Ulibarri points out that much of the misunderstanding between Chicano clients and Anglo-American professionals concerning appointments and spending patterns is a lack of understanding of cultural aspects. The problem lies in the professional worker's not being aware that the Chicano's regard for exactness of time and his use of his money are contingent upon the requests of his family and friends.[14] Their needs will always come ahead of an agency appointment or the suggested budget worked out in careful detail by the caseworker.[15]

Robert Coles says that the middle-class doctor, when working with the poor, is "overwhelmed by finding that what he has always thought to be 'symptoms' occurring only in some people, now appear everywhere; they are unremarkable, virtually the order of the day."[16]

Without an awareness of the life experiences of the farm migrant, the professional person could well hold unreasonable expectations that would more appropriately apply to middle-class experiences.

Barriers Created by the Migrant's Interpretation of Service

Questionable Services as a Barrier to Their Use

Quite often the migrant feels that he does not receive services when he goes to an agency. This may be because the services offered are different from what he expected or it can be because his way of life does not seem much improved after the service. This latter feeling was found in a three-year study of applicants accepted by the Arizona Division of Rehabilitation.

> The acute financial need of some of the Mexican-Americans was an important factor in their background. Not only was almost fifty-five percent of the group below the poverty line at the time they came to the agency, but almost twenty-two percent of them were $2,000 below the poverty line. Furthermore, more than forty-three percent were still below the poverty line at the end of the study three years later.[17]

Sometimes the "lack of service" is more glaring because it involves a technicality such as an uncompleted form. Recently, an American Red Cross staff member told of a client who applied for dentures a year ago but heard nothing; the agency worker investigated and found the application in an inactive file because it was incomplete.[18] Although this situation does not involve a farm migrant, it is illustrative of what often happens when a migrant reaches out for help. Frequently, he too has difficulty answering questionnaires or applications, and in addition he is not in one place long enough to find an advocate who will follow through and see that his application is "taken out of the inactive file" and processed properly.

Application of "Knowledge" Becomes a Barrier to Use of Services

When a migrant learns the policy of one agency, he applies it to another—whether the service be social work, insurance, or employment. He expects that if he knows how one place operates, his knowledge should apply to other places. When it does not, he begins to question his own capability to get things done or to feel that he is discriminated against.

Lupe Valdez lost a finger in a packing shed accident. The company's insurance paid medical expenses, time lost from work, and some compensation for his finger. By the time the family was interviewed as part of a study conducted by Michigan State University's Center for Rural Manpower and Public Affairs, Lupe's hand had healed. He had returned to work. His family, however, was afraid the insurance company would find out that the finger had healed, would locate them, although they were now in another state, and would make them pay back the $333.33 they had received. They got the impression they would have to repay the company from hearing of "welfare chiselers" who "were" or "should be" forced to reimburse the agency when they got a job.[19]

The Service Itself as a Threat or a Barrier

The service which is offered may be a threat to the migrant, although he has a great need for it. Child welfare services are an example. The migrant may be afraid that if he uses any one of the many services of a child welfare agency he will lose custody of his children. Even more threatening for some parents than the fear of losing custody is the fear of having their children turn to a new love object and show affection for someone other than themselves.

The parent who already feels insecure may find it very difficult to accept the fact that his children respond with love and affection toward a teacher, a foster parent, a social worker, or a nurse. He may feel jealous and cheated that these adults are taking love which rightfully belongs to him. He may struggle between wanting to take his children away or withdrawing himself to punish them for loving someone else. His behavior may be related to his own deprived childhood when his needs for love were not met. His own unmet needs for love may be so great that he may not be able to tolerate the new situation. He may need "to move on to the next crop" and thus restore his relationship with his children.

Sometimes his culture is threatened by the new experiences the school or community provides. This is especially true of the Spanish speaking or the American Indian, as there may also be the language barrier in addition to the cultural barrier.

Barriers Created by the Migrant's Experiences and his Culture

Language as a Conveyor of Barriers

The migrant's words may convey a stronger emotion than he actually feels. He may have a tendency to exaggerate. Such exaggeration may be allowed within his culture or may come about because of his inability to translate certain words with the proper effect. He can say one thing, mean something else, and even convey a third and different meaning with his body language. The gestures of Spanish-speaking migrants may be "so subtle they are understood only by their own fellow Spanish-speaking migrants." It may be next to impossible for an Anglo-American "to differentiate between Mexican-American gestures indicating guilt and those indicating remorse"[20] because, when translated into the gestures of an Anglo-American, these same gestures may indicate neither guilt nor remorse.

Lack of Community Indentity as a Barrier to Use of Services

Regardless of his ethnic background, the migrant is part of a folk culture that has little or no conception of community. He has little or no experience in a community leadership role and usually has very little comprehension of how a community should function to involve all of its members. He sees the community in relationship to self, but not self in relationship to the community. He has difficulty delegating authority to a spokesman. He feels he is "as good as the next one" and is reluctant to accept leadership from his own group, even a family member, unless they are older. He may feel "any assertion of leadership is 'putting on airs' or an assumption of unwanted authority."[21]

Long-range plans, either individual or group, are difficult to carry out among migrant workers because their enthusiasm wanes.

Jack E. Weller describes this in his study of Appalachia: "When the group saw that a long period of cooperative effort would be needed before any progress toward economic renewal could take place, enthusiasm soon died out. . . ."[22]

Culture as a Barrier to Use of Services

The professional worker needs sensitivity in order to understand what the migrant's culture teaches about needs, about asking for help, or about sharing personal information outside the in-group. Many farm migrants are from cultural backgrounds where personal facts relating to family or self are just not discussed outside the family, the tribe, or the clan, especially with strangers. When questions get too personal the migrant may fall back on the protection of the defense mechanisms which are allowed by his culture. These culturally determined defenses may allow him to deny his real feelings by making derogatory comments about his spouse or child. A person from such a culture may say, "My old lady is a sorry sight, stingy and mean, she cannot even fix good slop for the pigs," or "my husband is the kind who is never satisfied unless his wife is pregnant and barefoot," or "that kid of mine is the most ornery, obstinate, and contrary kid I know." All of this may be the acceptable pattern of expression for conversation with a stranger or a researcher who asks too many personal questions. Such derogatory comments do not necessarily reflect how the individual feels. Confrontation, as another example, is not part of the Southern tradition and therefore is culturally defended against. Most farm migrants are from a Southern culture and it is easier for them to avoid subjects of conflict such as sex, race, religion, or family feelings, or to deny them, than it is to talk them through or to be confronted by them in a direct fashion.

It is difficult for a person from a folk culture to view experience in the framework of others. He sees himself as being acted upon. He is forced into situations because of others. He feels surrounded by those who are envious, jealous, or hostile and who give him no choice except to behave in a certain way. It may be very difficult to help such a person take responsibility for his own action. Usually he will hint that he played a part in his problem. He may describe what he did in terms of "I"; but should the caseworker or teacher begin to explore the motivation of the "I," he will shift immediately to "they," over whom the "I" has no control. Through the defense mechanisms of rationalization and projection his ego is defended. He does not have the anxiety-provoking experience of having to take full responsibility for his actions, or his position in life.

The migrant's dislike for formal organization is another cultural attitude that makes use of services difficult.[23] He does not trust big business, political structures, or the so-called "establishment," which includes the administrative bureaucracy of health, education, welfare, and employment agencies.

How to Overcome the Barriers

Most Effective Approaches

There are several effective approaches to breaking down barriers to service. Questions must be concrete. Social workers should ask for a direct description, not a conclusion of feelings, not an analysis of behavior. The most effective programs designed to meet the needs of the poor show an "absence of the traditional concept of eligibility. . . . When a client is reluctant to give information, service is not withheld. Workers visit the homes, go shopping with them, even demonstrate and recommend a course of action for them." Verbalization is regarded as a waste of time.

> The social worker must be able to follow through on details to help the client develop new patterns of behavior. It took four months of persistent attention before the parents and children in one family understood that schools, hospitals, and agencies have a different time orientation than theirs.[24]

A service may not be used because it is not seen as useful or because it is too removed from the actual needs of people. Sometimes the agency is hard to reach. Perhaps the attitude of the staff may be distant—"We know the services you need better than you do; we do not need your help in planning: we need only for you to come and take part in the program we have designed for you." Alfred J. Kahn states this a different way:

Apart from passing new legislation, developing new policies, and launching new programs, all of which are certainly needed in many fields, one can also achieve redistribution of arrangements that facilitate access to the established rights, benefits, services, and entitlements and that assure the actual delivery and use of intended services.[25]

Differentiation of Service Needs

Agencies that would help the poor, especially the rural poor, need to differentiate more accurately the services they offer on the basis of the needs of those they would reach. Many poor people, especially rural poor, need information or advice on how to obtain service, how to make out application forms, or how to enroll in school. With this sort of information they can proceed on their own. Most migrant farm workers fit this classification. They are motivated by a strong desire to take care of themselves. They need direction and encouragement.

Another group, larger this time in terms of the total poor, are those who need motivation. They lack confidence in their own ability to apply for a job, housing, or tuition or to follow through once an application has been made. Large numbers of nonmigrant poor families in rural areas fit this description. Those who left their home base, even to follow the crops, are usually younger, better educated, more highly motivated. Those left behind are less well fitted for competition, and among them, as among the poor of ghetto areas, there is a pervasive sense of defeatism and alienation. They have been out of work so long that they cannot tolerate a regular work pattern.[26] These are people who need supportive help, motivation counseling, or opportunities for improving their self-concept.

Still another group of the poor are those so disadvantaged that they may never be able to use any service other than direct financial support.

The poor need the whole range of services. Some can use long-range psychological services and some cannot. Even for those who can use such services, attention first needs to be given to meeting concrete survival needs. As choice of treatment and use of theory need to be differentiated according to needs, so too does the delivery of service.

Access as the Key to Use of Services

Access to advice and information is a real problem for the poor, especially the farm migrant. In an urban area such access is needed at the neighborhood level, at the housing complex. Access for the nonfarm migrant is the major role of a travelers aid society. Access to information for the migrant is at the point of entry into the state. At the present time only the United States Department of Labor has a booth or trailer at state lines providing information on job opportunities to be found within the state. Although such information is helpful, what really is needed is information on services beyond job opportunities. Information is also needed on other services, including health, education, and welfare, as well as information about policies, laws, and local regulations which might differ from those found in the migrants' home-base states. Access to such information is needed not only at the point of entry into a state but also in migrant camps and in communities and neighborhoods which contribute largely to the make-up of farm labor crews. It is safe to say that such information is needed throughout all areas inhabited by the rural poor.

Out-reach is a major step in service use, but an out-reach approach is effective only if the available services or work experiences are those which the migrant actually can use. In other words, it is cruel to motivate people to the point of acceptance of a program and then not deliver the service which is wanted, needed, and now expected. An honest appraisal of present and future services must be made using the following criteria:

—Does the organization (school or agency) differentiate among the needs of those it would serve, or use, in the case of employment?

—Does it, on the basis of differentiations, determine the type of service it will give (information and advice, legal advice, treatment, financial assistance, etc.)?

—Are the services of the organization accessible to those it would reach?

If the agencies that make up the network of community services are seriously interested in relieving the distress of the poor, the rural poor, and especially the migrant poor, they must dare to reach out and become accessible. The challenge to these agencies, if they want to be accessible, is to always go one step beyond and dare to provide the sustaining help (financial, psychological, or public support) that will indeed enable the needy farm migrant worker and his nonmigrant rural cousins to make use of their services.

A Few Farm Migrants Travelers Aid Has Known

These cases are taken from "Farm Migrants: Why Can't We Help Them Help Themselves?" *Shifting Scenes*, Summer, 1971. I will conclude with them to show what one social work agency needed to do in order to meet the needs of farm migrant clients and to overcome the barriers that stood in the way of community services being provided for some American citizens who are nonresidents.

A Stranded Migrant

Leon Roberts, Black, age fifty, was brought to Travelers Aid by the police after a doctor at a local hospital intervened and prevented his being arrested on charges of vagrancy and drunkenness. The middle-aged migrant had joined a crew in South Carolina, but he had become stranded in Baltimore after he was abandoned by his crew leader. Subject to epilepsy and having had a seizure in the truck, he was sent by the crew leader into a store after tobacco when they stopped in Baltimore. When he came out of the store the truck was gone and, although he looked everywhere, he never saw the crew or the leader again.

Leon had been in Baltimore for some months before his referral, and already he had had an unfortunate and traumatic experience with the police. Standing on a street corner next to a stranger, a man suspected of robbery, Leon was booked as an accomplice when the latter was arrested. Although he tried to tell the police that he had never seen the man before, that he was waiting beside him for a light to change, he too was charged with taking part in the robbery. He was held for two months until released for lack of evidence. After his release he sought work on the docks, found a temporary job, but was assaulted a few days later and robbed of all he had—$2.00. He was taken unconscious to a hospital, and it was after emergency treatment that police, who did not believe his story of assault and robbery, were stopped from arresting him by the resident physician who explained that the migrant was not drunk but had suffered a seizure brought on by the blow on the head.

When he was released from the hospital after emergency treatment, the police brought him to the Travelers Aid office where a worker arranged temporary housing for him while a plan could be worked out. Through another Travelers Aid in South Carolina the worker located Leon's family and gave them news of him; they had not heard from him for nearly a year. Travelers Aid then contacted the South Carolina Department of Public Welfare and discovered that, although Leon had once applied for assistance, he had never received any checks. The welfare department said he had not responded to their letters; they did not know he could not read. The department agreed that Leon qualified and arranged for him to receive needed continued medical treatment and assistance when he returned home.

Travelers Aid provided Leon with a ticket home and money for food during the trip. The South Carolina Travelers Aid met him and saw him home to his family, and continued counseling until the welfare department took over.

A Migrant in Need of Legal Assistance

Diaz Marquex, twenty-six, was in a New Jersey county jail awaiting trial on charges of arson. He had come to work in the New Jersey blueberries from Puerto Rico. The sheriff called Travelers Aid because he thought the young migrant was mentally ill and unfit to stand trial. Moreover, Diaz had no legal representation. By the next day Travelers Aid had obtained a volunteer attorney through the County Bar Association who agreed to represent Diaz. The same day it was arranged for two physicians to examine him in the jail, and he was committed to the state hospital where he was later diagnosed as a schizophrenic.

Working through a sister agency in San Juan, Travelers Aid contacted Diaz's family, who requested that he be sent home where they could look after him. Travelers Aid then approached the prosecuting attorney, and the judge who, after reviewing Diaz's medical and social history, dropped the charges against him on the condition that his family arrange for psychiatric treatment. The family agreed, and Diaz was released and sent home. Had Travelers Aid not become involved Diaz would probably have been convicted and sent to a prison where psychiatric treatment was not available.

A Migrant in Need of Medical Assistance

Mike Franklin, thirty-five, tried to hang himself and was saved by his wife. He was taken to a local hospital for treatment and, because he was a nonresident, Travelers Aid was called by the admissions' office.

The Travelers Aid worker visited Mike, his wife, and six children in the house they had been assigned by his employer—one of the largest processors of frozen foods in the United States—and for which they paid $60.00 a month. Only the loft was habitable. All the windows and doors on the first floor were broken. There was no running water and no bathroom. A triple hot plate was used for cooking, and a large oil-burning space heater was used to warm the sleeping area. There were three double beds, but no other furniture.

The Travelers Aid worker talked with Mike about the attempted suicide and learned that he was overwhelmed by his problems: medical bills for a sick child had accumulated; he had received a series of threatening dunning letters from a collection agency; and he himself was having severe headaches but had not sought treatment because he wanted to take care of his children's needs first.

The Travelers Aid requested that a health inspector examine the home. The home was condemned by the health department and the company provided Mike and his family with new rent-free living quarters until his job with them terminated. The agency worker also arranged for volunteers to drive Mike, who had no transportation of his own, to an out-patient psychiatric clinic for help with his headaches and depression. It developed that he did have a medical problem and that his headaches would respond to treatment.

The Travelers Aid worker turned over the threatening dunning letters to the county attorney, who declared them illegal and forced the collection agency to stop using them and to stop harrassing Mike. Arrangements were worked out whereby modest payments would be accepted on the medical bill instead of the full payment that Mike had no way of making. He could, however, pay off his debts on a monthly basis in accordance with his earnings. As Mike and his family wanted to settle in the community, the Travelers Aid worker helped him find a steady year-round job with a neighboring farmer.

What would have happened to Mike and his family had Travelers Aid not intervened? His attempt at suicide was a cry for help. Had there been no help forthcoming, his next attempt could have been fatal; and his wife and six children could have become public charges for many years to come.

The situations depicted in the above cases are not unique in the experiences of farm migrants. The fact is that farm migrants are frequently caught in conditions over which they have no control. Often they turn to helping persons only to find that those who are professionally trained have little understanding of the conditions under which the migrant works, travels, and lives. The net result is that migrants may feel they are worse off after they have been professionally evaluated than they were before they turned to the agency for help.

NOTES

1. George Simpson, *People in Families* (New York: Thomas Y. Crowell Co., 1960), p. 8.

2. Personal interview with migrant.

3. Myrtle R. Reul, unpublished material.

4. Personal interview with the social worker and the migrant.

5. Personal interview with the migrant and his family.

6. From U.S., Department of the Treasury, Internal Revenue Service, "1970 Internal Revenue Service Tax Guide," Circular A.

7. *Ibid.*

8. It was difficult to determine if the confusion was due to language, as Mr. Ramos speaks limited English and the welfare workers did not understand Spanish, or if the agency was as rigid as Mr. Ramos saw it to be.

9. Personal interview with the family.

10. Consensual marriages are found frequently among the Spanish speaking. See Julian H. Steward, "Culture Patterns in Puerto Rico," *Annals of the American Academy of Political and Social Science,* CCLXXXV (January 1963), 95-103, for a description of regional and class subcultures on the island. Also see Kathleen L. Wolf, "Growing Up and Its Price in Three Puerto Rican Sub-cultures," *Psychiatry,* XV (1952), 401-33.

11. Elliot Liebow makes a careful distinction between "legal marriage, common-law marriage and living with" as seen among lower-class Blacks. *Tally's Corner* (Boston, Mass.: Little, Brown and Co., 1967), pp. 103-16.

12. Hertha Riese, *Heal the Hurt Child* (Chicago: University of Chicago Press, 1962), pp. 46-48.

13. Myrtle R. Reul, "Migrant Education Needs Encouragement," *Detroit News Magazine,* June 4, 1967, p. 8.

14. Horocio Ulibarri, "Social and Attitudinal Characteristics in Spanish-speaking Migrants and Ex-migrants in the Southwest," *Sociological and Social Research,* L (1966), 361-70; Naomi Hayward, *Socio-Economic and Other Variations Related to Rehabilitation of Mexican Americans in Arizona* (Tempe, Ariz.: Bureau of Publications, Arizona State University, 1969), pp. 3-11; and also Robert G. Hayden, "Spanish-Americans of the Southwest, Life Style Patterns and the Implications," *Welfare in Review,* XIV (1966), 14-25.

15. These same characteristics are found among American Indians where the concept of time and the use of money are viewed within a different value system from that of the white middle class. They have also been attributed to other groups, but I think they are characteristics of social class or are individual responses to the environment rather than cultural characteristics.

16. "What Poverty Does to the Mind," *The Nation,* June 20, 1966, pp. 746-48.

17. Hayward, *Socio-Economic and Other Variations,* p. 72.

18. Personal interview with the agency worker.

19. Personal interview with migrant and his family.

20. Sister Frances Jerome Woods, "Cultural Conditioning in Mental Health," *Social Casework,* XXIX (1958), 3-7.

21. Dwight Sanderson, *Leadership for Rural Life* (New York: Association Press, 1940), p. 66.

22. *Yesterday's People* (Lexington, Ky.: University of Kentucky Press, 1966), p. 95.

23. Distrust of organizations is found mostly among Spanish-speaking migrants and white migrants from Appalachia, the Ozarks, and the rural South. Black migrants have had so many negative experiences with such things as tests and forms that they are often "turned off" at the idea of going through the usual agency channels to get service. The distrust of migrants comes from what they see as an ultimate and subtle discrimination in the application of rules and regulations. They feel they are getting the run-around and not the service they need.

24. Margaret C. Shea, "Serving Low Income Persons: New Demands on Social Workers," *Anti-Poverty Programs: Implications for Social Work Education* (New York: Council on Social Work Education, 1967), pp. 3, 4, 6.

25. "Perspectives on Access to Social Services," *Social Work,* XV (April 1970), 97.

26. For a more complete discussion on this subject see J. W. Lawrie, "Making It the Hardest Way," *Psychology Today,* III (November 1969), 29-31, 60.

PART VII

Epilogue

. . . one must understand both the condi-
tions which underlie the demands for
autonomy and economic improvement,
and the difficulties to be overcome in
changing them.

Annette Baker Fox, 20th century
American authoress
Freedom and Welfare in the Caribbean

35

Beyond the Present

In these final pages, I want the reader to become more than ever conscious of the most pressing problem facing our nation today—that of our undeveloped human resources, especially our rural human resources. Throughout this volume I have attempted to help the reader become aware of this problem by examining the territorial boundaries as well as the structure of rural poverty. But the issues I have raised apply to all society, whether rural or urban, and illustrate the misuse or lack of use of people, especially poor people. Some of these issues have included minority-majority relations, sexual equality, regional equality, and attitudes toward the poor. None of these issues are new to this decade; they were all identified long before the turn of this century. But the very fact that they have been allowed to exist so long, together with their current urgency, only proves more than ever that in spite of our scientific knowledge and expertise, we as a country still do not know how to maximize the use of our human resources or how to enable individuals to reach their real potential or even to use the strengths they have already identified.

609

Individual Differences

Although we have tended to continue to evaluate individuals according to their race, nationality, sex, and geographical location, we have failed to recognize what Clyde Kluckhorn and other social scientists have spelled out for us for years—namely, that each individual is like all other individuals in that some of the determinants of personality are universal to the species; that all personalities are similar insofar as they all experience both gratifications and deprivations; and that each individual is uniquely different from all other individuals in that his or her modes of perceiving, feeling, needing, and behaving have characteristic patterns that are not precisely duplicated by those of any other individual.[1] Therefore, each individual has a unique worth—regardless of sex, race, age, nationality, or creed—and should have the opportunity to develop as fully as possible.

Effect on the Individual

For individuals in a rapidly changing country like the United States, where even the territorial boundaries of rural poverty are in a state of flux, success or failure may appear less related to competence and effort and more related to forces over which they have seemingly little control.[2] Because of the extent of this sort of individual stress, today more than ever before it is necessary for us as a country to view change, or lack of change, as it affects human beings. And if we do that we must consider a new approach to our national productivity. Rather than being concerned with production for profit only, we then would be concerned with ways of enhancing the social functioning of all our people—in short, with human profit. To accomplish this transformation, we would be forced to find equality solutions to reduce the stress of the rural poverty described in this book. Reducing such stress is more than providing jobs for poor people; it is also providing human services and giving recognition to all contributions that are made, regardless of who makes them.

For example, because of regional inequality—that is, inequality in the opportunities available to rural areas compared to urban areas—we penalize individuals purely on the basis of their geographical location. To further such geographical discrimination, we add resident and legal domicile requirements. We also relegate females to subservient positions, label them as nonproductive if they remain there, and penalize them through lower wages and continuous criticism if they dare do otherwise. We tend to label races or ethnic groups as superior or inferior without seeming to realize, as Kluckhohn points out, that practically all differences disappear when individuals or families of the same socioeconomic levels are compared. We put the burden on the individual to improve his own situation or else to leave, especially in rural areas where, up to now, there have been few opportunities for improvement and so the only alternative is to leave.

New Emphases

The solution to rural poverty, we should know by now, is not the migration of poor rural residents to cities; that solution has been tried and it has failed. The solution to rural poverty is to provide opportunities for education, employment, good housing, health, and social services in local areas. Having solved the problems of production—we certainly know how to produce food and material things—we now face the real problem of more equal distribution and, beyond that, the greater need to turn our attention to the development of human potential. As a nation we have not begun to tap our human power, the unrealized capabilities of the poor, the nonwhites, females, or those living in rural areas. Although we have tapped some human resources—the rich and affluent, whites, males, or those who live in urban areas—we certainly have never used them to their full potential. In other words, our greatest resource—*human beings*—has also become in the 1970s our greatest *unmet need* and often our greatest *unrecognized need*. This neglect calls for a new approach to viewing and using human resources. Such an approach would have the potential for improving the quality of American life, but at the same time it would be extremely threatening to individual self-identity because it would demand change and new ways of examining old issues.

We live in a new era. What is really new today is a revolution in our aspirations for extending the full benefits of society to all—to rural areas as well as urban, to women as well as men, to the poor as well as the rich, to nonwhites as well as whites. We live today in an era of upheaval, of enormous problems but of great promise.[3] We are challenged to respond to a series of related rural, racial, moral, sexual equality, and political crises, and to realistically recognize their dangers. They do demand change and creative regard for the opportunities they present. In part, this means giving up ideas and attitudes suitable to the past but unrelated to the present. Most of these ideas and attitudes have to do with equality—racial, sexual, and regional—and paramount in the midst of all of this are attitudes toward rural equality.

We, as a nation, must see that our rural areas are supplied with resources, financial and otherwise, on the basis of the degree of human need represented there, in order that the vast territorial boundaries of rural poverty can be reduced. This will involve more than the federal government's obligation to budget more monies for rural expenditures; this will involve a nationwide recognition that we as a country can truly be only as strong as our poorest rural areas and the farm laborers who live there. The territorial boundaries of rural America and the people who live and work within them are still the foundation for our urbanization even as they were before we became an industrial society. The words of Oliver Goldsmith, the British writer of the eighteenth century, are as true of our country today as they were of England when he wrote.

> Ill fares the land, to hast'ning ills a prey,
> Where wealth accumulates, and men decay;
> Princes and lords may flourish, or may fade,
> A breath can make them, as a breath has made;
> But a bold peasantry, their country's pride
> When once destroyed, can never be supplied.

And if the words of Goldsmith are truly believed, they will carry a commitment to reduce the boundaries of rural poverty in this country and to provide opportunities for our rural poor equal to those found in other areas of America so that migration out of the rural sections is not the one-and-only choice.

NOTES

1. A. L. Kroeber and Clyde Kluckhorn, *Culture A Critical Review of Concepts and Definitions,* Vintage Books (New York: Random House, Inc., 1952).

2. Social classes and individual life styles are as varied, and sometimes even more so, in rural areas as they are in urban neighborhoods, reasons for which can be found when individual families are examined. For example, families with low incomes and a low standard of living, tend in rural areas to be provincial and more traditional, regardless of their race or ethnic culture, than those who have a higher income but who may also live in inadequate housing. In such a case, it might appear that those with higher incomes are less traditional, but a further examination will show that those who earn more money are usually younger, better educated, and more adaptable to change than are older and less educated members of the same rural neighborhood, who, because they do not change, are more traditional. Also within the same socioeconomic level and, therefore, identified as low-income individuals, are those who have had past leadership roles, who have known a higher standard of living, but who are now in a low-income bracket because of age, retirement, or illness. These individuals tend to be older, more dependent, and more concerned about the problems of their immediate living situation than they are with the broader concerns of their neighborhood.

Leadership in these rural areas tends to be in the hands of those who are near middle age or older, have lived in the area for some time, or whose families have lived there for a long time; they usually tend to be conservative. These rural leaders—such as bankers, landlords, or employers such as mill owners—come from backgrounds where they have always worked for themselves rather than for others, and they are usually in a position that influences the lives of others. They are the individuals most knowledgeable about the community and use of the community structure. Sometimes they are the only ones who really know how to get things done because they know and are part of the influential force behind the power structure.

3. For more information on this subject see John Romanyshyn, *Social Welfare: Charity to Justice* (New York: Random House, Inc., 1971), pp. 82-87.

Bibliography

Books

Allen, Hervey. *Anthony Adverse*. New York: Farrer and Rinehart, Inc., 1933.

Allport, Gordon W. *The Nature of Prejudice*. Anchor Books. Garden City, N.J.: Doubleday and Co., Inc., 1958.

American Annual Cyclopaedia and Register of Important Events of the Year 1861. Vol. I. New York: D. Appleton and Co., 1862.

American Annual Cyclopaedia and Register of Important Events of the Year 1867. Vol. VII. New York: D. Appleton and Co., 1868.

Ames, Jessie Daniel. *The Changing Character of Lynching: Review of Lynching, 1931-1941 with a Discussion of Recent Developments in the Field*. Atlanta, Ga.: Commission on Interracial Cooperation, Inc., 1942.

Arieti, Silvane, ed. *American Handbook of Psychiatry*. Vols. I and III. New York: Basic Books, Inc., 1959, 1966.

Astin, Helen S.; Suniewick, Nancy; and Dweck, Susan. *Women: A Bibliography on Their Education and Careers*. Washington, D.C.: Human Service Press, 1971.

Barrio, Raymond. *The Plum Plum Pickers*. New York: Century Press, 1969.

Basden, George Thomas. *Ibos of Nigeria*. Philadelphia, Pa.: J. P. Lippincott Co., 1931.

Beck, Aaron T. *Depression: Clinical, Experimental, and Theoretical Aspects*. New York: Harper and Row, Publishers, 1967.

Bell, Norman, and Vogel, Ezra F., eds. *A Modern Introduction to the Family*. New York: Free Press, 1968.

Bernard, Jessie. *Marriage and Family Among Negroes*. Englewood Cliffs, N.J.: Prentice-Hall, Inc., 1966.

615

Bertelson, David. *The Lazy South.* New York: Oxford University Press, 1967.

Bible. King James version.

Bigelow, Karl W., ed. *Cultural Groups and Human Relations.* New York: Bureau of Publications, Teachers College, Columbia University, 1951.

Bird, Caroline. *The Invisible Scar.* Pocket Books. New York: Simon and Schuster, Inc., 1967.

Bloom, S.; Davis, A.; and Hess, R. *Contemporary Education for Cultural Deprivation.* New York: Holt, Rinehart and Winston, Inc., 1965.

Bonner, James C. *The Georgia Story.* Oklahoma City, Okla.: Harlow Publishing Corp., 1961.

Bosman, William. *Description of the Coast of Guinea.* London: Printed for F. Knapton, A. Bell, R. Smith, E. Midwinter, H. Haws, W. Davis, C. Strahan, B. Lintott, T. Round, and F. Wale, 1705.

Bossing, Nelson L., and Martin, Robert R. *Solving Our Problems in a Democracy.* River Forest, Ill.: Laidlaw Bros., 1956.

Botkin, B.A., ed. *A Treasure of Southern Folklore.* New York: Crown Publishers, 1949.

Bourke-White, Margaret. *Portrait of Myself.* New York: Simon and Schuster, Inc., 1963.

Bowman, Mary Jean, and Haynes, W. Warren. *Resources and People in East Kentucky.* Baltimore, Md.: Johns Hopkins Press, 1963.

Bremner, Robert H. *From the Depths.* New York: New York University Press, 1964.

Brenner, Charles. *An Elementary Textbook of Psychoanalysis.* Anchor Books. Garden City, N.J.: Doubleday and Co., Inc., 1955.

Broom, Leonard. *The Japanese-American Family in World War II.* Berkeley, Calif.: University of California Press, 1956.

Brophy, William A., and Aberle, Sophie D. *The Indian: America's Unfinished Business.* Norman, Okla.: University of Oklahoma Press, 1966.

Brown, Claude. *Manchild in the Promised Land.* New York: Macmillan Co., 1965.

Brown, Dee. *Bury My Heart at Wounded Knee.* New York: Holt, Rinehart and Winston, Inc., 1970.

Brown, Francis J., and Roucek, Joseph Slabey. *One America.* New York: Prentice-Hall, Inc., 1945.

Brown, Ina Corinne. *Understanding Other Cultures.* Englewood Cliffs, N.J.: Prentice-Hall, Inc., 1963.

Burchinal, Lee G., ed. *Rural Youth in Crisis: Facts, Myths, and Social Change.* Washington, D.C.: U.S. Department of Health, Education and Welfare, 1964.

Burma, John H. *Mexican-Americans in the United States.* Cambridge, Mass.: Schenkman Co., Inc., 1970.

Butts, R. Freeman. *A Cultural History of Education.* New York: McGraw-Hill Book Co., Inc., 1947.

Cabrera, Y. Arturo. *Emerging Faces: The Mexican-Americans.* Dubuque, Iowa: William C. Brown Co., Publishers, 1971.

Caldwell, Erskine. *The Pocket Book of Erskine Caldwell Stories.* Pocket Books. New York: Simon and Schuster, Inc., 1949.

_____. *Trouble in July.* Signet Books. New York: New American Library, Inc., 1949.

Calvin, John. *Institute of the Christian Religion.* Translated by John Allen. Book III. Philadelphia, Pa.: Presbyterian Board of Christian Education, 1928.

Campbell, John C. *The Southern Highlander and His Homeland.* New York: Russell Sage Foundation, 1921.

Carawan, Guy; Carawan, Candie; and Yellin, Robert, eds. *Ain't You Got a Right to the Tree of Life?* New York: Simon and Schuster, Inc., 1966.

Carranza, Eliu. *Pensamientos on Los Chicanos: A Cultural Revolution.* Berkeley, Calif.: California Book Co., 1971.

Carter, Thomas P. *Mexican-Americans in School: A History of Educational Neglect.* Princeton, N.J.: College Entrance Examination Board, 1970.

Cash, W.J. *The Mind of the South.* Vintage Books. New York: Random House, Inc., 1941.

Caudill, Harry M. *Night Comes to the Cumberlands.* Boston, Mass.: Little, Brown and Co., 1962.

Cede, Toni, ed. *The Black Woman: An Anthology.* Signet Classics. New York: New American Library, Inc., 1970.

Chambers, William Trout. *Texas—Its Land and People.* Austin, Tex.: Steck Co., 1952.

Channing, Edward. *History of the United States.* Vol. II. New York: Macmillan Co., 1913.

Children and Youth in the 1960's. Washington, D.C.: White House Conference on Children and Youth, 1960.

Cleaver, Eldridge. *Soul on Ice.* New York: McGraw-Hill Book Co., Inc., 1968.

Close, Upton, and Burke, Merle. *The Ladder of History.* New York: Macmillan Co., 1946.

Coe, Michael D. *Mexico.* New York: Frederick A. Praeger, 1962.

Cohn, David L. *God Shakes Creation.* New York: Harper and Bros., 1935.

Coles, Robert. *Children of Crisis.* New York: Dell Publishing Co., 1967.

_____. *Migrant Farmer: A Psychiatric Study.* Atlanta, Ga.: Southern Regional Council, 1965.

Collier, John. *Indians of the Americas.* Mentor Books. New York: New American Library, Inc., 1947.

Commons, J. R. *Races and Immigrants in America.* New York: Macmillan Co., 1920.

Coopersmith, Stanley. *The Antecedents of Self-Esteem.* San Francisco, Calif.: W. H. Freeman, 1967.

Dale, Eberet. *The Indians of the Southwest.* Norman, Okla.: University of Oklahoma Press, 1949.

Danforth, Mildred E. *A Quaker Pioneer.* New York: Exposition Press, 1961.

David, Allison, and Dollard, John. *Children of Bondage.* Washington, D.C.: American Council on Education, 1940.

Deutsch, Martin. *Minority Group and Class Status as Related to Social and Personality Factors in Scholastic Achievement.* Monogram No. 2. Ithaca, N.Y.: Society for Applied Anthropology, 1960.

Dickson, Harris. *The Story of King Cotton.* New York: Funk and Wagnalls Co., 1937.

Diggory, J. *Self-Evaluation.* New York: John Wiley and Sons, Inc., 1966.

Dubofsky, Melvyn. *We Shall Be All.* Quadrangle Books. Chicago: New York Times Co., 1969.

Eaton, Joseph W., ed. *Migration and Social Welfare.* New York: National Association of Social Workers, Inc., 1971.

Echanove, Triyillo Carlos A. *Mexico: A Sociological, Economical and Political Approach.* San Diego, Calif.: Division of Research, San Diego State College, 1966.

Eleazer, Robert B. *Thy Neighbor as Thyself.* Atlanta, Ga.: By the Author, 1953.

Engel, George L. *Psychological Development in Health and Disease.* Philadelphia, Pa.: W. B. Saunders Co., 1962.

Embree, Edwin Roger. *Brown Americans: The Story of a Tenth of the Nation.* New York: Viking Press, 1945.

English, O. Spurgeon, and Finch, Stuart M. *Introduction to Psychiatry*. New York: W. W. Norton and Co., Inc., 1954.

English, O. Spurgeon, and Pearson, Gerald H. J. *Emotional Problems of Living*. New York: W. W. Norton and Co., Inc., 1955.

Erikson, Erik H. *Childhood and Society*. New York: W. W. Norton and Co., Inc., 1950.

Fagen, Richard; Brody, Richard A.; and O'Leary, Thomas. *Cubans in Exile*. Stanford, Calif.: Stanford University Press, 1968.

Fairburn, Ann. *Five Smooth Stones*. New York: Bantam Books, Inc., 1966.

Fairchild, Henry Pratt. *Immigrant Backgrounds*. New York: Wiley and Sons, Inc., 1927.

Faulkner, William. *As I Lay Dying*. New York: Random House, Inc., 1930.

Fenalson, Anne F. *Essentials in Interviewing*. New York: Harper and Bros., 1952.

Fenichel, Otto. *The Psychoanalytic Theory of Neurosis*. New York: W. W. Norton and Co., Inc., 1945.

Flynn, Elizabeth Curley. *Sabotage: The Conscious Withdrawal of the Workers' Industrial Efficiency*. Cleveland, Ohio: I. W. W. Publishing Bureau, 1915.

Ford, Thomas R., ed. *The Southern Appalachian Region: A Survey*. Lexington, Ky.: University of Kentucky Press, 1962.

Fox, John, Jr. *The Little Shepherd of Kingdom Come*. New York: Charles Scribner's Sons, 1903.

Freud, Sigmund. *Complete Works*. Standard ed. London: Hogarth Press, 1957, 1959, 1961.

Friedland, William H., and Nelkin, Dorothy. *Migrant: Agricultural Workers in America's Northeast*. New York: Holt, Rinehart and Winston, 1971.

Fromm, Erich. *Escape from Freedom*. New York: Rinehart and Co., Inc., 1941.

————. *Man for Himself*. New York: Rinehart and Co., Inc., 1947.

Galarza, Ernesto. *Barrio Boy*. Notre Dame, Ind.: University of Notre Dame Press, 1971.

————. *Merchants of Labor: The Mexican Bracero History*. Santa Barbara, Calif.: McNally and Loftin, 1964.

————. *Spiders in the House and Workers in the Field*. Notre Dame, Ind.: University of Notre Dame Press, 1970.

Gamio, Manuel. *Mexican Immigration to the United States*. Chicago: University of Chicago Press, 1930.

Geiser, Karl F. *Redemptioners and Indentured Servants in the Colony and Commonwealth of Pennsylvania.* New Haven, Conn.: Tuttle, Morehouse and Taylor Co., 1901.

Georgia Writers' Project. *Drums and Shadows: Survival Studies among the Georgia Coastal Negroes.* Athens, Ga.: University of Georgia Press, 1940.

Ginsburg, Sol W. *A Psychiatrist's Views on Social Issues.* New York: Columbia University Press, 1963.

Gittler, Joseph B., ed. *Understanding Minority Groups.* New York: John Wiley and Sons, Inc., 1964.

Glazer, Nona Y., and Creedon, Carol J. *Children and Poverty.* Chicago: Rand McNally Co., 1968.

Gordon, Margaret S., ed. *Poverty in America.* San Francisco, Calif.: Chandler Publishing Co., 1965.

Grebler, Leo; Moore, Joan; and Guzman, Ralph. *The Mexican-American People.* New York: Free Press, 1970.

Greenhut, Melvin L., and Whitman, W. Tate, eds. *Essays in Southern Economic Development.* Chapel Hill, N.C.: University of North Carolina Press, 1964.

Grey, Zane. *The Desert of Wheat.* New York: Harper and Bros., 1919.

Grier, William H., and Cobbs, Price M. *Black Rage.* New York: Bantam Books, Inc., 1968.

Griffin, John Howard. *Black Like Me.* New York: New American Library, Inc., 1960.

Haimowitz, Morris L., and Haimowitz, Natalie Reader, eds. *Human Development: Selected Readings.* New York: Thomas Y. Crowell Co., 1960.

Haley, Jay. *Strategies of Psychotherapy.* New York: Grune and Stratton, 1963.

Hall, Edward T. *The Silent Language.* Garden City, N.J.: Doubleday and Co., Inc., 1959.

Hammerton, J. A., ed. *Manners and Customs of Mankind.* Vols. I and II. London: Amalgamated Press, Ltd., 1935.

Hansen, Niles M. *Rural Poverty and the Urban Crisis: A Strategy for Regional Development.* Bloomington, Ind.: Indiana University Press, 1970.

Hart, John Fraser. *The Southeastern United States.* Princeton, N.J.: D. Van Nostrand Co., Inc., 1967.

Hayward, Naomi. *Socio-Economic and Other Variations Related to Rehabilitation of Mexican Americans in Arizona.* Tempe, Ariz.: Bureau of Publications, Arizona State University, 1969.

Heller, Celia S. *Mexican American Youth: Forgotten Youth at the Crossroads.* New York: Random House, Inc., 1966.

Hendricks, W. C., ed. *Bundle of Trouble and Other Tarheel Tales.* Durham, N.C.: Duke University Press, 1943.

Herrick, C. A. *White Servitude in Pennsylvania.* Philadelphia, Pa.: University of Pennsylvania Press, 1926.

Herzberg, Frederick, *et al. The Motivation to Work.* New York: John Wiley and Sons, Inc., 1959.

Hosokawa, William K. *Nisei: The Quiet Americans.* New York: William Morrow and Co., Inc., 1969.

Hough, Henry W. *Development of Indian Resources.* Denver, Colo.: World Press, 1967.

Houston, James. *The White Dawn.* New York: Harcourt Brace Jovanovich, Inc., 1971.

Howard, Helen Addison. *War Chief Joseph.* Caldwell, Idaho: Caxton Printers, 1941.

Jernegan, Marcus W. *Laboring and Dependent Classes in Colonial America, 1607-1783.* Chicago: Frederick Ungar, 1931.

Johnson, Charles S. *Growing Up in the Black Belt.* New York: Schocken Books, 1967.

_____. *Shadow of the Plantation.* Chicago: University of Chicago Press, 1934.

Josselyn, Irene M. *The Happy Child.* New York: Random House, Inc., 1955.

Kaplan, Bert, ed. *Studying Personality Cross-Culturally.* Evanston, Ill.: Row, Peterson and Co., 1961.

Keller, Suzanne. *The American Lower Class Family.* Albany, N.Y.: New York State Division for Youth, 1968.

Kitano, Harry H. L. *Japanese Americans: The Evolution of a Subculture.* Englewood Cliffs, N.J.: Prentice-Hall, Inc., 1969.

Kluckhorn, Clyde, and Murray, Henry A. *Personality in Nature, Society, and Culture.* New York: Alfred A. Knopf, 1953.

Kornbluh, Joyce L., ed. *Rebel Voices, an I.W.W. Anthology.* Ann Arbor, Mich.: University of Michigan Press, 1964.

Kreitlow, Burton W.; Aiton, E. W.; and Torrence, Andrew P. *Leadership for Action in Rural Communities.* Danville, Ill.: Interstate Printers and Publishers, Inc., 1960.

Krier, H. *Rural Manpower and Industrial Development.* Paris: Organization for Economic Cooperation and Development, 1961.

Kroeber, A. L., and Kluckhorn, Clyde. *Culture—A Critical Review of Concepts and Definitions.* Vintage Books. New York: Random House, Inc., 1952.

Landis, Paul H. *Our Changing Society*. New York: Ginn and Co., 1942.

Lazo, Mario. *Dagger in the Heart*. New York: Twin Circle Publishing Co., 1968.

Leacock, Eleanor Burke. *The Culture of Poverty*. New York: Simon and Schuster, Inc., 1971.

Lee, Dorothy. *Freedom and Culture*. Englewood Cliffs, N.J.: Prentice-Hall, Inc., 1959.

Lee, Harper. *To Kill a Mockingbird*. New York: Popular Library, Inc., 1960. Also New York: J. B. Lippincott Co., 1960.

Leeper, Robert, and Madison, Peter. *Toward Understanding Human Personalities*. New York: Appleton-Century-Crofts, 1959.

Leinwand, Gerald, assisted by Collins, Elsie. *Power and the Poor*. New York: Washington Square Press, Inc., 1968.

Lewis, Oscar. *Five Families: Mexican Case Studies in the Culture of Poverty*. New York: Basic Books, Inc., 1959.

_____. *La Vida: A Puerto Rican Family in the Culture of Poverty*. New York: Random House, Inc., 1966.

_____. *Life in a Mexican Village: Tepotzlan Restudied*. Urbana, Ill.: University of Illinois, 1951.

_____. *Pedro Martinez*. New York: Random House, Inc., 1964.

_____. *The Children of Sanchez: Autobiography of a Mexican Family*. Vintage Books. New York: Random House, Inc., 1961.

Lidz, Theodore; Fleck, Stephen; and Cornelison, Alice R. *Schizophrenia and the Family*. New York: International Universities Press, Inc., 1965.

Liebow, Elliott. *Tally's Corner*. Boston, Mass.: Little, Brown and Co., 1967.

Lincoln, C. Eric. *The Negro Pilgrimage in America*. New York: Bantam Books, Inc., 1967.

Linton, Ralph, ed. *Acculturation in Seven American Indian Tribes*. Gloucester, Mass.: Peter Smith, 1963.

MacDougall, D., ed. *Scots and Scots' Descendants in America*. New York: Caledonian Publishing Co., 1917.

MacGregor, Gordon. *Warriors Without Weapons*. Chicago: University of Chicago Press, 1946.

MacGregor, James H. *The Wounded Knee Massacre*. Baltimore, Md.: Wirth Bros., 1940.

Maddox, James G.; Liebhafsky, E. E.; Henderson, Vivian W.; and Manlin, Herbert M. *The Advancing South*. New York: Twentieth Century Fund, 1967.

Malcolm X. *Autobiography of Malcolm X*. New York: Grove Press, 1964.

Manuel, Herschel T. *Spanish-Speaking Children of the Southwest: Their Education and Public Welfare.* Austin, Tex.: University of Texas Press, 1969.

Matsumoto, Toru. *Beyond Prejudice.* New York: Friendship Press, 1946.

May, Edgar. *The Wasted Americans.* New York: Harper and Row, Publishers, 1964.

McLaughlin, James. *My Friend the Indian.* Boston, Mass.: Houghton Mifflin Co., 1910.

McLuhnan, T. C. *Touch the Earth.* New York: Outerbridge and Dienstfrey.

McWilliam*   Brothers Under the Skin.* Boston, Mass.: Little, Brown a   , 1943.

_____. *Factories in the Field.* Boston, Mass.: Little, Brown and Co., 1939.

_____. *Ill Fares the Land.* New York: Barnes and Noble, Inc., 1967.

_____. *North from Mexico.* Philadelphia, Pa.: J. B. Lippincott Co., 1949. Reprinted, 1968, Greenwood Press, New York.

_____. *Prejudice: Japanese-Americans.* Boston, Mass.: Little, Brown and Co., 1944.

Mead, Margaret, ed. *Cultural Patterns and Technical Change.* New York: New American Library, Inc., 1955.

Miller, Herman. *Rich Man, Poor Man: The Distribution of Income in America.* New York: Crowell Publishers, 1970.

Mills, C. Wright; Senior, Clarence; and Goldsen, Rose Kohn. *The Puerto Rican Journey.* New York: Harper and Bros., 1950.

Milt, Harry. *Trends in Psychiatry.* Vol. III. Rahway, N.J.: Merck and Co., 1966.

Moloney, James Clark. *The Magic Cloak.* Wakefield, Mass.: Montrose Press, 1949.

Morgan, Edmund S. *The Puritan Family.* New York: Harper and Row, Publishers, 1944.

Muzzey, David Saville. *A History of Our Country.* New York: Ginn and Co., 1943.

Nixon, Herman Clarence. *Possum Trot, Rural Community South.* Norman, Okla.: University of Oklahoma Press, 1941.

Norquest, Carrol. *Rio Grande Wetbacks.* Albuquerque, N.M.: University of New Mexico Press, 1972.

Opler, Marvin K. *Culture and Social Psychiatry.* New York: Atherton Press, 1967.

Padilla, Elena. *Up From Puerto Rico.* New York: Columbia University Press, 1958.

Parad, Howard, ed. *Crisis Intervention: Selected Readings.* New York: Family Service Association of America, 1965.

Parrington, V. L. *The Colonial Mind, 1620-1800.* New York: Harcourt Brace and Co., 1920.

Passow, Harry; Goldberg, Miriam; and Tannenbaum, Abraham J. *Education of the Disadvantaged.* New York: Holt, Rinehart and Winston, Inc., 1967.

Pearsall, Marion. *Little Smokey Ridge: The Natural History of a Southern Appalachian Neighborhood.* University, Ala.: University of Alabama Press, 1959.

Petersen, William. *Japanese Americans: Oppression and Success.* New York: Random House, Inc., 1971.

Plaut, R. L. *Blueprint for Talent Searching.* New York: National Scholarship Service and Fund for Negro Students, 1957.

Prescott, William H. *Conquest of Mexico.* New York: Book League of America, 1934.

Proceedings of the First Convention of the I. W. W. New York: Labor News Co., 1905.

Proceedings of the 1908 I.W.W. Convention. New York: Labor News Co., 1908.

Proshansky, Harold M.; Ittelson, William H.; and Rivlin, Leanne G., eds. *Environmental Psychology: Man and His Physical Setting.* New York: Holt, Rinehart and Winston, Inc., 1970.

Raab, Earl, and Selznick, Gertrude Jaeger. *Major Social Problems.* Evanston, Ill.: Row, Peterson and Co., 1961.

Raper, Arthur F., and Reid, Ira De A. *Sharecroppers All.* Chapel Hill, N.C.: University of North Carolina Press, 1941.

Redfield, Robert. *Tepoztlan, A Mexican Village.* Chicago: University of Chicago Press, 1930.

Redlich, Fredrick C., and Freedman, Daniel X. *The Theory and Practice of Psychiatry.* New York: Basic Books, Inc., 1966.

Reid, Ira De Augustine. *The Negro Immigrant.* New York: Ams Press, 1968.

Reul, Myrtle R. *Where Hannibal Led Us.* New York: Vantage Press, 1967.

Rice, John Andrew. *I Came Out of the Eighteenth Century.* New York: Harper and Bros., 1942.

Riese, Hertha. *Heal the Hurt Child.* Chicago: University of Chicago Press, 1966.

Riessman, Frank; Cohen, Jerome; and Pearl, Arthur, eds. *Mental Health of the Poor.* New York: Free Press of Glencoe, 1964.

Romanyshyn, John M. *Social Welfare: Charity to Justice.* New York: Random House, Inc., 1971.

Rosenberg, M. *Society and the Adolescent Self-Image.* Princeton, N.J.: Princeton University Press, 1965.

Rubel, Arthur J. *Across the Tracks: Mexican-Americans in a Texas City.* Austin, Tex.: University of Texas Press, 1966.

Ruesch, Jurgen, and Bateson, G. *Communication: The Social Matrix of Psychiatry.* New York: W. W. Norton and Co., Inc., 1951.

Ruesch, Jurgen, and Kees, Weldon. *Nonverbal Communication.* Berkeley, Calif.: University of California Press, 1956.

Samora, Julian. *Los Mojados: The Wetback Story.* Notre Dame, Ind.: University of Notre Dame Press, 1971.

Sanderson, Dwight. *Leadership for Rural Life.* New York: Association Press, 1940.

Saunders, Lyle. *Cultural Differences and Medical Care.* New York: Russell Sage Foundation, 1954.

Senn, Milton J. E., ed. *Symposium on the Healthy Personality.* New York: Josiah Macy, Jr. Foundation, 1950.

Simmen, Edward, ed. *The Chicano.* Mentor Books. New York: New American Library, Inc., 1971.

Simpson, George. *People in Families.* New York: Thomas Y. Crowell Co., 1960.

Smith, Bradford. *Americans from Japan.* New York: J. P. Lippincott Co., 1948.

Smith, Lillian. *Killers of the Dream.* Anchor Books. Garden City, N.J.: Doubleday and Co., Inc., 1963.

Smith, Walker C. *Sabotage, Its History, Philosophy, and Function.* Spokane, Wash.: By the Author, 1913.

Socio-Cultural Elements in Casework. New York: Council on Social Work Education, 1955.

Soustelle, Jacques. *The Daily Life of the Aztecs.* Translated from the French. London: Weidenfeld and Nicholson, 1961.

Spencer, Robert F., and Jennings, Jesse D. *The Native Americans.* New York: Harper and Row, Publishers, 1965.

Spinden, Herbert J. *Ancient Civilizations of Mexico and Central America.* New York: Anthropological Handbook Fund, American Museum of Natural History, 1928.

Standing Bear, Luther, Chief. *Land of the Spotted Eagle.* New York: Houghton Mifflin Co., 1933.

Steen, Marguerite. *The Sun Is My Undoing.* Philadelphia, Pa.: Blakiston Co., 1941.

Stein, Walter J. *California and the Dust Bowl Migration.* Westport, Conn.: Greenwood Press, Inc., 1973.

Steinbeck, John. *The Pearl.* New York: Viking Press, 1947.

————. *Grapes of Wrath.* New York: Viking Press, 1939.

Steinberg, Samuel. *The United States Story of a Free People.* Boston, Mass.: Allyn and Bacon, Inc., 1954.

Steiner, Stan. *La Raza: The Mexican-American.* New York: Harper and Row, Publishers, 1969.

Suddeth, Ruth Elgin; Osterhout, Isa Lloyd; and Hutcheson, George Lewis. *Empire Builders from Georgia.* Austin, Tex.: Steck Co., 1962.

Summer, William Graham. *Folkways.* New York: Ginn and Co., 1906.

Sweet, William Warren. *The Story of Religion in America.* New York: Harper and Bros., 1939.

Taylor, Paul S. *Mexican Labor in the United States: Imperial Valley* (1928). *Mexican Labor in the United States: South Texas* (1930). *Mexican Labor in the United States: Chicago and the Calumet Region* (1932). *Mexican Labor in the United States: Migration Statistics* (1929-34). University of California Publications in Economics. Berkeley, Calif.: University of California Press.

Taylor, Ronald B. *Sweatshops in the Sun: Child Labor on the Farm.* Boston, Mass.: Beacon Press, 1973.

Thomas, Dorothy Swaine, and Nishimoto, Richard. *The Spoilage.* Berkeley, Calif.: University of California Press, 1946.

Thomas, George, assisted by Stewart, Merrilee. *Poverty in the Nonmetropolitan South.* Athens, Ga.: Regional Institute for Social Welfare Research, University of Georgia, 1971.

Thomas, Jean. *The Blue Ridge Country.* New York: Duell, Sloan and Pearce, 1942.

Thurston, Henry W. *The Dependent Child.* New York: Columbia University Press, 1930.

Tireman, Lloyd S. *Teaching Spanish-Speaking Children.* Albuquerque, N.M.: University of New Mexico Press, 1948.

Tiryakian, Edward A., ed. *Sociological Theory, Values and Sociocultural Change.* New York: Free Press of Glencoe, 1963.

Tucker, George. *Essays on Various Subjects of Taste, Morals and National Policy.* Georgetown, Washington, D.C.: C. Wiley, 1822.

————. *The Valley of Shenandoah; or Memoirs of the Graysons.* Vol. I. New York: C. Wiley, 1824.

Tyler, Robert L. *Rebels of the Woods: The I.W.W. in the Pacific Northwest.* Eugene, Ore.: University of Oregon Press, 1967.

Vance, Rupert B. *Human Geography in the South.* Chapel Hill, N.C.: University of North Carolina Press, 1932.

Van Every, Dale. *Disinherited*. New York: Avon Library Books, 1967.

Van Kleeck, May. *Mines and Management*. Charleston, W. Va.: West Virginia Mine Association, 1934.

Valentine, Charles A. *Culture and Poverty: Critique and Counter Proposals*. Chicago: University of Chicago Press, 1968.

Vasconcelos, Jose, and Gamio, Manuel. *Aspects of Mexican Civilization*. Chicago: University of Chicago Press, 1926.

Vestal, Stanley. *Sitting Bull, Champion of the Sioux*. Norman, Okla.: University of Oklahoma Press, 1957.

Von Hagen, Victor W. *The Aztec Man and Tribe*. New York: New American Library, Inc., 1961.

Wallace, Anthony F. C. *Culture and Personality*. New York: Random House, Inc., 1961.

Wax, Murray L.; Wax, Rosalie H.; and Dumont, Robert V. *Formal Education in an American Indian Community*. Monograph No. 1. Notre Dame, Ind.: Society for the Study of Social Problems, 1964.

Webb, John N., and Brown, Malcolm. *Migrant Families*. Research Monograph XVIII. Washington, D.C.: Government Printing Office, 1938.

Weller, Jack E. *Yesterday's People*. Lexington, Ky.: University of Kentucky Press, 1966.

Wharton, Lane. *The Negro in Mississippi 1865-1890*. New York: Harper and Row, Publishers, 1965.

Whetherford, W.D., and Brewer, Earl C.D. *Life and Religion in South Appalachia*. New York: Friendship Press, 1962.

White, Walter. *Rope and Faggot*. New York: Arno Press, 1969.

Williams, Mary Wilhelmine. *The People and Politics of Latin America*. New York: Ginn and Co., 1945.

Wittke, Carl Frederick. *We Who Built America*. Cleveland, Ohio: Press of Case Western Reserve University, 1964 and 1967.

Woods, Sister Frances Jerome. *Cultural Values of American Ethnic Groups*. New York: Harper and Bros., 1956.

Woodward, C. Vann. *The Strange Career of Jim Crow*. New York: Oxford University Press, 1957.

Wright, Louis B., ed. *The Prose Works of William Byrd of Westover: Narrative of a Colonial Virginian*. Cambridge, Mass.: Harvard University Press, 1966.

Wright, Richard. *Black Boy*. New York: Harper and Row, Publishers, 1966.

Articles in Books and Periodicals

Alvarado, E. M. "Mexican Immigration to the United States." *National Conference on Social Work Proceedings.* New York, N.Y., 1920.

Armstrong, Ann W. "The Southern Mountaineers." *Yale Review,* XXIV (1935).

Ballagh, J. C. "White Servitude in the Colony of Virginia." *Johns Hopkins University Studies.* Baltimore, Md.: Johns Hopkins University Press, 1895.

Bearwood, Roger. "The Southern Roots of Urban Crisis." *Fortune,* August 1968.

Bennett, Lerone, Jr. " 'Jubilee,' The Making of Black America." Part III. *Ebony,* February 1972.

Bernstein, Basil. "Social Class, Speech Systems and Psychotherapy." *Mental Health of the Poor.* Edited by Frank Riessman, Jerome Cohen, and Arthur Pearl. New York: Free Press of Glencoe, 1964.

Boyce, George. "Why Do Indians Quit School?" *Indian Education,* May 1, 1960.

Brearly, H. C. "Are Southerners Really Lazy?" *American Scholar,* XVIII (1948-49).

Bruck, Max. "The Relationship Between Student Anxiety, Self-Awareness, and Self-Concept and the Student Competence in Casework." *Social Casework,* XLIV (March 1963).

Bruno, Hal. "Chicago's Hillbilly Ghetto." *Reporter,* XXX (June 4, 1964).

Calcott, F. "The Mexican Peon in Texas." *Survey,* June 26, 1920.

Coles, Robert. "What Poverty Does to the Mind." *Nation,* June 20, 1966.

Crinnell, Milton. "Rambling 'Round." *Michigan Farmer,* November 6, 1971.

Davidson, Helen H., and Lang, Gerhard. "Children's Perceptions of Their Teacher's Feelings Toward Them Related to Self-perception, School Achievement and Behavior." *Journal of Exceptional Education,* December 1960.

Deutsch, Helene. "Absence of Grief." *Psychoanalytic Quarterly,* VI, No. 12 (1937).

Doree, E. F. "Gathering the Grain." *International Socialist Review,* XV (June 1915).

Durand, Loyal. "Mountain Moonshining in East Tennessee." *Geographical Review,* XLVI (1956).

Elkin, Henry. "The Northern Arapaho of Wyoming." *Accultura-*

tion in Seven American Indian Tribes. Edited by Ralph Linton. Gloucester, Mass.: Peter Smith, 1963.

Erikson, Erik H. "Growth and Crisis of the Healthy Personality." *Symposium on the Healthy Personality.* Edited by Milton J. E. Senn. New York: Josiah Macy, Jr. Foundation, 1950.

Foster, George M. "The Dyadic Contract: A Model for the Social Structure of a Mexican Peasant Village." *American Anthropologist,* LXIII (December 1961).

Gornick, Vivian. "Why Women Fear Success." *Ms,* Spring, 1972.

Gray, David M. "Effect of Self-Esteem on Drawings of the Human Figure." *Journal of Consulting Psychology,* October 1962.

Greene, Sheldon L. "Wetbacks, Growers and Poverty." *Nation,* October 20, 1969.

Harvey, O. J.; Kelly, H. H.; and Shapiro, M. M. "Reactions to Unfavorable Evaluations of the Self Made by Other Persons." *Journal of Personality,* XXV (December 1957).

Hayden, Robert G. "Spanish-Americans of the Southwest, Life Style Patterns and Their Implications." *Welfare in Review,* XIV (1966).

Henninger, Daniel, and Espesite, Nancy. "Regimented Non-Education Indian Schools." *New Republic,* February 15, 1969.

Horowitz, Frances Degen. "The Relationship of Anxiety, Self-Concept and Sociometric Status Among Fourth, Fifth, and Sixth Grade Children." *Journal of Abnormal and Social Psychology,* September 1962.

Hundley, John R. "The Mountain Man in Northern Industry." *Mountain Life and Work,* XXXI (Spring 1955).

"Issei, Neisi, and Kibei." *Fortune,* April 1944.

Kahn, Alfred J. "Perspectives on Access to Social Services." *Social Work,* XV (April 1970).

Kohler, Max J. "An Important European Mission to Investigate American Immigration Conditions, and John Quincy Adams' Relation Thereto (1817-1818)." *Deutsch-Amerikanische Geschichtsblatter* (Chicago: University of Chicago Press, 1917).

Kubly, Herbert. "Where Is Tell?" *Holiday Magazine,* July-August, 1971.

"La Causa Chicana." *Social Casework,* May 1971.

Lawrie, J. W. "Making It the Hardest Way." *Psychology Today,* III (November 1969).

Lewis, Oscar. "The Culture of Poverty in Mexico City—Two Case Studies." *Economic Weekly of Bombay,* June 1960.

_____. "The Culture of the Vecindad in Mexico City." *Actas del*

33 Congresso Internacional de Americanistas. San Jose, Costa Rica: ICA, 1959.

Lindemann, Erich. "Symptomatology and Management of Acute Grief." *Crisis Intervention: Selected Readings.* Edited by Howard Parad. New York: Family Service Association of America, 1965.

Lorens, David L. "Natural Hair: New Symbol of Race Pride." *Ebony,* December 1967.

Martin, Richard. "City 'Hillbillies.' " *Wall Street Journal,* September 30, 1965.

McCormac, E. I. "White Servitude in Maryland, 1634-1820." *Johns Hopkins University Studies.* Baltimore, Md.: Johns Hopkins University Press, 1904.

McGill, Ralph E. "Cultural Growth and Domestic Problems." *Cultural Groups and Human Relations.* Edited by Karl W. Bigelow. New York: Bureau of Publications, Teachers College, Columbia University, 1951.

Merton, Robert K., and Barber, Elinor. "Social Ambivalence." *Sociological Theory, Values and Socio-cultural Change.* Edited by Edward A. Tiryakian. New York: Free Press of Glencoe, 1963.

Miller, Herman P. "Who Are the Poor?" *Nation,* June 7, 1965.

Montiel, Miguel. "The Chicano Family: A Review of the Research." *Social Work,* March 1973.

Porter, E. Russell. "From Mountain Folk to City Dweller." *Nursing Outlook,* II (June 1963).

Reul, Myrtle R. "A Preview of the Migrant as a Rehab Client." *Rehabilitation Record,* November-December 1969. Reprinted in Loewenberg, Frank M., and Dolgoff, Ralph, eds. *The Practice of Social Intervention: Roles, Goals and Strategies.* Etasca, Ill.: F. E. Peacock Publishers, Inc., 1972.

_____. "Communication with the Migrant." *Child Welfare,* XLIX (March 1970). Reprinted in *Legal Aid Briefcase,* XXXVII (July 1970).

_____. "Migrant Education Needs Encouragement." *Detroit News Magazine,* June 4, 1967.

_____. "What It Is Like to Be Hungry." *School Foodservice Journal,* May 1973.

Rowan, Carl T. "Indian Is Outcast in City of Hope." *Minneapolis Tribune,* February 9, 1957.

_____. "What Can Society Do to Help Set Free Today's Indians?" *Minneapolis Tribune,* March 3, 1957.

Sanchez, George I. "The Age-grade Status of the Rural Child in

New Mexico Public Elementary Schools, 1931-1932." *Education Research Bulletin.* Sante Fe, N. M.: New Mexico Department of Education, November 1932.

Senior, Clarence. "Movers, Migrants and the National Interest." *Migration and Social Welfare.* Edited by Joseph W. Eaton. New York: National Association of Social Workers, Inc., 1971.

Shea, Margaret C. "Serving Low Income Persons: New Demands on Social Workers." *Anti-Poverty Programs: Implications for Social Work Education.* New York: Council on Social Work Education, 1967.

Siebert, Wilbur Henry. "Slavery and White Servitude in East Florida, 1726-1776." *Florida Historical Society Quarterly,* X-XIII (July 1931).

Siggins, Lorraine D. "Mourning: A Critical Survey of the Literature." *International Journal of Psychiatry,* May 1967.

Silverman, Irwin. "Self-Esteem and Differential Responsiveness to Success and Failure." *Journal of Abnormal and Social Psychology,* July 1964.

Sininger, Harlan. "An Age-grade Study of the San Jose Training School and Its Two Control Schools." *University of New Mexico Bulletin School Series,* I, No. 2. Albuquerque, N.M.: University of New Mexico, 1931.

Spitz, Rene A. "Hospitalism." *Psychoanalytic Study of the Child.* Vol I. New York: International Universities Press, 1945.

Staines, J. W. "The Self-Picture as a Factor in the Classroom." *British Journal of Educational Psychology,* June 1958.

Steward, Julian H. "Culture Patterns in Puerto Rico." *Annals of the American Academy of Political and Social Science,* CLXXXV (January 1963).

Suin, R. M. "The Relationship Between Self-Acceptance and Acceptance of Others: A Learning Theory Analysis." *Journal of Abnormal and Social Psychology,* LXIII (July 1961).

Taft, Philip. "The I.W.W. in the Grain Belt." *Labor History,* I (Winter 1960).

Tharp, Roland G.; Meadow, Arnold; Lennhoff, Susan G.; and Satterfield, Donna. "Changes in Marriage Roles Accompanying the Acculturation of the Mexican-American Wife." *Journal of Marriage and the Family,* August 1968.

Thompson, Charles A. "What of the Bracero?" *Survey,* June 1925.

Ulibarri, Horocio. "Social and Attitudinal Characteristics in Spanish-speaking Migrants and Ex-migrants in the Southwest." *Sociological and Social Research,* L (1966).

Varon, Edith. "Communication: Client, Community and Agency." *Social Work,* April 1954.

Voas, R. B. "A Description of the Astronauts' Task in Project Mercury." *Human Factors,* III (1961).

Wax, Murray, and Wax, Rosalie. "American Indian Education for What?" *Midcontinent American Studies Journal,* VI (Fall 1965).

Wax, Rosalie. "The Warrior Dropouts." *Trans-Action,* May 1967.

Wesley, Clarence. "Indian Education." *Journal of American Indian Education,* I (June 1961).

Witt, Shirley Hill. "Right Flank and Left Flank: The City Indian and the Reservation Indian." *American Aborigine,* II, No. 1, Gallup, N. M. (1961).

Wolf, Kathleen L. "Growing Up and Its Price in Three Puerto Rican Subcultures." *Psychiatry,* XV (1952).

Woods, Sister Frances Jerome. "Cultural Conditioning in Mental Health." Social Casework, XXXIX (June 1958).

Yasumura, Jobu. "What Happens Next for Americans of Japanese Ancestry?" *Missions,* January 1946.

Zintz, Miles V. "Problems of Classroom Adjustment of Indian Children in Public Elementary Schools in the Southwest." *Education of the Disadvantaged.* Edited by A. Harry Passow, Miriam Goldberg, and Abraham J. Tannenbaum. New York: Holt, Rinehart and Winston, Inc., 1967.

Papers and Reports

Bird, Alan Jr., and McCoy, John L. "White Americans in Rural Poverty." Agricultural Economics Report No. 124 for the U.S. Department of Agriculture Economic Research Service, 1967.

Cronemeyer, Cora. "A Rural Manpower Strategy." Paper for the U.S. Department of Labor, Manpower Administration Rural Manpower Service, June 1971.

Jordan, Max F., and Bender, Lloyd D. "An Economic Survey of the Ozark Region." Agricultural Economic Report No. 97 for the U.S. Department of Agriculture Economic Research Service, 1966.

Kain, John F., and Persky, Joseph J. "The North's Stake in Southern Rural Poverty." Discussion Paper No. 30, Harvard University Program on Regional and Urban Economics, March 1968.

"Oglala Sioux Reservation Pine Ridge, South Dakota." Undated mimeographed report obtained from the Adult Education Department of the Pine Ridge Agency in 1964.

Reul, Myrtle R. "Level of Expectation Among Minority Groups." Mimeographed colloquium presented for the Michigan State

University School of Social Work, East Lansing, Mich., April 13, 1965.

————. "Sociocultural Patterns among Michigan Migrant Farm Workers." Center for Rural Manpower and Public Affairs, Michigan State University, East Lansing, Mich., 1967. (Mimeographed.)

Roberts, S. O. "Test Performance in Relation to Ethnic Group and Social Class." A report. Fisk University, Nashville, Tenn., 1963.

Upper Great Lakes Regional Commission. "Strategy for Development." 1968.

Young, Robert. "The Navajo Yearbook." Report No. VII. Arizona Navajo Agency, Window Rock, Ariz., 1958.

Public Documents

California, State of. Department of Industrial Relations. "Mexicans in California." October 1930.

U.S. Civil Rights Commission. *Report of United States Civil Rights Commission.* Vol. 5. Washington, D.C.: Government Printing Office, 1961.

U.S. Comptroller General. "Report to the Congress: Payment Limitation Under 1971 Cotton, Wheat, and Feed Grain Programs Had Limited Effect on Reducing Expenditures." April 12, 1972.

U.S. Congress. Joint Economic Committee. "Toward a Fundamental Program for the Training, Employment and Economic Equality of the American Indian," by Herbert E. Striner. *Federal Programs for the Development of Human Resources.* Vol. I. 90th Cong., 2d sess. Washington, D.C.: Government Printing Office, 1968.

U.S. Congress. House. *House Executive Document 184.* 44th Cong., 1st sess. Washington, D.C.: Government Printing Office, 1875.

U.S. Congress. Senate. *Senate Executive Document 51.* 51st Cong., 1st sess. Washington, D.C.: Government Printing Office, 1886.

U.S. Congress. Senate. *Senate Report 283.* 48th Cong., 1st sess. Washington, D.C.: Government Printing Office, 1882.

U.S. Department of Agriculture. Economic Research Service. *Domestic and Migratory Farm Workers: Personal and Economic Characteristics, and the Hired Farm Working Force of 1966: A Statistical Report.* Washington, D.C.: Government Printing Office, 1967.

U.S. Department of Commerce. Bureau of the Census. *Current*

Population Reports—Consumer Income. Series P-60, No. 76. Washington, D.C.: Government Printing Office, 1970.

U.S. Department of Commerce. Bureau of the Census. *Current Population Reports—Population Characteristics.* Washington, D.C.: Government Printing Office, 1970 and 1972.

U.S. Department of Commerce. Bureau of the Census. *Current Population Reports—Special Studies.* Series P-23, No. 33. Washington, D.C.: Government Printing Office, 1970.

U.S. Department of Commerce. Bureau of the Census. 1970 Census of Population. *General Population Characteristics.* Washington, D.C.: Government Printing Office, 1971.

U.S. Department of Health, Education and Welfare. *Equality of Educational Opportunity,* by J. S. Coleman, *et al.* Washington, D.C.: Government Printing Office, 1966.

U.S. Department of Health, Education and Welfare. *Perspectives on Human Deprivation: Biological, Psychological, and Sociological.* Washington, D.C.: The Department, 1968.

U.S. Department of Health, Education and Welfare. Office of Education. *Selected Programs in Migrant Education,* by George E. Haney. Washington, D.C.: The Department, 1963.

U.S. Department of Interior. *Impounded People.* Washington, D.C.: Government Printing Office, n.d.

U.S. Department of Interior. *The Indian Child Goes to School,* by L. Madison Coombs, *et al.* Washington, D.C.: The Department, 1958.

U.S. Department of Interior. *The Relocation Program.* Washington, D.C.: Government Printing Office, n.d.

U.S. Department of Interior. *The Wartime Handling of Evacuee Property.* Washington, D.C.: Government Printing Office, n.d.

U.S. Department of Interior. Bureau of Indian Affairs. *Answers to Your Questions About American Indians.* Washington, D.C.: Government Printing Office, 1970.

U.S. Department of Interior. Bureau of Indian Affairs. *The United States Indian Service: A Sketch of the Development of the Bureau of Indian Affairs and Indian Policy.* Washington, D.C.: The Bureau, 1962.

U.S. Department of Labor. *The Negro Family: The Case for National Action,* by Daniel P. Moynihan. Washington, D.C.: The Department, 1965.

U.S. Department of Treasury. Internal Revenue Service. "Internal Revenue Service Tax Guide, 1970." Circular A.

U.S. President's Commission on Migratory Labor, 1951. "Migratory Labor in American Agriculture." *Children in Migrant Families.* Washington, D.C.: U. S. Children's Bureau, December 1960.

U.S. War Department. *War Department Annual Report 1875.* Washington, D.C.: The Department, 1875.

U.S. War Department. *War Department Annual Report 1876.* Washington, D.C.: The Department, 1876.

Periodicals and Newspapers

Business Week, July 3, 1937.

Business Week, May 29, 1971.

Maryland Gazette, March 16, 1769.

Minneapolis Tribune, February 9, 1957.

Minneapolis Tribune, March 3, 1957.

Monthly Labor Review, December 1936.

New York Times, June 25, 1962.

Pacific Rural Press, February 13, 1926.

Press Scimitar (Memphis), January 27, 1921.

San Diego Tribune, March 1908.

Solidarity, June 4, 1910.

Solidarity, September 30, 1916.

Survey Graphic, May 1, 1931.

Virginian Magazine of History and Biography, XXXVI (1928).

Washington Historical Quarterly, XXII, No. 4. Seattle, Wash.: University State Historical Society, October 1931.

West Virginia Review, 1926.

West Virginia Review, September 1930.

Index of Subjects

Affect, defined, 411n6
Aggression
  among children, 378, 379n2, 421
  among migrants, 393
  and scapegoating, 379n4
  South a seedbed of, 98-99
Agriculture. *See also* Farm-labor management; Farm workers
  assets of, 543-44n1
  decrease of farms in, 428-29, 532-33
  Indians forced into, 68-69
  as an industry, 543
  Mexicans employed in, 128, 129,
    130-31
  poor, percentage of in, 32
  specialization in, 533
  stages of, 283n6
  systems analysis in, 542
  work in, fewer people finding, 476
Alcoholism, in rural areas, 160. *See
  also* Drunkenness
Allotment Act, The (1887), 78-79, 80
American Federation of Labor, 145
American Indian. *See* Indian, American
Anal stage, 493
Anger
  cultural expressions of, 560
  projected, as a characteristic of the
    disadvantaged, 555-56
Anomie, defined, 229-30
Anthony, Susan Brownell, 124n46
Apache Indian, and anger, 560
Apathy, among the deprived, 557-58
Appalachia
  and alienation, 229-30, 232, 244
  cultural aspects of
    child-rearing practices, 241-43

communication, 323, 567
family: extended, 247; loyalty to,
  246; roles in, 239, 242; size, 398,
  410n1
geography as part of culture, 493
gossip, 245-46
graves, importance of, 89n55, 402,
  412n8
homogeneous culture, lack of, 221,
  223
humor, 413n12
newcomers, attitude toward, 231-
  32, 245, 255, 406
prejudice toward Blacks, 266
psychological ties of native, 235-36
sex roles, 412-13n11
superstition, 521
women's roles, 239-41, 398, 412-
  13n11
geographical description of, 221,
  224-25, 250-51, 252-53
housing in, 236-39, 251-52
isolation in, 229, 236-37
lumbering in, 233
mining in, 230-32, 233-34, 252-53,
  260-62
out-migration from, 247-48
seasonal work in, 233-34
settlement of, 225-28, 230
snakes in, 237, 264
social classes of, 228-29
Apple sorters, 418-19
Association of Southern Women for
  the Prevention of Lynching, 113,
  123n46
Authority, fear of as a characteristic of
  the disadvantaged, 554-55

Index of Authors
and Titles

About the Author

Myrtle R. Reul is Assistant Dean of the School of Social Work and Professor of Social Work at the University of Georgia. She first became acquainted with culture and rural poverty in her early childhood environment. Born on what was the Great Sioux Indian Reservation in Montana to parents who had migrated there eight years before from their native state of West Virginia, Dr. Reul's preschool and early school non-Indian playmates were the children of European immigrants (representing countries from Scotland to Russia) or the children of migrants from Appalachia, the eastern states, and Canada. There were no Blacks in that section of Montana and fewer than twenty-five in the entire state, but in addition to the Sioux there were Pawnee, Crow, Blackfoot, and Cheyenne Indians who lived both on and off the reservations. Many of these people played an important part in Dr. Reul's orientation to culture. She was able from her earliest memories to see firsthand the poverty, the discrimination, the cultural differences and commonalities, as well as the cultural shock when Indian and non-Indian, native born and foreign born, migrant and nonmigrant suffered a loss of identity and then, through their interaction with each other, gradually came to have a new sense of being.

Dr. Reul received all of her college education in Michigan where she took an A.A. degree at the Jackson Community College, an A.B. degree from Albion College, the M.A., M.S.W., and Ed.D. degrees at Michigan State University, and did additional graduate work at the University of Michigan. She holds an honorary L.H.D. degree from Albion College for her work in the area of migrant farm labor. Before moving to Georgia in 1968 she was on the School of Social Work faculty at Michigan State University, where she coordinated the School Social Work Visiting Teacher Program with the College of Education and cooperated with the College of

Agriculture on projects for the Center for Rural Manpower and Public Affairs. Her nonuniversity experiences include, among others, working in family and child social welfare agencies and teaching in the public schools of Michigan.